Sta

YO-CAR-208

3/12/03

APR 1 0

Fourth Edition

The Sociology of Mental Illness

Bernard J. Gallagher III

Villanova University

Prentice Hall

Upper Saddle River, New Jersey 07458

Library of Congress Cataloging-in-Publication Data

Gallagher, Bernard J.
   The sociology of mental illness / Bernard J. Gallagher III.—4th ed.
     p. cm.
   Includes bibliographical references and index.
   ISBN 0-13-040868-9
   1. Mental illness—Etiology—Social aspects. 2. Psychiatry. I. Title.

RC455 .G23 2002
616.89'071—dc21

2001036899

Publisher: Nancy Roberts
Senior Acquisitions Editor: Chris DeJohn
Editorial/production supervision
  and interior design: Mary Araneo
Marketing Manager: Chris Barker
Editorial Assistant: Christina Scalia
Prepress and Manufacturing Buyer: Mary Ann Gloriande
Cover Art Director: Jayne Conte
Cover Designer: Bruce Kenselaar
Cover art: By Charles Manson from Vincent Bugliosi, Curt Gentry, *Helter-Skelter* (New York: Bantam
  Books, 1974).
Image Specialist: Beth Boyd
Manager, Image Rights and Permissions: Kay Dellosa
Director, Image Resource Center: Melinda Reo

This book was set in 10/11 New Baskerville by A & A Publishing Services, Inc.,
and was printed and bound by Hamilton Printing Co. The cover was
printed by Phoenix Color Corp.

© 2002, 1995, 1987, 1980 by Pearson Education, Inc.
Upper Saddle River, New Jersey 07458

Printed in the United States of America

10 9 8 7 6 5 4 3 2 1

ISBN 0-13-040868-9

Pearson Education LTD., London
Pearson Education Australia PTY, Limited, Sydney
Pearson Education Singapore, Pte. Ltd
Pearson Education North Asia Ltd, Hong Kong
Pearson Education Canada, Ltd., Toronto
Pearson Educación de Mexico, S.A. de C.V.
Pearson Education – Japan, Tokyo
Pearson Education Malaysia, Pte. Ltd
Pearson Education, Upper Saddle River, New Jersey

On November 4, 2000, I went to visit my mother. It was my birthday. My mother was in her usual good spirits, and I was complaining about making the deadline for this book. She said, "Bernie, just sit down and do it." She passed away two days later. Her words motivated me to finish the manuscript. Claire Marie Gallagher, neé Birnbrauer, was a wonderful woman and a great Mom. This book is dedicated to her memory.

Contents

PART II
COMMON FORMS OF MENTAL ILLNESS: PREVALENCE, SYMPTOMS,
AND CAUSES

6 Personality Disorders   129

PART III
THE SOCIAL EPIDEMIOLOGY OF MENTAL ILLNESS

7 Epidemiology: An Overview of Patterns of Mental Illness   157

10 Religion, Ethnicity, and Race   213

11 Migration, Place of Residence, and Age   231

PART IV
THE PSYCHOSOCIAL EXPERIENCES
OF MENTAL PATIENTS

12 Becoming a Mental Patient: The Prepatient Process   243

13 Treatment: The Inpatient Experience 266

14 After the Mental Hospital: The Social Role of the Ex-Mental Patient 293

Preface

There are countless forms of human suffering, but one of the most devastating is mental illness. It can rip the heart out of a person's opportunity for a happy life and it bewilders loved ones who try to help. This book has no single theme because mental illness has so many crippling dimensions—the symptoms, the social rejection, the routines of life in a mental hospital, the homelessness, the inability to cure, and, of course, the personal misery. The suffering knows no bounds, particularly in the case of the seriously mentally ill, who live hell here on earth in a fog of misery. They may be driven by delusions about pacts with satan or an overwhelming crush of depression and not know why. Although there is no single theme running through this book, there are two things that I hope to impart: an understanding of the sociology of mental illness and a sense of compassion for the millions of people in this world with psychiatric disorders.

Some feel that the causes of mental illness are a complete mystery. That used to be true centuries ago when mental illness was so misunderstood that it was relegated to poetry or sorcery because it was ignorantly confused with eccentricity or possession. Today there is a growing body of evidence that some mental illnesses are medical problems exacerbated by social stress. This book tracks that new knowledge, particularly the role of social stressors that can actually produce physical components of psychiatric ailments. I also try to untangle the chaotic turmoil politely referred to as *social policy,* a catchall phrase for treatment of the mentally ill. This is an especially pressing problem today as more and more patients are being released into the community.

This book is written with many engaging case examples from the world of everyday life. I wrote it to make the student *want* to go to the next chapter. I also wrote it as a reference book for professionals. To date, this text is one of the most comprehensive works about the sociology of mental illness. It includes thousands of studies from years of systematic research in psychiatric sociology spanning the microsocial problems within families to the macrosocial stresses of culture, war, and economy. This fourth edition has not merely been updated; it has been thoroughly reorganized as well. Two of its novel features are:

- A new emphasis on social stress theory, which is woven throughout the book
- Original sections centering on my recent research on social class, prenatal stress, schizophrenia, and sexual predators

I want to thank a lot of people for their help with this book and my career in general. My students at Villanova have been great, particularly those I met through the Honors Program who went on to do research and publish with me. They include Lamia Barakat, Suzanne Brixey, Meoghan Byrne, Mike Engle, Carolyn Everson, Maria Halluska, and Corinne Rita. Special kudos to Mike and Carolyn (my best students) for returning to Villanova and lecturing in my classes. And continued thanks to Corinne Rita for all of her work on the third edition of this book.

My course at Villanova goes by the name of Social Psychiatry. It is a popular course, partly because I am fortunate to have friends who give their time to lecture on their special areas of expertise. My best friend, Art Donato, a criminal defense attorney, joins Dan McDevitt, a district attorney, and Tony Pisa, a forensic psychologist, for an interesting (and unpredictable) class on psychiatry and the law. Barbara Cole, another "Honors student contact," gives a presentation on bipolar disorder that is masterfully creative. Mike Engle, who recently became a criminal defense attorney himself, delivers a riveting talk on serial murder. Lizzy Schmidt and Mike Gallagher speak to the students about their experiences growing up gay and further a sense of tolerance and open-mindedness. The highlight of the course is a trip to Norristown State Hospital, where the students obtain invaluable clinical contact with mental patients. More importantly, they are led through the trip by Laura Brobyn, a clinical nursing specialist, who imparts professionalism, compassion, and hope for the mentally ill—a forgotten population. Perhaps the best way to express what Laura means to my students is the statement they so often make about her: "I want to be like Laura." To all of these people my deep thanks for making the course fly.

More than 1,000 new studies were added to this new edition. They were partly compiled by two research assistants in Villanova's Sociology Department, Mary Martin and Melissa Pittaoulis. Louise Green, Acting Director of Falvey Library at Villanova, was also a huge help by providing exemplary literature reviews. Charlotte Vent completed numerous forms and mailings. My thanks to all of these fine people for helping me with this book.

I am also deeply indebted to some wonderful people at Prentice Hall. Nancy Roberts, my past editor, was central to the book being reorganized and published on time. Nancy and I go back a long time, traveling a route that has been nothing but pleasant and supportive. My new editor, Chris DeJohn, is ideal for the job. He is organized, understanding, knowledgeable, creative, and an all-around nice guy. His assistant, Christina Scalia, was not only there when I needed help but provided it in a way that was quick, smart, and friendly. I would also like to thank the following Prentice Hall reviewers for their input and suggestions: Gary A. Cretser, California State Polytechnic University, and John W. Fox, University of Northern Colorado.

Sue Jones is the one person who is most responsible for this edition's being completed accurately and on time. Sue is more than a typist. She is also "Ms. Speedy," who seemed to have finished chapters before I wrote them. Without her quality work and her optimistic attitude toward making the deadline, this book would not have happened. If I had not dedicated the book to my mother, I would have dedicated it to Sue. She was that inspirational.

I did not write this book simply to be the first to do so, way back in 1980; and I did not write it just because of the pride I feel from its quality. The most important reason for this book is to present all that is known about how sociological stressors can disfigure mental health by putting people adrift in a limbo of despair.

Bernard J. Gallagher III
Villanova, Pennsylvania

1

Mental Illness and Society

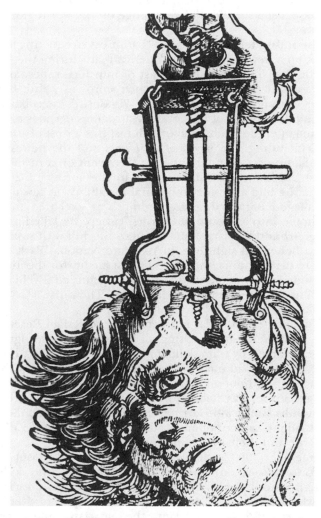

In early history, some believed that mental illness was caused by demonic forces. One "treatment" was trephination—drilling a hole in someone's head to allow the devil to escape. This artist's 1528 rendering shows what it may have been like when "surgery" was performed without the benefit of anesthesia.

THE SUBJECTIVE DIMENSIONS OF MENTAL ILLNESS

By the dawn of the twenty-first century, many branches of science, and medicine in particular, had made great advances in the understanding and treatment of an enormous array of ailments. However, mental illness has been a huge exception. What other major social problem is so widely misunderstood and stigmatized? Not only are the causes and treatment of mental illness elusive, but the very topic is often a cause for embarrassment to the American public in general and especially to the families of the afflicted. There are, of course, some groups, such as social scientists, that have an open-minded attitude toward people with mental health problems.[1] Social scientists, however, are just a small dot of knowledge on the world globe of ignorance and misinformation.

Part of this misunderstanding is the "bad press" frequently linked with mentally ill people. Pick up a newspaper in any American city during the last couple of years. What would you see? The usual horror list of murders, rapes, and fires. You would also see stories about people who evoke such words as weird, horrible, disgusting, crazy, macabre, outrageous, and deranged. Wisconsin's cannibalistic handyman, Ed Gein, had been found guilty of unspeakable atrocities decades ago. Yet his penchant for keeping human organs in his icebox still inspires a host of scary children's books and PG films, including *The Silence of the Lambs* and the newest version of *Psycho.* Richard Baumhammers, an immigration lawyer, went on a racially motivated killing spree of Jewish, Indian, and Asian victims in the spring of 2000. The headlines emphasized that he had a "history of mental instability." A few months before, Gary Heidnik, an alleged paranoid schizophrenic, was executed for turning his West Philadelphia home into a "house of horrors," where he killed and tortured women he lured there. Around the same time the news was hot with stories on Cary Stayner, who killed and beheaded sightseers in Yosemite National Park. And at Norristown State Hospital in Pennsylvania, the state's largest facility for the mentally ill, a hostage situation concluded in a victim's death when a disgruntled psychiatric nurse returned to retaliate against his supervisors who fired him. The nurse's "psychiatric instability" was promoted as the cause.

In 1999, a chameleon serial murderer named Rafael Resendez-Ramirez made the FBI's Ten Most Wanted List. Using all kinds of disguises, grooming styles, and aliases, Ramirez traveled by train, killing many midwesterners who were unfortunate enough to live near railroad tracks. Alleged to be "crazy," he was characterized by the FBI as a "changeling without a known motive." This was the same year when George Harrison, the ex-Beatle, was stabbed by a man recently released from a psychiatric clinic. A few months later, Paul Harrington, a former Detroit police officer who was a psychiatric outpatient, ran out of medication and killed his wife and son. He had also killed his first wife and their two children back in 1975.

Some remember 1999 as the year of deadly rage acted out through public violence—the poisonous resentments of two teenagers who killed 13 people at Columbine High School; the midwestern murder rampage of racist, anti-Semite Benjamin Smith, who left two dead; the paranoid disaffection of overwrought day trader Mark Barton that cost nine lives in Atlanta; the sectarian bias of Larry Gene Ashbrook, who slew seven worshipers at a Baptist church in Fort Worth. All of the attacks ended with the shooters' suicides.

Make no mistake about it—1999 was not a unique year for stories of "crazy" people acting violent. Pick another year at random, 1993. In the winter of 1993 the newspapers were jammed with stories of horror. A man named David Koresh, claiming to be God, was holed up in Waco, Texas, with 100 of his followers. The self-proclaimed leader of a religious cult known as the Branch Davidians was engaged in a bloody showdown with federal agents. The first day saw some 20 lives snuffed. This was in sharp contrast to Koresh's daily regimen in which he was treated as God as well as to the immediate availability of any of his estimated 20 "wives." This all took place in the name of the greater glory of God and it all ended in the fiery Armageddon he predicted.

The news from Europe was equally stunning. In London, one of Britain's so-called "Silent Twins" died unexpectedly after being freed from the top-security Broadmoor hospital. Jennifer Gibbons, 29, fell ill and died just hours after she and her sister left the hospital where they had spent 11 years following a bizarre spree of arson, drug taking, and burglary in Wales. The twins, described by physicians as "elective mutes," had made a pact of silence at an early age. They communicated with each other in an incomprehensible babble. At school they refused to read or write and retreated into their own world. Later it was discovered that they were prolific and secret writers who had taught themselves writing through a correspondence course. They were diagnosed as schizophrenic.

Serial and mass murder were also big topics that winter. In south Jersey, Matthew Heikkila, a psychiatric outpatient, was despondent and threatened to kill his pet cat. Instead, his feelings intensified and he shot and killed his mother and father with a shotgun. He had neatly written "Mom" and "Dad" in black ink on each shell. In Massachusetts, Wayne Lo, an 18-year-old talented music student, killed a teacher and a fellow student and wounded four others at an exclusive school for the gifted. He was described as withdrawn, angry, and "anti-everything." In Watkins Glen, New York, John T. Miller killed four workers in a county office, told deputies that "he killed everyone that he'd come to kill," and then shot himself in the head. On the West Coast, Lynwood "Jim" Drake III, apparently distressed over being evicted, went on a shooting spree across three central California towns. He took out six people, including his former landlord, and wounded another man before killing himself in front of a hostage.

Around the world reports were equally grim. The peaceful tranquility of Switzerland was shattered when a gunman stalked through three villages, ringing doorbells and shooting residents as they opened their doors. Six people were killed and six others were seriously wounded in one of the worst mass murders in Swiss history. In Russia, a "career" was finally coming to an end. Andrei R. Chikatilo, a 56-year-old innocuous-looking former schoolteacher, had finally been caught. Referred to in the press as the "Forest Strip Killer" and "The Crazed Wolf," he was convicted of 52 murders during a 12-year killing spree. The "world's worst serial killer case" centered about a man who dismembered women and children and ate their remains. Chikatilo's string of grisly murders resulted in the hauling in of tens of thousands of former mental patients for interrogation.

Back at home, Steven Brian Pennell calmly argued before the Delaware Supreme Court that he should be executed—as soon as possible. For years, the 34-year-old "family man" cruised highways, picking up prostitutes and other women to bind, torture, and strangle in his blue van. He delivered deathblows with a hammer. There had not been an execution in Delaware since 1946, but Pennell was set on changing that with his own demise by lethal injection. His eagerness was rewarded. And one last example of a newsmaker of the times—Jeffrey L. Dahmer. It was already known that he had eliminated 17 young males. But, in 1993, the word had spread that he had also attempted lobotomies on some of his victims while they were drugged. The newspapers reported that he drilled holes in their heads to deaden a portion of their brains and then poured fluids into their skulls. When his experiments failed, he strangled the victims and dissected the corpses. The list of highly visible abnormal people goes on.

Other headline crimes of the twentieth century in the Philadelphia region include:

- On September 6, 1949, Howard Unruh, a World War II veteran, walked through his East Camden neighborhood, fatally shooting 13 people, including two children, in a matter of minutes. Unruh, often described as the first of the modern rampage killers, was never tried for the crime because he was ruled mentally unfit. Now 83, he remains at Trenton State Hospital.
- On October 30, 1985, Sylvia Seegrist, 25, dressed in military fatigues and armed with an automatic rifle, opened fire in the Springfield Mall, killing three and wounding seven. Seegrist, a paranoid schizophrenic, was given three life sentences.
- On January 26, 1996, John E. du Pont, heir to one of the nation's greatest fortunes, shot and killed Dave Schultz, a champion wrestler working as a coach at du Pont's 800-acre Newtown Square estate. After a two-day siege, du Pont surrendered. Found guilty but mentally ill, he is serving a sentence of 13 to 30 years.

All of these stories make people feel as aghast as Londoners did in 1888 when Jack the Ripper was carrying out the "East End slaughters." The media are much to blame for the misperception of the mentally ill as dangerous and unpredictable. The book-turned-film *Awakenings* is a prime example, since it even fosters the belief that "crazy" people can just snap out of it.[2] A recent Jim Carey film, *Me, Myself and Irene*, trivializes mental illness as a joke.

Why is mental illness so subject to stigmatization? Fear is one factor. Mental illness is perceived to be dangerous, and the rare but widely publicized violent incidents, associated with mentally ill people, such as the accounts above, serve to fuel the fear enormously.[3]

Mental *illness* (a.k.a. mental *disorder*) is one of the most serious problems in the world today. Simply stated, it causes a living hell for both the afflicted people and those around them. This anguish was vividly illustrated by Charles Manson in a doodling he made while on trial for the famous Tate–LaBianca murders. It is uncertain whether Manson was purposely drawing his concept of a tortured person or actually uncovering a disorder of his own. Nevertheless, I was so impressed with how Manson's simple sketch emotionally represented the inner world of mental illness that I used the drawing for the cover of this book. Unfortunately, Manson was not so favorably impressed, as evidenced by the threatening phone calls I received from some of his "friends." The calls complained about my connecting Manson with mental illness. I thought the connection was obvious. I was also young, carefree, and more concerned about a good book cover than my own safety. But that is another story for another book. Ironically, legal permission to use Manson's sketch was given by Vincent Bugliosi, the prosecuting attorney in the Tate–LaBianca trial and co-author of *Helter Skelter*. Bugliosi is also number one on Manson's "hit list."

Clearly, people like Manson are deranged in some manner. But are they representative of the ways mentally ill people *typically* think and act? They certainly are not. What they represent is what makes a good news story—one that is interesting and unusual. Unfortunately, this gives the public the highly *subjective* impression that "crazy" people rant, rave, murder, and rape. In reality (or *objectively* speaking), mentally ill people typically are not dangerous or assaultive. They usually lead miserable lives (often in secret), have such uncontrollable feelings as worthlessness or anxiety, often cannot handle a job, and are faced with personal and social difficulties that seriously affect them, their family, and friends.

The real stories are more like Jane, a woman in her thirties, who lived in a community residential rehabilitation program for several years, receiving support from staff and peers. Having been abandoned by her family, she had a great deal of difficulty becoming stable while she was on medication but her treatment team worked closely with her to help her achieve her goal of living independently. Over time she progressed and was finally able to move into her own apartment.[4] Jane is a success story. For every one of her there are hundreds of mentally ill people who waste their lives away in the isolation of back wards or on the streets. These are the *real* faces of the mentally ill, not the faces of maniacal killers.[5]

The mass media do not have a monopoly on the subjective ways by which mentally ill people are perceived (or misperceived). Disturbed people themselves, mental health professionals, and society at large also play roles. But the roles are radically different. The shattered mind of a seriously ill person is an individual experience that no one can truly objectify. Psychiatrists and other mental health professionals *try* to objectify mental illness through diagnosis, in terms of specific symptoms, but they are regularly accused of employing art and not science.[6] And on a grander scale is the large web of society enmeshed with values and norms, all of which affect the very definition of normality and abnormality. Because the behaviors of the mentally ill are subjectively filtered through a biased lens, public attitudes toward the causes of mental illness are riddled with misunderstanding and stigma. For instance, a 1993 study by a National Advisory Mental Health (NAMH) affiliate reported that approximately 71 percent of respondents attributed mental illness to an "emotional weakness," 35 percent found it to be rooted in "sinful behavior," and 65 percent blamed "bad parenting." Additionally, 45 percent blamed the mentally ill themselves, stating that they "bring on their own illnesses." In sharp contrast with the opinions of psychiatrists, only 10 percent of the public believed mental illness can stem from a biological abnormality. Alternative perspectives on mental illness, as seen through the eyes of the individual mentally ill, health care professionals, and the general public will be detailed throughout this book.

Fear, misunderstanding and a host of myths about madness are major roadblocks on the path to effective care for people with mental illness.[7] There is a rough parallel with the way that the elderly are perceived by many in our society, namely, as worthless people who are expected to drop out of mainstream life.[8] The upside to all of this is that there appears to be a real change occurring in both Americans' attitudes toward acknowledging mental health problems and in their willingness to talk to others about them. This is evidenced in the general population by the appearance of new Web sites with such addresses as "schizophrenia.com". And it is visible at the federal level with legislation proposed to expand benefits for mental health care.

THE OBJECTIVE DIMENSIONS OF MENTAL ILLNESS

According to the World Health Organization, mental illness is not only an agonizing *personal* anguish but is also a major *social* problem, as evidenced by a large number of studies reporting that an alarmingly high percentage of the world population is mentally ill. Mental disorders are reported to account for four of the ten leading causes of disability in established market economies worldwide.[9] In addition, the size of the mentally ill population appears to be growing, as some of the same studies indicate that the rate of mental illness has increased sevenfold since the end of World War II. Part of this increase is due to a more liberal definition of mental illness in the post–World War II studies.[10]

Even these large numbers are questionable in that the massive Global Burden of Disease study, assessing risk factors for mental illness from 1990 to 2020, reports that the burden of mental illness on health and productivity in the United States and throughout the world has long been underestimated.[11] The same study reports that mental illness is more than the disease burden caused by all the cancers. In 1999, the first Surgeon General's report on mental health estimated that more than 50 million Americans suffer from some kind of mental illness each year. However, many fail to get treatment even though effective therapies are widely available.[12] It should also be noted that a significant comorbidity exists between mental health and physical health problems, although the chronological order of the problems is not known and probably varies widely from patient to patient.

Although there is a wide array of estimates, a 1993 update on the decade-long Epidemiologic Catchment Area (ECA) survey reported that approximately 22.1 percent of Americans had some kind of psychiatric disorder during that year and that 32 percent are at risk for serious mental illness at some point in their lives.[13] This roughly translates into one in five Americans.[14] This figure does not include the estimated 5 million American children under the age of 18 who suffer from a diagnosable mental disorder.[15] The issue of diagnosing children is another matter. Today some researchers are treating teenagers for schizophrenia before they are diagnosed. Some bioethicists think that is insane.[16]

There certainly are many agencies, mainly federal, that report mental health statistics. In 2001, the National Reporting Program for Mental Health Statistics collected a ton of information on mental health services and the people who receive them. As this book is being written, the National Institute of Mental Health (NIMH) is sponsoring a 5-year survey of 10,000 American adults to examine mental illness in the United States. All of the reporting services publish a unanimous conclusion: Mental health problems are a huge issue that often goes untreated. In a recent report, Surgeon General David Satcher said that there is no scientific reason to differentiate between mental health and other kinds of health. Mental illnesses are often physical illnesses and constitute the second-leading cause of disability and the second-leading cause of premature death in the United States.

The Surgeon General stated that the problem is exacerbated by the fact that people are embarrassed to admit that they have a mental health problem or cannot afford to see a professional to treat the ailment. To make things even worse, a 1999 report to the American Psychiatric Association estimated that 10 million Americans suffer from "extreme shyness." Embarrassment and shyness add up to a huge reluctance to seek help.[17]

A 1992 NIMH study of the *seriously mentally ill in treatment* estimates their number to be between 4 million and 5 million persons in the adult population. Those not in treatment linger at home or on the streets, where they constitute almost half of the social horror known as homelessness.[18] The problem has been compounded by the closing of state hospitals. In 1969, there were 36,745 mental hospitals; now there are about 3,800. This is the result of aggressive public deinstitutionalization policies, a movement that many see as a disaster that has resulted in widespread homelessness among the mentally ill.[19] They wander the streets of cities as Thorazine zombies in an ill-conceived outpatient program that can literally freeze them to death.

As Figure 1:1 shows, there has been an enormous increase in the number of people *treated* for mental disorder in recent decades. This increase was somewhat visible in terms of inpatients in various types of mental health facilities for short stays. It was very real at the "outpatient" level. Outpatients include people under the care of psychiatrists in private practice, clinical psychologists, various types of "counselors," or psychiatric social workers. Figure 1:2 presents a percentage breakdown of adults with mental illness categorized by level of severity.

The data in Figures 1:1 and 1:2 are drawn from studies using known treated cases as the criterion for the prevalence of mental disorder. Certainly many other people have real mental health problems and never receive help. How many of these people are there? Some researchers have tried to answer this question by studying large groups of people who are not being treated to see what the real rate (*true prevalence*) of mental disorder is. They report that between 20 million and 30 million Americans actually need some kind of mental health care, although only a fraction receive it. The rest go unrecognized.

Given the wide, objective spread of mental illness, logic would dictate that there

Figure 1:1   Inpatient additions per 100,000 civilian population, all mental health organizations and state and county mental hospitals: United States, selected years 1969–1988.

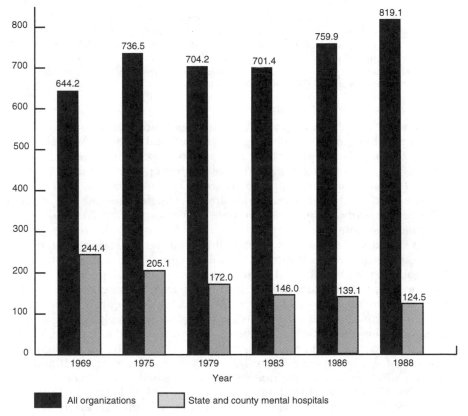

Source: Statistical Research Branch (SRB), Division of Applied and Services Research (DASR), National Institute of Mental Health (NIMH), 1990.

Figure 1:2   Adults with mental illness, categorized by level of severity.

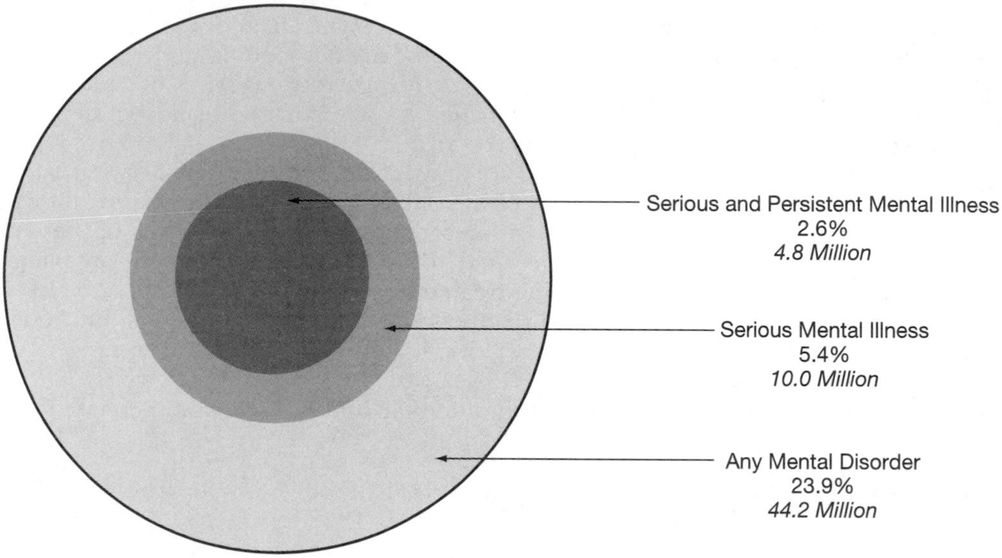

Serious and Persistent Mental Illness
2.6%
4.8 Million

Serious Mental Illness
5.4%
10.0 Million

Any Mental Disorder
23.9%
44.2 Million

One-year prevalence of mental illness and affected population. Adults, aged 18–54 DSM-III-R criteria. Pooled Baltimore Epidemiologic Catchment Area (ECA) and NCS data. Excludes homeless people and residents of institutions such as nursing homes, prisons, and long-term-care facilities; an additional estimated 2.2 million persons with serious mental illness, for 12.2 million in total population.

Source: Adapted from Kessler & Zhao (in press). Copyright 1999 by Cambridge University Press. Reprinted with permission of Cambridge University Press.

would be serious efforts in researching the roots and treatment of the problem. Here logic would lose. In 1989, for instance, the National Advisory Mental Health Council reported that only $11 per patient was spent on researching mental illness. Compare that to the $161 spent for every person suffering from multiple sclerosis and the $1,000 for each muscular dystrophy patient. The comparison is even more depressing in light of one additional fact: Schizophrenia, which is just *one form* of mental illness, is five times more common than multiple sclerosis and sixty times more frequent than muscular dystrophy.

The status of research on mental illness may be improving. Certainly more books are being published on the topic.[20] Additionally, a separate section of the Surgeon General's Report on Mental Health lists over 100 agencies centered about research and treatment of mental illness, reflecting growing awareness of the problem.

No point about the fiscal lack of concern for the mentally ill would be complete without mentioning that state funds for mental health facilities are going in one clear direction—downward. Given the absence of any universal federal health care or mental health care system, the role of the states in orchestrating public mental health services is critical. The curve in Figure 1:3 makes it clear, however, that the portion of state budgets allocated to this vital need is becoming smaller and smaller.

Some states do better than others. Take a look at Figure 1:4. You will note that New York allocates more dollars than Wyoming or Idaho. This is not simply the result of a greater sense of compassion on the part of the New York state legislature. Later in this book you will see that mentally ill people tend to be geographically clustered in

Figure 1:3 Total SMHA-controlled expenditures for mental health services as a percentage of total state government health and welfare expenditures.

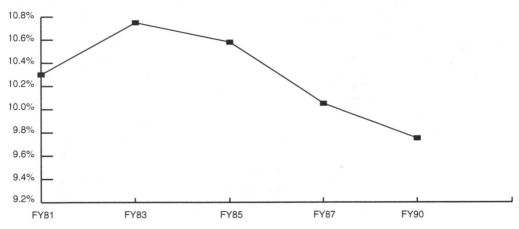

Source: State health and welfare expenditure totals are from the U.S. Bureau of the Census, Governments Division, 1991.

highly urbanized areas. That may explain some of the state-by-state variations but not all of them. New Hampshire, for instance, ranks high on the "expenditure hierarchy" but is commonly perceived as a sea of tranquility.

Perhaps no other issue better exemplifies the dramatic difference between the objective and subjective aspects of a social problem as mental disorder does.[21] Because so many victims go untreated, the objective dimensions of the problem are more widespread than any "official" statistics. Yet even the official statistics would shock most people because mental disorder has traditionally been denied, ignored, or explained away as something else. Only recently have magazine articles, television programs, and books on mental health helped to improve public awareness. Still, the gap between the actual extent of the problem and the average person's subjective awareness is enormous. In recent years, organizations have formed to increase objective awareness of the real facts about mental illness. One such group, Planned Lifetime Assistance Network of Pennsylvania (PLAN), offers support for the family of the mentally ill and helps to arrange financial help for the disordered person after his or her relatives are deceased.

The public is also unaware of the total economic costs of mental disorder to American society. Although the costs cannot be precisely determined, estimates have been offered. The National Foundation for Brain Research estimates the direct costs to be $136.1 billion annually. Additionally, alcohol abuse accounted for $90.1 billion, and drug abuse cost the nation $71.2 billion a year. These figures include both private fees and taxpayer dollars. The average annual cost of caring for each patient in a state mental hospital alone is approximately $135,000. If a patient is cared for in a forensic ward, the annual costs soar to $175,000. And a stay at a private mental hospital is billed at an astronomical rate: Would you believe hundreds of thousands of dollars a year? Believe it and you will understand why most patients in private mental hospitals do not stay very long. Some of the private hospitals are a rich man's psychiatric resort where families with means can tuck away their genetic inconveniences and embarrassments, their senile elders and poorly programmed kids.

Figure 1:4   State mental health expenditures as a percentage of total state government expenditures, fiscal year 1990.

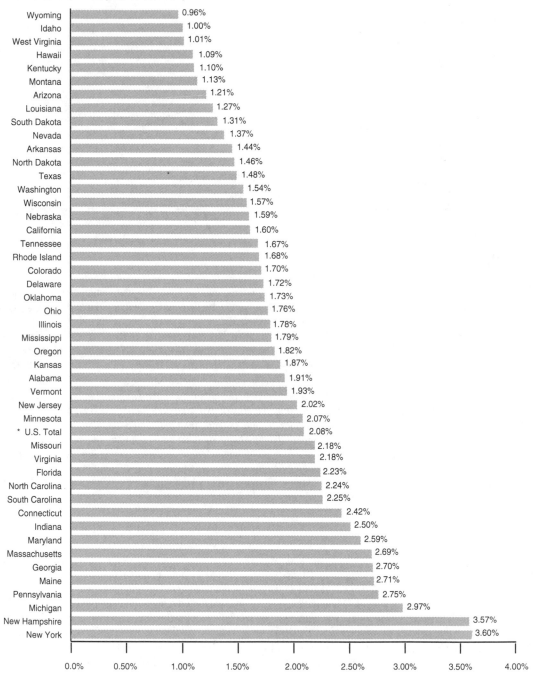

Source: Total state government expenditures are provided by the U.S. Bureau of the Census, Governments Division, 1991.

There are other indirect costs that should be added to the direct cost of patient care, such as a 25 percent loss of productivity to the work force due to employee illness and inefficiency. The monetary value of this loss is estimated to be approximately $79.3 billion per year, but this is an underestimation of the actual figure, given that the income lost because of drug and alcohol abuse and related psychoses is not included. It also fails to include the loss of productivity connected with the mentally ill who are homeless.[22] Figure 1:5 provides a breakdown of the distribution of the cost of treatment by type of provider.

The lack of concern of corporate America deserves special mention here at the end of this litany of objective facts about the plight of the mentally ill. In a nutshell, corporate America does not care. In fact, one study of Fortune 500 companies found that only a handful have policies specifically concerning psychiatrically handicapped employees.[23] Despite legislation that has encouraged equal opportunity for people with mental health problems in various types of vocational programs, the delivery of such services is next to nonexistent.

All of the statistics about the status of the mentally ill today paint a picture about an enormous problem that is relatively ignored. But that is not the entire picture. There are other objective dimensions that are more difficult to estimate, such as the increases in divorce, crime, drug addiction, and child abuse that stem from mental disorder. We also have a morbid approximation of the cost of suicide among the mentally ill. The most recent estimate of the indirect cost to the economy from suicide was $9.3 billion, or $233,337 per death.[24] Obviously, the emotional cost of such tragedies is

Figure 1:5 Percent distribution of mental health, alcohol, and other drug abuse treatment expenditures, by provider, 1996 (total – $79.3 billion).

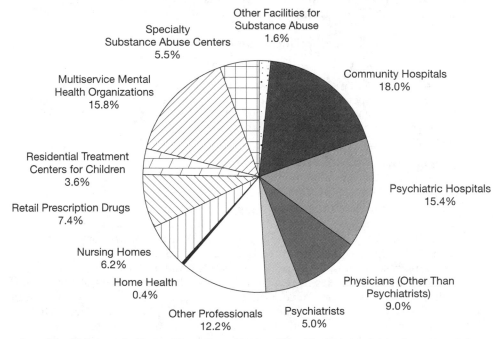

Source: Tami Mark et al., *National Expenditures for Mental Heaalth, Alcohol and Other Drug Abuse Treatment, 1996* (Rockville, MD: U.S. Department of Health and Human Services, 1998).

incalculable. Objectively, mental health problems may be the most extensive and expensive health maladies of all, yet the public knows very little about them. Often the path to knowledge starts with the devastating impact of seeing a close friend or relative disintegrating into the depths of psychosis.

MENTAL ILLNESS THROUGH HISTORY

Ancient Demonology

The different ways in which the mentally ill have been viewed and treated through history are hard to describe in a rational way. Words like "staggering" and "macabre" quickly come to mind. It has only been in the last 100 years that mental illness has been researched in any kind of scientific way. Primitive people viewed mental illness as magic. One of their doctrines was that an evil being, such as the devil, could control the mind of a person. This is called *demonology*. It was based on the widespread belief in *animism*—that everyone has a "soul" and mental disturbance is caused by evil spirits.[25]

Ancient Babylonians followed a religion in which there was a specific demon for every known disease. In the case of insanity, Idta was to blame. The course of treatment was to exorcise demons from the person by use of procedures that were often cruel and barbaric by modern standards. If less painful techniques failed, such as prayers, loud noises, and foul odors, the person would be whipped and/or starved. One particularly crude practice employed by Paleolithic cave dwellers was *trephination* in which the disturbed person's skull was chipped away to allow demons to escape. Although there is no written proof that this was the specific design of trephining, archeological evidence from this period includes many skulls with holes drilled in them.

William Cockerham succinctly summarizes primitive attempts to explain mental disorders:

> Most often, an illness, however, especially if its cause could not be directly observed, was ascribed to supernatural powers. In essence, primitive medical practice was primitive psychiatry, as humans applied subjective notions about their environment to ailments whose origin and prognosis were beyond their comprehension.[26]

The Greco-Roman Period

Ancient Greeks and Romans made a number of speculations about mental illness. They assumed that the cause of mental illnesses was a disturbance within the natural body itself. These people were so certain that mental illness was biologically caused that in A.D. 4, a Roman physician tried to cure the emperor's symptoms with an electric eel. This may have been the first use of "shock therapy." Around 700 B.C., the physician-priest Alcamaeon hypothesized that brain processes caused sensation and concluded that difficulties in reasoning resulted from an illness of the brain. During the sixth century B.C., the concept of asylum (therapeutic sanctuary) for the mentally ill reached a high point in Greece where a special place was erected at Epidauros. Patients were treated with diet, remedies, baths, exercise, fasting, prayers, and rituals, sometimes in combination with hypnotic and hallucinogenic drugs. Less fortunate patients were treated with flogging, bloodletting, and sheep dung mixed with wine.

Hippocrates (460–367 B.C.) stated that mental illness originated from an excess or imbalance among the four humors of the body. His classification of temperaments—choleric, melancholic, sanguine, and phlegmatic—corresponded to excesses in the four humors: yellow bile, black bile, blood, and phlegm, respectively. More specifically, he believed that a preponderance of black bile caused depression, too much yellow bile explained anxiety, an excessive amount of blood led to a changeable temperament, and a preponderance of phlegm made a person sluggish and dull. In addition, he believed that hysteria, a disorder involving the loss of use of a body part, was a uniquely female disorder caused by a uterus that wandered throughout the body! Similarly, the Roman philosopher Cicero (106–43 B.C.) held that imbalances among intellect (reason), appetites (instinct), and temper (passions) caused mental illness. He particularly emphasized the role of "violent desire" in abnormal behavior. Heraclitus (535–475 B.C.) also looked for the causes of abnormal behavior within the individual. Believing that fire was life's energy, he held that irrationality stemmed from the nature of the fire within the soul.

Plato (429–347 B.C.) departed from a purely physiological explanation and argued for the role of divine intervention. He described four kinds of madness, two of which implied possession by good spirits. These were prophetic madness, such as Apollo's oracle at Delphi, and poetic madness, which provided creative abilities. The other two types were erotic madness and ritual madness, which was induced by orgiastic religious ceremonies. Aristotle (384–322 B.C.) revitalized Hippocrates' emphasis on bodily functions. His theory, however, was far from progressive, since he claimed that the heart is the causal agent in mental illness.

Asclepiades (ca. 100 B.C.) rejected the biological theory of Hippocrates and stressed the importance of environmental factors. He differentiated among *delusions, hallucinations,* and *illusions,* as well as acute and chronic onsets. A delusion is a belief that is not consistent with reality. A hallucination is a sensory perception not associated with real external stimuli. An illusion is a false sensory perception of real external sensory stimuli. Some of Asclepiades' notions are comparable to many current theories of mental illness. Aretaeus (A.D. 30–90) is credited with the observation that mental illness is an exaggeration of the normal personality. He grouped illnesses according to patterns of symptoms, something that no one had previously considered.

In ancient Palestine, mental illness was connected with the supernatural. Little thought was given to medical or other aspects of mental illness. In fact, there is some evidence that magical practices were designed to cast out the demons of madness as primitive people had done centuries before. According to the Bible, Christ himself cured a man with an "unclean spirit" by casting out the devils within him and driving them into a herd of swine.

Middle Ages

During the Middle Ages treatment of mental illness was in the hands of priests who believed that demonic forces were at work in the mind of the afflicted. They would sprinkle the disordered person with holy water and shout obscene epithets at Satan to hurt his pride. Monks also prayed over the mentally ill, touched them with relics, or concocted exotic potions for them to drink during the last phase of the moon. Wild ideas involving humors, demons, and astrological "facts" characterized some of the speculations about demonic possession. Actually, two kinds of possession were recognized. In one form the person was unwillingly seized by the devil as God's punishment for sins. These people were considered to be mentally ill. In the second form, the person deliberately entered into a pact with the devil. These were witches with supernatural powers. By the end of the fifteenth century the distinction between these two forms of possession was blurred, and many unfortunates were labeled as witches and accused of causing pestilence and floods.

In 1484, Pope Innocent VIII issued a papal bull urging the clergy to search exhaustively for witches. This decree ushered in a violent and tragic period in Western history. Other actions by officials of the Catholic and Protestant churches furthered the belief in witches and prompted a multitude of arrests, hangings, and other grotesque executions of suspected witches, many of whom were actually suffering from mental illness. Pressing victims to death was one method of execution that is reported to have been used in Salem, Massachusetts, in the late 1600s. The actual number of people who were killed during the era of witchcraft mania is unknown, but the most widely cited estimate is about 200,000 people in Germany and France alone.

Many of the mostly female victims of the Middle Ages of politicoreligious fervor were probably mentally ill. They suffered from delusions, hallucinations, and such great emotional turmoil that they would "confess" to having sex with the devil and flying to sabbats, secret meeting places of their cults. Later we will discuss *hysteria*, a condition that can cause anesthesia of parts of the body. Back then, areas of insensitivity to pain were called the "devils mark." To identify witches, professional "witch prickers" went from town to town jabbing pins into the accused.

It is easy to see why the Middle Ages are often referred to as the Dark Ages. It clearly was a period of disenlightenment, horror, and despair. There was one refreshing note from that time, however. A Franciscan monk, in his thirteenth-century reference work *Encyclopedia of Bartholomaeus,* speculated that madness originated near fluid-filled cavities of the brain called lateral ventricles. As we will see in Chapter 4, this is very close to current thinking on the etiology of schizophrenia.

The Dutchman Johann Weyer (1516–1588) attacked demonology. He insisted that witches were ill and should be treated humanely. Although he formulated no theories of his own, he was skillful in describing disorders that are well known today. He was particularly instrumental in helping to counteract the barbaric treatment of mentally ill people who were constantly threatened with execution or expulsion from the community. Weyer's treatise, called "The Deception of Demons," was a major advance in the description and classification of forms of abnormal behavior. He actually formulated an early version of what is now known as *diathesis-stress theory,* which holds that a constitutional weakness (diathesis) may interact with environmental stresses to produce a mental illness. Little did he know how accurate his theory would prove to be.

Period of Reform

A sense of public outrage toward the abuses suffered by the mentally ill developed toward the end of the eighteenth century. Consequently, a "reform movement" started, first, by placing the mentally ill in jail rather than exterminating them. Later, more humane treatment came about largely through the efforts of three people—the Frenchman Philippe Penil, Vincenzo Chiarugi, an Italian, and the Englishman William Tuke.

In Europe, the mentally ill were no longer killed or tortured as common practice. Instead, they were chained and confined in jail with criminals. The places were literally dungeons where people were not even given the care that would be accorded an animal. The mentally ill lived in dark, cold cells with dirt floors, often chained to straw beds and surrounded by their own excrement. Although many feel that medical scientists were responsible for ending this practice, Foucault reports that the change was initiated by prisoners who were indignant at being forced to live with madmen.[27] They viewed their enforced association with the mentally ill as the ultimate punishment and humiliation. There were also separate asylums for the mentally ill, the most famous of which was St. Mary of Bethlehem in London. Conditions there were appalling. The moon-mad "lunatics" of Bethlehem, or Bedlam as it was called, were daily put on display for a small fee to amuse the public. It was the social equivalent of today's circus sideshow.

The situation of the mentally ill was roughly similar in the United States. By 1860, 28 of 33 states had public asylums for the "insane" to keep them isolated from society. This was a reflection of the belief that the causes of mental illness were diseases of the brain that should be treated by physicians. In both the European institutions and the American asylums, the mentally ill were condemned to lives of misery and, in most cases, permanent separation from society.

The reform movement started in Italy through the efforts of Vincenzo Chiarugi (1759–1820), the superintendent of a mental hospital in Florence called the Ospidale di Bonifazio. He removed the patients' physical restraints, provided them with activities, and spread the word through his writings about the need to make mental hospitals comfortable.

Humane treatment was initiated in France through the efforts of Philippe Pinel (1745–1826), a founder of modern psychiatry. Pinel invoked the concept of individual freedom, made so salient in the French Revolution, in calling for reforms in treating the mentally ill. At the Bicêtre Hospital, he removed patients' chains, allowed them access to hospital grounds, and instructed the staff to employ human kindness. Pinel's ideas were heavily influenced by a virtually unknown man named Jean-Baptiste Pussin, a hospital staff worker. Pussin had been a patient in the hospital where he was treated for a tubercular condition. After recovering, he became superintendent of the ward for "incurable" mental patients. In this capacity, Pussin instituted humanitarian treatment. The results of the efforts of these men were dramatic, as many people recovered who were considered incurable. Pinel's reform movements were formalized at the Salpetrière Hospital where personnel were trained to be more than custodians and were instructed in keeping systematic records on each patient. Record keeping itself reflected the new belief that the mentally ill could be cured.

The policy of nonrestraint, promulgated by Pinel and other reformers of the time, such as Tuke, was slowly adopted throughout the Western world.[28] Pinel's ideas were tested in the United States largely through the efforts of Benjamin Rush (1745–1813), the "father" of American psychiatry. Rush, concerned with social reforms, introduced methods based on moral treatment at the Pennsylvania Hospital. His views were not entirely consistent, however, since, in his widely used textbook on psychiatry published in 1812, he reaffirmed his beliefs in bloodletting, purgatives, and in the "tranquilizer," a special chair into which patients were tied and suspended upside down in midair. He believed that mental illness was caused by an excess of blood in the brain. Consequently he would draw great quantities of blood, as much as six quarts over a period of a few months. It was no great surprise that Rush's patients felt "different" after a trip to the chair or a good bleeding. Rush also believed in terror tactics in the cure of "madness." These included convincing a patient of his impending death. Needless to say, that also had an effect.

In 1752, the Pennsylvania Hospital in Philadelphia, the first institution in America to receive mental patients, was opened. Then, in 1773, the Williamsburg Asylum in

Williamsburg, Virginia, opened its doors. It was the first institution in America devoted exclusively to the care of the mentally ill.

Dorothea Lynde Dix (1802–1887) was called "Dragon Dix" by some, but her efforts were credited with saving many lives. In 1841, Dix, a Massachusetts school-teacher forced by tuberculosis into early retirement, investigated the deplorable and brutal conditions prevalent in asylums. For 40 years she worked diligently for the building of state-supported hospitals. She initiated the principle of public responsibility for the mentally ill. A measure of her effectiveness is the striking increase in the number of people treated in mental hospitals: from 2,561, or 14 percent, of the estimated ill in 1840, to 74,028, or 69 percent, of the estimated ill in 1890. In 1843, she addressed the legislature of Massachusetts with these words:

> I come to present the strong claims of suffering humanity. I come to place before the Legislature of Massachusetts the condition of the miserable, the desolate, the outcast. I come as an advocate of the helpless, forgotten, insane, and idiotic men and women; . . . of beings wretched in our prisons, and more wretched in our almshouses . . . I would speak as kindly as possible of all wardens, keepers, and other responsible officers, believing that most of these erred not through hardness of heart and willful cruelty so much as want of skill and knowledge.[29]

The reform period was a time of ups and downs. The efforts of Dix were a clear move in a progressive direction. She was directly responsible for extending or enlarging about 32 mental hospitals and she made sure that physicians were added to the staffs of many of those facilities. At the same time, some very backward thinking prevailed. In Illinois, for instance, a married woman could be committed to the state asylum at Jacksonville at the request of her husband without any evidence of mental illness required. Masturbation was a big topic. In fact, in some circles it was officially blamed as the cause of insanity, epilepsy, melancholia, and suicide. Recommended treatments of masturbation in children included branding the spine and genitals with a hot iron.

Somatogenic Views

From an etiological perspective, Hippocrates' original belief that all mental disorders were biological in origin was revived in the early nineteenth century when psychiatry was first scientifically organized. This period was characterized by the unquestioned belief that pathological bodily conditions and brain tissue dysfunctions were solely responsible for mental disorder. This perspective became known as the *somatogenic* view since it looked for the origin of mental illness in the body, or soma.

Western Europe was the center of psychiatric investigation during this period. Unfortunately, specialists in mental disorder did not concern themselves with each other's work due to their preoccupation with their own limited research. This was responsible for a rather chaotic approach to research on mental illness. Many did not recognize any difference between neurological and psychological phenomena, partly because the study of mental illness was undertaken exclusively by physicians. The French psychiatrist Morel (1809–1873), for example, worked on the premise that mental disease was the unfortunate result of hereditary neural weakness. Others, such as the German psychiatrist Griesinger (1817–1868) and the Frenchman Magnon (1835–1916), were oriented toward biological explanations of mental disorder simply because they studied only diseases involving overt somatic symptoms, such as paralysis and alcoholism.

Research in the late 1800s brought some empirical evidence to support the somatogenic hypothesis. *Dementia paralytica*, commonly known as *paresis*, was discovered in 1798 among patients at the Bethlehem Hospital in Pennsylvania. It was noted that paralysis, delusions of grandeur, and dementia (loss of mental powers) were associated with the disorder, but the cause of the illness eluded researchers.

There were many competing theories. In trying to account for the high rate of paresis among sailors, for example, some speculated that seawater might be the cause. In 1894, Fournier found that 65 percent of paretic patients had had syphilis. It was postulated that the syphilitic infection had impaired brain tissues, but researchers could not determine why syphilis was not found in all paretic cases. An ethically questionable experiment in 1897 by Krafft-Ebing laid that question to rest. He injected paretic patients who denied having had syphilis with the syphilitic virus! Surprisingly, none of them developed syphilis, which demonstrated that syphilitic infection leads to paresis. Apparently, Fournier had naively relied on patients' self-reports of having had syphilis, not a very useful way to detect a fact that many people would prefer to hide. If Krafft-Ebing were to try such an experiment in the United States today, he would be hit with a ton of lawsuits.

During the somatogenic period, the first organized attempt at classifying mental illness was undertaken by Emil Kraepelin (1855–1926). He noted that mental disorders tended to be expressed by a specific grouping of symptoms known as a *syndrome*. Kraepelin observed that there were two major types of disorder. One was a disorder of *mood* expressed by excited behavior (mania) or melancholic behavior (depression), which he called the *manic-depressive psychosis*. The other disease involved a disorder of *thought*, often progressive, what he called *dementia praecox* because it resembled premature senility. It is now known as *schizophrenia*. Kraepelin's classifications proved to be less controversial than his etiological beliefs because he viewed the manic-depressive psychosis as an irregularity in metabolic function and dementia praecox as an imbalanced chemical state caused by abnormal secretions of the sex glands.

Psychogenic Views

In the late nineteenth century, John P. Gray, superintendent of Utica State Hospital and editor of the *American Journal of Insanity*, became the chief advocate of the somatogenic position. Around this time, a great struggle was beginning between somatogenic theorists such as Gray and a new school of thought which suggested that mental disorders could be caused solely by a disturbance in the patient's psychological state. This approach to mental illness, known as the *psychogenic* view, first became established within modern psychiatry through the study of hysteria.

Hysteria is associated with somatic symptoms such as loss of sight, hearing, or partial anesthesia. For reasons that are still unclear today, many people in Western Europe during the late eighteenth century were subject to hysterical conditions. It was believed that hysteria was a purely physiological disorder until the application of hypnosis provided new insight. The Austrian physician Mesmer discovered hypnosis. In fact, hypnosis was originally called *mesmerism*. Widely regarded as a fraud, Mesmer promulgated the belief that magnetic fluid fills the bodies of all living creatures. He believed that mental illnesses were caused by an imbalance in this fluid. He would "cure" people in groups while they held hands around a tub filled with chemicals and iron rods that supposedly transmitted "animal magnetism." The whole charade did produce one useful finding, namely, that the process of being put into a trance effected changes in the minds of his subjects. Thus the origin of hypnosis.

Hypnosis was first applied to hysterical patients in France by Charcot and his student, Janet, who demonstrated that "normal" people under a hypnotic state can exhibit symptoms identical to hysteria. This discovery, combined with the recognition that many hysterical patients had physical symptoms that were anatomically impossible, forced investigators to conclude that abnormalities of psychological processes alone can produce mental disorder. One example was "glove anaesthesia," where the patient loses feeling in the hand from the wrist to the fingertips. Anatomically, this is impossible since the nerves are not distributed in such a way that the entire hand can be anesthetized without losing feeling in part of the arm as well. These patients lost the feeling of their *concept* of the hand as a unit. The insight about the connection between thinking and mental illness was limited, however, in that it failed to specify the causal direction of the relationship; that is, does the abnormal psychological process produce mental disorder, or vice versa? "Chicken and egg" questions permeate psychiatric research throughout time, including today.

The causal link between psychological processes and mental illness was first described by Sigmund Freud (1856–1939), who, with the assistance of Josef Breuer in the late 1800s, studied the unconscious segment of the human mind. Freud was a brilliant physician with extensive neurophysiological training and a deep interest in the brain and the mind. He was impressed by the hypnosis-hysteria connection, and from it he developed an entirely new view of human behavior. Freud's discovery of the unconscious origin of psychological difficulties, along with his theory that the personality consists of three interdependent parts—the instincts (*id*), the seat of moral regulations (*superego*), and the agent that mediates compromises between the parts of the personality and the constraints of reality (*ego*)—is often viewed as the cornerstone of modern psychiatry. This school of thought, commonly known as *psychoanalysis*, served as both a theory of personality development and as a means to treat particular types of mental disorders.

From clinical observations, Freud postulated the sequential development of the personality through the satisfaction of specific needs at various stages of "psychosexual" development. He believed that mental illness results from an interruption of this process. Consequently, the aim of psychoanalytic treatment was to trace the origin of the experiences in earlier life that gave rise to the abnormality. Since Freud's theories were based on the importance of sexual and aggressive strivings of the unconscious id, he devoted a great deal of energy to developing techniques that would allow access to that part of the personality. His efforts led to the production of more sophisticated techniques than hypnosis, such as dream interpretation, free association, and a simple "talking out" technique known as *abreaction*. All of these methods allowed access to the unconscious, a previously unknown part of the human personality that had only been referred to by poets.

Around the beginning of the twentieth century, many ideas were espoused that stressed the role of the sociocultural environment in the development of mental illness. During the 1880s, as industrialization and urbanization were rapidly expanding, articles appeared in popular magazines pleading for Americans to wake up and avoid the loss of their moral fiber, which was being threatened by the competitive jungle of modern industrial society. As early as 1844, C. D. Hayden concluded that "[it is our] free institutions which promote insanity . . . life in our republic has all the excitement of an Olympic contest. A wide arena is thrown open and all fearlessly join in the maddening rush for the laurel wreath."[30] Many more articles appeared articulating the theme that the competition engendered by modern industrial society had debilitating effects on individuals. Before the turn of the century, G. A. Blumer, the distinguished editor of the *American Journal of Insanity*, warned: "Either the average brain of today has become a more unstable structure than the average brain of our ancestors; or else the average stress of environmental forces brought to bear on the brains of our generation has become more severe than formerly."[31] He believed that the alarming increase in the rate of mental illness in the United States was caused by the preoccupation of Americans with social mobility.

W. A. White suggested in 1903 that a return to a simpler lifestyle was desirable. He felt that "the frontiersman who takes his family and goes West to open up new territory, engages in legitimate agricultural pursuits, and grows up with the country, is pretty apt to be of hardy stock and insanity, if it appears at all, comes in later generations."[32] Dr. R. Jones, superintendent of the London County Asylum in Claybury, England, had a similar view. He asserted: "With the progress of civilization, mental breakdown becomes more serious, if not more frequent, and the varieties of insanity more chronic and less curable than when life was simpler and men were more content."[33] At this point in history it was becoming increasingly popular to believe that mental illness was importantly related to sociocultural forces.

The Mentally Ill in the United States Today: Homelessness and Prisons

Later in the book, I will describe the origins and rationale of what has come to be known as "community-based care." In a nutshell, it is an attempt to move people out of mental hospitals and into residences in the community where they may regain their social skills and avoid the dependency on the routines of hospital life. Although it has been successful for some patients, it has been a miserable failure for others, who have ended up on the streets or in prisons, as they did centuries before. Box 1:1 describes one released patient's experience from treatment to homelessness to jail.

The demographic characteristics of the mentally ill in state adult correctional facilities are roughly equivalent to the characteristics of the mentally ill in society as a whole.[34] There are, however, some alarming facts about the mentally ill in prisons aside from the fact that they are there. First, the police are now taking an increasingly larger role in handling mentally ill persons and making decisions about psychiatric referrals.[35] Police officers and judges are simply not trained to identify and deal with the mentally ill. These are people in need of the state's help, not a prison sentence.

A second startling fact is the size of the "mentally ill in prisons" problem. The prison's new role as mental hospital includes 283,800 inmates with severe mental illness, about 16 percent of the total jail population.[36] No wonder we have achieved the highest incarceration rate in human history for nonpolitical offenses.[37]

Mentally ill inmates are more likely than other offenders to have committed violent offenses, the Justice Department reported in 1999. However, disorderly conduct and public nuisance are the most typical charges. These are especially common patterns among young mentally ill offenders.[38] Mental health services provided by prisons vary enormously from state to state. They basically run the gamut from trying to keep people "on meds" to simple incarceration.[39]

Sending the mentally ill to a place like Rikers Island, a prison in New York City, is ignorant, insensitive, and inhumane. Human rights groups have asked that records of the treatment of mentally ill prisoners be made public. In 2000, a federal judge in New Jersey ruled in their favor. But that is a tiny victory in changing the criminal justice system from a revolving door for a person with mental illness—from the street to jail and back without treatment.

•••••••••••••••••••••••••••••••••••••   **Box 1:1**   ••••••••••••••••••••••••••••••••••••
Prisons Replace Hospitals for the Nation's Mentally Ill

Michael H. had not had a shave or haircut in months when he was found one morning sleeping on the floor of St. Paul's Episcopal Church in suburban Lancaster, next to empty cans of tuna and soup from the church pantry. There was little to suggest that he had once been a prosperous college graduate with a wife and two children—until he developed schizophrenia, lost his job, and, without insurance, could no longer afford the drugs needed to control his mental illness. Charged with illegal entry and burglary, Michael was taken to Los Angeles County Jail. The jail, by default, is the nation's mental institution. On an average day it holds 1,500 to 1,700 inmates who are severely mentally ill, most of them detained on minor charges, essentially for being public nuisances.

The situation in the jail, scathingly criticized as unconstitutional by the U.S. Justice Department, is the most visible evidence that jails and prisons have become the nation's new mental hospitals. On any day, almost 200,000 people behind bars—more than one in ten of the total—are known to suffer from schizophrenia, manic depression, or major depression, the three most severe mental illnesses. The rate is four times that in the general population. And there is evidence, particularly with juveniles, that the numbers in jail are growing.

Some of these people have committed serious, violent crimes. But many more are homeless people like Michael H., charged with minor offenses that are by-products of their illnesses. Others are picked up with no charges at all, in what police call "mercy arrests," simply for acting strangely.

The trend began in the 1960s with the mass closings of public mental hospitals. At the time, new antipsychotic drugs made medicating patients in the community seem a humane alternative to long-term hospitalization. States also seized the chance to slash hospital budgets. From a high of 559,000 in 1955, the number of patients in state institutions dropped to 69,000 in 1995. But drugs work only when they are taken—and when they work, patients are tempted to stop, because of unpleasant side effects. As states lagged in opening a promised network of clinics and halfway houses to monitor patients, obtaining treatment became harder. Health insurers restricted coverage, for-profit hospitals turned away the psychotic, and new laws made it more difficult to commit disturbed people. Thousands began to fall through the cracks.

Coincidentally, with voters willing to spend freely to fight rising crime rates, states were building more jails and prisons. Jails became the only institutions left open to the mentally ill, 24 hours a day.

Source: Fox Butterfield, *New York Times*, March 5, 1998, pp. A1, A26.

•••

CURRENT THEORIES OF MENTAL ILLNESS

The Medical Model

Treatment Techniques.   In the twenty-first century, psychiatry is much less in the dark about the causes of mental illnesses, although we are far from plotting the exact roots. Today there are a number of major schools of thought in terms of etiological perspective. The *medical model,* also known as the *biogenic model* or *sickness* (disease) *model,* was originally based on biological theories developed by the ancient Greeks. According to this view, mental illness is a physical disease like polio or cancer. Emphasis is placed on the recurring behavior, or "pathological symptoms," of a disease, as well as "diagnosis" and "treatment." The language and concepts of the medical model are clearly analogous to that of physical medicine. This model dominated twentieth-century psychiatry and continues to do so into the twenty-first partly because psychiatrists receive a medical school training that predisposes them toward organic views.

Some feel this is unfortunate because it hinders the development of an awareness of environmental influences on mental illness. Freud, for instance, warned against the employment of medically trained people as psychoanalysts, but physicians dominate that field as well.

Another factor leading to increased reliance on the medical model has been the discovery and steady expansion of psychotropic drugs, which are commonly used to treat many emotional conditions. These drugs were widely employed in the 1950s and proved to be an invaluable method for giving patients relief from their symptoms. Earlier, somatogenic forms of treatment had been successfully developed for psychotic people. These approaches employed applications of shock to the patient. Manfred Sakel developed insulin shock therapy in 1929 and used it to treat schizophrenics. Sakel accidentally discovered the effectiveness of insulin shock. He had been using insulin to lower the blood-sugar level of morphine addicts. In certain cases a standard dose had too strong of an effect, and the patient was thrown into shock. Sakel noticed that this experience sometimes improved the confused mental state of his addicts, so he began to apply the same treatment to schizophrenics, with good results.

In 1934, the Portuguese neurosurgeon Ladislas von Meduna believed that there might be some sort of connection between severe mental illness and seizures, the neurological "storms" underlying convulsions. He used the convulsant drug Metrazol to test the idea that seizures inhibit mental illness. In 1938, the Italian neuropsychiatrists Ugo Cerletti and Lucio Bini developed a technique by which the channeling of electricity into the body produced a coma followed by relief from the symptoms of manic-depressive illness. This technique is known as *electroconvulsive therapy* (*ECT*). However, today there is still no generally accepted theory that explains how any form of shock therapy works.[40] There is, however, plenty of controversy about whether ECT is ethical. Some assert that it is an effective intervention whose use has been limited as a result of social stigma. Others criticize ECT because of its disturbing side effects such as memory loss.[41] ECT is the equivalent of rebooting a computer as opposed to determining the reason for the errors. Though the end result may be a healthy reconnecting of brain pathways, the formatting "bugs" causing the problem will inevitably be forgotten and, possibly, forever lost. As a rule, ECT is not the treatment of choice for the young.

Since the beginning of the twentieth century, isolated efforts to treat abnormal behavior through psychosurgery had been carried out in Switzerland and Russia. In 1936, Antonio de Egas Moniz developed new techniques for calming highly agitated or depressed patients by making lesions in selected parts of the brain. Later, he won the Nobel Prize for his *frontal lobotomy* technique. Frontal lobotomy involved passing a wire loop through a hollow needle that had been inserted into the brain. The wire was pushed through the needle, expanded at the other end, and then rotated to produce circular cuts in brain tissue. The results were unpredictable. Like ECT, psychosurgery is also the center of a very stormy controversy today. Some see it as damaging the brain to save the mind.[42] Some assert that it is an invaluable intervention for certain kinds of seriously disordered patients. Still others argue that psychosurgical procedures rest on a shaky scientific foundation and cause irreversible brain injury.[43]

Causal Theories. Etiological support for the medical model has been offered in recent decades through studies of the frequency (*concordance rate*) by which both members of a pair of identical (*monozygotic*) twins exhibit the same abnormality. Identical twins can be alarmingly similar. For example, England's Chaplin twins seem to be halves of a single personality. They are identical twins in their fifties who dress alike, walk in step, take two-hour baths together, and frequently talk—and sometimes swear—in unison. If separated, even for a moment, they wail, scream, and wet their pants simultaneously.

The frequency rates among identical twins vary by type of mental illness and from study to study. For psychosis, the most severe kind of disorder, the rates are impressively high. These findings serve as the foundation for a particular school of medical thought, the *genetic school,* which holds that mental illness is transmitted through heredity. Recently, this view has been extended to criminal behavior as well.[44]

Another major medical view is the *biochemical school.* Researchers in this field believe mental illness is the result of an abnormal imbalance of neurotransmitters (chemical messengers) circulating within the brain. As a relatively recent development within psychiatry, biochemical hypotheses are still being tested. Some studies have shown rather convincingly that certain types of mental illness, particularly psychosis, involve an alteration of the normal biochemical state. The biochemical theories are subject to one very important criticism: simply because mental disorders and abnormal biochemistry are found together does not necessarily mean biochemistry is *causing* the disorder. It is quite possible that disturbed biochemistry is the *result* of the disorder rather than the cause. This criticism is particularly relevant in light of common knowledge of how emotions can cause physiological changes, such as when fear induces accelerated heart rate and sweating. This issue of cause and effect is one of many "chicken and egg" issues that nag modern psychiatry.

The third, and most recent, medical model of mental illness is *natality theory.* This intriguing line of inquiry investigates whether some kind of maternal prenatal illness may have crossed the placenta wall and caused an insult to the developing brain of the fetus. Natality theory also includes stressors shortly after or during birth such as obstetrical complications. My own research indicates that natality factors may indeed be involved in the origin of schizophrenia and that these factors appear to be related to social class.

Psychological Theories

The psychological perspective actually encompasses a number of theories that are bound by a common emphasis on the effect of life experiences. One theory is the *behaviorist* (social learning) *model,* which is oriented toward the study of *conscious* experience because its proponents contend that abnormal behavior is no different in origin from other behavior. Behaviorists reject the basic Freudian idea that symptoms are symbolic expressions of unconscious, conflict-ridden needs originating in childhood. In fact, they do not even believe in the existence of an unconscious. They posit that abnormal behavior, like normal behavior, is determined largely by environmental stimuli; it is not a problem within an individual but rather the result of interaction with other people. Thus, according to behaviorist spokesmen such as Watson, Pavlov, and B. F. Skinner, mental illness is a learned, or *conditioned,* behavior.

Another psychological theory is *psychoanalysis,* the Freudian perspective. This model views mental illness as the result of an excessive use of instinctual energy at a particular stage of psychosexual development that causes an arrest, or fixation, of personality. Each particular type of mental illness is linked with impairment at a specific stage. The experiences considered capable of causing fixations are essentially social, such as difficulty in fulfilling society's demands for anal control, the absence of a warm mothering figure, rejection by one's peers, and failure to achieve the expectations of significant others. The most debilitating illnesses are considered to originate within infancy and early childhood through severe frustration of the person's needs. These early pathologic influences are well hidden within the unconscious until they manifest themselves in the form of abnormal behaviors in later life.

The Sociological Perspective

The sociological perspective is the most recently articulated and serves as the central focus of much of this book. Known as *social psychiatry* or *psychiatric sociology,* it is the product of a concerted effort by socially oriented psychiatrists, sociologists, psychiatric social workers, social psychologists, and cultural anthropologists. Actually, the sociological perspective is more of a research focus than a separate causal theory, although some of the findings from this field uncover specific possible causes. In significant ways, it is a reaction to the failure of medical researchers to "deliver" in terms of discovering all of the causes of mental illness.[45]

The intervention of sociologists in the field of mental illness has not been without problems. One relentless issue is the ongoing debate between the sociologists and the psychiatrists concerning the domain of the discipline. This conflict has resulted in a split between the psychiatrically oriented and the sociologically oriented. Those who have entered the field from psychiatry call it *social psychiatry*, a subspecialty of psychiatry.[46] The psychiatrists view their function in practical ways, emphasizing *service* rather than *research,* and they consider social psychiatry as the study of methods by which society combats mental illness and of the psychiatric training given to social workers as well as the social training given to psychiatrists. There are differing opinions within this group regarding the magnitude of the services to be performed; some see social psychiatrists functioning only within the one-to-one therapist-patient relationship, while others envisage entire societies as patients.

Sociologists who have entered the field call it *psychiatric sociology,* a term coined by Arnold M. Rose. They view the discipline in theoretical, research-oriented ways. As in the social psychiatry branch, there is differing opinion concerning the scope of the research; some concentrate on studies of the one-to-one therapist-patient dyad, and others conduct basic etiological investigations of large populations. The most popular definition of psychiatric sociology focuses on *the role played by social factors in the causation of mental disorder.* Implicit in this definition is the inclusion of epidemiological analyses, which are important forerunners of etiological conclusions. In short, the major difference between social psychiatry and psychiatric sociology is that the former is service-oriented and the latter is research-oriented. Their combined efforts are responsible for forging new inroads into the origins and treatment of mental illness. This book addresses the literature compiled in both of these fields, particularly psychiatric sociology since its data examine a number of social aspects of mental illness beyond those encountered in treatment settings.

The Biopsychosocial Perspective

Much of mental illness remains a mystery. Pieces of information exist about the biology, psychology, and sociology of the problem. There is evidence accumulating that all of these factors interact with one another to influence the causes and treatment of psychiatric disorder.[47] As one researcher so aptly put it:

All medical disciplines, in their clinical/pragmatic aspects, deal with whole persons. Because the thrust of general biomedicine is to partition humanity into ever more basic and abstracted systems (e.g. organs, tissues, chemical processes), this has led to criticisms that seek to restore its true "biopsychosocial" basis. . . . However, psychiatry has a special emphasis on the whole behaving person because attributes of illness implicate social (symbolic) behavior. . . . Even if a key lesion or biological marker were found for each psychiatric illness, the social and symbolic importance of psychiatric illness would not diminish because realizations of psychiatric illness have far different meanings and consequences in modern contemporary society than, for example, realizations of diabetes or pneumonia, because the core of the self is affected by them.[48]

Clearly, it is impossible to assess abnormal behavior merely through such procedures as urinalysis, CAT scans, or electroencephalograms . Alternatively, psychological tests such as the Rorschach Ink Blot Test and Thematic Apperception Test (TAT) only serve to examine a piece of the picture. And a sociological snapshot of the social stresses in people's lives is also just a contribution. Dealing with the *whole* person is the essence of the biopsychosocial perspective—an effort to integrate rival etiological theories of mental illness. It is a very useful general approach that recognizes biological, psychological, and sociological components of abnormal behavior. Some see it as an orientation rather than a theory.[49] In this respect, it is a multifaceted approach rather than a model bound by theory. Regardless of what it is called, it appears to be a wise idea which recognizes that mental illness is too complicated to be understood by one viewpoint alone. This is a good idea to keep in mind while moving through the pages of this book.

PLAN OF THE BOOK

The chapters in this book contain the research findings of those involved in the study of mental illness over the past 70 years or so. It is important to note that the studies reported here have not been selected simply to support a sociological perspective. That would be unfair to the reader, irrelevant to some aspects of mental illness, and a scientific disgrace. Certainly it is not uncommon for an author to overemphasize a favorite theory while ignoring other explanations that are just as valid. In the case of mental illness, however, a purely sociological explanation will not suffice any more than a purely medical or psychological approach. Mental illness is a multidimensional phenomenon that must be considered from a number of different perspectives. This book is an attempt to evaluate the strengths and weaknesses of all of the theories—an *eclectic* exercise that I believe is the most reasonable approach to a phenomenon as mysterious as mental illness presently is.

There are, however, some aspects of mental illness that must be considered from a sociocultural perspective. One important issue is the question, "What is mental illness?" This is a difficult question to answer objectively because of problems in terminology and cross-cultural differences in how abnormal behavior is defined. These issues, as well as an examination of the common definitions of mental illness, comprise the major topics of Chapter 2. Included is a discussion of the most recent terminology of the American Psychiatric Association. Chapter 3 specifically details all of the environmental theories of mental illness with a special emphasis on social stress theory.

The second part of the book deals with the symptoms and theoretical causes of some of the major types of mental illness. The research evidence favors different theories for different types of illness; for some illnesses, medical explanations may be most valid while other disorders appear more related to sociological forces. The fact is that the etiology of mental illness is a patchwork of limited findings and educated guesses. Chapters 4 through 6 organize and critique all of the etiological theories.

One aspect of mental illness that is clearly sociological is the distribution of mental illness among various social groups. If particular groups have noticeably high rates of mental illness, it can be assumed that certain social roles are more stressful than others. Are there differences between males and females? Are single people more impaired than married persons? Do members of various religious and ethnic groups have different rates of mental illness? How does migration affect mental health? Are such factors as age and sibling position related to psychological status? What is the relationship between social class position and mental illness? The research on these and other questions related to the social epidemiology of mental illness is presented in the third part (Chapters 7 through 11).

The fourth part of the book examines the ways in which social factors affect a person during and after the onset of mental illness. Psychiatric sociologists view this as a *process* in which the prospective patient follows a sequence of experiences that together make up "patienthood." The status of the mental patient is separated into three chronological components. The prepatient status, examined in Chapter 12, includes the subjective onset of pathological feelings, the reactions of family and friends, experiences associated with seeking help from physicians, ministers, and the like, as well as the psychiatric and legal aspects of formal evaluation before commitment.

Chapter 13 evaluates the role of the psychiatric inpatient with an eye toward the ways in which health care delivery systems affect the patient's chances for final recovery. Research evidence clearly suggests that the organizational structure of the hospital and the interpersonal relations between staff and patient can worsen and extend the patient's symptoms during hospitalization. This finding has led to a new movement in psychiatry, commonly known as *community psychiatry*, to treat people without hospitalizing them. The utility of both approaches is considered.

The third phase of the patient process is release from a hospital to rejoin the outside world. This is the nexus of Chapter 14, which demonstrates that patients' chances for permanent recovery are chiefly determined by the type of social climate to which they are returned. In a nutshell, the central feature of this climate is the presence or absence of negative, primitive, and stigmatizing attitudes toward mental patients among family members, employers, and significant others. These are the factors that are important determinants of the need for rehospitalization or the resumption of a meaningful life in the community.

Concepts, Definitions, and Types of Mental Illness

A Cross-Cultural Perspective

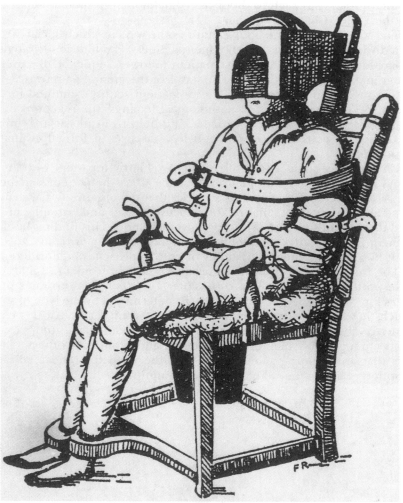

Benjamin Rush introduced reform treatment in the United States during the eighteenth century. Rush was a bit of a hypocrite, however, since some of his treatments involved bloodletting, terror tactics, and the "tranquilizer," a special chair in which patients were tied down and suspended upside down in midair. Small wonder his patients reported feeling different afterwards.

In many branches of medicine and science, few issues are involved in defining terms and reaching a consensus about causality, treatment, prognosis, and the like. Psychiatry is not like that at all. The world of mental illness is saturated with mysteries that run the gamut from causes to treatment. Included in these complex issues is the fundamental question of what separates mental illness from normal behavior. This chapter centers about that question and presents a multitude of arguments as to how mental illness should or should not be conceived.[1] One challenging goal in defining mental illness objectively is to include the ways by which culture shapes personality as well as the very ways in which "normality" is defined.[2] That is not the only challenge; there are legal, terminological, and diagnostic problems as well.

Before we tackle all of these complexities, let me point out that there are some "everyday" definitions of mental disorder that some people feel are useful, such as behavior that exceeds the tolerance of others. It is, for instance, all right to talk to God, but woe to the person who hears God talking back. Others view mental disorder as behavior that is inappropriate to the circumstances, such as laughing when a tragedy occurs. Still others feel the seriousness of the behavior separates the mentally disordered from people who are simply eccentric. Thus the person who babbles incoherently and walks naked in the street is seen in a different light than the old man who lives as a recluse. Of course, many people employ no definitions at all and indiscriminately label people as "weirdos," "nuts," "kooks," and "lunatics" (a term originally based on the idea that abnormal behavior was caused by lunar or astrological forces). These slang terms are still widely used in our so-called "enlightened" era.

INSANITY AND THE LAW

Psychiatry and the law are such worlds apart that they do not even speak the same language. Words such as "insanity," "grave disability," "due process," "mental competence," "involuntary commitment," and "mens rea" (guilty mind) are employed by the law. They are examples of what is known as *legalism* in the field of mental health. Thus we have codified two separate social processes that are at odds with one another: the legal rights of the courts and the rights of professionals to assess and treat mental illness.

Earlier, Jeffrey Dahmer, Gary Heidnik, and Ed Gein were mentioned. The violent acts of these people, and many others, have brought questions of *legal insanity* into the public limelight. But were these people actually mentally ill? This issue, central to the legal proceedings against many of them, has proved to be an area of particular confusion since it is difficult to render completely objective psychiatric diagnoses. As one University of Chicago law professor stated: "If your psychiatric labels aren't clear and the legal standards that you use to feed them into decisions are foggy, fog times fog equals fog squared."[3]

Laws are designed to separate criminal responsibility from criminal *non*responsibility.[4] Criminal responsibility is based on criminal intent, literally having a "guilty mind." This concept, known as *mens rea,* is a combination of willful malevolence and a comprehension of wrongdoing. Criminal *non*responsibility, on the other hand, involves two broad categories: immaturity and insanity. The immaturity concept is relatively straightforward, as in the case of a minor or a mentally retarded individual, people who, because of their chronological or "mental" age, are presumed to be unable to appreciate the nature of an illegal act. The term *insanity* applies to those rare cases of mental disorganization or irresistible impulse that can absolve a person from criminal responsibility. Insanity is a legal concept that has no technical status in psychiatry.

It is used most often to refer to persons who suffer from *psychosis,* a severe mental disorder involving loss of contact with reality. There are many different criteria for insanity. Many of them were established in the 1800s and still are used in different states today. I discuss some of them below.

Irresistible Impulse

In 1834, an Ohio court ruled that a pathological impulse could drive an otherwise competent person to commit a crime despite that person's comprehension of right and wrong. The impulse must be so great that the person would be driven to follow it even if a policeman were present. This could occur, for instance, when an individual is overwhelmed by a seizure-like fit of murderous rage caused by a brain abnormality.

The *irresistible impulse* criterion is rarely used today because of the difficulty of objectively ascertaining the difference between an irresistible impulse and an impulse not resisted due to culpable self-indulgence. In the case of a crime committed by something as obviously organic as a seizure, however, a defendant is likely to be exonerated.

M'Naghten Rule

One law designed to separate insane people who commit criminal acts from mentally competent people who do so is the widely used *M'Naghten rule.* It provides that a person may establish a defense of insanity if the person did not know he or she was doing something wrong in the eyes of society at the time of the offense.

The M'Naghten rule stems from an 1843 case in England involving a Scotsman named Daniel M'Naghten who was accused of killing Edward Drummond, secretary to Sir Robert Peel, the Tory prime minister of England. (For what it is worth, M'Naghten was a bad aim. He was shooting at Peel and hit Drummond instead.) Driven by the delusion that Tories were tormenting and endangering him, nine physicians testified that M'Naghten was "insane." Queen Victoria, enraged by the decision, set up a commission of 15 judges to review the case. Their deliberations produced the so-called M'Naghten rule, which provides that at least one of two criteria must be met to establish insanity: First, there must be confusion as to the nature of the act (shooting a person believing it is a rat) and, second, not being able to appreciate the wrongfulness of the act. Ironically, M'Naghten himself would probably have been judged guilty under the M'Naghten rule itself.

One of the problems with the "right-wrong" approach of the M'Naghten rule is that there are many people who suffer from mental disorder and realize that they are doing something wrong. Their problem is they do not care because they lack a conscience. Because of the decision-making process underlying the M'Naghten rule, they are sent to prison rather than a psychiatric facility where they might be helped. However, since research shows that people without a conscience can rarely be rehabilitated, some professionals feel that it may not really matter where they are sent. Our own research uncovered this depressing fact about "sexual predators."[5]

Durham Product Rule

In response to criticisms of the irresistible impulse and M'Naghten rules, the U.S. Court of Appeals forged a new rule in *Durham* v. *United States* in 1954. The court stated that "an accused is not criminally responsible if his unlawful act was the product of mental disease or defect."[6] Although it was designed to encourage maximum use of psychiatric testimony, it got bogged down in the ambiguity of terms like "mental disease" and "product." This made guilt or innocence hinge too much on the definitional whims of psychiatrists.[7]

American Law Institute Rule

In the late 1960s and early '70s, many jurisdictions adopted the American Law Institute (ALI) formulation of the insanity defense. It states that "a person is not responsible for criminal conduct if at the time of such conduct as a result of mental disease or defect he lacks substantial capacity to appreciate the criminality (wrongfulness of his conduct) or to conform his conduct to the requirements of the law."[8] The ALI further modifies mental disease or defect with the caveat "the terms 'mental disease or defect' do not include an abnormality manifested only by repeated criminal or otherwise antisocial conduct."

The *ALI rule* essentially liberalized the standards for establishing insanity while encompassing major components from earlier rulings. Irresistible impulse is reflected in the "conformity of conduct" criterion. M'Naghten is represented in the "appreciation of criminality"(wrongfulness) criterion and the "mental disease or defect" criterion ties in with *Durham*.

Widely publicized trials of defendants who plead the insanity defense—for example, John Hinckley, the would-be assassin of President Reagan, and serial murderer Jeffrey Dahmer—rivet the public's attention on the question of whether mental illness should be an "excuse" from punishment for crime. There is also the related concern that mental hospitals are being used as repositories for dangerous persons who cannot be cured, as well as the question of when the state must release a person confined to a psychiatric facility after being found not guilty by reason of insanity.[9] These are valid concerns, but others are not. John Hinckley, for example, successfully pleaded insanity and was sent to a mental hospital. Because the case was widely publicized, the public received the subjective impression that criminals frequently avoid jail through an insanity defense. The objective truth is that the insanity defense is rarely employed, and, when it is, it usually does not work. As one expert puts it, "The insanity defense is not an easy way to get clients off. Rather, it is a complicated defense that is seldom successful and is likely to result in a client spending significant time in a mental institution."[10]

In recent years, the insanity defense has veered far from the stereotype of guilty people literally getting away with murder. As legislators, juries, prosecutors and the public at large have grown increasingly impatient with violent crime, some states have rewritten their insanity laws to severely limit the use of the defense.[11]

TERMINOLOGICAL ISSUES

Some people feel that art outweighs science in any attempt to accurately classify and diagnose mental illness.[12] Because people are infinitely variable, the argument goes, diagnosis is fruitless and classification is difficult. Even the meaning of the term "diagnosis" is the subject of debate, since in many societies a psychiatric diagnosis has both legal and political significance. In the former, it may be a reason why someone is judged disabled and found eligible for welfare support. In the latter, it may alter a person's civil rights and responsibilities.[13] Thus psychiatry and the law clash again.

There are even differences in the meaning of "person" in different societies around the world.[14] Broadly speaking, the Western self is more autonomous and differentiated, and the Eastern self is more relational and interdependent. All of these complexities, however, have not stopped attempts to apply scientific methods to psychiatric *nosology* (classification). Basically, there are two predominant forms of psychiatric nosology—"the great professor principle" and "the consensus of experts." The great professor approach includes notable figures (Pinel, Freud, Bleuler) who developed their own particular classification systems. Today, however, there is an almost total reliance on the consensus of experts who formulate psychiatric criteria in committees of professional organizations.

The consensus of experts' approach has been used extensively in the United States, largely through the efforts of numerous committees and subcommittees regulated by the American Psychiatric Association (APA). Still there is controversy because advancing knowledge often complicates rather than simplifies an understanding of mental health and illness. The problem of the effect of personal values on diagnoses as well as terminological issues are together responsible for leaving the scientific concept of mental illness in a shaky condition. Indeed, at meetings of some of the leading American psychiatrists, sociologists, and anthropologists, the question, "What is mental illness?" is often received in silence. Some contend that mental illness is a mythical notion and cannot be satisfactorily defined. Others reply that such a position is ridiculous because disordered people can be clearly recognized. By any standard, psychiatric evaluation is not simple. Thus it is no mere accident that much of the psychiatric literature plainly skirts the definitional issue.

Mental illness cannot be approached in the same way as an illness of the body. The mind is an abstract concept, not a physical entity. Consequently there exists a qualitative difference between the subject matter of psychiatry and general medicine. Psychiatry investigates the origin and treatment of abnormal behavior, something that cannot be measured in objective, quantitative terms as physicians approach the study of physical sicknesses. Simply stated, mental illness is an invincibly obscure concept. As Sir Aubrey Lewis, the eminent British psychiatrist, pointed out, attempts to define mental illness use a host of terms, undefinable in themselves: lack of joy of life, no will to live, discontentment, inability to adjust, and so forth.[15] The very terms used to define mental illness are vague, thus creating a thicket of difficulties. One such difficulty is with the use of the term "illness," a term that perpetuates the belief that mental abnormality stems from physical ailments as exemplified by the following syllogism:

- Behavior disorders are mental illnesses.
- Only physicians should treat illnesses.
- Therefore only physicians should treat behavior disorders.

The logic is impeccable; nevertheless the conclusion is false because in the major premise "illness" is used literally when it should be used metaphorically. The term "mental disorder" is also problematic because it is employed in a multiplicity of senses. To some it is synonymous with mental illness. Others, however, distinguish between mental illness and mental disorder. They treat mental disorder as covering the whole range of abnormal conditions of the mind, including both states of psychological disorder and mental retardation, while they view mental illness as synonymous with mental retardation only. The terms continue to be used because no others convey a similar meaning to most readers. Rather than get lost in myriad possible meanings, the following terms are used interchangeably throughout this book: mental illness, mental disorder, psychopathology, psychological disorder, and abnormal behavior. They are used interchangeably by many psychiatric researchers as well.

CROSS-CULTURAL ISSUES

In 1999, a novel clash occurred between psychiatry and the law when a black man accused of bank robbery claimed he was innocent by reason of "cultural insanity" caused by longtime exposure to racism. It came as no surprise that the defense did not work, but the case did put the role of cultural factors in the legal limelight.

Many "models" of mental illness fail to include cultural variables in their equations. That is a mistake since biological, psychological, sociological, and cultural variables are interdependent and cannot be understood apart from one another. These connections are so important that a specific discipline has emerged within anthropology to examine the impact of culture on psychiatric issues.[16] Known alternatively as *cross-cultural psychiatry* or *psychiatric anthropology,* the discipline has gathered some provocative reports on how the symptoms, causes, diagnoses, course, outcome, and epidemiology of mental illness vary around the world.[17] Indeed, some contend that any theory of mental illness that does not account for the role of culture is a theory anchored by tunnel vision.[18]

Psychiatric signs and symptoms are partly shaped by a person's behavior and experience. Because these in turn are partly shaped by culture, it is not surprising that the very process of diagnosis is different around the world. British and American psychiatrists often render different diagnoses of the same essential symptoms. The British, for example, are predisposed to diagnose depression while their American counterparts are more likely to diagnose schizophrenia.[19] Additionally, culture affects such psychiatric phenomena as paranoid delusions of persecution.[20] Culture may even affect a person's biochemistry inasmuch as sociocultural stressors, such as deprivation, conflict, and confusion, can have an impact on hormones and neurotransmitters.[21]

Standards of mental illness are also relative *within* a culture because the social context in which a particular behavior occurs affects whether it is adjudged normal or abnormal. Depending upon the situation, the same behavior may be considered mentally ill, criminal, or even socially acceptable. For example, an adolescent who sets fires may seek psychiatric help, be labeled mentally ill, and receive psychotherapy. The same individual may have encountered the police, be labeled a juvenile delinquent, and be jailed.

Moreover, behavior that is usually considered abnormal may be accepted and even admired under certain circumstances. Examples of this are hallucinatory behavior in an LSD session or the production of unintelligible speech in a church in which speaking in tongues is common. Such practices as not wearing clothes, handling poisonous snakes, and even suicide are often positively sanctioned and honored by members of certain groups. The seventeenth-century religious leaders who had witches and heretics burned at the stake were considered respected members of the community, but today they would be committed to an institution. A sexually promiscuous woman is called a whore or a nymphomaniac, but the sexually active male is lauded for his "talent" with females and considered to be a real "stud." The list goes on.

Back to cross-cultural differences. In the United States, political dissent is often praised, but in the former Soviet Union many dissenters were sent to insane asylums. These included poets, writers, and intellectuals who would be highly revered in the West. Thinness provides another example of cross-cultural differences in acceptable appearance. The cultural preoccupation with thinness in the United States, for example, is far removed from cultures where fat is revered, although anorexia is spreading throughout parts of Eastern culture as well.[22]

CULTURE-BOUND SYNDROMES

There are numerous reports that a number of mental illnesses are found among a certain people of the world and nowhere else. Thus they are referred to as *culture-bound* or *culture-specific*. Some observers suggest that certain syndromes are considered culture-bound only because they are non-Western and hence more visibly influenced by culture than their Western counterparts.[23] Whatever the case may be, they certainly appear to be rare, exotic, and perhaps unclassifiable. It is interesting that these disorders are found more frequently among women in a number of societies. Below are brief descriptions of 11 such syndromes. Some of the names are well established in the literature. In one instance (Bena Bena syndrome), I took the liberty of applying my own label.

Spirit Possession

There are many examples of this phenomenon, including the belief among Liberians that they are possessed by a spirit called Mammy Water, and the notion among many Caribbean peoples that they may be possessed by any one of a host of gods. Possession syndrome is also reported throughout the lower castes in India.[24] Anthropologists report very specific forms of this condition, forms found only in tiny parts of the world. This is true in the case of *vimbuza*, which is specific to Malawi, Africa.[25]

Evil Eye

Closely related to spirit possession is a phenomenon that occurs in Algeria. The symptoms include an indifference to one's social environment such as social withdrawal or general loss of interest in other people. The "evil eye" is a precipitating factor that is used as a punishment against anybody who is perceived as overwhelming in wealth, health, beauty, and happiness. It is usually motivated by jealousy, but the "eye" may also be cast by an admiring enemy or friend.[26] A similar preoccupation with evil eye, black magic, and the like is found among Mexican Americans. Known as *susto*, it is characterized by irritability, insomnia, reduced libido, retardation, nightmare, diarrhea, and vomiting.[27]

Amok

Also referred to as *running amok,* the term *amok* is a Malaysian word meaning "to engage furiously in battle." Although it was traditionally associated with Malaya, it has also been reported in Africa, Laos, Thailand, New Guinea, and the Philippines.[28] It occurs in people who go berserk with little or no warning and for no apparent reason. Amok is a highly violent frenzied state in which the individual runs around aimlessly with a weapon and kills people or animals. Typically, the perpetrator is killed by others or kills himself.[29] Those captured alive are exhausted and claim no memory of the killing.[30]

Investigators describe a characteristic psychosocial profile of individuals who have run amok.[31] They are usually young or middle-aged men living away from home who have recently suffered a loss or an insult or have otherwise "lost face." They are often quiet, withdrawn individuals from a low socioeconomic background who are in, or recently discharged from, the military. The perpetrator (*pengamok*) is theorized to display distraught behavior by acting against others rather than himself because he comes from a culture that uses shame rather than guilt to maintain conformity.[32]

Although amok has been identified with similar syndromes in other parts of the world, it clearly became the most terroristic disorder in Laos, where grenades became the weapon of choice in the 1960s. The first case of "grenade-amok" occurred in 1959 at a religious festival known as *boun*. After this event, the number of incidents gradually increased, peaking at 20 reported episodes in 1966.[33] The frequency of grenade-amok has gradually decreased, although it still occurs in places like Thailand and the Philippines, particularly during episodes of social upheaval. Amok in the Philippines has also involved the use of other "nontraditional" weapons—automatic guns.

Amok does not always take the form of what American psychiatrists would call "isolated explosive disorder," as in the case of the disgruntled postal worker. It has occurred as an epidemic in a number of countries, a fact that underscores the importance of shared cultural beliefs in the genesis of the syndrome.

Latah

Latah is the term for a Malay condition involving compulsive obscenity precipitated by sudden fright.[34] A similar condition is reported among older women of the Ainu of Japan, where it is known as *imu*. It is frequently triggered by a sudden stimulus, such as loud noises or highly feared objects, including snakes, caterpillars, and snails. Wild, aggressive behavior results, followed by running away in panic. There is occasional loss of consciousness and the person often experiences considerable embarrassment upon recovery.[35]

Bena Bena Syndrome

Among the Bena Bena people of the Eastern Highlands of New Guinea, men are affected by daylong episodes during which they become deaf and aggressive toward clanspeople, including their wives and children. They run about randomly in circles and wield clubs and arrows in threatening gestures. Speaking is rare during these attacks. The episodes are quickly forgotten, and there is no social censure. The Bena Bena believe the attacks are the work of malevolent ghosts, who are the objects of intense fear.[36]

Pibloktoq

Also known as *Arctic hysteria,* this syndrome is reported among the polar Eskimos of the Thule district of northern Greenland. It follows a classic four-stage sequence. In the first stage, the victim is irritable and socially withdrawn. The onset of the second stage is sudden; victims become wildly excited with bloodshot eyes, foaming mouths, and elevated blood pressure. They may tear off clothing, break furniture, attempt to walk on ceilings, shout obscenities, throw objects, eat feces, or perform other irrational acts such as plunging into snowdrifts or jumping off icebergs. This excitement is followed by a third stage characterized by convulsive seizures, collapse, and stuporous sleep or coma lasting for up to 12 hours. In the final stage, the victim behaves perfectly normal and has complete amnesia regarding the experience.[37] As with latah, it occurs most frequently among women.

Windigo Psychosis

Also called the *whitiko psychosis,* windigo psychosis occurs among the Ojibwa Indians of the northeastern United States and Canada. It usually follows a failure in hunting. Victims believe they are possessed by the spirit of the whitiko monster, a huge skeleton of ice that devours humans. Symptoms involve depression, a distaste for food, nausea, and periods of semistupor. They become obsessed with the idea of being possessed by the spirit and are subject to homicidal and/or suicidal thoughts. They perceive those around them as fat, appetizing animals who they wish to eat. This condition may finally reach a state of homicidal cannibalism since the Objibwa believe that a craving for human flesh will never leave once it has been fulfilled.[38] Thus the victims are killed before they eat others.

Ataque

This peculiar group of disordered reactions to minor stress is reported in Puerto Rico. The behavior includes outbursts of verbal and physical hostility, regression to infantile behavior, forgetfulness, and loss of interest in personal appearance. It may also include hallucinations, screaming, self-mutilation, and mutism.[39] Generally, the episode may last only minutes. Physicians describe the outbursts this way: "The most outstanding reaction pattern is characterized by a transient state of partial loss of consciousness, most frequently accompanied by convulsive movements, hyperventilation, moaning and groaning, profuse salivation, and aggressiveness to self or to others in the form of biting, scratching, or striking, and of sudden onset and termination."[40]

Koro

This culturally specific disorder occurs among Cantonese males. It is also known as *shook yang.* According to Yap, koro is "an acute anxiety state with partial depersonalization leading to the conviction of penile shrinkage and to fears of dissolution."[41] This exotic disorder is connected with the Chinese belief that masturbation and nocturnal emission from erotic dreams prevent the normal change in yin and yang humors that accompanies sexual maturation. This causes an unbalanced loss of the yang-producing koro, and the person fears his penis is shrinking and will disappear into his abdomen, thereby producing death.

Bouffées Délirantes

Bouffées délirantes is found among Haitian peasants. It is a confused state of mind that often deteriorates into schizophrenia.[42] Native priests interpret the illness as a form of possession caused by an unwillingness to accept the call of the voodoo gods to join the voodoo church. Consistently, the recommended treatment is to attend services. The association of mental illness and supernatural powers in foreign cultures is not unusual. Portuguese immigrants (mostly uneducated) to the United States ascribe their abnormalities to the evil eye, encounters with sorcery, spiritual possession, or the devil.[43]

Magnan, a French physician, reported bouffées délirantes in former French colonies in North Africa, "black Africa,"[44] and in African immigrants in France.[45] It is interesting how many radically different forms of behavior have been dubbed bouffées délirantes. One type is "nuptial psychosis," which occurs after the wedding night as a result of the stresses involved in an arranged marriage. It is usually experienced by the bride.[46]

Falling Out

Griffith noted this condition among African Americans.[47] It is also called *blacking out* by Bahamians and *indisposition* by Haitians in Miami. Those who manifest this illness often simply collapse but without biting the tongue or losing bowel or bladder control. They are not able to speak or move, even though they hear and allegedly understand.

All of the illnesses reported here exemplify culturally specific manifestations of psychological disorder, but they do not necessarily differ from one another in causal origin. Langness has convincingly argued that a majority of the "strange" mental illnesses reported by anthropologists are all cases of hysteria.[48] The different symptoms simply manifest culturally conditioned modes of expression and belief systems, although the psychiatric origins and processes are the same.[49] There is a growing opinion among those who have researched mental illness in preliterate or non-Western cultures that the same types of illnesses are found in all cultures; only the symptoms and distribution vary.[50]

It is my opinion as well that a psychiatric equivalence underlies these externally unrelated types of illness. The dramatic nature of these disorders has simply distracted attention from the underlying psychopathology. The syndromes actually exemplify the ways in which disordered people in specific cultures conform to the behavioral patterns that that culture expects and encourages. They are, therefore, nothing more than *culturally recognized and accepted ways of becoming mentally ill.* This position is strengthened by evidence demonstrating that people from different cultures may not exhibit the same symptoms even though they are known to have the same disorder. For example, Mexicans are reported to have more severe symptoms than Americans who have an equivalent psychopathology and are at the same socioeconomic level.[51]

In addition, compared to schizophrenics from other cultures, Indian schizophrenics are usually withdrawn and rigid, an assumed reflection of their formal, hierarchical culture, which fosters introversion and emotional control. Even within the same society, the nature of the symptoms can differ sharply among people of various ethnic backgrounds. Irish American male schizophrenics, for example, are typically quiet and withdrawn whereas their Italian American counterparts are often loud and aggressive.[52]

WORLD PATTERNS

Are there forms of mental illness that exist in every society, or does culture have such a profound impact that no illness appears worldwide? While many disorders occur in only certain parts of the world, there are some that are found everywhere. These include organic brain disorders (such as epilepsy), schizophrenia, manic-depression (bipolar disorder), major depression, and a group of anxiety disorders such as obsessive-compulsive disorder, panic anxiety, and certain phobias.[53]

A number of studies report that schizophrenia is a cross-cultural universal.[54] The lifetime risk for schizophrenia is just over 1 percent around the world. This indicates that it is by no means a rare illness. In fact, in different populations of people and at any given point in time, at least 5 out of every 1,000 adults meet the clinical diagnostic criteria for schizophrenia. And they are just the ones who are visible.

To date, no population, demographic group, or culture has been known to be free of schizophrenia. That is the consistent part of the illness. Beyond that, there are some interesting cross-cultural variations in the type, onset, and outcome of schizophrenia. In the case of type, there are more diagnoses of catatonia (body rigidity) in developing countries like India, yet hardly any catatonics in Western Europe or North America. Schizophrenics in developing countries are also more likely to hear voices and experience visual hallucinations. The disorder is also more likely to have a rapid onset in less developed places like Nigeria or China than in the United States.[55]

A truly baffling finding has emerged that runs counter to conventional psychiatric reasoning. The course of schizophrenia is better for patients in the less developed societies and worse for those in the most advanced industrial societies! Why would the outcome be better in countries with fewer (or no) psychiatric facilities? Perhaps the research is flawed. Perhaps mental hospitals really do make people worse. One interesting hypothesis is that, where schizophrenia is popularly viewed as an acute problem, people are expected to recover just like those who suffer from other acute disorders such as influenza.[56] But how can that theory apply if schizophrenia is really a brain disorder? It may be that schizophrenia is more than a brain disorder and is actually influenced by different degrees of family support.

Depression is another complex and multiform phenomenon that can range from a basic human experience to a serious psychiatric disorder. Depressive disorders have been found in virtually all areas of the world where they have been searched. Their form, however, has an interesting connection with culture. One common depressive syndrome consists of sadness, disturbed sleep, fatigue, and feelings of emptiness in life. Another type of depression, mania, appears to be the exact opposite; hyperactivity, excessive talking, and grandiose delusions are some of the core symptoms of mania.

A number of studies of the transcultural aspects of depressive disorders report that mania is more common in underdeveloped societies such as some countries in Africa. Researchers refer to this as the "primitive" pattern.[57] It is in sharp contrast to the typical depressive pattern reported more frequently in Western cultures where guilt (Judeo-Christian influence?), worthlessness, and suicidal ideas are more common.[58]

What about suicide itself? Does it show much variation around the world? Take a look at Figure 2:1 and you will see an enormous difference in the suicide rate among cultures. Many of the countries with the highest suicide rates have typically undergone long periods of civil and economic upheaval.

It is especially interesting how patterns of mental illness are influenced by culture in the case of neighboring societies. In Northern Ireland, for instance, admissions to psychiatric hospitals are much higher than in England and Scotland.[59] This suggests that political violence is taking its toll on mental health. However, things are not all that jolly in British culture where, strangely enough, half of all bereaved people experience hallucinations of the dead person for years after the loss.[60]

In 2000, I had the opportunity to lecture in Ireland and Holland about new research in schizophrenia. In the process, I learned quite a bit about the mental health systems of the two countries as well. In Holland, there is a very progressive sys-

Figure 2:1   The prevalence of suicide around the world: countries with excessive rates.

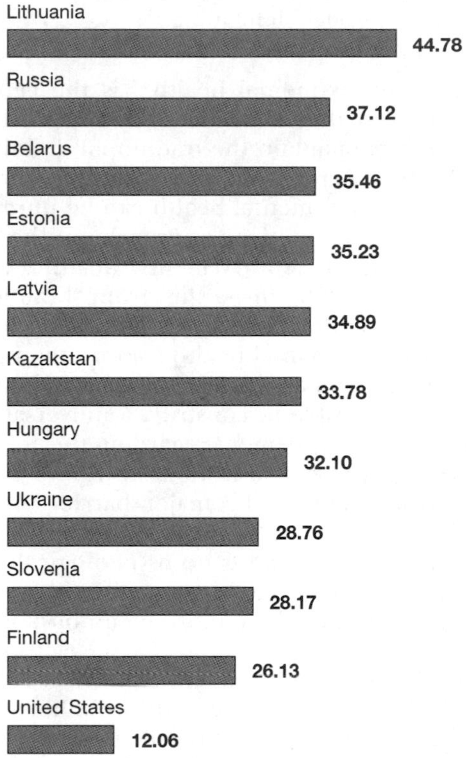

Suicide rates are based on the number of people who take their own lives per 100,000 members of the population.

Source: World Health Organization, 1998.

tem of research and treatment of mental illness.[61] Ireland, for as beautiful as its people are, is in bad shape. In fact, I arrived at the very time when the Inspector of Mental Hospitals issued a scathing report on the conditions of mental institutions.[62] Included in the report were case histories of people who had been involuntarily committed for decades by relatives seeking their land. Some of those who had been committed were not mentally ill, just unfortunate to have such manipulative kin. It reminded me of the "dungeon days" of centuries ago.

ALTERNATIVE DEFINITIONS OF MENTAL HEALTH

Culture can have an enormous impact on whether some forms of behavior are viewed as normal or deviant. There are both remarkable differences and similarities in the descriptions of mental health across cultures. As one team of authors put it:

> Cultures vary in their ideas about the relationship between mind and body and, hence, in their beliefs about the degree to which physiological processes are related to mental processes. Cultures also vary in the degree to which abnormal behavior is explained as the

result of inner- or outer-directed forces. In some cultures demons or ghosts or germs can invade individuals and cause their symptoms while in other cultures individuals bring on their own symptoms through sinful living.[63]

The question "What is mental health?" is the center of much debate in the United States and around the world. The continental European and Scandinavian approaches, for example, maintain the traditional definition established by Kraeplin in the nineteenth century. Actually the Kraeplin orientation is a number of definitions based on the assumption that mental health can be unraveled in various ways to produce different illnesses. The American approach, on the other hand, has shifted over time. Earlier in the twentieth century mental health was viewed as a state of mind. Today it is viewed as a state of brain—a shift from "brainless" psychiatry to "mindless" psychiatry.[64] Although it is difficult to say which definition is more accurate, it is a fact that a therapist's concept of mental health is more than philosophically important; it can have a profound effect on a patient's outcome as well.[65]

At present, it is impossible to construct a universal definition of mental health because there is so much disagreement regarding the components of "normal" behavior. As stated earlier, what is viewed as normal in one cultural context may be quite unacceptable in another. This is the major barrier to objectively defining mental health, although it is by no means the only obstacle. Every attempt to define mental health has failed because "there exists no psychologically meaningful and . . . operationally useful description of what is commonly understood to constitute mental health."[66] Following are some of the more common approaches to defining mental health.

From a medical perspective, mental health is a condition in which *parts of the brain are not malfunctioning*. The brain comprises billions of nerve cells, called *neurons* and thousands of billions of support cells called *glia*. Within the brain large groups of neurons form anatomically distinct areas (*brain regions*) and so on. The medical view contends that a malfunctioning brain is the primary cause of mental illness. As we will see in later chapters, a biological approach may be especially relevant to severe illnesses such as schizophrenia, but it fails to account for pathological states of *mind* that produce problems such as psychosexual disorders.

One of the earlier approaches simply viewed mental health as *the absence of mental disorder*. This perspective is limited for two reasons. First, while most would agree that the absence of psychopathology is a necessary condition for mental health, one must still define mental illness in order to understand, by contrast, mental health! Second, this approach fails to take into account cross-cultural differences in acceptable behavior. For example, is homosexuality to be viewed as an abnormality or as a lifestyle? It was a widely accepted lifestyle among the early Greeks, and it has gained acceptability among many people in the United States today. But these views contrast sharply with attitudes predominant among nineteenth-century Europeans, who viewed homosexuality in a number of negative ways ranging from "hereditary inferiority" to the result of "masturbatory insanity."[67] So, depending on the cultural assumptions of the evaluator, the same behavior can be viewed as normal, even laudable, or it can be viewed as perverted.

A third definition of mental health holds that a *correct perception of reality* is the key to mental health. In view of the cross-cultural variations in social norms, this approach holds little promise. What is "correct" depends on the way in which a given people perceive the world. For example, the Kwakuitl Indians of British Columbia have a perception of the world that American psychiatrists would diagnose as paranoid delusions of grandeur.[68] And the Buddhist self-absorptions of esteemed mystics in India are clinically equivalent to the withdrawn type of schizophrenia Western psychiatry has dubbed catatonia.[69]

These problems are often skirted by specifying that the correct perception of reality is the opinion of the "average person," but this fosters a belief in the "average" as correct and the "exceptional" as incorrect. The concept of averaging is simply unsatisfactory in defining mental health because one is then faced with a further definitional problem: "Who is average?" There are countless cases in modern society in which the opinion of a majority of people has not been linked with correctness but with ungrounded and pathological beliefs. The racist ideology of the southern states in the twentieth century and in Nazi Germany are cases in point. Conversely, the view of the uncommon as pathological is even less viable since it logically includes the great achievements of individuals and people with outstanding IQs.

A fourth criterion of mental health hinges on the concept of *adjustment to the environment,* which is generally taken to mean that a person has established a workable arrangement between personal needs and social relations. The absence of such an arrangement is a definite counterindication of mental health, to be sure. After all, mental stability cannot be enjoyed by a person who is hostile toward the everyday world.

In this sense the "adjustment" definition is useful in separating some obviously abnormal people from the rest of the population. But this approach would include some mentally ill people in the normal category since adjustment to one's environment is not always desirable. Some people are adjusted to a pathological environment such as that fostered by maternal deprivation, intrafamilial disharmony, or social isolation. The individual who adjusts to these conditions must do so at considerable psychological cost. This would be true in the case of people raised by abusive alcoholic parents. We would expect them to become adults with a sense of vengeance. This is exactly what happened to convicted serial murderer John Wayne Gacy. Such a view of mental health denies that life circumstances are better or worse and would dangerously conclude that passive acceptance of all environmental conditions constitutes mental health. Without specifying which environmental conditions are considered to be pathological, the "adjustment" definition suffers the same limitations as the "correct perception of reality" approach.

The psychoanalytic definition of mental health is an interesting formula that focuses on the state of the *self*.[70] Specifically, psychoanalysts believe that the mentally healthy person is in a state of *intrapsychic equilibrium,* one that is free from conflicts among its three constituent parts: id, ego, and superego. The person whose personality is integrated is not dominated by any one part. Thus only sensualists (id-dominated types), moralists (superego-dominated types), and those with rigid, nonadaptive egos are viewed as mentally disordered.[71] Those who do suffer from an intrapsychic imbalance are considered to have gained their health if the energies of the id become more mobile, the superego becomes more tolerant, and the ego becomes free from anxiety and its integrative function restored.

This is a particularly useful approach to the problem of defining mental health, but unfortunately it too has a shortcoming. There are some mentally ill people whose personalities are unified but whose view of reality is distorted and highly individualistic. This is true of many schizophrenics who are self-regulated and unified but live in a fantasy world that is radically different from the world of others.

A malfunctioning brain, absence of mental disorder, correct perception of reality, adjustment to one's environment, and intrapsychic equilibrium are the ideas that most frequently appear in attempts to delineate mental health and illness. Different theoreticians stress different aspects of mental health. But after all the verbiage has been sifted, certain themes recur: personal happiness, interpersonal adjustment, and ability to adapt to change. All of these criteria, however, are impossible to assess objectively, particularly on a cross-cultural level. Many of these themes express only the personal value judgments of their authors rather than scientifically established facts.

Of course, extreme cases do not cause difficulty when it comes to defining mental illness, as in the case of "the old man who no longer knows where he is, does not recognize his wife and children, and in his nightgown runs into the street to go to 'his' store which he had sold twenty years ago—this man, everybody will concede, is ill and needs protection."[72] But a large proportion of questionable behavior is not as overtly disordered as the behavior of this hallucinatory old man. It is these less extreme cases that pose the real challenge to objective diagnosis.

As stated earlier, there is currently a *medicalization* of mental disorder. That is, mental illness is a medical problem that should be treated by physicians only. This is partly a reflection of the inordinate political power the medical profession has to define its own area of responsibility. Alternative professions, such as clinical psychology and psychiatric social work, are not taken as seriously.

Another reason for the medicalization of mental health problems is the failure of social approaches to mental health care, such as community-based mental health clinics. As we will see later, the medical approach has provided some important discoveries about the causes and treatment of mental disorder. However, because it is a one-sided approach, it hinders an awareness of how social *and* psychological forces influence mental health. This is evident in an alarming increase in conservative definitions of mental disorder—a growing biological orientation that centers around physiological and genetic factors. At a time when psychiatric research is still in the dark regarding the real nature of mental disorder, any such unilateral view like the medical model can seriously impede progress. What we need today is a concept of mental illness that integrates the complex links between medical and environmental factors.[73]

Perhaps the "checklist" approach of the famous Menninger psychiatric research institute in Kansas is a useful guide to assessing mental health. The Menninger Clinic lists "criteria of emotional maturity." They include the ability to deal constructively with reality; the capacity to adapt to change; freedom from symptoms that are produced by anxieties; the capacity to find more satisfaction in giving than receiving; the capacity to relate to other people in a consistent manner with mutual satisfaction; the capacity to direct one's instinctive hostile energy into creative and constructive outlets; and the capacity to love.

THE RELIABILITY OF PSYCHIATRIC DIAGNOSIS

I asked Mr. Smith how I could help, and he told me: "I have seen four different people and gotten four different explanations for my panic attacks, so I came to you to find out who is right and who is wrong." He had had the symptoms for two years. At first he thought it might be his heart, so he consulted his family doctor, who found no heart problem and recommended a psychoanalyst. Mr. Smith believed that the analyst had helped him to understand himself better, but he became discouraged when the panic attacks were no better after six months. He went to a behavior therapist, who told him that the problem had nothing to do with the unconscious but resulted from conditioning that could be helped by relaxation training. That didn't work either, so he consulted a family therapist. This time he heard that the panic attacks resulted neither from sexual wishes nor from conditioned anxiety but from conflicts in his marriage. The therapy improved his marriage, but the panic attacks continued so he went to an anxiety clinic at a nearby university. There a psychiatrist told him that the symptoms resulted from a brain disorder of genetic origin and should be treated with medications. Mr. Smith said, "I will take the medicine if it will help, but before I do, I want to see if I can find two psychiatrists who say the same thing. It sure seems like none of you know what you are doing."[74]

The problems with defining mental illness become especially apparent when a mental health professional attempts to render a valid diagnosis and prescribe treatment. This is not always a smooth process, as is evident in the case of the highly frustrated "Mr. Smith." That is one reason why the American Psychiatric Association (APA) is regularly setting forth guidelines for diagnosing mental disorders, known secularly as the *Diagnostic and Statistical Manual of Mental Disorders*, or DSM. In the mid-1990s, the fourth edition—DSM-IV—was published. Although there are rumblings of discontent from some researchers and clinicians who are faced with these "biblical" rewrites every half-dozen years, the goal of objectivity is certainly legitimate. DSM also has an added practical importance because its diagnoses are often required by government and private insurers that pay for psychotherapy and other mental health services. Presently there is speculation as to the contents of the next DSM and what psychiatry in general will be like in the new millennium.[75]

DSM or no DSM, psychiatric diagnosis remains a difficult problem for a number of reasons. Prejudice is one. Black patients, for example, are especially likely to be overdiagnosed in some categories and underdiagnosed in others.[76] In fact, a white psychiatrist may attach different pathological significance to the same behavior in black and white patients. Gender also influences a psychiatrist's diagnosis.[77] So does a patient's obesity.[78] If you factor in cross-cultural differences in psychiatric training and orientation, diagnosis becomes a crap shoot. The American-British contrast mentioned earlier and later in this chapter is one blatant case in point.[79]

There is also a close relationship among social norms, diagnostic categories, and politics. Take the case of "self-defeating personality disorder." Proposed as a new diagnosis for inclusion in the DSM in 1984, it is characterized by involvement in abusive relationships and avoidance of success. The diagnosis never made it to the DSM because the APA Committee on Women strongly contested it on the basis that the diagnosis would be applied differently to men and women. A main concern was that it could be misused as a way of blaming women for being victims of marital abuse and other types of violence.

Early studies indicated that psychiatrists frequently disagree with each other regarding patients' (and pseudopatients') diagnoses. During World War II it became apparent that it is not always possible to distinguish normal persons from mentally ill ones, as indicated by an overwhelming lack of success with psychiatric screening.[80] In 1949, Ash ran an experiment in which normal persons and mental patients were presented to a group of psychiatric diagnosticians for their evaluation. In that study, the diagnosticians agreed with each other only 45.7 percent of the time.[81] Since then, other investigators have confirmed that psychiatrists disagree with one another much more than is commonly recognized.[82] This has led some to conclude that art outweighs science in ascertaining the presence or absence of mental illness.

Further evidence for the unreliability of psychiatric diagnosis comes from cross-cultural studies. For instance, a much higher proportion of schizophrenia compared to manic-depressive psychosis is found among hospitalized patients in the United States than in England. Consequently, it was generally assumed that the two cultures predispose their members to different types of psychotic breakdown. However, there is now evidence that much of the reported difference between American and English psychotics is the result of different diagnostic criteria employed in the two settings.[83] When the criteria are standardized, no important differences emerge between the two countries.[84]

Clearly, it is next to impossible to diagnose mental disorder in a completely objective and cross-culturally meaningful way, but how good are American psychiatrists at diagnosing members of their own culture? Practical experience has shown that certain sets of symptoms tend to occur together as a *syndrome.* Psychiatric diagnoses, however, are still much more difficult to render than traditional medical diagnoses. In fact, much of the diagnosis depends on the theoretical orientation and depth of knowledge of the psychiatrist. In addition, psychiatrists are susceptible to suggestions in their diagnoses. In one study, therapists were asked to diagnose interviewees who were normal. One group of therapists was given no prior information. A second group was told that the people were quite normal.[85] A third group was told the interview was part of a job selection process for an industrial research scientist. A fourth group was told that the interviewees were part of a sanity hearing, and the fifth group was told that the interviewees were mentally ill. Although the interviews were the same for all five groups, only the fifth group diagnosed the people as disordered.

Aside from suggestion, another reason diagnoses are often unreliable is that they are made on the basis of only brief personal contact. This is risky because symptoms can change over time, at least the symptoms seen at the first interview. Although diagnoses conducted under ideal circumstances (including a number of interviews) are usually more valid, the experiments to assess the validity of diagnosis rarely employ favorable conditions. They will, instead, parade normal people and disordered people before a panel of psychiatrists, give them a few minutes to ask questions, and then ask for a very specific diagnosis.

There is another side to the question of diagnostic reliability. Diagnoses by psychiatrists of the same patients are apparently more consistent when they use broad diagnostic categories as compared to when they are required to specify a subtype of illness. In one study in which broad categories were used, a team of psychiatrists agreed on their diagnoses 96 percent of the time.[86]

The problems of diagnosis received national attention in 1973 when David Rosenhan, a psychiatrist, studied admissions procedures at mental hospitals around the country.[87] Specifically, Rosenhan wanted to see what would happen if perfectly normal people applied for admission, so he arranged for some of his associates to present themselves at 12 different mental hospitals. They were instructed to complain of hearing a voice saying a word such as "hollow," "empty," or "thud." All of the pseudopatients were diagnosed as severely disordered and were admitted. The most alarming outcome, however, occurred when the fake patients acted normal after admission and no longer claimed to hear voices. Not a single staff member of any hospital realized they did not belong there! The only people who caught on to the experiment were the real patients. The pseudopatients were held for an average of 19 days. During that time, all their behavior was interpreted on the basis of their respective diagnoses. One woman, for instance, became so frustrated with the situation that she began taking handwritten notes about her experiences. She was further diagnosed as having "compulsive handwriting"!

After publishing his exposé, Rosenhan warned another mental hospital that he would be sending pseudopatients there between January and March. Of the 193 patients admitted during that period, 43 were designated as pseudopatients by the staff. Actually, Rosenhan had not sent any fake patients! Such imprecision in the diagnosis of mental disorder is a major obstacle to gaining accurate knowledge on how to effectively handle this major social problem.

As Rosenhan notes: "We seem unable to acknowledge that we simply don't know. The needs of diagnosis and remediation of behavioral and emotional problems are enormous. But rather than acknowledge that we are just embarking on understanding, we continue to label patients . . . as if in those words we had captured the essence of understanding. The facts of the matter are that we have known for a long time that diagnoses are not useful or reliable."[88]

Psychiatrists are also frequently unable to predict how patients will behave once they are released from a mental hospital.[89] This is especially evident in their inability to predict whether a person will be violent sometime in the future.[90] Of course, it is understandable that predictions of dangerousness are inaccurate. After all, predictions are made in an institutional setting, far removed from the time and situation in the open community where the dangerous behavior occurs. To compensate for this problem, psychiatrists tend to overpredict dangerousness.[91] This serves to protect them from censure by the community when a released patient causes harm. In search of better accuracy, researchers at New York University have developed a scale that includes a history of violence, socialization in a deviant family environment, history of a violent suicide attempt, and a measurable neurologic abnormality. The scale can predict dangerousness with a 70 percent degree of accuracy.

CURRENT PSYCHIATRIC NOMENCLATURE

Because there are so many instances where behavior and psychiatric diagnosis do not correspond, it is impossible to develop a single definition of mental health or mental illness that can deal with all of the cross-cultural, philosophical, and diagnostic questions discussed in this chapter. Perhaps a universal definition will eventually be developed, but it must include multiple criteria. Such an approach might consider mental health as an integrated personality that correctly perceives the world and is adjusted to a nonpathological environment and to changes within it. This definition draws together the most significant components of the major approaches today. However, it is not without its shortcomings, particularly with regard to the ambiguity of the word "correct," which can be clearly specified only in a culturally relativistic way.

Two additional points are pertinent here. First, Devereux suggests that the issue of what is normal has been overemphasized.[92] Even though certain patterns considered abnormal in one society are institutionalized in other cultures, they are not often commonly observed behaviors in these cultures. People who fill these roles are usually acknowledged to be on the periphery of the social system, as in the case of witch doctors. Second, Kiev has stated that, although mental illnesses are viewed differently cross-culturally, they are functionally equivalent in that the patient's symptoms are either distressing to him or the group.[93]

Kiev further suggests that the difficulties inherent in the cross-cultural study of mental illness can be overcome by intensive studies of singular cultures. This book is based on such an approach since it utilizes the psychiatric nomenclature painstakingly developed by the American Psychiatric Association. This classification system is chosen for a very practical reason: research in the field generally employs APA terminology. Therefore, there is not much choice in the matter since the APA's nomenclature has been used in almost every investigation of mental illness for the last five decades.

This framework is limited because it only considers mental illness within the

American context. It is not the purpose of this book, however, to delineate every known way in which humans have been considered disordered or healthy. That is more appropriately the responsibility of psychiatric anthropology. It *is* imperative, however, to be aware of the problems encountered in such an undertaking; the American view of mental illness is not necessarily shared by others, particularly those in other parts of the world.

DSM-IV

To many, the DSM-IV has certain limitations but represents a vast improvement over previously used systems and incorporates the most up-to-date knowledge available.[94] Others assert that the DSM-IV is flawed and that its usefulness should be seriously questioned. Gender bias is the most frequently voiced complaint.[95] Basically, the definition of a mental illness depends, in part, on social and cultural values, as well as what professionals say it is. Today the official position is that a condition qualifies as a disorder if it causes distress or disability to the person. Ideally, a classification system should be based on cause. However, because the causes of mental disorder are so elusive, classification is actually carried out on the basis of manifest symptoms, even though the very definition of "symptom" is riddled with cross-cultural controversy.[96]

The DSM has undergone tremendous changes since it was first published in 1952. Categories have been added and some, such as homosexuality, have been removed. Many of these changes occur through political activities and are decided by votes taken by official APA decision-making committees. But, for all of the furor and change, we have a growing consensus on the types and subtypes of psychiatric disorders largely due to the efforts of the World Health Organization (WHO). In 1994, the American Psychiatric Association (APA) published the fourth edition of the *Diagnostic and Statistical Manual of Mental Disorders* (DSM-IV). It represented a great expansion of the definition of mental disorder (see Table 2:1). While this may prove to be a real help in making more accurate diagnoses, some feel that the APA included too many behaviors and created a "psychiatric imperialism." This complaint is voiced especially loudly among health insurance companies, which, for obvious reasons, would prefer fewer categories. The major groups of the DSM-IV are briefly described below.

Disorders Usually First Diagnosed in Infancy, Childhood, or Adolescence.   A variety of classes are included here: mental retardation, attention deficit, conduct disorder, separation anxiety (from home or parents), and mutism (refusal to speak). Tourette's disorder also occurs among the young. The essential features are involuntary movements (tics) and an irresistible urge to shout obscenities. Other disorders in this group are stuttering, enuresis (bed-wetting), communication disorders, and autistic disorders.

Delirium, Dementia, Amnestic, and Other Cognitive Disorders.   The essential feature of this group of disorders is a psychological abnormality resulting from an actual impairment of brain tissue. This includes senility, a condition in which there is a loss of neuron cells, the brain cells that send nerve impulses to the body. There may be as many as 4 million persons suffering from senility in the United States, not all of whom are aged. Brain tissue impairment can also result from ingestion of a drug, head trauma, Parkinson's disease, and Huntington's disease.

Substance-Related Disorders.   These occur among people whose drug usage induces undesirable behavioral changes. There are many subtypes associated with the specific drug used.

Schizophrenic Disorders.   Sufferers of these disorders have severely deranged thinking processes and exhibit a wide array of bizarre symptoms. The forms and causes of schizophrenia are presented in detail in Chapter 4.

Mood Disorders.   Mood disorders are characterized by wide fluctuations in feeling (affect). Depression is the most common form. Some people have moods that alternate between mania and depression, the so-called bipolar disorder. Mood disorders are discussed in Chapter 4.

Anxiety Disorders.   This is a new term for what used to be called neuroses. It is important to realize that a certain amount of anxiety is normal. Many college students experience anxiety before final exams or before an oral report in class. That is normal. Students whose anxieties are so great that they are unable to take the exam or give the speech have an anxiety disorder. These and related problems are analyzed in Chapter 5.

Somatoform Disorders.   The essential features of this group of disorders are physical symptoms linked to psychological problems. This category includes hypochondriacs, as well as people who have real physical ailments (such as paralysis or blindness) for which there is no demonstrated organic cause (originally referred to as conversion hysteria).

Dissociative Disorders.   This is the contemporary term to describe people with memory loss (amnesia), as well as for the more dramatic case of multiple personality. Dissociative disorders used to be classified as simply "neurotic" but now are grouped separately because of their greater severity.

Sexual and Gender Identity Disorders.   People with these problems have either a socially unacceptable choice of sexual object or imagery (paraphilia) or a problem of gender identity. There are many varieties of psychosexual disorders, including people who prefer sex with children and those who are attracted to corpses.

Eating Disorders.   Eating disorders include anorexia nervosa, which involves an intense fear of becoming obese. Anorexic persons, almost always teen-age females, refuse to eat and consequently experience significant weight loss. Another eating disorder, often found among female college students, is bulimia. Bulimics go on eating binges (typically consuming about 40,000 calories) followed by self-induced vomiting or heavy use of laxatives.

Sleep Disorders.   This set of problems includes dysomnias (abnormalities in the amount, quality, or timing of sleep) and parasomnias (nightmares and sleep walking).

Impulse-Control Disorders.   People with disorders of impulse control are unable to resist an urge to perform some act harmful to themselves or others. Some may gamble. Others may steal (kleptomania). This category includes one of the few groups of disordered people who pose a real physical danger to others—those who suffer from

what is known as intermittent explosive disorder. The central features are gross outbursts of rage that are unpredictable and in sharp contrast to the person's usually
placid behavior.

Personality Disorders.   These disorders describe people whose personality traits are
maladaptive and cause significant impairment in social or occupational functioning or
subjective distress. Some of these conditions are discussed in Chapter 6, particularly
antisocial personality disorder. Antisocial people regularly violate social mores and can
rape, murder, or steal with no remorse because they lack a conscience.

These diagnostic categories are always subject to change as new information
about mental illness is acquired and more refined classifications are developed. Some
of the changes are the result of sociological forces that cause attitudinal changes. This
is particularly likely to occur in the area of sexual deviations, a blatant example of the
influence of societal opinion on the accepted view of the abnormal.

It is important to reemphasize that a behavior is considered "officially" ill in the
United States only if it is viewed as such by the APA. The APA makes these decisions
by polling the opinions of its members and resolving issues according to the majority
vote. This is not unlike the "averaging" approach to defining mental illness that was
criticized earlier, but at least here the population from which the vote is taken consists
of mental health professionals. It is certainly not the ideal foundation for objectively
studying mental disorder, but if we become so concerned with scientific purism that
we feel compelled to wait for value-free indices of mental illness to be developed, a
self-fulfilling prophecy will occur. It is self-fulfilling because idle waiting can never contribute to the development of indices that are pure, refined, and objectively scientific.
Those indices can be achieved only through continual effort.

With these problems and limitations stated, the data and theories presented in
this book should be considered as a portrayal of mental illness in the United States
today, recognizing that tomorrow's knowledge will be a result of today's efforts. When
you consider how far we have come from yesterday's ignorant theories and practices,
the future looks much brighter.

Table 2:1 DSM-IV Classification

NOS=Not Otherwise Specified.
An x appearing in a diagnostic code indicates that a specific code number is required.

An elipse (...) is used in the names of certain disorders to indicate that the name of a specific mental disorder or general medical condition should be inserted when recording the name (e.g. 293.0 Delirium Due to Hypothyroidism).

Numbers in parentheses are page numbers.

If criteria are currently met, one of the following severity specifiers may be noted after the diagnosis:

> Mild
> Moderate
> Severe

If criteria are no longer met, one of the following specifiers may be noted:

> In Partial Remission
> In Full Remission
> Prior History

Disorders Usually First Diagnosed in Infancy, Childhood, or Adolescegnce (37)

MENTAL RETARDATION (39)
Note: These are coded on Axis II.
317   Mild Mental Retardation (41)
318.0   Moderate Mental Retardation (41)
318.1   Severe Mental Retardation (41)
318.2   Profound Mental Retardation (41)
319   Mental Retardation, Severity Unspecified (42)

LEARNING DISORDERS (46)
315.00   Reading Disorder (48)
315.1   Mathematics Disorder (50)
315.2   Disorder of Written Expression (51)
315.9   Learning Disorder NOS (53)

MOTOR SKILLS DISORDER
315.4   Developmental Coordination Disorder (53)

COMMUNICATION DISORDERS (55)
315.31   Expressive Language Disorder (55)
315.31   Mixed Receptive-Expressive Language Disorder (58)
315.39   Phonological Disorder (61)
307.0   Stuttering (63)
307.9   Communication Disorder NOS (65)

PERVASIVE DEVELOPMENTAL DISORDERS (65)
299.00   Autistic Disorder (66)
299.80   Rett's Disorder (71)
299.10   Childhood Disintegrative Disorder (73)
299.80   Asperger's Disorder (75)
299.80   Pervasive Developmental Disorder NOS (77)

ATTENTION-DEFICIT AND DISRUPTIVE BEHAVIOR DISORDERS (78)
314.xx   Attention-Deficit/Hyperactivity Disorder (78)
   .01   Combined Type
   .00   Predominantly Inattentive Type
   .01   Predominantly Hyperactive-Impulsive Type
314.9   Attention-Deficit/Hyperactivity Disorder NOS (85)
312.8   Conduct Disorder (85)
          Specify type: Childhood-Onset Type/ Adolescent-Onset Type

313.81   Oppositional Defiant Disorder (91)
312.9   Disruptive Behavior Disorder NOS (94)

FEEDING AND EATING DISORDERS OF INFANCY OR EARLY CHILDHOOD (94)
307.52   Pica (95)
307.53   Rumination Disorder (96)
307.59   Feeding Disorder of Infancy or Early
Childhood (98)

TIC DISORDERS (100)
307.23   Tourette's Disorder (101)
307.22   Chronic Motor or Vocal Tic
Disorder (103)
307.21   Transient Tic Disorder (104)
Specify if: Single Episode/Recurrent
307.20   Tic Disorder NOS (105)

ELIMINATION DISORDERS (106)
___.___   Encopresis (106)
787.6   With Constipation and Overflow
Incontinence
307.7   Without Constipation and
Overflow Incontinence
307.6   Enuresis (Not Due to a General Medical
Condition) (108)
Specify type: Nocturnal Only/Diurnal
Only/Nocturnal and Diurnal

OTHER DISORDERS OF INFANCY, CHILD-HOOD, OR ADOLESCENCE
309.21   Separation Anxiety Disorder (110)
Specify if: Early Onset
313.23   Selective Mutism (114)
313.89   Reactive Attachment Disorder of Infancy
or Early Childhood (116)
Specify type: Inhibited Type/
Disinhibited Type
307.3   Stereotypic Movement Disorder (118)
Specify if: With Self-Injurious Behavior
313.9   Disorder of Infancy, Childhood, or
Adolescence NOS (121)

Delirium, Dementia, and Amnestic and Other Cognitive Disorders (123)

DELIRIUM (124)
293.0   Delirium Due to ... *[Indicate the General
Medical Condition]* (127)
___.___   Substance Intoxication Delirium (129)
*(refer to Substance-Related Disorders for
substance-specific codes)*
___.___   Substance Withdrawal Delirium (129)
*(refer to Substance-Related Disorders for
substance-specific codes)*

___.___   Delirium Due to Multiple Etiologies
(code each of the specific etiologies) (132)
780.09   Delirium NOS (133)

DEMENTIA (133)
290.xx   Dementia of the Alzheimer's Type,
With Early Onset *(also code 331.0
Alzheimer's disease on Axis III)* (139)
   .10   Uncomplicated
   .11   With Delirium
   .12   With Delusions
   .13   With Depressed Mood
Specify if: With Behavior Disturbance
290.xx   Dementia of the Alzheimer's Type, With
Late Onset *(also code 331.0 Alzheimer's
disease on Axis III)* (139)
   .0   Uncomplicated
   .3   With Delirium
   .20   With Delusions
   .21   With Depressed Mood
Specify if: With Behavioral Disturbance
290.xx   Vascular Dementia (143)
   .40   Uncomplicated
   .41   With Delirium
   .42   With Delusions
   .43   With Depressed Mood
Specify if: With Behavioral Disturbance
294.9   Dementia Due to HIV Disease *(also code
043.1 HIV infection affecting central nervous
system on Axis III)* (148)
294.1   Dementia Due to Head Trauma *(also
code 854.00 head injury on Axis III)* (148)
294.1   Dementia Due to Parkinson's Disease
*(also code 332.0 Parkinson's disease on
Axis III)*(148)
294.1   Dementia Due to Huntington's Disease
*(also code 333.4 Huntington's disease on
Axis III)* (149)
290.10   Dementia Due to Pick's Disease *(also
code 331.1 Pick's disease on Axis III)* (149)
290.10   Dementia Due to Creutzfeldt-Jakob
Disease *(also code 046.1 Creutzfeldt-Jakob
disease on Axis III)* (150)
294.1   Dementia Due to ... *[Indicate the General
Medical Condition not listed above] (also
code the general medical condition on
Axis III)* (151)
___.___   Substance-Induced Persisting Dementia
*(refer to Substance-Related Disorders for
substance-specific codes)* (152)
___.___   Dementia Due to Multiple Etiologies
(code each of the specific etiologies) (154)
294.8   Dementia NOS (155)

AMNESTIC DISORDERS (156)

294.0   Amnestic Disorder Due to . . . *[Indicate the General Medical Condition]* (158)
         Specify if: Transient/Chronic

___.__   Substance-Induced Persisting Amnestic Disorder *(refer to Substance-Related Disorders for substance-specific codes)* (161)

294.8   Amnestic Disorder NOS (163)

OTHER COGNITIVE DISORDERS (163)

294.9   Cognitive Disorder NOS (163)

Mental Disorders Due to a General Medical Condition Not Elsewhere Classified (165)

293.89   Catatonic Disorder Due to ... *[Indicate the General Medical Condition]* (169)

310.1   Personality Change Due to ... *[Indicate the General Medical Condition]* (171)
         Specify type: Labile Type/Disinhibited Type/Aggressive Type/Apathetic Type/Paranoid Type/Other Type/Combined Type/Unspecified Type.

293.9   Mental Disorder NOS Due to ... *[Indicate the General Medical Condition]* (174)

Substance-Related Disorders (175)

[a]*The following specifiers may be applied to Substance Dependence:*

     With Physiological Dependence/Without Physiological Dependence

     Early Full Remission/Early Partial Remission
     Sustained Full Remission/Sustained Partial Remission
     On Agonist Therapy/In a Controlled Environment

The following specifiers apply to Substance-Induced Disorders as noted:

     [1]With Onset During Intoxication/[w] With Onset During Withdrawal

ALCOHOL-RELATED DISORDERS (194)

Alcohol Use Disorders

303.90   Alcohol Dependence[a] (195)
305.00   Alcohol Abuse (196)

Alcohol-Induced Disorders

303.00   Alcohol Intoxication (196)
291.8   Alcohol Withdrawal (197)
         Specify if: With Perceptual Disturbances

291.0   Alcohol Intoxication Delirium (129)
291.0   Alcohol Withdrawal Delirium (129)
291.2   Alcohol-Induced Persisting Dementia (152)
291.1   Alcohol-Induced Persisting Amnestic Disorder (161)
291.x   Alcohol-Induced Psychotic Disorder (310)
   .5   With Delusions[1,W]
   .3   With Hallucinations[1,W]
291.8   Alcohol-Induced Mood Disorder[1,W] (370)
291.8   Alcohol-Induced Anxiety Disorder[1,W] (439)
291.8   Alcohol-Induced Sexual Dysfunction[1,W] (519)
291.8   Alcohol-Induced Sleep Disorder[1,w] (601)

291.9   Alcohol-Related Disorder NOS (204)

AMPHETAMINE (OR AMPHETAMINE-LIKE)–RELATED DISORDERS 204

Amphetamine Use Disorders

304.40   Amphetamine Dependence[a] (206)
305.70   Amphetamine Abuse (206)

Amphetamine-Induced Disorders

292.89   Amphetamine Intoxication (207)
         Specify if: With Perceptual Disturbances
292.0   Amphetamine Withdrawal (208)
292.81   Amphetamine Intoxication Delirium (129)
292.xx   Amphetamine-Induced Psychotic Disorder (310)
   .11   With Delusions[1]
   .12   With Hallucinations[1]
292.84   Amphetamine-Induced Mood Disorder[1,W] (370)
292.89   Amphetamine-Induced Anxiety Disorder[1] (439)
292.89   Amphetamine-Induced Sexual Dysfunction[1] (519)
292.89   Amphetamine-Induced Sleep Disorder[1,W] (601)
292.9   Amphetamine-Related Disorder NOS (211)

CAFFEINE-RELATED DISORDERS (212)

Caffeine-Induced Disorders

305.90   Caffeine Intoxication (212)
292.89   Caffeine-Induced Anxiety Disorder[1] (439)
292.89   Caffeine-Induced Sleep Disorder[1] (601)
292.9   Caffeine-Related Disorder NOS (215)

CANNABIS-RELATED DISORDERS (215)

Cannabis Use Disorders
304.30   Cannabis Dependence[a] (216)
305.20   Cannabis Abuse (217)

Cannabis-Induced Disorders
292.89   Cannabis Intoxication (217)
          Specify if: With Perceptual Disturbances
292.81   Cannabis Intoxication Delirium (129)
292.xx   Cannabis-Induced Psychotic
          Disorder (310)
   .11   With Delusions[1]
   .12   With Hallucinations[1]
292.89   Cannabis-Induced Anxiety
          Disorder[1] (439)
292.9   Cannabis-Related Disorder NOS (221)

COCAINE-RELATED DISORDERS (221)

Cocaine Use Disorders
304.20   Cocaine Dependence[a] (222)
305.60   Cocaine Abuse (223)

Cocaine-Induced Disorders
292.89   Cocaine Intoxication (223)
          Specify if: With Perceptual Disturbances
292.0   Cocaine Withdrawal (225)
292.81   Cocaine Intoxication Delirium (129)
292.xx   Cocaine-Induced Psychotic
          Disorder (310)
   .11   With Delusions[1]
   .12   With Hallucinations[1]
292.84   Cocaine-Induced Mood
          Disorder[1,W] (370)
292.89   Cocaine-Induced Anxiety
          Disorder[1,W] (439)
292.89   Cocaine-Induced Sexual
          Dysfunction[1] (519)
292.89   Cocaine-Induced Sleep Disorder[1,W] (601)
292.9   Cocaine-Related Disorder NOS (229)

HALLUCINOGEN-RELATED DISORDERS (229)

Hallucinogen Use Disorders
304.50   Hallucinogen Dependence[a] (230)
305.30   Hallucinogen Abuse (231)

Hallucinogen-Induced Disorders
292.89   Hallucinogen Intoxication (232)
292.89   Hallucinogen Persisting Perception
          Disorder (Flashbacks) (233)
292.81   Hallucinogen Intoxication
          Delirium (129)
292.xx   Hallucinogen-Induced Psychotic
          Disorder (310)
   .11   With Delusions[1]
   .12   With Hallucinations[1]

292.84   Hallucinogen-Induced Mood
          Disorder[1] (370)
292.89   Hallucinogen-Induced Anxiety
          Disorder[1] (439)
292.9   Hallucinogen-Related Disorder
          NOS (236)

INHALANT-RELATED DISORDERS (236)

Inhalant Use Disorders
304.60   Inhalant Dependence[a] (238)
305.90   Inhalant Abuse (238)

Inhalant-Induced Disorders
292.89   Inhalant Intoxication (239)
292.81   Inhalant Intoxication Delirium (129)
292.82   Inhalant-Induced Persisting
          Dementia (152)
292.xx   Inhalant-Induced Psychotic
          Disorder (310)
   .11   With Delusions[1]
   .12   With Hallucinations[1]
292.84   Inhalant-Induced Mood Disorder[1] (370)
292.89   Inhalant-Induced Anxiety
          Disorder[1] (439)
292.9   Inhalant-Related Disorder NOS (242)

NICOTINE-RELATED DISORDERS (242)

Nicotine Use Disorder
305.10   Nicotine Dependence[a] (243)

Nicotine-Induced Disorder
292.0   Nicotine Withdrawal (244)
292.9   Nicotine-Related Disorder NOS (247)

OPIOID-RELATED DISORDERS (247)

Opioid Use Disorders
304.00   Opioid Dependence[1] (248)
305.50   Opioid Abuse (249)

Opioid-Induced Disorders
292.89   Opioid Intoxication (249)
          Specify if: With Perceptual Disturbances
292.0   Opioid Withdrawal (250)
292.81   Opioid Intoxication Delirium (129)
292.xx   Opioid-Induced Psychotic
          Disorder (310)
   .11   With Delusions[1]
   .12   With Hallucinations[1]
292.84   Opioid-Induced Mood Disorder[1] (370)
292.89   Opioid-Induced Sexual
          Dysfunction[1] (519)
292.89   Opioid-Induced Sleep Disorder[1,W] (601)
292.9   Opioid-Related Disorder NOS (255)

PHENCYCLIDINE (OR PHENCYCLIDINE-LIKE)-RELATED DISORDERS (255)

Phencyclidine Use Disorders
304.90   Phencyclidine Dependence[a] (256)
305.90   Phencyclidine Abuse (257)

Phencyclidine-Induced Disorders
292.89   Phencyclidine Intoxication (257)
          Specify if: With Perceptual Disturbances
292.81   Phencyclidine Intoxication
          Delirium (129)
292.xx   Phencyclidine-Induced Psychotic
          Disorder (310)
    .11   With Delusions[1]
    .12   With Hallucinations[1]
292.84   Phencyclidine-Induced Mood
          Disorder[1] (370)
292.89   Phencyclidine-Induced Anxiety
          Disorder[1] (439)
292.9   Phencyclidine-Related Disorder
          NOS (261)

SEDATIVE-HYPNOTIC-, OR ANXIOLYTIC-RELATED DISORDERS (261)

Sedative, Hypnotic, or Anxiolytic Use Disorders
304.10   Sedative, Hypnotic, or Anxiolytic
          Dependence[a] (262)
305.40   Sedative, Hypnotic, or Anxiolytic Abuse (263)

Sedative-, Hypnotic-, or Anxiolytic-Induced Disorders
292.89   Sedative, Hypnotic, or Anxiolytic
          Intoxication (263)
292.0   Sedative, Hypnotic, or Anxiolytic
          Withdrawal (264)
          Specify if: With Perceptual Disturbances
292.81   Sedative, Hypnotic, or Anxiolytic
          Intoxication Delirium (129)
292.81   Sedative, Hypnotic, or Anxiolytic
          Withdrawal Delirium (129)
292.82   Sedative-, Hypnotic-, or Anxiolytic-
          Induced Persisting Dementia (152)
292.83   Sedative-, Hypnotic-, or Anxiolytic-
          Induced Persisting Amnestic Disorder (161)
292.xx   Sedative-, Hypnotic-, or Anxiolytic-
          Induced Psychotic Disorder (310)
    .11   With Delusions[1,w]
    .12   With Hallucinations[1,w]
292.84   Sedative-, Hypnotic-, or Anxiolytic-
          Induced Mood Disorder[1,w] (370)
292.89   Sedative-, Hypnotic-, or Anxiolytic-
          Induced Anxiety Disorder[w] (370)
292.89   Sedative-, Hypnotic-, or Anxiolytic-
          Induced Sexual Dysfunction[1] (519)
292.89   Sedative-, Hypnotic-, or Anxiolytic-
          Induced Sleep Disorder[1,w] (601)

292.9   Sedative-, Hypnotic-, or Anxiolytic-
          Related Disorder NOS (269)

POLYSUBSTANCE-RELATED DISORDER
304.8   Polysubstance Dependence[a] (270)

OTHER (OR UNKNOWN) SUBSTANCE-RELATED DISORDERS (270)

Other (or Unknown) Substance Use Disorders
304.90   Other (or Unknown) Substance
          Dependence[a] (176)
305.90   Other (or Unknown) Substance
          Abuse (182)

Other (or Unknown) Substance-Induced Disorders
292.89   Other (or Unknown) Substance
          Intoxication (183)
          Specify if: With Perceptual Disturbances
292.0   Other (Or Unknown) Substance
          Withdrawal (184)
          Specify if: With Perceptual Disturbances
292.81   Other (or Unknown) Substance-
          Induced Delirium (129)
292.82   Other (or Unknown) Substance-
          Induced Persisting Dementia (152)
292.83   Other (or Unknown) Substance-
          Induced Persisting Amnestic Disorder (161)
292.xx   Other (or Unknown) Substance-
          Induced Psychotic Disorder (310)
    .11   With Delusions[1,w]
    .12   With Hallucinations[1,w]
292.84   Other (or Unknown) Substance-
          Induced Mood Disorder[1,w] (370
292.89   Other (or Unknown) Substance-
          Induced Anxiety Disorder[1,w] (439)
292.89   Other (or Unknown) Substance-
          Induced Sexual Dysfunction[1] (519)
292.89   Other (or Unknown) Substance-
          Induced Sleep Disorder[1,w] (601)
292.9   Other (or Unknown) Substance-
          Related Disorder NOS (272)

Schizophrenia and Other Psychotic Disorders (273)

295.xx   Schizophrenia (274)

The following Classifications of Longitudinal Course applies to all subtypes of Schizophrenia:

Episodic With Interepisode Residual Symptoms
(specify if: With Prominent Negative
Symptoms)/Episodic With No Interepisode
Residual Symptoms/Continuous *(specify if:*
With Prominent Negative Symptoms)

Single Episode In Partial Remission *(specify if:*
With Prominent Negative Symptoms)/
Single Episode In Full Remission
Other or Unspecified Pattern

.30	Paranoid Type (287)
.10	Disorganized Type (287)
.20	Catatonic Type (288)
.90	Undifferentiated Type (289)
.60	Residual Type (289)

295.40   Schizophreniform Disorder (290)
Specify if: Without Good Prognostic
Features/With Good Prognostic
Features

295.70   Schizoaffective Disorder (292)
Specify type: Bipolar Type/Depressive
Type

297.1   Delusional Disorder (296)
Specify if: Erotomanic Type/Grandiose
Type/Jealous Type/Persecutory Type/
Somatic Type/Mixed Type/Unspecified
Type

298.8   Brief Psychotic Disorder (302)
Specify if: With Marked Stressor(s)/
Without Marked Stressor(s)/With
Postpartum Onset

297.3   Shared Psychotic Disorder (305)

293.xx   Psychotic Disorder Due to ... *[Indicate the
General Medical Condition]* (306)
.81   With Delusions
.82   With Hallucinations

___.__   Substance-Induced Psychotic Disorder
*(refer to Substance-Related Disorders for sub-
stance-specific codes)* (310)
Specify if: With Onset During
Intoxication/With Onset During
Withdrawal

298.9   Psychotic Disorder NOS (315)

Mood Disorders (317)

*Code current state of Major Depressive Disorder or Bipo-
lar1 Disorder in fifth digit:*

1=Mild
2=Moderate
3=Severe Without Psychotic Features
4=Severe With Psychotic Features

Specify Mood-Congruent Psychotic Fea-
tures/Mood-Incongruent Psychotic Features

5=In Partial Remission
6=In Full Remission
0=Unspecified

*The following specifiers apply (for current or most recent
episode) to Mood Disorders as noted:*

[a]Severity/Psychotic/Remission Specifiers/
[b]Chronic/[c]With Catatonic Features/
[d]With Melancholic Features/[e]With Atypical
Features/[f]With Postpartum Onset

*The following specifiers apply to Mood Disorders as
noted:*

[g]With or without Full Interepisode Recovery/
[h]With Seasonal Pattern/[i]With Rapid Cycling

DEPRESSIVE DISORDERS

296.xx   Major Depressive Disorder, (339)
.2x   Single Episode[a,b,c,d,e,f]
.3x   Recurrent[a,b,c,d,e,f,g,h]

300.4   Dysthymic Disorder (345)
Specify if: Early Onset/Late Onset
Specify With Atypical Features

311   Depressive Disorder NOS (350)

BIPOLAR DISORDERS

296.xx   Bipolar 1 Disorder, (350)
.0x   Single Manic Episode[a,c,f]
Specify if: Mixed
.40   Most Recent Episode
Hypomanic[g,h,i]
.4x   Most Recent Episode
Manic[a,c,f,g,h,i]
.6x   Most Recent Episode
Mixed[a,c,f,g,h,i]
.5x   Most Recent Episode
Depressed[a,b,c,d,e,f,g,h,i]
.7   Most Recent Episode
Unspecified[g,h,i]

296.89   Bipolar II Disorder[a,b,c,d,e,f,g,h,i](359)
Specify (current or most recent episode):
Hypomanic/Depressed

301.13   Cyclothymic Disorder (363)

296.80   Bipolar Disorder NOS (366)

293.83   Mood Disorder Due to ... *[Indicate the
General Medical Condition]* (366)
Specify type: With Depressive Features/
With Major Depressive-Like Episode/
With Manic Features/With Mixed
Features

___.__   Substance-Induced Mood Disorder *(refer
to Substance-Related Disorders for substance-
specific codes)* (370)
Specify type: With Depressive Features/
With Manic Features/With Mixed
Features
Specify if: With Onset During Intoxica-
tion/ With Onset During Withdrawal

296.90   Mood Disorder NOS (375)

Anxiety Disorders (393)

300.01	Panic Disorder Without Agoraphobia (397)
300.21	Panic Disorder With Agoraphobia (397)
300.22	Agoraphobia Without History of Panic Disorder (403)
300.29	Specific Phobia (405) *Specify type:* Animal Type/Natural Environment Type/Blood-Injection-Injury Type/Situational Type/ Other Type
300.23	Social Phobia (411) *Specify if:* Generalized
300.3	Obsessive-Compulsive Disorder (417) *Specify if:* With Poor Insight
309.81	Posttraumatic Stress Disorder (424) *Specify if:* Acute/Chronic *Specify if:* With Delayed Onset
308.3	Acute Stress Disorder (429)
300.02	Generalized Anxiety Disorder (432)
293.89	Anxiety Disorder Due to ... *[Indicate the General Medical Condition]* (436) *Specify if:* With Generalized Anxiety/ With Panic Attacks/With Obsessive-Compulsive Symptoms
___._	Substance-Induced Anxiety Disorder *(refer to Substance-Related Disorders for substance-specific codes)* (439) *Specify if:* With Generalized Anxiety/ With Panic Attacks/With Obsessive-Compulsive Symptoms/With Phobic Symptoms *Specify if:* With Onset During Intoxication/ With Onset During Withdrawal
300.00	Anxiety Disorder NOS (444)

Somatoform Disorders (445)

300.81	Somatization Disorder (446)
300.81	Undifferentiated Somatoform Disorder (450)
300.11	Conversion Disorder (452) *Specify type:* With Motor Symptom or Deficit/With Sensory Symptom or Deficit/With Seizures or Convulsions/ With Mixed Presentation
307.xx	Pain Disorder (458)
.80	Associated With Psychological Factors
.89	Associated With Both Psychological Factors and a General Medical Condition *Specify if:* Acute/Chronic
300.7	Hypochondriasis (462) *Specify if:* With Poor Insight
300.7	Body Dysmorphic Disorder (466)
300.81	Somatoform Disorder NOS (468)
300.xx	Factitious Disorder (471)

Factitious Disorders (393)

.16	With Predominantly Psychological Signs and Symptoms
.19	With Predominantly Physical Signs and Symptoms
.19	With Combined Psychological and Physical Signs and Symptoms
300.19	Factitious Disorder NOS (475)

Dissociative Disorders (477)

300.12	Dissociative Amnesia (478)
300.13	Dissociative Fugue (481)
300.14	Dissociative Identity Disorder (484)
300.6	Depersonalization Disorder (488)
300.15	Dissociative Disorder NOS (490)

Sexual and Gender Identity Disorders (493)

SEXUAL DYSFUNCTIONS (493)
The following specifiers apply to all primary Sexual Dysfunctions:

Lifelong Type/Acquired Type/Generalized Type/Situational Type/Due to Psychological Factors/Due to Combined Factors

Sexual Desire Disorders

302.71	Hypoactive Sexual Desire Disorder (496)
302.79	Sexual Aversion Disorder (499)

Sexual Arousal Disorders

302.72	Female Sexual Arousal Disorder (500)
302.72	Male Erectile Disorder (502)

Orgasmic Disorders

302.73	Female Orgasmic Disorder (505)
302.74	Male Orgasmic Disorder (507)
302.75	Premature Ejaculation (509)

Sexual Pain Disorders

302.76	Dyspareunia (Not Due to a General Medical Condition) (511)
306.51	Vaginismus (Not Due to a General Medical Condition) (513)

Sexual Dysfunction Due to a General Medical Condition (515)

625.8	Female Hypoactive Sexual Desire Disorder Due to ... *[Indicate the General Medical Condition]* (515)

608.89   Male Hypoactive Sexual Desire Disorder Due to … *[Indicate the General Medical Condition]* (515)

607.84   Male Erectile Disorder Due to *[Indicate the General Medical Condition]* (515)

625.0   Female Dyspareunia Due to … *[Indicate the General Medical Condition]* (515)

608.89   Male Dyspareunia Due to … *[Indicate the General Medical Condition]* (515)

625.8   Other Female Sexual Dysfunction Due to … *[Indicate the General Medical Condition]* (515)

608.89   Other Male Sexual Dysfunction Due to … *[Indicate the General Medical Condition]* (515)

___.___   Substance-Induced Sexual Dysfunction *(refer to Substance-Related Disorders for substance-specific codes)* (519) *Specify if:* With Impaired Desire/ With Impaired Arousal/With Impaired Orgasm/With Sexual Pain *Specify if:* With Onset During Intoxication

302.70   Sexual Dysfunction NOS (522)

PARAPHILIAS (522)
302.4   Exhibitionism (525)
302.81   Fetishism (526)
302.89   Frotteurism (527)
302.2   Pedophilia (527) *Specify if:* Sexually Attracted to Males/ Sexually Attracted to Females/Sexually Attracted to Both *Specify if:* Limited to Incest *Specify if:* Exclusive Type/ Nonexclusive Type
302.83   Sexual Masochism (529)
302.84   Sexual Sadism (530)
302.3   Transvestic Fetishism (530) *Specify if:* With Gender Dysphoria
302.82   Voyeurism (532)
302.9   Paraphilia NOS (532)

GENDER IDENTITY DISORDERS (532)
302.xx   Gender Identity Disorder (532)
   .6   in Children
   .85   in Adolescents or Adults *Specify if:* Sexually Attracted to Males/ Sexually Attracted to Females/Sexually Attracted to Both/Sexually Attracted to Neither
302.6   Gender Identity Disorder NOS (538)
302.9   Sexual Disorder NOS (538)

Eating Disorders (539)

307.1   Anorexia Nervosa (539) *Specify type:* Restricting Type; Binge-Eating/Purging Type

307.51   Bulimia Nervosa (545) *Specify type:* Purging Type/ Nonpurging Type
307.50   Eating Disorder NOS (550)

Sleep Disorders (551)

PRIMARY SLEEP DISORDERS (553)

Dyssomnias (553)
307.42   Primary Insomnia (553)
307.44`   Primary Hypersomnia (557) *Specify if:* Recurrent
347   Narcolepsy (562)
780.59   Breathing-Related Sleep Disorder (567)
307.45   Circadian Rhythm Sleep Disorder (573) *Specify type:* Delayed Sleep Phase Type/ Jet Lag Type/Shift Work Type/ Unspecified Type
307.47   Dyssomnia NOS (579)

Parasomnias (579)
307.47   Nightmare Disorder (580)
307.46   Sleep Terror Disorder (583)
307.46   Sleepwalking Disorder (587)
307.47   Parasomnia NOS (592)

SLEEP DISORDERS RELATED TO ANOTHER MENTAL DISORDER (592)
307.42   Insomnia Related to … *[Indicate the Axis I or Axis II Disorder]* (592)
307.44   Hypersomnia Related to … *[Indicate the Axis I or Axis II Disorder}* (592)

OTHER SLEEP DISORDERS
780.xx   Sleep Disorder Due to … *[Indicate the General Medical Condition]* (597)
   .52   Insomnia Type
   .54   Hypersomnia Type
   .59   Parasomnia Type
   .59   Mixed Type
___.___   Substance-Induced Sleep Disorder *(refer to Substance-Related Disorders for substance-specific codes)* (601) *Specify type:* Insomnia Type/Hypersomnia Type/Parasomnia Type/Mixed Type *Specify if:* With Onset During Intoxication/ With Onset During Withdrawal

Impulse-Control Disorders Not Elsewhere Classified (609)

312.34   Intermittent Explosive Disorder (609)
312.32   Kleptomania (612)
312.33   Pyromania (614)

312.31	Pathological Gambling (615)
312.39	Trichotillomania (618)
312.30	Impulse-Control Disorder NOS (621)

Adjustment Disorders (623)

309.xx	Adjustment Disorder (623)	
.0		With Depressed Mood
.24		With Anxiety
.28		With Mixed Anxiety and Depressed Mood
.3		With Disturbance of Conduct
.4		With Mixed Disturbance of Emotions and Conduct
.9		Unspecified

Specify if: Acute/Chronic

Personality Disorders (629)

Note: These are coded on Axis II.

301.0	Paranoid Personality Disorder (634)
301.20	Schizoid Personality Disorder (638)
301.22	Schizotypal Personality Disorder (641)
301.7	Antisocial Personality Disorder (645)
301.83	Borderline Personality Disorder (650)
301.50	Histrionic Personality Disorder (655)
301.81	Narcissistic Personality Disorder (658)
301.82	Avoidant Personality Disorder (662)
301.6	Dependent Personality Disorder (665)
301.4	Obsessive-Compulsive Personality Disorder (669)
301.9	Personality Disorder NOS (673)

Other Conditions That May Be a Focus of Clinical Attention (675)

PSYCHOLOGICAL FACTORS AFFECTING MEDICAL CONDITION (675)

316	… /Specified Psychological Factor] Affecting … [Indicate the General Medical Condition] (675)

Choose name based on nature of factors:

Mental Disorder Affecting Medical Condition

Psychological Symptoms Affecting Medical Condition

Personality Traits or Coping Style Affecting Medical Condition

Maladaptive Health Behaviors Affecting Medical Condition

Stress-Related Physiological Response Affecting Medical Condition

Other or Unspecified Psychological Factors Affecting Medical Condition

MEDICATION-INDUCED MOVEMENT DISORDERS (678)

332.1	Neuroleptic-Induced Parkinsonism (679)
333.92	Neuroleptic Malignant Syndrome (679)
333.7	Neuroleptic-Induced Acute Dystonia (679)
333.99	Neuroleptic-Induced Acute Akathisia (679)
333.82	Neuroleptic-Induced Tardive Dyskinesia (679)
333.1	Medication-Induced Postural Tremor (680)
333.90	Medication-Induced Movement Disorder NOS (680)

OTHER MEDICATION-INDUCED DISORDER

995.2	Adverse Effects of Medication NOS (680)

RELATIONAL PROBLEMS (680)

V61.9	Relational Problem Related to a Mental Disorder or General Medical Condition (681)
V61.20	Parent-Child Relational Problem (681)
V61.1	Partner Relational Problem (681)
V61.8	Sibling Relational Problem (681)
V62.81	Relational Problem NOS (681)

PROBLEMS RELATED TO ABUSE OR NEGLECT (682)

V61.21	Physical Abuse of Child (682) *(code 995.5 if focus of attention is on victim)*
V61.21	Sexual Abuse of Child (682) *(code 995.5 if focus of attention is on victim)*
V61.21	Neglect of Child (682) *(code 995.5 if focus of attention is on victim)*
V61.1	Physical Abuse of Adult (682) *(code 995.81 if focus of attention is on victim)*
V61.1	Sexual Abuse of Adult (682) *(code 995.81 if focus of attention is on victim)*

ADDITIONAL CONDITIONS THAT MAY BE A FOCUS OF CLINICAL ATTENTION (683)

V15.81	Noncompliance with Treatment (683)
V65.2	Malingering (683)
V71.01	Adult Antisocial Behavior (683)
V71.02	Child or Adolescent Antisocial Behavior (684)
V62.89	Borderline Intellectual Functioning (684)

Note: This is coded on Axis II.

780.9	Age-Related Cognitive Decline (684)
V62.82	Bereavement (684)
V62.3	Academic Problem (685)

V62.2	Occupational Problem (685)
313.82	Identity Problem (685)
V62.89	Religious or Spiritual Problem (685)
V62.4	Acculturation Problem (685)
V62.89	Phase of Life Problem (685)

V71.09	No Diagnosis on Axis II (687)
799.9	Diagnosis Deferred on Axis II (687)

Additional Codes

300.9	Unspecified Mental Disorder (nonpsychotic) (687)
V71.09	No Diagnosis or Condition on Axis I (687)
799.9	Diagnosis or Condition Deferred on Axis I (687)

Multiaxial System

Axis I	Clinical Disorders
	Other Conditions That May Be a Focus of Clinical Attention
Axis II	Personality Disorders
	Mental Retardation
Axis III	General Medical Conditions
Axis IV	Psychosocial and Environmental Problems
Axis V	Global Assessment of Functioning

CONCLUSIONS

It is next to impossible to define mental illness objectively. Semantic issues are partly responsible for the problem; alternative use of words such as insane, mental disorder, psychopathology, and, particularly, mental illness, can often result in substantially different interpretations by different people. Another nagging element is the lack of a cross-culturally meaningful definition of mental health and illness. Often one culture's deviants are another culture's heroes.

Attempts to define mental health and mental illness have been limited by one-sided approaches that often reflect a value endorsed only by a particular group of people. The more well-known definitions of mental health (a healthy brain, absence of mental disorder, adjustment to environment, correct perception of reality, unity of personality) are not sufficient by themselves. Their most outstanding flaws are their inability to fit with anthropological data evidencing culturally specific expressions of disorders and lack of reliable diagnostic techniques. The cross-cultural phenomenon may be less of a problem than originally believed since evidence now suggests that what appear to be exotic illnesses may simply be reflections of different ways of exhibiting psychopathology. Thus exotic things like spirit possession, amok, and the evil eye may have the same underpinnings.

The American Psychiatric Association has developed a very detailed system of classifying types of illnesses. This nomenclature is based on frequently occurring syndromes that are distinct from each other in kind and degree. Some of the major types of disorders serve as the focus of this book because of their relationship with sociological factors. The disorders that are clearly biological, such as Alzheimer's disease, are found in traditional sources, such as textbooks in abnormal psychology and psychiatry, dealing with all forms of mental illness.

3

Environmental Theories of Mental Illness

The Influence of Social Stress

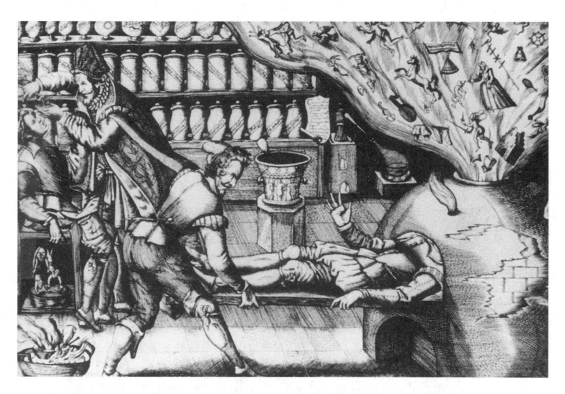

In the seventeenth century, psychiatry was very much in the dark. This illustration of the "French School" shows physicians employing exotic techniques to cure "fantasy and folly."

There are many ways to divide the great number of causal theories of mental illness. The approach that I use in this book is a three-part breakdown: sociological, psychological, and medical. Each of these theoretical branches has its own subdivisions. There is, however, a common theme that runs through almost all theories—the important role of *social stress*. Social stress is especially relevant to environmental theories, those that center about the influence of negative life experiences. In this chapter I summarize the central tenets of the five major environmental theories of mental illness: social stress theory, family systems theory, labeling theory, social learning theory, and psychoanalytic theory. *All are bound by a common recognition of the role of social stress.*

THEORIES AND TYPE OF MENTAL ILLNESS

The biopsychosocial model of mental illness is the safest theoretical bet in psychiatry today. On the other hand, the biological and environmental approaches to explaining the roots of mental illness are not equally relevant to different *types* of mental illness. Below I explain this point and summarize the main differences among the three groups of disorders dissected in the second part of the book—the psychotic disorders, the anxiety disorders, and the personality disorders.

Evidence to date favors the idea that the medical model is more relevant to serious mental illnesses marked by psychosis and not as applicable to the less debilitating illnesses, such as anxiety (neurotic) disorders. There are some important differences that separate anxiety disorders from more severe psychotic disorders, such as schizophrenia and bipolar disorder. If mental illness is regarded as a continuum, anxiety disorders fall between normal behavior and psychosis. Important criteria differentiate the two. Psychoses are profound disturbances that involve more disorganization and misinterpretation of reality than the anxiety disorders. For this reason, the overt behavior of the psychotic is a more accurate manifestation of the underlying disturbance. In addition, psychotics usually do not realize that they are disturbed, whereas people with anxiety disorders are frequently aware of their problems.[1]

Another difference between the anxiety disorders and the psychoses is the benefit that people with anxiety disorders may receive from having symptoms. This phenomenon, known as *secondary gain*, usually takes the form of sympathy from others, which some patients exploit to their best advantage.

The anxiety disorders are not to be confused with the personality disorders, which are deeply ingrained maladaptive patterns of behavior. Personality disorders are closer to normal behavior on the mental illness continuum. The major difference is in degree rather than kind since many of the personality disorders are conditions that lead to anxiety disorders. In later chapters we will examine the psychoses that fit better with medical theories. With these distinctions as background, keep in mind that the theories presented here are generally considered to be most relevant to the anxiety and personality disorders. However, because the causes of many forms of mental illness are presently a mystery, no one theoretical perspective can completely explain anything. In fact, stress is also known to play a role in the genesis of psychotic disorders, such as schizophrenia, which are traditionally viewed as biological problems.[2]

The chapters in the second part of this book present the symptoms and causes of some of the common mental illnesses. Some of this material is not *directly* representative of the sociology of mental illness because it is clinical and medical. However, it is necessary to understand this material in order to comprehend the pure sociology of mental illness presented in the last two parts of this book. Without knowing the symptoms of the different illnesses and, particularly, how they can arise in an individual, the fact that they are found (or reported) more frequently in certain social groups has much less meaning.[3]

SOCIAL STRESS THEORY

The *social stress theory* of mental illness complements psychology's focus on the individual by viewing abnormal behavior within the context of social and cultural forces.[4] Like psychological models of mental illness, social stress theory is based on experiences within the psychosocial environment. However, the parameters of social stress theory are more broadly based in large social groupings.

Recently, a case has been made that the problem of psychiatric illness is a *sociopolitical problem*, a question of public order over people who do not confirm to society's rules of behavior.[5] On a less philosophical level, extreme attitudes like that and more general sociological models of mental illness fill a gap created by strict medical views that omit interpersonal and social factors, especially those based on social differences, conflicts, and power differentials. *Environmental stress* is one of the many important examples of such an external factor.[6] Stress comes in many forms. It may be fortuitous, as in a natural disaster, intentional, as in a concentration camp, chronic, as in a dysfunctional family, or simply a natural part of the life cycle.

Social stress impacts differently on members of various social groups as in the case of race, gender, ethnicity, religion, and social class, to name a few. Alcoholism and suicide among Native Americans, for instance, can be attributed to the stresses imposed by prejudice and lives of hopelessness. Suicide is also common among homosexual adolescents whose sexual preference is mired in widespread social disapproval. Gender clearly imposes different stresses on men and women. Anxiety and depression, for instance, are diagnosed about twice as often among women than among men, a phenomenon explained in later chapters. The large influence of cultural values on gender is also apparent in the growing prevalence of eating disorders that stem from the Western aesthetic ideal of feminine thinness.

Traumatic events, such as sudden deaths, car jackings, and vicious murders, call into question basic human relationships and breach the attachments of family, friendship, love, and community. They violate the victim's faith in a natural order and cast the victim into a stress-induced state of crisis. Children are especially vulnerable and, as school shootings become more common, many school districts have developed plans to deal with catastrophe and trauma.[7] Children involved in traffic accidents can develop posttraumatic stress disorder, even if their injuries are minor. In fact, the effects of severe trauma have become the focus of so much concern in recent years that they are the center of many research studies, publications, and workshops.[8]

Stress has a complicated relationship with mental illness. Some believe that stress leads to the perception of mental illness and the seeking of help, not to illness itself. Others contend that mental illness causes stress, and another group feels that some unknown factor causes both the stress and the mental illness. We will look at the well-established relationship between numerous social stressors and mental illness. Since the 1950s, for example, empirical research has consistently shown both an inverse association between mental illness and social class (more mental illness in the lower class) and a direct association between mental illness and being female and/or unmarried (more mental illness among women and single people).[9] Stay tuned for the explanations. They involve a lot of "chicken and egg" issues.

As I noted, social stress takes a different psychiatric toll on members of separate social classes. In fact, rates of severe psychiatric illness are three times as frequent in the lower classes as in the higher classes. Lower social class life is filled with stressful life experiences, such as limited educational opportunities, poor health care, over-crowding, unemployment, and crime. These horrors simply add up to small hells on earth, hells that can translate into disordered minds.[10]

One of the curious things about the effects of stress in general, and traumatic life events in particular, is that some people do not seem to be affected by them at all. Why is that? It could lie in the "hardiness" of each individual's personality, or it could be related to social support from others. Much research has shown that social supports, also referred to as "social networks," are protective because of the interpersonal engagement, sympathy, advice, and overall satisfaction that they provide.[11] But having other people around does not always mean that "quality" support is available. While the general importance of an individual's support network has been recognized in the field of community mental health for some time, more detailed studies show that dif-ferences in social networks affect functioning.[12] Those who look to friends for sup-port, for example, do not function as well as those who look to immediate family members and professional contacts.[13]

Social stress may also be engendered by social change. It is interesting to note that the "change" appears to be the source of the stress rather than the nature of the event. In Chapter 12, there is a discussion of the impact of life events on mental ill-ness. The discussion includes the famous Holmes and Rahe Social Readjustment Rat-ing Scale. Curiously enough, an unpleasant event, such as a personal injury, generates a similar amount of stress as a pleasant event, such as getting married. Change, per se, appears to be the culprit or what some call the "trigger."

Change, such as unemployment, connects with loss of economic security and a blow to self-esteem. In societies ravaged by economic depression, suicide and clinical depression often show dramatic increases. Rapid urbanization accompanied by fast-paced technological change, social isolation, and migration are further examples of stress imposed by change. The bottom line is that some psyches are pushed too far. And the pushes stem from such societal forces as the economy, war, and the wide net of culture. Each of these is delineated below.

The Economy

Experts on the dynamics of unemployment have noted a dramatic increase in concern by sociologists and policymakers over the causes and consequences of job loss. That makes sense since some of the central consequences of unemployment are physical health problems, decline in psychological well-being, and family disruption. More violent results include suicide and homicide, a patterned response to job loss that is reported cross-culturally.[14]

The list of negative effects of unemployment is enormous. In fact, the Peruccis, one of the most respected research teams in psychiatric sociology, report that the loss of economic security associated with plant closings can destroy the social cohesiveness of entire communities.[15] The effect of job loss on mental illness is especially apparent during economic downturns when the unemployment rate is high.[16] Brenner, exam-ining admissions data to New York state mental hospitals over more than a century, found that admissions increase significantly when unemployment climbs,[17] a pattern later reconfirmed by Catalano, Dooley, and Jackson.[18]

A more dramatic example of the effect of unemployment on mental health is reported by Srole, who found the psychological status of people raised during the Great Depression to be significantly worse than those raised later.[19] The psychiatric costs of recessions and depressions have been explained in a number of ways. It may be that economic change causes *new* disorders by imposing stress. It is also possible that economic downturns affect the tolerance and ability of family and friends to care for people who are *already* disordered. It is interesting to note that unemployment is especially likely to cause depression among men, particularly those without supportive marital relations or ties to the extended family or peer groups.[20] Once again, the importance of social networks on reactions to stress rears its head. There is a lot to be learned about how unemployment can affect the human psyche. Future research must place greater attention on such issues as how the severity of unemployment (e.g., income loss, duration) is related to mental health, as well as the role of intervening variables (e.g. reduced self-esteem, loss of social contacts, family conflicts) that link unemployment to mental illness.

War

Certainly no list of the impact of social stress on mental disorder would be complete without mention of the devastating effects of war. These are particularly evident in long-term war zones such as Northern Ireland, Israel, Lebanon, Cambodia, and Bosnia. The list goes on. The personality effects of extended chaos are immeasurable. The risks are especially great for the "children of war," the ones raised in environments where fear, torture, mutilation, bombings, and hatred are part of their "normal" lives.[21] One of the most striking illustrations is the work of the Hampstead Clinic in London with children rescued from the death camp at Auschwitz during World War II. They survived because they were attractive and docile enough to be chosen as pets by female guards. As a result of being treated like dogs or cats rather than members of a human community, their personalities were arrested at infantile levels.[22] Psychiatric treatment of children from such horrible backgrounds is a frustrating, if not impossible, task. For example, an assessment of the treatment of Lebanese children exposed to heavy extended fighting reported *some* improvement but only for a limited period of time.[23] And the psychological damage may be even more deep-seated for small children when parents try to protect them by denying the facts of war.

It is well documented that a war experience has serious psychiatric ramifications for soldiers as well as civilian populations living in a war zone. During World War II the greatest loss of manpower was not from combat-related injuries but from combat stress (then referred to as "shell shock"), which led to a variety of mental disorders. Consider some of the common stress reactions to combat. They include (a) guilt about actions; (b) shame over some failure; (c) excessive drinking or drug abuse; (d) uncontrollable or frequent crying and other extreme reactions to stressful events that would normally be handled more calmly; (e) sleep problems (too much or too little); (f) depression, anxiety, and anger; (g) stress-related physical illness (e.g., headaches, gastrointestinal disorders, upper- and lower-back pain, poor stamina or resistance); (h) inability to forget scenes of horror from the war; (i) difficulty concentrating or excessive ruminating; (j) uncharacteristic social isolation; (k) blunting of emotions; and (l) suicidal thoughts and plans.

In addition to these symptoms, a number of characteristic symptoms of family stress should be watched, such as (a) family conflict that does not come to resolution; (b) any signs of verbal or physical violence; (c) family members isolating themselves from one another; (d) extreme dependency and clinging; (e) making one or two family members (often children) scapegoats for the family's difficulties; and (f) children's discipline or academic problems.[24]

And the war does not end when the shooting stops. The psychological toll can be lifelong. Indeed, clinicians and researchers assert that Holocaust survivors suffer from some degree of posttraumatic stress disorder until they die.[25] It is also noteworthy that many of their children suffer from a milder version of similar symptoms even though they were born after the experience. This "transgenerational traumatization" is not limited to those who survived the Holocaust of the Third Reich.[26] It is also reported in children of parents interned in Japanese civil internment camps during World War II in the Dutch East Indies and in the United States.[27]

The Vietnam War clearly wreaked its own special havoc. In a sense, the words "Vietnam vet" and "posttraumatic stress" have become synonymous. It is no secret that soldiers' experiences lead to depression and interpersonal problems. The culture shock of the foxhole-to-front porch transitions, the reorganization of financial and work responsibilities, and the general unpopularity of the war were not rewarding experiences for those who didn't come home in a box. Factor in the depression, anxiety, repressed anger, and sleep disorders of the wives of prisoners of war and the psychological damage to the countries involved was (and is) immeasurable.

The Vietnam War certainly exacted a heavy toll on Asian people as well. Posttraumatic psychosis among Cambodian refugees was disruptive to those directly affected as well as their families.[28] Consequently, many Asian American survivors of mass violence migrated to the United States with the hope of saving their lives and minds.[29]

It is interesting to note that at the end of World War II there was a conspicuous lack of awareness by the psychiatric profession of the rehabilitative needs of Holocaust survivors. In fact, there was not even a reference to the problem in major psychiatric textbooks of the time.[30] Such is not the case today. The mental health of soldiers exposed to combat in the Persian Gulf and in Bosnia has been deeply scrutinized. In fact, a special task force on war-related stress was convened to develop strategies for prevention and treatment of disorders associated with the Persian Gulf War.[31] Although the war was won with relative ease, negative psychological patterns still became apparent in family disruption, the overall stress of war, and financial difficulties. In short, all wars are hell in more ways than one.

Culture

What is culture? Hunt's definition is especially accurate:

The most powerful social influence on human behavior is the culture in which the individual lives, works, procreates, and dies. Culture can be viewed as the aggregate of all beliefs, customs, language, history, and technological achievements of a people. Culture influences not only directly observable behavior but also the values and beliefs that govern that behavior. It provides us with a notion of what is right and wrong and gives meaning to our actions.[32]

Culture may also induce stress and affect the *rate* of mental disorder in different societies. Freud expressed the view that culture directly interferes with mental health by frustrating human instincts.[33] He held that this occurs to a greater degree in civilized, sophisticated cultures such as our own. In these settings, culture exists and continues to exist only through individuals' renouncement of their instinctive desires. The whole structure of culture, with its elaborate set of norms and values, puts prohibitions on people's instinctual drives of aggression and egoistic self-satisfaction. Freud believed that the pursuit of culture is responsible for human misery because that pursuit requires the repression of instinctual needs and desires. He also held that civilized people would be much happier if they gave up the perpetuation of culture and returned to more primitive conditions! This thesis astonished many people in Freud's time and continues to raise some eyebrows today. There are, of course, those who do not believe that modern industrial society is generative of more mental disturbance than any other kind of society.[34] However, empirical evidence shows that fast-paced, industrial societies, particularly the capitalistic ones, are least conducive to mental health. One possible correlate of these societies is less interaction and support among family members, a condition that reportedly has led more children to seek psychiatric help.

Culture can also affect mental health by the stressful restrictions it places on people in particular social roles. In American culture there are numerous examples, all of which are presented in part three of this book. One is the connection between the female sex role and menopausal depression. Some women during their "change of life" experience a sudden breakdown and assert that their lives are not worth living. Why? A medical explanation holds that biological changes are responsible for the change in mood. But it may also be that these women react to menopause with depression because of the limited definition of the female sex role in American culture.

Consider the derogative phrase "change of life" itself. This is a sexist phrase that defines women solely in terms of their reproductive utility, implying a dramatic downturn in the quality of life following loss of capacity to give birth. This denies the potential value of those years following menopause. If women have based their lives on a narrow range of fulfilling experiences, such as childbearing and child rearing, they have fewer alternatives through which to gain satisfaction when childbearing is no longer possible. They feel then that they have lost an important asset, and depression often results.[35]

Of course, a list of cross-cultural (and intracultural) differences in mental illness is lengthy and cannot always be explained by different levels of stress. Many of the cultural differences are the result of the very fabric and values of a particular culture. The wide range in attitudes toward homosexuality is part of that list. The facts that groups such as Puerto Ricans are reported to exaggerate their symptoms while the Chinese and Japanese behave stoically are also chunks of the "cross-cultural point." Even therapy looks oddly different around the world. If you are a troubled American, it would be common to consult a psychiatrist or clinical psychologist. But somewhere else you may be directed to a "shaman," a healer who uses "magical" modes of treatment. These same shamans are the stuff of novels here in the United States.[36]

There is one further note to be added to the whole issue of the influence of stress on mental health. Stress may not just be a psychosocial problem that simply affects the mind. There may also be a biosocial basis of stress as evidenced by the suspicion that social stressors can also be precursors of physical health problems such as heart attacks and even death.[37]

Evaluation of the Social Stress Model

The social stress model of mental illness is a prime example of the sociology of mental disorder since it examines the psychological impact of different social roles. Nowhere is this connection clearer than in the case of social class. Numerous studies report that lower social class membership is a mental health hazard; lower-class people not only have the highest rate of mental illness, but they are also subject to the worst form, psychosis. One weakness of the social stress model is that it cannot certify that social stress preceded mental illness. It may be that people who are predisposed (biologically?) toward psychopathology may end up in stressful social roles. This would be true in the case of a person from a higher-class family who became schizophrenic, no longer could function in higher occupational roles, and skidded *down* the social class ladder. This is a "chicken and egg" issue that haunts the social stress view.

FAMILY SYSTEMS THEORY

Family system theorists propose that the structures and rules of some families may cause a member to behave abnormally in order to keep the familial system together, a condition referred to as *homeostasis*. Although relatives may appear to be acting abnormally according to outsiders' definitions of deviance, within the family the behavior is regarded as normal because it prevents disruption of a well-established system.[38]

Schizophrenia is a good example. Early family system theorists proposed that families in which "double-bind communication" occurs (giving simultaneous mutually contradictory messages) were more likely to produce schizophrenic offspring. Most commonly the "schizophregenic" mother was blamed for such mixed communications, for example, "I love you, don't touch me." Essentially the child continuously exposed to these kinds of messages simply cannot win parental approval. He grows increasingly suspicious of the world around him and may eventually deteriorate into paranoid schizophrenia. According to family systems theorists, double-bind messages permit the family to stay together at the expense of one or more of its members who serve to maintain balance. Sound crazy? Not when you factor in the fact that there are a lot of parents who are unfamiliar with normal family values such as love, nurturing, and trust. In essence, family systems theory centers on the effects of a disturbed person(s) raising children.

There are many types of stressful influences on mental illness, but perhaps those within the nuclear family are most frequently responsible for abnormal behavior. These can range from "disturbed communications" to total neglect.[39] Among those families that remain together, a number of pathological family patterns have been uncovered. One is what is called "family schism." Here the family is divided into two warring camps headed by the parents. This forces the children to choose one side, often causing a concomitant splitting of their own identities into two antagonistic parts. Where the family is "skewed," one parent dominates the group usually through excessive dependency on the other parent. This type of relationship typically proceeds at the expense of parental satisfaction of the children's needs. In a nutshell, the kids are ignored.

One of the problems in identifying the influence of family stressors on mental health is the ambiguous way in which "stressors" and "troubled" are identified. So many people claim that they had a "troubled childhood" but go on to become happily married parents.[40] That's probably a case in which "troubled" can mean anything. Where children are raised by parents who are clearly abnormal, a happy outcome is not likely. Such is the case in children of clinically depressed mothers. The influence that a depressed mother has on the developmental outcome of her child is overwhelmingly negative.[41]

Other potentially damaging familial experiences include the lack of a mother figure, especially during the first years of life. Here the child is denied the warmth and

affection necessary for normal personality development. Observations of such mater-
nally deprived children make it clear that "when deprived of maternal care, a child's
development is almost always retarded—physically, intellectually, and socially—and
symptoms of physical and mental illness may appear."[42] Aside from parental absence,
institutionalization (such as living in an orphanage) can also exert a heavy psychiatric
toll.[43] On the other hand, a mother-child relationship that is *too* cohesive is reported
to jeopardize mental health by creating a personality that is pathologically dependent
on others and not able to function adequately alone.[44]

The examples cited here are about families that remain together, although they
may be bound in pathological ways. What about families that break up? Nothing positive here. In fact, the some 40 percent of American children whose parents divorce
before they reach age 18 are more emotionally troubled, have more behavior problems, and perform less well in school than the average.[45]

After years of studies, there is a growing number of reports that divorce exacts a
far severer and longer-lasting toll on the nation's children than previously believed. As
a result, some research analysts are questioning whether divorce can continue to be
viewed primarily as a right of adults, without weighing the potential detriment to children and society. In the 1950s, half of young mothers believed couples with children
should stay together even if they did not get along with their husbands. Today fewer
than one in five feel that way.

The emotional difficulties and misbehaviors of children of divorce are part of
the visible aspects of the problem. Another factor is that, after a divorce or separation,
children are almost twice as likely to be living in poverty than they were before their
parents separated. Not all children of divorce are damaged by the experience, of
course. For some, life improves after warring parents separate. Many parents also go
out of their way to minimize the impact of divorce on their children. On a related
note, children in single-parent families and stepfamilies have higher rates of emotional problems than those in mother-father families.[46] Of course, it would be simple-
minded to hold that divorce itself is the entire problem since the roots of the
difficulties are often evident much earlier.

No discussion of the relationship between abnormal behavior and the family
would be complete without mention of the devastating impact of violence. Consider
these statistics. One and a half million aggravated assault and a half million incidents
of child abuse are reported each year. Much of this violence, including a third of all
homicides and up to 75 percent of assaults, occurs within families. In divorce proceedings, about a third of couples mention physical abuse. One study of 290 pregnant
women found that 8 percent had been battered during their current pregnancy.[47] As
many as 10 percent of women may have been raped by their husbands. These are very
depressing statistics, especially in light of the fact that they only represent *reported*
cases.

The impact of violence on children is enormous not only in terms of impaired
mental health but also in the danger that abused children will grow up to repeat the
pattern in their own relationships and families.[48] Clearly, the family can provide love,
stability, and a sense of identity to its children. Too often, however, it is also the scene
of violence.[49]

The effects of family violence are myriad and sometimes macabre. Experts
report that a violent childhood is a common experience among those who grow into
adult sexual predators.[50] Can witnessing violence actually alter the way the brain develops? Researchers at the Baylor College of Medicine report that it can. Their explanation is that the brain organizes itself in response to experience, becoming "the stored

reflections of the collective experiences of the developing child." In other words, stressful experience can become biology.

What can stop the increase in the number of families in which violence is the norm? Certainly the profile of batterers may provide a predictive clue.[51] But what about stopping it now? One creative approach has been developed to stop parents who deliberately harm their children so that they will gain attention from being hospitalized, a mental illness known as Munchausen syndrome by proxy. An Atlanta hospital hid video cameras in 41 rooms in an attempt to confirm physicians' fears that certain children's illnesses were being intentionally caused by their mothers. In more than half of the cases, the cameras recorded evidence that the mothers were injecting their children with urine, switching their medication, and even suffocating them to keep them sick.

There are many other ways to examine the role of the family such as through the singular impact of marriage itself. Unmarried adults of all ages have higher death rates and higher rates of psychiatric and physical illness.[52] But mental health and companionship is a very complicated relationship. Marriage, for instance, is not as good for women as it is for men. Although many married women are happy and adjusted, they suffer far greater mental health hazards (both in frequency and severity) than married men.[53]

The list of intrafamilial experiences that lead to mental illness is well documented and growing constantly. It is no longer a body of knowledge shared exclusively by mental health experts but is rapidly disseminated to the public through a number of popular publications. In fact, psychiatric knowledge has entered into legal conflict situations in which children have charged their parents with raising them improperly. In 1992, for example, an 11-year-old British girl was granted a "divorce" from her mother and stepfather and given permission to live with her grandparents. That same year a Florida court allowed a 12-year-old boy to divorce his parents and be adopted by his foster family. Dozens of child divorce cases are presently pending in Britain and here. In the chapters that follow, a number of intrafamilial theories of mental disorder are presented and evaluated. Keep these ideas about the role of the family in mind when you judge them yourself.

Evaluation of Family Systems Theory

Family systems theory is based on the observation that people with mental illness often come from families headed by people with their own disturbances. Thus children may be raised in tense, abusive ways that lay the foundation for pathological personality development. That may be true, but, like any single theory of mental illness, the family systems model certainly does not provide all of the answers. One question left unanswered is: "If pathological upbringing leads to mental disorder, why do some become disordered while their brothers and sisters are mentally healthy?" Perhaps the disordered one was raised in a unique way. Perhaps.

LABELING THEORY: THE SOCIETAL REACTION MODEL

Members of the *labeling theory* school view mental illness as the result of an unfortunate experience of a socially powerless individual who committed a deviant act, much like those committed by everyone at one time or another during a lifetime. This individual, however, was caught by socially powerful others and assigned the label of mentally ill. Some extend this observation to the belief that *mental illness is simply social misbehavior.* As noted earlier, psychiatric diagnosis is a relativistic endeavor, dependent upon the accepted dominant model of illness or disease within a society.

Some labeling theorists claim that mental illness is nothing but a myth. A penetrating voice from within traditional psychiatry is Thomas Szaz, who argues that psychiatric theory rests upon unproven assumptions.[54] Additionally, G. W. Albee has stated that the medical model of mental illness is responsible for a gross waste of time and funds "to support the urine boilers and myelin-pickers looking for the defective hormone or the twisted synapse."[55] Labeling theorists also take issue with psychiatric nomenclature, contending that DSM diagnostic labels are alarmist and threatening. Members of this movement feel that a damaging stigma attaches to these labels, a stigma that fosters the public belief that mental patients are not merely sick but to be feared and scorned. It is no surprise that labeling theory is sometimes called the "antipsychiatric model."[56]

Labeling theory contends that mental illness is a status with a prescribed set of role-related behaviors that are acted out by those who have been so labeled. Individuals who acquire the label may have simply failed to manage their lives comfortably within the demands of their social environment. They may be irritable, bad-tempered, or aggressive, and others urge them to seek medical advice—especially if they are young and still at the mercy of their elders. In these cases, it is often the socially obnoxious behavior that leads to psychiatric treatment. Simultaneously, the fact of the illness is inferred from the behavior so that the behavior itself *is* the illness. According to Szaz, the behavior, which is nothing more than "problems in living," results in conduct that violates rule-following prescriptions. As long as the criteria for mental illness are conduct and personal beliefs, evaluations of diagnosticians will always reflect their own moral, ethical, and political standards.[57]

Although labeling theory was highly influential during the 1960s, it has now fallen out of fashion.[58] Still it offers some solid ideas for thought. Sarlin, for instance, argues that the concept of "illness" came to include unacceptable behavior during the sixteenth century to save unfortunate people from being labeled witches. It was more humane to treat persons who exhibited different kinds of misconduct as if they were ill.[59] But what was useful in an earlier historical era has, according to labeling theorists, been continued into a harmful myth.

Labeling theory rests on the propositions of the classic sociological theories of personality (*symbolic interactionism*) developed by Charles Cooley and George Herbert Mead. Both believed that one's personality is largely a reflection of how an individual interprets other people's reactions to him. More recently, Scheff and Szasz have pioneered in applying this concept to mental illness in general.[60]

The labeling theory of mental illness holds that, if the reactions of others to a person are generally negative, and if the person perceives and accepts this negative evaluation, she suffers a high degree of anxiety and eventually develops a disorder.[61] Note that labeling theorists consider abnormal behavior to be a process by which an individual moves from *primary deviance* to *secondary deviance*, a distinction made by Lemert.[62] Primary deviance is the original deviant act, which may have a wide variety of causes. Secondary deviance results from being labeled a deviant. In other words, a primary deviant act is followed by negative social sanctions that cause the person to be hostile and resentful toward those doing the penalizing. Then the person reacts to others' stigmatization and penalties, not by stopping the deviance but by accepting the deviant status.

The acceptance of a negative self-attitude must occur over a period of time in order to produce a disorder. It is one's self-concept that underlies mental illness, and one's self-concept depends on the attitudes that others have toward the person. If others blame him, he will blame himself. If they accept him, he will accept himself. It is the *negative self-image* that creates feelings of inadequacy and forms the core of a later problem. For example, children are likely to become disordered if they are taught to seek perfection in themselves because they will feel compelled to spend their lives trying to achieve the unattainable and to win the approval of everyone. Ellis, for instance, reports on the case of an unusually good-looking, 17-year-old female, an accomplished dancer and sculptor, with a tested IQ of 178. She considered herself ugly, untalented, and stupid. The origin of this distorted self-concept was her parents, who always complained that their daughter was a failure in school because she received a 98 in a subject rather than 100![63]

Criticism can also engender a negative self-image because it is often perceived as disapproval, a sign of one's worthlessness. Competitiveness can inflict the same damage as perfectionism and criticism, since by promoting the belief that a child should be better than other children, the child with average skills feels deprived relative to other talented peers.

Forcing competitiveness, criticism, and perfectionism on a child are some of the ways by which a second type of self-disparagement can occur. This is a selective process by which the individual gives the negative reactions of others prime importance while disregarding any positive evaluations since the negative reactions are consistent with a sense of self-deprecation. People who have suffered extreme criticism or who have perfectionistic attitudes often overreact to slight blows to their ego. These are people who go through life preoccupied with feelings of worthlessness that grow until the perception of their own worthlessness makes them unattractive to others. It is a cycle of mounting tension that deteriorates into chronic anxiety.

One of the best fits of labeling theory with the development of mental illness is with the psychosocial experience known as "patienthood," the central topic of the last part of this book. A huge amount of research makes one thing very clear: being labeled as mentally ill affects all phases of the patient process, including diagnosis, commitment, treatment, and the horrible stigma attached to people who are released from a place like a state mental hospital. Their attempts to rejoin mainstream society are often sad horror stories.

Evaluation of Labeling Theory

The labeling theory of mental illness clearly places the origin in disturbed interpersonal relationships and therefore points out the important effect that social stress can have on psychopathology. However, one weakness of the theory is that it is deterministic in assuming that negative evaluations by others are automatically accepted by an individual. Certainly some people ignore others' criticisms and live mentally healthy lives. What is peculiar to those who accept the label? Is there an inherited weakness or an unconscious problem that leads some to respond poorly to others' evaluations? Clearly, these questions remain to be answered.

SOCIAL LEARNING THEORY

Both the psychoanalytic and social learning perspectives reject the disease metaphor of psychopathology, as espoused by the medical model. The theoretical assumptions of both schools hold that abnormal functioning originates from the same processes as normal human development. While psychoanalysts describe intrapsychic processes, social learning theorists examine the source of overt stressful experiences.[64] They theorize that mental disorder results from *learning*, a change of behavior that takes place through experience.[65] Behaviorists do not differentiate the symptoms of mental illness from the underlying cause; they are considered to be one and the same. This view, championed by Dollard and Miller, argues that mental illness is nothing more than a set of observable symptoms.[66] Thus, the principles of social learning theory can be applied to abnormal as well as normal behavior.

Social learning theory centers about the principle of *conditioning*, an approach to abnormal behavior developed by B. F. Skinner.[67] Skinner contends that learning an abnormal pattern of behavior is not acquired by the simple pairing of a stimulus with a response, but by producing new responses under conditions of reinforcement from the environment. A reinforcer is essentially any event that strengthens the response that it follows. Reinforcement may be positive (e.g., food, money, attention) or negative (a stressful life event). The reinforcements are contingent on what a person does. If, for instance, a child receives a reward from her parents when she exhibits excessive cleanliness or orderliness, she is likely to repeat such behaviors in the future. Over time the process continues until the behavior becomes a regularly occurring part of the person's actions, which, in the case of the child, would approximate obsessive-compulsive disorder.

Social learning theorists propose that the degree of abnormal behavior exhibited by the mentally ill may be influenced by conditioning.[68] Such may be the case when psychotic behavior is acted out and the attention given to the mentally ill individual acts as a reinforcement for that behavior. Studies of schizophrenic patients have demonstrated that severe psychotic symptoms decrease when socially desirable behaviors are rewarded with attention or privileges and deviant behavior is ignored by the psychiatric staff. Substance abuse may also be linked with conditioning since the initial use of drugs can bring comfort. Although a person may be aware of the long-term risks involved with drug use, the immediate jolt of positive reinforcement can be very seductive. Social learning theory has been most clearly formulated in the work of Julian Rotter[69] and Albert Bandura.[70] Learning occurs through both the observation and imitation of models (other people) whose patterns of response are acquired through repetition of their behaviors.

Abnormal behavior may follow from this type of experience. Rotter and Bandura postulate that a common reason for pathological anxiety is that the individual's environment directly encourages it. Inadequate parental models who induce stress are often seen as a cause of maladaptive behavior. Essentially, the child is exposed to parents who are themselves poorly functioning in some way. Sometimes the encouragement is quite blatant, as in the case of overprotective parents who urge their children to be habitually on guard. It is also visible in the case of parents who chronically feel guilt themselves and thereby provide a guilty role model for their children. Another common example of direct encouragement of anxiety is the parent who creates a sense of unworthiness in a child through constant criticism. Sometimes the encouragement is more subtle, as in the case of overpermissive parents who do not provide their children with a stable framework with established limits of acceptable behavior, a situation that can create feelings of insecurity.

Modeling extends beyond the family framework. Bandura, for instance, conducted an experiment where stressful (aggressive) behaviors in adult models were observed by young children.[71] The kids exposed to an adult model abusing a doll learned to abuse the doll themselves. Children who had no such exposure did not behave aggressively toward the doll. Essentially, it was the authority of the model as an adult figure (not necessarily a parent) that affected the children's aggressiveness. This classic experiment has led to questions about the effects of other extrafamilial models of authority, such as television characters, particularly violent ones.[72]

One variation of social learning theory is *cognitive-behavioral theory*. Cognitive theorists recognize that learning also involves the influence of privately held thoughts and beliefs (*cognitions*). Cognitive-behavioral theory emphasizes the unique ability of human beings to actively reflect on the nature of their beliefs. Both normal and abnormal behaviors are determined primarily by an individual's thoughts and interpretation of beliefs. Cognitive behaviorists believe that disturbed thinking processes are the root of abnormal behavior because emotions are the product of cognitions.[73]

From the perspective of cognitive-behavioral theory, mental illness results from habitual patterns of illogical, self-defeating thinking processes that lead to such pathological consequences as depression. Aaron Beck, for example, has observed that depressed people tend to engage in *overgeneralization* when a stressful but insignificant event is expanded to include a broad negative interpretation of all events. Depressed people are also prone toward *selective perception,* as in the case of a person who limits her or his interpretation of things to only the negative features of life. And there is also *magnification,* where the importance of undesirable events is exaggerated. The bottom line is that counterproductive thinking causes abnormal behavior. It is not caused by "illness" in the medical sense.[74]

Albert Ellis proposed an entire category of maladaptive beliefs ("basic irrational beliefs") that create counterproductive thinking. The anxious person who spends life consumed by questions of self-doubt and fear may be a victim of the irrational belief that it is necessary to be approved of by virtually everyone. In seeking approval, he may distort a listener's yawn into a message of boredom or dislike. Irrational beliefs are generally extreme, unrealistic, and illogical. Other examples include the idea that human unhappiness is externally caused and that people have little or no ability to control their lives.[75] The list goes on—a list of the beliefs that embody the "all or nothing thinking" characteristic of some abnormal minds.

Evaluation of Social Learning Theory

One problem with the social learning theory of mental illness is that it may examine only surface behaviors and therefore ignore underlying causes. The theory holds that a stressful social experience or sets of experiences cause symptoms through a learning process. A fear of being in attics, for example, is linked to an earlier experience where an attic was associated with something unpleasant or painful. But this does not elucidate the way in which the specific learning experience may be generalized to anxiety about other situations as well.

Social learning theory, like any theory of human behavior (normal or abnormal), is limited by its own vision. Certainly there is plenty of evidence that children mimic adult role models, particularly parents. Logic would dictate that the natural process of modeling is partly responsible for the way certain character traits run in families. A parent who is phobic toward insects, for instance, may very well instill a similar fear in children who see the adult having a panic attack if a wasp flies into the house. However, there is much more to the intergenerational transmission of character flaws than mere modeling. In the case of a severe disorder, such as schizophrenia, family patterns may be the sheer result of genetic endowment, something that has nothing at all to do with modeling.

Cognitive-behavioral theory is interesting. However, it seems most relevant to understanding the origin of clinical depression and much less applicable to other illnesses, such as multiple personality disorder. Even as a theory of depression, it may fall short because it fails to answer the fundamental question of why a particular person would fall victim to illogical thinking while someone from a similar background maintained rational thought.

PSYCHOANALYTIC THEORY

Sigmund Freud proposed that the mind (psyche) contains a *tripartite* personality structure consisting of the id, ego, and superego. The process of continuous interaction among these structures is an *intrapsychic* phenomenon, occurring below the tangible surface of observable behavior, as expressed by the term *psychodynamics*. The psychoanalytic school emphasizes the specific intrapsychic pathways by which social stressors are transformed into disordered patterns of behavior. The origins of psychopathology are considered to result from the interaction among the three parts of the personality and their reaction to interpersonal stress.[76]

According to psychoanalytic theory, two parts of personality are diametrically opposed: the selfish, pleasure-seeking id and the moral, straitlaced superego.[77] The ego acts as an executive by mediating the needs of the instincts, the constraints of reality, and the strictures of the superego, commonly known as the *conscience*. Mental illness is considered to originate in a conflict among these interdependent parts during childhood when the personality is being formed. These years are crucial because the *social* experiences that occur then can have lasting effects on the individual's psyche. Psychoanalysts believe that the most important experiences are those connected with *libidinal* needs, those stemming from the sexual urges of the id. Thus, their view is also known as *psychosexual theory*. Unlike other models, psychoanalytic theory emphasizes unconscious mental activity and is therefore oriented toward the way in which an individual interprets an event rather than toward the external, visible aspects of the event. The theory analyzes the symptoms of abnormal behavior in terms of how psychiatric symptoms symbolically represent intrapsychic conflicts. Psychoanalytic theory holds that mental illness, particularly the anxiety and personality disorders, is largely the result of the responses of the unconscious to the social experience (and stresses) of individuals seeking libidinal satisfaction. Specifically, traditional psychoanalysts believe that abnormal behavior develops from problems (often sexual) originating in interpersonal difficulties, particularly with the parents.

Mental illness results from a conflict between instinctual impulses arising within the id or from a conflict between an id impulse and the ego or superego. Since the ego represents the external social environment and the superego represents cultural values, *abnormal behavior is essentially the result of the stress generated by a conflict between innate human needs and societal norms*. The conflict often arises from a threatening childhood experience that imposed severe stress on the ego. Typically this is a disturbed parent-child relationship. The painful early childhood experience establishes a potential to become disordered. However, this experience must be reactivated in adult life if abnormal symptoms are ever manifested. How? When the individual encounters a situation in life that is perceived as similar to the earlier one.[78] For instance, an individual may experience anxiety working within a rigid bureaucracy just as he did growing up under the domination of a strict father.

The mechanisms of this process have been formalized in psychoanalytic theory under the terms *fixation* and *regression*. Fixation means that personality growth is arrested at a particular developmental stage as the result of an unresolved childhood conflict, usually with the parents. It can cause difficulties in functioning later in life because the fixation remains as a scar in the person's psychological structure. To depict the phenomenon of fixation more clearly, psychoanalysts use the analogy of an army that leaves strong garrisons behind en route to conquering new territory. This serves to both forward supplies and allow for a place of retreat in case insurmountable difficulties are met ahead. The retreat is the military parallel to the psychoanalytic concept of regression whereby the personality returns to an earlier developmental stage, the stage at which it is fixated. The specific type of mental illness is determined by the point at which the personality is fixated.

Freud held that anxiety disorders result from a "learning excess."[79] This was based on his observations that fixation was often associated with unusually harsh treatment of the child by the parents. This can result in an excessively severe superego that impedes the healthy gratification and development of instinctual drives. Others since Freud have supported the proposition that stressful infantile experiences can have a traumatic effect on personality development. But harsh parental treatment and unnecessary taboos on instinctual needs are not the only pathways to abnormal behavior; sexual abuse by adults, seduction by older siblings, and seeing or overhearing sexual play between adults may be dangerous for personality development as well.[80]

In addition to frustrations, there is a minority opinion in psychoanalytic theory which holds that the opposite of frustration, namely, excessive satisfaction (spoiling) of an instinctual need, can also underlie fixation.[81] The rationale for this opinion is that childhood overindulgence makes the person unable to bear frustrations at a later age. Thus, in painful frustration and pleasurable satisfaction, there is a common element: an excessive amount of libidinal energy is used at a particular stage leaving an insufficient amount for normal development through the remaining stages. It has also been hypothesized that sharp transitions from one developmental stage to the next may lead to fixation. This is caused by forcing the developing ego into a stage before it has mastered the challenges and requirements of an earlier stage. It is usually caused by impatient parents who also place difficult expectations on their children. Psychoanalysts hold that these different types of experiences arrest personality development, and the resultant "weak spot" predisposes the person toward regression later.

Evaluation of Psychoanalytic Theory

The traditional Freudian psychoanalytic theory of mental disorder has been criticized on a number of points.[82] One problem with the theory is that it is too deterministic; it assumes that a person's entire personality is chained to the past. Childhood experiences may play an important role in personality formation, but if they determine everything, there is no room left for individual growth and change. This is a very pessimistic view that has yet to be proven.[83] Freudian theory overemphasizes the role of the parent-child relationship so that one gets the impression that full responsibility for the child's makeup falls on the parents, as if other forces in the social environment play no active role.[84] This criticism seems particularly relevant in contemporary American society where the cohesiveness of the nuclear family has been weakened by the forces of industrialization. Today the mass media and educational institutions, as well as parents, play an important role in socialization.[85]

How much value can a "stage sequence" theory have if an individual was genetically programmed to be mentally ill? Although psychoanalytic theory directly relates biological maturation to the intrapsychic conflict generated from physical motiva-

Is Freud Dead?

Many are the ways of coping with the world's vicissitudes. Some people fear and propitiate evil spirits. Others order their schedules according to the display of the planets across the zodiac. There are also those who assume that they carry, somewhere inside them, a thing called the unconscious. It is mostly invisible, although it can furtively be glimpsed in dreams and heard in slips of the tongue. But the unconscious is not a passive stowaway on the voyage of life; it has the power to make its hosts feel very sad or behave in strange, self-destructive ways. When that happens, one recourse is to go to the office of a specially trained healer, lie down on a couch and start talking.

The first two beliefs can, except by those who hold them, easily be dismissed as superstitions. The third—a tenet of the classic theory of psychoanalysis devised by Sigmund Freud—is this century's dominant model for thinking and talking about human behavior. To a remarkable degree, Freud's ideas, conjectures, pronouncements have seeped well beyond the circle of his professional followers into the public mind and discourse. People who have never read a word of his work (a voluminous 24 volumes in the standard English translation) nonetheless "know" of things that can be traced, sometimes circuitously, back to Freud: penis envy; castration anxiety; phallic symbols; the ego, id, and superego; repressed memories; Oedipal itches; sexual sublimation. This rich panoply of metaphors for the mental life has become, across wide swathes of the globe, something very close to common knowledge.

But what if Freud was wrong?

This question has been around ever since the publication of Freud's first overtly psychoanalytical papers in the late 1890s. Today it is being asked with unprecedented urgency, thanks to a coincidence of developments that raise doubts not only about Freud's methods, discoveries and proofs and the vast array of therapies derived from them, but also about the lasting importance of Freud's descriptions of the mind. The collapse of Marxism, the other grand unified theory that shaped and rattled the twentieth century, is unleashing monsters. What inner horrors or fresh dreams should the complex Freudian monument topple as well?

That may not happen, and it assuredly will not happen all at once. But new forces are undermining the Freudian foundations. Among them:

- The problematical proliferation, particularly in the United States, of accusations of sexual abuse, satanic rituals, infant human sacrifices and the like, many of them guided by therapists, who suddenly remember what they allegedly years or decades ago repressed. Although Freud almost certainly would have regarded most of these charges with withering skepticism, his theory of repression and the unconscious is being used—most Freudians would say misused—to assert their authenticity.
- The continuing success of drugs in the treatment or alleviation of mental disorders ranging from depression to schizophrenia. Roughly 10 million Americans are taking such medications. To his credit, Freud foresaw this development. In 1938, a year before his death, he wrote, "The future may teach us to exercise a direct influence, by means of particular chemical substances." Still, the recognition that some neuroses and psychoses respond favorably to drugs chips away at the domain originally claimed for psychoananlytic treatment.
- The Clinton health care reform proposals, oddly enough, which are prompting cost-benefit analyses across the whole spectrum of U.S. medicine, including treatments for mental illness. Whatever package finally winds its way through Congress, many experts concede that insurance will not be provided for Freud's talking cure. (A 50-minute hour of psychoanalysis costs an average of $125.) Says Dr. Frederick K. Goodwin, director of the National Institute of Mental Health: "It's clear that classical psychoanalysis, which is four to five times a week for a four-to-five year duration, will not be covered. It won't be covered because there is no real evidence that it works." Goodwin, for the record, professes himself an admirer of Freud the theoretician.
- A spate of new books attacking Freud and his brainchild psychoanalysis for a generous array of errors, duplicities, fudged evidence, and scientific howlers.

Source: Paul Gray, "The assault on Freud," *Time*, November 29, 1993. By permission of publisher.

tions, it appears to ignore the effect of pathological biological maturation as predetermined by genetics or created by hormonal imbalances.[86] The theory is also criticized for overlooking the effect of traumatic experiences that occur during adulthood, as if the personality is hardened like concrete by that time and therefore not subject to change.

From a sociological perspective, the psychoanalytic theory of mental illness has often been criticized for assuming that the psychosexual stages occur in an invariant order. More specifically, the theory is criticized for being oriented toward Western culture and not accounting for child-rearing practices of other societies, particularly preliterate ones. Certainly the oral period is quite different when children are allowed to suckle at the breast until 5 or 6 years of age. It is also obvious that the anal phase of development takes on a different character in a society that does not stress toilet training, or perhaps does not even have toilets. And what happens if a child is raised in an environment in which adults encourage sexual relations between boys and girls as young as 7 years old? Such societies do not fit the psychoanalytic formula very well. This may be because the theory is limited to a particular social stratum in a specific cultural context. Much of the theory stems from the original work of Freud, and his findings were largely based on observations of middle-class Europeans. Thus it is questionable whether the psychic life of these people is altogether relevant to non-Western peoples, particularly in regard to sexuality, a key factor in psychoanalytic theory.

The cross-cultural criticism of psychoanalytic theory has limited relevance to mental illness in the United States since it is a Western society. As such, it is more important to know whether the major propositions of the theory make etiological sense. Generally speaking, there is evidence that mental illness, particularly anxiety disorder, can stem from early childhood experiences. The fact that anxiety and insecurity are noticeably greater among children raised in institutions and deprived of normal parenting demonstrates this.[87] Even those who had parents but who underwent a series of humiliating childhood experiences, such as a preference of the parents for other children, often develop deep-seated personality disturbances. Some of these disturbances manifest themselves in socially acceptable ways, such as a drive for upward mobility even though the drive may be a pathological quest for power by a vindictive person who seeks to humiliate others.[88]

Another criticism of Freudian thought is his formulation of feminine development.[89] Feminists are clearly ill-disposed toward such ideas as "penis envy." However, Freud was reproached within his own male-dominated psychoanalytic circle by Karen Horney, who discarded Freud's assumptions about women and counteracted his assertion of "penis envy" with a model of "womb envy" on the part of the male.[90] She rejected the idea that women resent and blame their mothers for their lack of a penis and proposed that such theorizing stems from chauvinistic males who may unconsciously desire to bear and nurse children. Aside from all of these speculations about the unconscious, Horney's work is sociologically critical to current feminist thought in Western culture and etiological attitudes toward female depression.[91] She asserted that "penis envy" represents the overvaluation of masculinity in Western culture. Back in 1926, Horney maintained that the neurotic needs observed in male-female relationships in many ways stem from the role conflicts generated by male-dominated social systems. These are "systems" that ascribe roles of marriage and dependency to women while celebrating the liberating force of careers and independence enjoyed by men. The desire to "be a man" is synonymous with the desire for status and power.[92]

Perhaps the biggest problem with traditional psychoanalytic theory is that it is not very popular among social scientists because it presents mental illness as an intrapsychic phenomenon. It may be true that the theory is not consistent with a purely environmental perspective, but that does not make it invalid, only unpopular. It seems obvious that any discussion of the etiology of mental illness, particularly anxiety disorder, would be incomplete without the intrapsychic perspective that psychoanalytic theory offers. Because of its originality and attendance to possible unconscious processes underlying human behavior, it is included (and criticized) in relevant parts of this book. It is also widely criticized by many contemporary social scientists. Box 3:1 includes some of the issues surrounding psychoanalytic theory today.

There are no neutrals in the Freud wars: admiration on the one side; skepticism on the other. A psychoanalyst who is currently trying to enshrine Freud must contend with a relentless critic who believes that Freud is a charlatan. There is, however, one thing on which the contenders agree: for good or ill, Sigmund Freud, more than any other explorer of the psyche, shaped the mind of the twentieth century. The deep-rooted hostility and persistence of his detractors are a wry tribute to the staying power of Freud's ideas. Aside from his theories of mental illness, Freud gave us the first scientific method for showing the meaningfulness of dreams. This has affected the way we think of ourselves ever since, and it has also affected the practice of many psychotherapists and researchers. *Frankly, I had mixed feelings about including so much of Freudian theory in this chapter for fear that it would be misinterpreted as an endorsement. However, it would be intellectually dishonest not to provide the reader with an account of the theory since no one can fairly reject ideas unless they are familiar with them.*

CONCLUSIONS

There are five major environmental theories of mental illness: social stress theory, family systems theory, labeling theory, social learning theory and psychoanalytic theory. Social stress theory examines the impact of belonging to different social groupings, such as race and social class. It also examines the wider impact of such macrosocial forces as the economy, war, and culture on mental health. Family systems theory holds that some families have structures and rules that are abnormal. They may mesh with the pathological minds of the head(s) of household, but they can have a devastating impact on the children. The central proposition of labeling theory is that mental disorder stems from internalizing the negative reactions of other people. The result is a highly negative self-image.

Social learning theory examines the source of overt behaviors. There is no room in this model for an unconscious. Human behavior (both normal and abnormal) is theorized to stem from conditioning. Social learning theory centers about a special form of conditioning called modeling. Psychoanalysts recognize that social forces play a role in the origin of mental illness, but they believe that the instincts and the unconscious are also involved. The central proposition of psychoanalytic theory is that disorder originates from conflicts that arose during a particular stage of psychosexual development.

Although these five theories have radically different components, they are bound by two important factors. One is the belief that mental illness can stem from life experiences. The second is that the experiences that put a person at risk for mental illness involve some form of stress.

At this point, it should be emphasized that the causes of mental disorder are still mysterious. All that exists are *theories*, each with its own pile of supporting evidence. However, not one single view can explain any type of disorder. In the face of such uncertainty, the only safe view is an *eclectic* perspective, one that combines all of the approaches into a broader sociomedical view. For example, there are probably many people who are genetically and/or biochemically vulnerable to schizophrenia, but environmental factors such as stress determine which ones will actually be affected and how they will react.

4
Schizophrenic and Mood Disorders

Genetics and environment can contribute to schizophrenia in mysterious ways. Here are two identical twins. The one on the left did very well in college. Her twin developed schizophrenia and ended up in a mental hospital. Cases of discordant identical twins provide a real challenge to understanding the roots of schizophrenia.

UNDERSTANDING PSYCHOSIS

If mental illness can be viewed as a continuum where the most debilitating disorders are on the extreme left, then that is where the psychoses belong. This chapter is about the most devastating states of the mind and brain. Although they are often biological in origin, their onset and progress are affected by the stress of sociological forces. The psychopathological conditions known as the "major psychoses" include the most severe and bizarre mental aberrations: schizophrenic disorders, major depression with psychotic features, and bipolar disorder. These conditions are presented here in terms of their prevalence, symptoms, and etiology. Together, the psychoses account for a major portion of the hospitalized mentally ill in the United States today.

Other psychoticlike states exist but are not considered here because they are uncommon and, in some instances, unclassifiable. Some of these, such as pibloktoq and running amok, were discussed in Chapter 2. In addition to these conditions, which appear to be culturally specific, there are other psychotic states that have been noted in the literature.[1] For example, some people develop the belief that a person, usually a relative, has been replaced by a double. This is known as the *Capgras syndrome*. In the *couvade syndrome*, husbands, during their wives' pregnancies, suffer symptoms that are ordinarily associated only with pregnant women. There is also what is known as *voodoo death* or *thanatomania*. Here a person *actually dies* after transgressing a taboo or from the fear of being bewitched. These are very exotic disorders.

Regardless of whether a particular syndrome is exotic or common, it is considered to be a psychosis if it involves a *loss of contact with reality*. In psychosis, a person replaces reality with a world of fantasy and is unable to differentiate between the external world of others and the internal world of his own mind. The bizarre symptoms of the psychoses most often include false beliefs (*delusions*) and false sensory perceptions (*hallucinations*), both of which demonstrate the central feature of psychosis: an impaired and distorted ability to perceive, process, and understand the everyday world.

Psychotic behavior is often described by "positive" symptoms that suggest excess and "negative" symptoms suggesting deficiency. Schizophrenia, for instance, is typically characterized by both positive and negative symptoms of varying degree. DSM also lists a group of problems known as "delusional disorders." These are very unusual cases in which a person has false beliefs, does not display any positive symptoms, and is otherwise normal. Because of their rarity, delusional disorders are not included here.

Major depression with psychotic features may involve both hallucinations and delusions. In addition, the manic phase of bipolar disorder exhibits many positive symptoms of psychosis whereas its depressive variant expresses only negative symptoms. The overlap in symptoms among these disorders suggests a common biological origin (diathesis), although one has yet to be demonstrated. The social stressors that can trigger a psychosis are numerous and varied. They are described throughout the chapter as part of environmental theories.

The epidemiology of psychoses indicates some definite patterning; some appear most frequently among lower-class people and some among certain age groups. Although the symptoms and epidemiology of psychotic disorders are richly defined, what is less well documented is their etiology. A wealth of causal theories exists, however. Some theories, especially those with empirical support, are more compelling than others, but no one theory can presently account for all cases of any particular psychosis. Although the medical theories do not involve environmental factors, per se, it is important to note that medical information is vital to *all* students of psychiatry, including students of psychiatric sociology, since it allows for a fuller understanding of the sociology of mental illness.

ETIOLOGICAL APPROACHES TO PSYCHOSIS: AN OVERVIEW

The Medical View

There is a growing body of evidence that psychoses may result from vulnerable brain systems such as the frontal lobes.[2] The evidence is hard to ignore, especially when it comes in the form of color brain scans that show that something is clearly wrong in schizophrenics compared to normal people.[3]

The medical model of psychosis partially relies on the measuring of the coincidence (*concordance rate*) of a disorder among family members in order to pinpoint the role of genetic agents. This method suffers some methodological problems because it overlooks the effect of common social stressors among members of the same family. To mitigate this factor, some studies have limited their samples to identical and fraternal twins. A genetic hypothesis is then supported when a disorder is shared more often among identical twins than among fraternal twins. However, this assumes that both types of twins have similar environmental experiences. This is a questionable assumption since identical twins often cling together and are treated more similarly by their parents and others than are fraternal twins. Thus only those studies of identical twins raised in different environments allow for a *relatively pure* assessment of genetic forces.

In 1990, the now famous Minnesota Twin Study was published. The research followed identical and fraternal twins separated in infancy and reared apart.[4] Although this was not a study of mental illness, per se, but of personality traits in general, the results were astounding. Indeed, the conclusion was that a large part of IQ, occupational interests, leisure-time activities, and even religiosity is genetically based. Needless to say, the Minnesota study caused quite a ruckus in the scientific community.

Biochemical theories are another part of the medical perspective. They examine relationships between psychosis and an abnormal state of body chemistry, such as unusual agents in the blood, irregularities in metabolism, or a disruption of the nervous system. The medical model also includes natality theory, which involves any "insult" to the fetus from conception (prenatal) to shortly after birth (perinatal). From my perspective, the "environment" can start at conception. Therefore, drug-addicted or alcoholic pregnant women and obstetrical complications are some of the environmental stressors that can affect brain development in an abnormal way. And they are just a few from a very long list.

The Environmental View

Some environmental theories of psychosis are purely social and others are intrapsychic. Included in the socially oriented approaches are those that stress the causal influence of such stressors as threatening life changes (social isolation, retirement, or divorce) and lower-class impoverishment. In addition, there are theories that locate the origin of the disorder in the structure of the family.

The intrapsychic environmental theories are largely psychoanalytic. Psychoanalysts view psychosis as the result of a severely deprived childhood resulting in fixation.

Psychosis, then, is considered to be a regression to the childhood state at which the person is fixated. Typically, these are the earliest stages of psychosexual development, stages in which the child's mind is normally full of fantasy as is the mind of the adult psychotic. Additionally, psychoanalytic interpretations of psychosis suggest that some of these mental conditions are the result of the repression of unacceptable sexual drives. Even here a social factor is involved since the disorder could not develop without the existence of negative attitudes in society toward certain sexual urges.

There are other intrapsychic theories that are not purely psychoanalytic. Some of these view psychosis as an extreme response to the loss of a highly prized person (love object). Some theories place the origin of psychosis in the specific ways in which people in different sibling positions are socialized, particularly in large families. Both medical and environmental theories are presented in this chapter since it would be unwise to discount any theory while the origins of psychosis remain such a mystery.

SCHIZOPHRENIC DISORDERS

Prevalence

DSM-IV reports that estimates of the prevalence of the schizophrenic disorders in the United States range from 0.2 to 2.0 percent across many large studies. One percent is the most commonly used figure. Slightly less than half of all admissions to mental hospitals are diagnosed as schizophrenics, but because of their relatively poor chances for recovery, these people tend to remain institutionalized for long periods, particularly in state hospitals. Thus they constitute a clear majority of the state hospital population.

Some have charged that the prevalence of schizophrenia is typically overestimated because of broad diagnostic standards and misdiagnoses. It is certainly difficult to know the true extent of schizophrenia since there may be as many schizophrenics outside of hospitals as there are inside of them (*ambulatory schizophrenics*). DSM-IV has narrowed historically broad classification standards by requiring that the diagnosis of schizophrenia include symptoms of the "active phase" persisting for at least one month rather than one week. It also requires that continuous signs of the disorder must be present for at least six months. The active phase includes at least two of the following symptoms: delusions, hallucinations, disorganized speech, grossly disorganized behavior, and negative symptoms.

Schizophrenia is primarily a disorder of the young. It begins early in life, often during adolescence. Admission rates for schizophrenia are concentrated in the age range of 20 to 40 years, with most cases occurring between 25 and 34 years. The median age at onset is in the early to mid-20s for men and in the late 20s for women.[5] Because the age of *onset* may be in the 20s, many children destined to become schizophrenic often go unrecognized.[6]

In 2000, the NIMH reported the following facts about schizophrenia. More than 2 million adult Americans are affected. Most people with schizophrenia suffer chronically throughout their lives. And the most depressing "number": one out of every ten people with schizophrenia eventually commits suicide.

Schizophrenia is known to be heavily concentrated among lower-class people. There are also reports that the disorder advances differently between men and women as they grow older.[7] Hartmann and his colleagues found that, in childhood, there are behavioral indicators of eventual schizophrenia, such as difficulty in interpersonal relationships, lack of goal-directed behavior, and unusual anxiety.[8] But regardless of the course and regardless of childhood warning signs, one fact remains: schizophrenia is a devastating mental illness found throughout the world.[9] Travel north to Canada, for instance, and you will find that the problem has the same dimensions.[10]

Symptoms

My friend Laura Brobyn has been treating schizophrenic patients at Norristown State Hospital for almost 20 years. To her, the condition is so horrible that, if she were forced, hypothetically, to choose between schizophrenia and cancer, she would take the cancer. Laura is not alone. Many mental health professionals agree that schizophrenia assaults much of patients' "humanness" in the prime of life.[11] As you will see later, it is equally aggravating because of its mysterious origins.[12] There is help out there for families trying to cope with a schizophrenic relative, but typically the information only reaches the more educated who are connected with the literate community and/or go "online."[13]

To many, schizophrenic disorders are the most fascinating of all psychopathologies. Thousands and thousands of professional articles, books, and films have been written about them, evidencing that schizophrenia is the subject of lively controversy and much speculation. Part of this fascination lies in the bewildering variety of symptoms exhibited by schizophrenics. Schizophrenia is chiefly expressed through *disordered thought processes,* which, in turn, lead to difficulties in communication, interpersonal relationships, and reality testing.[14] As a consequence of these difficulties, schizophrenics withdraw from the world of others and retire into their private world of thoughts and fantasies.

Delusions.   To have a *delusion* means to be paranoid. Paranoid impulses include suspiciousness, jealousy, hostility, and accusing others of evil acts or intentions. The symptoms may occur in a variety of mental disorders, particularly schizophrenia and occasionally mood disorders. The most common delusions are *delusions of persecution.* A delusion of persecution is a belief that a person is the victim of some organized conspiracy or the prey of a particular person. The "enemy" is believed to be damaging the person's reputation, keeping the person from attaining a goal, or even threatening her or him with physical harm.

Closely related to persecutory delusions are *delusions of jealousy,* also known as *conjugal paranoia.* These people become overwhelmingly suspicious about a spouse or lover who is believed to be in love with someone else or to be promiscuous. The delusion, sometimes referred to as the *Othello syndrome,* typically deteriorates into persecutory ideas that the loved person is spying on or secretly attempting to kill the paranoid.

Paranoid *delusions of grandeur* are less common than persecutory beliefs. These are people who believe that it is their mission in life to achieve great fame and success. Cases include those who insist that they are the heir to a large fortune, that they are God, or some well-known important figure, such as Napoleon, Hitler, or Jennifer Lopez. Another recurring grandiose delusion includes the belief that one is the mastermind of a new scientific theory or invention.

There is also a *grandiose* delusional system, which includes erotic features and is most common among females. In this instance, the person is certain that someone of the opposite sex is trying to seduce her. The seducer is usually someone who is famous and extremely attractive but one with whom the woman is not even acquainted. This is known alternatively as *erotomania* or *De Clerambault's syndrome,* and is sometimes expressed by a belief that many people are overcome by the person's charm.

One other delusional subtype involves bodily functions or sensations. These are *somatic* delusions, which can occur in several forms. Most common are the person's conviction that he or she emits a foul odor, that there is an infestation of insects on or in the skin, and that certain body parts are ugly or not functioning.

The Four A's.   In addition to disordered thought processes and social withdrawal, there are more specific symptoms commonly known as the "four A's" of schizophrenia.[15] The first "A" is an *affective* disturbance, which usually takes the form of a flatness of affect, a lack of outward display of emotion. This may also be manifested by an apparent dissociation between affect and thought content, as when a schizophrenic laughs when describing a tragedy. The second "A" is *looseness of association,* which refers to a lack of continuity of ideas and an inability to move orderly from one group of thoughts to another. For example, if a schizophrenic is asked how old he is, he may respond with a completely irrelevant answer, such as "a colonial home." *Autism* is the third "A"—a self-centered type of thinking that is filled with fantasy. Schizophrenic humor is often autistic; no one gets the joke other than the schizophrenic. The fourth "A" of the schizophrenic syndrome is *ambivalence.* This refers to having two opposite feelings or emotions toward the same object (person, situation, goal) at the same time. This in itself may not be abnormal, as most people experience a number of ambivalent feelings. However, some schizophrenics are ambivalent toward everything, and their ambivalent feelings tend to be half positive and half negative. To this list some would add a fifth "A" of schizophrenia—*anhedonia,* a marked incapacity to experience pleasure.[16]

Schizophrenic Types.   The general symptoms of schizophrenia are found in many different combinations. However, there are certain constellations of symptoms that occur with some regularity. In the *disorganized (hebephrenic)* type, for example, the psychosis is characterized by primitive, uninhibited behavior that is best described as "silly" since it usually includes unpredictable grinning and giggling. *Catatonic* schizophrenia involves marked psychomotor disturbance, alternating between symptoms of excitement and withdrawal. There are two types of catatonic schizophrenia. The *catatonic excited* patients manifest excessive and sometimes violent motor activity. They often talk continually in incoherent streams of speech. They can be destructive and assaultive and for that reason are frequently considered dangerous. By contrast, the *catatonic withdrawn* patient is inhibited and manifests stupor, mutism, a refusal to eat, and an attempt to retain feces. These patients will often maintain uncomfortable physical positions for an extended period of time, regardless of whether they assume these positions themselves *(posturizing)* or are placed there by others *(waxy flexibility).* The *paranoid* form of schizophrenia is characterized primarily by the presence of persecutory or grandiose delusions, often accompanied by hallucinations. The patient's attitude is frequently hostile, and behavior is consistent with the delusions. Excessive religiosity is sometimes present.

There are other forms of schizophrenia as well.[17] One category includes patients who show a mixture of schizophrenic symptoms and mood swings. This is the *schizoaffective* type. There is also a special category for cases in which the symptoms appear before puberty, the *childhood* type, often incorrectly referred to in the popular literature as the autistic child. Many schizophrenic patients have symptoms that are a mixture of other types. These cases are designated as *undifferentiated,* a label that is frequently used and often criticized as a diagnostic wastebasket. Case 4:1 leaves no doubt as to which type of schizophrenia Mr. Simpson suffers from. He has many of the classic features of paranoid schizophrenia.

Case 4:1
Under Surveillance

Mr. Simpson is a 44-year-old, single, unemployed, white man brought into the emergency room by the police for striking an elderly woman in his apartment building. His chief complaint is, "That damn bitch. She and the rest of them deserved more than that for what they put me through."

Mr. Simpson had been continuously ill since the age of 22. During his first year of law school, he gradually became more and more convinced that his classmates were making fun of him. He noted that they would snort and sneeze whenever he entered the classroom. When a girl he was dating broke off the relationship with him, he believed that she had been "replaced" by a lookalike. He called the police and asked for their help to solve the "kidnapping." His academic performance in school declined dramatically, and he was asked to leave and seek psychiatric care.

Mr. Simpson got a job as an investment counselor at a bank, which he held for seven months. However, he was getting an increasing number of distracting "signals" from co-workers, and he became more and more suspicious and withdrawn. It was at this time that he first reported hearing voices. He was eventually fired, and soon thereafter was hospitalized for the first time, at age 24. He has not worked since.

Mr. Simpson maintains that his apartment is the center of a large communication system that involves all three major television networks, his neighbors, and apparently hundreds of "actors" in his neighborhood. There are secret cameras in his apartment that carefully monitor all his activities. When he is watching TV, many of his minor actions (e.g., getting up to go to the bathroom) are soon directly commented on by the announcer. Whenever he goes outside, the "actors" have all been warned to keep him under surveillance. Everyone on the street watches him. His neighbors operate two different "machines"; one is responsible for all of his voices, except the "joker." He is not certain who controls this voice,

which "visits" him only occasionally, and is very funny. The other voices, which he hears many times each day, are generated by this machine, which he sometimes thinks is directly run by the neighbor whom he attacked. For example, when he is going over his investments, these "harassing" voices constantly tell him which stocks to buy. The other machine he calls "the dream machine." This machine puts erotic dreams into his head, usually of "black women."

Mr. Simpson describes other unusual experiences. For example, he recently went to a shoe store 30 miles from his house in the hope of getting some shoes that wouldn't be "altered." However, he soon found out that, like the rest of the shoes he buys, special nails had been put into the bottom of the shoes to annoy him. He was amazed that his decision concerning which shoe store to go to must have been known to his "harassers" before he himself knew it, so that they had time to get the altered shoes made up especially for him. He realizes that great effort and "millions of dollars" are involved in keeping him under surveillance. He sometimes thinks this is all part of a large experiment to discover the secret of his "superior intelligence."

At the interview, Mr. Simpson is well-groomed, and his speech is coherent and goal-directed. His affect is, at most, only mildly blunted. He was initially very angry at being brought in by the police. After several weeks of treatment with an antipsychotic drug failed to control his psychotic symptoms, he was transferred to a long-stay facility with the plan to arrange a structured living situation for him.

Source: Robert L. Spitzer, Miriam Gibbon, Andrew E. Skodol, Janet B. W. Williams, and Michael B. First, *DSM-III-R Casebook.* (Washington, DC: American Psychiatric Press, 1989), pp. 28–29. By permission of the publisher.

Positive versus Negative Symptoms.   I know that I run the risk of sounding too clinical in a book about the *sociology* of mental illness, but there is something so potentially important about schizophrenia, it would be irresponsible to let it go. The "it" is the distinction between positive and negative symptoms of schizophrenia, which were sketched earlier. Positive symptoms are pathological features *added* to the personality such as hallucinations. Negative symptoms are normal traits that are *missing* such as the ability to interact with others.[18] The distinction is more than academic; it may be related to cause and outcome.[19]

Type I (*reactive*) schizophrenia is typically described as sudden onset, environmentally induced, and with a better chance of recovery. In *Type II* (*process*) schizophrenia, the personality deteriorates over a long period of time. Type II has a poor prognosis and is considered to be biological doom.

I do not want to give the impression that schizophrenia falls into two neat categories of bad and worse. Things like that rarely occur in the world of mental illness. In fact, there is not even complete agreement that a clear-cut case of schizophrenia with negative symptoms is always indicative of a poor outcome.[20] You can always find some report somewhere that is "contrary to common opinion."

The Medical Model of Schizophrenia

There is a huge controversy over whether schizophrenia is biological or environmental.[21] Frankly, the issue may be moot since it appears that schizophrenia is not a simple choice between medical and sociological explanations but is instead a multidimensional problem. The fact that some patients exhibit brain abnormalities when photographed by sophisticated brain imaging techniques certainly weighs heavily on the side of biology.[22] And the fact that it appears to be concentrated in certain sociodemographic groups favors the social stress view. Both perspectives are examined below.

Research into the etiology of schizophrenia is extensive, but in many ways, contradictory; nearly 20 distinct explanations have been proposed as causes of the disorder. Some researchers have attempted to order the different theories by noting common themes among them and then creating workable subgroups. Siegler and Osmond, for instance, developed a theoretical framework consisting of "models" of schizophrenia.[23] They describe six models: medical, moral, psychoanalytic, family interaction, conspiratorial, and social. Soskis uses a similar approach by dividing the causal hypotheses into genetic, psychodynamic, family-learning, social, biochemical or neurological, and existential.[24] However, many of these overlapping perspectives fail to deal directly with the long-lived controversy between those who contend that schizophrenia is caused by biological forces and those who stress the impact of environmental influences. The evidence for both sides of that debate is presented here—from mind to molecule.[25]

Genetic Theory.   In 2000, researchers at Rutgers University reported that they were narrowing the search for one gene in the human DNA code that induces schizphrenia. It may not be that simple because searching for the *genes* that cause schizophrenia is like looking for a light switch in a dark theater. Make that several switches—and all in different places.[26]

Is schizophrenia inherited? It might be obvious by now that such a simplistic question does not do justice to the complex, multidimensional nature of the "cancer of mental illnesses." There has been much passionate debate on both sides of the nature-nurture controversy, but presently no singularly definitive explanation of the etiology of schizophrenia exists.[27] There is, however, persuasive evidence that schizophrenia is at least partially caused by genetic factors. The children of schizophrenics have an unusually high probability of becoming schizophrenic themselves. Approximately 10 percent of children with one schizophrenic parent and 50 percent of those with two schizophrenic parents also develop the disorder. Of course, it is possible that this is the result of being raised by schizophrenics rather than heredity, per se.

The preferred method to assess the role of genes is the study of concordance rates for schizophrenia in monozygotic (identical) and dizygotic (fraternal) twins. The concordance rates in the several studies of monozygotic twins range widely from 0 to almost 90 percent. The rates of concordance for the dizygotic twins range from 2 percent to around 15 percent. The fact that concordance is much greater among monozygotic twins than among dizygotic twins strongly suggests the influence of genetic factors. However, genetic transmission does not comprise the complete picture. If it did, the concordance rates would never be less than 100 percent among identical twins.

By their own assumptions, the genetic studies have forced the conclusion that schizophrenia involves more than genes. In fact, many genetic researchers feel their findings indicate that both genetic and environmental factors are significant in schizophrenia.[28] It is important to note that studies of the rate of schizophrenia among identical twins do not necessarily provide a vehicle to directly test the contribution of genes because the twins are not always identical. For instance, they may not equally share the placenta, as evidenced by differing birth weights. In some cases they are actually in separate placentas.

Genetics and schizophrenia intersect in an interesting way when identical twins are discordant.[29] What happened to the twin who ended up schizophrenic that did not happen to the co-twin? We do not know for sure, but in some cases, it is clear that brain abnormalities may be involved.[30] Using magnetic resonance imaging (MRI), one group of researchers scanned the brains of 15 pairs of monozygotic twins, in each of which only one twin was schizophrenic. When compared with the healthy twin's brain, the brain of the schizophrenic twin showed signs of atrophy in almost every case.[31]

E. Fuller Torrey analyzed a case of discordant identical twins in some detail.[32] You should read it. It really hits the psychic home of college students. One of the twins is doing quite well in college, academically and socially. The other one is a completely different story—in and out of institutions and on what looks like a permanent pathway to psychosis. The twins even look different—on the outside of their bodies and in the interior of their brains. If cases like this are brain abnormalities, then which part of the brain is affected? Again, plenty of educated guesses. At this writing, temporal lobe asymmetries are receiving some research attention.[33]

One early genetic researcher is F. J. Kallman, who found a concordance rate of 86.7 percent among monozygotics.[34] He pointed out that this concordance was an *average* over monozygotic twins who had been separated for some years as well as for those who had not been separated. In the nonseparated group, the concordance rate was 91.5 percent, but it dropped to 77.6 percent in the separated group. In other words, concordance decreased when the social environment was changed. There has been some controversy over the validity of twin studies because some feel that they confuse genetics and environment and thus are not an accurate test of the role of genes.[35]

Some research designs counter the criticism of twin studies. Heston, for example, followed up 47 people who were born to schizophrenic mothers in state mental hospitals.[36] The infants were separated from their mothers at birth and raised in foster homes. This group was compared to 50 control subjects who were also residents of the same foster homes. Psychiatric diagnoses were made on members of each group. None of the control subjects was schizophrenic, but 16.6 percent of the offspring of schizophrenic mothers were diagnosed schizophrenic. Other studies of the adopted-away offspring of schizophrenics also support the idea that there is a *vulnerability* to schizophrenia that is transmitted genetically.[37] Controversy remains, however, because some contend that the findings are contaminated by inaccurate diagnoses.[38]

Since there is only a significant tendency for schizophrenia to occur among children born to schizophrenic mothers and not an invariant relationship, it is likely that a vulnerability to schizophrenia is inherited rather than schizophrenia, per se. The vulnerability must then be mixed with sufficient environmental *stress* to produce schizophrenia.[39] This is the position taken by well-known genetic researchers. Paul Meehl, for instance, considers an inherited brain defect to be the necessary but not sufficient cause of schizophrenia. According to Meehl, a person with this defect (*schizotaxia*) displays only mild schizophrenic symptoms (*schizotypic*) and will not decompensate into schizophrenia unless the psychosocial environment is stressful. This is an early version of what we now call diathesis-stress theory.[40]

Research by Gottesman and Shields resulted in an important refinement in the assessment of the role of heredity.[41] They started with 57 schizophrenics who had an identical twin. They then divided the twin sets into four categories graded in terms of degree of concordance with respect to *severity* of schizophrenic symptoms. They uncovered a significant direct relationship between concordance and severity of symptoms. This suggests that only severe cases of schizophrenia are attributable to a genetic defect while milder forms of the disorder may not be related to genetic factors at all.

Many more refinements of the role of heredity in schizophrenia are to be derived from future studies, such as the way in which schizophrenia is actually transmitted genetically. Currently there are several positions on this issue, some favoring a dominant gene, others a recessive gene, and still another that favors the operation of different genetic mechanisms for each of the schizophrenic types. When you consider all of the evidence for a hereditary explanation of schizophrenia, you cannot help but be impressed. You also cannot accept the notion that schizophrenia is completely genetic.[42] Take a look at Table 4:1 and you will see what I mean.

Table 4:1   Lifetime Risk for Developing Schizophrenia by Genetic Relationship

Relationship	Genetic Relatedness	Risk
Unrelated persons	0%	1%
Spouse	0	2
Nephew or niece	25	3
Full sibling	50	10
Son or daughter	50	13
Dizygotic twin	50	14
Monozygotic twin	100	46

Note: The data are an average of numerous studies conducted throughout the United States and Europe over the last 50 years.

Biochemical Theories.   Is schizophrenia biochemical? There certainly has been a lot written in favor of biochemical views. But even these reports cannot be separated from the threatening role played by social stress. In fact, thanks to recent advances in biology, scientists are able to see how stress, an emotional phenomenon, can actually change the physical structure of one's brain. Stress causes cortisol levels to jump and, in high doses, it becomes toxic, destroying neurons.

A ton of research has been undertaken to identify all of the biochemical culprits that may underlie schizophrenia. The reports range from isolated cases of a specific biochemical abnormality to a theory that, like AIDS, schizophrenia is an autoimmune problem that disrupts the central nervous system.[43] Today's ideas sprang from research in the 1950s when studies of the effects of mescaline and LSD yielded some insight into the nature of the chemical alterations possibly involved with the schizophrenic state. Both of these drugs were found to produce temporary schizophrenic symptoms in normal people. Experimental subjects underwent considerable turmoil and confusion and experienced marked disturbances of thinking, perceiving, and feeling. Some subjects showed catatonic reactions; others hallucinated or exhibited paranoid suspiciousness, and several subjects reported losing their sense of personal identity and experiencing their bodies in peculiar ways.

All subjects under the influence of psychedelics suffered a loss in sociability. The psychotic-like episode lasted for only a few hours and normal subjects seemed none the worse for their brief visit to the schizophrenic-like state. The specific linkages between the components of these chemicals and their effects on the brain remain uncertain. Research in this area has been hampered by society's attitude toward LSD and mescaline, both of which became associated with the countercultural youth movement of the 1960s. It is interesting to note that LSD was discovered by accident in a Swiss lab in 1938 and then became a visible symbol of a political movement 30 years later. But that is another book.

A number of specific chemicals are considered to cause schizophrenia if they are present in abnormal amounts. One such chemical is *serotonin*. Early researchers postulated that schizophrenia stems from a cerebral serotonin hormone deficiency resulting from metabolic failure. A clue to the importance of serotonin came from the discovery that LSD blocked its normal effects on the involuntary muscles. This led to the hypothesis that drugs whose effects mimicked schizophrenia did so by inhibiting the action of serotonin.

More recently, another biochemical hypothesis has been put forth that links schizophrenia with excessive amounts of *dopamine*.[44] This theory stems from the observation that antipsychotic drugs produce side effects similar to the physical problems found in patients with Parkinson's disease. Parkinson's disease is caused by too little dopamine in the brain. Thus it was inferred that antipsychotic drugs work with schizophrenics by blocking the effects of excessively large amounts of dopamine.

The dopamine hypothesis is especially interesting when it is evaluated in light of Parkinson's disease.[45] Earlier in the book I warned about the side effects of psychotropic drugs. If they are overused they can produce irreversible problems such as *tardive dyskinesia,* a problem that mimics the movement disorders of Parkinson's patients.[46] Could it be that excessive medication reduces elevated dopamine levels in schizophrenics to the abnormally low levels of Parkinson's patients? Sounds logical, but logic is not always a useful tool in psychiatric research.

At present, the role of biochemical abnormalities in schizophrenia is not completely known. Some reports indicate abnormalities in the blood platelet activity of schizophrenics as well as altered glucose metabolism in the frontal cortex of the brain.[47] It is possible that such abnormalities may not be of etiological significance since they may simply be the *effects* of schizophrenia rather than the *cause*. In recent years biochemical research has turned toward the role of infections.[48] This coincides with related studies on abnormalities in neural development in schizophrenia.[49]

Before I leave the biochemistry of schizophrenia, let me pose one last question: Can schizophrenia, in part, be caused by drug abuse? That question used to be asked more frequently but is not heard as often today. My colleague Corinne Rita examined the social and medical histories of some 1,500 schizophrenics and found that a surprisingly high number had regularly abused "heavy" drugs such as speed and LSD.[50] In fact, she found that to be the case in approximately 30 percent of the cases. One immediately thinks of self-medication of symptoms, but these individuals were abusing drugs five years *prior* to the onset of schizophrenia. That placed their drug abuse in the 1970s and 1980s when many street drugs were laced with dangerous fillers. Either these patients were misdiagnosed with schizophrenia or the drug intake had a significant effect on the development of schizophrenia, coupled with other environmental stressors. Very few of these cases had a familial history of schizophrenia and almost all of the patients exhibited positive symptoms. Others report similar findings in the abuse of psychomimetic drugs.[51] This is not to say flat out that drugs cause schizophrenia, but it seems reasonable to believe that they could trigger the psychosis in those already predisposed. They certainly can be "stressful."

While we do not know the specific biochemical parameters of schizophrenia, we do know that new medications are regularly bringing hope to patients and their families.[52] High on the list of hopes is risperidone (Clozaril), which became available in 1990 in the United States. Posing fewer side effects than other drugs, it has been a godsend for patients who had been given a doomsday prognosis.

Natality Theory.   My colleagues and I recently uncovered a curious finding about schizophrenics—that they were likely to have been in their mother's womb (in utero) during January. Let me give you the background and details.[53]

Although the etiology of schizophrenia is multifactorial, our previous research indicated a statistically significant tendency for adult patients with schizophrenia to have been born during the winter months.[54] Some associate this risk factor with the high number of winter-related viruses, particularly influenza, which can interfere with normal fetal brain development.[55]

A number of other studies also report a "winter-born phenomenon" among patients with schizophrenia.[56] Evidence from a number of different countries throughout the twentieth century has established that people who become schizophrenic are especially likely to have been born during the winter.[57] This is also true in the Southern Hemisphere, where the seasons are the reverse of the Northern Hemisphere.[58] Some reports strongly suggest that winter-related viruses have a greater impact on individuals born in city areas where population density increases the probability of disease transmission.[59]

A few studies have not detected an overdistribution of winter births among schizophrenic samples, and it is important to note that some researchers report that seasonality of schizophrenic birth patterns may not exist at all. The contradictory findings of the minority reports may be the result of grouping all patients with schizophrenia into one homogeneous category rather than separating the patients into meaningful subgroups as some have suggested.[60]

One study did assess birth patterns among patients with schizophrenia by subtype and reported no difference between winter- and non-winter-born schizophrenic cases.[61] However, that study used an unusual classification scheme that separated schizophrenia into subtypes based on neurological evaluations such as developmental reflexes, neuropsychological scales, including the Wechsler Adult Intelligence Scale, and magnetic resonance imaging (MRI) scanning. Our study was specifically designed to assess the role of winter-related health problems on the etiology of Type I and Type II schizophrenia.

The monthly birth patterns of the 801 patients in our sample were compared to the monthly birth patterns of members of the general U.S. population born during approximately the same years, 1933 to 1963.[62] For example, the proportion of all births that occurred in January over this period (8.2 percent) was compared to the proportion of all the patients with schizophrenia in the sample who were born in January. The same comparisons were made for the 11 other months. Essentially our analyses were exploratory, although the study was motivated by the idea that the seasonal birth patterns of patients with schizophrenia may be different from the population at large.

Our data indicate that the excess of winter births is specifically relevant to Type I (reactive form with positive symptoms) schizophrenia. Type II (process form with negative symptoms) schizophrenia, on the other hand, has a notable birth spike in September. This finding places both groups of patients with schizophrenia in utero during the winter, particularly during January, and January has traditionally been the most common month for influenza exposure.[63] The excess of January births among patients with Type I schizophrenia is 29 percent greater than the population at large. The excess of September births among patients with Type II schizophrenia is 35 percent greater than the U.S. population as a whole. See Figure 4:1.

Figure 4:1   Type of schizophrenia and season of birth.

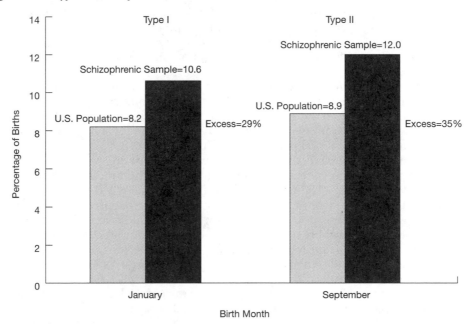

Source: Bernard J. Gallagher III, Joseph A. McFalls, Jr., Brian J. Jones, and Anthony M. Pisa, "Prenatal illness and subtypes of schizophrenia: The winter pregnancy phenomenon," *Journal of Clinical Psychology, 55* (7) (1999), 915–922.

Some hypothesize that Type I schizophrenia is likely to result from a biochemical disturbance, as evidenced by the fact that it is often responsive to medication.[64] This fits well with our data because experts in fetal brain development have reported that a great amount of biochemical processes are completed during the last trimester of pregnancy.[65] At this time much of final synaptic development occurs, although it is not fully complete until after birth. Thus, our findings on Type I schizophrenia are consistent with the theory that maternal illness during the third trimester may induce an insult to fetal brain development.[66] This, in turn, may result in pathological biochemical processes that are proschizophrenic.

Type II schizophrenia follows another theoretical pathway. This type of schizophrenia has been linked with an abnormality in the actual structure of the brain.[67] Once again, a winter-related virus may adversely affect brain development of the fetus, and the form of the brain abnormality appears to be related closely to the stage of development at which the insult takes place. Much of the research on fetal brain development is consistent with our findings that patients with Type II schizophrenia were likely to have been in utero in the winter during the first trimester. During this period of gestation there is a rapid acceleration in the growth of developing brain ventricles.[68] Thus, first trimester disturbances in development of the fetal brain may show most frequently as retardation in general growth of the brain, a phenomenon that is proschizophrenic.

Our findings support the research of others who have reported that disruption of fetal brain development by maternal antibodies can cause adult schizophrenia.[69] Specifically, the seasonal birth patterns of patients with schizophrenia are significantly different from those in the general population. The main difference is the greater propensity for preschizophrenics to have been in utero during the winter when numerous viruses are especially common. We hypothesize that a winter-related virus imposed upon a pregnant woman acts as an insult to the normal brain development of the fetus. We further hypothesize that the type of schizophrenia connects with the trimester of pregnancy during which the illness occurred. Therefore, what has been referred to as the "winter-born phenomenon"[70] should be retitled the "winter pregnancy phenomenon."

There is further indirect evidence of the relationship between maternal illness and later schizophrenia in the offspring. A major outbreak of influenza occurred throughout Europe in 1957. Nineteen to 30 years later (the typical age of onset, or diagnosis, for schizophrenia) the rate of hospitalization for schizophrenia in England, Wales, and Finland was 88 percent higher than normal.[71]

Phenomena such as the 1957 European epidemic suggest that there is a causal relationship between prenatal influenza suffered by the mother and eventual schizophrenia of the child. The fact that the influenza virus is airborne is consistent with reports that winter risk factors linked to schizophrenia predominantly operate in urban areas with high population density.[72] It is possible that the rate of influenza infection among mothers of different social classes is variable and could account for the high rate of schizophrenia in the lower social class.

Seasonality aside, there is plenty of evidence that a host of natality factors may also be linked with the incubation of schizophrenia. As I stated, viruses have been widely connected. Influenza is at the top of many researchers' lists.[73] Obstetrical complications, particularly those that result in fetal oxygen loss (*hypoxia*) are especially risky.[74] All of these problems may impact on brain development and its resultant structure and functions.[75]

Understand that *there is a sociology in all of this theorizing about natality*. I am not just talking about sketchy ideas about how "social deprivation" during gestation and early life predispose to later schizophrenia.[76] My own research has uncovered more blatant problems. When I examined the social and medical histories of over 1,000 schizophrenics, I found that their mothers frequently underwent a number of physical calamities when they were pregnant, including drug abuse, alcoholism, violence, health problems, and mismanaged deliveries. They were reported in about 20 percent of the cases,[77] and they are just the *reports*. The real numbers are obviously higher.

One last point about natality theory. *It is not a purely medical model.* The end result may be physical, but what are the pathways that expose people to these kinds of problems? *They are often purely sociological.* For example, which group in our society is most likely to be exposed to violence and poor health care? The lower class. Keep that in mind here and in Chapter 8 where there is immense documentation of an elevated risk for schizophrenia among the poor.[78] Not only are they more likely to develop schizophrenia but our own data indicate that they are especially likely to suffer from the worst form of schizophrenia, Type II.

The Environmental View of Schizophrenia

Despite a growing pile of evidence that schizophrenia is imposed by biological forces, there is still much to suggest that the psychosocial environment has an impact. Some well-respected researchers still claim that "schizophrenia is usually psychogenic."[79] But their views, which used to be the *only* view, are tempered today with a broader form of thinking. It is my impression that psychiatric sociologists generally have the broader form of thinking consistent with the diathesis-stress orientation.

What are the social stresses involved? They are a wide map from the general location that schizophrenia is "psychologically contagious"[80] to the specific locale of particular forms of "environmental stressors."[81] The urban environment is often targeted.[82] Specifically, the stresses of "big-city life" may push some people (the vulnerable) into this darkest paradigm of the human mind.[83] In fact, some report that, although a family history of schizophrenia is associated with a high risk of having the disorder, sociological variables such as place of birth account for more cases.[84]

Below I present a menu of these stressors associated with the risk of schizophrenia. They range from the pathological dynamics of family life to the bigger picture of social class. We will start historically—Freud first.

Psychoanalytic Theory. Freud attempted to bring schizophrenia into consonance with the concept of regression. In different patients, the regression may have had different causes, but Freud held that it always reached back to earlier times when the ego first came into existence. Specifically, psychoanalytic theory holds that the schizophrenic has regressed to a state of primary narcissism, a phase in the early oral stage before the ego has differentiated from the id. The differentiation of the ego coincides with the discovery that the self is distinct and separate from objects in the outside world. Therefore, the following etiological formulas of psychoanalysts mean one and the same thing: the schizophrenic's ego has broken down; the schizophrenic has regressed to narcissism; the schizophrenic has parted with reality. Through regression, the schizophrenic has effectively lost contact with the real world.

Psychoanalysts believe that the schizophrenic regression is caused by the personality being severely fixated at the oral stage either because of frustrating weaning experiences or from being denied the comfort of a warm mothering figure. The regression is manifested through social withdrawal, a major symptom of schizophrenia. Resemblances between schizophrenic thought processes and those of children are interestingly striking in that both are simplistic, concrete, and weakly governed by principles of relevance.[85] As schizophrenics regress, they revive fears, conflicts, and fantasies that they experienced during the earliest phase of psychosexual development.[86] In other words, they live in a dream world in which people and things lose their distinct identities and appear to merge. It is a world of fantasy-filled thoughts that we call *autistic*.

Because of the regressive nature of schizophrenia, psychoanalytically oriented researchers view it as the royal road to the unconscious since its study can yield information about the makeup of the unconscious as well as information about the dynamics of early childhood. In fact, many fruitful hypotheses concerning the early infantile period have been derived from the study of deeply regressed schizophrenic adults. Some feel that this kind of research is speculative and without empirical support. However, while it is true that many psychoanalytic propositions are difficult to assess, some evidence suggests that the schizophrenic mind is structurally equivalent to the fantasy-filled mind of the infant.[87] The minds may be equivalent, but today this kind of theorizing has fallen out of vogue.[88]

Cognitive Theory.   The cognitive approach centers on information processing and other aspects of cognition in an attempt to explain the origin of schizophrenia. Some cognitive theorists focus on associations while others focus on concepts. It has been clearly demonstrated that schizophrenics experience disturbances in both of these areas. Researchers who view schizophrenia as a cognitive dysfunction have increasingly endorsed the notion that *attention* is the key problem in schizophrenia.[89]

Studies in this area have been carried out by Shakow and, most notably, McGhie and Chapman.[90] Their basic assumption is that schizophrenia is the result of an inability to select, focus on, and regulate incoming information. Because schizophrenics cannot cope with elements in their environment, they become perplexed and disorganized. The psychotic symptoms are considered to stem from the cognitive problems. Andorfer advanced another theory of information processing based on the idea that schizophrenics misinterpret information because they cannot fit it into stable categories.[91]

The weakness of the cognitive theory is that it may simply be describing the altered mental state of schizophrenia rather than explaining its origin. Indeed, this approach appears to be more of an elaboration of the cognitive state that occurs in schizophrenia than of its cause. In the 1990s, however, this theory gained new ground when cognitive dysfunction was linked with brain pathology.[92]

Family Systems Theory.   Many environmental theories point to the family unit as the agent responsible for the schizophrenic breakdown.[93] One such view contends that schizophrenia is the result of mentally disturbed parents raising children. Because the parents are disturbed, their children are considered to learn disordered behaviors through the normal process of imitation. The parents reportedly seriously deviate from usual child-rearing patterns and breed psychopathology in their children in an emotionally bizarre and deprived familial context. In such settings the child is often subjected to rejection, hostility, and emotional abuse.

Schizophrenia has been linked to upbringing for a long time.[94] Through studies of schizophrenic patients and their families, Lidz and his colleagues concluded that schizophrenic patients virtually always emerge from homes marked by serious strife or eccentricity.[95] They contend that it is not the characteristics of a single parent but rather the disorganization fostered by an irrational strife between the parents that creates a family climate unfavorable to child rearing. Their studies classify types of intrafamilial structures and then correlate those structures with the incubation of schizophrenia. Two family types have been observed. One is the *schismatic* family (*marital schism*), which is divided into two antagonistic and competing factions. The other is the *skewed* family (*marital skew*) in which the serious personality disturbance of one parent sets the pattern of family interaction.[96] In either case, schizophrenia is viewed as the product of the family's failure to provide the psychosocial climate necessary for normal personality development of the children.

Others who support family systems theory have concentrated on the pathological traits of specific parents rather than their interactive effect. Studies of socially withdrawn children indicate that they are frequently raised by parents who are demanding, interfering, and overwhelming.[97] Today, the notion that "your parents did it to you" is not widely considered as a singular explanation of the origin of schizophrenia.[98] But, once again, it should be regarded as a dangerous social stressor.

Double Bind Theory. One variation of family systems theory was originally offered by Bateson and his colleagues. They described the specific intrafamilial origins of schizophrenia through their "double bind hypothesis."[99] According to them, schizophrenic thought disorder develops through the constant subjection of a child to contradictory messages from the parent(s). Of prime importance is the fact that the child can neither comment on the contradictory messages, ignore the messages, nor withdraw from the situation. One message is often verbal and the other nonverbal. An example would be beckoning someone to come through gestures and saying, "Go away," at the same time. Contradictory communications are particularly dangerous to children because the parent threatens the child, often in subtle ways, with rejection or disapproval if the child fails to respond to both messages. Escape is impossible because an infant or a small child has nowhere to go. Simply stated, they are damned if they do and damned if they don't.[100]

These kinds of parents attack the children themselves rather than criticize things they do; they habitually tell the child what the child's feelings and thoughts are rather than listening to what the child has to say. And the parents often speak ambiguously, saying one thing and then partly denying what they had said, leaving the child confused. Thus the origin of the term "schizophrenogenic mother."

Bateson and his associates contend that enough childhood double bind experiences can cause the person to perceive the total environment in double bind patterns, to the point that any part of what appears to be a double bind sequence is met with fear and rage. Such theorizing comes from the "blame mother" school of thought, popular in the 1950s. Although this explanation is extreme, parental disapproval has been demonstrated to play an influential role.

In a study comparing schizophrenic patients with their nonschizophrenic siblings, Lu uncovered a recurring form of the double bind pressure.[101] The parents' relationship with the preschizophrenics was significantly different from the way they interacted with their other children. The parents expected a higher degree of obedience, submission, and dependence from the preschizophrenic than from the nonschizophrenic child. Yet, while they expected the child to be more dependent, they simultaneously entertained the conflicting expectation that the preschizophrenic should assume responsibility for achievement and perfection. This placed the child in a stressful dilemma by being expected to play the contradictory roles of dependence and responsibility at the same time.

In adolescence, the dilemma was heightened after the child was confronted with two social stressors that precipitated the actual schizophrenic breakdown. The first stressor was a sudden, explicit expression by the parents that the child should assume concrete adult responsibility.[102] The second stressor was the loss of intimate relations with persons on whom the person depended for emotional support. Together, these two experiences traumatized preschizophrenics by placing them in a position of independence without the support of others—a position threateningly different from the way they were raised.

There is an additional aspect of the double bind theory of schizophrenia that includes the effect of being the last born child in a large family.[103] The youngest, by being allotted the special affections and privileges given to the family "baby," has difficulty acquiring the skills required for independent behaviors and is thus particularly prone to dependency. This hypothesis is consistent with the dependency facet of Lu's theory and is also supported by data demonstrating a higher rate of schizophrenia among last borns.[104] However, it is just a guess and, in my opinion, not a very good one. I looked at the sibling positions of some 2,000 schizophrenics and no such pattern emerged.

Social Class Theory.   One purely sociological theory of schizophrenia holds that the disorder is the result of belonging to the poorest socioeconomic class. It would be an oversimplification to say that poverty causes schizophrenia, but the fact is that schizophrenia is much more common in the lower class than in the working, middle, or upper classes.[105]

There are several explanations for the observed relationship between social class and the rate of schizophrenia. One is the *social stress hypothesis*—the notion that being a member of the lower social class may itself cause schizophrenia. Lower-class people frequently experience stressful situations in the form of broken homes, degrading treatment by others, the lack of opportunity for education, inability to achieve cultural goals, and the overall miserable conditions of deprived life circumstances.[106] Another explanation of the preponderance of schizophrenia in the lower class is that schizophrenics *drift* into poverty from higher social classes. The *drift hypothesis* holds that those who are already disordered lose their ability to function at higher class levels (e.g., occupationally) and eventually skid into the lower class, rather than being born into it.

Some early studies indicate that schizophrenics are downwardly mobile,[107] although other studies show that this is not the case.[108] The question of class-caused schizophrenia has also been addressed by determining whether the parents of schizophrenics are from the lower class. If they are, this would support the theory that lower-class life itself is conducive to schizophrenia. If the parents are not from the lower class, the drift hypothesis would then be supported. A study in England and Wales,[109] as well as one conducted in the United States,[110] found that male schizophrenic patients tended to be employed in lower-class occupations but that their parents held more prestigious jobs. These data lend support to the theory that schizophrenia produces social class, rather than the reverse. Further support of this proposition comes from a related set of data demonstrating that schizophrenics exhibit significant discrepancies between their status aspirations (supposedly developed through socialization in a higher class) and their actual accomplishments (lower-class status).[111] Such a discrepancy is consistent with the experience of skidding into the lower class. Presently, it would be foolish to pick between the stress hypothesis and the drift hypothesis as each may be relevant to *different groups* of schizophrenics.[112]

In the early 1900s, the high frequency of schizophrenia in the lower social class was explained ecologically as the result of living in a socially isolated environment.[113] Today there is ample evidence that schizophrenics live in such conditions because they frequently reside in the socially disorganized areas of cities. The relationship between social class and schizophrenia is etiologically important. It is also highly complex and impossible to delineate in a few paragraphs. The question is dealt with more thoroughly in Chapter 8.

Before I leave the huge question of social class and schizophrenia, I want to note some preliminary findings recently gathered by my colleagues and me. We have found that lower-class schizophrenics are more likely to suffer from the worst form of the psychosis, Type II. We are not sure why this is. Some may theorize that it results from a genetic pool at the bottom of the social class hierarchy. That may prove to be true. It may also be due to prenatal stressors since our data also indicate a huge birth spike in September among lower-class schizophrenics. That places them squarely in January, "influenza month," during the first trimester of their development.[114] This may all prove to be the result of poor health care among the poor, including a lower likelihood of being vaccinated for the flu.

Research on Schizophrenia: Changes Over Time

At the present time, the causes of schizophrenia are not clearly known. Researchers have expended considerable energy investigating possible origins, but not one of today's theories of schizophrenia is capable of explaining all cases of the psychosis. Schizophrenia appears to be a disorder that can be caused in a variety of ways, probably through the complex interplay of many biological and sociological forces.

Some studies have attempted to assess the relative importance of the major theories of schizophrenia by polling the views of psychiatrists. Twenty-five years ago, two such studies produced conflicting results. One was undertaken by Soskis, who uncovered a preference for biological theories among psychiatrists in his sample.[115] However, the findings of that study were limited because the sample was drawn from a census of psychiatrists practicing in only one specific county of New York State. I also conducted a national survey of members of the APA around that time and derived a final sample that was representative of psychiatrists from all geographic areas, in various types of treatment settings (private practice, state hospital), and of different theoretical leanings (psychoanalytic, behaviorist, etc.).[116]

I discovered that most psychiatrists were quite uncertain about the causes of schizophrenia and consequently were reluctant to endorse any particular etiological theory. However, those theories that were most frequently endorsed by psychiatrists were environmental. That was the 1970s. When I ran the same study in the late 1980s, things had really changed. Ten years later, I found that psychiatrists preferred biological theories *if they had to choose* one explanation.[117] However, most of the psychiatrists felt that schizophrenia is the combined result of biological forces and environmental stress. The thinking has really swung from the era of "bad parenting" to the present-day thinking of "diathesis-stress."

MOOD DISORDERS

Prevalence

Mood disorders (originally known by the older, more descriptive name of *manic-depressive illness*) are fundamentally severe disorders of feeling (*affect*). They are more frequently treated in private hospitals which cater largely to wealthier families who are more likely to receive this diagnosis than the poor. Depression may begin at almost any age, although the onset is fairly evenly distributed throughout adult life. Manic episodes typically occur before age 30.[118] Depression is much more common in women.[119] In fact, the best estimate is that depressive episodes occur twice as frequently in women as in men.[120] The NIMH reports that more than 2.3 million Americans aged 18 and over—about 1 percent of the population—suffer from mood disorder and that as many as 20 percent of these people die by suicide.

From a different statistical perspective, the DSM reports that approximately 18 to 23 percent of females and 8 to 11 percent of males will have a major depressive episode at some time in their lives. Approximately 6 percent of females and 3 percent of males have had a depressive episode sufficiently severe to require hospitalization.[121] Depression with a manic episode (*bipolar disorder*) strikes equally in men and in women.

Symptoms

It is amazing how many times the name for these conditions has changed over time. Toward the middle of the last century, it was recognized that mania and melancholia (depression) should be classified within the same group of disorders. Thus, the condition was originally designated *cyclical insanity*. Some researchers question the use of the term *psychosis* because there is not always a loss of contact with reality. This occurs only in severely depressed states and highly manic states.

There is also considerable disagreement among researchers as to whether the less severe cases should be termed *mild psychosis*. Unlike schizophrenia, in which there is typically a sharp break with reality, mood disorders vary in degree of impairment from person to person.[122] The number of attacks is also variable. One person may have only one episode in a lifetime while another individual may have numerous attacks.

The nature of the episodes also varies; a person may have alternating episodes of depression and mania or recurrent episodes of depression or mania only. Perhaps as many as 20 percent have only one attack. However, those who do have a second attack typically experience recurrences throughout their lives. The attacks are separated by periods ranging from a few months to several years, but the duration and the frequency of attacks tend to increase as the person grows older. Attacks of all types usually begin quite suddenly with little warning.[123]

Depression is more than having an occasional "off day." It is a much more serious and prolonged condition characterized by feelings of worthlessness, hopelessness, and guilt. Often these patients feel better in the evening than in the morning. Frequently there are appetite disturbances (loss or increase in appetite). Sleep is also commonly disturbed (insomnia or excessive sleeping). Symptoms must be present nearly every day for at least two weeks to warrant the diagnosis of major depressive episode. Culture can influence the symptoms of depression. In some cultures, depression may be experienced in somatic ways rather than as sadness or guilt. Thus we hear

··· **Case 4:2** ·······································
Down and Out

Mr. J. was a 51-year-old industrial engineer who, since the death of his wife five years earlier, had been suffering from continuing episodes of depression marked by extreme social withdrawal and occasional thoughts of suicide. His wife had died in an automobile accident during a shopping trip which he himself was to have made but was unable to because professional responsibilities changed his plans. His self-blame for her death, which was present immediately after the funeral and regarded by his friends and relatives as transitory, deepened as the months, and then years, passed by. He began to drink, sometimes heavily, and when thoroughly intoxicated would plead to his deceased wife for forgiveness. He lost all capacity for joy—his friends could not recall when they had last seen him smile. His gait was typically slow and labored, his voice usually tearful, his posture stooped. Once a gourmet, he had

lost all interest in food and good wine, and on those increasingly rare occasions when friends invited him for dinner, this previously witty, urbane man could barely manage to engage in small talk. As might be expected, his work record deteriorated markedly, along with his psychological condition. Appointments were missed and projects haphazardly started and then left unfinished. When referred by his physician for psychotherapy, he had just been released from a hospital following a near-fatal and intentional overdose of sleeping pills. Not long afterward, he seemed to emerge from his despair and began to feel like his old self again.

——————————

Source: Gerald C. Davison and John M. Neale, *Abnormal Psychology: An Experimental Clinical Approach* (New York: Wiley, 1974), p. 174. By permission of publisher.

···

of complaints of "nerves" in Mediterranean and Latin cultures, "imbalance" in Asian cultures, and problems of the "heart" in Middle Eastern cultures.

The most severe form of depression is referred to as *depressive stupor.* It typically includes psychomotor retardation (such as slow reaction time and underproductive speech) and a preoccupation with death. Although it is questionable whether suicide always indicates depression, it is important to note that the rate of suicide among young Americans 15 to 24 years old has skyrocketed since the 1960s. Case 4:2 sketches a common picture of depression.

Manic episodes are euphoric mood disorders, accompanied by delusions.[124] In a way, they are exaggerations of normal elation and often are initially mistaken for happiness. These people appear restless and overactive and usually do not realize that they are in an abnormal state. They speak rapidly and jump quickly from one idea to another (*flight of ideas*). In addition, they often joke and tease others but may suddenly become insulting and sarcastic.

Manics behave in a grandiose manner, are invulnerable to reason and logic, frequently allude to outstanding personal achievements, and bend every circumstance to the service of self-aggrandizement. Frequently, their unwarranted optimism and lack of judgment may lead to such activities as buying sprees, foolish business investments, and reckless driving. There is almost always a decreased need for sleep. Some manics seem to be as severely impaired as schizophrenics. The milder cases are called *hypomanic,* and the most severe cases are known as *acute mania* or *delirious mania.* Symptoms must be present for most of one week for the diagnosis of manic episode to be warranted.

Most manic people experience a transitory breakthrough of depressed feelings, thus the term *bipolar.* Some researchers suggest that this is because the mania acts as a substitute method of working through problems which threaten to precipitate depression. From this perspective, the *latent* content in mania is deeply depressive, although

· **Case 4:3** ·
Too Many Hats

Mrs. M. was first admitted to a state hospital at the age of 38, although since childhood she had been characterized by swings of mood, some of which had been so extreme that they had been psychotic in degree. At 17, she suffered from a depression that rendered her unable to work for several months, although she was not hospitalized. At 33, shortly before the birth of her first child, the patient was greatly depressed. For a period of four days she appeared in a coma. About a month after the birth of the baby she "became excited," and was entered as a patient in an institution for neurotic and mildly psychotic patients. As she began to improve, she was sent to a shore hotel for a brief vacation. The patient remained at the hotel for one night and on the following day signed a year's lease on an apartment, bought furniture, and became heavily involved in debt. Shortly thereafter Mrs. M. became depressed and returned to the hospital. . . . After several months she recovered and . . . remained well for approximately two years.

She then became overactive and exuberant in spirits and visited her friends to whom she outlined her plans for reestablishing different forms of lucrative business. She purchased many clothes, bought furniture, pawned her rings, and wrote checks without funds. She was returned to a hospital. Gradually, her manic symptoms subsided, and after four months she was discharged. For a period thereafter she was mildly depressed. In a little less than a year Mrs. M. again became overactive, played her radio until late in the night, smoked excessively, took out insurance on a car that she had not yet bought. Contrary to her usual habits, she swore frequently and loudly, created a disturbance in a club to which she did not belong and instituted divorce proceedings. On the day prior to her second admission to the hospital, she purchased 57 hats.

———————

Source: L. C. Kolb, *Noyes' Modern Clinical Psychiatry* (Philadelphia: Saunders, 1973), p. 376. By permission of publisher.

· ·

the *manifest* content is superficially boastful, happy, and overactive. Cameron has compiled some evidence to support this position. He found that depressive and manic states are very much alike at the biological level when such measures as basal metabolism, blood pressure, blood sugar level, and rate of blood flow are compared.[125]

Case 4:3 exemplifies the behavior of a person with moods alternating between mania and depression. Originally known as the circular type, the DSM-IV label is *bipolar disorder.*[126]

The Medical Model of Mood Disorders

There is a lot of evidence that biology plays a big causal role in mood disorders.[127] Comparisons of psychotic depressives with those suffering from less severe depression are one important clue. The psychotic depressives respond much more favorably to somatic treatments including electroshock and antidepressant pharmaceuticals, particularly lithium carbonate, monoamine inhibitors, tricyclic antidepressants, and serotonin reuptake inhibitors (e.g., the controversial Prozac). The most widely researched medical theories are genetic and biochemical.[128]

Genetic Theory. There is clear evidence of a genetic factor in mood disorders, especially the bipolar kind.[129] Both twin and adoption studies support a very strong case for diathesis. One study of genetic factors measured the concordance among people with mood disorders and their first-degree relatives.[130] The data indicated that the relatives are about 10 times more likely to have the same diagnosis than members of the general population. Another study found a particularly high risk for mood disorders among first-degree relatives where the disorder appears early in life.[131]

The rates of mood disorders among monozygotic and dizygotic twins whose co-twins are known to have similar problems are revealing. It is well documented that the concordance rate in dizygotic twins is approximately 13 percent while the rate in monozygotic twins is over 60 percent.[132] The fact that the pathology is substantially higher among relatives of people with mood disorders than in the general population, and that it increases as genetic similarity increases, lend support to the idea that genes may be an important cause.

All of these findings are subject to the same criticism as are the genetic studies of schizophrenia, namely, that the similarity of the social environment is also greater among members of the same family (particularly identical twins) than among members of the general population.

Biochemical Theories. With the introduction of Prozac, the biochemistry of mood disorders got a lot of press. One biochemical hypothesis is that mania and depression stem from autonomous fluctuations in the metabolic system. This idea is suggested by a variety of somatic disturbances, including loss of appetite, insomnia, cessation of menstruation, heart rate and circulatory alterations, skin difficulties, and gastrointestinal disorders. In other words, symptoms may appear because the autonomic nervous system is operating in a deranged manner.[133] In turn, the adrenal glands are not stimulated normally, resulting in an abnormal production of epinephrine. Depression is considered to be caused by a deficiency of epinephrine and mania by an excess of the same substance. Schildkraut compiled indirect evidence for this position by noting these effects in persons receiving drugs known to cause abnormal production of epinephrine.[134]

A related biochemical hypothesis involves electrolyte metabolism. Two of the electrolytes, sodium chloride and potassium chloride, play an important role in the functioning of the nervous system. Alterations in the distribution of sodium and potassium affect the excitability of the nerve cell. The level of intracellular sodium has been found to be elevated in people with mood disorders.[135] This is probably why lithium carbonate has been so effective in treating these problems. It acts to restore sodium levels to normal states.

More recent biochemical explanations include alterations in glucose metabolism as well as abnormal cortisone levels. Manic episodes are reportedly correlated with increased glucose activity in the right temporal region. Additionally, in depressed patients, there may be an overproduction of cortisone, the "stress hormone."[136] Of course, these biochemical theories are subject to the criticism that observed metabolic fluctuations may not be autonomous occurrences but simply biochemical responses to life stressors.[137]

I mentioned Prozac a few times in this chapter. It deserves special mention. I cannot think of another drug that has been so sociologically visible and medically controversial. Opinions on Prozac include the strong conviction that it cures mood disorder to the equally strong feeling that it kills the patient. Box 4:1 relates parts of the Prozac story, including the question of whether it does more harm than good.

The Environmental View of Mood Disorders

To some, these are depressing days for behavioral science. Researchers in psychology and psychiatric sociology want badly to transform their sometimes impressionistic disciplines into a hard, quantifiable science that is on a par with medical research. Some of the theories discussed here may be old, or they may be unproven.

·   **Box 4:1**   ··
Prozac: Killer or Cure?

Prozac was on "Nightline" when you went to sleep and on the "Today" show when you woke up. How could a medicine preoccupy us, stimulate us so? The news stories, the sober ones that tried to describe what the drug does, told little. Prozac, they said, has fewer side effects than other antidepressants. But why did we care about side effects? Since when had we taken to reading day after day about the fine points of a medication for mental illness? No, the news was not side effects. The news was takeoff. Prozac enjoyed the fastest acceptance of any other psychotherapeutic medicine ever—650,000 prescriptions per month by the time the *Newsweek* cover appeared, just over two years after Prozac was introduced.

And then the backlash began, in the great American tradition of tarnishing the idol's luster. The occasional column or feature story asked why we had jumped on the bandwagon. People were taking the drug for weight loss and for binge eating, for premenstrual tensions and postpartum blues. These were women mostly, and the question arose, was Prozac another Miltown or Librium, the "mother's little helper" from which we expect too much and about which we know too little?

Just before *Newsweek* made Prozac a star, an ominous report had appeared in a scholarly journal. Six depressed patients experienced urgent suicidal thoughts while on Prozac. Yes, some had considered suicide before. But when they took Prozac, their self-destructive drive was more persistent and more intense. Lawyers began to venture the Prozac defense in murder trials. Prozac was implicated in the suicide of a celebrity, the rock star Del Shannon. Lawsuits sprouted like toadstools after rain.

On the talk shows, there was word of Prozac Survivor Support Groups, as if the pill were an abuser—a molesting parent, perhaps. The Scientologists came whooping in, seeing in Prozac conspiracy, coercion, evil incarnate. Fear reigned: Macy's barred a man from a Santa Claus job because he was taking Prozac.

Time began the backlash to the backlash, with a cover exposé of the Scientologists, who were shown to be fomenting much of the anti-Prozac hysteria. Then "60 Minutes" weighed in with a balancing piece: Lesley Stahl confronted women who claimed not to have been suicidal before taking Prozac—leaders of the anti-Prozac movement—with a medical report and doctor's letter saying they had.

By now, new drugs had entered the market—Prozac wannabes. They were not Prozac, but perhaps Prozac was no longer what it had been. The craze was over. And we were free to wonder, what had the fuss been about?

———————

Source: Peter D. Kramer, *Listening to Prozac* (New York: Viking, 1993), pp. xvii–xviii.

· ·

But to toss out the idea that life stress, such as marital disruption,[138] does not induce mood disorder is to toss out the proverbial "baby with the bathwater." To do so would ignore the important role that environmental experiences can play as *social stressors*. Each of the theories centers about the concept of stress. The main difference among the theories is the form that the stress takes.[139]

Psychoanalytic Theory.   The idea that maternal loss or separation, especially during infancy, can produce mood disorder is as old as Freud. According to classical psychoanalytic theory, the potential for mood disorders is created during the first two years of life, the oral stage.[140] During this period the infant's oral needs are insufficiently gratified. This causes fixation at the oral stage and a dependency on the instinctual needs that are peculiar to it. These are the kind of people who remain excessively dependent on others, particularly for feelings of self-esteem. In people with mood disorders, ordinary personality defenses fail to keep feelings of dependency and helplessness in the unconscious. As a result, the feelings eventually reemerge and cause the personality to regress to the state of helplessness found in infants.[141] The theory is similar to the psychoanalytic theory of schizophrenia except that the stressors leading to fixation are different.

The precipitating factor is the loss of an important "love object" such as a parent. This the individual cannot tolerate. Some psychoanalysts feel that the loss does not have to be experienced early in life. It may be the loss of a loved one through death or desertion in adult life as well. The precipitating event may also be a *perceived* loss, such as an imaginary cooling of interest on the part of a person's spouse.

Whatever the nature of the loss, it is significant because it reanimates the childhood experience of separation from maternal affection. The mood disorder is considered to be a cry for love and a display of helplessness that is an appeal for lost affection and security. The loss is considered to be particularly important because it is perceived by the person as rejection, which, in turn, causes anger. The feeling of anger toward a loved one cannot be tolerated, and it is turned inward onto the self in the form of self-blame and causes the person to feel unworthy and depressed. This sequence of events is highly likely to occur in dependent personalities and is fostered by traumatic infantile experiences. These are people who cannot loosen their emotional bonds with the lost love object, and they castigate themselves for the loss. *Depression, then, is anger turned against oneself*—according to the theory.

Psychoanalysts who have researched the etiology of the mood disorders have not treated mania and depression separately because they feel that mania is a reflection of an underlying depression. The manic's behavior is considered to be a way of defending against depression by denying its existence. Although manics may appear self-confident, they are basically dependent on others. They deny the existence of every fact and thought that engender depressed feelings and behave in a way that is the exact opposite of their real feelings. This defense mechanism (*reaction formation*) is often found in a variety of situations involving depression. In tragic bereavement, for example, some people immediately immerse themselves in work and even amusements to convince themselves that they are not grief-stricken over a person's death. Thus, the manic state has an adjustive purpose in affirming that all is well. Depressed states, on the other hand, do not involve any such struggle to rectify the situation. Both mania and depression are considered equivalent psychologically. For this reason, psychoanalysts believe that discoveries about the origin of depression simultaneously shed light on the origin of mania.

The central proposition of psychoanalytic theory is that mood disorders have infantile origins. There is some evidence for this. Spitz has described depressive reactions in infants who experience a loss or reduction of the "emotional supplies" that had been provided by the mother.[142] When removed from a mothering environment, the children showed signs of social withdrawal, loss of appetite, difficulty in sleeping, and a slowdown of mental development. All of these symptoms parallel features of the adult depressive syndrome and suggest that in infancy the stage is set for later depressive reactions. However, early parental loss may not necessarily mean an eventual mood disorder but may, as some suggest, create a personality weakness that is conducive to it.[143] Diathesis-stress again.[144] And it all stems from early social stress in the form of the loss of a loved person.

Cognitive Theory. The cognitive theory of mood disorders emphasizes the effect of thought processes on emotions. This is a reverse of the psychoanalytic contention that emotions affect beliefs. Cognitive theorists believe that individuals suffer depression because they commit *errors of logic*. This idea is chiefly advanced by Beck, who noted that his patients tended to distort normal experiences in the direction of self-blame.[145]

In Beck's view, people with mood disorders operate within a set of logical principles that dispose them to conclude that they are fools whose lives are hopeless.[146] They tend to draw sweeping conclusions on the basis of a single, often trivial, event (*overgeneralization*), to see themselves as losers in spite of a series of achievements (*minimization*), and to draw conclusions on the basis of one minor, negative element in a situation (*selective abstraction*).

The basic assumption of Beck's theory is that thoughts determine emotions rather than the reverse. Although this is difficult to prove, there is some relevant evidence from experimental psychology. In one study of normal people, it was discovered that individuals become less fearful when they are led to believe beforehand that they will experience pleasure even when this belief is not confirmed.[147]

At the present time, there is no direct empirical evidence which shows that mood disorders follow from illogical thought patterns. Certainly, depressed people exhibit a very negative view of the world, but this could well be the result of a psychological abnormality rather than the cause of it. In fact, Beck himself suggests that childhood experiences, such as the loss of a parent, establish the potential for the illogic.[148]

Social Learning Theory. This theory of mood disorders mainly deals with the origin of depression, not mania. The loss of accustomed positive social reinforcements is held to be the causal culprit. Once people lose an important source of rewards, they begin to behave differently, and this new type of behavior (depression) may itself be reinforced. When, for example, depressed people receive sympathy and special dispensations from others, they may continue to feel depression long after it is appropriate because of the rewarding *secondary gains*, the benefits a person enjoys from having emotional problems. The gains often take the form of attention from other people.

According to this perspective, depression need not be preceded by the loss of a loved one, although such a loss is one way by which a person's positive social reinforcements may be eliminated. Therefore, this theory is not inconsistent with the psychoanalytic theory; it is simply more general in that it interprets loss in a less specific way than psychoanalytic theory. The loss that engenders depression may be the loss of a job or of a person's credit standing as well as of a loved one. Whatever the nature of the loss, it leads to stress.

Family Systems Theory. Another environmental theory of depression centers on the family.[149] It has been documented that the families of depressives can be unusually concerned with social approval.[150] The parents have often failed to reach their desired status level, and consequently they place expectations on one of their children to change this through the child's achievement. Case histories frequently reveal that the depressive's family was set apart, usually economically, from other families in the community.[151] The family felt this difference keenly and reacted to it through attempts to raise their prestige by excessive adherence to conventional standards to proper behavior, particularly by expecting one of their children to be successful in school and the world of work.[152]

Family systems theory helps to explain why only one of the children in these families typically develops depression. This is the child who occupies a special place among the siblings—often, the most talented member of the family. He feels different and alone because his special position exposes him to the envy of his siblings.

The Status of Present Research

At present, the causes of mood disorders have not been entirely determined. There is considerable evidence that they can be caused by biological factors or environmental experiences, or both. The only conclusion that can be drawn from the existing evidence is that mood disorders, like schizophrenic disorders, can be caused by a variety of factors. Evidence also indicates that the severe cases are more likely to be associated with medical problems.

Treating mood disorders is as important, perhaps more important, than understanding their causes. Here the current state of things is much more positive and hopeful as new forms of therapy are discovered and evaluated. Like theories of mood disorder, the forms of treatment really run a large gamut from new medications to new psychotherapies.[153] One consistent finding about both causes and treatment of mood disorders is the role of *social networks*.[154] Social support systems can be both a source of distress and an aid to recovery. It all depends on the structure of the support system.

CONCLUSIONS

Schizophrenic and mood disorders involve a variety of symptoms that are only matched by a diversity of opinion about their causes. With schizophrenia, for instance, some data indicate that it is biological, and there is evidence supporting environmental causes. The medical model has three major components. First, there is the proposition that the disorder is genetic, as evidenced by a marked concordance among monozygotic twins. Second, there is the argument that schizophrenia results from a biochemical abnormality that in turn disturbs the central nervous system. Third, there is the theory that the psychosis may come from insults to the fetus (prenatal) or adverse events shortly after birth (perinatal).

Environmental theories of schizophrenia are numerous. According to psychoanalytic theory, severe fixation at the oral stage of psychosexual development is the cause of schizophrenia. The cognitive view of schizophrenia appears to be more descriptive of the mind-altering nature of the disorder than a real causal theory. Cognitive theorists see schizophrenia as a breakdown in communicative abilities, but they do not explain what caused the breakdown.

A number of theories of schizophrenia emphasize the social environment. Social learning theorists, for example, believe that the disorder is the result of being raised by mentally disturbed parents. Other intrafamilial theories include the double bind hypothesis—the notion that schizophrenia is fostered by parents who treat their children in inconsistent and mutually exclusive ways. For instance, they expect their children to develop feelings of autonomy, yet, at the same time, they also expect the children to be overly dependent on them. Some contend that this experience is particularly likely to happen to those born last in a large family.

One view linked with macrosocial forces is social class theory, which explains schizophrenia as the psychotic result of the everyday misery of lower-class life. A significant proportion of the schizophrenic population is lower class, but there is much debate as to whether membership in the lower class precedes schizophrenia or whether schizophrenia causes a drift into the lower class.

There is also evidence that genes play a role in the development of mood disorders since concordance rates among monozygotic twins are high. Biochemical hypotheses of mood disorders center about problems such as metabolic dysfunctions and cortical levels.

The psychoanalytic theory of mood disorders is similar to the psychoanalytic theory of schizophrenia in that fixation at the oral stage is believed to lay the foundation for depressive reactions later in life. But the nature of the fixation varies in the two disorders. The depressive's fixation results in a sense of dependency on others that is normal for infants but pathological for adults. This orientation toward dependency, coupled with the loss of an important loved one later, triggers depression.

The cognitive school holds that people with depression are individuals who illogically conclude that they are worthless. Social learning theorists contend that depression is a reaction to a loss of rewarding reinforcements. Thus this proposition is not inconsistent with psychoanalytic theory since both consider a loss to be important. There is also the family systems theory of depression. According to this view, depressives are those who had unrealistic expectations placed on them by their parents. Often this resulted from an excessive concern with status attainment by parents who failed to achieve their goals and placed the burden of the accomplishment on one of their children.

5

Anxiety Disorders

Sigmund Freud (1856–1939), the founder of psychoanalysis. Although Freud's theories are widely criticized today, his list of credits include recognizing how social and cultural forces can influence mental health.

AN OVERVIEW

In 2000, the National Institute of Mental Health reported that more than 16 million adults aged 18 to 54 in the United States suffer from some type of anxiety disorder. Anxiety disorders cost the U.S. economy close to $50 billion each year. They are frequently complicated by depression, eating disorders, or substance abuse. Many people have more than one anxiety disorder.[1] Traditionally, anxiety disorders have been known as the neuroses. However, the term *neurosis* no longer appears in the current literature. The APA recognized that the word confers causal significance, since it literally means "an illness of the nerves." Most evidence indicates that these problems are not neurological.

The major symptom of these disorders is an intense experience of *anxiety*, a feeling of subjective distress. Anxiety is similar to fear, both subjectively and in objective terms of physiological disturbance. Fear, however, is an appropriate reaction to a real danger, whereas anxiety is not related to a real, external threat or is grossly disproportionate to any such threat. In essence, anxiety warns of an internal danger caused by a stressful feeling. Anxiety is considered to be a normal correlate of aging and experiencing new and untried things.[2] Children often experience anxiety on their first day in school, as do old people contemplating impending death.[3] Pathological anxiety, on the other hand, is a response inappropriate to a given situation. For example, almost anyone would experience unpleasant feelings in the presence of a man-eating beast, but some people with anxiety disorders would be similarly upset by a docile dog. This self-created terror is known as pure anxiety or free-floating anxiety when it is severe, persistent, and experienced directly without the use of a defense mechanism. Because these problems are so common, there is a huge number of publications about them, as well as workshops and seminars on how to understand and treat them.[4]

In DSM-IV, the term *anxiety disorder* refers to problems "in which the predominant disturbance is a symptom or group of symptoms that is distressing to the individual and is recognized by the person as unacceptable and alien (*ego-dystonic*); reality testing is grossly intact; behavior does not actively violate gross social norms (although functioning may be markedly impaired); the disturbance is relatively enduring or recurrent without treatment and is not limited to a transitory reaction to stressors; and there is no demonstrable organic etiology or factor." Physiological problems include trembling, increased heart rate, dry mouth, nausea, goosebumps, hot and cold sensations, dizziness and faintness, urinary urgency, fatigue, muscular tension, restlessness, insomnia, and sexual dysfunction.

Psychological symptoms are even more varied. Most affected people are chronically unhappy.[5] Other common features are indecisiveness, feelings of inadequacy, hostility, guilt, hypersensitivity, rigidity, shyness, excessive concerns with physical health, and self-centeredness. Some have difficulties at work, which are generally related to a fear of being rejected or humiliated.

In this chapter, I discuss a number of different forms of anxiety disorders, including phobic disorders, generalized anxiety disorder, and obsessive-compulsive disorder. Other forms include panic disorder (unpredictable anxiety attacks) and posttraumatic stress disorder (symptoms following a psychologically traumatic event). Whatever the form, certain patterns run through the anxiety disorders. On the serious side, these are states of mind that can lead to premature death through problems such as suicide and cardiovascular disease.[6] Alcoholism is also frequently associated with anxiety disorders, as is depression in general.[7]

In the next chapter, a group of mental illnesses collectively known as "personality disorders" is discussed. As you will see, personality disorders involve a wide range of bizarre behaviors. To add to the complexities in psychiatric research today, anxiety disorders are sometimes found together with personality disorders.[8] To make things even more complicated, anxiety is shaped by culture. Some of the "culture-bound syndromes" presented in Chapter 2, for instance, are linked by an underlying problem of intense anxiety.

Aside from all of these complex issues, one thing about anxiety disorders seems certain—they affect a lot of people. On the other hand, there is an enormous uncertainty about the causes of anxiety disorders. It is true that they often run in the same families.[9] To some, this suggests the influence of social learning and stress. Others contend that this is evidence for a genetic base to these problems that has been traditionally overlooked.[10]

THE PREVALENCE OF ANXIETY

Anxiety disorders are so common that many people confuse them with eccentric behavior. In fact, the twentieth century was dubbed the "age of anxiety." Books on the topic are frequently purchased as popular reading. Questions on how to detect the problem, avoid it, as well as live with it, rival issues of international news, sports, and entertainment. Undoubtedly, these problems are very much a part of our everyday world. Anxiety disorders are the most common mental illnesses in the United States. The millions of people treated for these disorders only represent the people who are diagnosed. There are many others not included who do not receive treatment. It is estimated that at least 24 million Americans suffer from an anxiety disorder during a given year.

Some of the psychiatric literature (psychoanalytic) suggests that suppression of instinctual drives can engender anxiety. For this reason, the relationship between civilization and anxiety disorder may be fundamental; the higher the level of cultural development, the more complete is the suppression of the instincts, particularly the sex drive.[11] Simply stated, these problems may be the price people pay for cultural advancement. Consistently, the anxiety disorders are reportedly not common in pre-literate societies that more fully allow for the expression of innate human needs.[12] In primitive society a person is not as likely to be subjected to radically different behavior standards as a child than as an adult. In developed society, however, as an individual passes from one age group to another, permissible behaviors become forbidden, and vice versa.

The United States epitomizes cultural discontinuity as a country becomes more developed. During the twentieth century, immeasurable complexities were added to the American cultural base. Many of these additions have come in the form of material culture, such as advances in science and technology. But these advancements have had covert impacts on interpersonal relationships by introducing increased competition and tension to the impersonality of urban living. This growth in cultural complexity has been accompanied by a reported increase in the prevalence of anxiety disorders.[13] Some feel that the true prevalence of these disorders is presently beyond statistical calculation, in part because different psychiatrists use different diagnostic standards and also because different types of methods are used to collect data. For these reasons, some mental health experts avoid the issue by saying that everyone has "neurotic potential" and will display such behavior under stress.

Culture influences the prevalence of anxiety disorder beyond the preliterate-developed differences noted above. Using various forms of anxiety as an indicator of these problems, Lynn reports a number of cross-cultural differences among developed societies.[14] France, Austria, West Germany, and Italy are reported as high anxiety countries while Sweden, the Netherlands, and Great Britain score low on Lynn's anxiety measures. Lynn constructs an interesting hypothesis to account for these differences by suggesting that climate has an effect on anxiety. He points out that the high anxiety countries have warmer climates and more frequent storms, both of which have a psychologically unsettling effect on people. That, of course, is just a guess.

THE ONSET OF ANXIETY DISORDERS

Gender differences in anxiety disorders are revealing. Not only is there a preponderance of females with diagnosed cases of anxiety disorder but the female preponderance emerges early in life. In fact, retrospective studies indicate that, at age 6, females are already twice as likely to have experienced an anxiety disorder than are males.[15] Of course, this may simply be a reflection of women's greater propensity to *express* a problem rather than a difference in *true* prevalence.[16] Consistently, females are reported to be more likely to seek treatment for anxiety disorders than are males with the same problems[17]

Although the onset of some of these disorders may be abrupt, the psychopathological process that culminates in symptoms has a long history. In fact, evidence of psychological difficulties is typically found in the childhood histories of people with anxiety disorders. These include feeding problems in early infancy, difficulties in toilet training, nightmares, temper tantrums, bed wetting (enuresis) persisting until age 8 or beyond, and thumb sucking or nail biting persisting into adolescence. The onset is often precipitated by a *stressful* event (see Chapter 12). Most of these involve some type of *change* that the individual perceives as threatening, such as pregnancy, divorce, or even an outstanding personal achievement.

Whether a particular event produces stress depends on a number of variables, including how the person interprets the event, as well as personal coping mechanisms. Individuals predisposed toward anxiety disorders are likely to interpret everyday events in threatening ways. Many life events are viewed by most people as inherently neutral or necessary for personal growth, but to others they become highly charged through processes such as social learning.

Full-blown anxiety disorders can occur in children, and when they do, they are typically preceded by stressful events within one month of the onset. Events commonly precipitating a childhood form include mild physical illness, change of school, reprimand for school performance, birth of a younger sibling, and separation or impending separation from a close relative. Clearly, change—particularly change in interpersonal relationships—is the central aspect of many precipitating triggers in childhood problems as it is in adult disorders. And interpersonal relationships are but one of the many factors that impact on the sociology of mental illness.

PANIC DISORDER

Symptoms

There are many manifestations of panic disorders, including fear of a *panic attack*, an intense experience of apprehension, fearfulness, or terror, often associated with feelings of impending doom.[18] During the attacks the person may be overwhelmed by palpitations, chest pain, shortness of breath, choking sensations, and a fear of "going crazy." It may reach the point of being afraid of dropping dead on the spot. Panic disorder also involves a recurring concern about having another panic attack.

Panic disorder is not just an unnecessarily severe form of ordinary nervousness or anxiety; it has its own distinct origins.[19] Panic attacks usually begin before the age of 30, often before 20, and sometimes in childhood. They are extremely rare after age 65. The typical attack lasts for five minutes to a half hour. Sometimes the anticipatory anxiety is more serious than the panic attacks themselves. Anxiety is a double-edged sword. If kept in check, anxiety will improve our performance in most situations. This is known as *eustress,* or positive stress. If allowed to rise above a certain healthy threshold, it may become *distress,* or negative stress. Panic disorder is distress to the nth degree, a feeling of having lost control.

The anxiety in panic disorder takes forms that are clearly distinct from other anxiety disorders such as *generalized anxiety disorder.*[20] Although some current research differentiates panic disorder by symptom profile, the big picture is homogeneous and pervasive.[21] It is a picture of people whose quality of life is seriously diminished. I mean this in every way possible—in the family, with friends, in the world of work, and in virtually every nook and cranny of the sociology of everyday living.

Prevalence and Onset

Epidemiological studies around the world consistently report the lifetime prevalence of panic disorder to be between 1.5 and 3.5 percent. One-year prevalence rates are between 1 and 2 percent.[22] Approximately half of these people also have *agoraphobia,* a socially crippling fear that causes some people to literally become housebound. In the United States, panic disorder is slightly less common among African Americans than among whites.[23] However, panic disorder has become a global issue during the last decade as evidenced by the fact that it has become the focus of worldwide research.[24]

The NIMH reported in 2000 that panic disorder typically strikes in young adulthood. Roughly half of all people with panic disorder develop the condition before age 24. Women are twice as likely as men to suffer from it, at least they are in the *reported* facts. Panic disorder, like many anxiety disorders, has a high connection (*comorbidity*) with depression and substance abuse.

What precipitates the attacks in panic disorder? That question has been answered in a variety of ways. Reports of physiological arousal are numerous,[25] but that seems to be stating the obvious. If you look deeper you will see that a host of conditions are precursors for panic. Most central to the sociological theme of this book, however, is the fact that *environmental stressors*, particularly interpersonal ones, often induce panic attacks.[26] Separation anxiety is one prime example of a socially stressful panic-inducing event.[27] Consistently, the most intense stages for everyday social life—public settings—are the most common locations for the actual attacks. The case story in Box 5:1 is about a woman whose problems were dangerously induced while driving on a highway.

The Medical Model of Panic Disorder

Although there are demonstrable physiological changes that occur with the onset of a panic attack, it is unclear as to whether the physiological problems cause the psychiatric symptoms, or vice versa—another chicken and egg issue awaiting further research. Some hypothesize that biochemical changes in the body trigger the psychological sensation of panic. In other words, the person with panic disorder has presumably been predisposed to conditions of panic due to a biological vulnerability.[28] For example, when panic-prone individuals are injected with sodium lactate in clinical studies, the infusion causes symptoms equivalent to a full-blown panic attack. Normal subjects similarly injected show no such response.

The causal role of sodium lactate levels is purely speculation. Similarly, some researchers think that panic-disordered people suffer from an excess of norepinephrine, a neurotransmitter normally activated under conditions of stress or danger. When panic-disposed subjects are injected with a drug stimulating norepinephrine activity, they are more likely to experience panic than do normal controls. Again, a sensitivity to a laboratory-induced biological change in no way provides a conclusive cause. It is possible that under experimental conditions people with panic disorder are already anxiety-ridden about participating in an experiment, and that alone could trigger a fear response. Other biochemical hypotheses about the etiology of panic disorder include the notion that symptoms such as hyperventilation are caused by a hypersensitivity to carbon dioxide.[29] That is an interesting alternative explanation to the frequency of panic attacks on the streets, but it is only an idea. So also is the notion that panic disorder, like so many other mental illnesses, has a connection with abnormal serotonin activity.[30]

In my opinion, the most interesting evidence to date for any biology of panic disorder is that it runs in families. According to DSM-IV, first-degree relatives of individuals with panic disorder have a four to seven times greater chance of developing the problem. If one of a pair of identical twins suffers from panic disorder, the chance that the other will also have it is as high as 40 percent. What makes people genetically vulnerable to panic disorder remains uncertain. And, as you know, the fact that it runs in families may be due as much to nurture as it is to nature. Genetics and social learning are very difficult to separate.

The Environmental View of Panic Disorder

A number of clues are available as to how social forces contribute to panic disorder. Several controlled studies have found a high level of *stress* in the lives of people with panic disorder in the months before the first attack. About 80 percent recall some event like an accident, a death or illness in the family, or some serious family conflict.[31] Other reports center about stressful situations earlier in life. Chief on the list is child abuse—but it is only on some lists and not others.[32] Some connect panic

Terror on the Highway

LOS ANGELES: Rose Deetra, an accomplished Hollywood film development executive, peered in the rear-view mirror, spotted a white big rig bearing down on her and floored the gas pedal in terror.

Ordinarily, Deetra never gets near Interstate Highway 405, which runs through Los Angeles. It so horrifies her that her heart pounds, her chest tightens. Panic sets in. This time, however, her therapist was in the passenger seat.

"Slow down!" commanded Gerald Tarlow as his patient leaned forward and hastily switched lanes, white knuckles clutching the steering wheel.

Deetra, 29, is an experienced driver with no history of mental illness. Six years ago, she was overcome with driving phobia, an overwhelming anxiety that can strike without warning, virtually paralyzing even longtime drivers.

Driving phobics worry about having an anxiety attack while behind the wheel. They fear losing control, needing help and being unable to get it. In rush-hour traffic or driving the lefthand lane, they often feel trapped. Bridges, tunnels, or just the distance between freeway exits can send them into a tailspin. For Deetra and others, the condition twists their lives, forcing them to avoid situations, including jobs, that entail driving or forcing them to spend countless hours on small roads as they bypass nerve-racking highways and faster routes.

At its worst, the phobia completely grounds drivers.

In Deetra's mind, each highway offers its own memento of battle, a spot where she wrestled overwhelming emotions. On Sepulveda Boulevard, there's the narrow tunnel near Los Angeles International Airport that she drove into and then backed out 400 feet, snarling traffic, because she could go no farther.

At a southbound I-405 on-ramp, she once sat in tears for 30 minutes and begged her therapist not to make her drive the freeway. On the northbound 405, a dip in the freeway sent her anxiety soaring. At dinner parties, she couldn't enjoy the food or conversation because she worried about driving back in the dark. As she fell asleep at nights, she dreamed she was driving off the road.

"It gets depressing; it's like you are incapable of normal everyday life. You feel like a total idiot," said Deetra, who asked that her real name not be used.

Only two of Deetra's friends know her secret. Her boss, colleagues, and secretary don't have a clue that she has this problem. Like many driving phobics, she experiences anxiety only when she is in her car—not when she rides in buses or cabs.

"Once someone has a panic attack driving on the freeway, the fear reinforces the fear and they can't get on the freeway at all," said David L. Fogelson, associate clinical professor of psychiatry at the University of California, Los Angeles. "These patients can't tolerate being in a situation where they feel they can't escape easily."

No one knows for certain why some people are stricken with driving phobia. Some are genetically prone to anxiety, experts say. Others say the condition can be brought on by the accumulation of stress or occasionally by an accident. While it can strike at any age, it's most likely to first occur in one's 20s, said Gerald Tarlow, an assistant clinical professor of psychiatry at UCLA and director of the Center for Anxiety Management.

Phobics resort to various techniques to get through the day. They carefully craft routes. They learn relaxation breathing methods. They develop their own secret weapons to help ward off panic or lessen its impact when it strikes. One driver taped a tranquilizer to the dashboard. Another put a teddy bear in the passenger seat when she drove alone.

Treatment often involves therapy—although not every therapist conducts sessions in cars—and sometimes prescription drugs. The majority of cases can be successfully treated, although symptoms sometimes return, Ross said. But fewer than one in four get help—either because people are too embarrassed to seek aid or the condition is misdiagnosed, she added.

Experts say treatment often depends on patients confronting their fears and getting behind the wheel.

With his voice steady, therapist Tarlow seemed unflappable even as a client recently crossed five lanes of traffic. One patient used to close her eyes when she felt anxious behind the wheel.

But that didn't bother him as much as the patient who insisted on driving 40 m.p.h. on the freeway. "You'd get these trailer trucks six inches from the back of the car," he said. "It scared the hell out of me. I certainly realized why she was feeling anxious—it made me anxious."

Source: Nora Zamichow, "Road holds terror for driving phobics; Some go to great lengths to avoid a certain bridge or highway; Some don't drive at all," *The Philadelphia Inquirer,* September 5, 1993, p. A02. By permission of publisher.

disorder with angry frightening parents while others find no connection between panic disorder and the ultimate form of child abuse—incest.[33]

The cognitive model of panic disorder proposes that panic patients interpret physical symptoms in a catastrophic way, thus precipitating panic attacks.[34] Of course, this still leaves us with the question of where the inappropriate thinking came from in the first place. When all the evidence for the environmental models is sifted, certain things are clear and others things are muddied. What is clear is the fact that social forces play a causal role. Why else would "talking-out" therapy be effective?[35] (Therapy is placebo?) And why else would patients separated from a loved one by death or divorce have the worst prognosis? The muddy part is the connection between the specific effects of particular events on the form and severity of the panic disorder.

PHOBIC DISORDERS

Symptoms

Phobias—irrational fears—appear more frequently as a psychiatric complaint than as a distinct syndrome. In fact, some psychiatrists feel that all psychiatric patients have phobias. This may be true, but studies of the prevalence of phobias in the general population suggest that a much more conservative conclusion is warranted. One early study in New England estimated that phobias are found in 77 people per 1,000 members of the population.[36] Most of these were mild phobias; only 2.2 per 1000 were rated as severely disabling. Many people have an irrational fear when they come in contact with something harmless, like an insect, but it does not have a serious impact on their lives. The diagnosis of phobic disorder is only warranted if the fear is a significant source of distress. Although phobic symptoms are widespread, it has been estimated that only about 5 to 10 percent of the U.S. adult population are actually diagnosed with severe forms of these problems. That is a huge number of people, especially when you factor in that some phobias are so strong that they keep the person housebound.[37]

Although people with phobias have an intense fear of some object or situation, they consciously recognize that their fear is irrational because no real danger is posed. They often say that they know what it is about the phobic object that arouses anxiety, yet they engage in ritualized ways to avoid contact with it. As long as they avoid the phobic object, no anxiety is suffered. Phobias often involve useful *secondary gains*. For example, a traveling salesman with a fear of flying may be able to avoid work.

A phobia should not be confused with a *natural aversion*. Many people feel uncomfortable in the presence of a vicious dog, but a phobic person may become extremely frightened around a docile cocker spaniel. A phobia is also not an *avoidance reaction*, which is a socially learned response whereby certain objects or environments are avoided because of some previous unpleasant experience with them.

In an odd way, phobias provide some definite "advantages" over other types of anxiety disorders. Since no anxiety is experienced when the phobic object is absent, the escape from anxiety is organized and controlled rather than diffused to a constant threat of catastrophe. The phobic may experience somatic symptoms, such as faintness, nausea, hyperventilation, and tremor. But since symptoms are localized to the phobic object or situation, these people can more easily engage in everyday activities without constant harassment from within. Phobias with panic attacks are another story, however. Symptoms such as palpitations, chest pains, excessive sweating, dizziness, hot or cold flashes, diarrhea, and fears of going crazy or vomiting in public may strike in the form of an overwhelming episode.

Some phobias are known to spread. If, for example, a person is terribly afraid of large groups of people, this fear may gradually extend to smaller groups to the point where the person feels comfortable only when alone. One "contagious" case is reported of a man who became phobic of the number 13.[38] Eventually, he stayed in bed on the thirteenth day of each month to avoid contact with calendar and newspaper dates. Then he began to stay in bed on the twenty-seventh day of each month when he discovered it contained 13 letters. Eventually, he avoided people entirely for fear that they would greet him with a 13-letter statement such as "good afternoon."

DSM-IV divides phobias into three groups: *agoraphobia* (fear of being alone, outside home, in closed or open spaces, or in public places from which escape might be difficult); *social phobia* (fear of public speaking, using public lavatories, eating in public, and so forth); and *specific phobia* (fear of specific objects or situations other than those included in agoraphobia and social phobia).

Agoraphobia. This is the most common of all of the phobias. Over 3.5 million people suffer from agoraphobia—enough people to fill the fourth largest city in the United States. It is often a secondary feature of panic disorder. In fact, it is estimated that close to 5 percent of the population is afflicted by panic disorder with agoraphobia. The central characteristic of agoraphobia is a feeling of impending doom without escape. So the agoraphobic avoids situations in which there is little chance of escape, relying instead on safety signals such as supportive people or familiar surroundings that protect her from overwhelming anxiety. I use the pronoun "her" because agoraphobia is twice as prevalent in women as it is in men. It is diagnosed most commonly in housewives (some of whom become housebound), but it strikes people from all walks of life, including those whose jobs require them to travel long distances, such as truck drivers. Apparently, the truck is a safe refuge from the outside world.

Agoraphobia can also occur without panic.[39] Although it is not unusual for some cultural or ethnic groups around the world to restrict the participation of women in public life, it is important to note that this has nothing to do with agoraphobia. Beginning in a person in the late teens or early 20s, agoraphobia almost always develops in response to what is perceived as a traumatic loss of control. The age of onset is significant, as this is the time when the pressures of adult responsibility begin to materialize. Once the cycle of fear starts, it is rarely halted unless treatment is sought. One such example is Case 5:1, which vividly demonstrates the well-documented fact that agoraphobic behavior can have a crippling effect on a person's life.[40]

Social Phobia. Social phobia may differ across cultures, depending on the sociological "rules of the game." In certain cultures (e.g., Korea and Japan), individuals with this problem may fear giving offense to others in social situations, instead of being embarrassed themselves. This may take the form of anxiety over eye contact or body odor. Approximately 3.7 percent of the American population is estimated to suffer from social phobia in a given year. Widely thought to be more common in women, it is curious that a higher proportion of men seeks help for the disorder. Although the onset is typically during adolescence, it is questionable whether it does not often appear earlier in the form of the all-too-familiar "grade school phobia."

Waldfogel describes the school phobia as "a reluctance to go to school because of acute fear associated with it. Usually this dread is accompanied by somatic symptoms with the gastrointestinal tract the most commonly affected. . . . The somatic

•••••••••••••••••••••••••••••••••••••• **Case 5:1** ••••••••••••••••••••••••••••••••••••
Too Far from Home

A 32-year-old, white, married housewife came to the clinic because of fear of either losing her balance and either fainting or falling. (She has, in fact, never fallen or fainted.) The current difficulties began one year ago, shortly after she and her family moved away from her mother's neighborhood. Her husband went into his own business, which kept him away from home much of the time. Before the move, she could walk to her mother's and sister's houses; now she lives so far from them that she knows they can't come over immediately if she needs them. At first, she avoided going out of her new house, but she eventually could go alone to small neighborhood stores and supermarkets if they were not crowded. Two months ago a man of 41, who was her friend, died of a brain cyst. Since then she

has been contiuously anxious, unable to go out, and comfortable at home only when she is with her husband.

The patient's condition is a recurrence of symptoms she first experienced 12 years ago, immediately after her marriage. She began to fear losing her balance and falling. The more frightened she became, the more unsteady she felt. She became unable to go anywhere. She remembers thinking, "Now that I don't want to die, God is going to answer my childhood prayers, and I will die."

———————————————

Source: Robert L. Spitzer, Miriam Gibbon, Andrew E. Skodol, Janet B. W. Williams, and Michael First, *DSM-III-R Casebook* (Washington, DC: American Psychiatric Press, 1989), p. 134. By permission of the publisher.

••

complaints come to be used as an auxiliary device to justify staying at home and often disappear when the child is reassured that he will not have to attend school. The characteristic picture is of a child nauseated or complaining of abdominal pain at breakfast and desperately resisting all attempts at reassurance, reasoning, or coercion to get him to school."[41] Waldfogel also states that it can last for years. This is important since school phobias may later develop into social phobias in adolescence. I know of a child who experienced a full-blown school phobia. During adolescence he suffered anxiety in anticipation of social events, particularly dating. The underlying threat emanated from a fear of failure in front of others. In childhood, vomiting was the typical beginning of a schoolday. This was also the major somatic symptom in adolescence. What is remarkable about this case is that the person chose to become a college professor. Vomiting continued to be the normal order of events before each lecture. After many years of hell, the phobia eventually subsided. Now it is back.

In social phobia, victims irrationally ruminate on the prospect that their social behavior will become the object of scrutiny and that, as a result, they will be criticized and mocked. The fear of being observed and humiliated is closely tied to low self-esteem, and many with this phobia consistently underperform relative to their ability because of fear of failure and ridicule. Interestingly, social phobics do not suffer when they are alone or unobserved. It is the social aspect of interaction that causes the intense anxiety. Much like agoraphobics, these people suffer from a fear of *public* embarrassment. And, like the panic-disordered, approximately half self-medicate their tension by the abuse of alcohol. To make matters worse, some 90 percent are occupationally impaired because of the paralysis of fear.[42]

Specific Phobia.   This category includes such things as a fear of closed spaces (*claustrophobia*), heights (*acrophobia*), and animals or insects. A number of phobic objects and situations are reported in the clinical literature. While the content of phobias varies with culture and ethnicity, the most common phobias are those beginning in childhood. Although most children experience fear of the dark and of imaginary monsters, these fears are generally outgrown. Fears of closed spaces, spiders, animals, and blood are not as easily shaken.[43] Childhood phobias are only some of the many fears afflicting adults. Flying in airplanes, thunderstorms and lightning, the sound of balloons popping, the feel of wool, velvet, and suede, the texture of some food, body odor—the list is enormous. For the sake of historical interest, Table 5:1 describes some of them along with their traditional labels. Some time ago there was a movement away from the use of the Greek prefix. Instead, phobias are described in plain English, such as fear of heights, fear of death, and so forth.

One of the most famous cases of simple phobia occurred in a 5-year-old boy who refused to go into the streets because of a fear of being bitten by the horses that pulled the street cars in Vienna of the early 1900s. This is the case of Little Hans, which was reported by Freud.[44] He interpreted Hans's fear of the horse as a displacement of the boy's fear of his father. Hans's fear of his father reportedly originated in castration threats, which are common during the phallic stage. Freud held that the horse came to represent his father for a number of reasons: the father had played "horsie" with Hans, the horse's bridle reminded Hans of his father's moustache, and so on. It was the analysis of this case that helped to develop the psychoanalytic theory of phobic disorders. Of course, it is also quite possible that Hans had had a frightening experience with horses and therefore was socially conditioned to avoid them. It would be interesting to know how the case would have been interpreted had Freud been a social learning theorist and not been predisposed to look for unconscious factors and sexual impulses.

Other famous cases of phobia include Augustus Caesar, the widely feared dictator of the Roman Empire, who was afraid to sit in the dark. King James I of England, who commissioned the modern version of the Bible, feared the sight of an unsheathed sword; his contemporary King Henry III of France was afraid of cats. Daredevil Evel Knievel reportedly has a phobia about planes, while the late Alfred Hitchcock, the master of film terror, admitted to a fear of policemen. Howard Hughes suffered from a morbid dread of germs carried by people around him. You do not have to look far and wide for examples of specific phobias. They are all around you. Math anxiety among college students (mainly females?) is one everyday example on campus.[45]

Table 5:1   Common Phobias

Phobia	Fear of	Phobia	Fear of
acrophobia	high places	necrophobia	dead bodies
agoraphobia	open places	nyctophobia	darkness, night
aichmophobia	sharp objects	pathophobia	disease
ailurophobia	cats	pecctaophobia	sinning
algophobia	pain	phonophobia	speaking aloud
aquaphobia	water	photophobia	strong light
astraphobia	thunder and lightening	pnigophobia	choking
autophobia	being alone	pyrophobia	fire
claustrophobia	closed places	sitophobia	eating
cynophobia	dogs	taphophobia	being buried alive
ergasiophobia	writing	thanatophobia	fear of death
hematophobia	sight of blood	toxophobia	being poisoned
lalaphobia	speaking	xenophobia	strangers
mysophobia	dirt & germs	zoophobia	animals

The Medical Model of Phobic Disorders

There is some evidence that social phobia may be caused by biological factors.[46] However, there have not been many studies to assess the rate of phobias among relatives to determine the effects of genetic influences. The mere fact that phobias may run in families is not sufficient support for a genetic perspective. Although some believe that the autonomic nervous system of people with phobic disorders may be easily aroused by environmental stress, concrete proof is far from available. Because agoraphobia is so closely linked with panic disorder, it is possible that biological factors playing a part in panic attacks may set up an agoraphobic "fear of fear." In other words, the agoraphobic becomes afraid of both the internal sensations of anxiety and the actual physical situations in which the panic attack occurred. However, this is more of a *social learning* explanation than a medical answer. Thus it is environmental and completely disconnected from biology.

The idea of biological *preparedness,* as an evolutionary artifact, may predispose humans to fear anything threatening the survival of the species. This theory is drawn from the observation that phobic reactions to animals, heights, and illness are much more common than fear of grass or houses, for example. The most prevalent phobias represent conditions that are historically more dangerous. In this respect, a phobia may be a response that played an adaptive role in the past by evolutionarily "preparing" us to respond to a feared stimulus. In a primitive setting, it would not have been unusual to fear animals, snakes, or fire since we learn to fear to survive. Although this hypothesis is entirely theoretical, animal studies have provided some empirical support. The fact is that, in 2002, biological markers for phobias have not been verified. Many think that they never will be.

The Environmental View of Phobic Disorders

The Big Debate.   The well-established theories of phobic disorders are environmental. However, there is considerable disagreement as to which environmental theory is most valid. The debate centers around differences between the psychoanalytic and social learning theories. Psychoanalysts consider phobias to have unconscious symbolic significance while social learning theorists contend that phobias arise from unpleasant experiences with the phobic object or situation. The debate is actually somewhat senseless because the two positions are really not analyzing the same psychiatric phenomenon. Psychoanalysts study a type of psychiatric fear known as *true phobias*—irrational fears of an object that have no apparent explanation. Social learning theorists, however, concentrate their research on the origin of strong fears of objects or situations that the person has actually encountered in some threatening way. These are not true phobias but another type of psychiatric fear known as *avoidance reactions* that are quite rational relative to true phobias. This is not to say that social learning theory is less valid than psychoanalytic theory because the latter has concentrated on the irrational type of fear. On the contrary, avoidance reactions can be just as debilitating as true phobias. The point is that the social learning—psychoanalytic debate exists largely because the two schools concentrate on different types of psychiatric fears.

Social Learning Theory.   This theory has been tested experimentally. Some of the early experiments were not successful in demonstrating that fear is simply acquired through exposure to stress.[47] However, a later experimental study did demonstrate the influence of modeling on the development of fear.[48] In that study, subjects watched others experience pain when a buzzer sounded. Eventually, the observer expressed a negative emotional response to the sound of the buzzer alone. It had the flavor of Pavlovian dogs.

Some question whether this experiment actually demonstrated the genesis of a phobia based on social learning inasmuch as it did not analyze an *irrational* fear but an avoidance reaction. However, because people with both types of fears seek psychiatric help, this distinction is largely theoretical, especially in light of the fact that behavioral therapists have been very successful in eliminating certain debilitating fears through principles of conditioning. For example, behavioral therapy "unlearns" a fear through *extinction* when a person is repeatedly exposed to a feared object and sees that it brings no harm. Thus, from a practical perspective, the etiology of these conditions may not be as important as how to effectively treat them, although it would be very helpful to differentiate between people with avoidance reactions and people with true phobias and send them to appropriate help sources.

Psychoanalytic Theory.   According to psychoanalytic theory, the emotion associated with an unconscious conflict is displaced onto a phobic object that comes to symbolize the conflict. In other words, the anxiety generated by the conflict is substituted for by fear of a specific object. The specificity of the displaced anxiety onto a particular object makes the anxiety more manageable; that is, if the person avoids the object, he or she also avoids anxiety. Thus, threatening forces from the unconscious are alleviated by an act of camouflage.

The phobia is a compromise between wishes that are repressed in the unconscious and the inhibiting forces that repressed the wishes. The person actually both wants and fears the phobic object at the same time or, more appropriately, wants that which the object symbolizes. Psychoanalysts contend that a phobic is not really afraid of the phobic object, per se, but is afraid of the wish for what the object *symbolizes*. The fear simply prevents the forbidden wish from being fulfilled. Therefore, the mother who has a phobia that she will harm her child unconsciously wants to do exactly that. The person who is irrationally afraid of dirt actually desires to be dirty but finds such temptations upsetting. Or people who have a phobia about knives are actually inclined to harm themselves.

Although it is impossible to know the origin of the anxiety by knowing only the phobic object, certain themes reportedly appear frequently among people with particular phobias. Claustrophobia, for example, is commonly interpreted by psychoanalysts as a fear of being left alone with one's own impulses and fantasies. This phobia may originate in the experience of being locked in one's room as a child. Some cases of claustrophobia occur in a confined space with others, such as in an elevator. Here, the etiology is considered to be different. People with elevator phobia are not afraid of physical harm if the elevator falls but feel threatened by being in close proximity to strangers.

Cases of school phobia have common characteristics according to psychoanalytic researchers. These children almost always become anxious when they are separated from their mothers. Some feel this implies a fault in the mother's relationship with her husband, since a mother in a satisfying marriage is not likely to have such a symbiotic relationship with her child.[49] Other phobias have recurring psychoanalytic themes as well. Acrophobia, for example, is not a fear of a physical fall but of a social fall and the loss of self-esteem that accompanies it. Sleep phobias are interpreted as fears of unconscious wishes that may arise during sleep. The fear of sleep is, therefore, a fear of dreams in which repressed material emerges. Fears of darkness are believed to be the result of witnessing the *primal scene* (parents having sex). Of course, many of these associations are obviously pure speculations.

GENERALIZED ANXIETY DISORDER

Symptoms

In contrast to a panic attack, which is sudden and acute, generalized anxiety disorder is chronic and can last for an extended period of time. Motor tension, hyperactivity, hypervigilance (constantly on the lookout)—these are some of the symptoms of generalized anxiety disorder. This condition is a problem among people who have an anxious overconcern extending to panic. It may occur under any circumstances and is not restricted to specific situations or objects.[50] In this condition, anxiety completely dominates the clinical picture. The anxiety is accompanied by a variety of somatic difficulties, such as fatigue, insomnia, tremor, diarrhea, headache, dizziness, choking sensations, nausea, appetite disturbances, heart irregularities, sexual difficulties, back pain, and a desire to urinate. As anxiety increases, somatic discharge accelerates.

Where one symptom occurs alone, the condition is designated *abortive anxiety*. Affected people also display emotional disturbances, such as irritability, expectant anxiety, a sense of weakness, a fear of impending death, and an inability to relax. Between periodic attacks, the individual may be comfortable, but more often there is some degree of tension. This is very similar to panic disorder except that the problems are more constant and less predictable.

There is considerable cultural variation in the expression of this type of anxiety disorder. For example, in some cultures, it is expressed through somatic symptoms, whereas in others, cognitive symptoms predominate. Regardless of one's background, to suffer from this problem is to be constantly on guard against an unknown danger. Because these people usually do not recognize the linkages between their psychological distress and their symptoms, they may begin to question their physical health. They often attribute their symptoms to a true medical illness and are, for example, very susceptible to suggestions of hidden illness made during public health campaigns. This free-floating form of anxiety disorder and its psychologically imposed health worries are apparent in Case 5:2.

The Medical Model of Generalized Anxiety Disorder

Anxiety as a trait has a familial association, but reports of family patterns for generalized anxiety disorder yield inconsistent findings. Several theories of this problem have been advanced, including a genetic explanation.[51] At least one biological study has shown that the intrafamilial pattern is consistent with a theory of genetic transmission. Slater and Shields compared 17 pairs of monozygotic twins in which one twin had been diagnosed as having this disorder with 28 pairs of dizygotic twins in which a co-twin was so diagnosed.[52] Concordance occurred in 49 percent of the monozygotic twin sets and in only 4 percent of the dizygotic twin sets. However, the study did not control for the effect of being raised by the same parents. A similar study found significant concordance among male monozygotics but not for female identical twins.[53] The difference is a mystery.

On a more specific level, some believe that the major etiological factor is an

••••••••••••••••••••••••••••••••••• **Case 5:2** ••••••••••••••••••••••••••••••
Edgy Electrician

A 27-year-old, married electrician complains of dizziness, sweating palms, heart palpitations, and ringing of the ears of more than 18 months' duration. He has also experienced dry mouth and throat, periods of uncontrollable shaking, and a constant "edgy" and watchful feeling that has often interfered with his ability to concentrate. These feelings have been present most of the time over the previous two years; they have not been limited to discrete periods.

Because of these symptoms the patient had seen a family practitioner, a neurologist, a neurosurgeon, a chiropractor, and an ENT specialist. He had been placed on a hypoglycemic diet, received physiotherapy for a pinched nerve, and told he might "have an inner ear problem."

He also had many worries. He constantly worried about the health of his parents. His father, in fact, had had a myocardial infarction two years previously, but now was feeling well. He also worried about whether he was a "good father," whether his wife would ever leave him (there was no indication that she was dissatisfied with the marriage), and whether he was liked by co-workers on the job.

For the past two years the patient has had few social contacts because of his nervous symptoms. Although he has sometimes had to leave work when the symptoms became intolerable, he continues to work for the same company he joined for his apprenticeship following high-school graduation. He tends to hide his symptoms from his wife and children, to whom he wants to appear "perfect," and reports few problems with them as a result of his nervousness.

Source: Robert L. Spitzer, Miriam Gibbon, Andrew E. Skodol, Janet B. W. Williams, and Michael First, *DSM-III-R Casebook* (Washington, DC: American Psychiatric Press, 1989), pp. 264–265. By permission of the publisher.

inherited unstable autonomic nervous system that is expressed in emotional overresponsiveness. Others consider this kind of anxiety to be related to the level of neural activity of the frontal lobes of the brain, the center of the sympathetic nervous system.[54] This has been demonstrated in a number of ways, including the use of the surgical procedure known as *prefrontal leucotomy*. The operation has been reported to reduce neurotic anxiety in some instances. The inference is that the frontal lobes maintain anxiety, since rendering them inactive can reduce anxious feelings. However, that is not always the outcome.

Research involving surgical alteration of the brain has rarely been attempted since the 1950s because the dangerous side effects of the surgery often outweigh any benefits. It is important to note, however, that even if the frontal lobes are involved in anxiety, it is probably because they simply provide the biological vehicle for anxiety, not because they actually cause the anxiety. In support of this idea, there is no evidence that the frontal lobes of people with anxiety disorders are qualitatively different from those of normal persons. All that can be said is that feelings are often altered when the lobes are severed. And saying that is stating the overwhelmingly obvious. Who would not feel different?

The Environmental View of Generalized Anxiety Disorder

Social Learning Theory. The environmental theories of this disorder hinge on a contention between social learning and psychoanalytic theories. The nexus of social learning theory is that this kind of anxiety is developed through imitation—anxious parents raise anxious children. Thus the parents provide concrete role models of anxiety and the child reflects the parents' insecurity by internalizing their behavior. This would be true in the case of a woman who reacts to life situations in exactly the same anxious ways her mother does.[55]

Wolpe reports that the cause of generalized anxiety is connected to the social environment.[56] According to Wolpe, anxiety is a learned response to external stressors. Thus, the person who is fearful of work and reacts with vomiting while traveling to his job does so because the anxiety attack is a conditioned response to the experience of being transported to a threatening environment. Interesting thought, but some view it as too simple-minded.

Psychoanalytic Theory.   The traditional Freudian explanation of generalized anxiety is that it stems from a disturbance in the parent-child relationship. The disturbance is most pronounced when the parent raises a child who has an excessive and distorted superego. Theoretically, the child becomes frightened of his own sexual or aggressive impulses due to a pathological fear of punishment. The stage is set for an anxiety attack when a situation arises in which anger or sexual demands become threateningly intense.

Some psychoanalysts believe that this kind of anxiety can be the psychological result of masturbation, which generates excessive guilt.[57] Another psychoanalytic opinion holds that sexual deprivation can cause generalized anxiety, since coitus interruptus, frustrated excitation, long abstinence, and the like are considered capable of producing very disturbed feelings. In each of these abnormal courses of sexual activity there is no discharge in orgasm and therefore no psychological gratification. This theoretically creates a sense of psychic helplessness that then engenders an anxiety attack. In my opinion, this kind of theorizing is such a stretch that it is helpless itself. Perhaps the same can be said of any theory of generalized anxiety disorder because it is just another item on the long list of etiological mysteries of psychiatric research at the dawn of the twenty-first century.

OBSESSIVE-COMPULSIVE DISORDER

Symptoms

Many of us have patterns in our lives. We follow routines during most days, taking the same route to work or school and spending our free time in much the same ways. Some of us read the Sunday papers in a certain order, or always eat our meat before our vegetables. We all have patterns of behavior, and most of us have reasons for doing things the way we do.

In some people, however, the patterns aren't just patterns. They are patterns run wild, patterns with a mind of their own. There are people in this world—many more than previously recognized—who take part in strange rituals. They wash their hands 40 times a day. They save things until their rooms are filled with junk. They check to see that the lights are turned off so many times that they are late for work or can't leave the house at all. To make matters worse, they are filled with unbearable anxiety or dread that something terrible will happen if they don't carry out these rituals.

These people have obsessive-compulsive disorder (OCD). This disorder causes people to become haunted by repetitive thoughts or compelled to perform senseless, time-consuming rituals, or both Not much has been known about this illness because people who have it felt ashamed of their thoughts and behaviors and have hidden their condition.[58]

Obsessive-compulsive "traits" are common in normal persons.[59] Many people have their favorite way of arranging their bureaus or closets or organizing their study habits. Others employ their own sleep-inducing gadgets as a nightly bedtime preparation. A certain degree of obsessive-compulsive drive may add a desirable quality to the individual and is partly responsible for the organization necessary to accomplish a diversity of goals. People with OCD, however, have a pathological exaggeration of these traits. They are not free to lead normal lives because they are excessively preoccupied with such concerns as cleanliness or an irresistible urge to perform daily tasks in certain ways. Some suffer from *obsessions,* which are recurring, unwanted thoughts that cannot be excluded from consciousness. The thoughts are *ego-dystonic,* that is, the person experiences them as senseless and repugnant thoughts that invade consciousness. Other persons are dominated by *compulsions,* which are recurring needs to perform a certain act. A compulsion is, in effect, an obsession put into action.

A central symptom of this disorder is constant doubting; afflicted people may check and recheck the front-door lock, the jets on the stove, the contents of pockets, answers on an exam, rewash their hands to guarantee their cleanliness, count or repeat the number of times they blink, or collect and hoard clothes, mail, and even trash. Freud aptly called this disorder a "private religion" because it is often characterized by elaborate ceremonies, self-denials, penances, and ruminative thoughts about sin. The symptoms of this disorder may be meaningless to an observer, but they are aggravating rituals to the person because they must be completed to avoid anxiety. Therefore, although obsessive-compulsives may not want to act upon their urges, and even feel a need to resist them, they have to act or suffer worse consequences. The necessity underlying some of the behaviors is dramatically evident in the case of people with "odd movement compulsion." Dr. Samuel Johnson, the famous eighteenth-century poet and playwright, could not pass through a door without whirling, twisting, and making bizarre hand motions. His friends were aghast.

Compulsive acts are symbolic rituals that psychoanalysts believe serve as a sort of self-punishment and atonement for unacceptable urges. Phobias frequently occur with compulsions, as exemplified by the common combination of a fear of dirt and repeated hand washing (*washing mania*). The hand-washing ritual is undertaken to alleviate the fear of contamination (*mysophobia*). This phenomenon is sometimes referred to as the "Pontius Pilate complex." Mysophobia may also be alleviated by opening doors with elbows or handling all articles while wearing gloves. The famous millionaire Howard Hughes suffered from mysophobia. He insisted that everything be handled by Kleenex and even made his barber use different scissors for different parts of his head to avoid germ buildup. In another case, a woman, every Saturday, washed the church pew she expected to occupy on Sunday!

OCD is not usually found together with any of the other major groups of disorders discussed in this book.[60] However, there are enough strange behaviors in this condition that many things seem possible. *Trichotillomania* is one of these unusual practices. It is found among people who have an irresistible urge to pull their hair out one strand at a time.[61] Some describe it as a basic mechanism of primitive grooming gone haywire in modern society.

Obsessive thoughts vary from such trivial acts as saying a word or phrase over and over or counting (*arithomania*) to more complex procedures such as reassembling the letters in words according to private equations. One such "word game" consists of spelling a word according to the alphabetical ordering of its letters (*alphabetizing*). In another type of obsession the person spends hours brooding about an abstract topic, usually religious or philosophical, to the exclusion of other interests. This is known alternatively as the *thinking compulsion,* the *obsessive-ruminative state,* and *Gruebelzwang.*

Ritualistic compulsions, which are undertaken to dispel obsessive thoughts, may be nonspecific and appear as qualities in all of the person's behavior.[62] This type of compulsive performs daily activities according to a rigid sequence. Other compulsives have more specific drives that can be dangerous, such as an impulse to jump off a high building, to leap in front of an approaching subway, or to act defiantly toward authorities. Some researchers believe that there is a compulsive drive toward eating that they consider to be a factor in some cases of obesity. Sometimes compulsions can lead to socially undesirable acts, such as compulsive promiscuity, arson, or shoplifting (*kleptomania*).

People with OCD suffer from a deep fear of not being able to control their environment completely. This may be the reason for the development of phobias in so many of these people. Like phobics, obsessive-compulsives feel that they would be in perfect control of the world were it not for the phobic object. Thus, the phobic object serves to capsulize their fundamental fear of losing control. Examples of this fear of loss of control abound; many obsessive-compulsives have difficulty in falling asleep because they are no longer in command while sleeping.[63] They are also frequently incapable of expressing affection toward others because of a perceived danger in committing themselves to others who are not entirely under their control. This is not to say that they shy away from sex as well. On the contrary, they often approach sex as a personal challenge to their endurance. Some male obsessive-compulsives, for instance, believe it is a failure not to prolong intercourse by maintaining a limitless erection. Salzman reports a case of a man who tried to achieve orgasm in a woman who had never been able to have one.[64] When he failed, he blamed himself.

Part of the reason an obsession can have so much power over the person with OCD is that these people cannot employ normal ways of getting rid of a threatening fear or thought. They do not seem to know anything with certainty. Nothing is "obvious." Their own senses—their own eyes and ears—do not convince them. They see that their hands look clean, but still they wash and wash. They may have to repeat the action 10, 20, or more times before they start to feel that "Now it's okay."

Obsessive-compulsive disorder is one of the most severe anxiety disorders. It offers a poor prognosis; obsessive-compulsives usually worsen as they grow older, and they may break down when stressful events occur, such as an accident, disease, or any abrupt *change* in lifestyle. When this occurs, depression with suicidal tendencies is a frequent outcome. They may also develop an addiction to alcohol or drugs if they realize that they cannot completely control their environment. The addiction represents the discarding of all controls and a movement to the opposite extreme—the binge. It can become so extreme that neurosurgery has been used to produce personality change.[65]

Not all cases end in such disaster. Some, in fact, develop to the point where the patient develops unusual skills, as exemplified in the following case.

> Jonathan G., a 28-year-old professional, often occupied his consciousness with obsessive thoughts. As a child, he used to count the number of letters in words. However, in an effort to make every word balanced, he would add vowels to the words at preconceived points so that the letters of each word added to a number divisible by 4.[66] Sometime in adolescence this process was altered in a more sophisticated way when he began to juxta-

pose the letters in words so that they were arranged alphabetically. By young adulthood, Jonathan was so well versed in this mental game that he could put a word in its alphabetical ordering before the average person could spell it in its normal form. He kept the whole thing a secret until he saw a celebrity (Dick Cavett) attempt to "alphabetize" on national television. This served to legitimize his obsession and allowed Jonathan to freely express his "talent" in front of others. He was a big hit at parties and bars.

Prevalence

Although DSM-IV reports that OCD is equally common in males and females, there are indications that, at least among college students, it is found more often in men.[67] The NIMH reports that, in 2000, about 2.3 percent of the U.S. adult population aged 18 to 54, or 3.3 million people, had OCD. The nation's social and economic losses due to OCD are approximately $10 billion a year.

Until the mid-1980s, OCD was considered rare. Later, more sophisticated epidemiological studies began to pick up on it.[68] In 1988, an Epidemiologic Catchment Area study estimated lifetime prevalence rates from 1.9 to 3.3 percent in the U.S. population.[69] More recent studies report that OCD increased in the 1990s to the numbers reached today.[70]

OCD affects adults, teenagers, and small children. It is found in people at all socioeconomic levels. About half of people with OCD begin having problems with the disorder before the age of 19. When it begins early in childhood, it seems to affect boys more often than girls.[71]

The Medical Model of Obsessive-Compulsive Disorder

In an earlier edition of this book I said: "Very little has been said concerning biogenic causes of obsessive-compulsive disorder." Scratch that. Much has changed since then. I was first struck with the "new biology of OCD" while scanning the newspaper in 1992. There was a story that was astounding. A 19-year-old college student, depressed over the cancerous growth of OCD in his life, decided to end it all. He shot himself in the head with a pistol. Not only did he survive, but all of his cognitive, intellectual, motor, and sensory functions remained intact. Guess what was gone: his compulsions to wash his hands, constantly count, and jump through doorways. In a sense, he cured himself with a bullet! In a larger sense, it was obvious that OCD is not always purely environmental.[72]

Researchers have been on the track of biological factors for some time now. Twin studies support a medical model. More specifically, high-technology brain-imaging techniques have found specific links between dysfunctions of particular areas of the brain and symptoms of obsessive-compulsive disorder.[73]

Some families seem to have a tendency for OCD to turn up in two, three, or even four generations in a row. About 15 to 20 percent of individuals with OCD come from families in which another family member has the same problem. Of course, OCD may only *appear* to be inherited; children may actually be copying the behaviors of relatives. However, when OCD shows up in the next generation it often takes a different form. A parent may be a "checker," for example, but the child may be a "compulsive washer." That fact, combined with successful treatment of the problem with medication, makes the medical model of OCD a promising area for future research.[74]

The Environmental View of Obsessive-Compulsive Disorder

Social Learning Theory.   This school of thought considers obsessions and compulsions to be learned and repeated over time because they are reinforced by their positive consequences.[75] The obsession is a learned response to feelings of anxiety, and a compulsive act is undertaken when the person realizes that the act can reduce anxiety attached to the obsessive thought. Eventually, the act becomes a fixed pattern of behavior. Sahakian summarized the social learning theory of OCD in the following way:

> An obsessional neurosis develops as the result of a mental conflict in which the neurotic vainly resists an overwhelming drive—not once, but repetitively—if not invariably, then at least with a degree of regularity. Actually, he is undergoing a state of conditioning of which he is not aware, amounting to the establishment of a mental habit of doing things that he chooses not to do.[76]

According to this position, the source of the original anxiety is relatively unimportant compared to understanding the pattern by which obsessive thoughts and ritualistic actions are developed. Some social learning theorists address the etiological question more directly by examining specific traumatic events in adulthood that can produce the disorder. Kardiner, for example, reports a case of a person who could not sleep at night until he performed an elaborate ceremony consisting of lying flat on his stomach with his nose in the pillow.[77] He also placed his face in his hands and held his breath as long as possible. This ritual was a reenactment of a battlefield experience during which he desperately tried to protect himself from an enemy attack at night. The enemy used gas as a weapon and the person made constant adjustments of his gas mask.

The major thrust of the social learning argument is that the origin of obsessive-compulsive behavior need not be in childhood, or, if it is, it is not necessarily connected with unconscious experiences, as psychoanalysts hold. Washing mania, for instance, may yield a direct reassuring effect to people simply because in childhood it protected them against being criticized by their parents for having dirty hands.

Psychoanalytic Theory.   Traditional psychoanalytic theory holds that obsessive-compulsive behavior originates in fixation at the anal stage. The foundation of this theory was the recurring observation that obsessive-compulsives exhibit a key feature of the anal stage—ideas associated with dirt. A preoccupation with dirt signifies anal tendencies because these impulses are normally modified in the remaining stages of development. However, in many obsessive-compulsives they remain as an engrained part of the emotional makeup. This is considered to be the result of unresolved conflicts during the anal stage, conflicts involving order and disorder, cleanliness and soiling.

Fixation at the anal stage is believed to be the result of toilet training that was begun too early or conducted in too demanding a way by the parents. This causes the child to become anxious. The anxiety is controlled by rigid performance standards that translate into ritualistic patterns.[78] Children who initiate such patterns are unable to please their parents by living up to their demands for sphincter control. Consequently, they are left with feelings of doubt and uncertainty, symptoms that frequently appear among obsessive-compulsive adults. The type of parents who are likely to bring about anal fixation in their children are well known. They simply cannot tolerate soil-ing by their child or any stubborn attempts by the child to maintain autonomy. The parents are typically rigid and compulsive themselves. This may be one reason why the disorder frequently appears among members of the same family.

Psychoanalysts believe that it is the harsh superego of obsessive-compulsives that causes the heightened sense of self-criticalness frequently found in these people. This can result in what Nunberg described as "those wrecked by success."[79] If they achieve a long-cherished objective, they become depressed. They cannot enjoy success because their superego "only permits them to await happiness but never to enjoy its fulfillment."[80] There are many people who have attained highly prized positions (per-haps partly due to their obsessive-compulsive tendencies) but are saddened immedi-ately afterwards. This is not uncommon among graduate students who have just completed the formal requirements for the Ph.D. In graduate school circles, it is known as the "postdoctoral syndrome." In its more general form, Maslow refers to it as the "Jonah syndrome," and he explains it is an incapacity of obsessive-compulsives to enjoy peak experiences for an extended time because of a fear of losing control and being shattered.[81]

Perhaps the most important sociological point to be made about the genesis of OCD does not center about the "modeling" of social learning theory or the "fixations" of psychoanalytic theory but, rather, the more general environmental fact that *social stress* is a frequent precursor of OCD. I am not saying that stress by itself causes OCD. I am saying that it can trigger symptoms or make them worse. In either event, stress appears to be a necessary but not sufficient condition.

POSTTRAUMATIC STRESS DISORDER

Symptoms

The term *posttraumatic stress disorder* (*PTSD*) often conjures up images of a Viet-nam War veteran who flinches violently at the sound of a firecracker or dives to the ground when a helicopter flies low overhead. This is the subjective perception. The objective facts about this syndrome are laid out in great detail in DSM-IV. There it is defined as "the development of characteristic symptoms following exposure to an extreme traumatic stressor involving direct personal experience of an event that involves actual or threatened death or serious injury, or other threat to the physical integrity of another person."[82] That certainly covers a wide range of life's horrors. It also extends to *learning* about a trauma, not just experiencing it. Case example: the police knock on the front door and tell you that your parents were just killed in a car accident.[83] Another case example: those victimized by the terroristic attacks on the World Trade Center and the Pentagon on September 11, 2001.

The real way to think about the events that can produce PTSD is beyond Viet-nam and is regularly featured in the daily newspaper in accounts of violent personal assaults (physical attack, sexual assault, robbery, mugging), kidnappings, hostage tak-ing, torture, terrorist attacks, natural or man-made disasters, severe car accidents, or diagnoses of life-threatening illnesses. These all exemplify the nasty ways that life can sneak up behind you and destroy a part of your psyche.[84]

When I set about to write this section on PTSD, I was struck by how all-encom-passing this mental disorder is. I was also impressed by the long list of psychiatric symptoms associated with it. They include reexperiencing the traumatic event through recurrent dreams, dissociative states lasting for seconds to days, and intense psychological distress when the person is exposed to triggering events that resemble an aspect of the original trauma (anniversaries, weather patterns, entering an elevator for a woman who was raped in an elevator). Other problems include guilt over survival, self-destructive behavior, hostility, social withdrawal, and phobias. Case 5:3 demonstrates how a traumatic event can trigger recollections of a previous experience that was even more horrendous.

In a nutshell, PTSD is a lengthy list of psychiatric outcomes to a lengthy list of horrible life experiences.[85] This is not to say that everyone who is traumatized so radically necessarily exhibits any of the symptoms described in Case 5:3. Many people are only temporarily damaged and are able to move on with their lives after a period of time. Who are the ones who do not? We are not sure, but a study by Fierman and his colleagues provides some insight. They report that many of the people described earlier in this chapter are prime candidates for a trauma-imposed stress disorder. With the exception of panic disorder, those researchers found a high prevalence of previously existing anxiety disorder (35 percent) among people with PTSD.[86] A connection

•••••••••••••••••••••••••••••••••• **Case 5:3** ••••••••••••••••••••••••••••••
Memories

Zelda Padlevner, a 59-year-old, married, Orthodox Jewish woman is referred to a psychiatrist for an evaluation in preparation for an appeal to the board that had previously denied her claim for Workman's Compensation. Zelda's problems began six months earlier, following a fire in the dress factory where she had been employed as a seamstress for 15 years. The fire was minor and easily contained, but the synthetic fabrics that burned produced an extremely acrid smell. After the fire, Zelda developed abdominal pains, nausea, and palpitations. She was hospitalized in an intensive care unit for a week because her doctor suspected asthma or a heart condition. A thorough medical evaluation revealed no evidence of physical illness.

In the psychiatric interview she appears mildly depressed, and says that whatever the decision of the appeal board, she cannot bring herself to go back to work. She feels comfortable and safe at home; but whenever she has to go out, she becomes apprehensive, though she cannot say exactly what she is afraid of. She feels more comfortable when her husband accompanies her to stores in the neighborhood; but when she has to travel to a different neighborhood (e.g., to go to a doctor's office), she feels uncomfortable despite his presence, afraid that his long sideburns and ethnic garments will attract hostile

attention from non-Jews. She has trouble sleeping because of recurrent nightmares of her experiences in a concentration camp over 40 years ago and finds herself dwelling on these memories during the day and unable to concentrate on reading.

The psychiatrist asks her to talk about her experience in the concentration camp and learns that she was in Auschwitz in 1943, at the age of 17. Having been young and healthy, she was selected by Dr. Mengele, the sadistic camp doctor, to be part of the work force. After the selection, she and hundreds of other women were told to undress and wait for instructions. As the camp was extremely overcrowded, they were shoved into a strange-looking empty hall without windows. The place had a peculiar odor. When they were transferred a few hours later, she found out that she and the other women had been temporarily kept in a gas chamber. She began to cry as she realized that the smell in the factory fire had brought back the memory of the gas chamber.

———————————

Source: Robert L. Spitzer, Miriam Gibbon, Andrew E. Skodol, Janet B. W. Williams, and Michael First, *DSM-III-R Casebook* (Washington, DC: American Psychiatric Press, 1989), pp. 7–8. By permission of the publisher.

between PTSD and borderline personality disorder is also reported by others. The bottom line appears to be that PTSD has a high comorbidity with other mental disorders.

Prevalence

People who have recently emigrated from war zones and areas of civil unrest have elevated rates of PTSD. Community-based studies reveal a lifetime prevalence ranging from 1 to 14 percent depending on the population sampled. If you return to Chapter 3, you will see a warning about long-term personality damage that can occur among children raised in war zones. That kind of violent setting is associated with the highest prevalence estimates. And remember, these are only estimates. The real numbers may be much greater when less visible, untreated cases are included. The NIMH reports that about 3.6 percent of adults, or 5.2 million Americans, have PTSD during the course of a given year. The same report also says that PTSD is more likely to occur in women than in men. That is consistent with the fact that women are more likely to be victims of violence. [87]

PTSD can occur at any age, including childhood. Symptoms usually begin within three months after the trauma. In some people there may be a delay for years. The likelihood of this disorder is directly linked to the severity, duration, and proximity of an individual's exposure to the traumatic event as well as to the quality of *social supports* available.

The Environmental View of PTSD

Notice that I have not included a section on the medical model of PTSD. That is a purposeful reflection of the fact that little is known about the biology of the problem. A few books have been written about PTSD and parts of the brain,[88] but a book does not make a fact. The real fact is that, because the core definition of PTSD is a reaction to an event, the etiology lies in environmental stressors and individuals' reactions to them.

At the risk of repeating myself, let me point out that for years psychiatric sociologists and clinicians have recognized that soldiers often develop severe anxiety and depression during combat. PTSD is a recognition of the *additional* effects of war after the shooting stops. During World War I, the syndrome was called "shell shock" because it was thought to result from minute brain hemorrhages caused by little explosions. During World War II and the Korean War, it was referred to as "combat fatigue."

You already know about the psychic tolls of the horrors of war. Everything that can be written has been written about war atrocities and detention camps from the Gulf War to Croatia.[89] Vietnam was a special hell. Call it PTSD. Call it "postservice suicide."[90] But never call it anything normal. Vietnam contrasts sharply with some other wars. British veterans of the Falklands war and Nicaraguan veterans from the contra war are functioning effectively and hardly in need of counseling.[91] Of course, much of the difference lies in the nature of the wars. American soldiers in Vietnam were caught in a jungle full of deadly surprises. Another difference lies in the *social* contexts of wars. Unpopular wars like "Nam" add the burden of social stigma and returning home to a hostile America.

When you think of PTSD, think horror in general, not just the horror of combat. Think of the stress disorders in survivors of a mass shooting such as the atrocity at Columbine High School.[92] Think of the lifelong developmental abnormalities of child victims of sexual abuse.[93] Posttraumatic response may have been most thoroughly studied in soldiers, but it may turn out that the heaviest and most lasting burden falls on abused women and children.[94] And when you think of PTSD, also think of the victims of bloody traffic accidents who may not have been an official "mortality" but definitely died a little psychologically.

CONCLUSIONS

Anxiety is a common experience of everyday life. You feel it before an exam, in a traffic snarl, and during a frustrating day at work. That is normal. Pathological anxiety is a felt fear that is completely inappropriate.

The topics in this chapter on anxiety disorders take a number of forms. They include panic disorder where people are victimized by attacks, apprehension, or terror with little warning. Phobic disorder is anxiety linked with a particular object or situation out of the safe confines of home. In that sense, phobic reactions are predictable. There is some evidence that panic and phobic disorders occur in people who are biologically vulnerable, but most of the etiological research centers on the effects of intrapsychic forces and social learning.

Generalized anxiety disorder is found among people who are so anxiously over-concerned about things in their life that they may panic. Unlike panic disorder, however, the anxiety is more constant. It may be an inherited condition, or it may result from a fractured upbringing. People with obsessive-compulsive disorder are anxious if they do not repeat private thoughts or engage in often bizarre ritualistic behaviors. For a long time, OCD was linked with childhood experiences such as severe toilet training. Today that thinking is beginning to look naive in light of new evidence that there is a biology of OCD.

Posttraumatic stress disorder is a new term for an old problem. The problem is the psychiatric response some people have to an overwhelmingly stressful life event. The life events are, unfortunately, too numerous and very common. They involve the carnage of war, rape, child abuse, torture, and violent accidents. Although the origin of PTSD is clearly an environmental experience, we do not yet know why some people react worse than others to the same trauma.

6

Personality Disorders

It is not unusual for mentally ill people to contemplate various forms of suicide. People with antisocial personality disorder, however, rarely take their own lives because they are often narcissistic.

Personality disorders are a curious group of problems with loose behavioral and causal connections. The caption to the photo at the beginning of this chapter states that a particular group of people with personality disorders rarely commit suicide. Yet there are other types of personality disorders in which suicidal behavior is common, especially among women.[1] There are also cross-cultural variations in the rate and expression of personality disorders. In Croatia, for example, sadistic behavior is especially common in this diagnostic category.[2]

The status of research on personality disorders today is a duality: much more has been written about the topic than ever before, yet these forms of mental illness are still very elusive.[3] The symptoms of these people are well delineated, but the course of their problems is not always predictable. Frequently, personality disorders lead to worse outcomes, as in the case of schizoid personalities who decompensate into schizophrenia. At other times, they are an end to themselves, an end that generally translates into a life of psychic hell and interpersonal malfunctioning.

Personality disorders are common, although the *true* prevalence is unknown.[4] It is apparent, however, that many mental patients with other primary diagnoses have a personality disorder as well. Because of the complexities in recognizing personality disorders and understanding them as psychiatric entities, they are especially difficult to treat.[5] The APA defines personality *traits* as "enduring patterns of perceiving, relating to, and thinking about the environment and oneself . . . exhibited in a wide range of important social and personal contexts."[6] When they become inflexible and maladaptive, causing either significant impairment in social or occupational functioning or subjective distress, personality traits evolve into *personality disorders.* They seldom result in hospitalization, for two reasons. First, they are not as disabling, relatively speaking, as most of the disorders discussed previously; second, one of the most common personality disorders, the *antisocial personality disorder,* is frequently found among criminals, people who are not likely to seek help.

Gender differences in personality disorders have been examined and reexamined to the nth degree.[7] Still there does not appear to be any reliable consensus as to which gender is most susceptible to these problems. In the past, women were traditionally reported to suffer more frequently from these conditions than men, with the exception of the antisocial personality disorder.[8] Now there are reports that the earlier reports were wrong.[9] To make things even more complicated, there are also reports that no one knows the true difference in the rates of personality disorders between the genders because there is a sex bias in diagnosis.[10]

DSM-IV groups personality disorders into three "clusters" with shared characteristics as described in Table 6:1. The first cluster includes *paranoid* and *schizophrenia-spectrum disorders.* People with these disorders often appear "odd" or eccentric. The second cluster includes *histrionic, narcissistic, antisocial,* and *borderline personality disorders.* Individuals with these problems often appear overly dramatic, emotional, or erratic. The third cluster includes *avoidant, dependent,* and *obsessive-compulsive disorders* in which people usually appear fearful or anxious.

The DSM "cluster" approach to classifying personality disorders has been criticized as a sure recipe for clinical confusion and gender bias.[11] Some have suggested that, since personality disorders are traits that are present to some degree in all people, they should only be considered as having reached inflexible and harmful extremes by very detailed diagnoses. The "five-factor model," for example, focuses on the extent to which personality traits vary across five broad dimensions: neuroticism, extroversion, openness to experience, agreeableness, and conscientiousness.[12]

In my psychiatric sociology class, I prefer to approach personality disorders as

Table 6:1   Symptoms of Personality Disorders

Cluster A

Paranoid Personality Disorder

- suspects, without sufficient basis, that others are exploiting or deceiving him or her
- is reluctant to confide in others because of unwarranted fear that the information will be used maliciously against him or her
- reads hidden demeaning or threatening meanings into benign remarks or events
- persistently bears grudges. i.e., is unforgiving of insults, injuries, or slights
- recurrent suspicions, without justification, regarding fidelity of spouse or sexual partner

Schizoid Personality Disorder

- neither desires nor enjoys close relationships, including being part of a family
- almost always chooses solitary activities
- little, if any, interest in having sexual experiences with another person
- appears indifferent to the praise or criticism of others
- emotional coldness, detachment. or flattened affectivity

Schizotypal Personality Disorder

- odd beliefs or magical thinking that influence behavior and are inconsistent with subcultural norms (e.g., superstitiousness, belief in clairvoyance, telepathy, or "sixth sense"; in children and adolescents, bizarre fantasies or preoccupations)
- unusual perceptual experiences, including bodily illusions
- suspiciousness or paranoid ideation
- behavior or appearance that is odd, eccentric, or peculiar
- lacks close friends or confidants other than first-degree relatives

Cluster B

Antisocial Personality Disorder

- failure to conform to social norms with respect to lawful behaviors as indicated by repeatedly performing acts that are grounds for arrest
- irritability and aggressiveness, as indicated by repeated physical fights or assaults
- impulsivity or failure to plan ahead
- deceitfulness, as indicated by repeated lying. use of aliases, or conning others for personal profit or pleasure
- reckless disregard for safety of self or others
- lack of remorse, as indicated by being indifferent to or rationalizing having hurt, mistreated, or stolen from another

Borderline Personality Disorder

- a pattern of unstable and intense interpersonal relationships characterized by alternating between extremes of idealization and devaluation
- identity disturbance: persistent and markedly disturbed, distorted, or unstable image or sense of self
- recurrent suicidal behavior, gestures, or threats, or self-mutilating behavior
- chronic feelings of emptiness
- inappropriate, intense anger or lack of control of anger (e.g., frequent displays of temper, constant anger, recurrent physical fights)

continued

Table 6:1   continued

Histrionic Personality Disorder
- is uncomfortable in situations in which he or she is not the center of attention
- interaction with others is often characterized by inappropriate sexually seductive or provocative behavior
- consistently uses physical appearance to draw attention to oneself
- style of speech that is excessively impressionistic and lacking in detail
- self-dramatization, theatricality, and exaggerated expression of emotion
- considers relationships to be more intimate than they actually are

Narcissistic Personality Disorder
- a grandiose sense of self-importance (e.g., exaggerates achievements and talents, expects to be recognized as superior without commensurate achievements)
- believes that he or she is "special" and unique and can only be understood by, should associate with, other special or high-status people or institutions
- requires excessive admiration
- is interpersonally exploitative, i.e., takes advantage of others to achieve his or her own ends
- arrogant, haughty behaviors or attitudes

Cluster C
Avoidant Personality Disorder
- avoids occupational activities that involve significant interpersonal contact, because of fears of criticism, disapproval or rejection
- is unwilling to get involved with people unless certain of being liked
- inhibited in new interpersonal situations because of feelings of inadequacy
- belief that one is socially inept, personally unappealing or inferior to others

Dependent Personality Disorder
- is unable to make everyday decisions without an excessive amount of advice and reassurance from others
- has difficulty initiating projects or doing things on his or her own (due to a lack of self-confidence in judgment or abilities rather than to a lack of motivation or energy)
- feels uncomfortable or helpless when alone, because of exaggerated fears of being unable to care for himself or herself
- urgently seeks another relationship as a source of care and support when a close relationship ends

Obsessive-Compulsive Personality Disorder
- preoccupation with details, rules, lists, order, organization. or schedules to the extent that the major point of the activity is lost
- perfectionism that interferes with task completion (e.g., inability to complete a project because one's own standards are not met)
- overconscientiousness, scrupulousness, and inflexibility about matters of morality, ethics, or values (not accounted for by cultural or religious identification)
- inability to discard worn-out or worthless objects even when they have no sentimental value
- adopts a miserly spending style toward both self and others; money is viewed as something to be hoarded for future catastrophes
- rigidity and stubbornness

Source: American Psychiatric Association, *Diagnostic and Statistical Manual of Mental Disorders*, Fourth Edition (Washington, DC: American Psychiatric Association, 1994) pp. 629–674.

be an extension of bragging/showing off connected with the "American male stereotype."[40] Unlike many of the other personality disorders, narcissistic personality disorder does not usually develop into something else. It does not seem to be caused by biology at all but instead appears to stem from psychosocial experiences during childhood.[41] These are people who have a grandiose sense of self-importance and an exhibitionistic need for constant attention and admiration. Like the histrionic personality, the narcissistic type is extremely self-centered. They overestimate their abilities and achievements and have fantasies typically involving power, wealth, or brilliance. They may expect special favors from others but will not reciprocate. They are manipulative people who take advantage of others with no regard for others' rights. As such, they are very similar to antisocial personalities, discussed in the next section.[42]

Research on narcissistic people is relatively new. To date, studies have made some interesting findings, including the hypothesis that future research will uncover significantly different kinds of narcissistic people.[43] One study of college students has identified a particular narcissistic style on campus and in the classroom.[44] Narcissistic people are also reported to be attracted to military life where certain roles confer an ostentatious glory.[45] Because these people enjoy the way they are, they are extremely difficult to treat.[46] Take a look at Case 6:3 and you will see what I mean.

· **Case 6:3** ·
My Fan Club

Nick is tall, bearded, muscular, and handsome. He is meticulously dressed in a white suit and has a rose in his lapel. He enters the psychiatrist's office, pauses dramatically, and exclaims, "Aren't roses wonderful this time of year?" When asked why he has come for an evaluation, he replies laughingly that he has done it to appease his family doctor, "who seemed worried about me." He has also read a book on psychotherapy, and hopes that "maybe there is someone very special who can understand me. I'd make the most incredible patient." He then takes control of the interview and begins to talk about himself, after first remarking, half jokingly, "I was hoping you would be as attractive as my family doctor."

Nick pulls out of his attaché case a series of newspaper clippings, his resumé, photographs of himself, including some of him with famous people, and a photostat of a dollar bill with his face replicating George Washington's. Using these as cues, he begins to tell his story.

He explains that in the last few years he has "discovered" some now-famous actors, one of whom he describes as a "physically perfect teenage heartthrob." He volunteered to coordinate publicity for the actor, and as part of that, posed in a bathing suit in a scene that resembled a famous scene from the actor's hit movie. Nick, imitating the actor's voice, laughingly, and then seriously, describes how he and the actor had similar pasts. Both were rejected by their parents and peers, but overcame this to become popular. When the actor came to town, Nick rented a limousine and showed up at the gala "as a joke," as though he were the star himself. The actor's agent expressed annoyance at what he had done, causing Nick to fly into a rage. When Nick cooled down, he realized that he was "wasting my time promoting others, and that it was time for me to start promoting myself." "Someday," he said, pointing to the picture of the actor, "he will want to be president of my fan club."

Source Robert L. Spitzer, Miriam Gibbon, Andrew E. Skodol, Janet B. W. Williams, and Michael B. First, *DSM-III-R Casebook* (Washington, DC: American Psychiatric Press, 1989), pp. 12–14. By permission of the publisher.

· ·

ANTISOCIAL PERSONALITY DISORDER

Symptoms

What compels a seemingly normal person to disregard a fundamental societal principle and commit an outrageous act like murder?[47] Much has been written about antisocial personality disorder (APD), including the specific DSM-IV criteria to accurately diagnose it.[48] No small wonder that there is widespread concern about this problem since these are people with a special capacity for dangerousness. No other disorder is more clearly related to society than the antisocial personality. This type of person suffers from a weak or absent conscience, the intrapsychic representative of society. DSM-IV reserves the term for individuals who are basically unsocialized and whose behavior repeatedly conflicts with society's expectations. Because of the blatant sociological nature of this disorder, and the fact that it is the most well researched of all the personality disorders, a considerable part of this chapter is devoted to it. For many reasons, it deserves special attention.

The central symptom is a defect in the conscience, technically known as *superego lacunae*. This lack of conscience allows the person to pursue a lifestyle that regularly opposes the laws and mores of society. Typically, immoral behavior is exhibited in many aspects of life, although, as children, antisocial personalities may have only been immoral in particular areas. They may have been thieves but not truants, or they may have set fires but behaved normatively otherwise. At that age, the superego appears to be "punched out" with regard to certain norms. Because these people lack a well-developed conscience, they can freely pursue antisocial activities without the pain of guilt. Psychiatrists typically report that antisocial individuals *act* as if they are indifferent to the social impact of their behavior. The truth is they are not acting; they really *are* indifferent. Since the conscience defect causes antisocials to be callous to societal norms, they live by the pleasure principle; their primary concern is immediate gratification of instinctual impulses. Freud recognized this personality type and referred to it as the "erotic type" because the person is hell-bent on seeking pleasure regardless of the welfare of others.

Since antisocial individuals persistently violate the laws and mores of society, it is other people who suffer rather than the violators themselves. The fact that they have no remorse for the harm they do others exacerbates the problem. In fact, they have an inner conviction that they are special people who are immune to society's rules, and in a sense, they are, for they have no internalized element of society. These attitudes, combined with a conscience defect and an extreme sense of narcissism, render antisocial personalities dangerous people. When they are frustrated, they can spontaneously commit a number of offenses, including robbery and rape. In fact, these are people who could become profit murderers or "hit men" because they feel no guilt in committing such crimes.[49] Rarely do they take their own life through suicide simply because they are self-loving.

Antisocial individuals do not experience any subjective discomfort from their condition as people with anxiety disorders do. Their only anguish stems from the fear of getting caught and being punished for moral or legal violations. If they are punished, they are likely to repeat their behavior. They do not learn from experience since punishment cannot create a conscience.[50] When they do get into trouble, they usually project all blame onto others. Unreliability and chronic lying are also common features.

Any goals the antisocial person may have are immediate and directed toward self-aggrandizement, the acquisition of money, and the use of others for pleasure. Using others is a particular skill of antisocial people since they are often gifted, intelligent individuals with superficial charm.[51] These skills, along with an attractive physical appearance, make it easy for them to carry out their plot adeptly. If antisocials are questioned about moral and legal principles, they can verbalize all the correct rules, but they do not really understand them or believe them in the way that others do. Cleckly calls this verbal façade the "mask of sanity."[52]

Serial murderers Ted Bundy, the handsome law student, and successful businessman John Wayne Gacy, are examples of those who wear "the mask of sanity"; you would never know about them from their appearance or lifestyle.[53] You would only know them from their conscienceless crimes. In the words of serial murderer Henry Lee Lucas:

> I've got 360 people. I've got 36 states and three different countries. My victims never knew what was gonna happen. I've had shootings, knifings, strangulations, beatings, and I've participated in actual crucifixions of the humans. All across the country there's people just like me who's set out to destroy human life. I was death on women. I didn't—didn't feel they—they need to exist. I hated them, and I wanted to destroy every one I could find. And I was doing a good job of it. I've tracked them from all over the United States almost just do it out of spite, you know. I want to torment 'em. Every time, they'd stop or go someplace, I'd be there. I'd follow them on the highway: I'd go around them, play with 'em, back up and let them go by me. A woman alone ain't safe at all.[54]

Until recently, there had never been a report of a female serial murderer. In 1991, Aileen Wournos changed all of that. Part of her story is told in Box 6:1.

Recognizing APD

Although there are an estimated 3 million psychopaths—1 person in 100—walking the streets of North America, there is a lot of confusion as to what constitutes the disorder. The syndrome has had a unique history in psychiatry. Originally, APD was called *moral insanity,* by Prichard in 1835. The label was later changed to avoid a moral issue that is foreign to modern psychiatry. In the latter part of the nineteenth century, the disorder was called *constitutional psychopathic inferior,* a reflection of the somatogenic orientation of the time. Other terms that have been used are *anethopathy, semantic dementia,* and, more recently, *psychopathic* and *sociopathic.* They all refer to the personality disorder now classified as antisocial.

The label for this condition continually changes because there is so much confusion about who should be included. Some feel that so many different types of personalities can be considered antisocial that the term has become a diagnostic wastebasket. This is true to an extent since individuals with any of a number of disorders may engage in occasional antisocial behavior, as in the case of some people with organic brain syndromes and schizophrenia. In these instances, however, the antisocial behavior is only a *consequence* of a qualitatively different condition. Other cases involving antisocial behavior and an additional disorder are more difficult to unravel. For example, many antisocial individuals indulge in alcohol and narcotics.[55] It is generally considered that the antisocial condition establishes a predisposition for drug abuse, but it is also possible that chronic drug intake can generate a disregard for social laws and customs.

America's First Female Serial Murderer?

Ocala, Fla.— On a lonesome stretch of Florida Interstate, Aileen Wuornos waited for just the right man.

A strong-willed woman of 34, with a brown purse and a heart full of betrayal, Wuornos chose her company with care. No truck drivers. No drug users. No one too young. She watched the whir of passing cars for a white, middle-aged man traveling alone—someone with money, someone she could hustle.

What happened next depended on a mysterious mix of chance and intention.

Would it be a "normal day" or a "killing day"?

On a normal day of hitchhiking through the forested countryside of central Florida, Wuornos might be picked up by 10 men. Once in the passenger seat, she worked her hustle, sometimes with a tale about a sick child and often by peddling sex—a fling in the woods.

On a "killing day," somebody got shot. And before long, a lot of men were turning up full of bullet holes on dirt roads in rural Florida.

Then, a retired police chief fell victim. And his improbable murder just off Interstate 75 got investigators to wondering whether the serial killer they were hunting for was a woman.

Wuornos has already confessed to seven highway murders in separate, detailed statements.

Police in Florida and points beyond are calling her the country's first true female serial killer—a fearless woman with a dark, troubled past who is likely to be studied by experts in criminal violence for years to come.

Women almost never kill strangers, and certainly not seven in a row.

"Sure I shot them, but it was self-defense," Wuornos said in a jail-house confession taken down by a police officer. "I've been raped 12 times in the last eight years and I just got sick of it. So I got this gun and was carrying it around. As soon as I got the gun, it got worse." . . .

Her mother had abandoned her at 6 months old. Her father raped a 7-year-old girl and then hanged himself in prison with a bedsheet. Her grandfather was an alcoholic who she said beat her. She was sexually abused.

She was a runaway before she was a teenager.

At 12, she was drinking. At 13, she was pregnant. No one believed her when she said she'd been raped. Her grandparents decided she was wild and boy-crazy, and they shipped her off to a home for unwed mothers.

Not long after she returned, her grandmother died of liver failure and the family fell apart.

At 15, she was fending for herself—sleeping in abandoned cars, selling her body in Rochester, Mich. She dropped out of ninth grade. She landed in juvenile homes. When she exchanged sex for money, she often gave the money away to her brother and sister, to stock booze parties for teen-agers in town.

In 1976, her grandfather died in an apparent suicide and her brother died of throat cancer. The same year, Wuornos, described as a "very attractive" 20-year-old, married a man who was nearly 70, a man who had picked her up hitchhiking.

Again, it wasn't for keeps. She said her marriage ended after a month because her husband beat her with a cane. He said Wuornos beat him.

Two years later, she shot herself in the stomach, her sixth suicide attempt in eight years. . . .

Aileen Wuornos was a child of the streets before she was a woman of the highways. She had been hustling and selling her body for 20 years. . . . It all ended at the Last Resort, a scruffy biker bar on the U.S. 1 strip south of Daytona Beach. There, on what regulars describe as a good night, a biker woman will fling off her shirt, bare her breasts, and staple her bra to the ceiling. . . .

In a statement while in jail, Wuornos reflected: "You know, after I killed the first couple I thought about quitting, but I had to make money to pay the bills. . . . "

One of the men, she recalls, fell down after being shot, crying out: "I'm gonna die. Oh my God, I'm dying."

"I said, 'Yeah, motherf—, so what,' and I shot him a couple more times."

_____

Source: Donna St. George, "A troubled woman and a trail of dead men," *The Philadel-phia Inquirer,* Sunday, August 4, 1991. By permission of the publisher.

•••

The most common difficulty in diagnosing this disorder is the fact that *not all criminals are antisocial.* Since the antisocial label is applied from the viewpoint of the host culture, behavior acquired in a deviant subculture is sometimes confused with the antisocial condition. Actually, many members of deviant subcultures, particularly delinquents, are conforming to the norms of their criminal environment, just as conventional people conform to the norms of mainstream society.[56] The activity of people who follow criminal pursuits but who are psychiatrically normal is called *dyssocial behavior.* This is a personality type that is different in important ways from the antisocial type in that the dyssocial person can form stable relationships with others, although they may be members of a crime gang. In addition, the dyssocial person can defer pleasure, learn from experience, and feel guilt. None of these qualities exists within the antisocial personality, at least not in the extreme form. Another diagnostic difficulty involves race or perhaps I should say *racism.* Studies show that the diagnosis of APD is applied arbitrarily, as evidenced by the fact that, if everything else is held constant, black people "qualify" for the diagnosis more easily than whites.[57] Psychiatry has been frequently accused of race and gender biases in diagnosing many mental disorders. This is just one example.

Legal Issues

Another controversy about antisocial behavior is the question of criminal intent and mental illness. These two concepts are incompatible in the United States. If a bank has been robbed or a woman brutally raped, *legally* there is no criminal act unless the perpetrator of the act is adjudged mentally responsible. The decision is often a function of the particular social circumstances involved in the case. For example, if each of two women is booked for her fourth shoplifting offense within a year's time, the court decisions about the two cases may be quite different. If one woman was on welfare with a large family, her shoplifting is seen as a rational act, and she becomes criminally responsible. She will be pronounced guilty and be fined or sentenced to jail. If the other woman is married to a rich physician, she is not considered to be in need and therefore must have shoplifted because of an "unreasonable need." The judge finds it impossible to perceive any criminal intent. The woman is "clearly" ill and is committed to see a psychiatrist once a week as an outpatient.

Certain laws are designed to separate mentally ill people who commit criminal acts from mentally competent people who do so. One such law, mentioned in Chapter 2, is the well-known M'Naghten rule. It provides that people may establish a defense of insanity if they did not know that they were doing something wrong in the eyes of society. A major difficulty with this principle is that it excludes those with antisocial personality disorders since they know that others disapprove of their behavior. Their sickness is that they do not care. This is an inappropriate way to define mental illness because many disturbed people are adjudged to have criminal responsibilities and are then punished with a jail term.

Because the M'Naghten rule is not sophisticated enough to detect various types of disturbances, antisocial personalities are sent to prison rather than a psychiatric facility where they might be helped, although rehabilitation is unlikely. In prison their condition usually deteriorates because they are placed with other criminals with whom they exchange tricks of the trade in "factories of crime." Some feel that discussions and debates about the insanity defense are a colossal waste of time inasmuch as the defense is used in less than 1 percent of criminal cases and is successful only about a quarter of the time.[58]

Prevalence

Although the number 3 million is often used as an estimate, it is impossible to know the real number of antisocial personalities in the United States. One reason is that they are not the type of people who seek treatment on their own, and if they are treated, it is usually after having been caught by authorities and referred for psychiatric evaluation. Thus those who are never arrested go unrecognized. Additionally, those who are arrested but not adjudged in need of psychiatric care are overlooked because of the unrealistic legal guidelines that determine criminal responsibility. It may be that the rate of this disorder is rising, if the national crime rate can be used as a rough barometer, although some crime is carried out by "normal" people. My colleagues and I examined the psychiatric histories of a large population of criminals. Consistent with what is stated here, only a minuscule percentage of the criminals had been diagnosed as APD.[59] The rest fell through the cracks.

From records of diagnosed antisocial personalities, it is known that many come from lower-class families living in slum areas. The prevalence by sex is predominantly male.[60] Estimates are that ten times as many males as females are diagnosed as antisocial.[61] Typically, the antisocial behavior is manifested before the age of 15. There is also a high rate of antisocial personality types reported among adopted children. More recently, there are reports of a relationship between APD and homelessness.[62]

THE MEDICAL MODEL OF ANTISOCIAL PERSONALITY DISORDER

APD Today

Today there is a plethora of biological theories of APD.[63] Perhaps the word "theories" is too heavy; the word "correlates" is actually more appropriate.[64] Among these are constitutional factors as suggested by high rates of APD among male adoptees from biological parents with criminal backgrounds.[65] Biochemical abnormalities are again being reported in the literature as they were in earlier years.[66] And neuroimmunological studies are searching for brain pathways.[67]

The big topic in the biology of APD today is brain abnormalities. The reports are interesting. One set of studies suggests that antisocials have unusual forms of brain lateralization that impair their ability to understand emotion and experience full empathy.[68] This may stem from experiences shortly before or after birth,[69] or possibly may develop from a brain insult, such as a tumor, later in life.[70]

The idea that APD may result from brain and not mind has been around for a long time. It is just recently, however, that sophisticated medical research has made many people (sociologists included) think in terms other than adverse environmental influences. Below I sketch a brief history of biological research on antisocial personality disorder.

Early Research on APD

EEG Abnormalities.   There have been a number of attempts to assess whether antisocial disorder is caused by biological factors. Some researchers note that criminal antisocials frequently have a history of head injury or epilepsy. The relationship between antisocial behavior and brain tissue impairment has been further demonstrated by a number of studies using electroencephalographic (EEG) procedures to record the electrical activity of the brain. In a majority of the studies, antisocial individuals showed some form of EEG abnormality.[71] The proportion of subjects with abnormal patterns of brain activity ranged from 31 to 58 percent from study to study. In this connection, one report further finds that EEG abnormalities vary with type of antisocial traits; fire-setting is associated with high EEG abnormality while stealing is associated with low EEG abnormality.[72] However, it is questionable whether the EEG procedure is a valid way of assessing those activities of the brain related to thought and behavior since it records only a small sample of activity from the brain surface. If the EEG procedure is valid, I find it interesting that the early studies reported high EEG abnormalities with the more severe forms of antisocial behavior such as arson.

Genetic Theory. In the 1930s, studies of hereditary influences were conducted on monozygotic twins. In Germany, Lange found 13 antisocial criminals each of whom had an identical twin. Ten of the 13 co-twins were antisocial themselves.[73] However, a study of 19 monozygotic twin pairs in the United States did not support a genetic explanation of antisocial disorder.[74] The twins in the U.S. study had been separated at an early age and raised separately. No significant concordance for the antisocial disorder was demonstrated, leaving the theory of genetic transmission open to serious question.

The results of another German study, this one by Kranz, also point toward the importance of environmental factors.[75] Kranz found a 54 percent rate of concordance among fraternal twins of the same sex but only a 14 percent rate among fraternal twins of the opposite sex. The marked difference between concordance rates of same-sex fraternal twins and opposite-sex fraternal twins is critical because it demonstrates the greater effect of differing child-rearing practices over genetic similarity. Genetic factors were reinvestigated in the 1980s. One study found that genes may contribute to antisocial behavior in the presence of adverse environmental factors.[76] Another report suggests a biological link between schizophrenia and antisocial personality.[77]

Probably the most interesting (or controversial) genetic theory is the XYY proposition. The central thesis of this theory is that antisocial people, who are usually males, have an extra male (Y) chromosome. This chromosomal abnormality (XYY) is believed to cause aggressive behavior that can lead to antisocial acts. However, the XYY pattern, considered to produce "supermales," does not account for many cases of antisocial disorder. Perhaps only 1 percent of antisocial criminals have this chromosomal makeup. In fact, any link between the antisocial diagnosis and the XYY pattern may be due to the physical traits exhibited by these men; they are frequently large and riddled with acne, both of which traits may predispose evaluators (such as judges) to see them as deviants. Additionally, many males born with the XYY factor do not turn to a life of crime. The whole theory was kick-started by mass murderer Richard Speck, who went on a bloody rampage in Chicago in the late 1960s. Speck was diagnosed with the XYY syndrome. Years later it was discovered that the diagnosis was a laboratory error.

Biochemical Theory. Another medical explanation of antisocial behavior is biochemical. Lykken has demonstrated that antisocial personality types experience less anxiety about socially unpleasant situations than do normal people.[78] It is possible that antisocials are less sensitive to social mores due to a defect in the autonomic nervous system that in turn reduces arousal levels. If this is true, then they should act like normal people in their response to socially unpleasant situations when their anxiety levels are increased.

This idea was tested by Schachter and Latone, who injected a group of antisocial personalities with adrenaline, a chemical agent that stimulates the autonomic nervous system.[79] Under the influence of adrenaline, individuals in the group exhibited increased anxiety in response to socially unpleasant situations. It may be that their thirst for excitement and their inability to deal with boredom and routine may be the result of a biochemical state of lowered arousal. In this view, then, their "thrill-seeking" behavior may be extreme because it takes more for them to feel satisfied.[80]

Some experiments demonstrate that antisocial people perform less well than do normal people in tedious, monotonous tasks.[81] Studies also show that they prefer novel situations over familiar ones.[82] It is clear that antisocial people do not have the same emotional makeup as most people because they feel no anxiety in response to behavior that normally elicits guilt. It is unclear, however, whether this is a direct result of a neural dysfunction. If it is, the specific biochemical alterations have yet to be uncovered. It is more likely that any abnormalities in their nervous systems are in response to pathologic factors in the psychosocial environment. There are simply too many common family background features among antisocial individuals to justify a purely biochemical explanation.

THE ENVIRONMENTAL VIEW OF ANTISOCIAL PERSONALITY DISORDER

Psychoanalytic Theory

Psychoanalytically, antisocial behavior is viewed as the improper response of the ego to id impulses, resulting from a poorly formed superego that leaves the ego at the mercy of the instincts. Consequently, the ego is not able to tolerate instinctual tension or to postpone instinctual gratification.[83] Because the superego is defective, there is no inner mechanism to regulate life activities according to moral principles or social norms. Antisocial personalities have only an "external superego," that is, a fear of being caught by the law.

Because they lack a healthy superego, these people are constantly overwhelmed by the need for pleasure. This is the psychoanalytic explanation of their "thrill-seeking" behavior. Consistent with this theory, one researcher estimates that 90 percent of antisocial males are driven by sexual tension.[84] What causes the superego defect? The common psychoanalytic explanation is that, as a child, the antisocial was denied the normal opportunity to form a close relationship with a parental figure. Thus, the individual never incorporates the set of moral standards that usually result from identification with the same-sex parent. Numerous situations can create this type of deprivation. For example, when a child is repeatedly moved from one foster home to another, he is not provided with any stable parental figure after which to model himself. This kind of parental deprivation appears quite frequently in antisocial personality types. In fact, one study revealed that 60 percent of a sample of antisocial personalities had lost at least one parent during childhood.[85]

Psychoanalysts believe improper parenting is the primary cause of the antisocial disorder. Some research does report a marked association between the disorder and a lack of parental affection. One such study compared attitudes of antisocial boys and normal schoolboys toward their fathers.[86] A significantly larger number of the antisocial boys felt that their fathers were disinterested in them. Further evidence suggests that the antisocial individual is often a child born to parents who did not want him.

He is frequently either an illegitimate birth or a child born to parents with a bad marriage. As a result, he may be passed among a series of temporary "caretakers" or institutionalized. Additionally, one 1990s study of young adults who spent much of their childhood in large group homes reports a high degree of criminality.[87]

Social Learning Theory: The Parental Hypocrisy Model

The central proposition of the parental hypocrisy model is that children learn antisocial behavior from parents who encourage and reward it. In this sense, the disorder develops through social learning. The other part of the theory is that parents who encourage antisocial behavior do so because they achieve vicarious gratification of their own forbidden impulses through their child's acting-out behavior. Therefore, the *latent* antisocial parent produces the *manifest* antisocial child.

This theory assumes that the conscience develops through the incorporation of the parents' covert behaviors as well as their manifest behaviors. For example, the parent who immediately checks to see that a child has followed an order and who constantly warns of dire consequences simultaneously conveys an unstated alternative to the order, namely, disregard for authority.[88] Thus, it is *parental hypocrisy* that corrupts. The parents condemn antisocial behavior overtly while they simultaneously encourage it covertly. One team of researchers states, "It is possible in every case adequately studied to trace the specific conscience defect in the child to a mirror image of similar type and emotional charge in the parent." The same researchers cite some common examples of the ways in which the parents of antisocial individuals encourage immorality such as, "'Here is an extra quarter, but don't tell your father'; 'You can get into the movie for half-price, since you certainly don't look 12 years old'; 'Fires are dangerous but if you must get it out of your system, then we'll set some in the yard.' . . ." Children hear their parents gloating about shortchanging the grocer; naturally they sense the parental pleasure."[89]

Clinical observations of antisocial children who are being treated together with a parent support the theory of parental hypocrisy. In some cases the parent showed unmistakable joy while the child was telling the therapist about misdeeds. Immediately after the report, however, the parent became moralistic and condemned the child's behavior.[90] In other instances, the parent encouraged the child to relate misdeeds in graphic detail, provided missing pieces of information, and appeared to be openly enjoying the lawbreaking of the child.

It is not difficult to understand how parental hypocrisy can foster a defective conscience. Parents who verbally support one set of values but who act according to another cannot hope that their children will respect moral principles. A mother who lectures on honesty while bragging about an ability to evade income taxes or a father who appears to be astounded when he hears a four-letter word but who promiscuously performs the act it symbolizes is likely to raise children who harbor resentment toward authority figures.

Social Class and APD

The psychoanalytic emphasis on rejecting or absent parents seems to be a useful explanation of antisocial behavior in the lower classes in which there are *entire families* of antisocial personalities. The parental hypocrisy model, however, may be more appropriate to the genesis of the disorder in middle-class families where often only *one sibling* (the "black sheep") in a family manifests the disorder and the other siblings are well adjusted.[91] This may be the result of a single child being selected as the scapegoat for the parents' own forbidden desires.

The latter explanation makes particular sense in light of the high rate of antisocial behavior among adopted children.[92] The attitudes that parents manifest toward adopted children may be quite different from their attitudes toward their natural children. Such parents are often hostile toward each other as well. This hostility may either lead to childlessness or be the consequence of it. In either case, adopted children cannot overcome the problem of childlessness because they do not verify the biological and sexual identities of the parent. Rather, they serve as a living reminder of the parent's own inadequacies. Small wonder they are often not cared for lovingly. In Chapter 9, the high rate of mental illness in general among adoptees is more thoroughly discussed.

Labeling Theory

It is no small wonder that antisocial behavior, such as violent crime, occurs so frequently among urban youth who are regularly exposed to violence.[93] Consistently, labeling theorists contend that the family is not the exclusive source of social norms but part of the larger community whose norms it reflects. Children who are reared in the slum of a city are raised in a community that rewards crime and pleasure-seeking while ignoring ethical standards of the larger society.

Since there is a high rate of antisocial behavior among poor people living in slum areas, this theory certainly has considerable value. Some antisocial people may simply be acting out a role rewarded by their community. This argument is even more compelling when the city slum is contrasted with life in an entirely different setting. The religious sect of the Hutterites provides such a contrast. The Hutterites are an isolated Anabaptist sect who live a simple rural life in the western United States. The children are raised with strict discipline, suffering penalties for any infringement of moral law. Among these people there is a complete absence of antisocial behavior.[94] This suggests that the moral fiber of the community in which the child is socialized is an important etiological factor. Why else would APD be completely absent in an environment centered about moralism?

APD: CAN IT BE CURED?

It is important to examine the chances for recovery from APD in a book about the *sociology* of mental illness because of the important impact antisocial personalities have on society. In the next section there is a very dismal report on the hopes for rehabilitating violent sex offenders. Is the same true for all people with APD? The reports are not very encouraging, particularly because the disorder appears to be so deeply entrenched from early in life. The antisocial disorder begins in early childhood when a number of indications of the psychopathology appear. These children are emotionally immature and often react to small frustrations with violent temper tantrums. They are frequently deceitful, boastful, destructive, quarrelsome, and defiant. Their condition reaches a peak in adolescence and may start to subside in the late 20s. There are only a few older antisocial individuals in society. This occurs for one of two reasons. First, many have been placed in prisons or mental hospitals before they reach middle age, and second, for unknown reasons, some "level off" or "burn out" in later life and cease to exhibit antisocial behavior.

In general, the chances for recovery from APD are very poor because the condition is particularly difficult to treat and often intractable. For this reason, many mental hospitals avoid admitting antisocial people. If they are admitted, hospitals are unwilling to treat them for long periods of time because they often upset other patients. In the literature there are only scattered reports of successful treatment of antisocials. Those who do report success typically use a therapeutic approach involving discipline and punishment. In short, creating a conscience in an adult appears to be impossible. There are some therapy programs that may work. In Oregon, for instance, a controversial program for teenage murderers offers hope for rehabilitation. It centers about group therapy in which people are forced to confront their crimes, cease their denial, and feel genuine remorse. Some see it as having real potential; others see it as a waste of tax dollars.[95]

VIOLENT SEX OFFENDERS: A SPECIAL GROUP WITH APD

I am taking the liberty here of departing from the traditional listing of personality disorders to discuss recent research by my colleagues and me on a special group of people commonly referred to as "sexual predators." Our investigation found that these are almost always men who, when diagnosed, manifest APD and constitute a lethal threat to society.[96] In the first chapter, I stated that the public has the popular misconception that the mentally ill are assaultive and dangerous. Like most generalizations, that is not universally true. Sexual predators are the blatant exception.

The term *violent sex offender* elicits a multitude of horrendous opinions among Americans, many of whose attitudes are shaped primarily by the media. Are these attitudes an objective reflection of the real nature of this type of criminal offender, or are they a subjective misperception stemming from media accounts written for shock value? Is it true that people who have a history of repeated violent sex offenses can never be "cured"? Certainly much of the public believes that these people are hopeless and should be locked up indefinitely, but what are the *real* facts?

What are the opinions of mental health professionals who treat violent sexual offenders? Do they comport with public perception, or are they radically different? Curiously, this has been a very difficult question to answer because no systematic study of the attitudes of those who treat violent sex offenders has been undertaken to date. This may be due to a reluctance of people who treat them to be interviewed about a sensitive topic, or it may be the result of a failure of other research teams to gain access to membership lists. Whatever the reasons may be, it is important to note that our study is the first comprehensive analysis of sex offender therapists that addresses their attitudes and opinions concerning treatment, release, and recidivism. It is not only noteworthy that this study stands alone but also that its findings are alarming.

Definitional Issues

One serious problem in studying sex offenders is the basic difficulty in generating a definition for such a broad category of perpetrators. There are many types of sex offenses and various kinds of sexual offenders with a host of similarities and differences. For example, the Federal Bureau of Investigation's *Crime Classification Manual* identifies 16 primary categories of offenders who commit rapes and sexual assaults.[97] The offenses are classified by the kind of motivation underlying the offense, the victims' age, or the nature of the victim/offender relationship. One aspect of the classification dilemma is identifying different types of child molesters, as well as distinguishing between pedophiles in particular and child molesters in general. Since not all pedophiles are child molesters, and not every molester is a pedophile, the terms are not always synonymous. Our study defines violent sex offenders as those who have an insatiable predilection for committing violence during an act of nonconsensual sex. Since their behavior is of a chronic nature, they conform to the personality type commonly referred to as a "sexual predator." In our study, the terms *violent sex offender* and *sexual predator* are used interchangeably.

Does Treatment Work?

In addition to the inherent difficulty in *classifying* violent sex offenders, the mental health field also struggles with the task of *treating* individuals who many people feel should simply be locked away in prison facilities for the rest of their lives. Consistently, the efforts of those who undertake the difficult task of treating violent sex offenders are rarely appreciated by the public at large. Treatments are currently administered in a number of forms ranging from traditional group therapy to more radical measures such as chemical or surgical castration. It is generally unclear as to which treatments prove most effective for each individual or class of sex offender. In fact, the term *cure* is almost never used in the same context as sex offender treatment. Robert A. Prentky, director of clinical and forensic services at the Joseph J. Peters Institute in Philadelphia, indicated in an interview that, with respect to pedophilia, "We don't use the word 'cure.' We don't think of pedophilia in the same way we think of curing a fever. . . . The predisposition will probably always be there. So the treatment is to control it as effectively as possible."[98]

The question of whether violent sex offenders fail to respond to treatment modalities and eventually recidivate generates a storm of controversy and contradictory opinions. For example, William Plantier, superintendent of the Avenel, New Jersey, prison facility for repeat sex offenders, reports that some of the inmates at his facility are "completely untreatable."[99] Conversely, an early report from Philadelphia General Hospital found that only 1 percent of sex offenders treated there were arrested again for a sex offense within two years of release.[100] Additionally, the Sexual Abuse Clinic in Portland, Oregon, reports that over a 17-year period, 95 percent of its heterosexual pedophile population have not left the treatment program or reoffended after release. The same clinic also reports that 73 percent of all rapists at the facility have been successfully treated.[101] On the other hand, a separate seven-year evaluation study at another clinic reports that 43 percent of 136 extrafamilial child molesters committed another violent sexual offense after release.[102]

Predicting future dangerousness is very difficult and in no way constitutes an exact science, leading some to believe that lengthy and/or indefinite periods of incarceration are the answer. There are those who argue that violent behavior and overall dangerousness are situational and "the mere fact that an individual is a model prisoner has very little to do with what he'll do once he's no longer in a closely observed, highly structured situation."[103] On the other hand, Fred Berlin, founder of the Sex Disorders Clinic at Johns Hopkins University, contends that a sexual orientation such as pedophilia cannot simply be "punished away."

Recent Legislation

In the 1990s there have been waves of legislation around the United States designed to protect society from violent sex offenders. These new laws seek to further institutionalize offenders or to inform the general public of their whereabouts. California, for example, has created a CD-ROM tracking system that details information about some 64,000 sex offenders including their locations within state boundaries.[104] Additionally, some version of "Megan's law" has been enacted in all 50 states since similar legislation was passed as a federal statute in 1996.[105]

Megan's law requires, among other things, that a convicted sex offender register with local law enforcement authorities, who in turn notify the community of the offender's presence in a particular neighborhood.[106] The law has been widely challenged across the United States as a modern-day "scarlet letter" that arguably violates fundamental constitutional notions of due process, double jeopardy, and protection from ex post facto laws.[107] Courts throughout the country have split on the constitutionality of Megan's law, leaving the ultimate resolution to the U.S. Supreme Court.

In 1997, the U.S. Supreme Court upheld the Kansas "sexually violent predator law," another piece of preventive legislation that allows for the indefinite commitment of some sex offenders.[108] In *Kansas* v. *Hendricks*, 521 U.S. 346 (1997), the Supreme Court (in a 5 to 4 decision) upheld the constitutionality of a law that permits a state to involuntarily commit offenders (civilly) to a mental health facility if they satisfy the requirements for characterization as a "sexually violent predator." Generally, this commitment proceeding occurs after a full prison sentence has been served.[109] In order to commit the offender, the government must prove, beyond a reasonable doubt, that the individual is a sexually violent predator who poses a danger to himself and/or the community.[110] In Kansas, a "sexually violent predator" is defined as "any person who has been convicted of, or charged with, a crime of sexual violence and who suffers from a mental abnormality or personality disorder which makes the person likely to engage in predatory acts of sexual violence."[111] This kind of legislation has been adopted in many jurisdictions, beginning with Washington, California, and Minnesota. These laws have been challenged by the argument that such legislation involves a second punishment, constituting gross violations of the ex post facto and double jeopardy provisions of the U.S. Constitution.[112]

The recent legislative trend in precautionary lawmaking has clearly taken an unusually punitive stance against violent sex offenders. The need to protect society from these offenders is seen by many as very real. The same group asserts that violent sex offenders forfeit their rights to individual liberty. Conversely, others argue that the new legislative measures are a "knee-jerk" reaction to a media-fueled frenzy that has created widespread and ungrounded fears of released sex offenders.[113] Which position is accurate? Is it true that some sex offenders can never be "cured" and invariably pose a threat to others upon release? Our study is designed to answer these questions by posing them to those responsible for the treatment of sexual predators.

The ATSA Study

Our data were obtained through responses to a confidential mail survey sent to members of the Association for the Treatment of Sexual Abusers (ATSA). ATSA is a national organization of professionals from a variety of fields, including psychiatry, psychology, social work, corrections, and parole. This diverse group of individual works with and/or studies sex offenders of all kinds in many different settings from private treatment facilities to prisons. The research instrument was sent to each of the 1,040 members on the list provided by ATSA, of which 540 (52 percent) responded. The response rate was surprisingly high and unanticipated. The large response rate may be due to the fact that this study is the first of its kind, making members of ATSA likely to be especially interested in sharing their experiences in treating violent sex offenders. In our study violent sex offenders are defined as those who have a predilection for committing violence during an act of nonconsensual sex—violence (e.g., assault or murder) that goes above and beyond the inherently violent nature of any sex crime.

In general, members of ATSA do not feel that it is safe to release *some* sexual predators into the community. In fact, approximately 88 percent of the sample express this reservation. Additionally, over 70 percent are concerned about the legal and/or moral ramification of patients controlling their sexual urges upon release. The respondents also agree (81 percent) that sex offenders should be treated differently than other felons. However, their opinion is divided as to whether they should be treated in separate facilities.

Two other questions in our survey elicit respondents' opinions about the interrelated issues of causality and diagnosis. The item on etiology states: "Mental health professionals have a clear understanding about the causes of violent sex behavior." The responses to this statement are overwhelmingly negative; almost 70 percent disagree or strongly disagree. It is clear that members of ATSA feel that the origin(s) of violent sex behavior are a mystery. This is consistent with their responses to the question on diagnosis which asks: "Which official psychiatric diagnosis is most frequently associated with violent sex behavior?" An overwhelming majority of the respondents (69.6 percent) believe that violent sex offenders suffer from APD in either its pure form or together with other psychiatric syndromes such as narcissistic personality disorder.

Our study was an especially difficult undertaking because the topic of sexual predators is so delicate and controversial. Everyone seems to have an opinion on how to deal with this group of mentally ill offenders. The fact that those who treat them report such an overwhelmingly negative opinion about the likelihood of rehabilitation is alarming. There clearly is no simple answer in treating sexual predators. The Jesse Timmendequas case, which was the impetus for the creation of Megan's law, illustrates the tragedy that can result from ineffective treatment. He liked the softness of young girls' skin—at least that is what he told the police after he raped and murdered 7-year-old Megan Kanka. By the time of the murder, Timmendequas, who had twice before been convicted of sexual offenses involving young girls, had been getting "those same old feelings for little girls" for some time and that night, the defense contended, he lost any control over his pedophilia.[114] This was after six years of treatment at Avenel, New Jersey's prison facility for repeat compulsive sex offenders.

No silver bullet exists even for those who want to stop. Take the case of Mitchell Gaff who has been designated by the state of Washington as a sexual predator—someone who "suffers from a mental abnormality or personality disorder which makes [him] more likely to engage in predatory acts of sexual violence if not confined in a secure facility." He is now at Washington's Special Commitment Center after being incarcerated at various penitentiaries since the mid-1980s. He has been in therapy *voluntarily* since 1992. He claims that he wants to get better because he believes that evil is a condition that can be eliminated. Yet, after numerous forms of therapy, as well as studying books and taking courses on stress management, anger management, family dynamics, human sexuality, victim empathy, understanding sexual assault and relapse prevention I, II, and III, his desire to savagely rape young girls remains intense.

The cases of Timmendequas and Gaff reached different legal conclusions—execution and continued confinement, respectively. Today, laws dealing with sex offenders seem to be clearly moving in a singular, punitive direction both in the United States and around the world. In 1997, Britain announced new guidelines allowing police to warn people about the movement of convicted pedophiles. Sex offenders are required to inform authorities where they live and if they change their name or address. The police pass on details to employers, community organizations, and the public if the abuser is considered to be a threat to children. In the United States, the 1994 Crime Bill authorized states to create registration programs for the thousands of sex offenders who are released from jail each year. Some states, such as Washington and Kansas, have enacted laws that attempt to prevent offenders from returning to society all together by having them involuntarily committed through civil proceedings after their period of incarceration has been completed. While some states, such as Pennsylvania, debate such legislation, some individual judges have chosen not to wait for new laws by handing out lengthy sentences, thereby rendering release issues moot.

Why are the findings of our study so overwhelmingly negative? Why is there such a high response rate from members of ATSA? The answers to both questions are interrelated. First, there has never been a study of those who treat violent sexual predators. Therefore, there is no comparison point. Second, it is a good bet that the therapists in the study were chaffing at the bit to vent their frustrations and fears. The authors were not out to prove anything. The goal was simply to conduct scientifically based survey research and to report the findings. The fact that the findings are shocking is simply a fact. This is not said out of defensiveness but because there may well be a heap of criticism directed toward this study when it is published. Indeed, a preliminary press release of the results triggered one sex offender therapist to accuse the authors of contriving the entire study and its results!

The bottom line on rehabilitation and recidivism of sexual predators is alarmingly clear; those who treat them report little success at cure and great trepidation upon release. Given that almost 70 percent of those sampled report that sexual predators suffer from antisocial personality disorder—either alone or in combination with another personality disorder—the terminal attitude of the therapists is no surprise. While these men are clearly dangerous, their motivation is a mystery. To characterize them as attention-seeking, sadistic, and lacking a conscience is only an emotional blueprint for a dangerously different person who is callous to society's values and goals. It is far from a full explanation because the root cause(s) of APD are not completely known. Theories range from genetics to early abuse to physiological defects in the brain; but since etiology is a mystery, treatment modalities may be way off the mark. All of the counseling, occupational training, and social support may not make one iota of difference. Indeed, studies of federal prisoners with APD report that they are twice as likely as other prisoners to commit more crimes after release.[115] This is especially true for violent sex offenders with APD whose rate of recidivism is three times that of non-APD criminals.[116]

If all of the above sounds like unadulterated doom and gloom that is because the findings *are* overwhelmingly pessimistic. However, the study does uncover glimmers of hope for treatment. The literature is filled with thick volumes of comprehensive guides for treatment techniques that act as "problem solvers."[117] Aside from the literature, a separate section of the questionnaire mailed to ATSA members deals with specific forms of treatment (interactive psychotherapy, behavior therapy, cognitive restructuring, and antilibidinal treatment). The results hold some promise as therapists reported little success with certain treatments and significant success with others.

BORDERLINE PERSONALITY DISORDER

The reason why this personality disorder is called "borderline" is because these people move back and forth between neurotic behavior and outright psychosis. Little was known about this condition until recently. In the mid-1990s, however, there was a growing pile of information about the symptoms and origins of borderline personality disorder. I should add that I personally have witnessed an increasing number of these cases reported at my "research hangout," Norristown State Hospital. This is especially true among females.[118]

Borderlines manifest a wide variety of abnormal behaviors including shifts of attitude toward others, inappropriate anger, and impulsivity in self-damaging areas such as sex, spending, gambling sprees, and shoplifting.[119] They are also characterized by uncertainty about identity issues (self-image, gender identity, friendship patterns), mood shifts lasting only a few hours, intolerance of being alone, and chronic feelings of boredom.[120] If there is one thing that is especially dramatic, it is self-mutilation. Borderlines almost wear this diagnosis on their bodies. Cigarette burns and scars from cutting often cover their arms and legs. Shirtsleeves on a hot August day are common among borderlines who are ashamed of what they have done to themselves.[121]

Low self-esteem is obviously intertwined with borderline personality disorder (BPD). Is this why so many of these people are women?[122] Is it a truly "female" affliction?[123] Is this a reflection of how the traditionally subordinate status of women in American society translates itself into psychopathology? Maybe, but it may run deeper than that, deep into traumas in early childhood. These include sexual abuse, physical abuse, witnessing violence, and early separation experience.[124] Of all of these horrors, sexual abuse, particularly its incestuous form, may be the most common feature.[125] This links with the high prevalence of BPD among women since girls are the most frequent victims of sexual exploitation.[126] It also fits with the noticeably high number of borderline personalities who display symptoms similar to posttraumatic stress disorder.[127] There may also be cases of BPD associated with a brain dysfunction.[128] Although these may be rare cases (or misdiagnoses), new research on the biology of BPD is well underway in the early 2000s.[129]

If childhood sexual abuse is an important etiological factor in BPD, then why does the same experience lead to particular disorders in some people and different problems in others? We do not know the answer to that question, but there are some clues. BPD, for instance, may be a special risk for sexual abuse victims of limited intellectual skills as opposed to multiple personalities who typically are reported to be of high intelligence.

The little bit of psychiatric sociological guesswork I am providing here certainly does not tell us much, but it is a lot more than the etiological speculations prior to the 1990s. What is known about BPD is that, like many other psychiatric conditions, it imposes a psychic hell on its victims. Many turn to suicide to terminate the pain.[130] Others stay alive but alter their reality through drug abuse.[131]

BPD, like paranoid delusions, may be one of those mental illnesses that are frequently found together with another illness.[132] Or it may be so difficult to accurately identify that it is mistakenly confused with other disorders such as schizotypal, histri-

· **Case 6:4** ·
Hurting

A 26-year-old unemployed woman was referred for admission to a hospital by her therapist because of intense suicidal preoccupation and urges to mutilate herself with a razor.

The patient was apparently well until her junior year in high school, when she became preoccupied with religion and philosophy, avoided friends, and was filled with doubt about who she was. Academically she did well; but later, during college, her performance declined. In college, she began to use a variety of drugs, abandoned the religion of her family, and seemed to be searching for a charismatic religious figure with whom to identify. At times massive anxiety swept over her, and she found it would suddenly vanish if she cut her forearm with a razor blade.

Three years ago she began psychotherapy, and initially rapidly idealized her therapist as being incredibly intuitive and empathetic. Later, she became hostile and demanding of him, requiring more and more sessions, sometimes two in one day. Her life became centered on her therapist to the exclusion of everyone else. Although her hostility toward her therapist was obvious, she could neither see it nor control it. Her difficulties with her therapist culminated in many episodes of cutting her forearm and threatening suicide, which led to referral for admission.

Source: Robert L. Spitzer, Miriam Gibbon, Andrew E. Skodol, Janet B. W. Williams, and Michael B. First, *DSM-III-R Casebook* (Washington, DC: American Psychiatric Press, 1989), p. 233. By permission of the publisher.

· ·

onic, narcissistic, and antisocial personality disorders.[133] All of the etiological and diagnostic issues surrounding BPD make it one thing for certain—very difficult to treat.[134] Case 6:4 has many attributes of this perplexing condition, one of many in psychiatric sociology today.

AVOIDANT PERSONALITY DISORDER

This problem occurs among people who are hypersensitive to rejection, humiliation, or shame, and, as a consequence, they are socially withdrawn and unwilling to enter into relationships unless they are guaranteed uncritical acceptance.[135] Do you know people like this? I think they are common. People who are easily hurt by criticism and have no close friends or confidants are a sad part of the sociology of everyday life.[136] They are especially sad since their fears prevent them from living up to their potential, especially in the world of work.

Unlike people with schizoid personality disorder (who are socially isolated because they have no desire for interaction with others), avoidant personalities actually yearn for affection and acceptance. Although a reportedly common disorder, little is known about the etiology of avoidant personality disorder.

DEPENDENT PERSONALITY DISORDER

Dependent personalities are so lacking in self-confidence that they passively allow others to make major life decisions for them.[137] For example, they may allow a spouse to decide what kind of job they should have, where they should live, and whom they should choose for friends.[138] The problem may proceed to the point where a person with dependent personality disorder may tolerate a physically abusive husband for fear that he will leave her.

It is not unusual for these people to lack self-confidence, so much so that they constantly demean themselves as being "stupid." This disorder is apparently common and is diagnosed more frequently in women.[139] Little is known about its etiology, although it is known that it overlaps extensively with other personality disorders found more often among women, such as depression.

OBSESSIVE-COMPULSIVE PERSONALITY DISORDER

Obsessive-compulsive personality disorder (OCPD) is characterized by excessive concerns with neatness, orderliness, and punctuality. These people are social conformists who have a strict adherence to standards of conscience. They are not merely hard-working individuals; they neglect other aspects of life for the sake of work. When they help others, they do so not for purely altruistic reasons; it is a sense of duty that motivates them, rather than affection or true altruism.[140]

People with OCPD are unable to relax easily outside of work. As a consequence, they have few recreations. When they do join a social organization, they are attracted to roles that reflect their personality, such as secretary, treasurer, or other positions requiring organization and detail. Their preoccupation with detail, rules, and regulations dampens their creativity and restricts their aspirations to nonleadership positions. As Eaton and Peterson state, "These are not people who 'fail to see the forest for the trees'; they fail to see the tree while counting its leaves."[141]

Compulsives cannot tolerate ambiguity and have difficulty making decisions.[142] For these reasons, they avoid or delay marriage because a suitable mate must have precise qualities. When they do marry, the spouse is typically a compliant, dependent person who perceives the compulsive as strong and self-reliant.

When their organized system of living breaks down, these people may develop obsessive-compulsive disorder, the more extreme problem. If a stress occurs during the middle-age years, depression is a more likely result. OCPD differs from obsessive-compulsive disorder in that there is an absence of severe obsessions and compulsions in the former. As such, OCPD is less debilitating.[143]

These people are unique in their tendency to mix a compulsive characteristic with its opposite; compulsive disorderliness may coexist with compulsive neatness; a compulsive spendthrift may be compulsively stingy at other times. Like the obsessive-compulsive disorder, some link this condition to fixations from a childhood struggle with toilet training. This produces the so-called "anal character," who is excessively neat and stubborn. The other popular explanation is the social learning view that compulsives imitated parents who were hardworking and inflexible themselves. The disorder is reportedly more common among men. There is no evidence that it has a biological base.

One of the difficulties of OCPD that faces modern psychiatry is how to help a person with such deeply ingrained habits.[144] Problems are compounded further when other problems such as hypochondriasis coexist.[145] Case 6:5 demonstrates just how rigid and fixed these people can be—patterns that are highly resistant to change.

································ **Case 6:5** ································
The Workaholic

The patient is a 45-year-old lawyer who seeks treatment at his wife's insistence. She is fed up with their marriage: she can no longer tolerate his emotional coldness, rigid demands, bullying behavior, sexual disinterest, long work hours, and frequent business trips. The patient feels no particular distress in his marriage, and has agreed to the consultation only to humor his wife.

It soon develops, however, that the patient is troubled by problems at work. He is known as the hardest-driving member of a hard-driving law firm. He was the youngest full partner in the firm's history, and is famous for being able to handle many cases at the same time. Lately, he finds himself increasingly unable to keep up. He is too proud to turn down a new case, and too much of a perfectionist to be satisfied with the quality of work performed by his assistants. Displeased by their writing style and sentence structure, he finds himself constantly correcting their briefs, and therefore unable to stay abreast of his schedule. People at work complain that his attention to details and inability to delegate responsibility are reducing his efficiency. He has had two or three secretaries a year for 15 years. No one can tolerate working for him for very long because he is so critical of any mistakes made by others. When assignments get backed up, he cannot decide which to address first, starts making schedules for himself and his staff, but then is unable to meet them and works 15 hours a day. He finds it difficult to be decisive now that his work has expanded beyond his own direct control.

Source: Robert L. Spitzer, Miriam Gibbon, Andrew E. Skodol, Janet B. W. Williams, and Michael B. First, *DSM-III-R Casebook* (Washington, DC: American Psychiatric Press, 1989), p. 80. By permission of the publisher.

CONCLUSIONS

Personality disorders are inflexible, maladaptive traits that can cause significant impairment in social or occupational functioning. They are widespread, rarely result in hospitalization, and are currently grouped into three "clusters." The first cluster involves people who are odd or eccentric. Included are those with paranoid personality disorder (unwarranted suspiciousness), schizoid personality disorder (defect in the capacity to form social relationships), and schizotypal personality disorder (oddities of thought, perception, speech, and behavior).

The second cluster involves people who are overly dramatic, emotional, or erratic. Included are histrionic personality disorder (overly reactive and attention-seeking), narcissistic personality disorder (grandiose sense of self-importance), antisocial personality disorder (conscience defect), and borderline personality disorder (instability in interpersonal behavior, mood, and self-image).

The third cluster includes people who appear fearful or anxious. The types are avoidant personality disorder (hypersensitivity to potential rejection), dependent personality disorder (pathological lack of self-confidence), and obsessive-compulsive personality disorder (perfectionism and excessive devotion to work).

Of all the personality disorders, the antisocial type is most directly linked with sociological forces. It is a condition that blatantly demonstrates the role of the intrapsychic agent of society, the conscience. Antisocial personalities have a conscience defect that leads them to violate other people and suffer no remorse. Although this disorder is considered terminal, there is an outside chance that it could be prevented and cured. If so, society has failed miserably to deal with it. This is partly due to laws that do not segregate antisocial individuals from others who commit crimes. As a result, these people often end up in jail where their condition worsens.

There is some evidence that the antisocial disorder is caused by biological factors. Additionally, psychoanalysts consider this pathology to originate in parental rejection and the concomitant lack of opportunity to form a normal set of moral values. Social learning theorists stress the etiological influence of parents who encourage immoral behavior in their children. Labeling theorists explain antisocial behavior as a response to the countercultural standards of lower-class life in the ghettos.

7

Epidemiology

An Overview of Patterns of Mental Illness

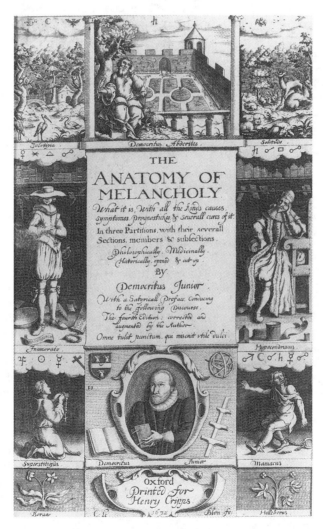

Early thinking about the causes of depression made for much speculation and interesting artwork, but today's diathesis-stress hypothesis is clearly much more on the mark.

DEFINING EPIDEMIOLOGY

> The most influential idea . . .—the idea that connects work on gender, socioeconomic status, race, ethnicity, age and poverty—is that social group differences in disorder are somehow linked to corresponding differences in exposure to the social conditions that cause disorder.[1]

Although this chapter concentrates largely on the United States, mental health is a major issue on the global public health agenda in the 2000s.[2] Widespread patterns of mental illness across U.S. society clearly demonstrate that some social groups are much more vulnerable to psychopathology than others.[3] That fact is at the heart of psychiatric sociology.[4] Although some believe that mental illness is a myth, some real numbers suggest otherwise.[5] One highly useful test of the influence of social and cultural factors on mental illness is the epidemiological approach. *Epidemiology* is the study of the distribution of an illness within a carefully delimited area or population group. This is the type of investigation most frequently undertaken by psychiatric sociologists, who, by measuring the occurrence and distribution of mental illness, uncover important clues about the role of social and cultural factors in etiology. Epidemiological investigations include the effects of a host of variables, such as race, gender, marital status, and age, on the development, diagnosis, and treatment of mental illness.[6]

As Kessler and Zhao point out:

> The three stages of epidemiological investigation are descriptive, analytic and experimental. Descriptive epidemiology is concerned with the distribution of illness, onset and course, whereas analytic epidemiology is concerned with the use of nonexperimental data to elucidate causal processes involved in illness onset and course, and experimental epidemiology is concerned with the development and evaluation of interventions aimed at modifying risk factors to prevent illness onset or to modify illness course.[7]

One of the most important topics in this area is the well-established relationship between social class and mental disorder.[8] It is presented separately in Chapter 8. The most common epidemiological study involves measurement of the total number of psychiatric cases in a given population. This measurement is known as a *prevalence rate.* The other type of epidemiological study involves measuring the *incidence* of mental illness, that is, the number of new cases during a specified time period. Incidence studies are rare because it is very difficult to determine retrospectively when an illness began. Prevalence studies work on the assumption that, if there is a difference in prevalence between different population groups, then the social factors that differentiate the groups may be related to cause. If, for example, prevalence rates are different between males and females, then sex roles may be an etiological factor. Or, if married people have lower impairment rates than single people, this indicates that there is something about married life that may be conducive to mental health.[9] Additionally, if members of the lower social class are more frequently impaired than people from higher classes, this suggests that lower-class life is a mental health hazard.[10] Although epidemiological studies were carried out as early as the seventeenth century, it was not until the early nineteenth century that they were linked to social forces.

In this chapter and the four that follow, the major findings of epidemiological research conducted since the turn of the early 1900s are reviewed.[11] These include studies of the relationship between rates of mental illness and such demographic factors as migration, religious membership, ethnicity, place of residence, age, family size,

Figure 7:1 When mental illness strikes. In any one year, 22 percent of the population suffers from mental illness—28 percent if substance abuse is included.

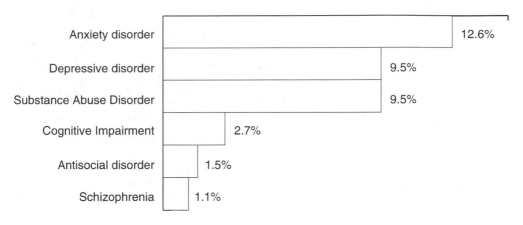

Anxiety disorder — 12.6%
Depressive disorder — 9.5%
Substance Abuse Disorder — 9.5%
Cognitive Impairment — 2.7%
Antisocial disorder — 1.5%
Schizophrenia — 1.1%

Note: Percentages exceed 28 percent because some people have more than one disorder.

Source: Department of Health and Human Services; National Mental Health Association; National Institute of Mental Health, 1990.

birth order, adopted child status, social class, and social mobility. Some of these demographic groupings have been investigated more thoroughly than others; social class, for example, has been the focus of considerable research whereas relatively few studies have examined the effects of religious affiliation. In Chapter 1, I discussed the various estimates that have been made regarding the size of the mentally ill population in the United States. An NIMH study offers a breakdown of the most common types of disorder as well. They are displayed in Figure 7:1.

METHODOLOGICAL PROBLEMS WITH EPIDEMIOLOGICAL STUDIES

One inconsistent aspect of epidemiological studies is the diversity of procedures used by different investigators to measure prevalence. Some studies use hospitalization records. Others use evaluations by psychiatrists of people in the community on the assumption that not all mentally ill people are or have been hospitalized. Both types of studies have been criticized on the grounds that psychiatric diagnosis cannot be made objectively because there are still many unsolved questions about the nature of mental illness.[12] *Thus, two sets of research findings may differ from each other simply because the investigators have different concepts of mental illness or use different methods to detect it.* This is a valid and very important criticism.

The data drawn from studies using hospitalization as the criterion of mental illness are less useful than those using a psychiatric evaluation of community members because the hospitalization definition is based on the shaky assumption that treatment rates evidence the amount of mental disorder in the general population.[13] The fact is that impaired people who are *treated* are only a part of the entire population of people with mental disorders. Consequently, figures based on treatment rates do not provide a satisfactory estimate of the real prevalence of mental illness in a society.

· **Box 7.1** ·
Nearly Half of Americans Have Mental Illness Some Time in Life

Mental disorders were called "part of life." Among the most common: depression and alcohol dependence.

Almost half of Americans experience mental illness at some time in their lives, and almost one-third are afflicted in any one year, according to the most comprehensive U.S. mental health study in a decade.

The study found mental illness more common than researchers had previously found. The findings point to a need to learn why more people do not seek help, the authors said. "It shouldn't be scary to say half the population has suffered from some mental disorder. That's part of life," said lead researcher Ronald C. Kessler, a sociology professor at the University of Michigan at Ann Arbor.

The study involved face-to-face interviews with 8,098 people aged 15 to 54 nationwide between September 1990 and February 1992. The findings are published in January's issue of the *Archives of General Psychiatry*.

The researchers looked for 14 of the most common mental illnesses. Forty-eight percent of respondents had suffered from at least one disorder at some time during their lives, and 29.5 percent had been afflicted within the previous 12 months, researchers said.

Results of the federally funded study do not change previous estimates that only 3 to 5 percent of Americans are in serious need of psychiatric help at any given time, Kessler said. Many mental disorders are mild, and people get over them without help, he said.

But the study made an important discovery: 79 percent of cases of mental illness are concentrated in a small proportion of people—14 percent of the population—with multiple psychiatric problems.

Multiple disorders are often "pileups" that accumulate over time. For example, adolescent anxiety can lead to teen drinking and then to adult major depression, Kessler said.

That finding suggests that early psychiatric treatment might prevent the later stages of the "pileup," Kessler said. "The trick is to figure out the nature of the pileups . . . before people crawl into the psychiatrist's office divorced and alcoholic," he said.

The study found that the most common disorders were:

- *Major depressive episode*, at least two weeks of symptoms such as low mood and loss of pleasure. More than 17 percent of respondents had suffered an episode in their lives, more than 10 percent in the previous 12 months.
- *Alcohol dependence.* More than 14 percent had experienced an episode in their lifetime, and more than 7 percent in the year before the interview.
- *Social phobia*, a persistent fear of feeling scrutinized or embarrassed in social situations, 13 percent lifetime, 8 percent in the previous year.
- *Simple phobia*, a persistent fear of objects such as animals, insects or blood, or of situations such as closed spaces, heights or air travel, 11 percent lifetime, 9 percent in the previous year.

The most persistent problems appeared to be anxiety disorders, which are marked by excessive worry for six months or more over such things as future events, past behavior, or competence.

———————————

Source: Brenda C. Coleman, "Study: Nearly half of Americans have mental illness some time in life," *Philadelphia Inquirer*, January 14, 1994, p. A22. By permission of the publisher.

· ·

A number of studies have demonstrated that treatment rates are a function of the availability of treatment facilities, public awareness of the facilities, public attitudes toward their use, the attitudes of the providers of psychiatric treatment, as well as administrative factors.[14] Studies of patient records suffer further from the fact that they frequently do not include patients treated in private facilities. Typically, state mental hospital records are used as this is one source that has been readily available over the years. The use of state hospital populations may bias results because admission rates to these facilities vary across social classes. The higher social classes, for instance, are better able to afford private hospitals or private practitioners. Another general handicap in using admission records is that they often record only the *total number* of admissions. Thus the researcher frequently has no way of knowing whether a single person is admitted three times or three persons are each hospitalized once. At this point, it should be emphasized that the numerous problems with prevalence studies make it difficult to draw inferences with any degree of certainty. Thus, *the research reported in these chapters on epidemiology should be interpreted with caution.* [15]

STUDIES OF NONHOSPITALIZED POPULATIONS

Epidemiological studies that evaluate nonhospitalized populations give a clearer picture of real prevalence by seeking information about the "hidden" part of the iceberg rather than just the "tip." The investigators who collect these data detect more cases, as would be expected. Based on these studies, the estimate of "one in five" is most often used to refer to the number of mentally ill persons in the U.S. population. Compared to the alarmingly high rates of well over 50 percent reported in some studies, that figure is a rather conservative estimate. One analysis of the overall prevalence of serious mental illness in the United States estimates that 3.3 million adults are affected. The specifics are presented in Table 7:1.

Because of methodological differences among studies, various investigators report findings that are radically diverse. Since this has caused much confusion, two epidemiologists, Bruce P. Dohrenwend and Barbara Snell Dohrenwend, have spent a considerable amount of time painstakingly trying to impose order on a disorganized body of literature. They report that about 60 different investigators or teams of investigators have attempted to count treated and untreated cases in more than eighty studies since the turn of the twentieth century.[16] These attempts to measure both treated and untreated cases are known as *true prevalence* studies. They have been conducted all over the world—in North and South America, Europe, Asia, and Africa.

The rates are quite varied; in some communities rates of 1 percent and less are reported and in others the rates exceed 50 percent. Some of these differences are the result of different data-collection techniques and contrasting conceptions about the definition of mental illness. However, one consistent result is that only a minority of the cases has ever received treatment. This is painfully clear in two landmark studies conducted in North America. One of these measured the prevalence of mental illness in a random sample of residents of Midtown Manhattan.[17] The other used a similar approach among residents of rural Sterling County in Nova Scotia.[18] Both the Midtown study and the Sterling County study concluded that there is a great unmet need for psychiatric treatment since a considerable portion of the untreated residents of both communities were evaluated as impaired to some degree. The interview and questionnaire data that were compiled on the 1,660 residents of Manhattan revealed that "less than one-fifth of the population is well, about three-fifths exhibit subclinical forms of mental disorder and . . . 23.4 percent exhibit some impairment in life functioning."[19] The Sterling County study estimated that about 50 percent of the population is psychiatrically impaired. Canada[20] and New York City[21] are still favorite sites for epidemiological investigators in 2000, just as they were 40 years before.

In the 1980s, the National Institute of Mental Health started a decade-long study that is the most comprehensive report ever assembled on the prevalence rates of mental disorders in the United States.[22] Known as the ECA (Epidemiologic Catchment Area) study, it is a comprehensive, community-based survey of mental disorders and

Table 7:1 U.S. Household Population with Serious Mental Illness
Number and percent distribution of the adult household population, adults with serious mental illness, and rate per thousand, adults currently limited by serious mental illness and percent limited, by selected characteristics: United States, 1989

CHARACTERISTIC	Adult Household Population		Adults with Serious Mental Illness					
			Total			Currently Limited by SMI		
	Number in Thousands	Percent Distribution	Number in Thousands	Percent Distribution	Rate per Thousand	Number in Thousands	Percent Distribution	Percent
Total[1]	179,529	100.0	3,264	100.0	18.2	2,571	100.0	78.8
Age[1]								
18–24 years	25,401	14.2	361	11.1	14.2	291	11.3	80.6
25–34 years	42,814	23.9	707	21.7	16.5	501	19.5	70.8
35–44 years	35,982	20.0	744	22.8	20.7	600	23.3	80.6
45–64 years	46,114	25.7	919	28.2	19.9	749	29.1	81.5
65–69 years	9,903	5.5	142	4.4	14.3	99	3.9	70.0
70–74 years	7,925	4.4	102	3.1	12.9	82	3.2	79.8
75 years and over	11,391	6.3	288	8.8	25.3	249	9.7	86.6
Sex[1]								
Male	82,257	47.5	1,320	40.4	15.5	1,105	43.0	83.7
Female	94,272	52.5	1,944	59.6	20.6	1,466	57.0	75.4
Race[1]								
White	153,763	85.6	2,812	86.1	18.3	2,194	85.3	78.0
Black	19,932	11.1	393	12.0	19.7	325	12.7	82.8
Other	5,834	3.2	59	1.8	10.1	52	2.0	87.1

Poverty Status[2]							
Below poverty threshold	15,464	9.5	609	21.0	39.4	525	23.1	86.3
or above poverty threshold	147,070	90.5	2,284	79.0	15.5	1,750	76.9	76.7
Education[2]							
Less than 12 years	39,809	22.4	1,083	33.8	27.2	937	37.3	86.5
12 years	68,563	38.6	1,120	34.9	16.3	866	34.5	77.4
More than 12 years	69,369	39.0	1,002	31.3	14.4	708	28.2	70.7
Respondent-Assessed Health Status[2]							
Excellent	62,277	34.8	337	10.3	5.4	192	7.5	56.9
Very good	50,941	28.5	620	19.1	12.2	414	16.1	66.7
Good	43,769	24.5	812	24.9	18.6	617	24.1	75.9
Fair	15,565	8.7	755	23.2	48.5	648	25.3	85.9
Poor	6,207	3.5	734	22.5	118.3	695	27.1	94.7

[1]Includes persons with unknown poverty status, education, and/or self-assessed health status.

[2]Percent denominators exclude persons with this characteristic unknown.

Source: Peggy R. Barker, *Serious Mental Illness and Disability in the Adult Household Population, 1989* (Hyattsville, MD: U.S. Government Printing Office, U.S. Department of Health and Human Services, 1992).

Table 7:2 Prevalence of Specific Disorders (Percent)

	Lifetime	*Active (One-Year)*
Phobia	14.3	8.8
Alcohol abuse/dependence	13.8	6.3
Generalized anxiety	8.5	3.8
Major depressive episode	6.4	3.7
Drug abuse/dependence	6.2	2.5
Cognitive impairment: mild or severe	a	5.0
Dysthymia	3.3	a
Antisocial personality	2.6	1.2
Obsessive-compulsive	2.6	1.7
Panic	1.6	0.9
Schizophrenia or schizophreniform	1.5	1.0
Manic episode	0.8	0.6
Cognitive impairment: severe	a	0.9
Somatization	0.1	0.1

[a]Not ascertained.

Source: Lee N. Robins, Ben Z. Locke, and Darrel A. Regier, "An overview of psychiatric disorders in America," in Lee N. Robins, Ben Z. Locke, and Darrel A. Regier, eds., *Psychiatric Disorders in America* (New York: The Free Press, 1990), pp. 328–366.

uses of services by adults, aged 18 and older. Based on DSM criteria, diagnoses were obtained in five communities in the United States through lay interviewer administration of the National Institute of Mental Health Diagnostic Interview Schedule.[23] Results from the survey provide the public health field with data on the prevalence and incidence of specific mental disorders in the community, unbiased by the treatment status of the sample. Based on the survey, it is estimated that one of every five persons in the United States suffers from a mental disorder in any six-month period, and that one of three persons suffers a disorder in his or her lifetime. Fewer than 20 percent of those with a recent mental disorder seek help for their problem, according to the survey. Table 7:2 presents a breakdown of the ECA study by specific form of mental disorder.

CHANGES IN PREVALENCE OVER TIME

It is important to note that, among those studies that evaluate a nonhospitalized population, there is a substantial difference in results between the studies published before 1950 and those published in 1950 or after. The later studies show an average prevalence rate about seven times greater than those published before 1950.[24] This finding led some to what seemed to be an obvious conclusion—that there is an increasing amount of strain in modern life. However, the conclusion is not actually that simple since psychiatric diagnostic procedures and forms of treatment have changed considerably since 1950. One such change has been an alteration in the concept of what constitutes a case of mental illness. On the basis of psychiatric screening experiences during World War II, there was a great expansion of the psychiatric nomenclature, as exemplified by the creation of DSM-I.

Psychiatric Epidemiology: Some Methodological Issues

In pursuing diverse goals over the years, psychiatric epidemiology has produced a rich variety of enterprises. There have been community studies of the prevalence of single disorders and their correlates, in particular senile dementia and depression. There have been studies of the psychiatric status of special populations such as adoptees grown up, Harvard sophomores followed to mid-life, the homeless, prisoners, and poor nondelinquent youngsters grown up. There have been studies of attempted and completed suicides, and of the psychological consequences of life events such as disasters and wars. There have also been many epidemiological studies of social problems that have relevance to psychiatric concerns, for example the distribution in the population of heavy drinking and use of illicit drugs.

But the core concern of psychiatric epidemiology from its earliest days has been the estimation of the overall prevalence of psychiatric disorder in the total population, in an effort to estimate need for services and to identify demographic correlates of disorder as clues to possible etiologic factors. . . .

The principles of sampling have not changed since the days of the Midtown Manhattan study, but as the focus has shifted from mental health as a unitary concept to specific disorders, power analyses based on expected prevalences have found that sample sizes had to be increased considerably if correlates of the rarer disorders were to be detected. Modern studies often have samples greater than 3,000, because even in a general population sample of 3,000, there should only be approximately 30 persons who have ever had a schizophrenic episode. . . .

Sampling designs have grown more complex since the days of the Midtown Manhattan study. It is now standard practice to oversample subpopulations of special interest, whose numbers would otherwise be too small to study separately. . . .

Modern studies of adults, unlike earlier studies, rarely collect information from records or informants other than their primary subjects. Privacy regulations make collecting record data difficult, and costs of interviewing collaterals have soared as sample sizes have increased. Relying exclusively on information provided by the adult study subject means trusting a source of uncertain reliability and validity. Since data were first gathered directly from members of the community, questions have continued to be raised about their accuracy. On the face of it, it seemed hard to believe that people would report socially disapproved behavior and intimate psychological symptoms to a stranger. Yet in studies where interviews were compared to records of treatment, military disciplinary actions, and arrest, socially disapproved behaviors were found to have been reported with surprising honesty.

If these studies have laid to rest the concern that respondents intentionally falsify memorable but socially disapproved behavior, they do not tell us whether even the respondent who intends to be honest can recall past subjective experiences once they have been abated. And if he is currently in the midst of a depression, will that color his memories so that he exaggerates past problems? These concerns have prompted many studies of the reliability and validity of reports by community respondents.

Source: Lee N. Robins, "Psychiatric epidemiology: A historic review," *Social Psychiatry and Psychiatric Epidemiology,* 25 (1990), 16–26. By permission of the publisher.

In short, the new nomenclature was based on a much broader definition of mental illness. Consequently, a greater proportion of test subjects was rated as impaired in the post-1950 studies. In addition, there have been notable changes in psychiatric diagnoses since the 1950s; the proportion of patients diagnosed with mood and schizophrenic disorders has increased while the proportion of patients diagnosed with anxiety disorders has significantly declined.[25] This may be due to shifts in the patient population, increased treatment of neurotic patients on an outpatient basis, changes in diagnostic categories due to increased clinical knowledge, or an increase in diagnoses more consistent with medical treatment.

The introduction of tranquilizers, antidepressants, and other forms of chemotherapy, as well as an increase in outpatient facilities, has reduced the length of stay in mental hospitals and allowed many people who at one time would have remained in institutions to be treated in the community. Yet, while the proportion of the total population that is hospitalized at a given time has dropped steadily since 1950, the rate of admission has been increasing since the same year. This is sometimes referred to as the "revolving door phenomenon"—more people come and go for shorter stays. The upturn in admission rates is also the result of a growing tendency to label behavior as mentally ill, which was formerly unrecognized or designated as eccentric or criminal. In addition, African Americans and the poor, who previously went untreated, are now being admitted more frequently to mental hospitals and clinics. Because the rate of discharge has crept ahead of the rate of admission, the overall size of the mental hospital population has declined since the early 1950s. Recently, the decline has been enormous as patients have been placed in community treatment settings.[26]

CROSS-CULTURAL DIFFERENCES

The International Consortium in Psychiatric Epidemiology (ICPE) was established in 1998 by the World Health Organization (WHO) to carry out cross-national comparative studies of the prevalences and correlates of mental disorders. To date, surveys have been undertaken in seven countries in North America, Latin America, and Europe.[27] The prevalence estimates varied widely from 40 percent lifetime prevalence of any mental disorder in the Netherlands and the United States to levels of 12 percent in Turkey and 20 percent in Mexico.

One important way to determine the effect of cultural factors on mental health is to compare the prevalence of mental illness in different societies, particularly societies that are quite divergent from one another. A comparative analysis of differences between industrial and preliterate societies is the best way to do that. Unfortunately, epidemiological studies of preliterate cultures have been uncommon as a result of the once popular belief that mental illness is so different in primitive areas that the psychiatric nomenclature of industrial, Western societies is inapplicable.[28] Recently, this belief has been contradicted by psychiatric research of anthropologists and sociologists in preliterate societies. In fact, the research done on primitive societies has generated some interesting (but very preliminary) hypotheses.

There are reports, for example, that mental illness is less common among homogeneous, preliterate cultures than in heterogeneous, technologically complex industrial societies. Others believe that the prevalence of mental illness is consistent throughout the world but that the symptoms are shaped by the customs of each culture.[29] In this instance, both the perception and presentation of psychiatric illness are seen as socially determined, not the existence of the illness. This appears to be at least partially correct; culture can affect the symptoms of mental disorder, but it can also affect prevalence.

Today there is a call for more research on the mental health problems in "underserved" populations.[30] In the 1970s there were studies in what were then referred to as "primitive" societies, but there has been a huge gap in research since that time. The few studies that were conducted reported the lowest rates of mental illness in very underdeveloped groups: 0.8 percent in two isolated aboriginal groups in Taiwan[31] and 5.4 percent and 6.8 percent in two studies of aboriginal groups in Australia.[32] Native

Americans appear to be an exception: they have the highest rate reported in any study to date— 69 percent in one group in the northwestern United States.[33] However, Native Americans no longer exemplify a culturally homogeneous nonindustrialized group. On the contrary, they are a people who have been uprooted by what has become their host culture, the highly industrialized United States.

Presently, available evidence suggests that mental illness is less common among people living in an uncomplicated, underdeveloped setting than among those living in a complex industrial society.[34] However, this must remain a hypothesis until more research can be conducted. One study of Yoruba villages in Nigeria, for example, found prevalence rates of about 40 percent, much higher than would be expected if the mere fact of living in a preliterate culture immunized people against mental disorder.

One interesting aspect of the cross-cultural epidemiology of mental illness is the unusually high rate of alcoholism among the Irish. No one has satisfactorily explained this phenomenon. Some feel that, because Ireland offers little social life other than the pub, alcoholism inevitably results. Others believe that the epidemiology of mental illness in Ireland is similar to that of other countries but that nonalcoholic disorders go unrecognized because they are masked by more visible drinking problems. A third explanation, and perhaps the most useful, suggests that alcoholism is so common among the Irish because they are one of the most sexually repressed groups of people in the world. Indeed, empirical data demonstrate an unusually high rate of celibacy among the Irish population,[35] which may be due to the ability of the Roman Catholic Church to control the personal lives of the Irish. The Catholic teachings on sex have been interpreted by the Irish in very rigid ways, as evidenced by a censorship on sexually arousing literature and a ban on the sale of contraceptives. Traveling through Ireland can give one the impression that sex is the "third rail" among the Irish. But all of these explanations are purely speculations.

CONCLUSIONS

The major reason why prevalence studies of mental illness have often produced inconsistent results is because different researchers use different techniques of measuring prevalence. Methodology aside, a number of demographics appear to be related to rate and type of mental illness. Cross-cultural research indicates that there may be less mental illness in underdeveloped societies than in industrialized settings. Numerous epidemiological analyses of the U.S. population make it clear that a large number of people in U.S. society will develop mental illness at some point in their lives. As the following chapters document, this risk is not equally shared by all social groups.

8

Social Class
and Social Mobility

The mental anguish of schizophrenia can be seen in the doodlings of mental patients. Schizophrenia strikes people from all walks of life, but it is found most frequently in the lower class.

As long as inequality exists, it is likely to be associated to some degree with the extent of mental disorder in society. Changes in socioeconomic structure will lead to consequent changes in the mental structure of society, including rates of mental disorders. Thus, research describing the relationship will always be central to sociology's interest in the causes and consequences of inequality.[1]

DEFINING SOCIAL CLASS

Social class is a term that has been thrown around in a number of different ways.[2] When it is used in the proper sociological sense, it is clear that membership in a specific class has an important effect on the lives of Americans.[3] The chances for a long life, for example, are positively related to social class; the higher one's social class, the longer one's life expectancy.

In recent years, there has been an enormous increase in research focusing on the relationship between social class and physical health. In fact, social class differences in health actually appear to be widening.[4] In addition to limited health care outcomes among the poor, general unhappiness with life is greatest in the lower social class.[5] There is simply an endless list of studies that have uncovered important relationships between social class and such phenomena as fertility rates, sexual behavior, political ideology, religious beliefs, and work satisfaction, to name just a few. As a result of these findings, it is now commonplace for social scientists to consider social class in many investigations of human behavior.

Social class has particular relevance for epidemiological analyses of mental health since many differences exist among social classes in the structure of interpersonal relationships, especially parent-child interaction patterns. It is these family interaction patterns that are partly responsible for different rates and forms of mental illness across social classes. This chapter examines the ways that members of different classes view the world and raise their children. These distinctions are then used to explain why people of various social classes have different rates and types of mental illness. But child-rearing differences are only part of the picture. The horrors and stresses of lower-class life in general may be much more important.

What exactly *is* social class? In many ways, the classes that compose highly industrialized, capitalistic societies, such as the United States, are made up of individuals who are similar to other members of their class yet significantly different from people of other classes. While there is little disagreement among social scientists regarding the use of the concept of social class, there is plenty of controversy concerning the techniques used to measure social class, as well as the number of discrete classes that exist. The most accepted method of assessing social class is an objective ranking of the occupational, educational, and financial standing of the head(s) of a family. Most scales measuring class center around these interrelated characteristics, particularly occupation, because education and income can usually be inferred from occupation. Customarily, the stratification system of the United States is described in terms of five major classes. It is the most manageable approach to differentiating social classes. Other scales are more specific, but often their specificity sacrifices practical usage. Some, for instance, recognize that income, education, and occupational status are the most widely used indicators of social class but contend that each indicator is distinctive and not interchangeable with the others.[6]

The Upper Class

This group comprises wealthy families whose money is passed down from one generation to the next. Upper-class families occupy positions of high social prestige and frequently have members who are community leaders and philanthropists. At the very least, they are college graduates. Despite their reverence for the past, these are people who have the social security to be individualists and indulge their idiosyncrasies. The Kennedy, du Pont, and Ford families serve as modern examples. Although these people are less than 1 percent of the U.S. population, their social and political influence is huge.

The Upper Middle Class

These families are headed almost entirely by adults who are college educated. They are well-to-do, but their income is acquired from executive and professional work not from an inheritance. These are self-made men and women who do not possess the ancestry and inherited wealth for membership in the upper class. Common occupations include medicine, law, corporate management, and university teaching.

The Lower Middle Class

This group includes small proprietors, white-collar workers, and many skilled manual employees. The lower middle class has expanded to almost half of the nation's population. These people are predominantly high school graduates who may have completed some college. Their incomes are modest but large enough to support a comfortable lifestyle. Their strivings for upward mobility are especially projected onto their children, who are attending college in increasing numbers.

The Working Class

This stratum consists of manual workers who have finished the elementary grades and, in many cases, high school as well. The boundary line between working class and lower middle class is blurred since many blue-collar workers earn more than lower-middle-class people in clerical and sales jobs. The force of ethnic tradition is more of a differentiating factor in the working class because they are closer to their European or Asian roots than those from the lower middle class.

The Lower Class

Lower-class adults are either semiskilled or unskilled workers or among the ranks of the unemployed. They differ from members of the working class in terms of the instability of their employment and the kind of work they do. Most have not completed elementary school and are more than familiar with the hardships of poverty and ghetto living. These are people who are inundated with life's miseries, including powerlessness, poverty, and mental illness.[7]

SOCIAL CLASS, CHILD REARING, AND PERSONALITY

People's views of life are affected by their position in the social class hierarchy. In general, there is a feeling of autonomy among members of the higher classes while those in the lower classes express a sense of being controlled by others. This is no surprise in light of the fact that the privileged classes enjoy more power and freedom, a luxury rarely experienced among the relatively powerless working and lower classes. This phenomenon was well described by Melvin Kohn in his early analysis of social class and values.

> The essence of higher class position is the expectation that one's decisions and actions can be consequential: the essence of lower class position is the belief that one is at the mercy of forces and people beyond one's control, often, beyond one's understanding. Self-direction—acting on the basis of one's own judgment, attending to internal dynamics as well as to external consequences, being open-minded, being trustful of others, holding personally responsible moral standards—this is possible only if the actual conditions of life allow some freedom of action, some reason to feel in control of fate. Conformity—following the dictates of authority, focusing on external consequences to the exclusion of internal processes, being intolerant of non-conformity and dissent, being distrustful of others, having moral standards that strongly emphasize obedience to the letter of the law—this is the inevitable result of conditions of life that allow little freedom of action, little reason to feel in control of fate.[8]

A major psychological difference among social classes is a feeling of *autonomy* among the middle and upper classes and a preoccupation with *conformity* among the working and lower classes. How are these differences fostered? An important agent for their development is the specific expectations placed on children of different social classes by their parents. There is much evidence that some of the differences in the personalities of children can be explained by the social class position of the child's family. The resultant personalities reflect the specific child-rearing practices with which they were tempered. Lower-class parents, for instance, place more emphasis on teaching their children obedience than do parents of higher social class position. Consequently, these parents transmit to their children an orientation that is inflexible and less capable of dealing with change.

In the higher social classes, parents place an emphasis on *developmental* ambitions, which involve raising children to be individualistic and self-directing, rather than conforming. Other social class differences in parental values express the *internally oriented,* autonomous concerns of higher social classes and the *externally oriented,* conformity needs of lower social classes. Middle-class parents, for example, see consideration for others and achievement as admirable traits for their children, whereas working-class parents see obedience and physical neatness as highly desirable. Research on disciplinary practices demonstrates that punishment techniques are structured quite differently among classes, consistent with parental expectations. The *internally oriented* parent tends to use psychological punishment, and the *externally oriented* parent typically employs physical forms of punishment.

The physical disciplinary techniques of lower social classes have typically been viewed as a dangerous approach to raising children. But few have considered that the psychological techniques employed by the middle class may also be damaging to the child's developing personality. It may be possible that the middle-class environment is even less conducive to healthy personality formation since the parent manipulates the child's fragile self-concept by threatening the withdrawal of love.[9] Some feel that this approach to raising children may create a "slavish dependence" on the parents because the personality of the child is partially absorbed by them. This is not to say that corporal punishment in the lower classes does not produce unhealthy personality traits as well (or more). It is possible that class differences in child-rearing practices may produce different *rates* of mental illness as well as predispose members of different classes toward specific *types* of disorder. Differences uncovered in the rate and type of mental disorder should be considered in light of the *internal-external* social class variations in worldview, parental expectations, and punishment techniques.

OCCUPATION AND MENTAL ILLNESS

The Effects of Unemployment

It is one thing to talk about how mental illness varies among people in different lines of work, but the question of even *having* a job is much more important. Later in this chapter you will read about the mental health miseries of people in the lower class. Many of their problems stem from unemployment. Research on the mental health effects of involuntary unemployment has produced consistent and strong results demonstrating the devastating psychological consequences of an inadequate income or a loss of income.[10]

Economic problems are a central energizer in the *social stress theory* of mental illness presented in Chapter 3. Another linkage between mental health and unemployment may not simply center about the likelihood/onset of a mental illness but its outcome as well. Indeed, Weich and Lewis report that the financial strain of both poverty and unemployment also increase the *duration* of common mental disorders as well.[11]

Mental Illness and Occupational Prestige

Studies to date indicate an inverse relationship between occupational prestige and rate of mental illness, even Alzheimer's disease.[12] This relationship holds within occupational categories as well. An early study by Blauner examined the degree of alienation among industrial workers. He found that the most alienated workers were those whose jobs were connected to the repetitive assembly line as opposed to those workers whose jobs allowed some sense of freedom and creativity.[13] Automobile workers, for instance, suffer a greater sense of meaninglessness in life than do workers in a craft industry such as printing. Even within the auto industry, there is a relationship between mental health and job type. Kornhauser found that mental illness is most common among autoworkers in the low-prestige jobs, which were highly repetitive, dirty, offered little opportunity for advancement, and required almost total isolation from other workers.[14] These workers are most susceptible to the *automation syndrome*, a pattern of depression and somatic symptoms associated with workers' attempts to deal with the constrictions brought about by the monotony of the workplace.

One problem with the literature on occupation and mental illness is that, while it is known that psychiatric impairment increases as one moves down the occupational prestige continuum, a more pressing question is left unanswered—namely, does occupation cause mental illness, or do people with certain personalities choose particular types of jobs? It seems likely that occupation and mental health can affect each other.

Some people seek out a job that suits their particular personality. The belief that the mentally disturbed are the very ones attracted to mental health occupations may not be just a myth since these jobs can prove attractive to those who are curious about their own makeup. Dentistry may provide another example of personality preceding occupational choice. Common sense dictates that an occupation like dentistry, which demands attention to fine detail and order, would appeal most to those with obsessive-compulsive needs. Consistently, dentists do have a high suicide rate. This may not be simply because the job is stressful but because obsessive-compulsives are prime candidates for suicide because they are too inflexible to cope with the changes associated with aging.

The other side of the coin is how an occupation can affect behavior, although not necessarily mentally ill behavior. The high reported rate of lesbian behavior among strippers is probably partly due to the conditions provided by the occupation such as the lack of opportunity for romantic relationships with men. The males who do cross their path typically view the women only as sex objects, as evidenced by their masturbatory behavior in the audience.[15] Another example of occupation affecting personality is the proliferation of the use of drugs by rock musicians and those in jobs that give them access to narcotics, such as physicians and nurses. Estimates are that the narcotics addiction rate is 100 times greater for physicians than the addiction rate for the public at large. In both instances, deviant behavior connects with specific working conditions.[16]

Education interacts with mental illness in an inverse way just as occupation does; those with higher levels of educational attainment have a lower reported rate of psychiatric impairment.[17] This is probably a true relationship and not simply due to reporting biases, for it is known that more educated persons are more likely to seek psychiatric help for personal problems. There are some exceptions to this norm—those whose educational and occupational statuses are dissimilar. This is a phenomenon known as *status inconsistency*, discussed later in this chapter.

THE PREVALENCE OF MENTAL ILLNESS BY SOCIAL CLASS

Early Studies

The combined effect of occupation and education on mental illness has been measured in a number of studies that examine patterns of mental disorder among members of different social classes. One of the earliest studies was conducted in 1934 by researchers at Johns Hopkins University in the eastern section of Baltimore, Maryland. It was a community study that reviewed the records of all people admitted to a mental hospital, sent to a mental hygiene clinic, or recorded by any agency as "exhibiting some mental defect or disorder."[18] The researchers found an "unmistakable association between personality problems and low socioeconomic status, with the lowest income groups having about six times the number of problems as the highest income groups."[19]

In 1950, August B. Hollingshead and Frederick C. Redlich undertook a landmark study in psychiatric sociology that analyzed the relationship between social class and mental illness in the urban community of New Haven, Connecticut. That classic study is used as the nexus for discussion here because it serves as a common reference to evaluate other relevant studies and also because its findings have been replicated time and again.

The social class breakdown of a 5 percent random sample of New Haven households was compared to the class breakdown of the psychiatric population, which consisted of people currently receiving psychiatric care on both an inpatient and outpatient basis. The study centered about diagnosed or treated prevalence rather than true prevalence. True prevalence figures, while theoretically more desirable, may not be as useful in studies of social class since methodological problems encountered in estimating those figures can bias the findings. This is due to the fact that the researchers' evaluations are a vital part of their studies of mental illness, and their own social class can affect their evaluation of who is mentally ill.[20]

The New Haven population was divided into five social classes equivalent to those outlined at the beginning of this chapter. A major hypothesis of the study was that the *expectancy* of a psychiatric disorder is significantly related to an individual's position in the class structure of society. Simply stated, a person's chances of being mentally disordered, regardless of the type or severity of the illness, are related to social class. This hypothesis was strongly supported by the New Haven data.

The New Haven researchers compared the social class distribution of the general population of New Haven with the social class distribution of the psychiatric part of the community, at least that part which had been diagnosed. If there were no relationship between social class and the prevalence of mental illness, then each social class would comprise the same percentage of the psychiatric population and the overall population. The data in Table 8:1 demonstrate that this was not the case. In New Haven, the upper class made up 3.1 percent of the community's population but only 1.0 percent of all known psychiatric cases. Upper-middle, lower-middle, and working-class individuals were also underrepresented in the patient population but not to the same degree as upper-class people. On the other hand, the percentage of lower-class people in the patient population was more than twice that which would be expected on the basis of their representation in the general population.

The researchers further tested their finding that social class is related to the likelihood of a person becoming a mental patient by controlling for the specific effects of sex, age, race, and marital status. In doing so they discovered some interesting ways in which these four demographic factors interact with social class. They found that there is a particular abundance of female patients in the lower middle class and a concentration of male patients in the lower class. Age is especially related to being mentally

Table 8:1   Distribution of Normal and Psychiatric Population by Social Class

Social Class	Normal Population		Psychiatric Population	
	Number	Percent	Number	Percent
Upper	358	3.1	19	1.0
Upper middle	926	8.1	131	6.7
Lower middle	2,500	22.0	260	13.2
Working	5,256	46.0	758	38.6
Lower	2,037	17.8	723	36.8
Unknown	345	3.0	72	3.7
Total	11,422	100.0	1,963	100.0

Source: Reprinted from August B. Hollingshead and Frederick C. Redlich, "Social stratification and psychiatric disorders," *American Sociological Review, 18* (1953), 167. By permission of the authors and publisher.

ill in the lower middle class, where adolescents and young adults were overrepresented in the psychiatric population. This may be related to excessive upward mobility ambitions, which are likely to be the particular burden of young people striving to surpass their parents' class position by aspiring for more prestigious lines of work.

In the New Haven study, blacks exhibited the same pattern as whites by social class, although, as a group, they were found more frequently in the lower social classes. Therefore, if the chance of becoming mentally ill were assessed on the basis of race alone, one would have to conclude that blacks were more predisposed. But the real truth is that race itself is unrelated to the likelihood of being in treatment. Rather, it is membership in the lower social class that is responsible for excessive mental illness among blacks. Blacks belong to the lower class, not because of an innate tendency to be lower class but as a result of prejudicial treatment in the United States.

Married members of the four higher classes were less likely to be mentally ill than separated, widowed, divorced, or unmarried members of these same classes in New Haven. In the lower class, however, married patients were as common as unmarried patients, suggesting that marriage does not function as a mental health haven in the miserable, deprived conditions of lower-class life. The New Haven study concluded that a definite association exists between social class and the chances of being mentally ill; the lower the class, the greater the proportion of people in the diagnosed population. The greatest difference was between the four higher classes and the lower class; the lower class had a much higher ratio of people diagnosed as disordered to the normal population than other classes.

Other early studies also reported an inverse relationship between social class and the rate of mental illness. One study conducted by the Selective Service reported on 60,000 male registrants examined at the Boston Area Induction Station in 1942.[21] The psychiatric rejection rates were noticeably greater among lower-class registrants. The Midtown Manhattan study tested the class-impairment relationship among members of a population not in treatment (true prevalence) and also found that lower social class carries a larger risk of impaired mental health.[22] The Midtown researchers estimated that 47.3 percent of the lowest social stratum was mentally impaired contrasted to only 12.5 percent of the highest stratum. The Dohrenwends also analyzed the findings of all studies of the *true prevalence* of psychopathology to the mid-1970's.[23] They found that the most consistent result reported was an inverse relationship between overall rates of mental disorder and social class. In fact, of 33 communities examined by different researchers to that time, 28 yielded the highest rate of mental illness in the lowest class.

This relationship holds for both rural and urban areas but may not always be valid outside of the United States. One study of the prevalence of mental illness by class in Lebanon found the highest concentration of cases in the lower and upper classes while the middle class showed the lowest rate.[24] However, other studies indicate that the usual relationship also holds in India[25] and even in Sweden, a country with a minimal social stratification.[26]

Recent Studies

Does the relationship between social class and mental illness still hold true today? Are the poor still more at risk for mental health problems? Absolutely. Consider some reports from recent decades. One review of studies documenting psychopathology among different social classes reported that, among 42 studies, 35 found the highest rates of mental illness among the lowest social class.[27] In the early 1980s the

National Epidemiologic Catchment Area Surveys (ECA) conducted by the NIMH reported that mental disorder was 2.9 times greater among members of the lowest socioeconomic group as compared to the highest socioeconomic group. This was especially true for schizophrenia.

The persistence of these social class differentials is sound evidence that the patterns of prevalence of mental illness are far from random. Follow-up studies continue to abound and report the same finding. Two huge studies in the 1990s provided even more evidence for the strong inverse association between social class and rate of mental illness. These include the National Comorbidity Survey conducted in 1990–1992 and the Epidemiologic Catchment Area follow-up conducted in 1993–1996.[28]

The most current "reviews of reviews" also confirm the familiar finding of "more mental illness in the lower class,"[29] as well as the especially stressful effect of unemployment.[30] And, to add more misery to the "lower-class finding," chances for recovery are also least likely among the poor.[31] The geographic basis of the "lower-class finding" still appears to be consistently strong in different countries and cities, from London [32] to New York.[33]

Today, studies relating inequality (poverty) to mental disorder are sorting out more refined aspects of the connection. These include the additional effects of ethnicity,[34] as well as how the connection between poverty and mental illness may be related to different stages in the life course.[35] The bottom line in all of these studies spanning 60 years constitutes one of the strongest findings in research in psychiatric sociology to date—an enduring relationship of social class to mental distress.

The Societal Reaction Hypothesis

The concentration of mental illness in the lower class is generally viewed as a well-established fact. What is not fact, however, are the theoretical *opinions* behind the relationship. Some blame the stress of lower-class life. Others believe mental illness causes a person to slide into the lower class. Still others feel psychiatrists are at fault by using biased diagnostic techniques. These three major theoretical explanations are still being debated and untangled.[36]

Some have concluded that the reported relationship of the prevalence of mental illness by social class is partly due to a middle-class bias that pervades psychiatric diagnosis. The middle-class prototype and the prototype of mental health are equivalent in many respects. This is a reflection of the large proportion of middle-class people who enter the mental health field and in turn project their own class-based values onto the evaluations of who is mentally ill. Attitudes toward problem solving, the control of emotions, and planning ahead vary significantly by social class.[37] These are all traits found more commonly in the higher classes. So also is self-expression, a skill highly valued by psychiatrists. Wilkinson uncovered a strong tendency for middle-class people to rate a lower-class patient as more seriously impaired than an equally disordered member of their own class.[38] He interpreted this as support for the *societal reaction hypothesis* and concluded that part of what is seen as a psychiatric disorder among lower-class people is actually their social class characteristics. This perspective is highly consistent with labeling theory.

The inherent biases of psychiatric diagnosis against lower-class people are particularly apparent in the projective tests used to assess mental health. Projective tests typically involve telling a story about a picture that is presented to the subject. These instruments rely on test-taking experience, motivation to perform, familiarity with the vocabulary of the tester, and reading ability, in all of which lower-class people are less skilled than their higher-class counterparts. It is these social class differences in abilities and norms that can be confused with pathological symptoms. In addition, higher-class individuals may be more aware than lower-class persons of what are considered to be the most socially desirable responses to questions used to assess mental health. However, not all projective tests are class biased; the Rorschach inkblot test, for example, involves a formalistic system that reportedly has no class content whatsoever. As you may know, the Rorschach technique involves free associating about an inkblot design, an ambiguous stimulus that allows the subject to reveal unconscious motivation.

Some work has been done by the NIMH to educate the public and increase their credence in mental health counseling. But such efforts have had an impact only on the pamphlet receiving and reading group, which is composed almost completely of middle- and upper-class people. The result is a network of mental health communications disseminated and received by the higher social classes. This problem, which functions to maintain lower-class ignorance regarding mental health and illness, may be partly responsible for the reported inverse relationship between social class and prevalence of mental illness. My feeling is that it is probably a very small part.

The Social Stress Hypothesis

Sociological interest in elevated rates of mental illness among the poor partly centers about stressful life circumstances in the form of harsh, difficult, or traumatic life conditions.[39] The social stress theory of the preponderance of mental illness in the lower class holds that the miserable conditions of lower-class life generate stress that, in turn, fosters psychiatric impairment. Social stress in the lower class takes many forms, including childhood deprivation, broken homes, degrading treatment by others, violence, social isolation, and resource deprivation that prevents educational and occupational attainment.[40] Of utmost importance is the fact that unemployment is highest in the lower class. Unemployment can have a devastating effect on feelings of self-esteem and cause estrangement from family and friends.[41]

A number of studies of mental illness and social class have been interpreted as supporting the *social stress hypothesis*, or *social causation hypothesis*.[42] The social stress explanation is very plausible in light of the finding that the most disadvantaged members of the lower class have the greatest degree of impairment; blacks and Puerto Ricans, for example, common objects of discrimination in the United States, are more frequently and severely impaired than their lower-class Irish peers.[43] Ethnicity aside, lower-class life is simply riddled with risk factors for mental illness, including feelings of hopelessness, anger, and hostility.[44]

Melvin Kohn has developed an interesting proposition regarding the predominance of one form of mental illness, schizophrenia, in the lower class. He contends that schizophrenia is caused by the stresses of lower-class life on genetically susceptible people.[45] The stresses that lower-class people experience are not alterable by individual actions because many of the stresses arise from economic circumstances over which there is little control. This is true for the lower-class person, who is typically socialized to have a conformist orientation system so rigid that he has a difficult time dealing with stress or change. The genetic component of Kohn's theory of schizophrenia in the lower class is consistent with existing medical evidence. It also explains why few studies have found important differences in patterns of parent-child relationships between schizophrenics and normal persons of lower social class background. Genetic predisposition coupled with the rigid orientation system programmed into lower-class children may cause schizophrenic breakdown when stress is imposed.

Others, however, take issue with Kohn's theory because it fails to consider that the lower-class person may be equally capable or even superior to higher-class persons in dealing with stress.[46] Perhaps it is more challenging to discover why many lower-class persons do so well in facing adversity, rather than why some fail. Some believe that the stresses of lower-class life give people greater opportunity to develop coping mechanisms rather than rendering them psychologically inoperative—a type of *robustness*. To others, that is an idea without a logical foundation.

The Social Drift Hypothesis

An alternative explanation of the high rate of mental illness in the lower class is the opposite of the social stress hypothesis. This theory, known as the *social selection hypothesis*, or *drift hypothesis*, holds that social class is not a cause but a *consequence* of psychopathology. According to this view, mentally disordered people are likely to be members of the lower class because mental illness did not allow them to function at a higher-class level. As a consequence, they became downwardly mobile and drifted into the lower class. This theory is consistent with a medical orientation to etiology, whereas the social stress hypothesis is consistent with an environmental orientation. Social drift theory is also consistent with reports that a mental disorder, such as depression, can affect a person's educational and occupational aspirations.[47] The theory also fits with data indicating that about 14 percent of high school and 4 percent of college dropouts are caused by mental illness.[48]

The social selection view gained respect from sociological researchers who previously denied its validity. Dunham, for instance, has argued against his and Faris's earlier interpretations of the high concentration of schizophrenia in socially and economically disadvantaged communities.[49] Previously, he offered a social stress interpretation that emphasized the isolated conditions of inner-city living. Since that time, a number of studies have impressively argued that social selection processes play a part in etiology, particularly for schizophrenia and antisocial personality disorder.[50] All of these studies employ a similar logic: if the parents of mentally ill people are in higher social classes than their offspring, then mental disorder preceded social class, and the social selection hypothesis is supported. One team of researchers examined the social class of fathers of mental patients in Great Britain. They found that the social class distribution of patients' fathers did not differ from that of the general population. The patients, however, were often downwardly mobile, particularly the schizophrenics.[51] On the other hand, a World Health Organization study of Dutch schizophrenics favored social selection theory.[52]

A study by Harkey and others presented a different twist on the relationship between mental illness and downward drift into the lower class.[53] They used a wide index of psychological health that essentially measured a person's general ability to function in society and administered it to more than 16,000 individuals in southern Appalachia. Their results partly supported the social selection hypothesis, as they found that the primary effect of psychological disorder is to retard upward mobility rather than contribute to downward mobility. This may result in two schools of thought within social selection theory: *those who believe mental illness causes downward mobility* and *those who believe that mental illness limits upward mobility*. Whatever the real direction may be, it is clear that severe disorders like schizophrenia lower cognitive ability and social skills.

One unique test of the social selection–social stress controversy contrasted stress levels of whites, African Americans, and Mexican Americans at the same social class level.[54] If the social stress model were correct, stress would be greater among African Americans, Chicanos, and other minority group people than among whites of similar social class because minority groups confront added stress in the form of racial bigotry and discrimination. If the social selection model were correct, there would be less impairment among disadvantaged minorities than among whites of the same class. The reason for this is that opportunities for upward mobility are more restricted, and downward pressures are much greater among disadvantaged groups compared to whites, who are not forced into lower classes by racial constraints. Therefore, lower-class whites should be more likely to be impaired since some psychological dysfunction caused their social class position. The data from that study strongly support the social selection hypothesis since the disadvantaged ethnics had appreciably fewer symptoms of mental illness than whites of similar social class. It seems that, for every study supporting the social stress model, there is another verifying the social selection model. Recent studies are still inconclusive and contradictory.[55] This is really not surprising because the two models are not mutually exclusive; *class can determine illness in one case and illness can determine class in another.*

SOCIAL CLASS AND TYPE OF MENTAL ILLNESS

The literature is rich with studies reporting a relationship between types of mental illness and social class. Unfortunately, the classification system used by the New Haven researchers was simplistic in that they divided all psychiatric cases into only two possible types: the neuroses and the psychoses. Obviously, other types of illness are ignored by such a breakdown, such as the personality disorders. In addition, the New Haven classification system did not treat the different types of psychoses and neuroses separately. Although the New Haven methodology was limited in this respect, the study did find a sharp contrast in the distribution of these two gross categories of disorders by social class. Specifically, it reported a concentration of psychoses in the lower class and the neuroses in the higher classes.

Results from the 1993–1994 Baltimore ECA follow-up study are revealing. Table 8:2 explores differences between two types of mental disorders, major depression and a group of anxiety disorders. Contrary to other studies, these two groups of disorders were also found more frequently in the lower social class. Traditionally, anxiety disorders are reported more commonly in the higher classes, as is depression in general. The Baltimore findings are presented here because they employed a community survey approach with a sophisticated breakdown of the components of social class.

Other early studies confirmed the major findings of the New Haven study. One investigation reported a higher rate of hospitalized psychoses in a lower- and working-class area of Boston than in an upper- and middle-class section.[56] Another study of psychiatric disorder in Baltimore found that psychotic disorders decreased as income increased.[57] The preponderance of psychoses, particularly schizophrenia, among the lower classes has also been found in similar research outside the United States, including studies conducted in England[58] and Lebanon.[59]

Research findings on the relationship between social class and type of mental disorder are not entirely consistent, however.[60] Clausen and Kohn, for example, found no relationship between the prevalence of schizophrenia and social class in a small

Table 8:2 Prevalence (in percent) of Major Depression and Anxiety Disorder by Social Class, Baltimore ECA Follow-up, 1993–1994 (*n* = 1,865)

Measures of Social Class	Major Depression		Anxiety Disorder	
	Percent	*OR*	*Percent*	*OR*
Education of Respondent				
Less than high school	1.2	1.0	16.0	1.0
High school graduate	2.5	1.9	14.8	1.3
Some college	2.7	3.5	7.6	0.3
College graduate	2.7	6.5	13.3	0.8
Graduate school	0.7	1.9	13.9	0.8
Household Income				
< $17,500	1.2	16.2*	19.1	2.9*
$17,500–$34,499	3.8	11.5*	16.3	1.6
$35,000+	2.0	1.0	10.8	1.0
Household Physical Assets				
Does not own car	1.8	0.6	19.3	1.6
Owns car	2.1	1.0	13.0	1.0
Does not own home	2.2	1.3	19.3	1.1
Owns home	1.8	1.0	12.1	1.0
Household Financial Assets				
No dividend income	2.0	1.0	16.3	1.0
Dividend income	2.1	2.9	11.6	1.2
No savings income	2.9	1.5	18.3	1.2
Savings income	1.5	1.0	13.3	1.0
No property income	2.0	1.0	15.7	1.0
Property income	1.9	1.8	4.7	0.1*
Respondent Occupation[a]				
Labor	2.9	—[b]	14.8	0.5
Craft	1.9	1.1	8.5	0.3
Service	0.9	0.6	14.1	0.6
Technical	2.7	0.6	19.0	0.8
Professional	2.6	1.0	14.7	1.0
Respondent Organizational Assets[a]				
Nonmanagement	1.4	0.5	15.7	2.1
Supervisor	3.6	2.9	15.7	2.6*
Manager	1.0	1.0	8.1	1.0

Note: OR = odds ratio—adjusted for age, gender, and race/ethnicity, as well as for other variables in the table.

*Statistically significant (95% confidence interval).

[a]The sample for measures of occupation and organizational assets is limited to 877 respondents who were in the labor force at the time of the interview.

[b]There were no sample respondents with major depressive disorder in this occupation category.

Source: William W. Eaton and Carles Muntaner, "Socioeconomic stratification and mental disorder," in Allan V. Horwitz and Teresa L. Scheid, eds., *A Handbook for the Study of Mental Health: Social Contexts, Theories and Systems* (New York: Cambridge University Press, 1999), p. 282. Reprinted with the permission of Cambridge University Press.

Maryland town.[61] In a study of the black population of Philadelphia, Parker found an increase in the rate of schizophrenia as social class decreased, but anxiety disorders showed no social class differences.[62] Prevalence studies in Australia,[63] Norway,[64] and Formosa[65] also failed to confirm the New Haven findings of more psychosis and less anxiety among lower-class people. Perhaps these differences exist because the New Haven findings are appropriate only for the type of population from which the sample was drawn, that is, white, urban America. The Parker study examined a black population, and the other studies dealt with populations outside of the United States. However, the Baltimore ECA follow-up study is a serious exception because of its sophistication. The only safe conclusion that can be made in 2002 is that there is a *significant tendency* for serious mental illness, particularly schizophrenia, to be concentrated in the lower class, whereas anxiety disorders are *typically* reported more often in higher classes.

Types of Psychosis

In addition to the New Haven investigation, other researchers have examined the relationship between social class and types of mental disorders. These investigations have been more specific than the New Haven study in that they have researched particular types of anxiety disorders and psychoses rather than only the two gross categories utilized by the New Haven researchers. One early study by Fuson analyzed the social class distribution of two major types of psychosis: schizophrenia and the manic-depressive illnesses (mood disorders).[66] From an examination of the records of 1,496 mental patients, Fuson found relatively more schizophrenia in lower-class groups and relatively more manic-depressive illness in higher-class groups. It is important to note here that schizophrenia involves a greater break with reality than the manic-depressive psychoses, which are typically more internal. At the risk of repeating myself, I want to caution the reader that the report of concentration of schizophrenia among the poor and of the overrepresentation of higher-class people with mood disorders is simply the typical *report*. Certainly there are many lower-class people with mood disorders, such as clinical depression, who suffer deeply and are very much in need of help.[67] However, because their symptoms are more internal they are less easily recognized and often overlooked in the depressive quagmire of life in the ghetto.

The social class gradient in schizophrenia has been examined in about 100 studies to date. With few exceptions these studies have found a preponderance of schizophrenia at the lowest social class levels of urban society. One exception to the "more schizophrenia among the lower class" finding is reported by Goodman and others.[68] However, the overall evidence strongly supports the notion that the poor are particularly vulnerable to schizophrenia. Some of this evidence even comes from research conducted in a number of countries outside of the United States, including England, Denmark, Finland, Canada, Norway, Sweden, and Taiwan.

Kohn's etiological argument is relevant here; he explains the preponderance of schizophrenia in the lower class as the result of the interaction of genetics and a psychological inability of lower-class people to deal with stress because of an inflexible, conformist conception of reality grounded in their socialization experiences.[69] Kohn's stress hypothesis has some opposition because others found that first admissions for schizophrenia tend to come from more affluent communities while readmissions tend to emanate from poorer communities.[70] This indicates that the schizophrenic condition occurs in all classes and causes a *drift* down the social class ladder over time. Psychiatric sociology—chicken and egg time and again.

Anxiety and Personality Disorders

Given the large number of studies showing that there are certain tendencies by which members of different classes become psychotic, is there a particular way in which the various classes develop anxiety or personality disorders? Some researchers have found suggestive differences among the social classes in this regard.[71] The most common anxiety disorder in the higher classes is the obsessive-compulsive disorder, a relatively internal type of problem compared to the phobic disorder, which occurs more frequently among those lower in the social hierarchy. Additionally, it is not by chance that the antisocial personality disorder is found among lower-class people since this also involves external symptoms in the form of social disobedience.

The Logic of Social Causation: Internal vs. External Symptoms

The relationships between social class and type of mental illness lend support to a major hypothesis of this chapter: *there is an increasing predisposition toward external forms of mental disorder among those lower in the social class hierarchy*. Perhaps this is best exemplified by the high rate of psychosis in the lower class. One essential difference between an anxiety disorder and a psychosis is the role of the ego in acting against two different agencies of the personality as a means of resolving intrapsychic conflict. Freud held that ". . . one of the features which differentiates a neurosis from a psychosis . . . (is) that in a neurosis the ego, in its dependence on reality, suppresses a piece of the id (of instinctual life), whereas in a psychosis, this same ego, in the service of the id, withdraws from a piece of reality. Thus, for a neurosis the decisive factor would be the predominance of the influence of reality, whereas for a psychosis it would be the predominance of the id."[72]

It seems logical that a response against social reality and in support of one's instinctual drives (a psychosis) is more likely to be found among those whose real world is unfulfilling. This is the everyday experience of lower-class life. On the other hand, a response against instinctual drives and in support of social reality (an anxiety disorder) is more consistent with the relatively desirable conditions of life in the higher classes.

The explanation of social class differences in type of mental illness that I prefer is the *social stress* proposition that people from lower-class settings develop *antireality types* of illnesses because their world is miserable and they were socialized as children toward external reactions. People from higher classes lead more rewarding lives, have less reason to retreat from that reality, and are not as prone to act out their feelings because of an upbringing that emphasized internal control. For these reasons, *antiinstinctual types* of illnesses are their most common way of exhibiting mental disorder.

This theory is useful beyond explaining the general neurosis/psychosis breakdown by social class since it is also possible to differentiate *within* these two categories in terms of the degrees to which specific disorders reflect a discontent with the real world. For example, both schizophrenia and the mood disorders are considered to be a withdrawal from reality, but schizophrenic fantasies are much less associated with the real world than are the unexplained changes of people with mood disorders, many of whom can get through the basic requirements of everyday living.

Within the anxiety and personality disorder categories, the instinct/reality distinction also holds. The lower classes are more susceptible to antisocial disorders that are a clear-cut rejection of the social structure. The obsessive-compulsive tendencies of the higher classes, on the other hand, are experienced in more internal ways. *This is not to say that the end result of psychological conflict is a simple function of social class.* It would be true only if all higher-class people developed specific types of anxiety disorders and all lower-class people developed only severe psychotic reactions. This is not the case. There is, however, a significant relationship in that direction which compels psychiatric researchers to regularly consider social class as an important factor in the etiology of all forms of mental disorder that are not known to be completely biological, such as Alzheimer's disease.

It may well be that the internal/external differences in type of disorder found in various social classes are linked to known differences in child rearing discussed earlier. In support of this, some report that lower-class families are less able to resolve conflicts than higher-class families.[73] This could lead to greater frustration in lower-class children and an increased likelihood of acting-out behavior. Consistently, higher-class patients suffering from depression are reported to have been overprotected by their parents.[74] These are interesting social class correlates that make the diathesis-stress model of mental illness especially viable.

DIFFERENCES IN PSYCHIATRIC TREATMENT BY SOCIAL CLASS

Do mental patients from different classes receive different kinds of treatment? The New Haven study examined treatment differences by social class. All treatments were grouped into three categories: psychotherapy, organic therapy, and custodial care. Psychotherapy includes any technique that rests on verbal interaction between the patient and someone else in a helping role. This ranges from the highly individualistic and lengthy psychoanalytic approach to the cheaper, group method technique typically employed in state hospitals. Organic therapy includes anything directly affecting the body and brain. Some major types of organic therapy are chemotherapy (the use of drugs, such as tranquilizers, to maintain temporary psychic equilibrium) and shock treatment (ECT). Custodial care is a polite term for no treatment at all. The custodial approach is based on the assumption that the patient cannot be rehabilitated but must be separated from the rest of society for security reasons.

The New Haven study found a roughly equal distribution of these three therapeutic approaches over the entire patient population, but the percentage of persons who received organic therapy or custodial therapy was greatest in the lower class. Psychotherapy was used more frequently in the higher classes, and, within the psychotherapy category, there were important differences in the *type* administered by class. Psychoanalytic techniques were predominant among upper- and upper-middle-class patients. The few patients in the lower class who received psychotherapy were typically administered a group method approach. The breakdown of type of treatment received by patients of various social classes is presented in Table 8:3.

The New Haven findings caused considerable controversy because some regarded the report as a blatant indictment of prejudicial systems of psychiatric care that favor higher-class patients with expensive, individually oriented therapy and relegate lower-class patients to inexpensive, less effective therapeutic programs. This charge has been strengthened by other studies showing that lower-class patients are socially disadvantaged in treatment settings. One study of depressed patients found that only 17 percent of depressed lower-class patients were referred for psychotherapy, in contrast to 33 percent in the middle class and 100 percent in the upper class.[75]

Table 8:3   Distribution of the Principal Types of Therapy by Social Class

Social Class	Psychotherapy		Organic Therapy		No Treatment	
	Number	*Percent*	*Number*	*Percent*	*Number*	*Percent*
Upper	14	73.7	2	10.5	3	15.8
Upper middle	107	81.7	15	11.4	9	6.9
Lower middle	136	52.7	74	28.7	48	18.6
Working	237	31.1	288	37.1	242	31.8
Lower	115	16.1	234	32.7	367	51.2

Source: Reprinted from August B. Hollingshead and Frederick C. Redlich, "Social stratification and psychiatric disorders," *American Sociological Review, 18* (1953), 169. By permission of the authors and publisher.

Another study of prospective patients at a psychiatric outpatient clinic found that lower-class people are more frequently misdiagnosed and less likely to receive psychotherapy than higher-class persons.[76] Many are claiming that equality of care is far from the norm, especially in the case of lower-class people who are also members of minority groups.

Before examining the bases of this alleged bigotry, *it is important to note that usually the psychotic illnesses found in the lower classes are not effectively treated through psychotherapeutic techniques.* This is particularly true in the case of psychoanalysis, which requires transference for successful treatment. *Transference* is the process by which a patient sees in the psychoanalyst the return—the reincarnation—of some important figure from childhood and consequently transfers onto the analyst feelings and reactions that originally applied to the past figure. Not only does this seem impossible to accomplish with any psychotic, but it is particularly difficult to achieve between a lower-class patient and an analyst from a higher class.

In addition, psychoanalysis relies on the patient's assuming an active role in the therapeutic process by verbalizing thoughts and feelings. This is not likely to occur with lower-class patients, who typically are not self-expressive. Psychotherapeutic techniques in general are most useful with higher-class, nonpsychotic patients, who are better able to engage in a "talking-out" approach. Unfortunately, psychiatry seems to be hamstrung in its effort to treat the most severely disturbed patients through talking-out therapies. Some feel that the "behavior control" approach of organic and custodial treatments is simply the only alternative. Perhaps medication *and* psychotherapy is the best combination for people with serious mental illness. But, even then, social class may get in the way of effective psychotherapy. This may be a huge problem when the patient is in the lower social class.

LOWER-CLASS PATIENTS IN TREATMENT

It may well be that psychoanalysis, which originated in nineteenth-century Viennese culture and flourished in twentieth-century American society, appealed to people living in a highly individualistic culture of opportunity. If that is true, it is doomed to failure among the impoverished.[77] But that cannot explain why *psychotherapy in general* does not seem to work with lower-class patients. In an effort to explain the underrepresentation (and failure) of lower-class patients in psychotherapy, some have suggested that lower-class people simply do not understand the psychotherapeutic process and are uninterested in it. On the other hand, some fault therapists, who are believed to stereotype negatively lower-class patients and relegate them to medical or custodial forms of therapy on the simple basis of social class characteristics. Some report that therapists consider lower-class persons as poor candidates for psychotherapy, not because they are lower class, per se, but because they typically lack "insight-verbal ability."[78] It may be true that lower-class patients often lack verbal skills, but it is important to realize that this is frequently the result of family and peers discouraging the person from talking about feelings. Thus, the absence of talking-out skills among lower-class persons is a *trained incapacity*. For this reason, perhaps it is the lower-class patients who really should be favored with psychotherapy since they can learn new skills from it. Or perhaps this is all "pie-in-the-sky" thinking about people who are too conditioned to be able to change.

Lack of verbal ability among lower-class persons is not the only reason why they are so frequently considered poor candidates for psychotherapy. Other forces are at work as well. One of these is *status homophily*, a term that refers to the degree of social similarity between two individuals. From this perspective, therapists are believed to select patients who have social class characteristics similar to their own. This was demonstrated some time ago by Kandel, who found that psychotherapists have an elitist bias toward higher class patients.[79] They prefer to treat patients socially similar to themselves, and they screen their patients in terms of an old adage that underlies many forms of social interaction—that "birds of a feather flock together."

Participation in psychotherapy is directly related to the extent of class discrepancy between psychotherapists and potential patients (more discrepancy, less participation). This appears to also be true of psychotherapists from the lower social classes since at least one study found that even this group of therapists tends to underselect lower-class patients.[80] These biases are found in state mental hospitals as well as among psychotherapists in private practice.[81] In inner circles, psychotherapists refer to the patients they prefer as "YAVIS"—young, attractive, verbal, intelligent, and successful. Call it what you may but the end result is that psychotherapy is treatment for the privileged. Even community mental health centers, which were established to give everyone equal access to treatment, are victimized by the middle-class bias that defines a "good patient" on the basis of social worth. To make matters worse, there is evidence that lower-class patients are much more likely to be misdiagnosed because "typical" lower-class behavior may be seen as abnormal.[82]

All of the findings on status homophily come from studies of psychotherapists in organizationally based practices, such as state mental hospitals. Marx and Spray also tested the "homophilic hypothesis" among psychiatrists and clinical psychologists in private practice.[83] They found that college graduates are clearly preferred as patients by all psychotherapists. More specifically, psychotherapists from higher social class origins have a much greater concentration of college graduates as patients than their colleagues from lower-class backgrounds. Marx and Spray also evaluated another component of status homophily—religiocultural values. They found that therapists also prefer patients from their own religious origins, even when the therapist is an apostate. This partly accounts for the large number of Jewish Americans receiving psychotherapy; although only 2 percent of the U.S. population is Jewish, about a third of psychiatrists are Jewish.[84] Catholic patients, on the other hand, typically seek treatment from clinical psychologists, who tend to come from Christian backgrounds.

The literature convincingly demonstrates that what happens therapeutically to people who become psychiatric patients is partly determined by their social class. However, this may not be true in all types of treatment settings, such as community mental health centers, which are publicly funded to serve the needs of all persons in a geographic area. Community health centers offer a variety of treatments, which are supposed to be chosen democratically. In fact, patient charges are scaled to a person's ability to pay.[85] However, much of what is *written* about community mental health centers is a function of the specific centers a researcher chooses to investigate since there are also reports that lower-class patients are typically assigned to the least competent therapists.[86]

The community mental health center may be dealing more effectively with another class-related problem in psychotherapy—the high attrition rates of lower-class patients. The patient characteristics commonly associated with attrition are poor verbal ability, lack of introspection or emotional responsiveness, and a lack of concern about interpersonal relations, all of which are associated with low social class. Some community mental health centers have reduced attrition among lower-class patients by using techniques designed to increase their comfort and reduce their fears.[87] The techniques include an informal atmosphere in the clinic and the selection of motivated therapists and employees drawn from the community. Now there are reports which indicate that even psychoanalytic treatment is trickling down to the lower class.[88] But such reports are rare, and understandably so.

Those who defend the selective tendencies of psychotherapists are not entirely wrong in stressing that "good patients" are required for successful treatment and that the likelihood of finding this type of patient declines with social class. On the other hand, those critical of these selective admission standards seem justified in taking issue with the intellectually sophisticated definition of a "good patient," which often rests on evaluations of social worth. The diagnosis and treatment of mental illness are not unique in social judgments of any kind of patient. These issues are part of a more general phenomenon that is prevalent in many facets of the medical world. Judgments include a multitude of issues related to the definition of a "good patient," including the ability to verbalize problems, hold common values, and pay bills.[89] What is the resolution to the dilemma? The answer lies in educating psychotherapists who understand lower-class people. How? I am not sure because, even if a poor person moves through college, medical school, and psychiatric training, he or she frequently ends up with a higher-class view of life and dissociates from their lower-class background. The answer is that there presently is no answer except for chalking it up to "life is not fair." That is not really much of an answer; it is just a cliché to end uncomfortable topics.

SOCIAL MOBILITY

Does movement up or down the social class ladder cause stress, which, in turn, leads to mental illness? A number of studies have tested this proposition, but the results have been inconclusive and contradictory.[90] One reason for this is that mobility studies often use different measures of social class. Because mobility is typically measured in terms of the difference between the subject's attainments and that of the parents, those studies that use education as the sole criterion of social class are especially problematic. Educational opportunities have changed so much over time that intergenerational differences in educational levels are common and thus are no real index of mobility.

Durkheim first reported an association between economic change and abnormal behavior in his classic study of suicide. He reported that the suicide rate increases during periods of economic depression *and* prosperity. He concluded that any type of economic change produces a state of normlessness, which leads to feelings of frustration. During an economic crisis, the downwardly mobile individual is forced to restrain desires, a requirement that some persons are not able to tolerate. Durkheim postulated a similar process operating in upwardly mobile people who find themselves with unexpected wealth resulting from an economic boom. Although some persons react with happiness, others fail to perceive the practical limitations of the situation, and they begin to strive for unrealistic goals. Thus they are frustrated by "the futility of an endless pursuit."

Since Durkheim's study of suicide, others have reported a direct relationship between any type of social mobility (upward or downward) and a number of psychological problems.[91] At the same time, some studies have shown no important relationship between social mobility (regardless of direction) and mental illness.[92] Fox, for instance, examined a number of studies and concluded that they provide little support for social mobility differences between seriously mentally ill and general population groups.[93]

The Pathology of Upward Mobility

In the 1930s, the psychoanalytic researcher Karen Horney reported that deep-seated personality factors are involved in the drive for upward mobility.[94] She believed that persons who sought power, prestige, and wealth were likely to be neurotics who were deprived of affection during childhood. Typically this took the form of a "series of humiliating experiences," such as parental preference for other children, unjust reproaches, rejection by parents, jealousy of a parent or sibling, and minority group membership. These experiences wounded the child's self-esteem and created a sense of unconscious hostility toward others whom the person desired to humiliate. According to Horney, the drive for upward mobility occurs in people who vindictively strive to rise above others. This, of course, is just a theory with little empirical support.

Horney's hypothesis that upward mobility is frequently inspired by emotional drives generated by unsatisfactory early family relations was tested by Ellis, who compared the backgrounds of upwardly mobile and nonmobile women.[95] She found that mobile women had a significantly larger number of humiliating experiences during childhood, more often rated their childhood as "less than average," and were considerably more lonely as adults than nonmobile women. A later study found that psychological disturbances are common only among upwardly mobile individuals at relatively high social class levels.[96] Apparently status climbing may have pathological effects for those who are unprepared for it. However, it would be unreasonable to hold that upward mobility is concretely linked with mental illness since there are many people who are upwardly mobile and display no signs of psychopathology. For them, sound mental health is either a preparatory asset that helps them improve their position, or the rewards of upward mobility improve their mental health. Chicken and egg again. Today, it is highly unlikely whether Horney's theory will undergo further testing because psychoanalytic research does not receive much attention.

The Pathology of Downward Mobility

The most consistent finding in the mobility literature is a positive association between downward mobility and mental illness. This has been verified by a number of studies using patient records,[97] as well as the Midtown Manhattan study of people in the community. The Midtown study found that impaired people were frequently downwardly mobile in relation to their parents' class level. Most of the studies reporting downward mobility to be commonplace among disturbed people have been limited to hospitalized schizophrenics, who undoubtedly are prone to drift into the lower class because of the severity of their condition. However, some researchers believe that the downwardly mobile experience *itself* generates sufficient stress to cause psychiatric impairment of varying degrees.[98]

Some reports specify that impairment rates for the downwardly mobile are only high at the lowest status level and for the upwardly mobile at the high end of the status scale.[99] All of these mixed reports make it apparent that Durkheim's assumption of an invariant association between *any* type of mobility and abnormal behavior is untenable. Downward mobility appears to be a greater mental health hazard than upward mobility, but this is only *generally* true. Much depends on the way the person perceives the experience. For some people status climbing may have costly effects in the form of shifting reference groups and concomitant interpersonal experiences that would have been avoided had they remained stationary. For others downward mobility may stabilize mental health by permitting an escape from taxing stresses at higher class levels. These are complicated relationships that appear to vary enormously from person to person. Part of the variation is probably the person's existing predisposition to mental illness.

Status Inconsistency

Closely related to social mobility is what is known as *status inconsistency*. A status inconsistent individual is a person whose occupational, educational, and income attainments are incongruous. In a sense, this resembles social mobility, as in the case of an individual with high educational attainment who holds a lower-class job. Studies of status inconsistency and mental illness allow researchers to understand more thoroughly the relationship between mobility and illness by examining the particular effects of each component of class.

One early study of rates of first admissions to mental hospitals found rates to vary inversely with status integration; individuals with inconsistent statuses were more likely to require hospitalization.[100] However, not all types of status inconsistency cause stress leading to mental disorder. Schizophrenics, for instance, tend to have backgrounds with a particular type of status imbalance—their occupational level is lower than their years of education merit. This finding is substantiated by a number of studies.[101] In fact, the greater the magnitude of this type of inconsistency, the higher the rate of schizophrenia.[102]

The literature consistently notes that those with high education–low occupation inconsistencies are disproportionately diagnosed as schizophrenics. This discrepancy between the individual's educational and occupational attainment is consistent with the *social selection* explanation of the large number of schizophrenics who are members of the lower class. Their aspirations are linked to middle-class goals because of the achievement-oriented influence of their formal education, yet their psychological condition prevented them from functioning at occupational levels consistent with their training. The consequence is a drift into the lower class. However, it is also plausible that status inconsistency is a cause of schizophrenia as well as a consequence. In both instances, however, lower social class membership does not precede schizophrenia as *social stress* theory would predict.

It is important to note that only one type of status inconsistency—high education–low occupation—is associated with schizophrenia. The opposite type of inconsistency—low education–high occupation—is associated with a very different form of behavior. The first type of inconsistent individual may be prone to schizophrenia because of frustrations when investments (educational level) exceed rewards (occupational level). The second type of inconsistent individual may be more prone to anxiety disorder because of the guilt experienced when rewards (occupational level) exceed investments (educational level).

At this writing, the debate about the role of social class factors in the etiology of mental illness continues in many forms. There is the general question of the relative importance of social stress versus social drift.[103] There are more specific analyses and reanalyses of the general significance of social mobility as well as its direction. What are needed are well-controlled, longitudinal studies of large populations of mentally ill people compared to normal controls. The U.S. National Comorbidity Survey is a huge step in that very direction.[104] I predict that, when all the verbiage and studies are shifted, social mobility will show itself as a multi-faceted phenomenon with widely varying effects on different people.

CONCLUSIONS

Social class may be the single most powerful demographic predictor of becoming mentally ill. Epidemiological analyses of mental illness by class have revealed important relationships between social class and prevalence, type, and treatment of mental disorder. In general, rates of treated psychiatric cases are highest in the lower class while the working, middle, and upper classes are underrepresented in the psychiatric population. This finding is open to criticism because typically the rates are based on *known* psychiatric cases. This type of study may underreport mental disorders among higher social class individuals who have a greater ability to hide their problems. In addition, the types of illnesses that typically affect members of higher classes are not as likely to result in institutionalization since they are often less severe and visible.

It is well documented that higher social class people are more likely to experience mental disorders that are *internally oriented*, whereas lower-class people often suffer from more *externally oriented* disorders. This finding itself is sufficient cause to question whether the conclusions on rate of disorder by class are simply a reflection of the need to hospitalize disordered members of the lower class because their disturbances involve more overt, less controllable symptoms, whereas members of the higher classes display more covert, hidden symptoms.

There are three major explanations for the higher reported rates of mental illness among lower-class people. The *societal reaction* hypothesis holds that what is seen as a psychiatric disorder among lower-class people is actually their social class characteristics, which higher-class diagnosticians consider to be abnormal. The *social stress hypothesis* holds that lower-class people are more prone to become disordered because their lives are miserable and stressful. The *social selection hypothesis* considers the high rate of impairment in the lower class as the result of disordered people from higher classes drifting down the social class ladder. There is evidence that all three of these propositions are true to some extent but for different people.

Type of psychiatric treatment varies significantly among patients of different social classes. Patients of the upper and middle classes are more likely to receive psychotherapeutic care while their lower-class counterparts are generally treated organically or custodially. Much of this relationship can be explained by the fact that the types of illnesses prevalent among the various classes require different treatments. However, more refined investigations that hold type of illness constant have also found that patients of different classes often do not receive the same kind of therapy. This is because most psychotherapists come from the higher social classes and prefer to treat patients who are similar to them (*status homophily*). For this reason, fewer lower-class patients receive psychotherapy. In response to this problem, community mental health centers have worked to make psychotherapy a feasible alternative for the poor. So far, the results have not been very encouraging.

The literature on the relationship between mental disorder and social mobility is inconsistent. There are reports of no association between the two, of a positive relation between mental disorder and upward mobility, as well as a positive relation between psychopathology and downward mobility. The latter relationship is documented most frequently. It is also supported by studies showing that the high education–low occupation status inconsistent individual is particularly vulnerable to serious mental illness.

The research reported in this chapter should be evaluated in light of known social class differences in values and child-rearing practices. Children whose parents are favorably situated in the social class hierarchy are generally oriented toward inner needs. Lower-class children, on the other hand, are oriented toward external behavior. It is my belief that these differences in worldview and socialization patterns are at least *partly* responsible for the relationship between mental illness and social class.

9

Gender, Marital Status, and Family Relationships

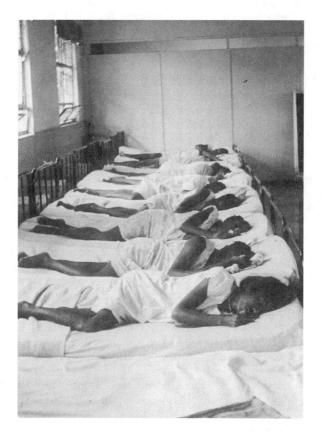

Around the world, depression is reported most frequently among women. These patients are recovering from electroconvulsive therapy at a hospital in the Caribbean in 1979. This is the ultimate treatment for severe depression. Although ECT is on the rise again in the United States, scenes like this are rare today.

GENDER DIFFERENCES

Structured inequality in the United States takes many forms.[1] This chapter examines some important relationships between inequality and mental illness, including differences by gender and marital status.[2] This is not to say that research findings in these areas is automatically caused by inequality, but oppression is considered to play a role by many sociologists. On a societal level, gender has become a huge issue. You do not have to look far for films centered about the special dimensions of women's lives both here in the United States[3] and around the world.[4] There are even special Web sites and research centers devoted exclusively to women's issues, including mental health.[5]

The question of gender and how it influences a host of life opportunities and experiences pervades many recent studies.[6] The topic is especially controversial in various fields of human behavior because noted differences in personality between men and women are haunted by the age-old "nature-nurture" dilemma.[7] The connection between gender and mental illness is especially delicate, although there is far from a paucity of research on the subject.

An early analysis by the Dohrenwends reported that studies of differences between male and female patterns of mental illness are inconclusive since 18 studies reported higher rates for females and 12 reported higher rates for males.[8] The difference did not seem large enough to establish a clear trend. However, a later tally by the same researchers demonstrates that rates of mental illness are highest for females; in 16 studies men show higher total rates of disorder, while in 27 studies women show higher rates.[9] This comes as no surprise since earlier research indicated that females expressed more distress than men in many areas of behavior, including phobias, constant worrying, concern over an impending "nervous breakdown," and a desire to seek help with a personal problem.[10]

Analyses of hospitalization records support the "greater illness among females" hypothesis. Female patients also outnumber males in private treatment. In fact, a greater proportion of females than males are said to be mentally ill, as indicated by first admissions to mental hospitals, psychiatric treatment in general hospitals, outpatient clinics, private outpatient treatment, and mental illness treated by general physicians.[11]

More relevant to estimates of *true* prevalence, community surveys of nonhospitalized populations find higher rates of psychiatric impairment among females. These surveys include both the Midtown Manhattan and Sterling County studies, as well as a number of other similar investigations.[12] Although studies of the prevalence of mental illness by gender examined by the Dohrenwends were conducted in North America and Europe, investigations of other cultural areas also find greater prevalence among females.[13] This is not to say that the relationship is a cross-cultural universal. Studies in Africa, for instance, report just the opposite; analyses of admissions to African psychiatric institutions unequivocally report higher rates for men than women. But here in the United States, estimates have been made that, for every male diagnosed as depressed, there are between two and six times as many women.[14]

Historical Changes

Women have not always had recognized higher rates of mental illness. In 1850, Edward Jarvis published a report on 250 hospitals in the United States and Europe.[15] He found that men were more prone to mental disorder than women, and he believed that this occurred because men experienced more stress than women did. Jarvis's find-

Table 9:1   Number of European and North American Studies Reporting Higher Rates of Psychiatric Disorder for Men or for Women According to Publication Prior to 1950 or in 1950 or Later

	Studies in which Rate Is Higher for (N)	
Date of Publication and Type of Psychopathology	*Males*	*Females*
Before 1950		
All types	7	2
Psychosis	3	3
Neurosis	1	2
Personality disorder	3	0
1950 or later		
All types	2	22
Psychosis	5	10
Neurosis	0	15
Personality disorder	11	3

Source: Bruce P. Dohrenwend and Barbara Snell Dohrenwend, "Sex differences and psychiatric disorders," *American Journal of Sociology, 81* (1976), 1449. By permission of University of Chicago, publisher.

ings do not stand alone; in a majority of prevalence studies published before 1950 (usually referred to as the "pre–World War II studies" because of the gap in publication between 1943 and 1950) the overall rates were higher for males. These findings contrast sharply with the post–World War II studies, which report higher rates among females. Table 9:1 summarizes the studies reporting rates of psychiatric disorder for men and women according to publication date. The differences are enormous.

The reported increase in rates of mental illness among women since World War II has been interpreted in a number of ways. One interpretation is that females have become increasingly ill since World War II because "women find their position in society to be more frustrating and less rewarding than do men and . . . this may be a relatively recent development."[16] In other words, there have been important changes in the female role during the post–World War II period, and these changes have created increased stress for women. Accordingly, more women than men now *actually* become mentally ill.

The Dohrenwends, on the other hand, do not believe that the dramatic reported increase in mental illness among women should be taken at face value. They argue that much of this change is due to differences in *methodology* between the two groups of studies and not to an actual increase in mental illness among females.[17] The studies published prior to 1950 relied on official records, particularly police files, to identify psychiatric cases. These types of records are most likely to record antisocial behavior, alcoholism, and drug addiction, the types of mental illness found more frequently among men. At the same time, those types of data sources are not likely to identify the more private "neurotic" problems that are disproportionately found among females. The later investigations use more inclusive data-collection techniques, such as interviews with community residents. These are more likely to uncover the anxiety disorders of women. Thus, the increase in rates of mental disorder among women may be the result of changes in methods for defining (and finding) a psychiatric case rather than the result of stress-inducing changes in the female role.

For a long time, the literature on gender differences and mental health consistently reported that women were more frequently disordered than men.[18] The situation may not be that simple.[19] An NIMH study concluded that the traditional impression that women have higher rates of mental disorder than men is erroneous. Past research often covered only selected disorders, such as depression and anxiety, which are more common among women. The NIMH study also included drug and alcohol abuse, as well as antisocial behavior, all of which are more common among men. Past research also reported that the emotional impact of undesirable life events is greater among women than among men, a presumed reflection of the larger vulnerability of the "weaker sex." Now there is evidence that the greater vulnerability of women to life stress is actually due to the fact that they are simply more involved in the lives of those around them.[20] A recent estimate of rates of mental illness among men and women indicates that much depends on the particular disorder in question. See Table 9:2 for the details. Taking all mental disorders together, some studies show that there really are no overall differences in men's and women's rates of disorder.[21]

Table 9:2   Lifetime and 12-Month Prevalence of DSM-III-R Disorders

Disorders	Male Lifetime %	Male 12 mo. %	Female Lifetime %	Female 12 mo. %	Total Lifetime %	Total 12 mo. %
Affective disorders						
Major depressive episode	12.7	7.7	21.3	12.9	17.1	10.3
Manic episode	1.6	1.4	1.7	1.3	1.6	1.3
Dysthymia	4.8	2.1	8.0	3.0	6.4	2.5
Any affective disorder	14.7	8.5	23.9	14.1	19.3	11.3
Anxiety disorders						
Panic disorder	2.0	1.3	5.0	3.2	3.5	2.3
Agoraphobia without panic disorder	3.5	1.7	7.0	3.8	5.3	2.8
Social phobia	11.1	6.6	15.5	9.1	13.3	7.9
Simple phobia	6.7	4.4	15.7	13.2	11.3	8.8
Generalized anxiety disorder	3.6	2.0	6.6	4.3	5.1	3.1
Any anxiety disorder	19.2	11.8	30.5	22.6	24.9	17.2
Substance use disorders						
Alcohol abuse without dependence	12.5	3.4	6.4	1.6	9.4	2.5
Alcohol dependence	20.1	10.7	8.2	3.7	14.1	7.2
Drug abuse without dependence	5.4	1.3	3.5	0.3	4.4	0.8
Drug dependence	9.2	3.8	5.9	1.9	7.5	2.8
Any substance abuse/dependence	35.4	16.1	17.9	6.6	26.6	11.3
Other disorders						
Antisocial personality	5.8		1.2		3.5	
Nonaffective psychosis	0.6	0.5	0.8	0.6	0.7	0.5
Any NCS disorder	48.7	27.7	47.3	31.2	48.0	29.5

Source: Lee N. Robins and Daniel A. Regier, eds., *Psychiatric Disorders in America: The Epidemiologic Catchment Area Study* (New York: Free Press, 1991).

Theories of Gender Differences in Prevalence

The controversy continues to rage over whether women are really more frequently impaired or whether this statistical finding is simply an artifact of biased techniques of data collection.[22] On one side are researchers who argue that there are *real* differences in levels of mental illness between the sexes.[23] They note that the high concentration of reported illness among females is consistent regardless of who is doing the selecting—"that is, women have higher rates when the patient is selecting, as with private outpatient care; when others in the community are selecting, as with most admissions to public mental hospitals; and when a disinterested researcher is selecting, as is the case in community surveys."[24] Researchers in favor of the idea that women truly do have higher rates of mental illness may favor biological explanations that separate males and females. There are reports that men and women differ in the specific ways in which they react to stress.[25] Cotton, for instance, found that women (married and single) have higher "tension levels."[26] If this is true, it may well be the result of lifestyles that are more frustrating than those of men rather than nature, per se.

On the other side, some contend that the higher reported rates of mental illness among women reflect the fact that it is more acceptable in American society for women to express their problems. Consequently, women are more likely than men to *admit* to feelings and behaviors that may lead to a psychiatric diagnosis.[27] Men in Western society are generally reluctant to admit to unpleasant feelings, whereas Western women enjoy much greater freedom in expressing their feelings and in seeking help in dealing with perceived emotional problems.[28] Not only are women more likely than men to show symptoms of distress, but they are also likely to be labeled mentally ill more often than men.[29]

Women are also more likely to play the role of "emotional monitor" for their families by going to help sources for family problems of which they are only a part. Thus, by seeking help for others, they can be mistakenly confused with the disturbed conditions of other people.[30] These sex differences are consequences of the socialization process. Males are socialized to ignore symptoms, while females are taught to be more sensitive to personal discomforts and to report their symptoms rather than overlook them.[31] Some women—in particular, housewives—also have fewer time constraints than do most men since they spend less time in the labor force. The bottom line is that nonworking women have more opportunity to bring their problems to the attention of a help source. In addition, the rates of mental illness among women may be artificially inflated due to the fact that women are more cooperative during health interviews and are better able to recall their symptoms than are men.[32] All of this weighs heavily on the side of nurture.

Another factor involved in reported gender differences in rates of mental illness is the heavy negative sanctions that men receive for abnormal behavior.[33] Studies utilizing case descriptions of disordered people have found that the male version of the case is rated as being more mentally ill than is the female version of the same case, regardless of whether the evaluators are men or women.[34] Since men suffer more stigmatization than women do, it is to be expected that they will admit to fewer psychological difficulties and therefore be underreported in epidemiological studies. The culturally defined male role tolerates less mentally ill behavior than does the female role. In addition, some research indicates that both males and females receive a more severe societal reaction when the deviant behavior is inconsistent with traditional gender norms.[35] If this all sounds very complicated, that is because it is.

Females recognize, admit, and seek help more frequently than males because they are traditionally granted greater emotional indulgence than men, who are expected to be more self-reliant.[36] For example, Table 9:3 shows that women generally seek treatment more often then men regardless of type of disorder. Males, particularly psychotic males, experience a prompter and more severe reaction from others than females do.[37] This runs counter to the labeling theory proposition that persons of low status and little power are most likely to be labeled deviant. If that were true, mentally ill females (in a sexist society such as the United States) would experience a more severe social reaction than their male counterparts. These sex-role biases are found not only among members of the general population, they are also common among clinicians who are said to have significantly lower standards of mental health for women.[38]

This double standard among clinicians appears in a number of studies which demonstrate that mentally ill males are hospitalized earlier than females and also spend more time in the hospital. Gender bias has also been leveled at the DSM-IV.[39] As sex roles continue to change, these prejudiced views of men and women should diminish, as will the reported relationship between sex and mental illness. In the future, males may be much less hesitant to admit to psychological problems if the current standards of masculinity are altered. In fact, one study indicates that the biases attached to sex roles began to wane significantly during the 1980s.[40]

Table 9:3   Treatment for Active One-Year Disorders in Persons with No Other Active Disorder (Household Sample)

| | Percent with Any Mental Health Care | | | | | |
| | Both Sexes | | Males | | Females | |
	N	%	N	%	N	%
None of these disorders	14,077	5	5,971	4	8,106	6
Any single disorder	4,385	13	1,836	10	2,549	16
Specific single disorders						
Somatization	22	67		—		—
Panic	38	47		—	30	50
Schizophrenia	49	40	21	29	28	50
Depression	300	36	68	29	232	37
Mania	17	34		—		—
Obsessive-compulsive	107	20	42	11	65	25
Phobia	1,291	12	378	18	913	21
Alcohol	520	10	439	9	81	14
Drugs	233	10	160	11	73	7
Cognitive deficit (mild or severe)	1,733	5	707	6	1,026	5
Antisocial personality	83	4	67	3		—

Source: Lee N. Robins, Ben Z. Locke, and Daniel A. Regier, "An Overview of Psychiatric Disorders in America," in Lee N. Robins and Daniel A. Regier, eds. *Psychiatric Disorders in America: The Epidemiologic Catchment Area Study* (New York: Free Press, 1991).

Gender Differences in Type of Mental Illness

Although it is difficult to determine whether the reported higher rates of mental illness among women reflect real differences in *true prevalence* by gender or nuances of gender roles that permit women to freely express emotional difficulties and require men to camouflage their problems, there is little doubt that the two sexes differ in the *type* of mental health impairments that they experience. One researcher states that:

> Females suffer more than males from internalizing disorders, including depression and anxiety, which turn problematic feelings inward against themselves. . . . More often than men, women live with fears in the form of phobias, panic attacks, and free-floating anxiety states. In contrast, males predominate in externalizing disorders, expressing problematic feelings in outward behavior. They more often have enduring personality traits that are aggressive and antisocial in character. Males also exceed females in substance abuse.[41]

The question of whether men and women have different rates of psychosis has not been fully resolved.[42] It is commonly believed that men are more susceptible to schizophrenia, while women have a higher prevalence of the mood disorders.[43] The Dohrenwends, however, reported that there is no clear sex differential among schizophrenics because half of the studies they investigated find schizophrenia to be more prevalent among men and the other half report it to occur more frequently among women.[44] This is also confirmed by a federal study of types of mental illness in all psychiatric facilities in the United States; approximately 22 percent of both male and female episodes are for schizophrenia.[45] However, contrary to earlier epidemiological data, other evidence points to significantly more men than women among schizophrenic patients diagnosed by restrictive criteria of DSM.[46] Reportedly there are also sex differences in the age of symptom onset and first hospitalization for schizophrenia; male schizophrenics are significantly younger than females at both onset and admission.[47] As noted in Chapter 4, males are more likely to develop the worst form of schizophrenia—Type II. In my psychiatric sociology class, I tell the students that the overall gender patterns of schizophrenia appear to be: (1) men develop it earlier than women; (2) men are more likely to suffer from Type II; (3) the overall rates are the same for both sexes.

Mood disorders reportedly affect women more often than men (18 of 24 studies reviewed by the Dohrenwends).[48] Kramer, using data from all U.S. psychiatric facilities, reported that depressive disorders make up 9.8 percent of the male psychiatric population and 21.1 percent of the female psychiatric population.[49] Studies in the late 1990s continue to report the same gender differences in mood disorders (higher rates among women, especially depression).[50] This is true for both the United States and Europe.[51]

Some believe that much of what is labeled "depression" includes both mood disorders and "middle-age depression" since the symptoms of the two disorders are quite similar. It is known that middle-age depression is more prevalent among females because menopause, a common correlate of the disorder among women, begins earlier in life than retirement, a typical trigger among men. Therefore, although women are *reported* to be overrepresented among depressives compared to men, this may partly be the result of clinicians diagnosing mood disorder when middle-age depression is in fact the proper diagnosis. Thus the higher female rates may result from researchers lumping the two disorders together into the same category.

There are some other facts about sex differences in depression. It is known that the diagnosis of mood disorder significantly increases the likelihood of suicide. This is particularly true of women; while male inpatients are five times more likely to commit suicide than the general population, female inpatients are ten times more likely to do so.[52] Additionally, women most vulnerable to depression are those who are not employed outside the home as well as those whose husbands are unemployed.[53]

Presently, the following conclusions can tentatively be drawn about the prevalence of type of psychosis by gender: schizophrenia is as common among men as it is among women, although there is some controversy about this; the mood disorders *appear* to be more common among women. Yet, while both sexes may be equally susceptible to schizophrenia, there are vast differences in the clinical symptoms of male and female schizophrenics. Male schizophrenics often adopt a "feminine" pattern of passivity, withdrawal, and submissiveness. Female schizophrenics, on the other hand, often adopt "masculine" patterns of aggression and hyperactivity. It is as if schizophrenia forces the person into behavior traditionally "appropriate" for the opposite gender. A survey of 30 psychiatrists (men and women) lends strong support to this "sex-role exchange" hypothesis among schizophrenics. The group of psychiatrists was in strong agreement that schizophrenic males are typically:

> Better organized; more distant; better to deal with in a room; quieter, cleaner, more controlled; more constrained; more organized socially; better behaved; they exhibited more camaraderie; were more amenable to commands, requests and instructions; were less exhibitionistic; less hysterical; showed less acting out; were less sick; there was less walking about, less screaming and crying; they were less hostile, more polite; clump in groups more; were less demanding, more cooperative, and better as a unit.[54]

The schizophrenic females were described by the same psychiatrists as:

> More explosive; violent; displaying more homosexual and more general acting out; being more hysterical; more exhibitionistic; exhibiting more physical activity and showing more overt hostility; more noisy and pesty; . . . more pent up; displaying more sexual material; more tearing of clothes; more disturbed; exhibiting more florid and interesting pathology; being more frenetic and volatile; more seductive; more agitated; more bizarre; more manipulative; more badgering; want to talk more; less conventional in approaching the doctor; grab your hand more; more clinging and dependent; there was more disrobing; they were less inhibited; "crazier," more psychotic, sillier, more expressive; had no group spirit; want more attention; were more outgoing and more imploring; displayed wider extremes of behavior; look more dilapidated, unkempt, and neglect themselves more.[55]

The prevalence of anxiety disorder by gender follows a clear pattern: women are reported to be more prone to these problems than are men. In fact, in 28 of 32 studies reviewed by the Dohrenwends, rates of neurosis were higher for females regardless of time (pre–World War II or post–World War II) or place (rural and urban settings in North America and Europe).[56] The overrepresentation of females in the neurotic population is particularly marked in the 30- to 50-year-old age group.[57] Because women are more susceptible to anxiety attacks, they are also more likely than men to develop psychophysiological disorders (psychological factors affecting a person's physical condition) in which anxiety is displaced onto a body organ mediated by the autonomic nervous system.[58] The vulnerability of women to anxiety disorders is especially prominent among women who are not employed outside of the home and among those with a poor marital relationship.[59] Both of these patterns are a logical fit.

The rates of personality disorders are reportedly higher for men than women. The Dohrenwends found this to be true in 22 of 26 studies conducted throughout the twentieth century in both North America and Europe.[60] This is particularly true of the antisocial personality, which has been the subject of most epidemiological research on personality disorders. In fact, many studies use the antisocial personality diagnosis interchangeably with the term *personality disorder.*

Overall, the DSM reports that men are more often aggressive or antisocial in a wide range of areas, beginning at an early age. What is *one* general conclusion to be drawn about patterns of gender and mental illness? Rosenfield states: "In summary, the evidence supports claims that males and females have different disorders because they encounter different social experiences *and* because they have different kinds of reactions to circumstances."[61] That is clearly an important part of the picture.

Age Differences in Gender Patterns

The prevalence of mental illness by gender is also related to age. All of the findings presented here refer to males and females beyond adolescence. Younger age groups, however, exhibit different patterns of mental illness by gender. Preadolescent males have higher rates of mental illness than do preadolescent females.[62] This is the result of a number of stress-producing problems that confront young boys. One of the problems is that the intellectual and physical development of boys is slower than that of girls, yet they are expected to achieve as much as girls.[63]

Another problem is that boys are more impulsive and aggressive than girls and have a lower frustration threshold, which involves them in quarrels.[64] This in turn generates anxiety through conflicts with parents and teachers. Another stress-producing factor is the stringent sex-role expectations placed on boys. Young boys are expected to act only in masculine ways, whereas girls are usually allowed to pursue masculine activities. Perhaps this is clearest in the different social reactions tomboys and sissies receive: the female tomboy is "amusing," but the boy who is a sissy is shunned.

At adolescence the situation of the sexes changes dramatically. During this period the girl experiences greater stress because suddenly she is expected to adopt the traditional feminine role and to drop any masculine traits she may have. Gove and Herb state: "It is clear that girls who once sought and were rewarded for academic success find, in adolescence, that they should not surpass men and they come to fear success and to feel anxious over competitive behavior."[65] However, evidence indicates that adolescent sex roles have changed somewhat since the 1980s in that at least one study reports that the sex ratio of mental disorder during adolescence has become equal.[66] Table 9:4 demonstrates how gender and mental illness interact with age and other demographic variables. What the table does not show are some very specific things about age, gender, and abnormal behavior. White men over 65, for example, are most prone to suicide.

MARITAL STATUS

We can conclude that marital status and parental status are associated with mental health. However, we must qualify any general conclusions about the degree and direction of those associations. Most importantly, the degree of benefit conferred by marriage is greatly dependent on the group (e.g., divorced, widowed, never-married, and remarried) against which the married are compared. Many studies demonstrate that the married

Table 9:4 Characteristics of Men and Women with Psychiatric Disorder

Characteristics	Male	Female	Total
Sex	177	275	452
Age			
<45	67	95	162
45+	110	180	290
Marital status			
Married	117	191	308
Not married	60	84	144
Employment status			
Employed	116	99	215
Not employed	61	176	237
Social status			
Higher	29	31	60
Lower	148	244	392
Educational level			
Higher	37	52	89
Lower	140	223	363
Area of residence			
Semiurban	46	93	139
Rural	131	182	313
Physical illness			
Physically ill	47	105	152
Not physically ill	130	170	300

Source: Lee N. Robins and Daniel A. Regier, eds., *Psychiatric Disorders in America: The Epidemiologic Catchment Area Study* (New York: Free Press, 1991).

exhibit lower levels of depression and psychological distress than the unmarried; this difference is greatest when the married are compared with the divorced or widowed.[67]

Marital status is associated with the likelihood of becoming mentally ill as well as the chances of recovering from it.[68] Single persons have a greater prevalence of mental illness than married persons, and they also have a poor prognosis in comparison with married patients.[69] Gove, reviewing 14 studies of the rate of mental illness by marital status, reported that the rates of single persons are higher than those of married persons in the majority of the studies.[70] Both community surveys and analyses of patient records show a higher rate of mental disorder among single, widowed, separated, and divorced persons than among the married population.

There is also a relationship between length of stay in a mental hospital and marital status: single persons have longer stays than those who are married.[71] Because of these associations, some consider marital status to be the best single demographic predictor of the chances of becoming mentally ill and recovering from it. Personally, I believe social class is the best predictor.

Theories of Differences between Married and Single People

Marital status may be a better predictor of mental illness for males than females due to the nature of the behaviors typically required of a man who marries. Gender roles may dictate that he show initiative, independence, and aggressiveness in courtship. These qualities are inconsistent with the development of many types of disorders, particularly schizophrenia. The schizoid female, on the other hand, may be passive and aloof, but to the untrained eye, her qualities are consistent with the dependency often expected of females during courtship. All of this, of course, is clearly sexist, but, nonetheless, that does not diminish its impact on the everyday lives of many people. Consequently, more mentally disordered males than females are likely to be recognized as mentally ill before they even get close to marrying.

One theory of the relationship between marital status and mental illness holds that the association is the result of a *social selection process* that prevents the mentally ill from marrying because they are not perceived as good mates, particularly the males.[72] From this perspective, mental illness precedes, and thereby influences, marital status; that is, those who are mentally ill are not likely to marry.[73]

There is another view in which the temporal sequence is reversed; marital status precedes mental illness. Proponents of this theory believe that marriage is a mental health haven that offers interpersonal security not available to single people.[74] Studies indicate that married persons are better adjusted and less depressed than single persons. Some interpret this as the result of more economic hardships and social isolation among single people.[75] Whatever the interpretation, marriage appears to be associated with a number of positive things, including greater happiness, less stress, lower rates of suicide, and diminished rates of mental illness overall.

Theories of Differences between Married Men and Women

Earlier I stated that female rates of mental illness are higher than male rates. This is quite apparent among married people, especially married men.[76] Married women have higher rates than married men, but single women have lower rates than their male counterparts.[77] These data shed suspicion on the hypothesis that the high rates of psychiatric impairment among females result from a greater willingness of women to *admit* to problems. If this hypothesis were true, then the prevalence of mental illness should be equivalent among females in different marital categories, but it is not. Thus, the difference in rates of mental illness between the sexes is importantly affected by marital status. Some see the high risk of mental illness among married women as a means of escaping the constraints of the housewife role.[78]

Why is it that married women are more prone to mental illness than their husbands?[79] One reason, stated earlier, is that the mentally disordered female, particularly the schizoid type, may not be recognized as ill during courtship. It is not until she becomes more severely disordered that others recognize an actual illness. Often this is well after the wedding.[80]

On the other hand, some researchers believe that married women are more likely to be mentally ill than their husbands, not because women are disordered before they marry but because women find marriage more difficult than men. Gove lists a number of factors about the female role in marriage that may be responsible for the unusually high rates of mental illness among married women. One factor is that the married woman's role has fewer sources of gratification than does the married man's role. The woman often has only her family to provide satisfaction, whereas the man has his family and his work. A second factor is that a common instrumental role of married women, keeping house, is frustrating. It requires little skill and offers little prestige but must be constantly performed. This, of course, has less relevance today as more women are entering the work force.

Gore also mentions a third factor—the lack of structure and visibility of the housewife role. This allows her to put things off and brood over her troubles in contrast to the jobholder, who must meet structured demands that draw his attention from his problems. Also, because the housewife role is only vaguely defined, the woman becomes responsible for "everything" that must be done in the house, while the husband has only a limited set of household duties. Thus, the wife may experience considerable anxiety concerning whether she has done "everything." Fourth, even the married woman with a job is less satisfied than the married male because she faces occupational discrimination in the form of low pay and underemployment. In addition, she puts in more hours than her husband because she must still perform household chores as well as job duties. The greater *total* number of work hours (home and job) per day places working wives under greater strain than their husbands.[81] A final factor involved in psychopathology among married women is that their lives may become less meaningful when their children grow up and move out of the home. At this time, the middle-aged housewife is no longer needed to nurture her children, a responsibility that was a meaningful source of gratification. Once again, this has less relevance to women with careers.

Although some feel that the happiest women are married and working, the impact of a wife's employment on her own and her husband's depression depends on whether it is consistent with their preferences. For instance, unemployed wives who want to work have high rates of depression, as do husbands who are opposed to their employed wives working. The various patterns of marital preference and depression are depicted in Figure 9:1. Depression can affect a marriage in a number of ways, including ruining it altogether, regardless of whether the wife or the husband is depressed.[82] Much has been written about stress and coping strategies in spouses of depressed patients and, for that matter, handicapped patients in general.[83] But theoretical writings and actual rehabilitation are often worlds apart.

Among married women, the highest rate of mental disorder occurs among lower-class females, especially those with little education.[84] This occurs for a number of reasons. First, the lower-class woman is more likely than the middle-class woman to fill only one aspect of the housewife role, that of mother.[85] Yet, while motherhood is more central to the lower-class housewife, she is less likely to feel gratified by being a parent than is the middle-class housewife because she is prone to view her children as persons to be controlled rather than developed.[86] In addition, the lower-class housewife may also be frustrated by her husband, who, compared to the middle-class husband, helps less with household duties and care of the children and is more likely to desert his wife in the first place.

Presently, the greater prevalence of mental disorder among married women compared to married men seems to be largely due to the high concentration of mental illness among lower-class women with less than a high school degree. Among women who are at least high school graduates, the differences between married and

Figure 9:1 Marriage patterns and depression.

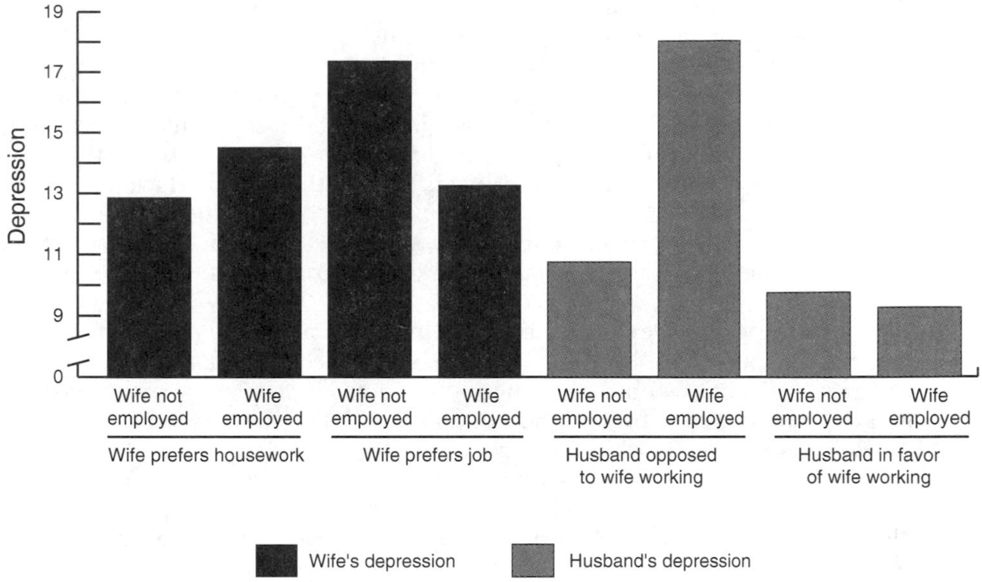

Source: Catherine E. Ross, John Mirowsky, and Joan Huber, "Dividing work, sharing work, and in-between: Marriage patterns and depression," *American Sociological Review, 48* (1983), 817. By permission of the publisher.

never married are much smaller.[87] In addition, the differences between unmarried men and women disappear after the male retires.[88] At retirement the male's social network shrinks, and his status becomes comparable to his wife's—limited and isolated. This fits with reports of depression and other mental health problems among older couples.[89] And, once again, many of the statements made about depression among married women are not likely to apply to those with meaningful jobs.

Theories of Differences between Single Men and Women

There are also differences in rates of mental illness between unmarried men and women, but, contrary to popular opinion, unmarried men are more frequently disordered than unmarried women. The stereotypes of the carefree bachelor and the rejected spinster are not reflected in the mental health statistics. Of 15 studies of the rates of mental disorder among men and women who have never married, 4 studies found single women to have higher rates and 11 found single men to have higher rates.[90] Why is it that single men are more impaired than single women? One possible reason involves the man's dominant role in courtship. If a man fails to get married he is more likely than the single woman to feel that it is his own fault. If it is true that most women want to get married, then it is likely, as Srole suggests, that the man who is rejected may well suffer from the handicap of physical or personality defects.[91] Thus it is the inadequate man who may be left over after the pairing has taken place. That is one theory.

A second possible reason for the higher rates of mental illness among single males is that they are more introverted and socially isolated than are single women who have closer interpersonal ties. One team of researchers studying this issue reports that "being unmarried creates 'expressive hardships' for a man at least as important as a single woman's economic hardships. Men's lesser ability to form and maintain personal relationships creates a need for a wife, as the expressive expert, to perform this function for them, just as the wife needs a husband, the economic expert, to function for her in the economic sphere."[92] Single women may be happier than bachelors because they are better able to form attachments with others and avoid the anguish of social isolation. While this may sound very sexist to some, it does not necessarily make it untrue, especially for older generations. Age aside, a number of recent studies indicate that women have larger social networks and both give and receive more support than men.[93]

A third possible reason for mental illness among single males may involve early childhood experiences. Knupfer and others collected information on the childhoods of a group of single men and women; they found that a larger proportion of single men experienced stressful childhood situations.[94] They also found that single women had more favorable childhood environments than married men and women. Perhaps there is some truth to the old saying that "Happy marriages produce old maid daughters." The Knupfer group believes that their findings "lend support to the idea that men who remain single are more apt to do so because they are handicapped to begin with, whereas single women do not give evidence of being handicapped in these ways."[95] In today's world, much of these speculations tread on thin sexist ice.

The Once-Married

The residence patterns in mental hospitals correspond to the sex differences between marrieds and singles discussed earlier; there are more married women than married men and more single men than single women. However, in addition to married persons and never-married persons, there is another marital grouping to consider —the once-married.[96] At the turn of the century Durkheim noted that severing the marital tie is particularly dangerous to mental health, as indicated by a high suicide rate among widowed and divorced persons. Since that time, almost all of the studies comparing the mental illness rates of widowed and divorced males and females with the rates of married males and females found higher rates of mental illness among the divorced and widowed.[97] That much is certain. What is not known is how much of the problem results from mental illness *causing* divorce.[98]

The rates of the widowed are slightly lower than the rates of the never-married, but the rates of the divorced are higher than most other marital status groups. Mental illness is particularly high among divorced men; they have higher rates than divorced women. The only other marital status group with more psychiatric impairment than the divorced are the separated—those en route to divorce.[99] Research also indicates that separated women are more likely to be mentally ill than separated men.[100] Because impairment is greater among those closest to the disruption of a marriage (the separated as opposed to the divorced), we can conclude that there is something about the marital breakup itself that causes stress and high rates of mental illness, rather than that unstable people had been involved in the marriage. Otherwise, the divorced and separated rates would be the same. Table 9:5 presents many of the interconnections between marital status and mental disorder.

Table 9:5 Marital Status of Those with Active Mental Disorders

	Number with Active Disorder	Currently Divorced/ Separated (%)	Single (%)	Widowed (%)	Married (%)	Divorced/ Separated of Those Ever Married (%)
Schizophrenia	229	26	36	5	33	41
Depressive episode	812	22	26	8	44	30
Panic	196	22	22	6	51	28
Somatization	64	21	25	26	28	28
Generalized anxiety	359	20	25	5	49	27
Manic episode	112	20	37	5	39	31
Alcohol abuse/dependence	1,018	18	39	3	40	30
Antisocial personality	295	18	35	2	44	28
Phobia	2,118	16	22	7	55	21
Obsessive compulsive	385	16	25	7	52	21
Drug abuse/dependence	602	14	61	1	24	36
Cognitive impairment						
Mild or severe	2,039	12	16	27	45	14
Severe	421	12	23	37	28	16
None of the diagnoses	5,777	8	23	8	61	10

Source: Lee N. Robins, Ben Z. Locke, and Daniel A. Regier, "An overview of psychiatric disorders in America," in L. N. Robins and Daniel A. Regier, eds., *Psychiatric Disorders in America: The Epidemiologic Catchment Area Study* (New York: Free Press, 1991).

Marriage and Mental Illness: Some New Findings

Although the relationship between marriage and positive mental health is one of the most established findings in the literature on psychiatric sociology, it is also one of the most complicated.[101] Consider this short list of recent findings.

1. It is people's *beliefs* about the permanence and durability of marriage that impact mental health.[102]
2. The mental health benefits of marriage are still significantly greater for men than for women.[103]
3. The *quality* of a marriage impacts mental health, not marriage, per se.[104]
4. Married men are more likely to have positive mental health *if* they perceive their marital partners to be meeting their interactional, emotional, and sexual needs.[105]
5. Alternatives to marriage, particularly *cohabitation,* provide mental health benefits that are very similar to those provided by marriage.[106]

FAMILY RELATIONSHIPS

Family Size

There is much controversy in the scientific community regarding whether a large or small family is more conducive to mental health.[107] Some argue that the material and emotional needs of the child are met better in a small family in which the child receives considerable parental attention. Others argue that the child in a large family has more opportunity to develop social skills through interaction with brothers and sisters. A minority opinion holds that there is no significant relationship between family size and mental health.[108]

There is some evidence that a person's mental health is threatened as a member of a large sibship (five or more siblings). This was first argued in the early 1900s, when Pearson noted an increased prevalence of "insanity" and criminality in unduly large families.[109] The hypothesized relationship between large family size and mental illness may not be the simple result of the *amount* of attention children in large families receive from their parents. It may be that the *quality* of interaction between parents and children in large families is undesirable, since at least one team of researchers reported that the mental health of mothers and fathers declines as family size increases.[110] However, it is not clear whether the mental health status of the parents led them to have an excessively large family, or whether the strains of raising a large number of children caused the parents to become disturbed. One study refutes the "large family" idea; it found that children from larger families exhibit a lower prevalence of mental disorders than children from smaller families, a presumed reflection of the greater availability of social support in big families.[111]

The relationship between social class and sibship size is marked and highly significant; lower-class families have larger sibships than families from higher social classes. Therefore, any interpretation of the observed relationship between sibship size and mental illness must take into account the close relationship between social class and mental illness, which was discussed in Chapter 8. Studies indicate that anxiety disorders usually occur among people from sibships of five or less,[112] and it is anxiety disorders rather than psychosis that are most common among those from higher social classes.

Much of the research on sibship size and mental illness has concentrated on the mental health status of the only child. Popular opinion has it that this child is most likely to be "spoiled" by parents and thus develop a pathological sense of insecurity and dependency. Despite evidence that the child in a two-child family is more likely to be spoiled than is the only child,[113] the stereotype of the only child persists. The major difficulty in assessing the validity of this stereotype is a lack of objective data.

The methodologies of some studies are suspect because they combine only children with firstborns into the same category so that it is impossible to determine which accounts for any results. Furthermore, it is not psychologically valid to couple the two groups. Indeed, Reiss and Safer found only children to have a significantly higher rate of anxiety, depression, and sexual disorder than a comparable group of firstborns.[114] Other studies define the only child in peculiar ways; one study considers a child "only" if raised to the age of 5 as a single child in an adult household without living siblings or the immediate prospect of a sibling.[115]

Despite the lack of objective data, controversy over the mental health status of the only child continues to rage. On the one hand, some professionals believe unequivocally that being an only child is a disease in itself. In support of this is a study comparing normal and psychiatrically disturbed soldiers which found that the only child was more frequently a member of the disturbed group.[116] Of course, it is possible that the temperament of only children is not suited to army life. If this is true, the disturbance may be caused as much by army life as it is by being an only child.

Other studies of the only child report that they are more apt to be referred for psychiatric help,[117] and to return for help more frequently than are children with siblings.[118] However these "findings" are also open to question, since it is likely that only children require psychiatric help so frequently because their overprotective parents rush them to help sources at the slightest sign of a problem.[119] Certainly there is a linkage between maternal overprotection and submissiveness in the case of only children. But it is far from clear whether such overprotection fosters children who truly need psychiatric care, or whether the overprotective attitude leads only children into treatment channels where they become registered as "cases" more frequently.

It is also possible that being an only child affects mental health in a positive way, as much evidence in everyday life suggests. Some have documented the fact that eminent scientists, scholars, and other great achievers tend to be only children.[120] In the early twentieth century, Stuart gave mental hygiene tests to random samples of only children and children with siblings and concluded that only children are not more prone to mental illness and that in fact they are more generous, more gregarious, independent, and responsible.[121] Ingham found no excess of only children among neurotic university students compared with a matched control group.[122] Glueck and Glueck, comparing 500 delinquent boys and an equal number of matched controls, discovered that delinquents were less likely to be only children than controls .[123] Some of these studies are old and need to be replicated today.

Obviously, research on the only child is highly polarized. Neither position has convincing evidence, creating the impression that the personal biases of the investigators color their findings since many researchers wholeheartedly support one or the other extreme. The debate still continues, and it probably will for a long time. Box 9:1 details some of the central "questions" of the only child.

Birth Order

So much has been written about birth order and personality traits that it could fill a small library. Some contend that the firstborn is the "most favored birth position."[124] Then there are researchers who report that "middle-born" siblings are most likely to be psychiatric patients.[125] There are also reports of inconclusive findings.[126] Frankly, it seems like *everything* has been reported or rejected. Following is a sampling of the literature on birth order and psychological traits. Much of it is speculative.

Barry and Barry uncovered a "double-branched relationship" among birth order, sibship size, and schizophrenia.[127] They note that stress is greatest for late-born members of large sibships who may be subject to parental rejection or neglect. This in turn can lead to the "shut-in" personality, which incubates full-blown schizophrenia. Other studies of schizophrenic patients also indicate an increasing trend toward later birth order with sibship size.[128] Schooler examined religion as a variable that may affect the relationship between birth order and schizophrenia. He found a last-born effect to be more pronounced for Catholic and Jewish patients compared to Protestant patients.[129] Other evidence suggests that the paranoid and catatonic forms of schizophrenia are most common among last-born children.[130]

Studies of the birth order of patients suffering from severe depression are few and contradictory. Grosz observed that, in sibships of three, those from the first two

••••••••••••••••••••••••••••••••••••' **Box 9:1** •••••••••••••••••••••••••••••• ••
The Question of the Only Child

Child-rearing experts may have neglected the psychology of sibling ties, but they have never been hesitant to warn parents about the perils of siring an only child. Children unlucky enough to grow up without brothers or sisters, the professional wisdom held, were bound to be self-centered, unhappy, anxious, demanding, pampered and generally maladjusted to the larger social world. "Being an only child is a disease in itself," psychologist G. Stanley Hall concluded at the turn of the century.

Recent research paints a kinder picture of the only child—a welcome revision at a time when single-child families are increasing. The absence of siblings, psychologists find, does not doom a child to a life of neurosis or social handicap. Day care, preschool, and other modern child-care solutions go far in combating an only child's isolation and in mitigating the willfulness and self-absorption that might come from being the sole focus of parental attention. And while only children may miss out on some positive aspects of growing up around brothers and sisters, they also escape potentially negative experiences, such as unequal parenting or severe aggression by an older sibling. Says University of Texas at Austin social psychologist Toni Falbo, "The view of only children as selfish and lonely is a gross exaggeration of reality."

Indeed, Falbo goes so far as to argue that only children are often better off—at least in some respects—than those with brothers and sisters. Reviewing over 200 studies conducted since 1925, she and colleague Denise Poli conclude that only children equal firstborns in intelligence and achievement, and score higher than both firstborns and later-borns with siblings on measures of maturity and leadership. Other researchers dispute these findings, however. Comparing only children with firstborns over their life span, for example, University of California at Berkeley psychologist B. G. Rosenberg found that only children—particularly female—scored lower on intelligence tests than did firstborns with a sibling.

Rosenberg distinguishes between three types of only children. "Normal, well-adjusted" onlies, he says, are assertive, poised and gregarious. "Impulsive, acting-out" only children adhere more to the old stereotype, their scores on personality tests indicating they are thin-skinned, self-indulgent, and self-dramatizing. The third group resembles the firstborn children of larger families, scoring as dependable, productive and fastidious.

Perhaps the only real disadvantage to being an only child comes not in childhood but much later in life. Faced with the emotional and financial burdens of caring for aging parents, those without siblings have no one to help out. But as Falbo points out, even in large families such burdens are rarely distributed equally.

_____

Source: Erica E. Goode, "Only children: Cracking the myth of the lonely, pampered misfit, " *U.S. News & World Report, 116* (1) (1994), 50.

•••

birth ranks are most vulnerable to a depressive breakdown.[131] Birtchnell's investigation, however, failed to replicate Grosz's findings, leaving the question of the relationship between birth order and depression unanswered.[132] But Grosz's hypothesis concerning three-person sibships may have revealed an important linkage since there is some evidence that the personalities of first-, second-, and third-born children manifest specific sets of characteristics.[133] Further, children in higher birth ranks may repeat these character types, fourth-borns resembling firstborns, fifths resembling seconds, and sixths resembling thirds. Indeed, Reiss and Safer, investigating the effect of birth order in a large outpatient population, found significant differences in diagnostic type among first-, second-, and third-born children.[134] They also found that the first- and fourth-born children tended to receive similar diagnoses, as did second- and fifth- and third- and sixth-borns. Remember, these reports are relatively sketchy and require further replication.

Some social psychologists have focused on personality differences between first-borns (including only children) and later-borns. Schachter first discovered a relationship between birth order and affiliative response in an anxiety-provoking situation.[135] Firstborns become more anxious than later-borns when exposed to an anxiety-arousing experience, such as being led to believe that they are about to participate in a physically painful experiment. In that kind of threatening situation, firstborns show more symptoms of psychological distress when they are not in the company of others. Later-borns, on the other hand, show more symptoms of distress when they are forced into social interaction.

Conditions of social isolation seem to be particularly threatening to firstborns, who have stronger dependency needs, than later-borns, who prefer socially isolated situations, presumably a manifestation of their self-reliance. You should note that these characterizations of firstborns and later-borns are not derived only from Schachter's experiment. A number of researchers, including the Dohrenwends, have found firstborns to be socially dependent and later-borns to be more isolated.[136] This holds true not only in an experimental setting but in outside situations as well. The 1965 power failure in New York City provided an opportunity to test the experimentally derived notions of the relationship among birth order, anxiety, and affiliation. Firstborns stranded alone (on elevators and in other situations) in the blackout were more anxious and more affiliative than were their later-born counterparts.[137] This relationship was stronger for firstborn women than for firstborn men. When the elevator doors finally opened, the firstborns stranded alone exited like a stampeding herd of one cattle.

Considering all of the studies on birth order and psychopathology, is there any evidence that a consistent relationship exists between the two? Some feel that the research is so contradictory that it is time to call a moratorium on the topic. It is true that many of the investigations are inconclusive, but this is not true of the studies that simultaneously consider sibship size *and* birth order. A number of these studies have found a concentration of youngest children from large sibships in patient populations. This is particularly true for schizophrenia. In addition, studies involving large samples of people in treatment have uncovered an overrepresentation of eldest children from small families. This is particularly true for anxiety disorders.

Hare and Price examined the family size and birth order of more than 10,000 patients attending the Bethlehem and Maudsley hospitals in England from 1958 to 1966.[138] In sibships of two and three, there was an excess of firstborn patients over last-born. In sibships of five or more, there was an excess of last-born patients over first-born. It appears that *the firstborn in a small family and the last-born in a large family are particularly vulnerable to mental disorder.* However, one should be cautious here as this is only a *tendency* over a large number of people and certainly not a universal. Evidence also indicates that the spacing between siblings may affect mental health. Schubert and others report a significantly higher percentage of psychiatrically abnormal adolescents having a sibling less than two years older compared to those with greater spacing between themselves and their siblings.[139] The authors suggest that this phenomenon may be connected to "unwantedness by parents," associated with unplanned pregnancies.

It seems like every feasible connection between birth order and mental illness has been investigated. There have even been studies of whether the connections vary cross-culturally.[140] The studies which report that birth order has no *direct* effect suggest that what really determines whether a child has a mental health problem is the parents' *belief* that their child needs help.[141]

The Adopted Child

The effects of adoption on the emotional and behavioral adjustment of children have been an issue in psychiatric research for many years. In a nutshell, studies have shown that adopted children are overrepresented in mental health settings.[142] One problem with research on adoptees is ascertaining what is cause and what is effect. Does adoption, per se, have a disturbing effect on personality development, or are children of mentally ill people more likely to be adopted away?[143] Both types of causal relationships seem possible but, of course, for *different* children.

There is considerable evidence that the adopted child is especially vulnerable to mental disorder as measured by treatment rates.[144] Indeed, Schecter claimed that adopted children are 100 times more likely to receive psychiatric care than would be expected on the basis of their numbers alone.[145] Although Schecter's study has been criticized for its methodological design,[146] his dismal view was supported by Toussieng, who also reported very high treatment rates for adoptees at a psychiatric treatment center.[147] In addition, children who were registered for adoption ran a greater risk than their classmates of developing mental disorder, regardless of whether they were growing up in an adoptive home, a foster home, or with their biological mother.[148]

Among adoptees, there is a high frequency of personality disorders, particularly the antisocial type.[149] A number of factors can account for this. Antisocial tendencies can result from neglectful parenting, which produces a deficient superego in the absence of adequate role models. In the case of the adoptee, this may happen when the child is adopted by parents who raise him incorrectly because they adopted for the wrong reasons in the first place.

Another reason for the high rate of psychiatric impairment among adoptees is the fact that many of these children are institutionalized (in an orphanage or a group foster home) for a period of time before they are adopted. During that time, they lack the intensive one-to-one relationship between infant and caretaker that is required for normal personality formation. Instead, they are shifted from one institution to another and are deprived of the opportunity for normal parenting. For this reason, the risk of impairment increases as the time span between birth and adoption lengthens. In the case of adoption closely following birth, the child is more likely to be mentally healthy, provided she is adopted by stable parents.

On the other hand, adoption can be particularly risky if the infant has already established a relationship with an individual who has been specifically identified as the nurturing figure. Such is the case when a child loses the parents through death after knowing them for years. The transition to another nurturing figure is an unsettling experience that can engender a psychiatric disturbance. If, however, there is a similarity between the original nurturing figure and the replacement, the experience may not be problematic at all. For this reason, adoption by a relative carries less risk for mental illness than adoption by a stranger.[150]

Socioeconomic factors also play a role in the high rate of reported disturbance among adoptees. Generally, adoptive families are from relatively high socioeconomic groups, and it is these groups that can afford private psychiatric and counseling services. Therefore adoptees may be more likely to become patients partly because their relatively wealthy parents bring them to treatment centers with little hesitation.

Another factor involved in the mental health of the adopted child has been emphasized by the adoptees themselves. Reflecting on their upbringing, some adoptees feel that their emotional difficulties stem from the void created by their lack of a personal history.[151] They use such words as "conspiracy" and "underground" to describe the emotional dishonesty they were subjected to as children. These feelings may be created by adoptive parents who either repeatedly tell the child not to ask about the natural parents or lie to the child about them. Since the 1980s there has been a trend making it increasingly possible for adolescents to locate their biological parents. This has led some therapists to consider the involvement of the biological parent in the treatment of disturbed adoptees.[152]

The whole issue of adoption can be a very complicated phenomenon. Should the child know about his biological parents? Do agencies have a right to withhold information about the child's background? In 2000, this issue reached a head when the adoptive parents of a confessed killer sued Los Angeles County, saying that they never would have gone through with the adoption if they had known that their son's birth mother was diagnosed as a chronic schizophrenic. They claimed that the county and several adoption department workers engaged in "despicable conduct," fraud, and breach of contract in the 1980 adoption.

CONCLUSIONS

While social class may be the sociodemographic factor most strongly related to mental illness, it is certainly not the only one. Being male or female is another factor. And a host of family variables also connect with mental illness (and mental health). There is more mental illness reported among females than males, although this may be changing. Females are either under greater stress or they are more likely to admit to emotional problems than are men, who are stigmatized for appearing weak and in need of help. Schizophrenia is reported to be equally common among men and women. Severe depression is held to be more common among females, who are especially vulnerable to depression during middle age. Anxiety disorders are reported to be more common among women. Personality disorders, particularly the antisocial type, are found more frequently among males.

Married persons have lower reported rates of disorder than do nonmarried persons. Within marital categories, there are important differences by sex. Married women are known to be more disordered than married men, either because women prone to mental illness are not as visible before marriage as are disordered men or because women find marriage more difficult than men due to the particular strains placed on those in the housewife role. Single females are reported to be less disordered than single males. This is generally taken to indicate that women are better able to form attachments with others and thus avoid the anguish of social isolation through larger social networks.

The question of the mental health status of the only child has not been resolved. It is true that only children have higher treatment rates than do children with siblings, but these rates may result from overprotective parents who rush their child to treatment centers more spontaneously than do parents of larger families. Birth order must be considered together with family size. Combining the two, a few patterns stand out: a concentration of schizophrenia among those born late in a large sibship and a concentration of anxiety disorders among those born early in a small sibship.

Adopted children have an unusually high rate of mental illness, particularly the antisocial personality disorder. This may stem from a number of forms of improper parenting. In some cases the child was adopted for the wrong reasons and functions as an outlet for the adoptive parents' needs. Other children become disordered because they were adopted after having formed a relationship with a nurturing figure from whom they were suddenly separated. It is also feasible that mental disorder among adoptees stems from a lack of personal history and identity. Additionally, adoptees may be in treatment more often because they are typically adopted by people who can afford counseling in the first place. There is also the possibility that adoptees were born to mentally ill parents and are therefore victimized by "genetic loading."

10

Religion, Ethnicity, and Race

Members of religious cults are often bound by psychopathology. Here is an extreme example. In 1978, hundreds of bodies were found at the People's Temple cult headquarters in Jonestown, Guyana. Authorities found many people clutching each other as they died from cyanide poisoning for the "cause." In 1994, a similar tragedy occurred among members of the Order of the Solar Temple cult, who ceremoniously burned themselves to death in various locations in Canada and Switzerland. The year 2000 saw even more of this behavior.

Religious, ethnic, and racial memberships are some of the master determinants of an individual's life experience. They affect power and wealth, crime and health. And they make an impact on a host of other things that translate into happiness or misery. This chapter examines their effects on a specific form of human misery—mental disorder.

RELIGION

One of the central issues concerning the role of religion in human affairs has been its relationship to constructs such as mental health, emotional well-being, and adjustment. While debate concerning the positive versus negative contributions of religion to mental health and related concepts is long-standing, it is only recently that theory and research have addressed these issues in a systematic and vigorous manner.[1]

Religion and Mental Health

While it is true that the connection between religion and mental health is a virgin research area, many studies have been conducted recently.[2] Some of them report that religious acts, such as personal prayer, can positively affect psychological well-being.[3] Others report a general connection between religiosity and health in general.[4] Although there is a growing feeling that religion connects with mental health,[5] the specific ways in which "being religious" are defined are still being formulated.[6] This is an especially tedious task in light of the fact that the content and meaning of religion vary so much around the world.[7] In fact, a review of the literature in 2000 revealed that research on the relationship between religion and mental illness was being conducted within eight different religious perspectives—Protestant, Catholic, Mormon, Unity, Jewish, Buddhist, Hindu and Muslim.[8]

Although formal research on the role of religion in mental health is relatively new, the question of religion and personality has been debated for a long time. Are religious people more mentally healthy, or does a belief in God imply less rationality? That is one of the questions. Where do religious interests originate? For a long time socialization was considered to be the obvious answer to that question, but recent research on identical twins indicates that it may be genetic. At the present time, the relationship between mental illness and religious experience has not been fully delineated, although there is a growing opinion that the interrelationships between the two should be further studied.[9] One basis for the connection between mental illness and religion is the religious imagery and delusions often found among psychotics in mental hospitals.[10] This may be especially common in the form of beliefs in possession or demonic influence.[11]

Many behavioral scientists firmly believe that religiosity is either pathological, per se, or it originates in an abnormal state of mind. Freud subscribed to such a view. He held that religion is an "obsessional neurosis" used by people as a means of repeating infantile experiences.[12] Other critics contend that religion is an escape from reality, a tactic originally used by primitive peoples to explain natural events that were mysteries at the time. In today's world, the critics hold that religion no longer serves such a purpose but instead is accepted by those who lack a rational perspective. Of course, it is quite possible that those behavioral scientists who think religious people are mentally disordered are reflecting their own biases against religion.[13] In fact, some evidence suggests that mental health professionals are biased by inadequate understanding of religion and differences in levels of religious involvement.[14] It is indeed quite a tangle.

With all of these opinions in mind, recent sophisticated scientific analyses of the effect of religion on mental health report a very positive influence. Specifically, individuals with strong religious faith report higher levels of life satisfaction, greater personal happiness, and fewer negative psychosocial consequences from traumatic life events. Current reports also indicate that religious people live longer[15] and are less vulnerable to mental health problems and substance abuse.[16]

Perhaps religion, per se, is not as important as the individual's response to it. In this sense, the way in which religion is taught by the family may be the key as to whether or not it is simply a body of beliefs about the divine. Certain mental health experts hold that a body of beliefs is the *true* nature of religion. They dispute the views of their colleagues who believe religion is abnormal. There is evidence that they may be right. Kendler and his colleagues found that religious behavior, such as personal devotion, can buffer the effects of stressful life events.[17] Consistently, others report a direct linkage between religion and the general ability to "cope" with life.[18]

How can this issue be resolved? One useful approach is to distinguish between *traditional* religious commitment and *pathological* forms of commitment. The form of religious commitment examined by those in support of psychopathological theories is usually abnormal—people obsessed with holiness, extreme fears of the devil, or the belief that one has been given divine inspiration. This type of commitment existed among members of the People's Temple, a religious cult led by the Reverend Jim Jones, who had the power to direct some 900 people to suicide-murder in the jungles of Guyana. In addition, leaving a cult, such as the Unification Church ("Moonies") can itself cause serious emotional problems.[19] Some of the questions about the powerful lure of cults are examined in Box 10:1. Evidence for the strong relationship between abnormal personalities and cult membership continues to grow. It does not require an academic genius to see the connection. Just pick up a newspaper and read about the horrors. One example occurred in Uganda in 2000. A doomsday cult, known as the Movement for the Restoration of the Ten Commandments of God, resulted in 979 murder-suicides when the world did not end as predicted.

In its conventional form, religious commitment may not be associated with mental illness at all. Indeed, an early analysis of personality differences between religious and less religious persons found no significant differences.[20] Investigations of religious affiliation (church membership) among mental patients and a random sample of normal people found that mentally ill people were less religiously committed. A few report that mental illness and religious commitment are inversely related, but it is questionable whether church membership indicates true religious commitment.[21] A number of studies have shown that church membership declines as social class declines, and, since lower-class people are overrepresented in mental hospitals, it is logical to expect that mental patients (in contrast to normal people) are reported more frequently to lack a religious affiliation.

Differences between Religious Denominations

Although the nature of the relationship between religiosity and mental illness will be argued for some time, there has been some empirical research on the prevalence of mental illness among members of the nation's three major religious denom-

•••••••••••••••••••••••••••••••••••• **Box 10:1** ••••••••••••••••••••••••••••••••••
Cults: A Matter of Mind Control

As she watched the televised drama of the Texas cult siege from her Broomall home last week, Lucy Volpe was gripped by a sense of doom and familiarity.

Just 15 months ago, Volpe, 46, made her own escape from what she describes as an eerily similar armed doomsday cult in Pennsylvania.

Now living with her parents, Volpe said that as a member of the Church of Our First Love she became a "robot"and sacrificed her middle-class Drexel Hill home, her 25-year marriage, her dignity and nearly her life for reaons she now finds absurd.

"We almost wanted to die, because we didn't care," said Volpe, whose three daughters were also in the group.

According to Volpe, her cult leader, Anthony Marcolongo, tried to rape her. Another former member, a 29-year-old Juniata Park woman who did not want her name used, said that Marcolongo menaced the group's children with a gun.

Volpe said Marcolongo finally lost his grip on his band of 28 followers after he started abusing drugs on the Clearfield County farm where the cult was awaiting the end of the world.

"We were able to get a little of our senses back," Volpe said. "I've been out now 15 months and it's been wonderful.

"I have my mind back."

For millions watching the federal government's siege of David Koresh and his followers, there is this puzzling question: How does a person get drawn into a cult?

In her case, Volpe said it was a gradual process that took years and stemmed from her own deep desire "to serve God with everything that I had in me." Volpe was associated with Marcolongo for six years, and moved to the western Pennsylvania commune when it was established in 1988. But at the nadir of her afffliation with Marcolongo, Volpe said, she was experiencing physical and mental abuse, the rape attempt by her spiritual leader, and fasting "until your mind shuts down—I mean you're mindless."

Experts say an unknown number of Americans are involved in hundreds, maybe thousands, of groups—secular as well as religious—that can be loosely labeled as cults because of the extreme degree of control they exert over their members' lives.

But there is disagreement over the psychology of cult membership.

Some anti-cult organizations say cults use brainwashing or mind-control techniques to get and keep members.

Others who study cults say otherwise reasonable individuals are susceptible because they crave emotional support or the group holds seemingly simple answers to life's big questions. Once inside the group, members remain, often despite disillusionment, because the cult provides identity and fulfillment, some researchers say.

Today, the lure of cults is believed to be stronger than ever because of the impending millennial change with the year 2000 approaching.

Source: Reid Kanaley, "Trying to understand the powerful lure of cults," *Philadelphia Inquirer,* March 7, 1993, pp. E1–E2.

••

inations—Protestantism, Catholicism, and Judaism. A landmark study by Roberts and Myers examined the religious affiliation of mentally disturbed people in New Haven, Connecticut. In that study, Protestants were slightly underrepresented in the psychiatric population compared to their number in the general population (31 to 33 percent). Catholics appeared in the psychiatric population in proportion to their numbers in the general population. What was noteworthy about the Catholic group, however, was an inordinately high rate of alcoholism and epilepsy. Catholics were 68.5 percent and 71.5 percent of the alcoholic and epileptic populations, respectively. Jews were overrepresented in the psychiatric population (12 to 9.5 percent), much of which was due to a high rate of anxiety disorders (two and a half times above expectation). At the same time, it was remarkable that few Jews suffered from alcohol and drug addiction.

Why was there such a high rate of neurosis (anxiety disorders) among Jews? Why is it still reported today?[22] One factor is that Jewish parents provide extremely ambitious goals for their children. However, it is unclear whether a failure to achieve these goals produces neurosis or whether neurosis produces the failure.[23] Another explanation involves Jews' positive attitudes toward psychotherapy. Since psychiatric treatment does not conflict with their religious doctrine, Jews seek treatment more readily than do other groups. Catholics, for instance, are often taught to deal with life problems through prayer and the counsel of priests. In the Midtown study, respondents were asked what they would do with a hypothetical psychiatric problem. About half of the Jewish respondents felt that psychotherapists were the most appropriate help source compared to only 23.8 percent of Catholics and 31.4 percent of Protestants.[24]

Most of the Catholics and Protestants said they would not go to any type of professional, including a physician. The Midtown study also found that Jews have the highest treatment rate of the three major religious affiliations. In that study, Jews had an outpatient rate more than twice that of Protestants and approximately ten times that of Catholics. Of course, many psychotherapists are Jewish. This partly accounts for the high rate of treatment among Jews who can readily find psychiatric help from a "similar other," a phenomenon related to status homophily.

Still another reason for the high rate of psychiatric treatment among Jews probably lies in educational and occupational differences that separate Jews from Catholics and Protestants. Jewish people are concentrated in the upper echelons of the American stratification system and thus are more able to pay for treatment than are Protestants and Catholics. They are typically professional people who are well educated, and it is the educated mind that is most sensitive to the nuances of human psychology. It is also the educated mind that is oriented toward a sophisticated, scientific approach to problem solving. Thus Jews who feel distressed are simply cautious and educated enough to take the problem to the most scientific help source available—the psychiatrist. In the process, they become registered patients. However, because they are more often *registered* as patients does not make them more disordered than other groups.[25]

Psychiatric research over the last 100 years suggests that Jews are at higher risk for mood disorders than members of other religious groups.[26] This is reported to be especially true for Jewish males. But there are a number of reports to the contrary. Zieba and others report no correlation between religion and mood disorder.[27] New reports indicate the highest rates of depression among Jews,[28] but a 1992 study by Meador and others shed some interesting light on the relationships between religious affiliation and severe depression. Using data from the Duke Epidemiologic Catchment Area study, they examined rates of depression among 2,850 adults in the community who were categorized into six groups: mainline Protestant, conservative Protestant, Pentecostal, Catholic, other religions, and no affiliation. Controlling for gender, age, social class, race, negative life events, and social support, one pattern clearly stood out: the likelihood of major depression among Pentecostals was three times greater than among persons with other affiliations.[29] Clearly, Jews do not have a monopoly on these problems.

Religion and Treatment

Religion, religiosity, spirituality, and everything else connected with religious values have not been utilized very much in therapy.[30] This may be unfortunate since some clearly warn that it is dangerous for psychiatry to treat religion as a nonconsequential factor in the treatment of mental disorders.[31] Part of the problem may be a reluctance to pursue these issues because of an absence of widespread dissemination of research findings.[32] But that is no excuse in light of recent reports that religion is intimately entangled with mental health problems. Consider two examples. First, some religions are especially prone to stigmatize mental illness, rendering the whole issue of treatment inoperable.[33] Second, religion can affect successful mental health adjustments in a number of areas in life, including academic performance in college.[34]

THE MEANING OF RACE AND ETHNICITY

Race and ethnicity are complicated concepts: complicated to define; complicated to understand the hostility they generate; and complicated to explain in terms of the driving forces behind intergroup relations. Biological, legal, and social definitions of race are arbitrary and contradictory. Basically, racial membership is a subjective, social perception of what people *say* it is.[35] And *racism* is what it *is*—divisive and still very much alive.[36]

Like race, there is wide variation in the meaning of the term *ethnic group*. It ranges from small, isolated "kin and culture" groups to large categories of people defined as similar on the basis of one or two shared characteristics. Ethnicity is often used interchangeably with country of origin, but it most commonly refers to cultural features that are handed down from one generation to the next. These may include dress, religion, language, food preferences, historical identity, *and* national origin.

Ethnic groups share a sense of "peoplehood" within a larger society. They are not necessarily a numerical minority within the larger society, although the term is sometimes used that way. It is most importantly a sense of group identity, an identity that is based on distinctive cultural patterns *acquired* through socialization in a particular psychosocial environment.

Race and ethnicity are different. *Race* is often more of a biological concept, whereas *ethnicity* is a cultural one. Sometimes the two are confused with each other, as in the case of Jews (an ethnic and religious group but not a race); and sometimes the two go hand in hand, as in the case of Asian Americans, who have distinct physical characteristics as well as common cultural traits. This is also true of African Americans and Native Americans. Religion is sometimes a qualifying factor in ethnic identification. Irish Protestants, for instance, are ethnically different from Irish Catholics, and Hungarian Catholics differ from Hungarian Jews. Given all of these issues and questions, the listing of ethnic and racial groups in this chapter is somewhat arbitrary.

RACE, ETHNICITY, AND PSYCHIATRY

In 2000, there was a call for research to allow for a better understanding of the positive and negative influences of ethnic characteristics and racial differences on mental health.[37] In Chapter 2, we saw how mental illness can take so many different forms around the world, but the call for greater awareness of the connection among race, ethnicity, and mental health is clearly an American need. That is not to say that it is not a world need as well, but that it should be examined intraculturally.[38]

Ethnic group influences on beliefs about mental illness are of huge importance in the United States.[39] They affect the likelihood of whether mental illness is understood or simply stigmatized.[40] This, in turn, affects the very decision even to seek help for mental health problems.[41] Studies also show that diagnosis and treatment relate to race and ethnicity; African Americans, for example, are less likely to receive extensive treatment at mental health centers.[42] This is especially true for young patients. Perhaps the most central fact about race, ethnicity, and mental health is that members of lower social or ethnic groups have lower levels of well-being and higher levels of distress. Much of this, however, can be explained as a result of belonging to the lower social class, a mental health hazard delineated in Chapter 8.

ETHNIC DIFFERENCES

Popular opinion has it that the United States is a melting pot in which people of different national extractions are homogenized into Americans. In time that may be true, but presently there is a considerable number of ethnic groups that still maintain an identity separate from that of the host culture. The mental health status of some of these ethnic groups is reviewed here. In a nutshell, the patterns are quite different.[43] One notable difference is the disadvantaged position of immigrants of Hispanic origin compared to others.

Hispanics

The term *Hispanic* has a nebulous meaning that is applied to an ever-changing group of U.S. residents. It includes people from Cuba, as well as people from the nations of Central and South America. While little is known about the mental health of some of these people, psychological profiles are available about those from Puerto Rico and Mexico.

As a group there are few nationally representative samples of the mental health patterns of Hispanics. Larger studies with larger samples are missing. Thus we do not have a clear picture except for Puerto Ricans and Mexican Americans. The need for more studies is not simply academic; it is estimated that in the twenty-first century nearly half of the clientele seeking mental health services will be members of ethnic minority groups. That is especially important to note in light of the fact that Hispanics are the most rapidly growing population in the United States.

Puerto Ricans

It is sometimes impossible to isolate the singular effects of ethnicity on mental illness because ethnicity is often intimately associated with religion, as in the case of Puerto Ricans, who are disproportionately Catholic. This makes it difficult to determine how much ethnicity contributes and how much religious membership contributes to mental health problems. However, unlike Catholics in general, Puerto Ricans in the United States have a relatively high rate of mental illness. The reasons are unknown.

There are higher reported rates of symptoms among Puerto Ricans than among Jews, a group known to overreport symptoms.[44] Specifically, Puerto Ricans are especially prone to develop somatic problems.[45] This is not that surprising since many Puerto Ricans are not well educated, a common characteristic among people who suffer from somatic symptoms (psychologically imposed physical ailments).[46]

Mexican Americans

Research on Mexican Americans (Chicanos) is contradictory. On the one hand, it is reported in south Texas that Mexican Americans make up a large part of the patient population in public psychiatric facilities.[47] Yet others describe them as relatively free of mental illness. However, the "low rate reports" outnumber the "high rate reports."

In a study of the comparative rates of mental illness among Mexican Americans and Anglo Americans living in Texas, Jaco found Mexican Americans to have 50 percent less psychosis than Anglo Americans.[48] Another study of admissions to California state hospitals also uncovered a low rate of illness among Chicanos.[49] A number of hypotheses have been generated to explain these low rates. One theory is that the Mexican American male is filled with feelings of insecurity and inferiority because of his subordinate social position in the United States. This stress is not visible, however, because it is masked by the Mexican machismo complex.[50] Another view suggests that some Mexican Americans have primitive concepts of mental illness. Consequently, they are resistant to psychiatry and frequently use "witch doctors" rather than professional therapists, a practice most frequently found in the Southwest.[51] Thus they are not registered as cases.

A third theory is that the strongly cohesive Mexican American family is very tolerant of abnormal behavior and thus avoids or delays treatment. If this "postponement thesis" is true, then those Chicanos who actually are hospitalized should be more disorganized and more severely psychotic than patients of other ethnic strains. There is evidence that this is the case.[52] But it is also possible that Chicanos feel alienated in Anglo hospitals and appear more ill as a result. A fourth theory holds that the reports of low rates of mental illness among Chicanos reflect the fact that there really is less mental illness among Mexican Americans than among Anglo Americans. It is argued that all members of the tightly knit Chicano family share the same values. This, in turn, provides the Mexican American with a clearer sense of identity and fewer role conflicts than Anglos.[53] In addition, the Mexican American view of the world allows them to avoid guilt and self-doubt by placing the blame for failure on witchcraft or fate rather than on themselves.[54]

Some researchers have investigated specific symptomatic differences between Chicano females and Anglo females in treatment.[55] Comparisons of diagnoses showed a relatively higher prevalence of personality disorders among the Anglo patients and a relatively higher rate of anxiety disorders among the Chicano patients. A recurring symptom among the Mexican American patients was depression. It may be that the depression results from the highly subordinate role of the Mexican American female, who is often expected to be a good mother, uncomplaining, and subservient to the males of the household. The women may be frequently troubled by their husbands' "acting-out" behavior, which includes sexual promiscuity, drunkenness, episodic desertion of the family, and physical assaults upon the wife and children. In contrast, the central symptom of the Anglo patients is guilt and defensive detachment from others, a presumed reflection of the Anglo societal ethic that holds individuals responsible for their own failures. Consistent with this, the Anglo patients are frequently troubled by economic matters, the symbols of personal achievement. Remember, these are only *theories.*

European Groups

There are only a few well-documented mental health characteristics for the many groups who emigrated from Europe since the early 1900s. One group is the Irish. As noted earlier, their rate of alcoholism is exceedingly high. In fact, it may be the specific contribution of the Irish that is largely responsible for the high rate of alcoholism among Catholics in general.[56] In many ways it is remarkable that the Irish can find an outlet for psychological conflict in this single form of escape. But, as noted earlier, the Irish version of the teachings of the Roman Catholic Church is exceptionally rigid, leaving few forms of behavior as socially acceptable. This is especially true in matters about sex.

Malzberg reports that admission rates for the Irish to American hospitals are the highest of all European groups.[57] Polish immigrants also have above average rates, but one must be careful to separate the Slavic and Jewish streams. The high rate for immigrants from Poland is due to the Slavic element, not the Jewish stream. The lowest rates are found among English, Italian, and Russian (disproportionately Jewish) immigrants while Germans have an average admission rate.

RACIAL DIFFERENCES

> The growing racial and ethnic heterogeneity of the U.S. population will require mental health researchers to think more seriously about sociocultural variation. To date, researchers have not given sufficient attention to how race, ethnicity and culture are linked to one another and to mental health. For instance, race can be an important factor in predicting exposure and vulnerability to stress, coping strategies, social support, and, in turn, mental health status. Race, however, grossly aggregates people and often hides subtle, and not so subtle, variations in mental health status and functioning.[58]

These words ring especially true today in light of the fact that race is a complicated issue in many ways. In the 2000 census, race was particularly elusive because many people identified themselves as members of more than one race. Racism, however, rears a particularly visible head in the form of ideologies of superiority to, and negative attitudes and beliefs about, outgroups, as well as discriminatory treatment of members of those groups by individuals and societal institutions.

Asian Americans

Very few large epidemiologic surveys include representative data on psychiatric disorder among Asian Americans. The one exception is the large study of 1,700 native-born and immigrant Chinese living in the Los Angeles area.[59] Known as the Chinese American Psychiatric Epidemiological Study (CAPES), it uncovered some clear mental health patterns. Overall, the rates of mental health problems of Chinese Americans are low when compared with the reported rates of other groups. This is especially true for panic disorder and anxiety disorders in general. However, the rates of major depression were reportedly higher than the ECA study results.[60]

Although, like Hispanics, Asian Americans are usually discussed as an entity, they are the most diverse ethnic group in the United States. They come from over two dozen different countries and do not share a religion, language, or even a common cultural background. More than 80 percent of Asian Americans trace their roots to one of five countries: the Philippines, China, Japan, India, or Korea. Approximately 40 percent of Asian immigrants came from Vietnam, Cambodia, and Laos. Recent immigration has significantly changed the composition of this part of the American population. Not only is the meaning of "Asian American" complicated by so many changing conventional subgroups, but it is further confused by the inclusion of Pacific Islanders in the census. This is especially odd in light of the fact that some Pacific Islanders, such as Hawaiians and Guamians, are born with U.S. citizenship.

Asian Americans constitute the fastest-growing minority in the United States today. In 2000, they numbered 4.5 million, up from 1.4 million in 1970. The Asian American population grew by 80 percent in the 1980s alone—twice the growth rate of Hispanics, 6 times the rate of African Americans, and 20 times that of whites. This is a phenomenal increase among a group with radically different histories. As in the case of Hispanics, mental health research has concentrated only on specific groups of Asian Americans. Studies of Japanese and Chinese Americans dominate the literature on the Asian American population. The plight of other Asian American groups is examined in Box 10:2.

Japanese Americans. Japanese Americans have puzzled behavioral scientists over the years because they appear to be an exceptional group in that they are free of antisocial tendencies, as evidenced by an immeasurably small rate of delinquency. The Japanese have not reacted to discriminatory treatment in the United States with high rates of crime and mental illness. For this reason, they are rarely considered to be a "problem minority." Kitano's investigation of hospitalization rates among the Japanese found that mental illness is not a major problem for them, compared to other groups. Those Japanese who are hospitalized are typically single, old, lower-class males suffering from schizophrenia. The hospitalization rates and symptomatic patterns are similar for the Japanese in Japan *and* in the United States.

One hypothetical reason for the low rate of disorder among Japanese Americans is their tightly knit family structure. Like the Chicano family, the Japanese family is very cohesive and exerts a high degree of social control over its members. This not only functions as a mental health haven by offering interpersonal security, but it also reduces the likelihood of outside "experts" being used to handle behavioral problems. Consequently, few Japanese become registered in the official mental illness statistics. Another control on the expression of mental illness among the Japanese is their strong belief in directing reactions to stress and frustration inward without showing any external signs. This tendency among the Japanese to internalize problems and not bother others with them is known as the concept of "*ga-man*." It may also connect with a high suicide rate.

Certainly the strong sense of social solidarity within the Japanese family and in the Japanese community as a whole reduces the need for professional help with psychiatric problems. But other factors are at work as well. Kitano notes that Japanese Americans are typically unsophisticated regarding the causes and treatment of mental illness.[61] Because of this, they have no clear conception of what mental illness is and consequently rarely use psychiatric facilities. In addition, there is the "*Kibei*" custom, whereby American-born children are sent to be raised by relatives in Japan. Often these are children with behavioral problems who are never treated here and therefore not included in the U.S. mental illness statistics.

The differences between Eastern and Western cultures are enormous and well documented. Although diverse in scope, traditional emphasis on the family and interdependence illustrated the similarities among Eastern cultures and their estrangement from the predominant values of Western culture. Western cultures like ours are known for their emphasis on independence, personal achievement, and upward mobility. A place like Japan is far removed from U.S. values. In Asia, people are more likely to be raised with an eye toward group orientation, altruism, and sacrifice.

Imagine the culture shock experienced by people who leave Asia and migrate here. Below are some pieces of information available about the mental illness patterns of people from Korea, the Philippines, and Indochina.

Korean Americans

Although no systematic epidemiologic studies have been conducted on the prevalence rates of psychiatric disorders among Korean Americans in the United States, a study of Korean Americans *seeking* mental health care indicates a wide range of mental health problems: Schizophrenic disorders, 17 percent; manic-depressive disorders, 9 percent; major depression, 8 percent, dysthymia, 22 percent; adjustment disorders, 13 percent, anxiety disorders, 9 percent; psychosomatic disorders, 8 percent; conduct disorders, 8 percent; alcohol abuse, 3 percent, and parent-child problems, 18 percent.

Similarly, suicide attempts, posttraumatic stress disorders, marital problems, intergenerational conflict, juvenile delinquency, spouse and child abuse, and violent behavior were prevalent in this study. However, the impact of problems of acculturation on mental health can only be guessed at since most Korean patients seek psychiatric help only as a last resort. Cultural obstacles such as the shame of exposing one's own problems to outsiders and the fear of mental illness as the stigma of "being crazy" inhibits Asian groups from utilizing mental health services. In this study, it was noted that only 9 percent of clients came for treatment on a self-referral basis.

It is likely that Eastern traditions of herbal medicine, acupuncture, or Christian religious counseling would be tried before seeking Western psychiatric help.

Philippino Americans

The incidence of paranoid schizophrenia has been noticeably higher among Philippinos as compared with other Asian groups. Psychophysiologic and other somatization disorders are also high in comparison with white Americans and African Americans. Depression is believed to be underestimated because of the value that Philippinos place on the virtue of endurance. Anxiety and related disorders are believed to approximate, if not exceed, the incidence rate for the general population in the United States. Suicide and alcohol and drug abuse are believed to be well below the national average, although there are indications that this may be changing, especially among third-, fourth-, and fifth-generation Philippino Americans.

Indochinese Americans

A series of catastrophic events over the last 50 years have formed the background of the arrival of Indochinese in the United States: the Japanese occupation of Indochina, the wars of liberation from the French, the devastation caused by American involvement in Southeast Asia, the fall of governments in the region, the establishment of reeducation camps, and the horrors of Pol Pot. Finally, there were the difficult experiences many faced while escaping Indochina, living in refugee camps in a second country, and enduring refugee status in the United States. The Indochinese have suffered a history of trauma, social and cultural breakdowns, and the loss of family members, country, language, and culture.

With all of the traumas imposed on these people through long-term war, social dislocation, immigration to what is essentially a new world, and the resentment many Americans harbor toward them, it may be more appropriate to ask why some still are the seat of mental health rather than why so many are disturbed. There is no

continued

Mental Health Problems of Korean Americans

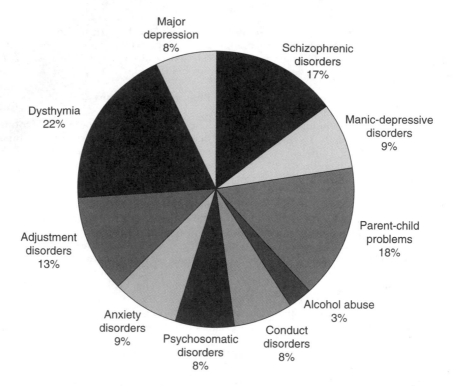

Note: Percentages add up to more than 100 percent because some people seek help for multiple problems.

doubt that many are disturbed. In fact the numbers are alarming.

The mental health needs of Indochinese Americans in California were assessed in a thorough community study indicating that the need for psychiatric services was moderate to severe for 31 percent of the Vietnamese, 54 percent of the Hmong, 50 percent of the Laotians, and 48 percent of the Cambodians. An estimated 10 percent of the refugees met the criteria for having posttraumatic stress disorder, 16 percent of whom were Cambodian.

In a community survey of Cambodian adolescents who were nonpatients, psychiatrists uncovered a particularly high rate of mental illness: 50 percent had PTSD, 53 percent at least a form of depressive disorder, and 65 percent had at least one major DSM-III diagnosis. Both affective disorders and PTSD are highly prevalent in both community and clinical populations. Almost all studies indicate that Cambodians and/or Hmong have the highest level of distress and the greatest needs. It is possible that as many as 50 percent of the general population of Indochinese Americans have severe needs and/or are impaired by their psychiatric symptoms. The Vietnamese tend to be the least impaired of all the Indochinese groups studied; even so, their needs are quite significant when compared with those of mainstream Americans. . . . The most significant psychiatric disorders among Indochinese are caused by traumatic experiences to which they were subjected.

Source: Adapted from Albert C. Gaw, *Culture, Ethnicity, and Mental Illness* (Washington, DC: American Psychiatric Press, 1993), pp. 284, 286, 366, 406. By permission of the publisher.

Chinese Americans. The Chinese in the United States exhibit mental illness patterns that in some ways parallel those of Japanese Americans. Chinese Americans have particularly low rates of antisocial behavior and alcoholism.[62] However, research indicates that the mental health status of Chinese Americans has worsened throughout the last century. During that time, trends in mental hospital commitments among Chinese in California, for example, have changed significantly.[63] There has been a twofold increase for the general population compared to a sevenfold increase among the Chinese in that state. Like the Japanese, the Chinese commitment rates are especially high for aged males, particularly those who emigrated from China.

Certainly, the Chinese have suffered much physical and social violence in America. Until the 1950s, the Chinese experience in America was one of blatant discrimination. Since that time, discriminatory behavior has assumed subtler forms. In 1882, however, discrimination was official government policy when Congress passed the Exclusion Act, which prevented further Chinese immigration. The psychiatric impact of this social policy was painfully clear; the rate of diagnosed paranoid schizophrenia (with persecutory content) increased from 3 to 9 percent.[64] This lends support to the sociological perspective that behavior labeled as delusions of persecution is often a realistic reaction to actual social rejection. Such a formula seems to fit the early Chinese experience in the United States quite well.

There was an interesting change in the mental illness trends of Chinese Americans from the 1850s to the 1950s. In the 1850s, 65 percent of Chinese mental patients committed to California hospitals were diagnosed as depressives.[65] Less than 7 percent were so diagnosed in the 1950s; instead, the diagnosis of schizophrenia rapidly increased to the point where 85 percent of Chinese patients were labeled as schizophrenics.[66] If schizophrenia is a more disturbed state than depression, and it certainly seems to be, then the shift from depressive to schizophrenic conditions can be interpreted as a growing deterioration of the mental health of Chinese Americans. However, the recent CAPES report raises serious questions about any alleged deterioration of Chinese Americans.

African Americans

Of all of the minority groups in the United States, the black experience has been most riddled by a tortured history. You already know that. There is a ton of evidence documenting the miseries of prejudice, discrimination, violence, unhappiness, and urban squalor which have been the plight of African Americans for hundreds of years. Because it is such a lengthy list of horrors, my short synopsis of the psychological problems of blacks only touches the surface. Below are just *some* of the central facts about their mental health makeup.

Nineteenth-Century Racism. Patterns of mental disorder among African Americans roughly conform to what is known about mental illness patterns among economically deprived persons in general. In the 1800s, there were a number of reports that blacks were relatively free of mental illness because of the special care they received as slaves.[67] These beliefs were strengthened by the 1840 census, which reported higher rates among northern blacks than southern blacks. Interpreting these data, Edward Jarvis, a Massachusetts physician, endeared himself to the southern slave states by declaring: "Slavery must have a wonderful influence upon the moral faculties and intellectual powers of the individual, for in refusing many of the hopes and responsibilities which the free, self-thinking and self-acting enjoy and sustain, of course it saves him from some of the liabilities and dangers of active self-direction. The false position of the Negro in the North had a disturbing effect on his 'character.'"[68]

Although the census report was falsified and Jarvis later issued a complete repudiation of his statements, the harm was already done and proslavery interests were strengthened. The 1860 census also reported some suspicious findings; only 766 "colored insane" were reported out of a total black population of 4,441,830. The number increased to 6,776 in 1890, a rate change from 17.5 per 100,000 in 1860 to 88.6 per 100,000 in 1890. The racist mentality of the era linked this increase with the abolition of slavery which altered the "peaceful" conditions blacks had enjoyed as slaves and introduced them to the stresses of competitive life.

It is disheartening to realize that ethnocentrism was so common even among social science researchers at that time. Many of them either did not recognize mental illness among blacks, or they attributed it to the "natural inferiority" of the race. One prominent nineteenth-century physician invented two psychiatric diseases to which he believed slaves were vulnerable: *drapetomania*, a condition that caused slaves to run away, and *dysaethesia aethiopica*, which he claimed caused slaves to waste and destroy everything they could handle. Only since the civil rights movement of the 1950s has the idea been challenged that blacks are happiest in their "place."

Rates of Mental Illness Today.   The Dohrenwends reported that of eight studies of black-white differences in rate of mental illness, four reported higher rates for blacks and four reported higher rates for whites.[69] However, the methodologies of many of those studies were poor since they were conducted at a time when statistical analyses were underdeveloped. The Midtown Manhattan study did not suffer such weaknesses; it uncovered higher rates among African Americans. It is curious that the Dohrenwends are more critical of the Midtown study than the less sophisticated designs of earlier studies. They suggest that the results of the Midtown study were affected by using white interviewers and by asking questions that better-educated people would know how to answer on the basis of social desirability.[70] That was in 1969. Studies are still confounded by that problem today. In the comprehensive Epidemiologic Catchment Area (ECA) survey, the rate of both lifetime and active disorder was higher for blacks than for whites or Hispanics. See Table 10:1 for a brief summary.

Researchers noted that scores on the Mini-Mental State Examination used to diagnose cognitive impairment are strongly correlated with education and social status. How significant is the effect of poor education and subsequent low social status on

Table 10:1   Race, Ethnicity, and Psychiatric Disorder

	Lifetime Prevalence	*Active cases in Last Year*
White	32%	19%
Black	38	26
Hispanic	33	20

Source: Lee N. Robins and Darrel A. Regier, eds., *Psychiatric Disorders in America: The Epidemiologic Catchment Area Study* (New York: Free Press, 1991).

reported rates of illness among African Americans? In my opinion, and in the arena of good common sense, it is *very* significant.

Overall, most recent studies of the relationship between race and mental illness have consistently found that *blacks have more mental illness than whites, but the differences are minimal when social class is held constant.*[71] In other words, much of the greater prevalence of mental disorder among African Americans is due to the fact that they are overrepresented in the lower social class which is known to be hazardous to mental health.

I cannot emphasize enough how important it is to consider social class when examining for differences in the mental health patterns between blacks and any other race. The relationship between socioeconomic status and race is extremely strong.[72] As you know from Chapter 8, lower-class membership is intimately tied with poor mental health—both by type and rate of mental illness. Racial discrimination is simply inherently stressful.

Many studies report that blacks have higher rates of mental illness than whites in every age, sex, and marital status group.[73] But these data are based on records of admissions to public institutions, the type of help source the poor are likely to utilize. Affluent whites, on the other hand, can better afford private care. As a consequence of these socioeconomic differences between blacks and whites, African Americans are more likely to appear as cases in studies using public records. To control for this, one study used the Monroe County case register, which includes not only all patients seen by public and private hospitals and clinics but also patients treated by psychiatrists in private practice.[74] Using these data, the prevalence rates were still higher for blacks than whites (11.55 per 1,000 population for blacks, 8.39 per 1,000 population for whites). Another study applied a "general psychopathology scale" to a nonhospitalized population and found that blacks were significantly more impaired than whites.[75] Additionally, one study of 2,000 randomly chosen adults living in the South found a higher percentage of blacks (38 percent) than whites (28 percent) were disordered.[76]

The higher rates of mental illness among African Americans can be accounted for in two ways. First, since blacks are overrepresented in the lower social class, it is expected that they will manifest more impairment than whites as a group. Second, even *within* the same social class, stress situations are more frequent and severe among disadvantaged blacks than among their relatively advantaged white counterparts. This just adds to the psychic hell. Another part of the problem was discussed in Chapter 8—the issue of treatment. What happens to black people who go for help? The experiences of some who did are described in Box 10:3.

Types of Mental Illness.   There are many differences in type of mental illness by race that closely follow known differences between social class groups. Schizophrenia appears more frequently among blacks than whites. Aside from differences in the rate of schizophrenia between blacks and whites in the United States, Adebimpe and others report that black schizophrenics are more likely to be angry and experience hallucinations.[77]

The mood disorders appear less frequently among blacks as they do in the lower social class in general.[78] But when the rates for depression are compared between blacks and whites of the same social class, these differences disappear.[79] Consistent with the labeling theory perspective that paranoia is often diagnosed among people who suffer actual social exclusion, it is reported that paranoid tendencies are more common among blacks than among whites.[80] African Americans are also more sus-

····················· **Box 10:3** ·····················
The Color of Therapy

They could not have been a more professional, or a more unhappy, couple. He a surgeon, she an attorney.

They sought the help of a psychologist.

The couple was black, the therapist white. Too busy to see them, she referred them to a student-intern psychologist.

Insulted, the couple wondered if they would have been sent to an intern if they had been white. . . . They went anyway.

The therapy sessions were a disaster. The couple's relationship was volatile, and the bitterness and resentment between them terrified the intern. The intern "acted as if she were scared to death" by it.

The couple decided they needed a black therapist.

Marlene Watson is the black therapist they saw, and the teller of the tale.

"What's significant about them is that they saw that race was getting in the way of getting proper treatment," said Wilson, a senior staff member and assistant director of training for the Marriage Council of Philadelphia.

She says that "we have to dare to speak the unspeakable and acknowledge that there is racism in the treatment process."

But the racism she speaks of is not simple mistreatment. It is treating someone with indifference because of race. It is failure to acknowledge cultural differences. And it is ignorance, the failure to accept that stereotypes, even odious ones, may be rooted in real life experience. . . .

Close family members, extended family, friends-who-are-like-family, and clergy are usually the consultants of choice. Kenneth Hardy, a Syracuse University counselor, said that the therapist often ignores the religious underpinnings and prominent role of the church in the lives of African American couples. "Therapy is on a collision course with spirituality and religion."

A family's emotional or psychological woes are dirty laundry and African American couples are usually unwilling to wash that laundry in front of strangers. . . .

"In some couples, the issue is chronic unemployment of the man, but so many of us are afraid of offending African American couples that we don't deal with the issue. We try to be politically correct, but we fail to effect change."

Another highly charged issue is fidelity.

"Sometimes, women believe they can't have a man of their own. Sometimes, African American men's only success is the sexual conquest. . . . We have to reframe that."

Hardy said that therapists, black and white, often commit "micro-aggressions" in therapy, such as ignoring the African American male. Author Nancy Boyd-Franklin says that the women usually come to the therapist first, whatever the race or ethnicity, but that the importance of "engaging the African American male" could not be overemphasized.

"Often, you have to go to him and that's not taught in graduate school," she said.

─────────────

Source: Murray Dubin, "The color of therapy," *Philadelphia Inquirer,* December 23, 1992.

···

ceptible to antisocial reactions, which are known to be more common among people in the lower classes.[81] Organic disorders also appear more frequently among African Americans. Organic brain syndromes, for example, due to the consequences of chronic alcoholism, are reported to be nine times as high for blacks than for whites. Many of the organic brain syndromes may originate from poor prenatal health care, a problem found more frequently among the poor.

It is important to note that alcohol abuse in the African American community does not represent an age-old pattern. During the 1840s and 1850s, abstinence from alcohol was synonymous with freedom from slavery and moral uprightness; slavery and demon rum both were seen as examples of moral depravity. It was not until Reconstruction and the association of the temperance cause with African American disenfranchisement and white supremacy that the drinking patterns of African Americans changed. The migration of blacks in the 1920s and 1930s during Prohibition and the Great Depression resulted in African Americans becoming more involved with the production, sale, and consumption of alcohol. Alcohol became a public health problem in the black community with the employment of African American entertainers in northern clubs and speakeasies and their involvement in the "nightlife."

Although substance abuse, psychotic illness, and affective illness can all produce changes in cognitive functioning, blacks are at increased risk for fixed deficits in cognitive functioning because of . . . dementia and alcohol dementia. This increased risk is attributable to the prevalence of obesity, diabetes, hypertension, and alcohol abuse in the population.[82]

African Americans also have higher rates of mental retardation, a disorder known to be associated with premature birth and complications of pregnancy, both of which are more likely to be encountered in lower-class groups. Consistent with their prevalence in higher classes, whites are more susceptible to anxiety disorders, with the exception of the phobic reactions, which appear more frequently among blacks, as they do in general among people in the lower class. Whites also have higher rates of psychosomatic disorders, which may be a consequence of the greater propensity of higher-class persons to report symptoms that fall into this diagnostic category.

The social class element underlying the mental health status of African Americans is most apparent when they are compared with Jews, a group overrepresented in the higher classes. The black and Jewish populations manifest psychic strain in radically different ways. Jews have high rates of anxiety disorder but low rates of alcoholism and antisocial reactions. The Jew turns stress inward, possibly because of the internally oriented socialization practices common among higher-class families and because of taboos in Jewish culture against the outward expression of hostility. This taboo apparently transcends social class constraints since there are also low rates of antisocial behavior among the few Jews in the lower class.[83]

Black-Jewish differences even occur when members of the two groups suffer the same illness. African Americans are most susceptible to the paranoid form of schizophrenia, a reflection of the outward expression of aggression and actual assault found in American black culture.[84] The Jewish schizophrenic, on the other hand, is usually diagnosed as simple, disorganized, or catatonic, diagnoses sometimes called "dependency schizophrenia" because these types of schizophrenic patients are usually in need of greater care and direction by the hospital staff than the more independent, paranoid schizophrenic.

The Effect of the Civil Rights Movement.   Ironically, there has been a tremendous reported increase in the black mental hospital admission rate since the advent of the civil rights movement. The change in the social status of African Americans has apparently not been without its costs as African Americans have been transformed from a deprived but homogeneous group to one riven with divisions based on newfound identities and ambitions. For many African Americans, the result has been an unsettling sense of marginality because they find themselves somewhere between black society and white society. This is particularly apparent in the case of blacks who were educated for prestigious occupations and used their acquired wealth to move to the white suburbs.[85] Here they may find themselves burdened with racist stigmas and labeled as "block busters." It is no small wonder that mental illness has grown among African Americans, given the frustrations and insecurities middle-class blacks face from breaking with their own cultural traditions while simultaneously suffering isolation as a result of their rejection by the white world. Whoever first said, "Life is not fair," must have had black people in mind.

The psychiatric effect of the marginal position of the African American is perhaps best exemplified by the high rate of impairment among younger African Americans. They followed the social change from the civil rights movement and in the struggle for desegregation. Yet their opportunities for sharing in the lifestyles and material benefits of the wider society are still limited compared to their aspirations. This frustration is probably responsible for a substantially higher rate of impairment among young blacks compared to young whites.

If, through integration, African Americans eventually become fully accepted members of American society, their mental illness patterns will change as they become more evenly distributed throughout the stratification system. Then they will be more subject to the psychological environment of traditional middle-class life, which in turn will increase anxiety disorder and decrease schizophrenia, antisocial behavior, and the organically based syndromes to which lower-class people are subject. Since racism seems to be so deeply entrenched in the United States, those days are probably a long time off.

CONCLUSIONS

Religion, ethnicity, and race all connect with the chances of becoming mentally ill in interesting and complicated ways. Overall, however, certain patterns emerge, patterns that clearly indicate high risks for some groups and low risks for others. One pattern from the research on religious denomination and mental illness is a high rate of alcoholism noted among Catholics. Some of this may be accounted for by the specific contribution of the Irish strain of Catholics. Another important pattern is the overrepresentation of Jews in the overall psychiatric population. The high prevalence of disorders among Jews is due in part to the fact that they seek and can afford treatment more readily than other groups.

The mental health status of different ethnic groups in America is far from homogeneous. High rates are reported among Puerto Ricans, whereas the Japanese and Mexicans, both with tightly knit family structures, have relatively low rates.

African Americans have higher reported rates of mental illness than whites. Even within the lower class, stress is more severe among blacks, who are disadvantaged compared to their white counterparts. African Americans are also more likely to develop more severe disorders, including schizophrenia, mental retardation, and organic brain syndromes. Much of the high reported rate of mental illness among blacks is the result of limited opportunities for socioeconomic advancement. In other words, blacks manifest the mental health patterns of lower-class people because they frequently are just that.

11

Migration, Place of Residence, and Age

Mental health problems are noticeably high among international migrants, particularly those who are forced out or escape from home. Culture shock is a factor in this phenomenon. What psychological fate awaits these Haitian refugees as they leave an antiquated, voodoo-based culture and enter U.S. territory?

It is important (and interesting) to note the sociodemographic characteristics of who is most likely to become mentally ill, as well as the type of psychopathology most common in different groups. As we saw earlier, social class and other life circumstances have a big impact on mental health. This chapter completes the "epidemiological investigation" by examining the effects of migration, place of residence, and age. Together, they add more pieces to the complicated jigsaw puzzle of mental illness.

GEOGRAPHIC MOBILITY

International Migration

In many ways, migration affects the lives of people everywhere both here in the United States and around the world. Today more people are traveling farther and for longer periods of time, sometimes permanently, than ever before. This can have major mental health implications for the physical and mental health of migrants because moving often involves a break from the past and from family.[1] This is a problem that is quite visible.[2] In fact, the International Centre for Migration and Health (ICMH) was established in Geneva, Switzerland, to evaluate the health effects of migration, particularly *involuntary* migration.[3]

"Social stress" is a common concept running through many sociological theories of mental disorder. One factor believed to produce stress is geographic mobility of which there are two types. One is international mobility, or *external* mobility. In this case, a person moves from one country to another; and the other is *internal* mobility, whereby a person moves to a different area of the same country. Since the two types of mobility may have different mental health effects, they are considered separately here.

What are some of the specific forms of stress that are most frequently encountered by immigrants? The list is long, but at the top are problems stemming from learning a new language, seeking employment, rebuilding social supports, and redefining roles.[4] These problems have taken their toll on the mental health of immigrants for a long time. In fact, an overrepresentation of foreign-born people in the mental hospital population was noted as early as 1910. In that year, native-borns constituted 69.8 percent of the population of New York State but only 52.6 percent of admissions to state hospitals. The foreign-born, on the other hand, constituted 30.2 percent of the general population and 47.4 percent of the hospital admissions, exceeding their "quota" by 17 percent.[5] In 1939, Faris and Dunham reported a similar finding in Chicago—a pronounced overrepresentation of foreign-borns in mental hospital admissions.[6]

From 1949 to 1951, admissions for schizophrenia in New York State among the foreign-born exceeded those of the native-born by 28 percent.[7] The corresponding statistics for Canada from 1950 to 1952 are similar to those of New York.[8] And in New Haven, Connecticut, in 1954, immigrants into the United States constituted 20.5 percent of the general population and 23 percent of the psychiatric population, a small overrepresentation of foreign-born compared to other studies but still consistent with the usual observed pattern.[9]

A review of studies of the prevalence of mental disorder among immigrants to the United States concluded that the rate of schizophrenia is markedly higher among the foreign-born than among the native-born.[10] The same review also noted that immigrant patients are often diagnosed as schizophrenic, paranoid type, a possible reflection of the suspiciousness that a person can develop living among unfamiliar people. This diagnosis is also very evident among immigrants to Great Britain and elsewhere.[11] A 1984 study of Indochinese refugees in Australia also uncovered significant levels of psychiatric dysfunction, especially among refugees lacking social support.[12]

A number of factors characterize the type of immigrant most vulnerable to mental illness. One factor is the duration of residence in the host country. Consistent with the concept of culture shock, those immigrants who have the shortest period of residence have the highest rate of hospital admissions.[13] Another factor is age, as older immigrants are particularly prone to mental disorder.[14] Other studies indicate that immigrants are especially vulnerable to specific problems such as paranoia[15] and depression.[16]

The central etiological question of the international migration studies is, "Do individuals who emigrate become mentally ill because of the stresses involved in adjusting to a new environment, or are individuals who are predisposed to mental illness more likely to emigrate?" The theories based on these two positions are known as the *stress model* and the *migration model*, respectively.

The Stress Model.   The stress model holds that mental illness among the foreign-born results from the strain of adapting to a new environment. Many are placed in a double bind relationship with society because they are offered inducements to social mobility while at the same time they face barriers to achieving such success. They are expected to strive but not to succeed. In fact, if people migrate to improve their social status, it is likely that they will first experience a decline in social status, a factor known to play an important role in the etiology of mental illness. Such is the case among Puerto Ricans who move to New York City. Many of them dream of a new life in the "Big Apple" where they think there are good economic opportunities. However, when they arrive they find themselves at the bottom of the socioeconomic structure.[17] They also find themselves in a novel cultural environment while lacking the psychosocial sources necessary to adjust, a condition known as *acculturative stress.*[18]

The mental health problems of international migrants vary from group to group depending on a number of circumstances. Migrant children in Western countries are especially prone to psychological problems, particularly if their physical features hinder their assimilation into the mainstream of society.[19] Vietnamese "Americans," on the other hand, have lower prevalence rates than originally expected even though many of them were refugees.[20] There are even some immigrant groups whose mental health is better or at least the same as that of the indigenous population. This is true for Muslim immigrants to Western Europe.[21] Curiously, Mexican-born immigrants to the United States have *better* mental health profiles than do U.S.–born Mexican Americans. Some interpret this as the result of U.S.–borns having easier access to abused substances and suffering the attendant problems that may ensue.[22]

The Migration Model.   The migration model posits that mentally disturbed people are more prone to emigrate than those with stable personalities. Consequently, they leave their native country to escape a society in which they are considered deviant. Consistently, one study reports that harsh and restrictive childhood socialization practices foster the development of a personality unable to deal with everyday life.[23] Actually there is not a lot of evidence to support the migration model over the stress model. One investigation of immigrants to Hong Kong, however, does favor the notion that disordered people are more likely to move. In that study over half of the immigrants had paranoid symptoms that had already been treated when they lived in their native country.[24] Some of the common sources of severe stress include fear of being repatriated, barriers to work and social services, separation from family, and issues related to the process of pursuing refugee claims.[25] But these seem to be more related to the stress of the move, not the personality that preceded it.

Evaluation of Stress vs. Migration Models.   One important factor in favor of the stress model is the discrimination the immigrant faces in attempting to obtain housing and jobs in the United States. It is not just a U.S. phenomenon. In Germany, for example, there are very stringent regulations against immigration, particularly of black people. In fact, intolerance of foreigners runs so deep in Germany, particularly East Germany, that there were 746 violent xenophobic crimes in 2000 alone. All of these facts weigh in favor of the stress model over the migration model.[26]

Some have concluded that the struggle between the stress and migration models is fruitless since mental illness may not be more common among the foreign-born than the native-born. Only a few empirical studies support this proposition. However, the fact that some studies report less mental illness among the foreign-born than among the native-born raises some interesting questions about intervening variables in the relationship between international migration and mental disorder. Not all international moves need be stressful as, for example, where the cultural practices of the original country are similar to those of the new environment. Thus, an individual who migrates from London to Boston is not as likely to be socially disoriented by the move as is the person who moves from the forests of New Guinea to the concrete jungle of New York City. As the cultural gap widens, the chances of mental illness increase.

Other intervening variables have been examined by Morrison, who believes that the contradictory studies on migration and mental illness cannot be integrated by grappling with the stress and migration models alone. Instead, Morrison insists that other factors should be examined to determine the ways in which migration affects different people.[27] One factor is the reason for leaving the old environment. A refugee who is forced to leave has no rationale for choosing a new location and thus is more vulnerable to psychological problems than a voluntary migrant. Another factor is the attitude of the new country toward the migrant. Israel, for instance, has a very positive attitude toward immigrants, which is reflected in lower rates of mental illness among the foreign-born than among the native-born. All of these factors indicate that the relationship between international migration and mental illness varies according to the nature of the move.

Some of the more recently identified issues in international migration include physical living arrangements. Overall, distress levels are reported to be lower among recent immigrants who live in government-supported housing than among those in community residence.[28] Additionally, Ritsner and Ponizovsky found that psychological distress through immigration follows a two-phase temporal pattern.[29] The first phase ("escalation") is characterized by an increase in distress levels until around the 27th month after arrival. The second phase ("reduction") leads to a decline in mental health problems, which eventually return to normal levels.

To summarize: three factors determine the likelihood of an international move being experienced as a stressful event:

1. The degree of cultural difference between the country of origin and the host culture

2. The reason for the move
3. The attitude of the host culture toward immigrants

Like many issues in psychiatric sociology, psychopathology among migrants is a complicated web composed of many issues, theories, and questions.[30] Now there is new research centered on *predicting* whether international migration will engender mental disorder including regrets about coming, female gender, and younger age.[31] Of all of these variables, perhaps age is the most salient because parents may decide to leave their homes, either willingly in the hope of improving their lives or involuntarily to escape danger. But it is never a voluntary decision for a child.[32]

Internal Migration

The question of whether moving from one part of the United States to another precipitates mental illness is highly relevant since about 20 percent of the U.S. population changes residence each year. However, research in this area has not produced consistent results. Some have found that internal migration causes adjustment problems, which in turn precipitate psychological disorder. Others have found that this holds true only under certain conditions. There are also reports about an inverse relationship between moving and mental illness; that is, people who move tend to be better adjusted.

One of the earliest reports suggesting a positive relationship between internal migration and mental illness was Malzberg's analysis of interstate migrants in the United States.[33] He found higher rates of hospitalization among migrants into New York State than among non-migrant natives. Later investigations by other researchers supported Malzberg's findings in different states.[34] Freedman, using census data, defined migrants as persons who moved from one county to another in Illinois between 1935 to 1940.[35] He found high admission rates among this type of migrant population for mood disorders but not for schizophrenia. A later investigation of patients using psychiatric facilities (state hospitals and psychiatric clinics) in Los Angeles County found a much higher proportion of migrants in the patient group than in the general population.[36]

Some of the studies reporting a preponderance of mental illness among internal migrants found an association only for certain *types* of moves. For instance, most of the studies that differentiate between migration from one city to another and mobility within a city found that high rates of mental illness were more common among *intracity* migrants.[37] This is probably because intracity migrants are often rootless individuals who move to avoid bill collectors and landlords. They may also be mentally ill people who were released from state hospitals and drift from one place to another. The *intercity* migrant, on the other hand, is more likely to move in conjunction with upward occupational mobility such as a job promotion. Additionally, those who migrate from one urban community to another have fewer adjustment problems than those who migrate from a rural to an urban area.

Some investigators who report high rates of mental disorder among internal migrants explain their results by drawing an analogy between the needs of a person new to the community and the needs of a newborn infant. Both need to belong and to be loved. A protracted absence from home decreases the fulfillment of these needs. Another line of reasoning is that migrants must struggle to maintain their identity, a task that can weigh heavily on insecure people. However, it is risky to assume that migration typically engenders mental disorder; indeed, a number of studies have reached the exact opposite conclusion.

One of the first studies by A. O. Wright, using 1880 census data, noted that the hospitalization rate for "insanity" was higher in Massachusetts than in any other state. The rate declined in rough proportion to the distance from that state traveling in any direction. He concluded that the more recently settled areas of the country are inhabited by "a selected population, mostly young and middle-aged people of sound minds and bodies. The insane are left behind."[38] That was the thinking way back when.

Studies in the twentieth century reported either an insignificant or an inverse relationship between internal migration and mental illness.[39] Kleiner and Parker, for instance, compared rates of admission to mental hospitals of interstate migrant and nonmigrant blacks in Pennsylvania.[40] They found lower rates among the southern black migrant population than among northern natives. They hypothesized that this was due to a greater discrepancy between level of aspiration and goal attainment among northern black natives than among southern migrants who had fewer ambitions.

Another team of researchers investigated mobility patterns among a group of mental patients in Louisiana.[41] They found geographic mobility and mental illness to be inversely related as the mobility rate of the study population (4 percent annually) was much lower than the national mobility rate (20 percent annually). The researchers concluded that "today the ability to be flexible, to move with the times, and to change one's life circumstances is indicative of good mental health. Moving to another environment can be an opportunity to test one's skills and mettle in competition with others for money and prestige."[42]

The large variation in research findings makes it clear that internal migration, like international migration, does not always precipitate mental illness. Instead, it requires adjustments that, depending on the conditions of the move and the characteristics of the individual, may improve or worsen mental health. Such factors as the characteristics of the place of destination, the personalities of the migrants, and the circumstances under which the move occurs (voluntary or involuntary) affect the amount of change experienced by the person. And it is change that is the crucial mental health hazard for those unprepared for it.

PLACE OF RESIDENCE

Rural-Urban Differences

It is widely believed that the strains of urban living lead to high rates of mental disorder.[43] A number of studies have tested this proposition by comparing rates between rural and urban dwellers. In a majority of those studies the urban rate is higher than the rural rate, but the differences are not large. An epidemiological survey in New Haven, Baltimore, and St. Louis uncovered higher levels among rural residents,[44] while a similar study of a Spanish community found the exact opposite.[45] However, the fact that, in most studies, the difference is greater than one would expect to occur just by chance indicates that living in the country or in the city can have a singular effect on mental health as measured by hospital admissions. Not all groups living in urban areas are susceptible to the reported mental health hazards of city living. A few groups have managed to preserve some aspects of rural life by creating small communities with traditional extended families within the larger city such as the Italian Americans of Philadelphia and Boston.

Some types of mental disorder are more prevalent in urban settings and others are found more frequently in rural settings.[46] The total rates for all the psychoses combined are higher in rural settings. This is largely due to the greater rural prevalence of mood disorders, not schizophrenia, which is more evenly distributed between the two areas. The rates of anxiety and personality disorders, on the other hand, are higher in urban settings in a majority of the studies.

Why is there apparently more mental illness in urban areas? A number of answers to this question have been offered. One explanation centers on the methodologies of the investigations that purport to measure rural-urban differences. Because most of the studies use hospital admissions as the measure of prevalence, it is to be expected that urban areas will have higher reported rates of mental disorder inasmuch as treatment facilities are more readily available in and around cities.[47] Mental illness is also less stigmatizing among urban dwellers, who, on the average, are more highly educated than their rural counterparts. Thus, seeking professional help in the city involves fewer social costs than in the country. Additionally, cramped urban living conditions make disordered people more visible. Consequently, they are more likely to be brought to treatment centers than are rural dwellers living in isolated farmhouses where their families may try to care for them at home. All of the above translates into the idea that rural rates of mental illness are probably underestimated.[48]

Another theory of rural-urban differences suggests that the quality of life varies between the two areas. The country is popularly viewed as a more benign environment in which human relationships are based on love, understanding, and an intimate concern with others, a *Gemeinschaft* type of community. Life in urban areas is said to be quite different; relationships between people are characterized by impersonality, tension, and competition, a *Gesellschaft* type of community. Additionally, the *nature* of urban and rural suicides differs, as evidenced by the fact that urban suicides are more likely to be chronically mentally ill.[49]

Not only is the quality of interpersonal relationships different between *Gemeinschaft* and *Gesellschaft* dwellers, but there is an added feature of urban living that affects mental health—population density. Various animal studies have shown that high population density creates stress that exhausts the vitality of animals. Studies of humans also conclude that high density leads to social disorganization and emotional stress. Research on men in the armed services correlated mental illness with population density. In one such study, people from sparsely settled regions were found to have better mental health than those from more populated areas. In fact, psychological tests of Selective Service inductees uncovered a rate of failure (rejection from the military) three times higher for those from the most populous states than for their counterparts from the least populated states.[50]

Aside from the methodological and quality of life theories, a third explanation has been offered. According to this view, mental health differences between rural and urban dwellers are not attributable to the characteristics of one's home community but to a self-selection process whereby unstable people are more likely to settle in urban than in rural areas.[51] Therefore, higher rates of mental illness among urban dwellers may be due in part to the unstable migrating from the country to the city, where they partially constitute a large part of our present crisis of "street people." Deinstitutionalization is partly responsible for this situation.

Zones of the City

Early in the twentieth century, Burgess divided Chicago into five *concentric zones* which he contended were related to social problems of the city: (1) the central or business district; (2) the zone of transition, also called the zone of disorganization; (3) the zone of working-class families; (4) the wealthy residential zone; and (5) the suburbs. He noted that the greatest concentration of social problems is in the second area, the zone of transition. It is this part of the city that is typically occupied by rootless transients who lead lives of loneliness in the anonymity of their surroundings. Today, it is where we typically find the street people.

Faris and Dunham later examined the spatial distribution of psychotics in Chicago to determine the nature of the relationship between type of psychosis and zone of the city.[52] They discovered that mental illness, like other social problems, varies across the ecological zones of the city. Specifically, they found that the highest rates of schizophrenia were found in zone 2, the zone of transition, and the rates of schizophrenia declined in all directions toward the periphery of the city. Although there was a tendency for the mood disorders to be found in the wealthier sections (zones 4 and 5), most of these cases were scattered randomly throughout the city. This landmark study in psychiatric sociology led to the development of a new etiological theory of schizophrenia. Since the highest rates of hospitalized schizophrenia in Chicago were found in the inner-city rooming house areas, Faris and Dunham offered their "social isolation hypothesis" to account for their findings. Their theory held that the anonymity of life in inner city areas creates an extreme sense of isolation that, in turn, incubates schizophrenia. However, with today's evidence that schizophrenia is often medical, this view has limited value.

Levy and Rowitz retested the Faris and Dunham findings in Chicago and found essentially the same spatial distribution: a concentration of schizophrenia in the inner city and a random distribution of depressive cases throughout the city.[53] Another study, in Worcester, Massachusetts, supported the Faris and Dunham findings as well.[54] However, that study found that the great number of schizophrenic cases in the lower socioeconomic areas of the city were predominantly single, separated, or divorced men living alone. There was little schizophrenia among inner-city dwellers who lived with their families.

Other studies were conducted in St. Louis, Milwaukee, Omaha, Kansas City, Rockford, Peoria, Cleveland, and Providence. All of these investigations confirmed the pattern observed by the Chicago researchers. The only notable exception is Clausen and Kohn's study of schizophrenics in Hagerstown, Maryland.[55] They argue that their data show no relationship between zone of the city and hospitalization for schizophrenia. However, in light of the overwhelming evidence in support of the Faris and Dunham findings, the Hagerstown data must be considered an exception, possibly because Hagerstown is not large enough to have well-defined city zones. Another analysis of this issue also found childhood disorder of various kinds to be very high in the inner cities.[56]

The inner-city concentration of mental illness as measured by hospital admissions has rarely been tested outside of the United States. One study of the Montreal metropolitan area, however, found a considerable amount of disorder among suburbanites.[57] In that study, prevalence was estimated through the use of psychiatric interviews of a random sample of Montreal residents. Because of a high rate of depressive symptoms among suburbanites, the researchers concluded that the high-income outer-city group is nearly as disordered as the low-income inner-city dwellers. The Montreal researchers hypothesized that, while suburban life may be materially rich, it is socially impoverished, particularly in the case of the isolated suburban housewife. Additionally, the higher-class suburbanite is more likely to develop depressive symptoms than is the lower-class inner-city dweller. This all fits with the concentration of reported mood disorders among the higher classes.

Although the concentration of depression among suburbanites needs further clarification, it is not a surprising finding since the research on American cities hinted at such a relationship. The American city research did not uncover the strong association between outer-city life and depression found in the Canadian city research because the former used hospital admissions as an index of prevalence and the latter used interviews with community residents. Since suburbanites appear to be most prone to depression, a disorder that does not necessarily require hospitalization, the suburban cases are not as likely to be discovered in research using hospital data. There is another matter about the suburban-urban issue that is changing: the "first-ring" suburbs—those communities just outside the city limits or even suburbanlike neighborhoods inside the boundary—are now suffering many of the problems found in the inner city.

The concentration of schizophrenia among inner-city dwellers has been the source of much etiological controversy. Medical theorists believe that a predisposition to schizophrenia influences place of residence and socioeconomic status. On the other hand, sociological theorists contend that the stresses involved in inner-city life directly contribute to the onset of schizophrenia. It is not necessary to choose between these two positions since both may be correct. In one case schizophrenia may precede residence, and in another case residence may exert *some* causal influence on schizophrenia. It is also possible that residence and illness may exert an interdependent influence on one another, as in the case of people who are already disordered and choose to live in a socially isolated section of the city. Once there, they become increasingly disordered by the surroundings.

MENTAL ILLNESS AND AGE

A necessary first step in devising a viable sociological explanation for mental disorder in late life is to describe the prevalence and age of onset for mental health problems. This point of departure is important because data on the age distributions of disorder and the age of onset provide hints about potential explanatory factors. If mental disorders emerge early in life and tend to taper off as people grow older, then it makes sense to search for causal mechanisms in the earlier decades of life. However, if mental health problems increase substantially as people get older, then the focus should be shifted to factors that are encountered in late life.[58]

The words in the quotation express a number of possibilities, but one theme is central—the importance of analyzing mental health and social circumstances.[59] Here we consider the circumstances associated with age and movement through the life cycle. This is a tricky endeavor because we do not always know whether current symptoms have emerged in late life for the first time, or if they represent a lifelong recurrence of problems.

In earlier chapters, reference was made to the average age of particular types of patients. But is there an overall relationship between mental illness and age? Is there a particular age group that is most vulnerable to mental disorder? A number of studies have analyzed this question, but the results have not been consistent. Because the results are discrepant, it is difficult to identify any particular age group as the most susceptible one. However, since more studies show a minimum rate of illness in the youngest group, it is safe to assume that *the chances of becoming disordered increase with age.*[60] This is certainly true of organic disorders and suicide. Indeed, one report on research in this area shows that "one of the most consistent patterns in rates of admissions to mental hospitals is the general tendency toward higher rates with increasing age." Another report on mental health problems of old age suggested that this is the result of negative social attitudes toward the elderly.[61]

The following account by a 70-year-old woman explains how she came to the conclusion that without confronting ageism it is impossible to have a good old age. It at least offers a glimmer of hope.

> The equation of old women with undesirability is so pervasive that no one is immune from its destructiveness. The fear about age, reaching phobic proportions among white skinned women of European background, has grave repercussions for us as we experience our own aging. We can attempt to deny our aging for a while at least, through the almost universal practice of trying to pass for younger; we can accept the ugly stereotypes about ourselves and become increasingly depressed and alienated; or we can embark on the struggle to confront the ageism of our culture as well as our own internalized ageism. As an old woman who has chosen this course, the impact on my life has been tremendous. I speak of my struggles against my own internalized ageism and how this path led me to a renewed social activism, sense of purpose, and inner exploration. I have been forced to explore the actuality of my aging vs. my ageist expectations, which I have found repeatedly to cloud my ability to experience my life. This process has brought excitement and fullness to my life, making my old age a time rich in learning and insight.[62]

There is another side to the reportedly higher prevalence of mental illness among older people: they simply have been around longer than others and consequently have had more time to experience a problem. This is particularly cogent in light of the fact that most syndromes emerge early in life. In fact, Robbins and her associates report that the median age of onset for any DSM disorder is age 16.[63] The same investigators state that 90 percent of people with psychiatric problems in the ECA study experience first symptoms by age 38. But these reports suffer from some methodological problems, including the possibility that prevalence rates may be underestimated in elderly populations. Depression is a case in point, as evidenced by a comorbidity between physical health and depression in late life, when risk for physical illness rises.[64] On the other side of the coin, some personality disorders, particularly antisocial personality disorder, mysteriously remit with age.[65]

Mental illness among the aged is a growing problem simply because the size of the elderly population is rapidly expanding. Since 1900 there has been an 80 percent increase in the proportion of persons 65 years of age and older. The social and psychological consequences of such longevity are not always favorable. Hospitalization rates for the over-50 age group have increased alarmingly, in part because it is difficult to care for old people at home in an urbanized society. This sharp increase in admissions with age holds true for all ethnic groups in the United States.[66] A similar pattern is also reported in Great Britain.[67] In Canada, the prevalence of mental illness increases rapidly with age; a longer life span allows more years of exposure to the risk of mental illness. The Canadian male who survives to age 90 has a 24 percent chance of being admitted to a mental hospital. The Canadian female who lives to the same age has a 20 percent chance of being hospitalized.[68] The difference in rate of admissions between elderly men and women may be the result of the greater ability of women to cope with single life (discussed in Chapter 9).

Why is there a high risk of mental disorder among people of 55 years or older? Part of this risk stems from changes in physical appearance and strength, loss of childbearing ability, and retirement, important factors in the origin of disorders such as depression. However, older persons are also high mental illness risks because they are socially dislocated. The attitudes of Americans toward aging persons add to this problem by often funneling the elderly into isolated warehouses to live out their remaining years.[69]

The subjective and objective qualities of life typically decline with age.[70] The sense of control over life diminishes as older age groups feel a shift from control over their lives toward a sense of helplessness.[71] But only some elders get caught in this downward spiral. Others are able even to thrive as they grow older. This is particularly true for those who have quality social support systems, enabling "these more fortunate individuals to age successfully."[72]

Does religiosity have any bearing on the mental health of the elderly? Apparently it does, as evidenced by research reporting that religious beliefs have a significant positive influence on the psychological well-being of older adults.[73] But the real predictors of mental health in old age are a complicated web of various factors. As Mirowsky and Ross state: "Late in life, in old age, people walk a narrowing path. Those who proceed with health, function, wealth and marriage intact find old age an enjoyable time of relaxation and companionship. Even those who lose a spouse or suffer a medical crisis often rebuild a gratifying life within a year or two. But physical impairment can impose demoralizing limitations; the shorter and less certain life appears, the less it seems possible to recover and rebuild."[74]

Older people need social supports for feelings of psychological well-being just as much, if not more so, than do younger people. Community prevention programs are especially in order.[75] One study found that psychological well-being among elderly people is *directly* related to the number of significant others in their lives.[76] Unfortunately, this social support is often missing during the later years of life because Americans display a great deal of disinterest toward the aged. This disinterest is found in the scientific community as well, as evidenced by a significant lack of basic information on mental health and illness among the elderly. Further, there is a good deal of misdiagnosis of patients in later life because the medical community often confuses functional and organic forms of mental illness among the aged. As mentioned earlier, depression probably occurs more frequently than most know because it is confused with senile deterioration, cerebral arteriosclerosis, and other organic disorders.[77]

The suicide statistics yield some interesting information on age and mental health. Although some consider it risky to assume that a person who commits suicide is mentally ill, it is safe to assume that a suicidal person is at least *temporarily* disturbed. Since Durkheim's comprehensive investigation of suicide patterns in the earlier part of the twentieth century, a countless number of studies have found that the risk of suicide, like mental illness, increases with age. Since the 1960s, however, there has been a new surge of suicides among American youth, particularly among those in college.

Depression among the young has been rising, as evidenced by clinical studies, suicide data, and the widespread use of mood-elevating drugs. Admission rates to mental hospitals have followed the same pattern. Since the early 1960s, the hospitalization rate among those aged 15 to 24 has skyrocketed. However, it is not certain that this is purely the result of a heightened rate of disorder among the young or simply the consequence of earlier detection and treatment of mental illness.[78] It cannot be explained by the fact that there are more young people today since the overall *rate*, not just the absolute *number*, has increased.[79] One of the problems about many of the mental health statistics about the "young" in general is a confusion of the "adolescent" age group with "young adults."[80]

Admission rates have also increased slightly among those in their 30s and 40s. It is this group that is reported to be most disturbed by economic and occupational anxieties, which may be the prime reason for their high rate of somatic disorders.[81] *Perhaps* it is "middle-age" people who have the greatest sense of well-being. They are at the peak of their earnings. Their jobs are usually secure. The tensions and conflicts of young adulthood have lessened and the problems of old age have not yet arrived. *Perhaps.*

A Potpourri of New Findings

The literature on age and mental illness is finally starting to intensify. Below is a short list of some of the more interesting findings from recent years.

- Highly educated people have fewer problems with aging.[82]
- Early childhood trauma is causally linked to other types of stress that subsequently emerge over the life course.[83]
- There is a sharp upturn in depressive symptoms that emerge at about age 60.
- The mental health needs of grade school children are largely unmet.[84]
- Older and younger mental patients are diagnosed with a similar degree of accuracy.[85]
- Disability from schizophrenia is greater among older and middle-aged adults than among their younger counterparts.[86]
- Adolescents who had been physically or sexually assaulted are more likely to be substance abusers.[87]
- The outlook for elderly depressed patients is poorer than for younger patients.[88]
- There is an increased risk of death among the elderly who are mentally ill.[89]

CONCLUSIONS

Those who migrate from one country to another are overrepresented in the mental hospital population. This is either because of the stress of moving to an unfamiliar environment or because mentally ill people are more likely to migrate. The research on internal migration is contradictory. This type of move can have a positive or negative effect on mental health depending on the nature of the move and the personality of the individual.

Aside from physical mobility, geographic place of residence is related to mental illness in other ways. Rural dwellers are reported to have lower rates than urban dwellers. Although this is commonly interpreted as indicating a better quality of life in rural areas, it is also possible that the greater availability of treatment centers in urban areas results in more urban than rural dwellers becoming registered cases. Within urban settings there is a concentration of schizophrenia in the area near center city, whereas depression is distributed more randomly with a noticeable concentration among suburbanites.

The overall relationship between prevalence of mental illness and age is direct; there are higher rates among increasingly older age groups. Although this may simply be the result of having more time to develop an illness, it may also be connected with the negative experiences that accompany aging, such as loss of loved ones through death, diminished physical vitality, and societal attitudes that ostracize the elderly. Recently there has been a rise in psychiatric disorder among adolescents, although this may be the result of earlier detection and treatment. Research on mental health and aging is still in its early stages.

12

Becoming a Mental Patient

The Prepatient Process

Humane treatment of the mentally ill was initiated in France through the efforts of Phillipe Pinel (1745–1826), a founder of modern psychiatry. Here he stands in the courtyard at the hospital of Salpetrière surrounded by patients. There is more hope for a cure for people who become mentally ill today, although that hope remains limited.

Sometimes my students smirk over the title of this chapter. After all, "Becoming a Mental Patient" can be literally misinterpreted as a recipe for becoming mentally ill. However, that is one of the few times in class that anything approaches humor. As you know by now, the situation of the mentally ill is grim. Symptoms can be overbearing, and cure may never come. Actually, things are even worse than what has been depicted to this point in the book. I am speaking here of the "social experience of patienthood."[1] What happens to people as they become mentally ill in the United States? What awaits ex-patients as they attempt to rejoin outside society? Those questions are the focus of this last part of the book.

Psychiatric disorders vary widely. Even within specific categories of illness, the reported experience of mentally ill individuals is diverse. Beyond these differences, however, are common social experiences that lead to the recognition of psychiatric conditions. These processes constitute the focus of this chapter, which centers about the *behavioral, interpersonal,* and *legal* events that prospective patients confront as they seek help. Together they compose the *prepatient process.*[2] More specifically, the temporal sequence of events preceding treatment consists of four stages. The first stage is the personal onset, which includes the subjective experience of pathological feelings that frequently occur after a stressful life event. The second stage involves the reactions of relatives and friends as they attempt to cope with a person's changed behavior. The third stage of the prepatient process is the community response, that is, all experiences associated with seeking help from the larger community, mental health experts included. The final stage consists of the psychiatric and legal aspects of formal evaluation, including possible commitment.

The social organization of mental health contacts is a complicated relationship among social, cultural, and economic factors, as well as the idiosyncrasies of the personalities involved. These include both the troubled person and those trying to help.[3]

> Since social scientists first directed their attention to understanding how individuals recognize and respond to mental illness, they have struggled to capture both the underlying process or dynamic that drives the search for care and the social, cultural, medical, and organizational characteristics that shape the fate of persons dealing with mental health problems.[4]

THE PERSONAL ONSET

Life Events

The influence of stressful life events has been under scrutiny for a long time. Adolph Meyer pioneered in the development of a systematic framework of the influence of psychosocial events in the early decades of the twentieth century. He constructed a "life chart" that showed the relationship between major events of a patient's life and the onset of psychiatric disorder. Subsequent work by others has more succinctly elaborated the mechanisms by which social events can influence the inner state. Holmes and Rahe devised a scale to gauge the specific influence of various social events on stress. Not all of the events on their scale are intrinsically unpleasant, but all reportedly involve some impingement on the steady state of the individual's life. The rank ordering of these events according to the amount of stress each produces (as measured by the subjective feelings of test subjects) is presented in Table 12:1. A high

Table 12:1 Social Readjustment Rating Scale

Rank	Life Event	Mean Value
1	Death of spouse	100
2	Divorce	73
3	Marital separation	65
4	Jail term	63
5	Death of close family member	63
6	Personal injury or illness	53
7	Marriage	50
8	Fired at work	47
9	Marital reconciliation	45
10	Retirement	45
11	Change in health of family member	44
12	Pregnancy	40
13	Sex difficulties	39
14	Gain of new family member	39
15	Business readjustment	39
16	Change in financial state	38
17	Death of close friend	37
18	Change to different line of work	36
19	Change of number of arguments with spouse	35
20	Large mortgage	31
21	Foreclosure of mortgage or loan	30
22	Change in responsibilities at work	29
23	Son or daughter leaving home	29
24	Trouble with in-laws	29
25	Outstanding personal achievement	28
26	Wife begins or stops work	26
27	Begin or end school	26
28	Change in living conditions	25
29	Revision of personal habits	24
30	Trouble with boss	23
31	Change in work hours or conditions	20
32	Change in residence	20
33	Change in schools	20
34	Change in recreation	19
35	Change in church	19
36	Change in social activities	18
37	Small mortgage or loan	17
38	Change in sleeping habits	16
39	Change in number of family get-togethers	15
40	Change in eating habits	15
41	Vacation	13
42	Christmas	12
43	Minor violations of the law	11

Source: Reprinted from T. Holmes and R. H. Rahe, "The social readjustment scale," *Journal of Psychosomatic Research, 11* (1967), 213–218. By permission of Pergamon Press, Ltd.

score (mean value) indicates that a particular life event produced a greater amount of stress (as measured by readjustment) than an event with a lower score.

The Holmes and Rahe study hypothesized that those individuals who had a very high life crisis score during a given period of time would be more likely to become ill than those who had a low score during the same period. For example, a person would be more likely to become disturbed over sex difficulties (mean value of 39) than from a change in sleeping habits (mean value of 16). Other investigations have confirmed the basic hypothesis. Rahe and his associates also tested the scale on a navy population and found that subjects in the highest decile of life crisis scores developed illnesses twice as often as did those in the lowest decile.[5]

The Holmes and Rahe scale was further developed by a group of researchers who expanded the list of 43 life events to 102 in a measure called the Psychiatric Epidemiology Research Interview (PERI) Life Events Scale.[6] However, others have criticized life event scales for failing to consider the quality of life events, particularly the "desirability-undesirability" of the change. Additionally, these same critics report that only *undesirable* changes are significantly associated with psychological impairment while desirable events are hardly related at all.[7]

A study by Samuelsson indicates that undesirable life events increase with the number of children a woman has.[8] While the debate continues, other questions remain unanswered, such as the issue of individual differences in reactions to major life changes. Do some people have an "emotional insulation" to these changes? If so, who are most susceptible to change—the genetically vulnerable, the biochemically imbalanced, or those who were improperly socialized? Perhaps the influence of life changes is different for each of these groups. That is why the external character of the stressful life event may be less important than the fact that it is *perceived* as stressful by the person.

Another unresolved issue is the nature of the causal linkage between life changes and psychiatric symptoms. It is generally assumed that life changes can cause symptoms, but it is also possible that certain types of symptoms can lead to self-induced stressful events. Being aware of the existence of stress and how it can adversely influence a person's life is another clue to the nature of the complicated relationship between life events and mental illness and how they can influence each other.[9]

Social Support, Personality, and Life Events

Life events and stress have been studied in every way possible. Their connection with mental illness is well documented. In fact, there have been so many studies of the relationship between life events and social stress that Paykel and Cooper conducted a separate study of how frequently researchers in this area produce consistent results.[10] There is no doubt that stressful life events can deteriorate mental health over time. But why is it that only certain people are vulnerable to stress while others are hardly affected? A number of studies report that the reaction to stress depends on whether the person has adequate social supports, such as friends and relatives.[11] Some believe that supportive people can act as a buffer against stressful events by providing sympathy and advice.[12]

Inadequate social support may be why certain groups (such as the lower class and single people) have high rates of mental disorder. In other words, *life events have a greater impact on certain groups because supportive others are not available to mediate the effects of the stress.*[13] A similar point can be examined in a different way. If mentally disabled people are more vulnerable to stress, then we would expect their mental health to deteriorate further when significant change occurs in their lives. This expectation is supported by the data in Figure 12:1. There you see the differing impacts of stress in 1985, 1990, and 2000, when the Center for Disease Control and Prevention targeted the problem through better mental health care systems designed to minimize the impact of change.

The reaction to stress is an important determinant of mental health. In fact, it is so important that it can even affect the development of the unborn. Nuckolls and others found that the pregnancy complication rate is much higher among women who experienced many life events during pregnancy but had few social supports (such as a good marriage) than for those who experienced as many life events but had supportive others.[14]

Personality characteristics are also involved as possible mediators between life events and mental disorder.[15] Some propose that *hardy people* are more resistant to stressful life events because they thrive on personal development through change. Hardy individuals have a lot of curiosity and find life events interesting and meaningful. They *expect* change, and they believe they can be influential through what they imagine, say, and do. This is an interesting finding that has been tested on university campuses. College students who feel in control of their lives, for instance, are less likely to feel stressed by life events than those who feel that they are controlled by others.[16] Another correlate of stress is place of residence. Those who live in the Middle Atlantic states (New York, New Jersey, and Pennsylvania) report more stress (and less happiness with life) than those who live in other parts of the country. This may be related to high levels of achievement orientation and competition.

Figure 12:1   Persons 18 years and over with adverse health effects of stress in the past year: United States, 1985, 1990, and year 2000 target for objective 6.5.

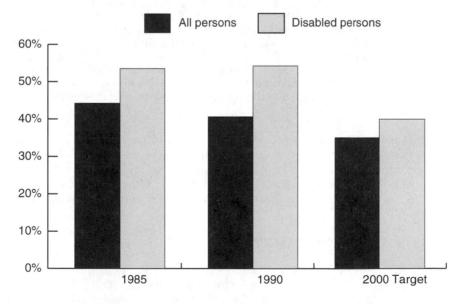

Source: Centers for Disease Control and Prevention, National Center for Health Statistics, National Health Interview Survey, 1993.

One group in American society that is especially likely to experience a number of life events is teenagers. Perhaps this is one reason why there is an epidemic of adolescent suicides. Newcomb and his colleagues report that teenagers experience about nine life events annually.[17] Some common events among teenagers include falling in love, deciding whether to go to college, and starting work. The process of applying to college can be especially stressful. This is evident in a number of ways, including a notable increase in blood pressure.[18] Certain groups of students are especially stressed by preparing for college, such as class leaders, high achievers, and those under inordinate pressure by their parents to succeed. The preoccupation with the almighty SAT score does not help either.

Autobiographical Accounts

Although the influence of social events on the beginning of an illness is more relevant to sociological analysis than an autobiographical perspective, personal accounts of distress are central to understanding the emotional costs involved. Accounts primarily describe the subjective experience of becoming mentally ill, and most of these portray radical alterations in the character of the consciousness and emotions of the person. Consider, for example, the following reports by schizophrenics describing the changes they underwent:

> Case 1: I began to think of myself as two people. One I referred to as "she." "She" was the Egyptian princess—a constant voice in my head telling me what to do to help the prince find his kingdom. One day she told me I was to have a special part in her future, and that I should brand myself to make this clear. I used a hot iron to burn a scar into my arm that happened to resemble a lightening bolt. I knew this was the right thing to do because the burn did not hurt.[19]

> Case 2: I felt distinctly different from my usual self. I would sit for hours on end staring at nothing, and I became fascinated with drawing weird, disconnected monsters. I carefully hid my drawings, because I was certain I was being watched. Eventually, I became aware of a magical force outside myself that was compelling me in certain directions. The force gained power as time went on, and soon it made me take long walks at 2 or 3 o'clock in the morning down dark alleys in my high-crime neighborhood. I had no power to disobey the force. During my walks I felt as though I was in a different, magical four-dimensional universe. I understood that the force wanted me to take these walks so that I might be killed.[20]

It is not uncommon for severe symptoms to go unrecognized by other people even though they wreak havoc in the individual's mind. Sometimes the symptoms reach extreme dimensions before they are noticed and then it may be too late. Such is the case of the woman portrayed in Box 12:1. Other times the problems may be noticed in childhood when there is still hope for effective intervention.[21]

THE CRISIS WITHIN THE FAMILY

More recently, research in this area has extended the analysis of burden to focus explicitly on the experience of caregiving for family members with psychiatric illnesses. With the continued trends toward the deinstitutionalization of individuals with mental illness, an increasing number of discharged patients return to live with their families. Consistent

The Satanic Voices: The Mother Who Stabbed Her Children

That night in bed, Eun Sook Kim watched the shadows playing on the bedroom wall, convinced they embodied evil. Already she believed that Satan possessed her and that the devil wanted her to spill innocent blood.

Seeking spiritual help, the Korean-born mother of three had temporarily left Philadelphia to stay at the home of her minister in Wyndmoor, Montgomery County. Together their families spent the evening praying and singing religious songs before going to bed.

At 1 A.M., the minister heard soft singing and murmurs of "Hallelujah" coming from Kim's room—a hopeful sign, he later told detectives.

But by 3 A.M. on Aug. 28, the "Hallelujahs" were being screamed hysterically from downstairs. That's where the minister found Kim with a bloody, 12-inch kitchen knife, alternating between frenzy and calm.

She had stabbed herself three times in her leg. She had stabbed her son Jason, 9, once in the side. She had stabbed her son Kwang, 7, five times in the back. Most seriously hurt was her daughter, Hyo, 5, stabbed in the stomach and back. . . .

Her thinking at the time was that if she killed the children and herself, they would not become slaves of the devil and there would be salvation. . . .

Kim's children have recovered from their wounds and remain in the custody of the Department of Human Services in Philadelphia. They speak with their mother frequently, said Kim's public defender, Elayne Bryne.

Kim had no previous history of violence or mental illness, testimony showed. She had attended college in Massachusetts and West Chester, had bought a home and a laundry business in Philadelphia, and struggled to keep both acquisitions after her husband left for California.

But two days before the stabbings, her head pounding with pain, Kim found herself unable to function at work, witnesses said. She gathered her children and went to stay with their minister.

When police arrived after the stabbings, they found the minister's wife, Hye Joo Kim, struggling with Eun Sook Kim on the bloodied carpet near an overturned potted plant. A knife lay a few feet away.

It took two Springfield Township police officers to handcuff the woman.

"Most of the time she was screaming 'Hallelujah' and singing," testified Cpl. Joseph Mellon. "It wasn't so much a resistance to arrest as a constant frenzy."

After her arrest, Kim was interviewed by Detective Daniel Diedel of Springfield Township. "She was like in another world," Diedel testified. "She told me that the devil was inside her, that the devil wanted blood."

During the interview, Diedel said, Kim stood up, grabbed a paper punch and started beating herself in the head. She fell rigid to the floor, her mouth frothing, as officers struggled to subdue her.

"I really don't think she knew where she was or what she was doing," Diedel said. "She just wasn't there."

Source: Larry King, "Mother who stabbed children found not guilty by reason of insanity," *The Philadelphia Inquirer,* March 11, 1992. By permission of the publisher.

•••

with earlier research, studies of these families reveal that the caregiving role is characterized by high levels of chronic strain.[22]

The Tendency to Ignore

The next set of events on the path to treatment occurs within the prepatient's interpersonal world. A number of published findings explore the reactions of the family in attempting to cope with the behavior of one of its members who later becomes a mental patient.[23] All of these studies have consistently documented "the monumental capacity of family members, before hospitalization, to overlook, minimize and explain away evidence of profound disturbance in an intimate."[24] In short, *the person's illness is typically ignored at first and then tolerated.* The high tolerance for abnormal behavior in certain types of families seems to be caused, at least in part, by "shameful" attitudes toward mental illness. The feeling of shame is more frequently found among less educated families who try to hide their mental illness problems. This phenomenon of hiding mental illness among the lower classes partially explains the tendency of these same people to develop the more disturbed illnesses; since persons from these families are left untreated longer, their sicknesses fester as a consequence. Lower-class circumstances strike again.

Geographic area of residence also affects the tendency of families to ignore behavioral disturbances, because it is much easier for a family to look after a mentally disturbed member in an isolated farmhouse than it is in the cramped living conditions of an urban area. Mental illness is simply more visible in urban than in rural areas because of greater population density. This affects the likelihood of a mental illness being treated because certain cases, particularly the visible ones, are more difficult to ignore.

Types of Family Response

Before I review the studies on the typical ways in which families react to a disturbed relative, I should point out that there really is no "typical" response. I learned that lesson the hard way when I responded to a plea for help from a family from my old neighborhood. The details are in Box 12:2. They are not pretty.

Box 12:2
Trying to Help Out: The Case of the Frustrated Family

It had been 30 years since I had heard from my childhood friend, Bobby V. We had had a lot of fun together as kids growing up next door to each other. Those days were gone. In the summer of 1992, Bobby's father called me. He knew that my occupation centered about mental illness, and he needed help desperately. Bobby's life had been a mess. He had been married numerous times, was an alcoholic, and had been diagnosed as schizophrenic and manic-depressive. At the time of Mr. V's call, Bobby was in the psychiatric ward of a general hospital after a suicide attempt.

The family was outraged at Bobby. Having paid his bills to the point of remortgaging the house, they were fed up. Could I help? Would the welfare or state hospital system support him? I did everything I could, making dozens of calls to agencies, representatives of mental hospitals, and a list of people that could fill this page. Every agency, it seemed, had some rule that disqualified him for help. I was frustrated but I didn't give up.

I went to see Bobby at the hospital. It was a shocking sight. The vibrant 10-year-old I remembered from childhood was an aging shell of a man who was bed-ridden. It was like visiting a person in an "old-age home." He remembered me. His spirits lifted. I promised to try to help. That proved to be a mistake.

After Bobby was released, he called me from a motel. He was living there with a nurse he had met at the hospital. I thought that was odd. I was also stunned when he asked me to co-sign an apartment for him. I couldn't reach his father for advice. My wife said I would be a moron to sign. I phoned Bobby's sister and she agreed with my wife. The chat with Bobby's sister, Ginny V., was helpful. It was also kind of enjoyable reminiscing with her about the old neighborhood. But guess what? The next day, Mr. V. called and told me off for "bothering" Ginny. That was the end of the story for me. Ungrateful family? Perhaps. Certainly they were confused. But, whatever they were, I will never stop worrying about Bobby's life.

The social psychological styles employed by different families to deal with the bizarre behavior of a loved one are varied and complex. Sampson and his associates looked at families in which the wife was eventually hospitalized for schizophrenia.[25] They detected two types of family response in that kind of situation. In the first case, the marital relationship was characterized by the mutual withdrawal of husband and wife and the construction of "separate worlds of compensatory involvement." This usually took the form of the husband becoming increasingly involved in his work or in other interests outside of the marriage. In fact, one case is reported where the husband would tinker in the basement every evening while his wife engaged in conversations and arguments with imaginary others upstairs! Over time, the husband became even less concerned with his wife's behavior and accepted it as a matter of course.

The second type of family response differs from the first in that family life was organized around the presence of a maternal figure (the wife's mother) who took over the wife's domestic and child-rearing functions. The wife's mother established a relationship with her daughter essentially based on helplessness. The husband, on the other hand, "withdrew to the periphery of the family system, leaving the wife and mother bound in a symbiotic interdependency."[26]

The multitude of feelings generated within a family toward the prepatient cannot adequately be summarized by observing behavioral patterns. In fact, an entire spectrum of feeling exists ranging from sympathetic understanding to overt hostility. There are those who vent anger as well as those who express chagrin, puzzlement, fear, and guilt. If there is any *typical* response it is probably confusion and ambivalence. In fact, a considerable number of families manifest these uncertainties by viewing the illness as physical or by denying that the person is ill at all.

In general, most families seek an adjustment by reducing their expectations of the prepatient and by reassigning the responsibilities formally assumed by the troubled person to other family members. This is particularly likely to occur when another family member is able to act as a functional equivalent, such as the son who assumes economic responsibilities previously held by his now-disordered father.

Factors Affecting Help Seeking

The decision to seek treatment is based on so many factors that a computer would be required to predict whether a specific individual would reach out for help or be led to it. Somewhere in the software of that computer program must be a file on the particular effect of such social factors as age, gender, race, social class, and ethnicity. If it is somehow convenient to think in terms of the "typical," then note that the typical intrafamilial patterns of *accommodation* and *denial* fail to preserve harmony permanently. Usually situations worsen as the person's illness progresses and the ability of the family to tolerate disturbing behavior decreases. At this point, the outside community may be called on for assistance.

Often members of the community are the first to recognize the problem as a mental illness. One study reports that this is true for 85 percent of the cases it investigated.[27] In that study, the community member most likely to spot the disorder was a physician, although this varied by social class; policemen, ministers, judges, and other community authorities accounted for bringing a larger proportion of lower-class people to psychiatric help sources than disturbed people from higher classes.

A number of factors affect if and when people realize that a relative is mentally disturbed. Zola outlined five "triggers" that relate to the decision to seek professional help.[28] They all involve reaching the "end of the line."

1. The first is an *interpersonal crisis* that calls attention to the symptoms, such as hostile behavior on the part of the prepatient toward the family.
2. The second involves *social interference*, which brings the disorder into conflict with a socially valued activity
3. The third is *sanctioning* in which others actually tell the person to seek help.
4. The fourth involves the prepatient seeing the symptoms of the illness as a *threat to himself and/or those around him.*
5. The fifth is the *actual recognition* by the person of the mental nature of his illness.

Mechanic has also dealt with the question of how people recognize the existence of a mental disorder and which factors affect the likelihood of a prospective mental patient seeking help outside of the family.[29] He developed a list of factors related to help seeking, all of which are associated with a high probability of soliciting assistance. Some of these are:

1. *The visibility and recognizability of deviant signs and symptoms.* Visible symptoms are more likely to engender help outside of the family.
2. *The extent to which the prepatient perceives the symptoms as serious.* This is an estimate of the present and future probabilities of something physically or socially dangerous occurring.
3. *The extent to which symptoms disrupt family, work, and other social activities.* The more disruptive they are, the more likely it is that others will become aware of the problem and either offer assistance or suggest a professional help source. This is related to the visibility of symptoms as well.
4. *The frequency of the appearance of deviant signs or symptoms, or their persistence.* Many families can tolerate bizarre behavior that is infrequent or transient. But ability to tolerate decreases as the family is faced with psychiatric symptoms on a regular basis.
5. *The tolerance threshold of those who are exposed to and evaluate the deviant signs and symptoms.* This threshold naturally varies from one person to another. There are important differences, however, as a function of the person's familial relationship. Spouses, for example, tolerate less from their mates than do parents from their children.
6. *The information available to, the knowledge of, and the cultural assumptions and understanding of the evaluator.* Social class is important here since lower-class people are less informed regarding the nuances of mental illness than their higher-class counterparts. As mentioned earlier, this results in more lower-class cases going untreated.
7. *The degree to which autistic psychological processes are present.* These are perceptual processes that distort reality and alarm others by their visible departure from the commonly accepted view of the world.
8. *The availability of treatment resources, their physical proximity, and the psychological and monetary costs of taking action.* This includes not only physical distance from the treatment center and investments of time, money, and effort but also such costs as stigmatization and feelings of humiliation resulting from being considered "crazy" and in need of help. These costs are less in higher social classes, because they are better able to pay fees, and they are less prone to stigmatize mental illness.

It is amazing how some studies in psychiatric research have uncovered findings that were implausible 50 years ago. New discoveries about the medical bases of schiz-

Figure 12:2   Family process preceding hospitalization of a relative.

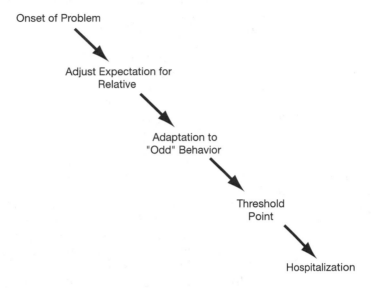

Onset of Problem

Adjust Expectation for
Relative

Adaptation to
"Odd" Behavior

Threshold
Point

Hospitalization

Source: Adapted from Bernice A. Pescosolido, Carol A. Boyer, and Keri M. Lubell,"The social dynamics of responding to mental health problems," in Carol S. Aneshensel and Jo C. Phelan, eds., *Handbook of the Sociology of Mental Health* (New York: Klurver Academic/Plenum, 1999), p. 444.

ophrenia are a case in point. Some things, however, never seem to change. Take a look at Figure 12:2. It is a diagrammatic representation of the process by which the onset of a psychiatric problem is recognized and managed over time. It was put forth by Clausen and Yarrow in 1955. It could possible apply forever.[30]

THE COMMUNITY RESPONSE

The Recognition Process

There are four important aspects of dealing with mental health problems. . . . First, mental health problems are poorly understood by most people. Typical "symptoms" of schizophrenia and more so those associated with depression, are not easily or quickly recognized as illness. Families often normalize situations, adapting to and accommodating behavior. Second, others beyond the family (e.g., police, bosses, teachers) are often the first to see the person's behavior as a mental health problem. Third, the image of entering treatment voluntarily is not entirely accurate. Fourth, the idea of an orderly progression through well-defined and logical stages is contradicted by the stories of people who faced, either for themselves or their family members, mental health problems.[31]

Although relatives tend to "normalize" bizarre psychiatric symptoms, there is a limit to this rationalization process. The limit is a function of the family's willingness to tolerate disruptive behavior. There are vast differences in toleration capacities, but few relatives can cope with a person who is suicidal, homicidal, hallucinatory, or disoriented. When such situations develop, in most states the police have considerable leeway in arresting on an "emergency basis." This is based on the principle of *parens patriae*, which enables the state to make decisions that both protect the individual from self-harm and promote his best interests. This may include involuntary hospitalization under extreme circumstances such as:

1. An indication of violence by the individual,
2. Incongruous behavior in physical appearance, such as odd posturing or nudity,
3. Evidence of attempted or potential suicide,
4. Disruptive behavior, such as creating a nuisance in public places, and
5. Situations in which the police have been summoned by a complainant in the family or a physician, employer, and so on.[32]

These circumstances are linked by a behavioral characteristic common to those who are most likely to be treated—*visible symptoms that engender public recognition.* These are situations in which individuals typically become labeled as mentally ill because they have evoked the judgment of others. It is important to note that prepatients displaying visible symptoms are not necessarily more disordered than those with more hidden psychopathologies. If this were so, the transvestite, for example, would be considered more disordered than the psychopath. On the simple basis of symptoms, the transvestite is more visible because cross-dressing is quite overt. A man in a prom gown is a case in point. But the psychopath does not always exhibit such external signs. Those who *do* display visible symptoms, however, are more likely to experience enduring problems because of the greater stigmatization associated with the public display of psychopathology. Following are some representative cases of this "publicly disordered" group.

J.P.C., a 38-year-old single man, had been arrested on a charge of drunkenness, growing out of an incident in which he was behaving in a very strange way near a neighbor's apartment building. When questioned by the police he said that he was looking for his sister, who he believed was in the tree, and said that she had dropped her child in a culvert and that he had retrieved the baby. He explained that his sister, while changing the baby's diaper, was snatched up into the tree.[33]

R.U., a 21-year-old married man, was referred to the courts after an incident in which he was arrested in a downtown department store dressed in women's clothing and sitting in the fitting room of the dress department. Upon examination by the police physician, it was discovered that he was completely dressed in women's clothing including padded bra, women's hose, and so on.[34]

In these two cases, the recognition process proceeds rapidly. This is particularly true of mentally ill people who are both severely *and* chronically disordered since they are frequently unable to provide good reasons to account for their actions. Many cases of mental illness, however, are not both severe and chronic. In such instances, the recognition process becomes more complex, and the degree of agreement among observers concerning the existence of an illness diminishes accordingly.[35]

The procedures by which people in need of psychiatric treatment are identified are frequently unclear, largely because their first source of help is usually a nonprofessional. Even if the help is a physician, the criteria a physician applies to deviant behavior are at times indefinite and the physician who practices in large treatment centers often *must assume the illness of the patient* who appears before him and then proceed to prescribe treatment. The consequences are that the initial decisions about mental illness take place prior to the patient's examination by mental health experts. Although this is an important phase of the recognition process, it is essentially man-

••••••••••••••••••••••••••••••••••••• **Box 12:3** •••••••••••••••••••••••••••••••••••

If Dahmer's Not Ill, Who Is? Persuading People That Eating People Isn't Insane

For almost three weeks recently, Americans were invited to observe the Wisconsin insanity defense being applied to a cannibalizing serial killer. Unfortunately for Wisconsinites, *State v. Dahmer*, F-914245 (1992), probably has convinced many that, at least in Wisconsin, a man is not crazy even when he drills holes in his living victims' heads, pours in chemicals to "zombify" them, has sex with the corpses' viscera and keeps some body parts in his refrigerator, occasionally eating them. As Mr. Dahmer's defense counsel said, "If that's not crazy, I don't know what is."

While Mr. Dahmer's conduct may indeed warrant the label "crazy," it did not compel a finding of nonresponsibility. In this area of criminal defense, perhaps more than any other, semantics is key. If we were to establish a negative formula for this defense, it would look something like this: colloquial "crazy" does not equal medical insanity does not equal legal nonresponsibility.

So, yes, people in Wisconsin, probably including the jurors and certainly including the court-appointed experts in *Dahmer*, think a person performing Dahmer's acts is crazy; most of the experts and at least the dissenting jurors in *Dahmer* consider him to be suffering from a mental disease and therefore medically insane; almost no one, however, with the exceptions of his counsel and the relatively inexperienced defense experts, considered Mr. Dahmer to be anything but responsible for the horrendous acts he described in 60 hours of police confessions.

Given the virtually stipulated facts in *Dahmer*, and the absence of any novel legal issues, it is not surprising that most of Wisconsin's criminal bar found the trial mundane. What gave the case such significance as it had were two interlocked issues: the somewhat arcane medical question of whether one of the paraphilias (necrophilia) is a mental disease; and the real, political question: Could the Wisconsin insanity defense survive a verdict of nonresponsibility? Because the required five-sixths of the jury answered "no" to the first question, the second question, fortunately, was mooted.

————————

Source: Stephen M. Glynn, "If Dahmer's not crazy, who is?" *National Law Journal*, March 9, 1992.

•••

aged by nonprofessionals, who lack the time and psychiatric insight to render a valid diagnosis. This is especially true of nonpsychiatric physicians (general practitioners, family specialists, internists, obstetricians, and gynecologists), who rarely even bother to send a disturbed patient to other persons or agencies for psychiatric care.[36] The police and judicial systems do not have a better record; they commonly fail to refer those with obvious psychological problems, particularly young, lower-class males.[37]

I do not suppose there is anything more directly related to recognizing that a person is disturbed than the visibility of his or her behavior. Today's world is loaded with examples, but one case that will go down in the annals of American psychiatry is Jeffrey Dahmer. Here's a person who ate people, yet there was still much debate over his mental condition. Dahmer is a classic case of the conflict between psychiatry and the law (discussed in Chapter 2). Box 12:3 is a brief synopsis of his story.

The Jeffrey Dahmers of the world are, fortunately, rare. The person chronically deteriorating at home is closer to the norm. Are there common first "everyday" warning signs of mental illness? What should a family look for? A comprehensive list of warning signs would fill an entire chapter. Below are a few of the more common ones:

- Social withdrawal
- Excessive fatigue and sleepiness or an inability to sleep
- Sudden shift in basic personality
- Hyperactivity or inactivity or alternations between the two
- Indifference, even in highly important situations

- Hostility or suspiciousness
- Inability to concentrate or cope with minor problems
- Dropping out of activities
- Decline in academic or occupational performance
- Devastation from peer or family disapproval
- Deterioration of personal hygiene
- Inability to express joy
- Inappropriate laughter
- Bizarre behavior
- Strange posturing
- Peculiar use of language
- Irrational statements
- Development of strange or unbelievable ideas
- Hearing voices or seeing visions
- Thoughts of suicide

Community Rejection

Those who are diagnosed as mentally ill often resist the label because it involves a negative change in their self-image. This is not an ungrounded fear in light of evidence that there is a social penalty exacted from the mentally ill, especially when they are considered to be violently dangerous, a condition that may be diagnosed much too frequently. The price that these people pay for "being different" is often rejection by others in the community. Of course, it is also possible that community rejection is a possible *cause* for seeking help. Derek Phillips investigated the factors involved in the social rejection of those seeking mental health counsel.[38] He found that the degree of rejection by others in the community is a function of the type of help source utilized. Individuals are increasingly ostracized as they go to more professional help sources. This ironic phenomenon is portrayed in Figure 12:3.

This partly explains why such a large number of disturbed people try to live with their problems rather than pay the costs in ostracism and self-image that are a consequence of seeking help. It can also account for the findings of other studies that have discovered a high percentage of people *reporting* that they were helped more by the clergy or physicians than by psychiatrists or mental hospitals.[39] These people may *say* nonprofessionals are more helpful, but they may be reacting to differences in social cost by type of help source. In other words, the clergy do not actually *help* more than psychiatrists; they just engender less social rejection of the disturbed person by others.

Figure 12:3 Degree of social rejection of individuals seeking mental health counsel by degree of professionalism of help source.

Professionalism of Help Source				
No Help	Clergy	General Physician	Psychiatrist	Mental Hospital
Social Rejection of Patients				

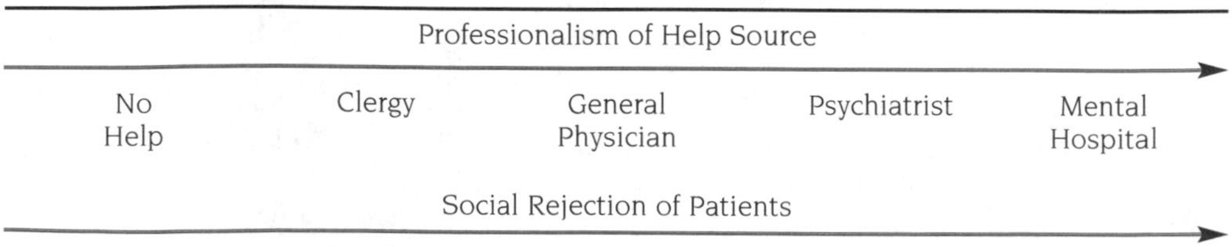

THE SOCIAL PSYCHOLOGY OF LEGAL COMMITMENT

Early Mental Health Laws

When prepatients reach the point at which commitment to a mental hospital is a real possibility, they will then be exposed to the professional evaluation of psychiatrists and legal experts. There is a historical conflict between psychiatry and the law that is dark, painful, and too lengthy to recount here in detail. Simply stated, the psychiatrist is involved with the commitment of patients to mental hospitals on the basis of specialized knowledge of mental illness, whereas legal experts are involved on the basis of the principle of protecting citizens' rights. This conflict is exemplified in the case of the prospective patient who requires hospitalization from the psychiatrist's point of view but who is seen as a criminal in need of a prison stay from a legal point of view.

Psychiatrists may possess the expertise to support their opinions, but the law possesses all the power to institutionalize or incarcerate. Judges and lawyers often view psychiatrists as interfering with the operation of the law, and psychiatrists view lawyers as skeptics who question the wisdom of psychiatric treatment. While these stereotypes may hamper cooperative efforts between the two professions, they do exist and are the inevitable result of involving both medical judgments and legal issues in the decision to commit a person to a mental hospital. It is a real tangle.

During the nineteenth century, the United States began to grapple with the question of the legal rights of the mentally ill. The era was chaotic, particularly in regard to the best means of ascertaining whether a person was disordered and in need of treatment. The problem of properly committing patients to institutions ("the propriety of confinement") is intimately woven into the history of psychiatry because it is a question that must be resolved before any treatment requiring hospitalization can be undertaken. Laws were passed, tested, evaluated, and often repealed when they failed to deal with the problem adequately.

In the 1890s, in Illinois, for example, a law was in effect that decided on commitment by jury trial with the patient present. It was also a law that permitted barbaric treatment of the mentally ill. The result was a return to the old and ugly procedures of dealing with mentally ill people that had supposedly ended ages before. The inhumane aspects of this law were graphically expressed by a respected physician of the time:

> I have seen a man suffering, unfortunately for him from acute mania, shackled hand and foot and then placed in a great canvas sack which was tied around his neck, and in that condition, carried thirty miles to the county seat and subsequently, in the same day, brought fifty miles to the asylum without an opportunity to attend to the calls of nature. I have found that man one mass of bruises from the top of his head to the soles of his feet, and I have seen him succumb in six days, and I attribute it to this treatment. When you have seen such things under this law it needs no argument to show that it is not the law for this time and this community.[40]

Laws change slowly, particularly the laws governing the commitment of the mentally ill. As late as 1933, there were still 14 states in which potential mental patients were jailed while they waited for commitment proceedings. This clearly supported the contention that those reported as disturbed are presumed to be just that before they are formally evaluated.

Commitment in More Recent Times

Although the idea of voluntary commitment was first given legal recognition by Massachusetts in 1881, the procedure did not become a common practice until well into the twentieth century. Today each state has its own laws governing commitment. Consequently, there is great diversity among the states regarding legal procedures, many of which still subject the patient to indignities and humiliations.

In 1949, the National Advisory Mental Health Council developed a "Model Act" governing hospitalization of the mentally ill in an attempt to create uniformity among the states. The thinking reflected in the provisions of the proposal was gradually incorporated into some state laws as they were modified. At this writing, considerable interstate variation still exists. Many states do not require that the person be present at the commitment hearing. Other states require only the sworn statement of a legal guardian or close relative to enact commitment. Almost all states have laws that permit a person to apply voluntarily for admission to a mental hospital, but the number of people who do so is negligible.

Because of the great diversity of state laws, a person can be committed by a court order based on the findings of an "insanity" commission, the conclusions of one or more medical examiners, or a jury trial. These approaches have been designed to protect the legal rights of the prospective patient by attempting to ensure that normal people are not railroaded into mental hospitals. Arthur P. Noyes, the original author of one of the leading psychiatric textbooks in the United States, contends that railroading is theoretically possible but probably rare. There are numerous cases in the sociological literature, however, in which a person was forced into a mental hospital on the basis of unconventional behavior. Frequently the "behavior" was nothing more than a value conflict between the person and others who wield power, as is often the case between rebellious youths and revengeful parents. But many of those cases occurred in the 1960s, when commitment laws were looser. Today, railroading is nowhere near as common as it was then.

What are the current standards for involuntary commitment to a mental hospital? As noted later in this chapter, the standards for commitment may have little to do with the way commitments are actually carried out. But back to what is actually on the books. Here Paul Applebaum's summary is useful.

> Mental health professionals are generally allowed to commit patients to mental hospitals only after determining that they are both mentally ill and dangerous to themselves or others. Danger to self includes not only self-mutilation and suicide attempts but also serious neglect of one's safety, health or nutrition. The predicted danger to others must usually be serious physical injury, not property damage or merely psychological harm.
>
> These requirements have been modified in various ways. Some states allow involuntary commitment only when a recent act of the patient suggests that further dangerous behavior is likely. In many jurisdictions the anticipated harm must be "imminent" or "a clear and present danger." Less rigorous laws permit commitment based on threats or even the reasonable fears of potential victims. States also differ on how reliable the prediction of dangerousness must be. The United States Supreme Court has established a minimum standard of "clear and convincing evidence." Some states, however, demand evidence "beyond a reasonable doubt." Despite all the efforts at legal precision, clinicians often lack guidance on such issues as how likely violence must be if the patient is to be regarded as dangerous, what period of time the prediction of dangerousness should cover, how mental illness is defined, and whether the illness must be the cause of the danger.

Meanwhile, given that the courts and legislatures are not inclined to permit involuntary commitment for any reason except dangerousness, how can clinicians best meet their responsibilities? In general, past dangerousness is the best indicator of future dangerousness, unless the long-term and immediate causes of the dangerous behavior are no longer operating. If the patient has not behaved dangerously in the past, it may help to consider variables such as age, sex, drug use, alcohol use, and living situations, which statistically affect the risk of violence in any population, mentally ill or not.[41]

The Presumption of Illness

Each year thousands of people are committed to mental hospitals, including voluntary commitments, although they make up a small part of the total. Serious questions have been raised about the judgments that lead to commitments, particularly in regard to whether commitment procedures are psychiatrically valid and meet legal requirements. To deal with these questions, some investigators have turned their attention from the behavior of the mentally ill to the behavior of psychiatrists who have been accused of hospitalizing people for nonpsychiatric reasons. Thomas Scheff, for example, has data demonstrating that psychiatrists indiscriminately diagnose people as mentally ill.[42] Furthermore, Scheff has found that the commitment procedures are incomplete and the hearings perfunctory. He reports that medical examiners spend an average of only ten minutes deciding upon each case and nearly always recommend hospitalization. Others have supported Scheff's findings, discovering that psychiatrists who do not have "sufficient time," sign commitment certificates after little or no examination.

It is disheartening to discover that the decision to commit can be so routinely made since psychiatric diagnosis is such a crucial step in the treatment of mental illness. Scheff, a labeling theorist, explains this phenomenon as a reaction by psychiatrists to the ambiguities of mental illness. They *assume* illness and recommend commitment in order to play it safe. This was dramatically demonstrated by David Rosenhan, who, with a team of colleagues, feigned schizophrenia before commitment evaluators at 12 mental hospitals around the country.[43] Recall from Chapter 2 that not only were all of the fake patients diagnosed as schizophrenic and committed, but their guise was never detected, even though they acted completely "normal" immediately after admission. The findings of the Rosenhan study strongly suggest that Scheff and other labeling theorists are correct in their assertion that the label of mental illness is difficult to eradicate once it has been rendered.

Within sociological circles, some have taken issue with the "presumption of illness" findings by holding that hospitalization can be a *positive* experience because it shifts a person's label from "obnoxious" and "intolerable" to "being ill" and "in need of help." While this argument merits consideration, it does not answer the question at hand—namely, are commitment procedures conducted thoroughly and ethically? If they are not, and some evidence indicates that they are not, then obviously some who are committed may not be mentally ill. They may be troublesome people who are a great irritation to their family, but that does not put them in the DSM.

Others who have analyzed the "presumption of illness" phenomenon in greater detail conclude that, while the probability of being committed is suspiciously large for the *general* population, it varies substantially along socioeconomic lines. For example, those with greater individual resources and higher standing in the community are less likely to be committed.[44] This is supported by the fact that people from the lower classes are most likely to be committed,[45] particularly lower-class blacks.[46] It is also consistent with the *status resource hypothesis*, which states that persons with more socioeconomic resources are better able to control their fates and thereby resist legal coercion that would lead to hospitalization.

There is also a greater tendency to commit someone who has no relatives or others currently available for psychological support.[47] People who are referred for psychiatric evaluation by physicians are more likely to be committed than nonphysician referrals. Males are more likely to be committed than females. Those with no previous record of hospitalization are also committed more frequently than those who have previously been hospitalized.[48] To summarize, *the prime candidate for commitment is the lower class, single, black, male, who has no relatives, no previous hospitalization record, and is referred by a physician.* These selection biases are particularly noticeable in state hospitals. The psychiatric day hospital has different prejudices. In this setting, there is selectivity as a function of the person's symptoms. This type of hospital is more likely to admit the prepatient with less conceptual and perceptual disorder and greater interpersonal competence than is observed among inpatient admissions.[49]

The tendency to presume illness and recommend commitment, while not universal, is certainly widespread. How can this phenomenon best be explained? The explanations are different for judges and lawyers than they are for psychiatrists. Many judges consider it pointless to conduct extensive examinations on each prospective patient since they are busy with other cases and because most persons considered for commitment are unusual in either appearance or behavior. Mechanic contends that this fact, coupled with a tendency to see an accused person as a different type of individual, predisposes judges to rubber-stamp commitment papers.[50] Furthermore, there is a pervasive belief that mentally ill persons are dangerous and thus should be hospitalized for the safety of others. This attitude is commonly found among judges who view their function as legal guardians of society's welfare.

The "presumption of illness" phenomenon among psychiatrists, however, is more complex. Scheff interviewed diagnosticians who indicate that they perform hasty examinations in part because their pay is determined by the number of examinations they conduct. Aside from financial reasons, a set of ideological assumptions also accounts for the presumption of illness by psychiatric examiners. These assumptions are:

1. Unlike surgery, there are no risks involved in involuntary psychiatric treatment. It either helps or is neutral, but it can't hurt.
2. Exposing a prospective mental patient to questioning, cross-examination, and other screening procedures makes him liable to the unnecessary stigma of trial-like procedures and may do further damage to his mental condition.
3. There is an element of danger to self or others in most mental illnesses. It is better to risk unnecessary hospitalization than the harm the patient might do himself or others.[51]

In response to each of these assumptions, Scheff has constructed counterpoints. He holds that:

1. There is very good evidence that involuntary hospitalization and social isolation may affect the patient's life, his job, his family affairs, and so on. There is some evidence that too hasty exposure to psychiatric treatment may convince the patient that he is "sick," prolonging what may have been an otherwise transitory episode.

2. This assumption is correct, as far as it goes. But it is misleading because it fails to consider what occurs when the patient who does not wish to be hospitalized is forcibly treated. Such patients often become extremely indignant and angry, particularly in the case, as often happens, when they are deceived into coming to the hospital on some pretext.

3. The elements of danger are usually exaggerated. In a psychiatric survey of new patients in state mental hospitals, danger to self or others was mentioned in about a fourth of the cases. Furthermore, in those cases where danger is mentioned, it is not always clear that the risks involved are greater than those encountered in ordinary social life.[52]

The arguments continue over the dangers of commitment versus the dangers of keeping a prospective patient in the community, but one thing seems painfully clear: many of the patients involved in commitment proceedings are sick and in need of help, but the superficial and prejudicial inquiries conducted by medical examiners and judges result in the institutionalization of some who do not belong in a hospital. It seems likely that these "errors," so damaging to the lives of those affected, will continue until the laws on commitment are rewritten. But changes in the law depend on changes in the values and ideology of our culture. It is difficult to effect these changes because deeply ingrained beliefs are not easily altered. In 1993, the federal government made a move in the right direction by recommending that something as radical as involuntary commitment be reserved only for those with "serious mental illness."[53] Much of the negative reports about people being forced into mental hospitals come from the 1960s, when the social climate was different. In 2002, for example, the pendulum has swung so far in the other direction that it has actually become difficult to have someone involuntarily committed. If he or she is committed, it is usually not for long.

Mental Health Laws of the 1970s and 1980s

In the 1970s, concern for civil liberty increased as evidenced by the patients' rights movement and the resultant laws some states have passed to protect those rights. The patients' rights movement is legally embodied in the law of informed consent. The core of this legal doctrine is the concept that the psychiatrist must inform the patient of the risks and benefits of the proposed treatment and then accept the patient's decision about the appropriate course of action.

In Pennsylvania, the Mental Health Procedures Act (MHPA) was passed in 1976 and remains on the books today. It established new procedures and standards for voluntary and involuntary commitments and is considered to be a progressive state statute. The policy of the MHPA is to prefer voluntary commitment over involuntary commitment. Before a person is accepted for voluntary treatment, a full explanation must be made of the type of treatment procedures in which the individual will be involved.

Under the Pennsylvania law, involuntary commitments are limited to persons who pose a clear danger to themselves or others. A patient committed on an involuntary basis must be either (1) discharged within 72 hours, (2) admitted as a voluntary patient, or (3) certified for extended involuntary emergency treatment by a judge or mental health review officer after a hearing. Under the MHPA, a court-ordered involuntary commitment cannot extend for any longer than 90 days. Court hearings are open to the public unless the person whose case is being heard requests privacy. In addition, the person has the right to confront and cross-examine all witnesses and to present evidence in his or her own behalf. The MHPA also specifies that each patient must have an individualized treatment plan that is reviewed every 30 days by a treatment team.

Unfortunately, Pennsylvania's law created some new problems in its attempt to ensure that prospective patients are accorded full civil liberties. One main problem is that it has resulted in a growing number of severely disturbed people in the community, since it states that a person must commit some violent or dangerous act before being involuntarily committed. This type of law is a major reason why we have so many street people in our cities today. Clearly, there are a number of very disturbed people who are in need of treatment yet are not violent or dangerous in some way.

Additionally, since the law provides for short commitment periods, other disturbed people are being prematurely released. Of course, this may appear to be beneficial because it keeps people out of mental hospitals where their problems may be exchanged for another set of ills.[54] But there are not adequate community facilities to care for these people. Therefore, they are being forced to fend for themselves with little supervision in the community. The pendulum has swung too far in the direction of upholding civil liberties because the law actually makes it necessary for people to harm themselves or others to get help. If they are not presently violent, it must be overwhelmingly obvious that they will be violent in the near future.

The Pennsylvania law reflects a nationwide trend against treating mental patients against their will. I believe this means that the country is in deep trouble because this kind of extreme change can only mean added grief to patients, their families, and the community in the absence of adequate outpatient facilities. Under the previous law, families could spot warning signs and get professional help before the patient regressed to violence. Now treatment is withheld from many people who desperately need it.

The major problem with many of the mental health laws such as the one in Pennsylvania is that they are frequently formulated without the advice of mental health experts. Lawyers and state senators play a large role in passing these laws, and, because they are untrained in regard to mental illness, the result is a naive, unrealistic set of legal guidelines that may win political favors but certainly worsen the plight of the mentally ill.[55]

Mental Health Laws Today

What is the status of mental health laws today? In three words, the laws are simultaneously *promising, ambiguous,* and *backward.* This applies to laws related to commitment as well as those designed to provide patients with effective, affordable treatment. In 1986, Congress set the stage for changes in treatment by passing the Protection and Advocacy for Mentally Ill Individuals Act.[56] The act established in each state a system for rights protection and advocacy on behalf of persons with mental illness, particularly those residing in institutions. Although the act faced many bureaucratic obstacles, the National Institute of Mental Health has pushed for it as a top priority in mental health care reform.[57]

The Americans with Disabilities Act of 1990 had special significance for persons with mental illness.[58] The act addressed a number of troublesome issues, including discrimination in general and employment in particular. Its effect, however, was more in the spirit of reform than tangible change.[59] The Clinton administration promised real change, particularly in mental health care coverage. Some mental health experts described it as "historic" and "sea change."[60] But, as we all know, health care reform in general is more of a hope than a reality.

Today there is legislation proposed that would eliminate many discriminating features against mental health treatment found in existing insurance plans. All people with mental illness would be able to get insurance coverage. Medications for mental illness would be covered the same as other drugs, and insurance would be portable, enabling employed patients to shift jobs without fear of losing their coverage. The spirit behind such proposals is captured by a report by the National Advisory Mental Health Council to the U.S. Senate:

> Many myths and misunderstandings contribute to the stigmatization of persons with mental illness and to their often limited access to needed services. For example, millions of Americans and many policy makers are unaware that the efficacy of an extensive array of treatments for specific mental disorders has been specifically tested in controlled clinical trials; these studies demonstrate that mental disorders can now be diagnosed and treated as precisely and effectively as other disorders in medicine.
>
> The existence of effective treatments is only relevant to those who can obtain them. Far too many Americans with severe mental illness and their families find that appropriate treatment is inaccessible because they lack any insurance coverage or the coverage they have for mental illness is inequitable and inadequate. For example, private health insurance coverage for mental disorders is often limited to 30–60 inpatient days per year, compared with 120 days or unlimited days for physical illness. Similarly, the Medicare program requires 50% copayment for outpatient care of mental disorders, compared with 20% copayment for other medical outpatient treatment.
>
> These inequities in both the public and private sectors can and should be overcome. Estimates based on studies of current coverage and utilization suggest that, under health care reform, for an additional cost of $6.5 billion—representing approximately a 10% increase over current total direct costs of mental health care—the nation can provide coverage for adults and children with severe mental disorders commensurate with coverage for other disorders.
>
> Commensurate coverage for Americans experiencing severe mental illness will yield both human and economic benefits. Millions of Americans will be able to participate more productively at home, at work, and in the community. Substantial numbers will no longer need to impoverish themselves to obtain coverage under Medicaid. The enormous but often hidden costs of untreated or undertreated severe mental illness, which are now borne by the general health care system and society at large, can be appreciably reduced. In addition, commensurate coverage for severe mental disorders can be expected to produce a 10% decrease in the use and cost of medical services for individuals with these conditions. The annual saving in indirect costs . . . would amount to approximately $8.7 billion . . . and represent an estimated net economic benefit for the nation of $2.2 billion annually.[61]

Many of these legal shifts for reform are based on an important but rarely acknowledged reason why we have a dual system of care for the mentally ill—lack of adequate insurance. Only time will tell whether meaningful change will occur on a national level. Meanwhile, some states have taken their own lead. A California law, for example, requires group health insurers that issue policies covering "disorders of the brain" to provide equal coverage for several severe mental illnesses such as schizophrenia and mood disorders.

The part of mental health care laws associated with treatment and insurance coverage may have a rosy future, but are things also looking up with regard to more workable commitment laws? Not really. In fact, here things have moved in a more punitive direction. Much of what is on the legal books to safeguard people's rights is actually ignored at commitment hearings where clinical opinions take precedence over the law.[62] John La Fond and other experts in the field report that commitment policies today are a regression from anything gained during the 1970s and '80s. In fact, LaFond calls today's situation a move "back to the asylum."[63] Others have been even more critical. Turkheimer and Perry[64] believe that civil commitment procedures simply flat out fail to meet statutory requirements. Whatever the degree of the problem may be, one thing is clear—the time to put mental health into the mental health laws is way overdue.[65]

It appeared as if things were really going to change in a positive way during the Carter administration. But his efforts ended with the next president. Rosalyn Carter, who led the reform movement, sadly reflects on those times.

> Even those with the most severe mental illnesses could significantly improve through treatment with the new medications and rehabilitation. Yet the hope of recovery is denied to hundreds of thousands because of lack of access to care.
>
> Many who could benefit from advances in treatment remain incapacitated because they have no way to pay for care. Hundreds of thousands more and their families face serious economic hardship because of limited coverage under most existing insurance plans. I often receive letters from distraught family members describing their heavy financial burdens and their frustrating efforts at obtaining care for their mentally ill loved one. The stark reality is that our current system of public and private insurance discriminates badly against those in need of a broad array of mental health services.
>
> As most of you know, my greatest disappointment after leaving the White House was the failure to implement the Mental Health Systems Act. A wonderful opportunity to create landmark change in the financing and delivery of mental health services was lost. However I am proud and pleased that, because of the efforts of many mental health organizations, some of its most significant principles were incorporated into new or existing programs throughout the 1980s.
>
> Small but significant victories were achieved in the use of Social Security Insurance and Medicaid to support people with severe mental illness in the community, and such programs as the Green Door in Washington, D.C., became possible. The Fair Housing Act and the Americans with Disabilities Act now prevent discrimination against those with mental disabilities. Slowly, but much too slowly, those with mental or emotional problems are being specifically included in programs designed to protect and support them.
>
> Today we are at a crossroads. We have an opportunity to bring mental health into the mainstream of our nation's health care system. We cannot afford to fail.[66]

If this chapter reeks of pessimism about the widespread misunderstanding about the mentally ill and how they should be treated, then it obtained its objective. There simply is such an overwhelming challenge to identify and treat mental illness accurately and without discrimination that the chances of successful change are remote. Even if we had "perfect" laws on commitment and mental health coverage, families would still wallow in ignorance about the entire help-seeing process. If real changes ever occur, they are still not even visible on the horizon.

CONCLUSIONS

Social forces are central in the recognition and treatment of mental illness. Studies of the effect of these forces suggest damaging consequences for prospective patients. The mentally ill, often driven to seek help by stress-producing changes in their lives, first encounter the reactions of family and friends who typically deny that there may be something wrong. This can only act to complicate the disorder by extending its duration and delaying treatment.

When the outside community is called on for help, nonprofessionals generally respond first, and these people often assume that a disorder exists even though the person may simply be seeking advice on transitory life difficulties. Here the label of mental illness is first applied to a person who may then be further penalized with social rejection. These social costs exacerbate the trauma of the experience by creating feelings of inferiority and social isolation.

The formal process of commitment often proceeds at the expense of the prospective patient through decision-making actions that manifest haste, value judgments, and an inability to validly ascertain who is actually disturbed. Consequently, some people enter the mental hospital population who do not belong there. In an effort to guard the civil liberties of prospective patients, some states have passed laws that allow for involuntary commitment only if the person poses a danger to himself or others. Since this is generally taken to mean violence, many nonviolent people who are seriously disturbed are left in the community without treatment. Some of these constitute today's street people.

The social psychology involved in becoming a mental patient reflects some of society's inappropriate attitudes toward mental illness. Some of these attitudes are based on embarrassment, ignorance, shame, and an exaggerated fear of the behavior of mentally disordered people, beliefs that reflect an underlying view of mental illness that is a problem itself.

13

Treatment

The Inpatient Experience

During the eighteenth century, there were special asylums for the mentally ill, the most famous of which was St. Mary's of Bethlehem in London. Conditions were appalling. The moon-mad "lunatics" of Bethlehem, or Bedlam as it was called, were put on display daily for a small fee to amuse the public.

In the United States, four cycles of reform have developed and shifted responsibilities for administration of mental health services among governmental and private interests over the past 200 years. . . . These reforms focused on asylums in the early nineteenth century, mental hospitals in the early twentieth century, community mental health centers in the 1960s, and community support systems in the 1980s. A fifth cycle of reform, involving the growth and evolution of managed care, is currently generating important new questions about the organization and utilization of mental health service delivery.[1]

This chapter is depressing. Here I am writing about the treatment of the mentally ill today and I am unable to say that things have improved since this book was first published in 1980. In fact, if anything, things have gotten worse. If you go back and check the statistics in Chapter 1, it is obvious that funding for the mentally ill has declined and the patients themselves have followed one clear path—out of the mental hospital and into the streets.[2] Back in the 1950s, the decrease in the mental hospital population was viewed in a positive way; it meant that perhaps people could function in the community now that psychotropic drugs were available.[3] Today's exodus, however, is not a positive move but one based on unsubstantiated hope that, if patients are released, there will be effective programs awaiting them in the outside world.

The mental health system in the United States is so disorganized that we do not have just one mental health system; we have 50 state systems.[4] Things are even worse in other parts of the world. Despite the long-term efforts of the World Health Organization to develop mental health systems in countries of the developing world, it is primarily the wealthier countries that are even able to afford an attempt.[5] The National Institute of Mental Health used to play a leadership role in mental health policy and service delivery. Now services for the mentally ill are governed much more by health policy developments outside of NIMH's domain, such as Medicare, commercial insurance, and managed health care.[6]

THE MENTAL HEALTH SYSTEM

Economies of No Scale

The need and demand for mental health services are enormous.[7] Plenty of guides have been published as to how to deal with these needs administratively,[8] but organizational ideas are often far removed from the actual implementation of care.[9] Despite meteoric increases in mental health care expenditures, the social problem of mental illness is a long way from being cured by psychiatric hospitals.[10] Indeed, more than 60 percent of all inpatient episodes occur in general hospitals.[11] Inpatient mental health costs may be falling, but that is because of a decrease in the average length of hospital stays, not because of some actual gain in treatment effectiveness.[12]

The reason why I refer to the mental health care "system" as an economy of "no scale" is because it is clearly out of control. This is not just a financial problem. Consider some other facts. Most of the mentally ill are treated in general hospitals. That's a big mistake. They do not belong there, in the first place because even the psychiatric wards in those hospitals are typically underprepared. To make matters worse, "for-profit" hospitals (1) treat fewer patients with severe diagnoses, (2) provide less treatment for uninsured patients, and (3) are more likely to transfer "unprofitable patients" to other facilities.[13] The result is that general hospitals are becoming chronic care institutions for the mentally ill.[14] In addition, there is a severe lack of programs to deal effectively with mental patients who have more than one psychiatric problem. Such is the case of severe depression combined with substance abuse[15] or child sexual abuse.[16] Such is also generally the case with patients who have any kind of comorbidity.[17]

Other problems include reports that patients are "skimmed and dumped" according to whether they are projected to be financially profitable.[18] People of color, for instance, have higher rates of mental disorder than whites but use fewer services, in part due to their relatively low socioeconomic status.[19] Indeed, some call for a hospital system based on a profit motive as the only way to manage the beast.[20] McCue and Clement report that for-profit psychiatric hospitals have net profits and fewer expenses than state-supported hospitals.[21] That certainly does not mean that they are doing a good job.

Today there is a spread of "proprietary" psychiatric hospitals that are essentially for-profit facilities.[22] This movement goes hand in hand with "managed care," a term that equates to cost containment.[23] Some think it should be called "managed misery" because it represents a move away from patient care to patient costs. There is widespread concern that people with mental illness who are a vulnerable population will be placed at even greater risk by managed care which manages the bottom line with a "less is more" accounting mentality.[24] The concerns are grounded because managed health care is quite capable of making mental health treatment systems worse than ever. Some of the projected dramatic changes connected with managed care include a decrease in the number of mental health organizations, reduced use of inpatient care, and a shrinkage of financial resources to deal with a major social problem.[25]

All of this business about economics, profit, and expenses does no good to a severely ill person who is indigent. Even those with insurance have no guarantee of care. No small wonder that some commit suicide when their insurance coverage is withdrawn.[26] In fact, the mere *threat* of having their insurance coverage *reviewed* has led some to suicide attempts.[27] Many of these attempts are successful. And much of these personal horrors have resulted from managed care and its resultant effect of fewer people receiving formal treatment than ever before.[28]

Types of Hospitals

Here, I describe changes in the mental health care delivery system and evaluate the effectiveness of various treatment modalities for people with serious mental disorders, such as schizophrenia. Less disturbed patients may be treated on an outpatient basis. As Figure 13:1 demonstrates, millions of Americans seek the help of a private practitioner each year.

During the two-year period 1989 to 1990, an estimated 37.6 million visits were made to office-based physicians in the United States who specialize in psychiatry—an average of 18.8 million visits per year.[29] The number of people treated in public (state) mental hospitals has decreased enormously; the number of beds, for instance, has declined 80 percent since 1955.[30] But admissions have risen in those hospitals because of high recidivism rates. Over the last few decades, psychiatric wards in general hospitals have been overflowing. In fact, occupancy rates well over 100 percent are the norm, especially in inner-city hospitals.[31] I have mentioned throughout the book how much all of these different types of services cost—the total is an incomprehensible figure in the billions.[32] Combine those dollars with the fact that this monstrous system of psychiatric care is uncoordinated and mismanaged and you realize that mental health

Figure 13:1 Percent distribution of office visits to psychiatrists and to all other physicians, by patient's age: United States, 1989–1990.

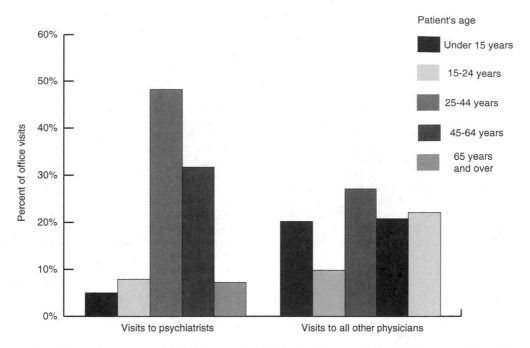

Source: Susan M. Schappert, "Office visits to psychiatrists: United States, 1989–1990," *Advance Data, 237,* December 28, 1993, 1–16.

care itself is just one more part of a major social problem gone awry.[33] The details in Box 13:1 document the problem even further.

For some time now in the United States, there have been two major types of psychiatric hospitals: the traditional "institution-centered," or custodial hospital, and the "patient-centered," or therapeutic hospital.[34] The custodial hospital is primarily concerned with segregating the mental patient from the rest of society. In this setting, the patient is expected to conform to the authoritarian routines of the hospital, passively accepting impersonal treatments such as medication. Electroconvulsive therapy (ECT) also used to be common, but it no longer is today for a variety of reasons including patients' rights. When ECT is administered in a state hospital, it must be with the patient's permission or through a court order. There is a strict ordering of power in the custodial hospital; the psychiatrist has the major therapeutic role, and the other personnel are merely ancillary and basically serve to control patients.[35]

The patient-centered hospital is concerned with rehabilitating patients rather than simply controlling them. In this setting, the needs of the patients are the focus around which the organization of the hospital is structured.[36] The patients' problems are treated individually, not impersonally. All hospital personnel, including the patients themselves, are expected to play active roles in the process of rehabilitation to normal social roles.

················· **Box 13:1** ·······················
Care (Miscare?) of the Mentally Ill

As most Americans increasingly suspect, care for people with serious mental illnesses is bad and getting worse. A trip downtown in any city shows the consequences of evicting hundreds of thousands of patients from state hospitals with no aftercare, no housing, and no rehabilitation programs. About 250,00 people with schizophrenia and manic-depressive illness are now living in public shelters, on the streets, in jails, and in prisons; only one fourth as many live in state mental hospitals. The largest "mental institution" in the nation is the Los Angeles County Jail, which has 3,600 inmates with serious mental illness in its population of 24,000. In Idaho, mentally ill people charged with no crime are routinely jailed while awaiting psychiatric examination or transportation to state mental hospitals.

With few exceptions, both inpatient and outpatient facilities for the seriously mentally ill are inadequate to atrocious. Hawaii State Hospital, nominated as the worst in the United States, was labeled by U.S. Department of Justice investigators in 1989 as "an abomination" with fire hazards, cockroaches, puddles of urine on the floor, inadequate food, and "patients often wrapped in blankets or sheets due to absence of adequate clothing." (Since then, conditions are said to have improved.) South Florida State Hospital has leaks in the roofs of half its buildings and a waiting list of six months. Nearby Broward General Hospital routinely shackles all psychiatric patients for as long as several days while they wait for a bed to become available in a public facility.

Community Mental Health Centers (CMHCs), originally designed to provide care for mentally ill patients discharged from state mental hospitals, have with few exceptions failed completely. Most have become counseling centers for the "worried well." Some, such as the Orlando Regional Medical Center in Florida, have built swimming pools and tennis courts with federal funds. Psychiatrists trained with public funds have abandoned jobs in the public sector for private practice among the rich and well-educated. Princeton, New Jersey, has one psychiatrist for every 250 residents, and Jersey City has one for every 13,600 residents; Berkeley, California, has one psychiatrist for every 900 residents, and Ontario, California, has one for every 57,000 residents. In South Dakota five CMHCs must share a single psychiatrist, and many CMHCs in Louisiana and Mississippi have no staff psychiatrists at all.

Source: E. Fuller Torrey, "Care of the mentally ill," *Harvard Mental Health Letter,* 7 (9) (1991), 8.

Not all hospitals can be classified as either institution-centered or patient-centered. Most large state mental hospitals are obliged to pursue the goals of custody-control and treatment simultaneously. The demand of custody-control for patients' conformity and the subordination of their needs to institutional routines sharply contrast with therapeutic treatment based on resolving patients' individual problems. Why are both of these conflicting goals pursued simultaneously? Schwartz and Schwartz believe that this dual function performed by the state mental hospital is the result of the ambivalence felt toward mental patients by society.[37] Because mental patients are viewed as dangerous deviants, the mental hospital is expected to isolate and restrain them. But since they are also seen as sick people in need of help, the mental hospital is supposed to rehabilitate them as well. Because of this dual mandate, the psychiatric staff is often split into two factions: psychiatric aides represent custody and control, and the professional staff represents treatment.

In the United States today there are between 700 and 800 mental hospitals.[38] Since 1980, the number has increased rapidly in the private sector, where there are 444 hospitals. State hospitals have declined; they now number less than 300 and are continuing to close.[39] Until 1955, most state mental hospitals were primarily custodial. Before then, hospitals had earned the reputation of being "snake pits." Treatment was brutal and inhumane, and physical restraints were commonly used. Under those conditions patients often deteriorated and became more disoriented and remote than they had been when they were admitted. The introduction of tranquilizers in the 1950s paved the way for reformers to control the negative effects of hospitalization by reducing the length of stay. Long-term hospitalization was widely abandoned, and mental hospitals became short-term treatment facilities. Some of this was good; some proved to be extremely bad.

State hospitals have had "snake pit" reputations for a number of reasons.[40] First of all, the design of the buildings is often so depressing that the patients may actually be emotionally harmed. The architecture is usually antiquated and bleak: huge wards with half-walls lined with rows of identical beds, long gloomy corridors, high ceilings, no privacy, drab colors, factory-type lighting, and, of course, the infamous glass observation cubicle in the dayroom where patients sit for hours on uncomfortable furniture, watch television, and smoke cigarettes to the butt. The closed wards for chronic patients are even worse because they are locked and offer little opportunity for change. Do not let me give you the impression that all state mental hospitals are depressing places where patients just sit and idle hours away. Some are much more progressive than others. For instance, at Norristown State Hospital, Pennsylvania's largest, the physical facilities are attractive, the staff is upbeat, and there is an atmosphere of optimism.

It is not really surprising that the condition of state hospital patients often worsens because sometimes they are simply ignored. In some instances, they are actually forgotten. In 1971, five patients were released from an Ohio institution. Although they had been sent there merely for observation, they had been kept for periods ranging from 21 to 41 years because the staff had forgotten about them! In Chicago alone, more than 300 patients died from neglect between 1977 and 1981. Some who had wandered away were found floating in rivers or dismembered on railroad tracks. Others died from exposure to the elements while still on hospital grounds. Some committed suicide while aides were busy with other patients.

Some ex-patients, such as Kenneth Donaldson, have politicized and demanded improvement of hospital conditions. Donaldson was involuntarily committed to the Florida State Mental Hospital by his parents. For 15 years he was forced to live in crowded conditions and work to the point of exhaustion. He spoke with psychiatrists for a total of only five hours in all that time. After his repeated attempts to gain release, a federal court ruled that the hospital knew that Donaldson did not belong there, yet continued to force a prison-like existence on him. He was released and awarded $38,500 in damages.

A U.S. Senate investigation report found shortcomings in virtually every level of the system of institutional care for the mentally ill, including violence, sexual harassment, neglect, and inept psychiatric care. The report described instances of unexplained deaths, rapes, patients routinely sleeping naked on bathroom floors, and foreign-born psychiatrists unable to communicate with their patients. In essence, the report described a nightmare.

Small private hospitals, usually regarded as being at the opposite pole from state mental hospitals in terms of quality and intensity of treatment, have higher rates of patient turnover. Much of this difference is due to the fact that state mental hospitals have a large number of patients and a small number of staff members to care for them. Another part of the variation in length of patient stay is due to differences in types of patients admitted: a greater proportion of private hospital patients are diagnosed with anxiety disorders, whereas state hospital patients are more likely to be psychotic. Perhaps the most important reason for differences in length of stay between state and private facilities is economic. Go back to Chapter 1 and check the annual fees at private hospitals. Most people can't afford such exorbitant rates for very long. If their insurance runs out and they are still in need of inpatient care, they may end up in a state hospital where costs are covered. But state hospitals have moved dramatically to short stays.

In addition to hospital type, quality and orientation of staff, and patient diagnosis, there is another reason why people spend a considerable amount of their lives in a mental institution: they may simply be destitute and not able to function in outside society.[41] However, this is becoming less common as the new mental health laws have *forced* the mass release of patients into society. Sound crazy? It does to me. What else can you call dumping patients into the streets while being "concerned" about their "rights" as citizens?

The Psychiatric Staff

As stated earlier, there is a hierarchy within the staff of the state mental hospital.[42] Psychiatrists occupy the position at the apex of the power structure; they make the final decision on all requests and recommendations. Next in power are the nurses, occupational therapists, and social workers. At the bottom of the hierarchy are the psychiatric aides. While this is the formal hierarchy of power in the state hospital, it does not necessarily represent the everyday reality of hospital life. Because the psychiatrists, occupational therapists, and social workers rarely appear on the ward, the head nurse occupies a crucial power position.

The nurse links the ward with the rest of the hospital world and is the immediate authority figure for the patients and aides. Student nurses also play important roles in the daily lives of the patients because they are responsible for individual patient care. The permanent personnel are often occupied with administrative functions and have impersonal contact with patients, while student nurses provide companionship, escort patients to off-ward activities, and help them in their personal hygiene.

The psychiatric aides are the low people on the staff totem pole. They are responsible for housekeeping functions, keeping records, and maintaining order on the ward. However, the aides themselves deemphasize these aspects of their work and stress their contacts with the patients. In fact, aides have been noted to have more contact and more *raw* knowledge of the patients than anyone in the hospital.[43] It appears to patients that they are under control of these nonmedical custodians because they seem to dominate such essentials as access to professional staff, ground privileges, and even eligibility for discharge. In fact, some studies of hospital life have concluded that the *real* control of a state mental hospital is exercised by the psychiatric aides because other staff members are so preoccupied with bureaucratic details. Because of time constraints, the psychiatrist may turn to a nonprofessional for an "educated guess" on a patient's condition. This practice is quite alarming in light of the fact that psychiatric aides are the least trained members of the entire staff, often recruited from the ranks of the uneducated.

The nursing staff enjoys a higher status than the aides because nurses are better educated. However, the unfortunate fact is that nurses typically have little knowledge about mental illness and its treatment because they rarely have formal training in psychiatry beyond a short affiliation as a student nurse. Consequently, psychiatric nurses do not have the sense of professional identity that their medical counterparts enjoy. Because psychiatric nurses feel undertrained, mental patients can pose a threat to them. This may cause the nurse to take on an authoritarian manner and endorse the use of control techniques such as heavy medication. One possible exception is the nursing program that is part of a full-time college curriculum. Here the student is usually exposed to sociological, psychological, and psychiatric concepts in the classroom. All of these act to increase compassion and understanding.

The problem of the quality of treatment administered to patients in large mental hospitals is, in part, the result of unfavorable staff-patient ratios. Few patients ever have as much as a five-minute conversation a week with the nurses. Psychiatrists, or "ward physicians," as they are called, have even less patient contact. A large part of the psychiatrist's time on the ward is spent writing medical orders and handling administrative duties. Because of the understaffing problem, actual contact between patient and ward physician may be limited to a bimonthly "ward round" in which all patients as a group meet in the dayroom where they are given the "opportunity" to present their problems. To avoid what state hospital psychiatrists see as a never-ending line of patient requests, the physician's office is usually located off the ward and often in a separate building.

Understaffing and undertraining are two important reasons for the impersonal atmosphere that typically pervades the state hospital ward. As Stone described it in the 1960s: "The system tends to reward standard performance by the staff, impartiality toward the patients, and the preservation of kindly but formal relationships. The system also arouses guilt in those staff members who find themselves responding in spontaneous ways to patients who have singled them out for attention."[44] There are, nevertheless, many personal adaptations that the staff employ to make the relationship with patients less impersonal. One technician, for example, suggests to patients that they "blow kisses" to each other. However, it would be inaccurate to describe the psychiatric nurse as universally impersonal and authoritarian since the nurse's behavior toward a patient is, at least in part, a function of the patient's behavior toward the nurse. If a patient derogates the nurse, the nurse's response may be total withdrawal.[45] On the other hand, the patient who approaches the nurse in a warm, interested manner is typically favored over the odd, indifferent patient.[46] It is simply a reflection of human nature.

A number of psychological and demographic variables affect nurses' attitudes toward patients, as well as the degree of social distance they maintain from them. The most negative attitudes toward patients are usually exhibited by the older, least educated staff members and those with the longest employment on the ward.[47] These nurses often display the greatest amount of authoritarianism and are prone to restrict themselves socially from the patients. Conversely, more humanitarian attitudes toward patients are found among nurses who are younger, better educated, and who have had experience in a number of different wards. It is not unusual for nursing personnel to become embittered toward mental patients over time. This is probably due to a sense of futility and helplessness that develops through treating people for whom there is no real cure.

At least one longitudinal study demonstrated that student nurses' attitudes toward the usefulness of psychiatric treatment become less favorable over time.[48] Views toward psychiatric treatment have also been linked with shift work. Day-shift staff members report more improvement in patient functioning over time as opposed to those working other hours. This may simply be because most therapy is scheduled during the day.

Relations among staff members also affect the quality of care patients receive. When coordination among staff members is high, there is a therapeutic atmosphere on the ward. If staff relations are weakened, staff members do not obtain support from one another, and they lose their sense of competence in dealing with the patients, who, in turn, can become agitated or depressed. In fact, conditions of weak relations among the staff are reported to be directly linked with patient suicides.[49]

A sense of futility and hopelessness among some staff members at state hospitals contributes to a host of other problems, including "nurse burnout."[50] Years of questioning the meaningfulness of work can lead to the obvious—quitting the job. This is not just a problem for the nurse but for patients as well because nurse cynicism lowers the quality of patient care.

Can nurse burnout and general staff dissatisfaction be controlled? Many methods for overcoming staff problems have been explored, but one relatively untapped help source is the college student volunteer. A number of benefits accrue to both patients and staff from the use of student volunteers. The enthusiasm of the students is contagious and often helps to renew or even initiate enthusiasm among patients and staff.[51] Perhaps the greatest strength the college student brings to the treatment setting is an ability to get close to the patient because the student is not viewed as a formal member of the hospital hierarchy. Students also benefit from being immersed in the hospital environment because they develop a greater sense of self-awareness and gain more knowledge about the mentally ill than books could ever offer. Unfortunately, there is a cost to all of this: at least one study reports that students often feel depressed after interacting with patients.[52] I frequently notice the same effect when I take my students to a state hospital as part of coursework. They arrive at the hospital gates with a sense of fear and alarm and they leave with a feeling of sadness and despair.

Types of Wards

Another factor that affects the quality of interaction between patients and staff is the organization of the mental hospital ward. Large wards that are organized according to a rigid status hierarchy in which authority and decision making ultimately rest with a few staff members are likely to produce staff conflict and unusual problems among patients.[53] For this reason, many large state hospitals are decentralized into small, semiautonomous units or buildings. The smaller treatment units establish closer ties between patients and staff, and they allow for easier evaluation and modification of therapy programs.

Decentralized staffs also have more personalized therapy programs than do the hierarchically controlled staffs.[54] Whether a hospital has a centralized or decentralized staff is largely a function of the staff's psychiatric ideology. A medically oriented staff typically employs organic forms of therapy and is usually organized according to a strict status hierarchy. On the other hand, the staff oriented toward psychotherapy is typically decentralized to allow for flexibility and individualism.

Perhaps the most important distinction between different types of patient wards is in terms of length of the patients' hospital stay. Chronic (long-stay) patient wards are traditionally separated from the acute (short-stay) patient wards. Some feel that it is more useful to define "chronicity" in terms of patient behavior rather than in terms of a specific amount of time spent in the hospital since the true chronic patients have become so dependent on the hospital that they can no longer function in the outside world.[55] However, the likelihood of this "dependency syndrome" is directly related to length of hospitalization.

It may be that being placed in a chronic ward is a self-fulfilling prophecy since living there calls forth the types of behavior that ensure a patient will become more and more dependent on the hospital and never leave. The atmosphere of the chronic wards is often depressing at best. Patients go through the same set of activities in a zombie-like state, day after day. They rise, they eat, they take their medication, and they idle their lives away within the sterile confines of the dayroom. They are stereotypically viewed by the staff as hopelessly ill and not quite human. However, that is the *stereotypical view*, it is not a universal fact. In some chronic wards real efforts are made to communicate with these lost souls and inject some hope into their lives. It is an immense challenge.

Over time, relatives and friends often stop visiting patients and eventually letters may end as well. One study reports that only 10 percent of chronic patients have visits from relatives and friends once a month compared to 42 percent of newly admitted patients.[56] Once again, the reports of patients being abandoned by their relatives is the stereotypical view that fails to recognize the agony family members experience when emotionally coping with a chronically ill loved one whose chance of remission is slim to nonexistent. What appears as abandonment may be the distance needed to defend against feelings of failure and despair on the part of the relative who cannot tangibly help to combat the chronicity of mental illness. Box 13:2 is an account of a mother with a daughter diagnosed with paranoid schizophrenia who vividly describes the pain involved in "letting go."

It is no small wonder that many patients on chronic wards feel alienated from outside society and are threatened by the idea of returning to the community. Can these problems be alleviated? One solution is to integrate the acute and chronic patients. This would help to eliminate the stagnant atmosphere of the chronic ward and combat the tendencies of the staff to treat all patients according to group stereotypes. A mixed ward more closely resembles the outside world and can also promote the patient's eventual return to it. "Solutions," however, are simply ideas that may be a complete failure when put to the test.

Patient Society

Erving Goffman's 1961 collection of essays, *Asylums: Essays on the Social Situation of Mental Patients and Other Inmates*, is one of sociology's classics. It has probably been read by more sociology students than any other single book in the field of mental health . . . the essays examine the nature of "total institutions" such as mental hospitals, the "moral careers" of patients, ways of "making out" in a mental hospital and the "vicissitudes of the tinkering trades," as he referred to psychiatry and other mental health professions.[57]

Is there a patient society, a system in which patients interact on the basis of prescribed statuses and roles? Erving Goffman, in his famous sociological examination of the conditions of mental health hospitals, portrayed the patient as such a dehumanized and embittered person that it seems unlikely that, if there is a patient society, it is modeled after anything resembling outside society.[58] Empirical investigations of patient attitudes toward hospital and staff support Goffman's descriptions. Over half of the patients in one study reported that the hospital unduly restricted their freedom,[59] and 99 percent of the chronic patients in another study viewed the psychiatric staff as oppressors.[60]

Because of the conditions found in many mental hospitals, there is little incen-

We walk on stiff dry grass, bare trees motionless, pointing to a near-perfect blue sky. The only stir is the rustling of the dry leaves beneath our feet. I listen to her and think: *Oh God, the pain. I had closed it off so well since the last time.* . . . "The staff is nice to us, very courteous and polite. The food's not bad." She kicks a stone in her path. "But they don't let us have seconds on meat or dessert. We get fresh fruit everyday, and with Christmas coming we'll get special things."

I glance sidelong at her, my sometime daughter, so beautiful, even in her sickness unto death. *Surely you've made a mistake, God, not her.* . . .

I say nothing, merely look at my feet as I walk and wait for her to speak again. I pray her words won't come out chaotic and irrelevant. Sometimes, I want to grab what she says out of midair and shove it back in her mouth, demand that she retract what she's saying and tell her, "No, no! You don't mean that!" But when I think it, the darkness around her eyes reproaches me. *Stop,* they say, *You don't know what you're asking. I've been there, I know.*

"It's really not bad here. Marie and I are good friends. She gave me a martini last night. She mixed it in a shampoo bottle."

You've got it all wrong, God, she doesn't belong here! You've made a mistake! She's intelligent . . . she's artistic . . . she's got talent. . . .

. . . On Tuesdays, she paints ceramic ashtrays in the shape of hearts and stars. . . .

With some animation, she tells me about her courses at the "University-Without-Walls." She is very tired, she says, because she was up late the past few nights studying and practicing chords on the piano, 156 of them. She has to be able to identify any one of them for her final exam. She expects to pass, even though she's never played the piano.

She leads me to what she calls her favorite place, a slab of concrete with a dozen picnic tables stacked away for the season, echoes that there once was a summer. She stops to extract a cigarette from the pocket of her jacket, but she has no match. She stops a fellow patient passing by for a light.

Why does her madness repel me? Why do I ache at the thought of her slipping into an oblivion where I cannot follow? She functions well here. She has everything she needs: food, shelter, friends, caretakers. Why can't I let her go? She's better off here, without me. They can give her what I and the world can't: permission to be crazy.

Here in the usually noisy and always smoke-filled C-2 recreation room, I deposit her, a fragment of my loss and helplessness, and then I walk to my car. I bury whatever grief I can in the night and the cold, knowing it will be resurrected the next time I come—just as surely as the picnic tables will be spread out in the spring and the waterfall will be turned on.

Source: Win Winship, "First person account: How do I let go?" *Schizophrenia Bulletin, 19* (4) (1993), 853–854.

•••

---

tive for patient interaction. However, some friendships and cliques do form among patients, and these have been the focus of some research.[61] On the open psychiatric ward, friendship choices are made on the basis of social similarity, much as they are in the outside world. But on a locked psychiatric ward, social similarity does not influence friendship choice at all, probably because the most severely impaired patients are placed in the locked wards and these patients are generally uninterested in friendships.[62] Unlike outside society, patients in a locked ward are apparently unconcerned about reciprocity of feeling since they frequently desire as friends patients who are uninterested in the friendship. In other words, liking does not beget liking, but rather begets interaction.

The likelihood of a patient having fellow patients as friends is significantly related to type of illness. Depressives and schizophrenics (without paranoid symptoms) have the greatest number of friends.[63] This is particularly true of depressives. They are most frequently chosen as friends by other patients.[64] Hostile patients, on the other hand, are more likely to be ignored. Hostility is most common among paranoids, a group of patients who rarely make friendships. When they do, they tend to select other paranoids.[65]

One unsettling aspect of friendships among mental patients is that popular patients have lower rates of contact with staff than do unpopular patients.[66] Assuming staff contact is positively related to recovery (and it may not be), the patient is almost forced to choose between social affiliations and recovery. This is a serious problem because patients need some rapport with each other to survive what is otherwise a very meaningless and undirected existence. Patient interaction helps to combat the boredom of ward living and to provide a means to assert independence and self-identity. Interaction among patients also serves as a reference point by means of which patients can judge their own recovery.

Patient and staff interaction are just two of a multitude of factors that affect patient improvement. What do the patients themselves say about their hospital experiences? Are they more often satisfied than not? We do not know for sure because, while one study reported that patients believed that they benefited from their hospital stay,[67] another report found just the opposite.[68]

The Sick Role

The "sick role" concept was popularized by Talcott Parsons. It is widely used in medical sociology to refer to the attitudes and behavior expected of people who become patients. Initiation into the sick role is begun early in childhood with physical illnesses. It is taught by parents and reinforced by physicians, all of whom expect the child to follow their orders submissively. This sick role is appropriate for medical patients who passively follow other's instructions, lest they injure themselves by independent activity.

The sick role of the psychiatric patient differs from the medical sick role. Not only does the psychiatric sick role last much longer than the medical sick role, but the expected behavior of the "good" psychiatric mental patient is radically different from that of the medical patient. To be a mental patient requires participation in one's own rehabilitation. Mental patients must actively deal with people in the environment to create a new concept of reality for themselves and gradually test their ability to fulfill autonomy, responsibility, and independence demands made on them. A common problem is that many mental patients perceive their role as a passive, dependent one because they transfer the role they learned during physical illnesses in childhood.[69] This inconsistency between the expectations of the medical sick role and the psychiatric sick role can cause difficulties in treatment. Typically, mental patients complain that the staff should be doing more for them or that the psychiatrist should be telling them what to do. This is a carryover effect from the dependent nature of the traditional medical sick role.

Psychiatric patients with a strong medical sick role orientation appear well adjusted to hospital life, but the adjustment is only apparent and actually dysfunctional since they are likely to become dependent on the institution and fail to anticipate discharge.[70] There is ample evidence that this problem is most common among lower-class patients, who have been socialized toward conformity and passivity. Consequently, they are not as able to shift from a submissive, medical role to an independent, psychiatric role as well as their higher-class counterparts do.[71] This is one of the reasons that lower-class patients tend to be hospitalized longer than higher-class patients.

Treatment Techniques

There has been over 50 years of sociological research on the use of mental health services. Tons of recommendations have been made on the role of social networks and reducing organizational impediments to utilization of help sources.[72] Given the debilitating effects of illnesses such as schizophrenia, patients need services that improve functioning, manage medications, and provide skills training for better community integration. The problem is that different types of treatment services produce unpredictable outcomes.[73] Some blame this on a failure to treat ethnic minorities with an "ethnic and language match" in therapy.[74] But there is more to it than that, including whether mental hospitals have the basic necessities to even *attempt* to rehabilitate effectively.

Mental hospitals do not always function as active treatment centers. This is particularly true of state mental hospitals that do not have a sufficient number of skilled personnel to administer intensive and individualized treatment. As a result, few patients receive psychotherapy oriented toward insight into their problems and eventual care. Instead, treatment techniques, such as medications that control psychotic symptoms, are employed. The drugs, however, make little contribution to permanent rehabilitation.

You can pick up a newspaper almost any day and read an account of a mentally ill person being sent to a county jail. There is the report of the mild-mannered surveyor's assistant who began hearing voices that directed him to put his roommate in a headlock, drag him into the street, and shout "Hallelujah! Hallelujah!" His delusional experiences earned him a trip to jail. There is the case of a young woman commanded by ethereal voices to take a bus to a bank and rob it with a toy gun and a broken voltmeter. The woman had a history of bizarre behavior, was clearly irrational at the time she pulled the bank job, but she remains in jail. Doing time for people like this is not easy. Because the mentally ill cannot cope in the general population they are isolated in psychiatric wings where jailhouse "shrinks" dispense antidepressant and psychotropic medication like candy, consigning them to a lonely, often zombie-like existence.[75]

Mental hospitals are frequently described as prisons for people who have not broken the law. In light of the types of treatment patients usually receive, this position seems justified. However, as the number of patients in mental hospitals has dropped over the past few decades, a greater effort has been made to give patients some psychotherapy. There is no doubt that being in psychotherapy can improve some patients' chances for recovery. This is particularly true of patients who receive individual psychotherapy over extended periods of time.[76] However, the patient-staff ratio in state mental hospitals never reaches the point where individual psychotherapy becomes a realistic option. Accordingly, group psychotherapy is used as a substitute for individual treatment. Group therapy is based on the idea that emotional disorders originate in pathological relationships with other people and, therefore, can best be worked through in a group setting that reproduces the original situation that led to the disorder. Those who criticize state hospitals for not providing individual therapy may be unfair since some patients, particularly schizophrenics, do not respond to individual therapy. There is even a new form of "brief therapy" designed to solve a patient's troubles as quickly as possible. Part of the approach is based on the idea of converting negative stories into positive stories.[77]

Many consider group therapy to be a poor substitute for individual therapy because the patient gets less attention, may be embarrassed in discussing some problems before a group, and is denied the confidentiality that only an individual therapeutic experience can provide. However, there are some positive aspects to group therapy. First of all, it is usually the only way that treatment needs can be met within an institutionalized setting. It also helps patients overcome feelings of isolation and provides them with some skill in interacting with others. Additionally, members of the group can point out each other's maladaptive behavior more readily than an individual therapist can. If a therapist bluntly confronts the patient with an unpleasant fact, the patient may feel hurt or angry and become less cooperative, but if a fellow patient in a group makes the same criticism, the therapist is then free to discuss it.

Related to group therapy is the community meeting in which all patients on a ward meet as a group with the staff. This exposes the staff to the social networks that operate on the ward. It can also help to provide the patient with an opportunity to obtain information about hospital life, as well as possible insight into their own problems. The meetings allow patients to participate actively in discussions about various aspects of the hospital. In the process, undesirable passive-dependent attitudes can be modified. The community meeting also fosters a team approach to treatment since different staff members can combine and integrate their treatment efforts after they interact with the patients. In turn, patients are less likely to be subjected to differing sets of expectations by different members of the staff.

Some feel strongly about the positive benefits of psychotherapy and believe that it will continue to occupy a prominent place in the future of treatments.[78] Conversely, others feel that it is a gross waste of time and money. The opponents of psychotherapy actually believe that it is counterproductive, particularly in the case of serious mental illnesses with medical origins.[79]

The primary goal of the community meeting is to increase patients' participation in their own care and treatment. In some hospitals, patients also participate in the administration of the hospital through patient government. This is a democratic organization composed of an executive council of patient-members who transmit patients' opinions about the administration as it affects their everyday lives. Generally, the issues decided on by the patient government are simple things, such as decorating the ward, but occasionally the patients are invited to express opinions on more important questions, such as admission and discharge policies. Both the community meeting and patient government help to take the despondent edge off mental hospital life by treating patients as people with social rights that are to be respected.

For some time now, token economy programs, based on the principles of behavior modification, have been increasingly used.[80] The aim is to elicit desired patient behavior by providing tangible rewards for acts viewed by the staff as adaptive. The rewards are tokens that can be exchanged for items selected by patients at a small in-hospital variety store. Token economy programs are reported to be beneficial in modifying a number of patient behaviors, including troublesome meal and bedtime behavior, as well as a number of personal care behaviors such as combing hair, making a bed, and bathing.[81] Many mental patients cannot perform these acts because of their impairment or as a result of an extended stay in a mental hospital, which deteriorates personal habits.

At least one study reports that token economy principles can also modify the delusional speech of schizophrenics.[82] Although token programs are reported to be positively related to hospital discharge,[83] most studies of token program efficacy examine only reported improvement in the patient's hospital behavior rather than the actual symptoms of illness.[84] Undoubtedly, token programs are useful in controlling the behavior of chronic hospitalized schizophrenics, but they clearly do not actually effect *cure* of psychotic symptoms.

Occupational therapy and other forms of therapy also provide opportunities for the development and expression of the patient's individuality, which is usually undermined by the restrictive world of the mental hospital.[85] By being encouraged to act spontaneously, patients can gain insight into themselves.

> Traditional avenues for fostering the expression of the patients' individuality are the ancillary therapies found in some form in most mental hospitals—occupational therapy, music therapy, recreational therapy, bibliotherapy and so forth. With the explicit aim of individualizing care and treatment, the patient may be given a plastic medium and told he may make with it anything he wishes. Neither usefulness nor excellence enter in, the objective being to help him find useful ways of expressing himself through the medium. His productions may be used both diagnostically and therapeutically; for example, the finger-paintings, drawings, or clay figures may be used as clues to his illness and his progress.[86]

I do not want to give the impression that the typical mental hospital provides a multitude of therapeutic activities. Many provide nothing but an excessively routinized, inactive, dehumanizing existence. Even when an effort is made to reach the patients individually, the results are largely a function of the staff person's skills. Since a large portion of the staff is undertrained, the benefits in terms of patient improvement are minimal. What else can account for the damaging ways in which some activities are conducted? For example, on a hospital tour with my students, I once witnessed "music therapy" that required the patients to individually sing about how "crazy" they were!

It would be dishonest to evaluate therapy within mental hospitals without mentioning the increasing numbers of reports concerning the dangerous and punishing practices that sometimes occur. There are still "seclusion rooms" where disagreeable patients are locked in solitary confinement to exhaust their energy, remove them from the stimulation of the environment, and to protect them from themselves or others.[87]

Coercion and restrictions are commonly used in psychiatric inpatient treatment. Methods include seclusion, mechanical restraint, forced medication, physical holding, and restrictions on leaving the ward.[88] Needless to say, the experiences of patients who have been secluded are mostly negative.[89] The same holds true for restraints.[90] There are reports, however, that patients, family, and clinicians have a common understanding of some aspects of coercion and share some sense of agreement on its utility.[91]

Patients with antisocial personality disorder pose a special problem to the hospital staff and other patients.[92] Because of their manipulative and cunning nature, they are especially likely to cause trouble in a variety of ways.[93] Conning other patients is one disturbing habit. Because they are so difficult to treat in conventional ways, antisocial patients may run the greatest risk of punishment to themselves. Although psychosurgery is supposed to be used only under careful guidelines and with the approval of the hospital board, a 1974 U.S. Senate report claimed that it was being used on patients who exhibited antisocial behavior. One "behavior-control experiment" implanted radio transmitter-receivers in the brains of known offenders to control their behavior through a computer. Another program used the drug Apomorphine, which can cause uncontrolled vomiting for up to an hour, on patients who used abusive language. In addition, another hospital tried to suppress assaults and suicide attempts with the drug Anectine, which causes prolonged seizure of the respiratory system and muscular paralysis. Don't get the impression that these techniques are used all the time. They are probably just isolated experiments, although psychosurgery is apparently used more frequently than is commonly believed. Speaking of experiments, I was shocked to learn that there are now plans to diagnose and treat people on the Internet! Now that is special.[94]

Collective Disturbances

Sometimes all the patients on a given ward become disturbed at once. These outbreaks are called *collective disturbances*, and they are not just chance occurrences.[95] Sometimes they are precipitated by a patient suicide, which, in turn, can set off a wave of suicidal acts by other patients. Suicide waves reportedly occur during periods of social disorganization within the hospital.[96] This anomic condition is frequently caused by weakened relations among staff members. As a result, the staff loses confidence in their ability to deal with patients who, in turn, develop feelings of hopelessness. Effective suicide prevention programs are a pressing need.

Staff resignations and conflicts are common causes of a breakdown in staff morale. In addition, Kahne's study of psychiatrists whose patients committed suicide found that psychiatrists who keep a great deal of social distance between themselves and their patients have high rates of patient suicide.[97] This problem is most common among psychiatrists of foreign birth or training. There is also a high rate of suicide among patients of psychiatric residents, not simply because of their lack of experience but also because the hospital often assigns high-risk cases to beginners.

Reported cases of collective disturbances occur mainly in private hospitals that have a high ratio of staff members (especially psychiatrists) to patients and that emphasize psychotherapeutic methods of treatment.[98] There are fewer disturbances in state hospitals because of a heavier use of drugs that tranquilize patients and minimize the effects of crowded wards.[99] Private hospitals are also more likely than state hospitals to have psychiatric residents in training. This can lead to constant turnover, which threatens the control system. It has also been suggested that the larger number of residents and students results in more *reporting* of collective disturbances in private hospitals. This may be because the greater interest of staff novices makes them respond more eagerly to a display of agitated behavior. Or perhaps the presence of concerned staff motivates patients to reveal bizarre symptoms because they feel that the staff will react with concern and tolerance. If the last hypothesis is true, more disturbances should occur on weekdays when more staff are present. Melbin tested this proposition and discovered that there is a timetable of collective disturbances; consistent with the prediction, patients behave "crazily" much more often during weekdays than they do during evenings or weekends.[100] Patient assaults against staff also follow cyclical variations; a much greater number of assaults occur during the summer months.[101] Also, certain conditions in the patient group seem to incite collective disturbances.[102] These include the admission of new disruptive patients, a concentration of schizophrenic patients, the lack of patient cliques, and the unique horror of patient rape. Unfortunately, there is no reliable way to predict patient violence except to rely on patients' histories of violence.[103]

The Relatives of Hospital Patients

No description of the life of the mental hospital patient would be complete without some consideration of patients' relatives since they can play an important role in increasing the patient's agony. In Box 13:2 there is the story of the woman who regularly visited her schizophrenic daughter. That woman may be the exception since there are so many reports that, over time, many relatives abandon the patient by terminating visits and even mail.[104] Yet, perhaps this is not as detrimental to the patient as it may seem because the painstaking results of weeks of work can easily be undone in half an hour by a relative's visit, as exemplified by the following case:

> A paranoid schizophrenic, with additional catatonic ailments, was treated quite successfully . . . at a state hospital. His social recovery was indicated by the fact that after nine weeks of treatment, he had progressed from a closed ward to an open, working ward and was making good at a hospital job. About this time, however, he received a visit from his wife, upon whom he was extremely dependent. During the course of the visit he questioned her, obviously in a paranoid manifestation, about her possible relations with other men. The wife's response was to belabor him with an umbrella. The following day found the patient . . . showing marked disturbance and complete loss of contact.[105]

As suggested by the medical and environmental theories of familial transmission of mental disorder, the relatives of mental patients may have as much psychopathology as the patients themselves. This allows some insight into the family dynamics involved in the patient's problems. In some instances, it is appropriate that the relative be treated as well. Frequently, it is important that the relative at least stay away from the patient, rather than risk additional stress or relapse. This is particularly advisable in light of reports that relatives have more pessimistic views toward mental patients than do nonrelatives. They view the hospitalized patient as unpredictable, hopeless, and unable to understand a letter or participate in a conversation. These negative attitudes are not reduced by more frequent visits. In fact they become immutable.[106]

It is no small wonder that staff members often feel hostile toward patients' relatives. They perceive the family as partly responsible for having produced a mentally ill member, and they commonly joke about the wrong family members being in the hospital.[107] The hostility between staff and relatives is mutual since the families often view the staff as being difficult to deal with and deliberately denying their rights, requests, and needs. The relatives may complain that the staff does not give them any information about the patient's treatment and progress, while the staff is frustrated by the family's reluctance to accept the authority of the hospital. All of this creates additional chaos, which further minimizes the patients' chances for recovery.

The Future of the Mental Hospital

In all likelihood, the archaic style of state hospitals will not continue. In fact, if present trends continue, state hospitals may soon be a thing of the past.[108] I personally have witnessed the shutdown of a large number of major buildings at Norristown State Hospital in recent years. Norristown is symbolic of a trend—a clear-cut movement of patients from long-stay hospitals into the community. Advances in medications are partly responsible for this move.

Psychiatric inpatients do enjoy some definite benefits from hospitalization. One is that derived from living apart from the family. This benefit removes the person from the demands and stresses of everyday living and allows for suspension of obligations as a spouse, parent, or worker. Hospitalization also allows treatment to be repeated, monitored frequently, and evaluated for its results. This may sound inconsistent in light of the negatives of mental hospital life, but many of those negatives are due to the attitudinal problems of a small and undertrained staff. If the staff were larger, better trained, and able to communicate openly with the patients, much better care would be available than has been the case.

From a practical point of view, the remarkable drop in mental hospital populations will probably lead to a major change in hospital functions or to total shutdowns. The hospital population decline was ushered in by advances in psychopharmacology in the mid-1950s. A moderate decline occurred until 1969, but since then, the total population has decreased dramatically. Today, some hospital buildings stand empty or have already been razed. If the size of the hospital staff can be maintained, the population drop will provide the opportunity to treat patients on the individual basis that good psychiatry requires. However, it is more likely that staff will be eliminated along with the buildings.

Some feel that releasing patients is a good thing with a predictable outcome. Is it? Is it possible to predict who will be readmitted and who can make it in the outside world?[109] In the next chapter you will see that this is largely a function of the setting to which the patient is returned. Here let me mention a few of the correlates of readmission. People who voluntarily continue on medication are not as likely to return.[110] The most powerful predictor of long-term outcome is diagnosis. Patients with schizophrenia, for instance, are especially likely to be readmitted while those with clinical depression have a better chance of rejoining the outside world and staying there.[111] But even the predictive ability of medication and diagnosis is affected by sociological forces such as race and ethnicity.[112]

Since the causes of the psychoses are often medical, it is not likely that mental hospitals will be *totally* abolished in the future. Medical treatment is absolutely necessary for controlling the symptoms of many psychotic patients. It simply is not feasible to administer treatment to some schizophrenics on an outpatient basis where the patient is not constantly monitored. Additionally, legal offenders, the confused, the acutely disturbed, those with actual brain diseases, and the potentially dangerous can only be housed in hospital wards inside locked doors. Anything short of institutional care for such patients poses a real threat to both the patients and the community.

Recently, many state hospitals, such as Philadelphia State Hospital at Byberry, have been closed. To many, this is a sign of hope, a movement away from archaic, prison-like institutions toward the development of better treatment programs in the community. Presently, some patients are living in state-paid group homes and doing rather well. The per patient cost of this type of arrangement is less than the cost of traditional state hospital care. Perhaps these homes will be the wave of the future. If they are developed further, funding may eventually shift from the state to the community itself. The main problem is not funding but whether community-based care can even work.

INSTITUTIONALIZATION

The Meaning of Institutionalization

The fact that mental patients in state hospitals are not treated individually but as a homogenous group of people is a routine feature of life in what Goffman calls a "total institution."[113] The features of this atmosphere include:

1. Barriers between the "inmate" and the outside world

2. Requirements that the "inmate" must show deference to the staff
3. Admission procedures that strip the "inmate" of personal possessions and a full name, and
4. Verbal and/or gestural profanations such as calling "inmates" obscene names, cursing them, and publicly pointing out their negative traits

The highly regulated style of life in the mental hospital can cause long-stay patients to develop a syndrome that is not part of their original mental disorder. The syndrome is usually referred to as *institutionalization,* although some prefer other labels such as *chronic institutional reaction, social breakdown syndrome,* or *dysculturation.* Institutionalization frequently develops in patients who have been hospitalized for two or more years. The syndrome consists of a varying combination of apathy, lack of concern for one's future, deterioration in personal habits, oversubmissiveness, and an excessive dependency on the hospital and staff.

One explanation of institutionalization is that it results from the authoritarian, impersonal routines in the mental hospital that force people to succumb to institutional demands and to minimize their individual needs for a prolonged period of time.[114] However, it is not clear whether patients become institutionalized because the hospital inducts them into a sick role by convincing them they are mentally ill or whether institutionalization is simply a passive acceptance of institutional life caused by an inability to cope in the outside world.[115] It is also not clear whether there is anything resembling a "uniform process of institutionalization" that affects all chronic patients.[116]

The Effects of Institutionalization

There can be little doubt that hospital expectations and requirements contribute to the institutionalization process. This is most pronounced in a custodial institution where the patient's most pressing need is often not how to cope with a disorder but how to emotionally survive the hospital experience. For this reason, some sociological discussions of mental hospitals imply that the patient is victimized by institutionalization.[117] Although it may take years to damage the patient's personality permanently, the process of institutionalization begins with admission experiences that diminish ego strength and can cause partial regression to a childhood stage during which the outer world is perceived as an extension of the self.

> Admission to the mental hospital is all too often a humiliating experience, reinforcing the patient's low self-esteem. In an atmosphere of impersonality and indifference, he waits for attention. He is stripped of clothes, spectacles, money, watches, and wedding rings. He is put in a shower. He is given a perfunctionary examination and is probably not told where he is and why and what will be done to and for him and why.[118]

Hospitalization can cause a loss in self-esteem and a loss of social identity. This is a result of a process of *self-mortification* that subjects the patient to a number of humiliating experiences.[119] Every detail of the patient's life comes under the scrutiny and control of the staff, including when to sleep, what to eat, what to wear, and how to behave. The hospital is a world of "unfreedom," particularly in the conventional state hospital where the patient is given no significant responsibility and little opportunity to make important decisions. Here patients are desocialized; that is, they are not helped to move back into the outside world since self-direction, as well as personhood, is virtually eliminated.

The factors that cause institutionalization have not simply been contrived by liberal social scientists observing from the outside; they have also been reported by researchers who have had themselves admitted as patients to observe firsthand the conditions of mental hospitals.[120] However, it only requires a tour through a state hospital to see the visible correlates of institutionalization. The lives of ward-bound patients are repetitive and boring. They are confined to the dayroom, which rarely contains anything more than uncomfortable chairs, a few ashtrays, and the ever-present television, the only contact with the outside world. In this setting, time becomes boundless, and some patients shrink into a vegetative state. In fact, some actually curl up in a corner and wither away.

Goffman argues that many long-term patients adjust to being hospitalized through what he calls *conversion*.[121] This is the process by which patients accept the hospital's definition of them as sick and belonging in an institution. To accomplish this, Goffman argues that the hospital discredits the patient's self-concepts so that they can come to view themselves simply as sick patients rather than as individuals. Goffman believes that conversion is most likely to occur in a patient-centered hospital that employs psychotherapy and group therapy, both of which are powerful tools in changing the patients' self-concepts. He states that "the more it (the hospital) attempts to be therapeutic and not merely custodial—the more he (the patient) may be confronted by high-ranking staff arguing that . . . if he wants to be a person he will have to change his way of dealing with people and his conceptions of himself."[122] It is a damned if you do and damned if you don't dilemma.

There is some support for Goffman's propositions concerning institutionalization and conversion. As logic would dictate, chronic patients exhibit more dependency on and identification with the hospital than do acute patients. As a result, these patients, particularly the females, become very anxious about returning to the community. On the other hand, a number of studies fail to demonstrate that mental patients think of themselves as mentally ill.[123] However, most of these studies examined the self-concepts of acutely ill patients, not the chronic patients that Goffman has studied.

Short-term patients tend not to change their self-concepts because they view their "apart state" as temporary and are therefore not likely to lose their social identities. But even short-term patients easily accept institutional life and believe that hospital routines are intended to benefit them. In one study, for instance, 66 percent of the short-term patients agreed with the statement, "Locked doors help you get well."[124]

Social learning theorists have analyzed institutionalization and conversion. Some researchers utilizing this approach define institutionalization in terms of behavioral symptoms that include a specific posture and gait. Interestingly, these behaviors can be modified by restructuring the physical environment of the hospital through rearranging the furniture or moving to a new building. These changes can have beneficial effects because they disrupt the monotony of hospital life. I am talking here about "simple" changes, such as plants, new wallpaper, and bright colors.[125]

Despite all of the talk about the dynamics of institutionalization, its meaning, and its alleged effects, some very visible signs indicate whether a released patient is really dependent on the hospital and not fit to be returned to the community. These include length of hospital stay, symptoms of psychosis, severe drug abuse, and problems obtaining regular meals.[126]

Providing a Therapeutic Milieu

Because social factors contribute to mental disorder, the mentally ill can often only be effectively rehabilitated in an environment that projects a remedial social character. Although it is probably impossible to totally avoid institutionalization, some steps can be taken to mitigate its effects. Maxwell Jones long ago recognized that the mental hospital is a community that can have a great therapeutic potential if it is properly structured.[127] His concept of *therapeutic community* hinges on a number of assumptions about improving mental patients without their developing a dependency on the hospital. One assumption is that patients do have certain conflict-free areas of their personalities that can facilitate recovery if programs can be geared to make use of them. A second assumption is the importance of pervasive staff involvement with patients, including nurses and aides, as well as psychiatrists and social workers. A third assumption is the constructive role that patients can play in designing their own treatment and influencing the organization of the hospital through patient government.

A fundamental component of the social organization of a therapeutic community is the daily community meeting with the entire patient and staff population of a ward or building. Jones reports that the community meeting activates patient tensions, which can then be worked through in smaller group meetings. In addition to patient-staff meetings, the therapeutic community also emphasizes treatment programs including individual therapy, psychodrama, and occupational-recreational therapy. Perhaps the most central component of the therapeutic community is delivering mental health services with a "continuity of care."[128] Without this consistent form of evaluation, treatment, and follow-up, the most well-designed modality of therapy (group therapy or otherwise) will be much less effective.[129]

A central feature of the therapeutic community is its attitudinal climate. The atmosphere created by personalized treatment, which encourages patient autonomy and social interaction without tolerating deviant behavior, reduces the risk of institutionalization. Patients are encouraged to express their anger and aggression openly. They share decisions with the staff regarding such matters as the discharge of patients, transfer to other wards, and actions to be taken with disagreeable patients.

A therapeutic community is impossible to obtain without a large staff that is properly trained, highly motivated, and of high morale. Presently, this is difficult to accomplish due to limited funding for mental health care. If therapeutic communities ever do become widespread, however, mental hospitals will no longer be places in which a horrible fate awaits patients. One model has been proposed by Kelly and her colleagues.[130] They suggest fostering self-help on a unit to address the problems of denial and the debilitating effects of mental illness by arranging patients into "self-help clubs." One of the features of the program is to use ex-patients who are successfully coping with their illnesses as guest speakers. Part of the success of a well-designed therapeutic community depends on the nature of the person's illness. Mood disorders, for example, respond more favorably to this approach.[131]

THE COMMUNITY MENTAL HEALTH CLINIC

Basic Services

I hope that I have made it clear that the mental hospital is often unable to effect proper care for the mentally disordered. As I mentioned earlier, a number of factors account for this inability, including the size and training of staff and the risk of institutionalization. Another problem is the tendency of psychiatrists, judges, and others involved in the commitment process to assume the person is ill. This floods hospitals with many people who do not belong there, although mental health laws are changing to correct this. Hospitalization itself may also unduly stigmatize mental patients because others in the community tend to view the hospitalized as qualitatively different from the rest of society. The stigma attached to institutionalized patients remains long after discharge, and, in some cases, is irreversible. All of these factors indicate that mental hospitals constitute as much of a problem as does mental illness itself. In fact, a number of studies, including the Midtown Manhattan study, have demonstrated that mentally disordered people can function more effectively in the community than those who have been hospitalized and released. Perhaps this is because the hospitalized person must unlearn hospital routines and become resocialized into the outside community while the never-hospitalized person has learned to adapt her illness to the routines of mainstream society. As a reaction to all of the problems connected with hospitalization, deinstitutionalization and community care are the most influential movements in the mental health field in recent decades.[132]

During the 1960s, the traditional mental hospital came increasingly under attack in the United States. In 1961, the Joint Commission on Mental Illness and Health placed the burden of treatment of the mentally ill on the community rather than psychiatrists and other mental health workers in hospitals. This ushered in *community psychiatry*, a movement based on the idea that community resources should be used for the treatment and prevention of mental disorder. The community psychiatry movement is commonly referred to as the "third revolution" in psychiatry, following Pinel's reform treatments and Freud's discoveries.

The focus of mental health care began to shift from the long-term care of chronic aspects of mental illness to short-term treatment of acute aspects. Short-term hospitalization and crisis-oriented outpatient care were added to the long-term approaches. Tranquilizers played a significant role in this change by easing the problem of otherwise uncontrollable behavior. However, some have criticized the mass prescription of antipsychotic drugs as being a "cheap fix." There were complaints about the aggressive marketing campaign by the drug company Smith Kline Beecham following the release of Thorazine. The company allegedly sold it as a "chemical straitjacket." Not only was it a cheap way to keep the mental wards silent, but it also acted as a substitute for ongoing, outpatient care. Suicide prevention centers were the original models of the principles of community action for mental health,[133] but later a number of different programs came about. These include day hospitalization, immediate crisis intervention at home by "flying teams," brief stays in a foster home, and, most recently, the multipurpose community mental health clinic.[134]

One of the functions of these clinics is to nurture adaptive behavior in individuals by promoting positive mental health attitudes in the community as a whole. A second purpose of the community mental health clinic is to shorten the length of illness through early evaluation and treatment, rather than ignoring symptoms until the illness becomes chronic. A third function is to assist chronic patients in their return from the mental hospital to the community. All of these goals are oriented toward avoiding or shortening hospitalization, since the longer patients stay in the hospital, the less chance they have of getting out and staying out.[135] The community mental health clinics are designed to offer disturbed people immediate action. An impetus for this approach came during World War II when it was found that quick intervention for the treatment of shell shock at the front lines was more successful than taking soldiers back to the States for long periods of hospitalization.

The typical community mental health clinic serves a population from 75,000 to 200,000 people, the size required to qualify for federal funding. This unit is a geographic area called a "catchment area." It may be a city, a county, or a neighborhood. Most clinics are located near the center of a large urban community. They may provide a number of services to persons of varying economic levels by setting fees on a sliding scale basis so that people pay what they can afford.

Community mental health clinics were formally established with the passage of the Community Mental Health Centers Construction Act in 1963 and its staffing implementation in 1965. Federal funds were awarded to assist in the development of over 800 community mental health centers, serving catchment areas representing 70 percent of the U.S. population. Each of these centers is somewhat unique because it serves a specific community with its own political structure, social system, and medical organization.

The most common type of clinic is the multiple agency center operated by from two to twelve agencies, each of which provides a basic service. The agencies include general hospitals, social work agencies, family therapy groups, and mental health programs affiliated with a university. Some clinics are part of a general hospital or a state mental hospital. All clinics are required to provide five basic services—inpatient, outpatient, partial hospitalization, emergency and consultation, and education. Some have special services for children, alcoholics, drug addicts, the suicidal, juvenile delinquents, geriatric patients, and the mentally retarded.

Consultation and education are often aimed at school systems. The clinic's staff can train guidance counselors, administrators, and teachers to provide mental health services in situations within their scope or ability. Psychiatric emergency services are helpful for less severely disordered persons who need immediate aid at times of crisis. During the 1970s, there was an astounding growth rate in these services, which include drug abuse clinics, suicide prevention centers, alcoholism programs, and hot lines.

"Partial hospitalization" is a treatment modality somewhere between inpatient and outpatient care. It includes day hospitals, night hospitals, and weekend hospitals. The day hospital, which provides care for those who are too disordered to be treated as outpatients, is the most common part-time facility.[136] Patients in day care hospitals participate in a full program of hospital activities during the day and return home in the evening. The average weekly cost of care for mentally ill patients in the inpatient setting is over twice the level of the cost of care for people attending a day hospital facility.[137]

The night hospital has the opposite treatment schedule of the day hospital: the patients work during the day and are treated in the evening. The night hospital is especially helpful for patients who do not function well during leisure time, such as alcoholics. The weekend hospital offers more intensive treatment than an outpatient clinic and is especially helpful to those who live far from treatment centers. Any of these forms of partial hospitalization may be sufficient for patients who need to be removed from temporary environmental stressors.

The major benefit of partial hospitalization is that it provides custodial care without the restrictive measures of full-time hospitalization. Patients are free to come and go as they choose. They are not forced to accommodate themselves to the needs of the staff. This approach can be useful with mildly disturbed patients who would otherwise endure miserable days. Recently, some new ideas for special treatment facilities are being put to the test. One is a combination of a state mental hospital and a community mental health clinic.[138] It is being used for difficult patients who are placed in locked community clinics. Closely related are involuntary outpatient commitments designed to make it more likely that people will keep their mental health appointments, take their medication, and stay out of the hospital.[139]

Effectiveness

If one measure of effectiveness of community mental health clinics is a reduction in admissions to mental hospitals, then they can be claimed a success: there has been a vast shift in care from predominantly inpatient settings to predominantly outpatient settings such as these clinics. Some of the community centers are psychiatric "halfway houses" in urban neighborhoods.[140] If the community response to local mental health care centers is another measure of effectiveness, then there is a clear sense of failure. Studies report that the public resists community-based programs, even when intensive educational campaigns designed to develop progressive attitudes toward mental illness are used. Many people simply fear a mass invasion of mental patients into their neighborhoods. Consequently, they often fight the establishment of community-based programs, particularly board-and-care homes for patients discharged from hospitals. Zoning ordinances, city ordinances, neighborhood pressures, fire regulations, and bureaucratic maneuvering have all been employed to fight off mental health programs in the community.

One of the questionable aspects of treating the mentally disordered in the community is the risk incurred with psychotic patients. The community clinics have been accused of handling the manageable patients and avoiding the difficult ones.[141] I do not know whether this is true, but, in some ways, it would be better if it were, since community clinics are not properly equipped to handle many psychotics. On the other hand, if community clinics do not intervene with the difficult ones, this can only contribute to the undesirable shift of patients from the back wards to the back alleys where they constitute a large part of our "homeless."[142] Programs to address unmet needs for mental health care, such as the ACCESS program for the homeless mentally ill, provide new models for service systems.[143]

A major problem of the typical community clinic is staffing.[144] In many instances, the clinics have even fewer professionals than do the state hospitals. One early survey revealed that 42 percent of full-time positions at community mental health centers were occupied by nonprofessional mental health personnel, most of whom were drawn from the catchment area served by the center.[145] This occurs, not by design but as a result of the fact that the community clinics are unappealing to many mental health personnel, particularly psychiatrists.

Psychiatrists are trained as medical specialists. As such, they often lack the training in the social sciences that good community psychiatry demands. In addition, the team approach by community clinics requires the psychiatrist to shift from individual-centered or family-centered therapy to group-centered or community-centered practice. All of this demands a mindset for which psychiatrists have not been prepared. They must accept the notion that they are only part of a team of caretakers that includes physicians, psychologists, social workers, and nurses, as well as family, friends, and neighbors, or anyone who can lend a helping hand at an opportune time. Psychiatrists also have difficulty performing consultation and education functions since these are rarely included in their training. Of course, no explanation of the under-representation of psychiatrists in community clinics would be complete without mention of the vital role of income factors. Income is an important determinant of professional contentment among psychiatrists and, since community psychiatry is a poor source of remuneration, most psychiatrists choose to work in more lucrative private practice settings.

Besides the staffing issue, community mental health clinics face other problems as well. One is the uncertain nature of funding from the federal government. Consequently, citizens and their local governments have had to raise much of the funding for these centers. Another nagging issue is how to deal effectively with patients who have returned to the community after a long stay in a mental hospital. Rooming-house programs are intended to provide these people with a comfortable place to live, but this is often not accomplished. One problem is the resistance encountered from nearby residents who resent ex-mental patients in their neighborhood. Another problem is the quality of life in the boarding homes. They can be as detrimental to the patient as state hospitals unless additional programs for reintegrating the ex-patient into the community are available. Without such programs, ex-patients will continue to waste away their lives in social isolation. Indeed, some contend that boarding houses are nothing more than small hospital wards in the community.

The real measure of the effectiveness of the community mental health clinics is whether they have significantly reduced the prevalence of mental illness. Unfortunately, it is not possible to answer that question objectively, although there is no shortage of researchers who have tried. Consequently, there are a number of conflicting reports regarding the supposed advantages and disadvantages of the community approach to treatment. On the positive side is the commonly cited fact that, since the creation of community clinics, hundreds of thousands of people have received care who would never have received it before, people whose emotional problems were not severe enough to warrant traditional treatment. Certain community clinic programs appear to be quite effective with these problems, particularly the problems that emergency services are equipped to handle.[146]

On the negative side, deinstitutionalization and the concomitant rise in community clinics have resulted in the growth of another social problem—"street people."[147] In urban areas, the homeless mentally ill pose special problems for health care workers who try to identify and treat them. They are an unwelcome result of the reduction in the number of large state hospitals. Estimates of the total number of homeless people in the United States range from as few as 250,000 to as many as 3 million. Whatever the real numbers are, they are probably five to ten times the number of people who live in state mental hospitals. Projections are that as few as 20 percent to as many as 90 percent of all homeless people suffer from some form of mental illness.

The large number of the mentally ill on the streets exemplifies what is wrong with the policy of outpatient care for people with serious mental problems.[148] It is not the only visible symptom, however. Many of the mentally ill go from a hospital to the streets to jail.[149] The United States has been accused of being especially willing to imprison the mentally ill rather than treat their problems.[150] But it is not clear that things are better in other parts of the world. A 1990 British report on the state of services for mentally disordered offenders identifies problems and makes 276 recommendations but has no provisions for putting them into action.[151] When you consider what such a lengthy report must have cost, it is clear that *talk is expensive.*

Big questions have been raised about the value of the community clinic idea both here in the United States and in Great Britain, where the community movement was first started. More specific questions center about the efficacy of short-term and day hospitalization, both of which require immediate prescriptions of high drug dosages for psychotics and allow little time for a careful observation of the patient's symptoms. Short-term hospitalization has increased the number of discharges to the point where they outnumber new admissions. There is, however, an undesirable side effect of this reform: readmissions have also increased dramatically since the initiation of short-term hospitalization. This is usually interpreted as a consequence of the ineffectiveness of the short-term stay approach for seriously ill patients. The label "revolving-door phenomenon" aptly describes the combined effect of shortened periods of hospitalization with a high probability of readmission.

The community mental health movement has its merits, as evidenced by the large number of people using community clinics who otherwise would go untreated. The underlying philosophy of the movement is also sound because it is based on the recognition that the effects of long-term hospitalization can be as debilitating as the mental disorder itself. However, the danger of the movement lies in the enthusiastic way in which some people have extended the community clinic concept beyond its appropriate sphere. As a consequence, many seriously disturbed psychotics are being treated as outpatients in clinics staffed by overambitious and undertrained people.

The list of problems of community mental health clinics is endless. Funding, of course, is the largest obstacle to overcome. In fact, spending for community mental retardation services alone has grown much more rapidly than spending for all other forms of mental health services combined.[152] Despite all of these pessimistic facts, the spirit of the community movement continues, even if it comes only in the form of neighborly assistance with everyday needs[153] or help in finding housing.[154]

CONCLUSIONS

The beginning of the twenty-first century does not appear to be any more promising for mental patients than the past. There is a lot written about new mental health services and laws, but much of this has been lip service, not actual change. The economics of treatment are out of control and the general situation in psychiatric treatment is confusion and caution.

Problems are rampant within today's system of psychiatric treatment, particularly the state hospitals. One problem is the infrequency of contact between patients and the generally untrained, nonprofessional staff. There is also not enough patient contact with the professional staff, which is often too small and primarily concerned with administrative functions. A second problem is the oppressive atmosphere of the typical hospital ward, which, in turn, minimizes interpersonal contacts among patients and between patients and others.

A third problem with psychiatric treatment is the inconsistency between the medical sick role and the psychiatric sick role. Most patients unconsciously assume that the submissive behavior of the medical sick role is appropriate for the psychiatric sick role. This interferes with recovery from mental illness since effective therapy requires patients to participate actively in their own cure. A fourth problem with today's mental hospitals is the lack of good therapy for treating large numbers of patients. There is virtually no psychotherapy in large hospitals; there is only group therapy, which is a poor substitute for individual therapy. The custodially oriented hospitals are especially problematic in this regard.

Other problems encountered within the mental hospital include collective disturbances among patients and the problems posed by the patients' relatives, who are frequently disordered themselves. Presently there is no way of alleviating the problems of traditional hospitals, although attempts have been made to reduce them, such as the use of decentralized wards, community meetings, and patient government.

A major difficulty that patients encounter in mental hospitals is that over time they develop an institutionalization syndrome that is distinct from mental illness, per se, although it is difficult to distinguish institutionalization from the actual pathology of the patient. The syndrome includes a sense of apathy, lack of concern for the future, extreme submissiveness, and overdependency on the hospital. This problem was a major impetus for the development of community mental health clinics where patients can receive treatment without being institutionalized full time. Community clinics were designed to provide a variety of services ranging from emergency and consultation services to part-time hospitalization. The community approach to treatment is based on the recognition that hospitalization can do more harm than good. While the problems of hospitalization are enormous, there is little evidence that the community clinics are doing a better job than the traditional hospitals, particularly in light of their staffing problems and their inability to care for many psychotics.

In summary, the present system of psychiatric care in the United States is far from ideal. On the one hand, the hospitalization approach subjects the patient to the risks of institutionalization and stigmatization by society. On the other hand, the community approach may be helpful for those who are not severely impaired, but it appears totally inappropriate for many psychotics who should be in residential programs. Hopefully, a mental health care system will evolve that channels milder cases to community centers staffed with more professionals and severe cases to an inpatient milieu that is truly therapeutic.

14

After the Mental Hospital

The Social Role of the Ex-Mental Patient

The mass release of mental patients into the community is an important cause of the size of our homeless population today. Their lives are wasted away on the streets begging for help, talking to imaginary others, or using odd gestures to fend off potentially dangerous strangers.

Mention the word "deinstitutionalization" in the United States and you invoke images of the government's abandoning vast numbers of people with serious psychiatric disorders and waves of homeless, helpless people flooding city streets. Few people remember that deinstitutionalization, when it was initially proposed, was conceived as a liberal proposal for *empowerment* of patients in mental hospitals.

In the United States the policy turned out horrifically, not least because deinstitutionalization at the hospitals was not accompanied by any meaningful follow-up to ensure housing, treatment, and social services for former patients in the community.[1]

I first wrote this chapter about what often happens to people after they leave the mental hospital in 1980. I am sorry to say that things are just as miserable for ex-patients in the early 2000s as they were in the 1980s. And, frankly, the 1980s were not much of an improvement on the '60s and '70s. As I said in the first chapter, mental illness is widely misunderstood by the American public. People who are or were in treatment engender feelings of horror, shock, and alarm and are typically viewed not only as undesirable but also as downright threatening. This chapter reviews the social experiences encountered by released patients. It looks at the criteria for discharge, which often are more arbitrary than objective. It also examines a host of aftercare problems, from complete neglect to ridding the mind of the chains of institutionalization.

It would be nice if I could say that at least these people have families to return to. But to do so would be a lie because the families typically prefer life without the troubled relative. If there is one word that best identifies the new psychic hell awaiting released patients it is "stigma." To refer to social stigma as "the social distance the public keeps from ex-patients" is a polite understatement. To tie it in with rejections released patients experience—as job applicants, from caring relatives, and human beings in general—is much closer to the reality of their lives as pariahs.

Stigma is a horrifying phenomenon. In a rough way, it parallels the lives of lepers, except that ex-mental patients do not have their own colonies. They live in some part of the outside community and are treated with disgust and fear *directly*. This is often such a devastating experience that victims and families say the stigma can be worse than the disorder.[2] We live in a society governed by mental health laws that, in many ways, have worsened the plight of the mentally ill. Instead of wasting their lives away inside the walls of institutions, some now wither away as "street people" and *die with their rights on*. At this point it should be clear to the reader that the methods used to treat people with mental disorders are far from scientific and are frequently non-therapeutic. The process by which prepatients are led to sources of help is typically complicated by the inappropriate reactions of others, such as family members who ignore the problem, physicians and clergy with no professional insight, psychiatric evaluators who generally presume the person is disordered rather than run any risks, and laws that release the chronically ill into the streets.

This ill-defined and subjective process can delay the treatment of the seriously disturbed, as well as result in the institutionalization of those who do not need it. Both types of patients are likely to deteriorate further during their stays in mental hospitals because there are no clear guidelines to curing mental illness. Instead, behavior is controlled by prescribed "meds" that may alleviate symptoms but often simultaneously produce new and undesirable side effects.[3]

Having examined the prepatient and inpatient experiences, let's look at the life of the ex-mental patient. Logic would suggest that this group of people would have fewer stresses than those headed for mental hospitals or those being treated within them. However, logic is a rather weak tool in understanding how the mentally

Box 14:1
Why the Mentally Ill Are on the Streets

Bedlam. The Snake Pit. The insane asylums: Warehouses for hollow-eyed humans. Their beards and hair infested with lice, clothes tattered and soiled, nails grown long as claws, bodies encrusted with excrement.

Exposés of conditions like these inside the walls of state mental hospitals led to the movement—begun in the idealistic 1960s and accomplished mostly in the cost-cutting '70s and '80s—to shut them down.

The result . . . is that our streets have become the new Bedlams. The pathetic, raving, dangerous, ill-equipped psychotics have been deinstitutionalized—and they are destroying the civility and order of urban life.

They who vacantly drooled tucked away unseen in hospitals years ago now drool right there on the sidewalk, on church steps, at the entrance to movie theaters, inside cash-machine alcoves and subway cars. And the homeless shelter has replaced the nineteenth-century poorhouse, critics say.

But is deinstitutionalization really the reason we have these urban zombies scavenging through trash cans, begging for change and muttering to themselves?

. . . The fact that deinstitutionalization saved the public money turned it into a cost-cutting strategy rather than a humane and innovative way of treating the mentally ill. . . .

Is it true that the ideas of liberation actually helped enslave the mentally ill poor by forcing them on the street? . . .

Consider the possibility that the growing numbers of homeless stem more from the nation's failure to understand and take responsibility for the social pathology of the underclass . . . (and) the difficult issues raised by court decisions that make it virtually impossible to obtain long-term involuntary hospital commitments of psychotics without clear evidence that these psychotics pose imminent danger to themselves or others. . . .

While it is true that the era of constitutional rights for the mentally ill has created difficulties for society, is it fair to blame the reform movers for these problems?

The demise of the big institutions did take away a place where the psychotic could be safely removed. Most of these people are living at home with their families. And their families can't handle them and have nowhere to go for help. . . .

While our leaders were so busy congratulating themselves for cutting costs and shutting down these places of shame—often after courts ordered them to do so—they failed to provide the safety net, an integrated system of local mental health services, group homes and humane hospital care.

Source: Henry Goldman, "Why the mentally ill are on the streets," *Philadelphia Inquirer,* March 3, 1991.

---

ill are treated in society. Perhaps this is most obvious in the case of ex-patients. People discharged from hospitals are expected to have shown notable signs of recovery, be protected from a setback by suitably tailored aftercare programs, and be accepted back into society as competent persons. Unfortunately, these expectations are rarely realized because the experiences of ex-mental patients are guided more by social accident than by objective standards. Consequently, ex-patients, like prepatients, undergo subjective and often negative experiences with discharge criteria, aftercare programs, and the problems of stigma and community readjustment. Each of these experiences is treated separately in this chapter. There is also a discussion and criticism of social policy designed to treat released patients. Some of the social consequences of ex-patienthood are described in Box 14:1. None of the social policies to date deal with mental health problems among mentally ill children, although organizations and institutes exist to *talk* about "high-risk" children.[4]

DEINSTITUTIONALIZATION

Deinstitutionalization was a lofty idea that simply did not work. Being in the community rather than the back ward may seem preferable, but cure can only happen if patients are released to therapeutic, supportive settings. That has been the central failure of deinstitutionalization: community care of the chronically mentally ill has been thwarted by a lack of preparation and interest on the part of community care providers, public hospitals, and community agencies.[5] The result has been devastating for mental patients who, though released from hospitals, still need some form of care. The failed policy has also been devastating for communities because they are unable to care for the mentally ill who roam their streets, often homeless and incoherent, and sometimes dangerous.[6]

As with most social problems, there are numerous studies and reports. Criticisms have been widespread, particularly as the relationship between deinstitutionalization and street people has become increasingly visible.[7] Some call the situation "hospitals without walls."[8] Actually, that may not be an accurate phrase since, for some patients, the community does have walls—and bars, police, and handcuffs. I am referring here to the fact that, since deinstitutionalization, U.S. jails are housing great numbers of the mentally ill.[9] Other criticisms place the blame on the spread of the biopsycho*social* school of thought.[10]

Are there certain groups of mental patients who have been especially victimized? Blacks are hit twice: once by being dumped in the community and once by all of the by-products of cultural insensitivity commonly referred to as prejudice and discrimination.[11] The elderly are also hard hit. At least one study shows that elderly patients (65 years and older) are more likely to die during the year following discharge than those who remain in the hospital.[12]

The horrors of deinstitutionalization are not unique to the United States. Other countries, including Denmark[13] and England,[14] have had similar problems. I would call it a global problem, but it really is not since, as you will recall from Chapter 2, in some parts of the world the mentally ill are not treated at all. Maybe we will eventually learn some lessons from the failure of deinstitutionalization in the United States.[15] Until that time, the present mental health policy will hobble along on wobbly crutches. Perhaps I am oversimplifying the situation as one homogenous mess. As Box 14:2 demonstrates, deinstitutionalization is a very complex program that has failed for *many* reasons.

CRITERIA FOR DISCHARGE

Some states, such as Pennsylvania, vow to use care in releasing state mental patients, but intentions do not always translate into airtight policies. One sad testimony to the fact that some patients should not be released is the high number of them who commit suicide after discharge.[16] The mental hospital simply does not have objective standards for evaluating patients for discharge, although some state laws require patients to have an understanding of what kind of shape they have to be in before they leave (such as no longer having delusions). Even the behavior of patients is not a useful standard because they may appear quite "well" in the hospital setting but "fall apart" in the outside world.

Deinstitutionalization Has Failed

Deinstitutionalization is a remarkably complicated concept. It has its roots in political ideology, economic reality, shifting social values, and clinical practice; housing juvenile offenders and the developmentally disabled as well as the mentally ill. Most simply, the idea behind deinstitutionalization is that optimal treatment of long-standing and chronic behavioral conditions will take place not in an institutional setting but in situations and under conditions most closely approximating the social and cultural norms that apply everywhere else. The term *deinstitutionalization* has come to connote both that underlying idea and, in a kind of clumsy corollary, its practical realization. This dual meaning can be confusing but is itself a clue to the very messy nature of the social problems deinstitutionalization seeks to address.

I believe that deinstitutionalization, particularly the deinstitutionalization of the mentally ill, never actually happened. While it is certainly true that at some point it became popular among social theorists and the more adventurous clinicians to believe that even the chronically mentally ill could benefit from community-based treatment rather than traditional custodial care, the chronically mentally ill were never removed from custodial care in any real way. For the most part, the chronically mentally ill who had been in state mental hospitals during the years of aggressive discharge—the state hospital census hit about 550,000 in 1955 and has been dropping ever since—were simply shifted to other custodial settings not run by the government. This paradoxical result, which might more appropriately be called *re*institutionalization, came about in large part because the drive to discharge was rooted in fiscal anxiety, not in concern for patients or their care. In 1949, representatives of the 48 state governments got together, agreed that for them to continue to foot the bill for the lifetime care of the chronically mentally ill was to risk bankruptcy, and decided to work together to seek alternatives to hospitalization.

At first, enthusiasm for emptying state mental hospitals ran high, and early reports brimmed over with success stories. Public and professional assumptions about mental illness had indeed changed, the public was generally receptive to new ideas about mental illness, and the first patients to be discharged mostly did just fine. Unfortunately, those first patients were the ones who had families to whom they could return or were those who had been hospitalized most recently—in short, those who were the easiest to place and had the most promising futures. Still worse, this same group of misleadingly successful discharges became the pool of subjects for research studies published in the early 1960s and used ever after to justify further depopulation of the state mental hospitals. The patients discharged afterward were not so easy to place—their families didn't want them or had died off long before—and so another custodial setting, the nursing home, was hastily adapted to fit the population. When the nursing homes were filled, the adult home, or board-and-care facility, was created to take up the slack. Census data tell the story:

Per 100,000 population:

YEAR	1950	1960	1970	1980
Mental hospital	407.2	351.3	213.4	108.2
Home for aged	196.9	261.9	456.2	629.6

Admittedly, the country had seen an overall increase in its elderly during these years, but that alone cannot account for the huge expansion of the nursing home population. In fact, a significant portion of today's nursing home residents are people who used to live out their days in mental hospitals, most notably the senile elderly and patients with Alzheimer's disease, while younger, more manageable mental patients are housed in privately owned and operated adult homes.

Source: Ann Braden Johnson, "Has deinstitutionalization failed?" in Stuart A. Kirk and Susan D. Einbinder, eds., *Controversial Issues in Mental Health* (Boston: Allyn & Bacon, 1994), pp. 215–216. By permission of the publisher.

The medical model logically postulates that patients should be released on the basis of the seriousness of their illness. This is not always possible, however, because mental health professionals have not proven to be good predictors of a patient's behavior in the community.[17] Psychiatrists argue that they can estimate a patient's readiness for life in the outside world, and they insist that the timing of discharge depends on the type and severity of the illness. Yet actual observations indicate that discharge decisions frequently do not relate to the patient's mental health status.[18] This is also true of patients discharged from day hospital aftercare programs.[19]

I do not want to give the impression that mental hospitals favor chronic patients for release. Actually, as one might expect, younger patients with less than two years of hospitalization are more likely to be released than their chronic counterparts.[20] However, there is a growing movement to release chronic patients exhibiting severe symptoms. The hospitals that are most likely to favor release of chronic patients to the community are often motivated by practical concerns, such as overcrowding or what some call "statistical pressure," typically motivated by fiscal concerns, rather than an interest in the patients' welfare.

The fact that criteria for release are not based solely on patients' present mental health conditions but more on their life circumstances is downright alarming. For example, whatever the pathology, patients have a better chance of release if they have a place to live and a job waiting for them. Among female patients, married women are more frequently discharged than single women, because the married woman is more likely to have a home to which she can return.[21] The sex of the patient may not be *directly* related to the probability of discharge but it is *indirectly* related as a function of life circumstances; a major prerequisite for male patients' release is employment, a condition not imposed upon women, who are more likely to be released if they have an acceptable level of self-care, housekeeping, and social contacts.[22] This is not just sexism; it is also a bad idea.

There is also evidence that the treatment of mental patients is partly determined by the judgments of nonprofessionals. Consider the very important role played by family wishes regarding release. The attitudes of the family toward the patient's release are more likely to affect length of hospitalization than is the degree of the patient's impairment.[23] The formal request for discharge nearly always comes from the patient's family. Furthermore, the attitudes of the family are the single most important determinant of when the patient is released; if the family is in favor of release, the patient's chances of exit from the hospital are improved and, conversely, release is delayed if the family does not favor it.

What determines the attitudes of the family toward release? Typically, the family wishes are based on factors totally unrelated to their relative's psychiatric condition, such as the need for help with child care, loneliness, guilt, social freedom without the patient living at home, or even the timing of a vacation. Perhaps a more important question is why are hospital psychiatrists so heavily influenced by the family's preferences? Greenley investigated this question and has found several possible reasons:

> First, the psychiatrist is much more likely to successfully place the patient in the home if the family supports his return. The family who wants the patient released is likely to be supportive and to help the patient reintegrate into the community; the reluctant family may undermine the plans of the psychiatrist, exacerbate the patient's symptoms, and drive the patient back to the hospital. Rational planning of treatment decision, such as discharge, may demand seriously taking into account the desires of the family. Second and possibly more important, the psychiatrist may follow the wishes of the family to avoid a range of possible family actions. At one extreme, the family may use the judicial system

in seeking a release or further retention. The psychiatrist may wish to avoid a hearing or other courtroom processes because they have a damaging impact on the patient or consume a considerable amount of his time and effort. The therapist may prefer to discharge the patient "Against Medical Advice" or to hold a patient while seeking a nonfamily placement in the community. Families may also place psychiatrists in awkward positions by taking their questions and demands to unit chiefs, department heads, or superintendents of the institutions involved. Institutional leaders both expect and easily tolerate a few such complaints. Yet if such complaints multiply beyond a scattered few, these leaders may come to question not the assertive families but the accused psychiatrists. This may give a family considerable leverage of which even it is unaware. Most commonly, a family's persistent questions and demands constitute a significant nuisance to the psychiatrist himself. In the state hospital studied, the work load was so heavy that a moderately interested and aggressive family could cause a substantial and disruptive drain on the psychiatrist's available time and energy. Under the pressure of too many patients, the psychiatrist appears to welcome the family which wishes to remove the patient from the hospital and the responsibility for him from the psychiatrist. On the other hand, if the family resists the patient's return, the overworked psychiatrist often redirects his limited energies toward patients whose return to the community seems more likely, thus continuing the hospitalization of the unwanted patient. Finally, the psychiatrist may seek to please the family, because he feels it to be as much his client as is the patient himself. The family is often the complainant, the patient only its symptom.[24]

Undoubtedly, the attitude of the hospital's "disposition staff" toward release is heavily influenced by the family's desires. This is not to say that patients do not influence their own release at all. In fact, before the disposition staff examination, which is supposed to determine discharge, patients are known to counsel each other on the "right" answers, which are usually based on stories of past successes and failures.[25] Patients who initiate their own release have a higher probability of discharge (particularly if their relatives are supportive) than patients who wait for initiation by the psychiatrist. Thus the most realistic view of discharge is as a process of *social negotiation* rather than as a simple process of psychiatric evaluation. Negotiation includes the expressed wishes of the family and the attempts made by the patient to be discharged. When both are oriented toward release, the resultant condition is the most powerful predictor of reentry into the community, even though the mental health of the patient may not warrant discharge.[26]

Speaking of predictors, are psychiatrists able to predict dangerousness after release? For decades this has been one of the major weaknesses of psychiatric evaluation, but recently some strides have been made. Researchers at New York University's psychiatric "violent ward" connect the likelihood of future violence not only to a patient's history of violence but also to such factors as a measurable neurological abnormality and being raised in a "deviant" family environment. Additionally, Lidz and his colleagues note that episodes of violent behavior occur among 53 percent of patients classified as *likely* to be violent.[27] Violent behavior was more difficult to predict for female patients than for male patients. The probability of violence was also higher among female patients and among younger patients as a group.

THE PROBLEMS OF AFTERCARE

It clearly is a long bridge from the mental hospital to the outside world, but there are some aftercare programs that make the journey a bit smoother. Effective programs are designed to ease the patients into the community. Medication monitoring and therapy are priority needs. So also are day and vocational activities.[28] Continuity of care over a long period of time is another guiding principle.[29] Support groups involving other released patients and relatives can be a big help.[30] And the quality of life can be especially enhanced by decent living conditions. In this regard, small group homes (12 or less) can be an invaluable source of social support.[31] Certain states, such as Massachusetts, have been especially progressive in providing a continuum of services for the chronically mentally ill who have been recently released.[32]

Regardless of how well designed aftercare programs are, they often do not work because many ex-patients are unfit to resume living in outside society since institutionalization has atrophied their social and occupational skills. In addition, many patients still exhibit the symptoms of their illness and, perhaps most importantly, refuse to continue their medication. Unfortunately, there is a deficiency of programs designed to provide discharged patients with the skills needed to function in ordinary life.[33] Consequently, many ex-patients, conditioned by long-term chronic care to be socially and economically dependent, fail to become functioning members of society and are either readmitted to the hospital or pursue a meaningless existence in a boarding home or on the street. Some of these problems can be minimized by an in-hospital treatment program that *prepares* chronic patients for return to the community. One such program allows patients to pass through a series of different living arrangements, each of which increasingly resembles a responsible lifestyle in mainstream society.[34] Patients are not completely and suddenly released from the hospital. Rather, they are prepared for reentry by a series of passes to go home for brief visits.

Another useful practice is to carry over some of the secure aspects of life in the hospital to the outside world. For instance, patients are often afraid to try to live outside because they do not know what will be expected of them, while expectations in the hospital are quite clear. The expectations of discharged patients in outside society are defined for them, and, if they are within the patients' capabilities, there is a greater chance that patients will feel useful, adequate, and successful.

Of course, the best approach to the problem of institutionalization is a program that involves a minimum period of hospitalization. For this reason, some advocate brief but frequent hospitalization as the means of sustaining the patient in the community. This approach is called "intermittent patienthood." It makes sense in terms of controlling the undesirable side effects of hospitalization, and there is evidence that a "short stay" approach minimizes the socially disruptive impact of mental illness upon the patient and family. At the same time, the short-stay approach is not realistic for seriously disturbed psychotics who require an extended leave from mainstream society because they are unable to care for themselves at all. These people must be hospitalized for an ample period of time, and it is these cases in which the problem of institutionalization is most apparent. Another problem with the short-stay approach is that more released patients still require some treatment for the symptoms of their illness. Thus, there is a trade-off between the symptoms of the mental disorder itself and the deterioration of social skills that accompanies long-term hospitalization.

Regardless of the length of hospital stay, it is highly probable that ex-patients have some kind of problem that interferes with their attempt to rejoin society. Thus, posthospital follow-up in the community can be used in reducing hospital recidivism and increasing occupational success and satisfaction.[35] Of equal importance is the role that aftercare programs can play in the patients' interpersonal world, an area of life that is often unsatisfactory to them, particularly because their social relationships may have contributed to their problems in the first place. To return the released patient to the same stressful situation that led to hospitalization is not good psychiatry; posthospital help in interpersonal relations is necessary if patients are to retain any progress they had made in the hospital.

Each aftercare program should be tailored to the particular needs of the ex-patient. However, there are some useful principles that can be used within any aftercare situation. One of these is what the Schwartzes call the process of "grading stress."[36] This is a strategy of providing opportunities for the graduated assumption of responsibilities. This simply means no more than the common-sense idea that one must learn to crawl before trying to walk. In regard to ex-patients, this principle can guide gradual reintegration into the community by giving increased doses of responsibility. Each new dose should go beyond the current level of performance. Higher expectations of oneself are necessary for improvement because they create the possibility of changing behavior, an essential condition for mental health progress.

Undoubtedly, aftercare programs are important in the treatment of mentally disordered people. This is evident from the high recidivism rates among ex-patients who do not receive some form of structured follow-up. However, it is often difficult to get ex-patients into posthospital programs simply because they are not motivated to follow through on the referral from the mental hospital.[37] This is not necessarily a dangerous behavior, however, since ex-patients who expect changes in their social and occupational lives constitute a large part of those who do not continue treatment.[38] Sometimes these people stop treatment because they were able to enter a life situation that itself was conducive to their rehabilitation.

Many ex-patients do not receive aftercare simply because there is often no concerted effort by hospital personnel or by the family to encourage them to do so. What kind of efforts are required? Certainly, aftercare programs should be integrated with inpatient care so that the patient will view a posthospital program as a natural next step. For example, an intake worker from the local community mental health clinic should see the patient in the hospital before release. This kind of personal contact helps to effect a successful referral.

Counteracting institutionalization and motivating patients to seek posthospital help are two major problems of aftercare programs. However, there are other problems as well. One problem is that, because aftercare programs are still being developed, only a few offer innovative programs that enhance the quality of life for chronically ill people. A second problem has been the failure to establish a liaison between hospitals and community-based facilities. As a result, some ex-patients have to fight through extensive red tape in order to be treated in the community.

A third problem with effecting posthospital treatment is that many patients do not have a family and home to return to, so they resort to living in substandard housing or are completely homeless. This group of isolated ex-patients then forms a new ghetto subpopulation. In other words, these patients are not actually being returned to the community but to a fringe element. Discussing readjustment of the ex-patient to the "community" makes little sense in this situation, especially because members of the "normal" community are often quite hostile toward ex-patients. They will use city ordinances, zoning codes, police arrests, and various informal approaches to exclude them from mainstream life. Consequently, ex-patients may be neglected more in the community than in state hospitals.

A fourth problem with effective aftercare is the risk of exchanging one set of ills for another, for providing the ex-patient with continued protection may foster overdependency and psychiatric hypochondriasis. In addition, the stigma of having been a mental hospital patient may be strengthened by this extended treatment so that ex-patients continue to consider themselves sick. It is a type of "lose-lose" situation.

There are other problems with aftercare such as the practical issues of transportation to a community clinic, and the heavy caseload of mental health workers. Perhaps the largest hurdles are the "residual impairment" and social deficits often found among released patients. These problems exist partly because the chronically mentally ill may never recover completely from their disorder. As a result, it is unrealistic to think that they are always rational enough to pursue treatment on their own. Consequently, some states have initiated "outpatient commitment"(OPC), which permits *compulsory* treatment of the mentally ill in the community.[39]

THE STIGMA OF MENTAL ILLNESS

> Psychiatric patients, and those who have spent time in psychiatric hospitals, may not be as routinely stigmatized today as in the past. Nevertheless, people diagnosed with a "mental illness" inhabit a different space in public perception from those hospitalized for "physical" conditions such as cancer or heart disease. Many cancer sufferers feel inhibited talking about their condition, but the inhibitions surrounding mental illness are more widespread and deeply rooted, with serious consequences to individual patients and their families. Though the legal, medical, and social status of patients has changed over the years, the legacy of stigma survives.[40]

These words were written by an author who almost had a book withheld from publication when her editor felt "uncomfortable" about the part of the book where she describes her time as a patient in a mental hospital. She had to alter the book to prevent legal action and ensure publication. This is just one person's encounter with stigma. Unfortunately, there are all kinds of inappropriate attitudes toward the mentally ill, including such notions that they cause their own problems.[41] Attempts are made to educate the public, but they are often futile. The federal government, for instance, declared a week in October 1993 as "Mental Illness Awareness Week," but very few people knew about it.[42] These are simply incredibly complicated problems to untangle, particularly when they present in the form of deep-seated prejudice against the mentally ill.

Much of the literature on the life of the ex-mental patient is couched in terms of the stigma attached to mental illness. The word *stigma* was used by the Greeks to refer to bodily signs that demonstrated something negative about a person's worth. Today stigma refers to the *disgrace itself* rather than any bodily evidence of it. People who are or were mentally ill are stigmatized because they are deeply discredited for their failure to live up to societal expectations and are frequently rebuffed whenever they attempt social intercourse. Some of the studies on stigma have centered on attitudes patients have about themselves.[43] For the most part, however, the attitudes of the public have been the focus of research.

Studies of public attitudes toward the mentally ill are polarized into two schools of thought: those who contend that society stigmatizes the mentally ill and those who believe that society accepts the mentally ill and is compassionate toward them. The former perspective is linked with the traditional view of mental illness that characterizes the mentally ill as unpredictable, bizarre, and violent. The latter perspective represents the "psychiatric ideology" that views the mentally ill simply as sick persons who can be treated and cured, just like people with physical ailments. The traditional view is usually learned during early childhood and reinforced by the mass media, whereas the psychiatric ideology is typically developed through higher education—simply *knowing* better.[44]

There are a few studies reporting that the public is somewhat tolerant of mental illness and does not automatically stigmatize mental patients. However, these findings usually apply only to people of a higher educational background or to those who were socialized in a more liberal cultural milieu, such as the 1960s. It takes no great insight to realize that the modal attitude of the American public toward the mentally ill is far from positive and accepting. Many people do not consider the mentally ill to be legitimately sick. They see them as a separate class of beings who are dangerous and incapable of cure.[45] These attitudes are largely responsible for the rejection of ex-patients. Even patients themselves fear the "mental patient."[46] This situation is depressing, particularly because neither patients nor ex-patients usually live up to their popular portrayal as uncontrolled monsters. In fact, ex-patients are less likely to act violently or commit crimes than people who have never been mentally ill.[47]

How have these inappropriate and damaging views toward the mentally ill been created? Much of the blame must be placed on the mass media, which reinforce the traditional view of mental illness by giving the public the impression that former patients harass their fellow citizens. The media are not interested in reporting on ex-patients who are good citizens because they do not make interesting news. Instead, concentration is on the sensational acts of ex-patients who may have broken the law. For this reason, the psychiatric background of former mental patients is frequently reported in news stories while the nonpsychiatric history of most people who commit crimes is conveniently ignored. If you go back to the beginning of Chapter 1, you will see numerous examples of this "exclusive" coverage.

The mass media have an enormous influence on societal opinion, to the point where attitudes created toward the mentally ill are particularly slow to change because they have been hardened through years of biased reporting. Consequently, ex-patients are relegated to extremely difficult lives in the community. They report that the fact of their illness was used as a threat or "club over their heads," which blocked communication with friends and family, resulted in feelings of low self-esteem, and seriously diminished their chances for meaningful employment.[48] Perhaps the difference between the mythical aspects of mental illness and the reality of mental illness is best summarized by the report of a patient's relative making her first visit to a mental hospital:

> I felt all the patients would be stark-staring mad and expected padded cells and screaming and shouting. When at last the time came for my first visit, I could hardly walk up the drive, my knees were shaking so. I wasn't afraid to visit my husband. I knew he wasn't mad but I did expect the others to be. I just couldn't believe my eyes when I saw it all. It wasn't only the place, . . . it was the amazing fact that the other patients all looked . . . normal. . . .[49]

As mentioned earlier, I take students to a mental hospital (Norristown State Hospital in Pennsylvania) as part of their coursework. The visit, combined with an intelligent, informed talk by Laura Brobyn, a dedicated psychiatric nursing specialist, clearly creates a more sophisticated attitude among the students toward the mentally ill. Many others would benefit from a similar tour. The students typically go to the hospital with trepidation and leave with a sense of sadness and compassion for the patients.

Changes in Public Opinion

On a recent television program, Kathy Cronkite, author and daughter of newsman Walter Cronkite, described her own battle with depression. "Stigma is only ignorance," said Cronkite. "Once we understand that these are medical illnesses . . . then there can be no more stigma. The real problem with stigma is that it keeps people from getting help." Can the stigma of mental illness be changed? To some, it is a daunting, if not impossible, task.[50]

Stigma has such a stronghold on the mentally ill that some have called the experience a "career" with long-run expectations and impossible hurdles.[51] Much has been written about how to reduce stigma, but talk and change are two different things.[52] Although the average layperson in the United States is uninformed about mental illness, there is less ignorance today than in past decades. Since World War II, the psychiatric movement has made a variety of attempts to educate the public about the nature of mental illness. At the beginning of the movement, fear, stigmatization, and rejection strongly characterized public feeling about the mentally ill.[53] Later studies have uncovered an increased awareness about the real nature of mental illness, as well as a more sympathetic understanding of it.[54] One large-scale study of public attitudes toward mental illness concluded that:

> People are almost unanimous in believing that the mentally ill are truly sick and thus require medical treatment "just as any other sick person" does. . . . They do not believe that most mentally ill are especially prone to criminal behavior. Quite consistently they do not believe that mental patients should be "locked up" or that mental hospitals should be fenced off and guarded. The public believes to the point of consensus that the mentally ill can be cured with proper treatment, and almost all are willing to accept people who have been severely mentally ill as neighbors, fellow club members, and workmates.[55]

It is not difficult to accept the proposition that there has been a growing acceptance of mental illness among Americans. However, the findings quoted above are far from consistent with the everyday experiences of ex-patients who are by no means welcomed back into the community with open arms. One study by Olmsted and Durham concluded that the liberalization of attitudes toward mental illness reached a plateau since they found no substantial differences in outlook from the 1960s on.[56] Studies around 2000 also show little change in public opinion.

Without waging an unnecessary debate over the actual progress the psychiatric movement has made in educating the public, it is important to point out some problems with this kind of survey research. First, attitudinal surveys tend to generalize about the entire population rather than to point out differences among social groups. For example, certain groups exhibit more enlightened opinions about mental illness and acceptance of the mentally ill. This tends to be true of younger, educated people; college students, for instance, are much less authoritarian about mental illness than is the public at large.[57] Second, an increased awareness of the psychiatric view does not imply a decrease in the rejection of patients returned to the community. People's responses to public opinion polls do not necessarily reflect their everyday behavior.

Opinion polls may measure beliefs to some degree, but they rarely capture emotions. Consequently, a growing number of Americans may *say* they do not stigmatize the mentally ill, even though they actually behave negatively toward them. Hence the shift in reported attitudes has not been accompanied by more humanitarian treatment of ex-patients. In fact, the problems of ex-patients are so great that the American Psychiatric Association felt compelled to issue a position statement on discrimination against ex-patients. Part of it reads:

> Knowledge of previous psychiatric treatment and/or the possession of a psychiatric label is blatantly used in a variety of settings to influence immigration, licensure, employment, insurance, the granting of permits, and credit. Such knowledge is not infrequently used prejudiciously to exclude individuals, as if society's institutions were attempting to protect themselves against what is felt to be a threat. Such exclusionary practices are arbitrary and prejudgmental, irrelevant to the purpose at hand, and subversive of fundamental needs for privacy, confidentiality, and the civil rights of individuals.[58]

The appeal from the APA was made in 1978. It rang on deaf ears, yet mental health agencies have not given up the crusade to educate the public. In 2000, the National Institute of Mental Health published a special plea on its Web site. The document, "What Can Be Done about Stigma?" made the following suggestions:

- Bring mental illness into the open and learn to think about it like other illnesses or conditions.
- Educate the community to overcome attitudes based on misconceptions.
- Encourage research into mental illness to assist understanding of how these illnesses affect people and how they can be prevented.
- Assist friends and relatives with a mental illness to obtain care and treatment.
- Eliminate discrimination in every area of life—including employment and education.

Stigma and Type of Illness

No account of the stigma of mental illness would be complete without pointing out that the degree of stigma is associated with the *characteristics* of a person's illness. One important characteristic is the severity of the disorder; the phobic, for instance, is not stigmatized to the same degree as is the psychotic.[59] A number of studies indicate that this difference occurs not because people evaluate a disorder according to the psychodynamics involved, but because more serious illnesses typically involve more bizarre, disruptive, and unpredictable behavior that is perceived as more *overtly* threatening by others.[60]

The relationship between external symptoms and degree of stigma was discovered in a 1950 national survey conducted by Star. That study involved interviews with 3,500 persons.[61] One of the key parts of the interview included six case descriptions of mentally ill people: a paranoid schizophrenic; a simple schizophrenic; an anxiety neurotic; an obsessive-compulsive neurotic; an alcoholic; and a child with a behavior disorder. Star found that only the paranoid schizophrenic was recognized as ill by a majority of the sample. This was also the only case described that included threatening, assaultive behavior. Some of the other cases involved equally serious pathology, but the symptoms were not as visible as the paranoid schizophrenic case, so they were not perceived as ill.

Another factor that influences the degree of stigma is the type of treatment the patient received. Although stigma declines somewhat when the patient is released from the hospital,[62] noticeably more stigma is suffered by those who have been patients in a state mental hospital than by those who have been in private hospitals.[63] This is especially true for those who were involuntarily committed.[64] The relationship between stigma and involuntarily commitment may be due to the tendency for more visible cases to be forced into treatment, a phenomenon discussed in Chapter 13.

Social Status and Stigma

A lot of people do not have the same compassion toward a depressed person or an anorexic girl who is starving herself that they have for victims of "conventional" illness like heart disease. The victims of mental illness are often erroneously distinguished from other sick people as being victims of their own weak characters and poor decisions. This flawed thinking does not cut across all groups of people evenly since a considerable number of studies report that attitudes toward the mentally ill are largely determined by social class. However, it is apparently not social class, per se, that affects attitudes but the educational component of social class. Studies measuring the specific effect of education on attitudes toward the mentally ill consistently show a positive relationship between education and the psychiatric ideology; as the amount of formal education increases, so does the likelihood of a psychiatric (informed) view of mental illness.

There is some debate as to whether a person who is *knowledgeable* about mental illness is also more *tolerant* of the mentally ill than an individual with less information about the topic. A sophisticated ideology may not necessarily imply a reduced tendency to stigmatize and tolerate psychopathology because knowledge is intellectually based, whereas stigmatization is an emotional phenomenon. Research on this question has not yielded consistent results. Some report that stigma decreases with higher levels of education; that is, better-educated people tend to have less derogatory attitudes toward the mentally ill *and* to be willing to tolerate more contact with them than do poorly educated people.[65] On the other hand, there is also evidence that knowledge of mental illness and stigmatization of the mentally ill do not vary together. Miller, for instance, reports that ex-patients living with grade-school–educated people report feeling less stigmatization than do those returned to more highly educated environments.[66] Others report greater tolerance of mental illness in less-educated groups as well.[67]

If future studies uncover less stigmatization among people of limited education, the reason for that relationship may prove controversial. Presently, two explanations have been offered. One suggests that, since less-educated people have little knowledge about mental illness, they have a narrow definition of it so that they consider only *extremely* disordered behavior to be abnormal. The other explanation is that mental illness is more common among less-educated (lower-class) people and consequently they are more tolerant of abnormal behavior because they are regularly exposed to it.

Other demographics are associated with stigma and knowledge of mental illness. All of them, however, are related to educational attainment and can thus be explained from that perspective. Older generations in the United States have less educational attainment than do younger age groups. Consequently, older people harbor more traditional, custodial views of the mentally ill.[68] They are also more prone to stigmatize the mentally ill than are younger people.[69] This is part of a process of aging that involves a movement toward authoritarianism, a personality type that is rigidly conventional.[70] These negative attitudes among older people are not ameliorated by exposure to the mentally ill since they are also found more prominently among older employees than younger employees in mental hospitals.[71]

Prevalence of Stigma

I do not want to give the impression that stigma is monopolized by certain social groups. It is found in varying degrees in different social settings, and is by no means limited to specific sectors of society. On the contrary, it is a widespread social problem that can cause considerable hardship to both ex-patients and their families.

There are many reports of the isolation of ex-patients from society. This affects their relatives as well; one study reported that over 70 percent of relatives experience stigma due to the presence of an ex-patient in the home.[72] What is particularly sad is that ex-patients frequently hold the same negative views of themselves that society does, because of the effects of labeling. Even more depressing are the ignorant views toward the mentally ill that nonpsychiatrically trained physicians maintain. One study found that physicians view neurotics as "foolish and twisted" and psychotics as "dirty and dangerous."[73] These physicians' attitudes are dangerous themselves not only because many physicians are mistakenly treating mentally disordered people but also because their views can influence those of many others. This is especially true in light of the exaggerated way that many Americans perceive physicians as tabernacles of knowledge. The hostility and despair that psychiatrists feel toward physicians in other branches of medicine are no secret.[74]

Unfortunately, for the ex-patient, stigmatization is not a temporary phenomenon. Years after former patients have been living in the community, their families still struggle with the burden of stigma.[75] Some ex-patients do manage to avoid the threat of stigma, but this is not because they return to a sympathetic community. On the contrary, those who do not feel that being an ex-patient is difficult are those who somehow have managed to keep their past hidden.[76] Others avoid stigma by moving to a new residence where they and their families are not known. Moving is most common among middle-class families, who tend to be more concerned with the visible deviance of the ex-patient than families of other social classes.[77] Moving, education, and type of mental illness aside, stigma is a killer. It's enough to be mentally ill without having to pay membership dues. One brave soul who stood up to the stigma says, "I'm mentally ill and that's O.K. It doesn't mean I'm a demon. It doesn't mean I'm a gorilla. It just means that I have emotional problems."[78]

I mentioned earlier that the APA and NIMH have attempted to reduce stigma through direct pleas, including messages on the Internet. The mentally ill themselves have also been at work on this problem. Witness the creation of the Web site MISANITY (the Mental Illness Stigma Action Network In Touch with You). In 2000, the site was funded by a number of foundations determined to promote recovery by confronting stigma. One of its themes is: "We need to do something to get better, not to wait to get better before we do something."

READJUSTMENT INTO THE COMMUNITY

Many of the patients released from state hospitals either have moved into inner-city areas or into neighborhoods near the hospital and created "psychiatric ghettos." They live in boarding homes that house only schizophrenics, manic-depressives, the retarded, alcoholics, drug addicts, and the marginally menacing. The boarders mostly wander aimlessly around mildly sedated, or lie on their beds sorting out bewildered thoughts. They have been simply dumped into the community, still hearing voices, still hallucinating, still paranoid, and still with the unmistakable look of the deranged. Over a quarter million of the mentally ill are incarcerated in prison or jail.[79]

This is a classic case of a social policy causing a new social problem. The U.S. Senate Subcommittee on Long-Term Care documented the horrible conditions of the boarding homes in these ghetto-like areas. Not only is there a blatant lack of therapeutic and rehabilitative care, but also most of the boarding homes' revenue comes from federal funds. The government is actually contributing to a very profitable industry that many see as legitimate. By the way, that Senate report was issued in the 1970s. It would read the same if it were conducted today.

Many of the problems associated with returning patients to the community are biological. One of these is the "residual impairment" often found among people who have been treated for schizophrenia. Closely related is the problem of compliance with medication directives, although it is not always clear whether patients stop taking their medication and get sick, or vice versa. The success or failure of the patients' attempt to rejoin society is also partly determined by sociological factors. Among these are employment and financial problems, the attitudes of relatives toward the patient, as well as the problems of stigma and effective aftercare programs. To be sure, psychiatric hospitalization alone does not ensure positive posthospital community adjustment to the extent that factors in the ex-patient's social world do.

Most of the studies of the determinants of adequate functioning in the community have used rehospitalization as the criterion for successful functioning. There is, however, some controversy over the use of rehospitalization as a measure of readjustment. On one side are those who argue that rehospitalization data do not take into account the special situation confronted by the released patient This argument seems particularly cogent today since patients are being hospitalized for shorter lengths of time and may require periods of respite to compensate for the brief treatment. If this is true, then rehospitalization may not necessarily be an index of community readjustment as much as an indication that the patient was released prematurely.

On the other side are those who feel that rehospitalization is a valid indicator of unfavorable community adjustment. They argue that "rehospitalization represents one of the most serious and clear-cut manifestations of the breakdown in social arrangements that are necessary for people to live together in toleration, if not harmony."[80] Most of these researchers agree that rehospitalization does not yield a *total* picture of ex-patients' functioning, since undoubtedly there are some who remain in the community but cannot perform the social roles expected of them. Studies using rehospitalization as an evaluation index overlook these types of individuals. But they do identify extreme groups of ex-patients, since the avoidance of rehospitalization is a minimum standard for evaluating the person's ability to cope with the real world.

Methodological issues aside, the fact is that studies of patients returning to the community usually use rehospitalization as a measure of functioning for the very practical reason that such data are readily available. However, another factor supports the practice—the high readmission rate that reportedly accounts for as many as 40 percent of all admissions to prolonged-care hospitals in the United States today. This is especially common among young males, who have rapid readmission rates. The factors that separate readmitted psychiatric patients from those who are not readmitted provide important clues to the social control of mental illness.[81] Are particular social roles conducive to eventual cure? Are these a function of family type, relatives' attitudes, and/or the ex-patient's occupational experiences? The findings of studies on these and related questions are presented next.

The Role of the Family

I have said before that the family of the mentally ill individual plays a vital role in the course and rehabilitation of the patient. I think that is worth repeating here. Some feel that people with a disturbed family member may suffer as much as the relative. Still others feel that, in a misguided effort to protect the rights of the mentally ill from involuntary commitment, the legal system often holds their loved ones "hostages to madness."[82] Whatever the real facts may be, there is no doubt that families have a crying need for mental health services for their disordered relatives.[83] There is also no doubt that the family life of the ex-patient is only one of the most important determinants of rehospitalization. Those with little involvement with others are particularly vulnerable to readmission, as evidenced by the unusually high rate of rehospitalization among discharged patients who live alone.

Interaction with significant others affects the adjustment and community tenure of ex-patients by encouraging them to perform normal roles. However, it is not the mere presence of significant persons in the ex-patient's life that aids readjustment as much as it is their behavioral expectation of the discharged patient to perform an active, normal social role. Evidence for this proposition comes not only from comparisons of ex-patients living alone with those living with others but also from studies of the effects of different types of family arrangements.

Being married is known to be a stabilizing influence on community adjustment for both patients released from state hospitals who were psychotically disordered[84] and for less severe cases discharged from community mental health clinics.[85] Married patients are less likely to return to the hospital than single patients. However, this is not simply because single patients are more likely to live alone; the phenomenon stems from deeper sources. Patients returned to parental (nuclear) families have much lower performance levels than patients returned to conjugal (marital) families.[86] Simply stated, the probability of rehospitalization is noticeably higher among patients returned to their parents than among those returned to a spouse.

Why is there a difference in rehospitalization rates between those who return to a spouse rather than those who go home to parents? Husbands and wives are simply less tolerant of deviant behavior than are mothers and fathers. Furthermore, spouses have higher expectations of the way in which the ex-patient should function in the community. The patient returned to the parental family may occupy the "child" role of son or daughter, which has low expectations of performance. In fact, some warn against the practice of releasing the patient to the parental family since that type of family setting can worsen the patient's condition by allowing deviant behavior that engenders regression. This is not to paint a picture of parents who always make things worse. On the contrary, it is more likely that they are people who fret and worry about what to do. The worries carry for a long time, even after their death. That is why some parents have written a kind of will to provide care for their mentally ill children after they are gone. See Box 14:3 for a description of one program that is presently spreading across the country.

There is also a significant relationship between family size and performance in the community. Male patients returned to large families are very likely to be rehospitalized.[87] This is not because the ex-patient is ignored in this type of family setting but because fewer expectations are placed on him due to the presence of other family members who are available as functional equivalents. Such is the case where a man has many sons or daughters who can assume financial responsibility for the household.

· **Box 14:3** ·
After the Parents Die

Conceived as a surrogate parent, PLAN of Pa. attempts to take the place of real parents when they die or get too old to care for their mentally ill or mentally retarded children.

It is a natural outgrowth of the nation's 30-year struggle to care for the mentally disabled in the community rather than in institutions. As that shift has occurred, parents have often found themselves providing housing for their mentally ill or retarded children, as well as acting as their de facto case managers—arranging benefits, coordinating treatment and monitoring their well-being.

Large numbers of these parents are now in their 60s, 70s and 80s, and as they've aged, they have begun to wonder what will happen to their children when they're gone.

The goal of the various PLANs is to carry on when a parent or sibling cannot, using money set aside for the disabled person—in Pennsylvania, typically through a family trust.

PLAN of Pa. is designed to be a kind of hovering presence. It surrounds the disabled person with a network of supports—day programs, friends, churches, YMCA programs, and the like—monitors the person's condition closely, and steps in quickly if a crisis arises.

During periods of stability, the client may need no more than one to three hours a month of a caseworker's time. At $50 an hour, "it ends up not being all that expensive at all," said PLAN executive Carol A. Caruso, a psychiatric social worker.

From the beginning, Caruso works with parents or siblings to develop a future plan for their mentally disabled relative. The centerpiece is a written account, by the family, of the person's life before and after becoming disabled.

Begun with a $150,000 grant from the van Ameringen Foundation, in New York, PLAN of Pa. currently serves about 40 clients, Caruso said. Another 20 or so are scheduled to receive services upon the death of a parent or other care giver.

One college professor calls it "the answer to a prayer."

Her son, a bright, athletic student while at Episcopal Academy, suffered his first psychotic episode in college. He was hospitalized eight times in two years. The diagnosis: schizophrenia.

He is 31 now. What he needs, said his mother, is a highly structured, supervised residence. But the mental health system in Chester County, where the family lives, doesn't have one. So he lives with his parents, both professors at Villanova University.

"I worried to death about what would happen to him when my husband and I aren't here anymore," said the professor. Two years ago, she heard about PLAN. She is now president of the board of directors.

Source: Henry Goldman and Carolyn Acker, "The assurance of care," *Philadelphia Inquirer,* February 9, 1994, pp. G1 and G4.

· ·

This reduces the expectations placed on the ex-patient as a breadwinner and simultaneously undercuts opportunities for independent action, so necessary for reintegration into society. Independent role expectations also affect the chances of rehospitalization among married women, as evidenced by the fact that mothers are less likely to be readmitted than childless wives.[88]

Of course, all of the research that reports a positive effect of the marital role on community adjustment of ex-patients is based on cases in which the conjugal family is intact upon release. Unfortunately, this is not always the case. An alarmingly high number of marriages deteriorate to the point of separation or divorce before release. This is particularly true when the patient is schizophrenic. A number of factors are responsible: long periods of separation result in loss of interest; financial burdens become too great for the nonhospitalized spouse; and discouragement stemming from the patient's lack of progress can lead to the spouse's denial of the patient's very existence.

Many family variables are related to community adjustment. One of these is place of residence; rural families provide a better milieu for rehabilitation than do urban families.[89] Although the researchers reporting the "urban-rural" finding explain it as a function of more realistic demands placed on ex-patients by rural families, it is also possible that the communal quality of rural life in general is simply more conducive to patient rehabilitation. Other family variables that affect recovery relate to the relatives' knowledge of mental illness and their propensity to stigmatize the ex-patient, as evidenced by reports that recovery is greatest among those returned to family members who are young and well educated.

One final note about families: siblings can play a very important role in recovery, and can be an immense source of social support.[90] Also, Riebschleger reports that they may want to be involved in treatment and appreciate an open system of communication with therapists.[91] In this instance, being an only child can be a liability.

Symptoms and Rehospitalization

Contrary to popular belief, the type and severity of the patient's symptoms at discharge may not always be useful predictors of rehospitalization. Early studies concluded that the extent to which the patient's symptoms are ameliorated in the hospital is not related to future readmission.[92] The fact that psychiatric variables may bear little relationship to case outcome is another indication of the extreme importance of the social milieu to which the patient is returned.

There is, however, one hospital-related variable that is definitely related to rehospitalization—a lengthy hospital stay. Long hospital stays are especially likely to produce institutionalization, which prevents reintegration into normal social roles. Those who spend less time in the hospital have a greater ability to function interpersonally regardless of the degree of their pathology. A number of investigations confirm this. However, this should not be interpreted as evidence for the utility of brief hospitalizations, because most of the studies compared patients hospitalized for a year or two with those who remained for five years or more. If comparisons were made between patients hospitalized for a year with those hospitalized for three months or less (a growing tendency today), I would expect poorer performance and more rehospitalizations among members of the short-stay group simply because the hospitalization period has not been long enough to monitor and treat symptoms adequately. This point remains to be tested.

The widely supported finding that type and severity of disorder during hospitalization are not useful predictors of readmission is only valid for some disorders. For the organic disorders, such as mental retardation and organic psychosis, there is a poor prognosis that worsens as the severity of the illness increases.[93] As a consequence, case outcome for some disorders may be more dependent on the social structure of the posthospital community, since organic disorders leave little hope for rehabilitation through socially oriented approaches. Additionally, the likelihood of rehospitalization is influenced by the state of the patient's physical health. Patients in poor health are less able to care for themselves or carry out expected roles in a community setting. In one study almost 70 percent of released patients with physical ailments were rehospitalized compared to 35 percent of those without such complications.[94]

The Role of Employment

It is amazing how deeply rooted stigma of the mentally ill is and how many different parts of a person's life it can ruin. There are plenty of people who are mentally ill, never hospitalized, and hold prestigious positions in professional occupations. Take the case of Dr. Steven H. Miles, a medical school professor.[95] One of his students committed suicide, allegedly because he feared career stigmatization from using mental health care. The next morning, at a scheduled lecture to a stunned class, Miles disclosed his own diagnosis of bipolar disorder. He told the students that such problems were not incompatible with a successful family or professional life—but that people should seek help. That proved to be a mistake that cost him thousands of dollars in legal fees to fight off a review by the Minnesota Board of Medical Practice.[96] It was feared that Miles was not fit to be on the faculty or even to be a physician at all. The standoff lasted more than two years.

Miles's experience is mild compared to the occupational horrors that ex-patients face. Jobs can give released patients a sense of purpose, particularly when purpose has been shadowed by the dark cloud of schizophrenia. Ex-patients have skills that can be tapped and developed into meaningful employment. This can be a great route to "reclaiming the community."[97] In fact, "job development centers" are offered to some as alternative mental health centers.[98] Unfortunately, these are not the typical opportunities of most released patients.

Steady employment in a fulfilling job is a meaningful form of social participation that simultaneously reduces the stigma of the patient label by demonstrating competence and an ability to interact with others in a normal fashion. Having a job is importantly related to successful functioning in the community, as evidenced by significantly higher readmission rates among discharged patients who are unemployed.[99] Unfortunately, many discharged patients *are* unemployed. This is particularly true for blacks, who face discrimination because of their patient status *and* their race.[100] If ex-patients do find work, it is typically in a job involving less skill, prestige, and pay than the one they had before they were hospitalized—not because they are unfit for employment, but because employers are leery of mental patients as is the public in general.[101]

Having been a mental patient directly prevents the discharged from seeking, obtaining, or holding a job. Indeed, more patients are occupationally active during their hospital stay (with in-hospital jobs) than during their stay in the community following release[102]—another example of the hostile way in which patients are treated by society. Too many people fall victim to the widespread myth that ex-patients are employment risks. The fact is that even the most disturbed group of released patients are employable in certain jobs, provided that they have the incentive to work.[103]

Employers' believe that mental illness connotes character weakness, and they have practical fears regarding the ex-patient's ability to handle an employment situation.[104] This is really a problem when the person describes his hospitalization to a prospective employer in terms of "mental illness" or "nervous breakdown" rather than in terms of "difficulty with interpersonal problems."[105] Some employers express a willingness to hire former mental patients, but these are usually employers connected with large manufacturing businesses that have many unskilled, repetitive jobs.[106] Receptive attitudes toward former patients are rarely found among employers in service companies or any job involving contact with the public.

Some have suggested that it is not unemployment, per se, that most significantly contributes to readmission but the humiliation suffered by having to depend on welfare. In fact, one study reported that 70 percent of a group of ex-patients on welfare were rehospitalized within a year of discharge.[107] Obviously, there is a real need for special employment centers staffed by mental health specialists to act as liaisons between ex-patients and prospective employers. This need should be met by the community mental health clinics, but, as noted earlier, these organizations have consistently failed to deal with the plight of ex-patients, including their employment needs. This situation is particularly depressing because the psychological, social, and economic rewards of employment can be invaluable to ex-patients seeking an accepted position in the community. Things are even worse in other parts of the world. In China, for instance, there is presently a law that forbids *children* of schizophrenics from holding government security positions such as policemen and ambulance drivers. This law applies to *all* children of schizophrenics, even though the children are completely normal.

Social Class and Readjustment

It is fitting that the final topic of this book concerns social class, since class is one of the most significant sociological influences on mental illness. In an earlier chapter it was noted that social class influences rate, type, and treatment of mental disorder. It also affects the ability of a returned patient to function in society. A follow-up of the patients in the landmark New Haven study revealed that lower social class patients have the highest rate of rehospitalization.[108] Not only were they readmitted more frequently than patients of other classes, but their instrumental performance in the community (steadiness of employment and extent of participation in social activities) was also more limited.[109]

There are several reasons for this relationship. One factor is family attitudes: since posthospital adjustment is related to the reactions of relatives, higher class ex-patients function better in the community because their relatives place greater expectations on them than do the relatives of those from the lower class. Another factor is stigma, which is more profound among lower-class people because they have little education. This in turn forces released lower-class patients into social isolation rather than subject themselves to possible ridicule or avoidance by friends and neighbors. Thus, low familial expectations, a high degree of stigma, as well as the generally depressing quality of the lower-class environment, are together responsible for the more frequent rehospitalization of lower-class patients. Lower-class life strikes again.

The community mental health movement should be directing some effort toward the plight of lower-class discharged patients through public education programs, employment counseling, and a variety of methods to enrich ex-patients' social lives. Unfortunately, this is not occurring. In fact, the community movement may have *worsened* the situation by pushing for the mass release of hospitalized patients into the community. This is particularly inappropriate for lower-class patients because their community environment is not conducive to rehabilitation. Consequently, they waste their lives away in the loneliness and anonymity of a boardinghouse, a rundown hotel, or out in the streets until they are either rehospitalized or die prematurely from social and physical neglect. Boxes 14:1 and 14:4 contain vivid descriptions of the everyday misery of mentally ill street people, the foresaken of America.

•••••••••••••••••••••••••••••••••• **Box 14:4** •••••••••••••••••••••••••••••••••
The Forsaken: America's Street People

Dawn was just beginning to brighten the eastern sky. It was a sunrise that went unnoticed by the man asleep on the steam grate opposite Rittenhouse Square, folded up between a concrete trash receptacle and a newspaper vending machine.

An electric digital display in a nearby bank window gave the time: 5:54.

The sleeping man was wearing baggy corduroy pants, a wool hat, a shirt and a dirty blanket worn over his shoulders like a shawl.

His eyes still closed, the man reached into his open shirt to scratch at the lice, as he had been doing all night. A bread truck roared by on Walnut Street, followed a few minutes later by a milk truck. Then it was quiet again.

The sidewalk, which in two hours would be crowded with people hurrying to their jobs, was deserted now. The only signs of life were the man and a lone car that waited obediently at an empty intersection for the light to change.

The man started to stir and, still without opening his eyes, pushed himself up to a sitting position, leaning back against the concrete trash receptacle. Joggers began to appear across the street, resolutely circling the park, too intent on their exercise to notice the solitary man.

It took a long time, maybe 15 or 20 minutes, for the man to wake up fully, but by 6:15 his eyes were open wide, staring down the elegant street that had been his home for three years. At first he did nothing but sit, stare, and scratch.

Another day was beginning for Jim Logue Crawford, 69, former mental hospital patient.

Despite appearances, Jim Crawford is neither an alcoholic nor a Skid Row bum too lazy to work.

He is instead a victim—a victim of a 20-year-old, $2.5 billion government program that didn't work right. A program called "deinstitutionalization."

Since it began, that program has released between 700,000 and 1.5 million mental patients from the state mental hospitals into the cities and towns of America.

Most are better off now than they ever were in the back wards of mental hospitals where they were warehoused and ignored.

But thousands of others were released into a world unprepared, or unwilling to care for them. They are now living, and occasionally dying, in alleys, parks, and vacant lots of America, with little more than garbage for food, rags for clothes, and no shelter or medical care at all.

In Philadelphia they are lined up like bundles of dirty clothing along 13th Street between Market and Race, camped out on steam vents and sometimes huddled under cardboard cartons for protection from the rain. Others sleep on the steps in the glassed-in stairway enclosure at 1234 Market St., and in the graffiti-encrusted caves of the subways, and on the steam vents of Walnut Street.

In Camden they seek refuge in the White Tower restaurant on Market Street, or in the double doorways of government buildings, or in boarded-up old houses.

In New York City an estimated 36,000 of them are attracted to the bus and railroad stations, to the steam tunnels that spread underneath the streets, and to doorways in the decaying neighborhoods where they are less likely to be chased away.

These are just the conspicuous ones. For every homeless mental patient on the street, there are probably 15 or 20 or 30 others equally abandoned but hidden from view in cheap hotels, boarding homes, and even in the homes of relatives.

First proposed by President Kennedy amid the idealism of the 1960s, deinstitutionalization promised to rescue hundreds of thousands of people like Jim Crawford from the nation's large mental hospitals, where they were shut away and forgotten.

It promised to give them care and psychiatric treatment in their own communities, where they could live better, more productive lives.

"We made promises to the patient when we deinstitutionalized him," said William Eisenhuth of the Philadelphia Advocates for the Mentally Disabled, a citizens group. "We said we will not forget you. That has been the biggest lie in mental health history. We have abandoned the worst and sickest of our entire society. And they have no voice to scream about it. They have no way to organize."

The big state hospitals were all but emptied of mental patients during the past two decades. About 85,000 such patients live in Pennsylvania communities, state officials estimate.

Eisenhuth estimates that more than 20,000 are living in Philadelphia. Dr. Melwyn L. Posternack, the assistant deputy health commissioner

continued

who oversees Philadelphia's mental care programs, puts the number at 5,000 to 10,000, half of whom, he says, need medication and considerable support from day hospitals to survive.

But instead of finding care, many ended up living on the streets.

Most of these people suffer from schizophrenia, a disease that causes its victims to talk to themselves, see and hear things that aren't there, and live in an unreal, often frightening world of the mind. Schizophrenia is the most common of all the severe mental illnesses, striking from 1 to 2 percent of the population. While it sometimes can be controlled with drugs, it is practically incurable.

To handle the problems of discharged mental hospital patients, an extensive community mental care system was established nationwide. It is not working for many patients.

In Philadelphia, in many ways, the system is almost as afflicted as those it serves. "There is a serious problem in the mental health and mental retardation system in Philadelphia," said City Health Commissioner Stuart H. Shapiro. "There is not a system of care available in Philadelphia. There are many excellent deliverers of care, but no integrated system."

Philadelphia's major problems are these:

People in severe mental distress are kept for days at a time in the cramped confines of neighborhood crisis centers, strapped to chairs or litters, while hurried officials search in vain for a hospital willing to admit them.

Psychotically ill people, unaware that they need care, or unable to get it, are deteriorating needlessly in both body and mind because the community system is too passive to reach out to them. The system responds mainly to those who are competent enough to make and keep appointments.

To get shelter or medical care, some mentally disabled people deliberately provoke the police to arrest them, by committing petty crimes such as shoplifting. As a result, hundreds of the mentally ill now reside in Pennsylvania's jails and prisons, where their mental condition may go undiagnosed and they may be beaten, raped, or otherwise abused by fellow inmates.

Hundreds of families in Pennsylvania are compelled to shelter mentally ill relatives in their homes—relatives who may rave uncontrollably, destroy property, or commit violence. A new state law, passed in 1976 to protect mental patients' civil rights, has discouraged an already reluctant system from committing these patients for treatment.

Thousands of patients are riding a therapeutic merry-go-round. They go into mental hospitals, are prematurely discharged, return to the streets, relapse without their medicine or other therapy, and are hospitalized again after creating a disturbance or breaking a law. The cycle recurs again and again, year after year.

State officials often accuse the communities of failing to care for men and women like Jim Crawford. Local officials say the state releases seriously ill patients faster than the communities can handle them.

"It's the state policy that deinstitutionalization is the final and ultimate good," said Posternack of the city's office of mental health. They get the patients out whether they can handle outside life or not. A lot of backward patients who shouldn't have been (locked away in the state hospital) were freed as a result of this policy. But a lot of people who couldn't survive were also released."

Crawford stood up and took off all the clothes above his waist, exposing an emaciated chest and a bloated belly.

It was midwinter and a heavy snowstorm had been predicted. The digital display in the bank window now gave the temperature: It was 28, but Crawford did not seem to mind the cold, even though his only clothing was baggy corduroy pants, ragged shoes, a wool hat, a shirt, and a dirty blanket that he wore over his shoulders like a shawl.

Standing half-naked on the streetcorner, as though under a shower, he started rubbing at his skin and picking off lice, invisibly tiny annoyances that he threw away with the contempt of a Charlie Chaplin character.

He spent many minutes trying to get the lice off his body. He reached over his left shoulder and scratched and then twisted his body in an awkward way so he could reach the small of his back and scratch. He scratched his armpits and scratched the back of his neck and scratched his bloated belly and his pale chest. Closing his eyes again, Crawford scratched away at his body again and again with long yellow fingernails that protruded two or three inches beyond his fingertips.

A newspaper truck pulled up at the corner, and the driver jumped out to put the morning papers into the vending machine. The man acted as though he did not see Crawford, who stood only a few feet from the vending machine. Crawford did not acknowledge the truck driver's presence either.

An unseen radio, probably a portable in the

continued

truck, blared into the quiet morning. An announcer's energetic voice said there was a 30 percent chance of snow. The driver drove off, taking with him the noise of the radio.

Crawford brought a small comb from his pants pockets and started combing the stubble on his face. Without a mirror, he had to feel his way across the contours of his face. He carefully pulled his comb through his crew cut, being sure to comb his entire head.

Completing this part of his morning preparations, he replaced the comb in his pocket, bent down and picked up the coat and blanket that lay at his feet, shaking them vigorously as though to get rid of something. He was probably trying to shake the lice loose.

It was almost 7 now, and men and women dressed in business clothes were starting to appear on the street. A man with an attaché case, who had just come from a nearby indoor parking lot, walked over to Crawford, handed him a dollar without speaking or smiling, and left. Crawford stuffed the money into his pants pocket and finished pinning the blanket shut around his head and chest.

Crawford was a short man with a round face that looked more boyish than old, despite his years, and he had no upper front teeth. The lines around his eyes went up rather than down, giving him an innocent if not happy appearance. His eyes were his most striking feature; they were pale blue, almost hypnotic, and added to the aura of contentment that seemed to surround him.

Once again dressed and comfortably pinned into his blanket, Crawford walked over to the curb. Although it was a one-way street, he looked in both directions for cars. Seeing none, he walked over to the park and crouched behind a stone entranceway, where he urinated.

It is ironic that Philadelphia has so many problems with deinstitutionalized mental patients; the city is abundantly supplied with treatment facilities.

Source: Donald C. Drake, "The forsaken," *Philadelphia Inquirer,* July 18, 1982. Reprinted by permission of the publisher.

MENTAL ILLNESS AND HOMELESSNESS

The recommendations of the American Psychiatric Association Task Force on the Homeless Mentally Ill (1984), if implemented, would probably greatly reduce the prevalence of homelessness among people with major mental illness. The task force saw homelessness as but one symptom of the problems besetting the chronically mentally ill generally in the United States and called for a comprehensive and integrated system of care . . . to address the underlying problems that cause homelessness. Such a system would include an adequate number and range of supervised, supportive housing settings; a well-functioning system of case management; adequate, comprehensive, and accessible crisis intervention, both in the community and in hospitals; less restrictive laws on involuntary treatment; and outgoing treatment and rehabilitative services, all provided assertively through outreach when necessary.[110]

Little has been done to implement the recommendations of the APA since they were put forth in 1984. That is part of the problem. The other part of the problem is that we would not even have the "mentally ill homeless situation" if it were not for deinstitutionalization.[111] The *typical* profile of the released patient who ends up in this kind of predicament is male, under 40 years of age, black, "residing" in a city with a schizophrenia-related diagnosis and a history of alcohol and drug abuse.[112] If you look into the childhoods of homeless patients, there are certain antecedents, including foster care, group home placement, and running away.[113] To some, this all adds up to a hopeless situation in which even the *thought* of aftercare is extremely unrealistic.[114]

One edition of the *Harvard Mental Health Letter* puts it this way:

> The conspicuous and growing problem of homelessness is not only a disaster but a scandal and an embarrassment. Because its persistence could be seen as a sign of incompetence or lack of compassion, responsibility is disputed, and the connection between mental illness and homelessness has become a political issue. How many of the homeless are mentally ill, how many of the mentally ill are homeless, whether mental illness causes homelessness, and how mental health institutions have failed—these are the questions of immediate concern to the general public as well as to mental health professionals. The issues at stake are decisions on how to distribute money, goods, and services and how to organize the working time of professionals and others.
>
> Even after settling on a definition, it is difficult to count the homeless. They move in and out of apartments, cheap hotels, subways and parks, jails, mental institutions and shelters. They often sleep by day and wander by night. They may deny that they are homeless or stay out of sight to avoid assault, arrest, or commitment to a mental hospital. The rural homeless are even less visible than those in urban areas. To add to these difficulties, various groups have been charged with exaggerating the number of homeless to dramatize the situation, or minimizing it as an excuse to ignore the problem. The National Coalition for the Homeless and other advocacy groups have estimated a total of two or three million; the Department of Housing and Urban Development, 300,000. Extrapolation from the most detailed survey so far, conducted on the streets of Chicago in the mid 1980s, suggests a figure of 400– to 500,000; but many consider the sampling methods used in that study inadequate and reject it as a serious undercount. The more extensive recent United States Census Bureau count has been criticized for similar reasons.
>
> Diagnosing psychiatric disorders in the homeless is difficult. Many are suspicious, reluctant to be interviewed, and inclined to deny their symptoms. The rate of mental illness found in a study also depends on where it is conducted—in a shelter, on the street, or in a psychiatric emergency ward. Quiet, withdrawn, chronic schizophrenics, for example, are less likely to appear in hospital emergency wards and shelters (the most convenient locations for study) than people who suffer more obviously or behave more disruptively. In other words, some of the most seriously ill may be out of sight. On the other hand, behavior that would be a sign of psychiatric illness in other circumstances might be an ordinary feature of life on the streets or a normal reaction to conditions there. Odd gestures and mumbles may be used to fend off potentially dangerous strangers; people who have no place to clean up are disheveled and dirty; many of the homeless are understandably depressed, anxious, and demoralized because of their poor living conditions and physical health (they have high rates of infectious diseases, skin conditions, high blood pressure, and many other illnesses). Some of their symptoms might be relieved by a few nights of comfortable sleep, an adequate diet, and social contacts.[115]

For many of the homeless, but especially for the mentally ill among them, living on the streets is not the result of a single crisis but the last stage in a long course of events that often begins at conception, is complicated in childhood, and erupts in adolescence. Certainly the mental health system is not well designed to serve these people. It is also true that psychiatric research is eons away from preventing mental illness in the first place. Reading about prevalence and social policy is not the same as the actual experience of life on the street. I can envision that life as a constant scare, humiliation and wish that it would somehow end soon.

IMPROVING SOCIAL POLICY

> The public saw the mental hospitals as snake pits. Some were and some were not, but closing them was supposed to save the states a nice pile of tax money. A little later, tranquilizing drugs speeded the emptying of the wards. But on the streets, without care or attention, the mentally disturbed did not take the drugs, and regressed rapidly.[116]

To give you some idea of how ineffective the community approach has been, I will close with mention of a dirty little secret among mental health professionals. In some American cities today, the mentally ill are being "treated" with a bus ticket to another city. Thus, one area's problems are reduced by shipping the mentally ill off somewhere else, an unethical and costly practice known as "Greyhound therapy."

What changes are needed to make community programs function better?[117] Certainly we need an organized, well-funded system that can properly diagnose the mentally ill and then refer them to the most appropriate help source. This type of operation exists in some European countries. If it were developed in the United States, the quality of the staff should improve as salaries would be more lucrative. It would also be very helpful if therapists were drawn from all class backgrounds, reducing the class and cultural differences between them and their patients. Psychotherapy could also be provided more evenly to people of all classes. The problem of public acceptance of community programs could be minimized through social programs by which patients and outsiders can mix and mingle. This would help to further close the gap between the objective reality and the subjective perceptions of the mentally ill. In fact, there is real evidence that this can lead to greater public acceptance of community programs.[118] But ideas and actual implementation are two radically different things.

We also need programs that really affect primary prevention rather than dealing with mental disorder after it begins. Specifically, we need ways of protecting individuals at risk (such as the poor and the children of mentally ill parents) from mental health hazards. Environmental and social design projects are necessary to change the situations that debilitate people, such as removing a child from abusive parents or providing social support to people undergoing stressful life events. Children in elementary schools should be exposed to issues in mental health. This would help to nip stigma in the bud. Until these changes come, and until the general public becomes more sensitive to psychological problems, mental disorder will continue to take what *could* be a normal life and twist it into a hellish nightmare that never ends.

CONCLUSIONS

The problems faced by ex-patients in the community are enormous and are largely responsible for the present high rate of readmission to mental hospitals. Often discharged on the basis of outside pressure rather than cure of their symptoms, they face a hostile community that offers only deficient aftercare programs. Employment opportunities are limited because ex-patients are perceived as dangerous, unpredictable creatures who disrupt work environments. Consequently, rather than being given a chance to rejoin society through occupational activity and the mental health benefits that flow from it, they are relegated to the ranks of the unemployed, the underemployed, or become welfare recipients.

One of the biggest problems faced by discharged patients rejoining society is the stigma attached to having been a mental patient. The public harbors such negative and hostile attitudes toward the mentally ill that ex-patients are doomed to permanent social ostracism before they leave the hospital, even if their symptoms are gone. The attitudinal climate in the United States appeared to have become more sophisticated and open-minded during the 1960s, but the change was pronounced only in certain groups such as the young and the educated. And the change never progressed much further.

Some people do leave mental hospitals and rejoin society as functioning members. Usually these are persons who are fortunate enough to be returned to a social environment that is conducive to reintegration. The most favorable environment is a higher-class, conjugal family with young members. However, most patients are not that fortunate. Many of them are poor people, without families, who are returned to a ghetto community and waste their lives away while on welfare. Clearly, this situation is a social problem that will grow as more states pass legislation resulting in the mass release of patients.

Ex-patients can assume a normal social role only with the help of agencies devised to educate the public (and reduce stigma), provide individualized aftercare counseling, and structure occupational programs, to name a few. Some of these tasks have been given to the community mental health clinics, which have failed miserably to provide anything of real value.

At the risk of sounding extremely pessimistic, the only real hope for remedying this crisis situation lies in compassionate federal, state, and community governments that are progressive enough to invest sufficient sums of money into community clinics. Without a considerable economic investment, these clinics will never attract the professional personnel required to deal with the problems ex-patients face in their attempt to rejoin society. And, without any of these changes, the mentally ill will continue to be treated as they have for centuries—*pariahs in a social wasteland.*

Endnotes

CHAPTER 1

1. Joseph A. McFalls, Jr., Michael J. Engle, and Bernard J. Gallagher III, "The American sociologist: Characteristics in the 1990's, *The American Sociologist, 30* (3) (1999), 96–100.
2. Oliver Sacks, *Awakenings* (New York: HarperCollins, 1990).
3. Astrid Jones, "Stigma of mental illness," *Lancet, 352* (9133) (1998), 1047–1050.
4. Carolyn S. Weiss, "A message from our executive director," *Newsletter of Planned Lifetime Assistance Network of Pennsylvania,* Spring 1998.
5. *Opposing Viewpoints, "How Should Society Respond to the Homeless Mentally Ill?"* (San Diego, CA: Greenhaven Press, 2000).
6. Thomas Szasz, "Noncoercive psychiatry: An oxymoron," *Journal of Humanistic Psychology, 31* (2) (1991), 117–125.
7. "Myths about madness: Challenging stigma and changing attitudes" (Princeton, NJ: Films for the Humanities and Sciences, 2000).
8. "Aging and paging" (Princeton, NJ: Films for the Humanities and Sciences, 2000).
9. National Institute of Mental Health, "The numbers count," *NIH Publication VIII,* June 1999, pp 99–458.
10. Gerald L. Klerman, "Paradigm shifts in USA psychiatric epidemiology since World War II," *Social Psychiatry and Psychiatric Epidemiology, 125* (1990), 27–32.
11. C. L. Murray and A. D. Lopez, eds., *A Comprehensive Assessment of Mortality and Disability from Diseases, Injuries and Risk Factors in 1990 and Projected to 2020* (New York: World Health Organization, World Bank, Harvard University, 1996).
12. *Opposing Viewpoints, "Mental Health"* (San Diego, CA: Greenhaven Press, 1999).
13. Stephen W. White, "Mental illness and national policy," *National Forum, 73* (1) (1993), 2–3.
14. Nicholas Zill and Charlotte A. Schoenborn, "Development, learning, and emotional problems: Health of our nation's children: United States, 1988," *Advance Data, 190* (1990), 1–20.
15. Peggy R. Barker, Ronald W. Manderscheid, Gerry E. Hendershot, Susan S. Jack, Charlotte A. Schoenborn, and Ingrid Goldstrom, "Serious mental illness and disability in the adult household population: United States, 1989," *Advance Data, 218* (1992), 1–10.
16. Dawn MacKeen, "The outer limits of schizophrenia treatment" (Salon.com, Health and Body, December 1, 1999).
17. For an interesting video presentation of the new research on shyness, see Philip Zimbardo, "Shyness" (New York: Insight Media, 2000).

18. E. Fuller Torrey, *Nowhere to Go: The Tragic Odyssey of the Homeless Mentally Ill* (New York: Harper & Row, 1988).

19. Howard H. Goldman and E. Fuller Torrey, "Has the deinstitutionalization of the mentally ill worked?" in Richard P. H. Halgin, ed., *Taking Sides: Clashing Views on Controversial Issues in Abnormal Psychology* (Guilford, CT: Dushkin/McGraw-Hill, 2000), pp. 262–275.

20. David Pilgrim and Anne Rogers, *A Sociology of Mental Health and Illness* (Levittown, PA: Open University Press, 1999); Allan V. Horwitz and Teresa L. Scheid, eds., *A Handbook for the Study of Mental Health: Social Contexts, Theories and Systems* (New York: Cambridge University Press, 1999).

21. Glenn O. Gabbard and Krin Gabbard, *Psychiatry and the Cinema* (Washington, DC: American Psychiatric Publishing Group, 1999); *Current Controversies: Mental Health* (San Diego, CA: Greenhaven Press, 1999).

22. Dorothy P. Rice, Sander Kelman, and Leonard S. Miller, "The economic burden of mental illness," *Hospital and Community Psychiatry, 43* (12) (1992), 1227–1232.

23. Brian J. Jones, Bernard J. Gallagher III, John M. Kelley, and Louis O. Massari, "A survey of Fortune 500 corporate policies concerning the psychiatrically handicapped," *Journal of Rehabilitation, 57* (1991), 31–35.

24. Rice, Kelman, and Miller, "Economic burden."

25. M. Martin, E. P. Seligman, and David L. Rosenhan, *Abnormality* (New York: Norton, 1998).

26. William C. Cockerham, *The Sociology of Mental Disorder* (Upper Saddle River, NJ: Prentice Hall, 1996), p. 5.

27. Michel Foucault, *Madness and Civilization* (New York: Vintage Books, 1973).

28. William E. Baxter and David W. Hathcox, *America's Care of the Mentally Ill: A Photographic History* (Washington, DC: American Psychiatric Publishing Group, 1994).

29. Thomas Szasz, *The Manufacture of Madness* (New York: Harper & Row, 1973), p. 306.

30. C. D. Hayden, "On the distribution of insanity in the United States," *Third Literary Messenger, 10* (1844), 178.

31. G. A. Blumer, "The increase of insanity," *American Journal of Insanity, 51* (1893), 310.

32. W. A. White, "The geographical distribution of insanity in the United States," *Journal of Nervous and Mental Diseases, 30* (1903), 267.

33. R. Jones, "Medico-Psychological Association of Great Britain and Ireland: Presidential address on the evolution of insanity," *Journal of Mental Science, 152* (1906), 632.

34. Jeffrey Swanson et al., "Demographic and diagnostic characteristics of inmates receiving mental health services in state adult correctional facilities: United States, 1998," U.S. Department of Health and Human Services, Mental Health Statistical Note No. 209, August 1993.

35. Linda A. Teplin, "Keeping the peace: Police discretion and mentally ill persons," *National Institute of Justice Journal* (July 2000), 1–14; George Watson, "Prisons dealing with mentally ill," *Hartford Courant,* June 7, 1999.

36. Fox Butterfield, "Experts say study confirms prison's new role as mental hospital," *New York Times,* July 12, 1999.

37. Rodger Doyle, "Behind bars in the U.S. and Europe," *Scientific American,* August 1999, p. 25.

38. Michael Rutter, Ann Hagell, and Henri Giller, *Antisocial Behavior by Young People* (New York: Cambridge University Press, 1998).

39. Joseph P. Morrissey et al., "Overview of mental health services provided by adult correctional facilities: United States, 1998, U.S. Department of Health and Human Services, Mental Health Statistical Note No. 207, May 1993.

40. R. D. Weiner, "Does electroconvulsive therapy cause brain damage?" *Behavioral and Brain Sciences, 7* (1984), 1–53.

41. Max Fink and Leonard R. Frank, "Is electroconvulsive therapy ethical?" in Richard P. H. Halgin, ed., *Taking Sides: Clashing Views on Controversial Issues in Abnormal Psychology* (Guilford, CT: Dushkin/McGraw-Hill, 2000), pp. 348–365.

42. Joanne Ellison Rodgers, "Psychosurgery: Damaging the brain to save the mind," in Joseph J. Palladino, ed., *Abnormal Psychology 98/99* (Guilford, CT: Dushkin/McGraw-Hill, 1998), pp. 219–224.

43. Fred Ovsiew, Jonathan Bird, and Frank T. Vertosick, Jr., "Should psychosurgery be used to treat certain psychological conditions?" in Richard P. H. Halgin, ed., *Taking Sides: Clashing Views on Controversial Issues in*

Abnormal Psychology (Guilford, CT: Dushkin/McGraw-Hill, 2000), pp. 166–182.

44. Jeffrey R. Botkin, William M. McMahon, and Leslie Pickering Francis, *Genetics and Criminality: The Potential Misuse of Scientific Information in Court* (Washington, DC: American Psychological Association, 1999).

45. John M. Townshend, "Psychiatric versus social factors: An attempt at integration," *Human Relations, 35* (1982), 785–804.

46. Leo Srole, "Social psychiatry: A case of babel syndrome," in Joseph Zubin and Fritz Freyhan, eds., *Social Psychiatry* (New York: Grune & Stratton, 1968), pp. 56–68.

47. Marvin Zuckerman, *Vulnerability to Psychopathology: A Biosocial Model* (Washington, DC: American Psychological Association, 1999).

48. Horacio Fabrega, "Cultural relativism and psychiatric illness," *Journal of Nervous and Mental Disease, 177* (7) (1989), 415–425.

49. Rosalind Dworkin, *Researching Persons with Mental Illness* (London: Sage, 1992).

CHAPTER 2

1. Samuel O. Okpaku, ed., *Clinical Methods in Transcultural Psychiatry* (Washington, DC: American Psychiatric Publishing Group, 1998).

2. Richard A. Shweder and Maria A. Sullivan, "Cultural psychology: Who needs it?" *Annual Review of Psychology, 44* (1993), 497–523.

3. Franklin Zimring, "Fog times fog," *Time,* October 20, 1975, p. 57.

4. Group for the Advancement of Psychiatry, Committee on Psychiatry and Law, *The Mental Health Professional and the Legal System* (Washington, DC: American Psychiatric Publishing Group, 1991).

5. Michael J. Engle, Bernard J. Gallagher III, and Joseph A. McFalls, Jr., "Violent sex offenders: The attitudes of members of the Association for the Treatment of Sexual Abusers toward treatment, release and recidivism" (under review, *Journal of Interpersonal Violence*).

6. Vincent J. Fuller, "Not guilty by reason of insanity," *Trial* (October 1984), 15.

7. Thomas G. Gutheil, *The Psychiatrist in Court: A Survival Guide* (Washington, DC: American Psychiatric Publishing Group, 1998).

8. Fuller, "Not guilty," p. 16.

9. Paul S. Appelbaum, "Foucha v. Louisiana: When must the state release insanity acquitees?" *Hospital and Community Psychiatry, 44* (1) (1993), 9–10.

10. Fuller, "Not guilty."

11. Richard B. Schmitt, "Insanity pleas fail a lot of defendants as fear of crime rises," *Wall Street Journal,* February 29, 1996, pp. A1, A8.

12. Herbert Weiner, "The illusion of simplicity: The medical model revisited," *American Journal of Psychiatry, 135* (1978), 27–33.

13. Arthur Kleinman, *Rethinking Psychiatry: From Cultural Category to Personal Experience* (New York: Free Press, 1988).

14. Paul Florsheim, "Cross-cultural views of self in the treatment of mental illness: Disentangling the curative aspects of myth from the mythic aspects of cure," *Psychiatry, 53* (1990), 304–315.

15. Aubrey Lewis, *Between Guesswork and Certainty in Psychiatry: The State of Psychiatry* (New York: Science House, 1967).

16. Arthur Kleinman, "Anthropology and psychiatry: The role of culture in cross-cultural research on illness," *British Journal of Psychiatry, 151* (1987), 447–454.

17. Horacio Fabrega, "Cultural relativism and psychiatric illness," *Journal of Nervous and Mental Disease, 177* (7) (1989), 415–425; Roland Littlewood, "From categories to contexts: A decade of the 'new cross-cultural psychiatry,'" *British Journal of Psychiatry, 156* (1990), 308–327; Alan Roland, "Psychoanalysis in India and Japan: Toward a comparative psychoanalysis," *American Journal of Psychoanalysis, 51* (1) (1991), 1–10.

18. Horacio Fabrega, "The role of culture in a theory of psychiatric illness" (part of a symposium on The Case of American Psychiatry), *Social Science and Medicine, 35* (1) (1993), 91–103.

19. R. E. Kendell, J. E. Cooper, A. J. Gourlay, J. R. M. Copeland, L. Sharpe, and B. J. Gurland, "Diagnostic criteria of American and British psychiatrists," in Juan E. Mezzich and Carlos E. Berganza, eds., *Culture and Psychopathology* (New York: Columbia University Press, 1984), pp. 321–342.

20. Christina E. Newhil, "The role of culture in the development of paranoid symptomatology," *American Journal of Orthopsychiatry, 60* (1990), 176–185.

21. A. J. Marsella, "Culture, self and mental disorder," in A. J. Marsella, G. DeVos, and F. Hsu, eds., *Culture and Self: Asian and Western Perspectives* (London: Tavistock Press, 1985); A. J. Marsella and A. Scheuer, "Coping across cultures: An overview," in P. Dasen, J. Berry, and N. Sartorius, eds., *Contributions of Cross-Cultural Psychology to Healthy Human Development* (Beverly Hills, CA: Sage, 1993).

22. Donald M. Schwartz, Michael G. Thompson, and Craig L. Johnson, "Anorexia nervosa and bulimia: The socio-cultural context," *International Journal of Eating Disorders, 1* (1982), 20–36.

23. Albert C. Gaw and Ruth L. Bernstein, "Classification of amok in DSM-IV," *Hospital and Community Psychiatry, 43* (8) (1992), 789–793.

24. Salman Akhtar, "Four culture-bound psychiatric syndromes in India," *International Journal of Social Psychiatry, 34* (1) (1988), 70–74.

25. Karl Peltzer, "Nosology and etiology of a spirit disorder (vimbuza) in Malawi," *Psychopathology, 22* (2–3) (1989), 145–151.

26. Ihsan al-Issa, "Culture and mental illness in Algeria," *International Journal of Social Psychiatry 36* (3) (1990), 230 240.

27. A. J. Rubel, C. W. O'Nell, and R. Collado-Ardon, *Susto: A Folk Illness* (Berkeley: University of California Press, 1984); C. Martinez, "Mexican-Americans," in L. Comas-Diaz and E. E. H. Griffith, eds., *Clinical Guidelines in Cross-Cultural Mental Health* (New York: Wiley, 1988), pp. 182–203.

28. Joseph Westermeyer, "Amok," in C. Freidmann and R. Faguet, eds., *Extraordinary Disorders of Human Behavior* (New York: Wiley, 1988), pp. 182–203; Ronald C. Simons and Charles C. Hughes, "Culture-bound syndromes," in Albert C. Gaw, ed., *Culture, Ethnicity, and Mental Illness* (London: American Psychiatric Press, 1993), pp. 75–93.

29. S. Arieti and J. M. Meth, "Rare, unclassifiable, collective, and exotic psychotic syndromes," in S. Arieti, ed., *The American Handbook of Psychiatry* (New York: Basic Books, 1959), pp. 543–563.

30. J. E. Carr, "Ethnobehaviorism and the culture-bound syndromes: The case of amok," in R. C. Simons and R. C. Hughes, eds., *The Culture-Bound Syndromes* (Dordrecht, The Netherlands: Reidel, 1985).

31. Al-Issa, "Culture and mental illness."

32. Gaw and Bernstein, "Classification of amok in DSM-IV."

33. J. Westermeyer, "Grenade-amok in Laos: A psychosocial perspective," *International Journal of Social Psychiatry, 19* (1973), 1–5; J. Westermeyer, "Sudden mass assault with grenade: An epidemic amok form from Laos," in R. C. Simons and R. C. Hughes, eds., *The Culture-Bound Syndromes* (Dordrecht, The Netherlands: Reidel, 1985), pp. 225–235.

34. Michael G. Kenny, "Paradox lost: The latah problem revisited," *Journal of Nervous and Mental Disease, 17* (1993), 159–167.

35. W. Winiariz and J. Wielawski, "Imu—A psychoneurosis occurring among Ainus," *Psychoanalytic Review, 23* (1936), 181–186.

36. L. L. Langness, "Hysterical psychosis in the New Guinea Highlands: A bena bena example," *Psychiatry, 28* (1965), 258–277.

37. Anthony F. C. Wallace, "Mental illness, biology and culture," in Francis L. K. Hsu, ed., *Psychological Anthropology* (Cambridge, MA: Schenkman, 1972), pp. 363–402.

38. R. Landes, "The abnormal among the Ojibwa Indians," *Journal of Abnormal and Social Psychology, 33* (1938), 14–33; S. Parker, "The whitiko psychosis in the context of Ojibwa personality," *American Anthropologist, 62* (1960), 603–623.

39. Marlene Steinberg, "Transcultural issues in psychiatry: The ataque and multiple personality disorder," *Dissociation Progress in the Dissociative Disorders, 3* (1) (1990), 31–33.

40. M. Rubio, M. Urdaneta, and J. L. Doyle, "Psychopathologic reaction patterns in the Antilles command," *United States Armed Forces Medical Journal, 6* (1955), 1768.

41. P. M. Yap, "Koro—A culture-bound depersonalization syndrome," *British Journal of Psychiatry, 111* (1965), 69.

42. Ari Kiev, "Transcultural psychiatry: Research problems and perspectives," in Stanley C. Plog and Robert B. Edgerton, eds., *Changing Perspectives in Mental Illness* (New York: Holt, Rinehart & Winston, 1969), pp. 106–127.

43. Ferreira Mario De Barros, "The evil eye, sorcery, and bodily possession by spirits in

immigrant psychiatry," *Evolution Psychiatrique, 47* (1982), 985–996.

44. R. A. Pierloof and M. Ngoma, "Hysterical manifestations in Africa and Europe: A comparative study," *British Journal of Psychiatry, 152* (1988), 112–115.

45. E. C. Johnson-Sabine, A. H. Mann, R. J. Jacoby, et al., "Bouffee delirante; An examination of its current status," *Psychological Medicine, 13* (1983), 771–778.

46. Al Issa, "Culture and mental illness."

47. Ezra E. H. Griffith, "Psychiatry and culture," in John A. Talbott, Robert E. Hales, and Stuart C. Yudofsky, eds., *The American Psychiatric Press Textbook of Psychiatry* (Washington, DC: American Psychiatric Press, 1988), pp. 1097–1116.

48. L. L. Langness, "Hysterical psychosis: The cross-cultural evidence," *American Journal of Psychiatry, 124* (1967), 143–152.

49. Norman Jacobs, "The phantom slasher of Taipei: Mass hysteria in a non-Western society," *Journal of Social Problems, 12* (1965), 318–328.

50. Bruce P. Dohrenwend and Barbara Snell Dohrenwend, "Social and cultural influences on psychopathology," *Annual Review of Psychology, 25* (1974), 431–432.

51. Horacio Fabrega and Carole Ann Wallace, "How physicians judge symptom statements: A cross-cultural study," *Journal of Nervous and Mental Disease, 145* (1967), 486–491.

52. M. Opler and J. L. Singer, "Contrasting patterns of fantasy and mobility in Irish and Italian schizophrenics," *Journal of Abnormal and Social Psychology, 53* (1956), 42–47.

53. Arthur Kleinman, "The psychiatry of culture and the culture of psychiatry," *Harvard Mental Health Letter, 8* (1) (1991), 4–6.

54. Assen Jablensky, "Epidemiology and cross-cultural aspects of schizophrenia," *Psychiatric Annals, 19* (10) (1989), 506–510; Assen Jablensky and Norman Sartorius, "Is schizophrenia universal?" (Berzelius Symposium XI: Transcultural Psychiatry), *Acta Psychiatrica Scandinavica, 78* (344, suppl.) (1988), 65–70.

55. Kleinman, *Rethinking Psychiatry.*

56. N. Waxter, "Is outcome for schizophrenia better in non-industrialized societies?" *Journal of Nervous and Mental Diseases, 167* (1977), 144–158.

57. K. Singer, "Depressive disorders from a transcultural perspective," in Juan E. Mezzich and Carlos E. Berganza, eds., *Culture and Psychopathology* (New York: Columbia University Press, 1984), pp. 360–384.

58. H. Lefley, "Culture and chronic mental illness," *Hospital and Community Psychiatry, 41* (3) (1990), 277–286.

59. S. Orbell, K. Trew, and L. McWhirter, "Mental illness in Northern Ireland: A comparison with Scotland and England," *Social Psychiatry and Psychiatric Epidemiology, 25* (1990), 165–169.

60. Lefley, "Culture and chronic mental illness."

61. A. J. Olderhinkel, "Time trends in mental health care utilization in a Dutch area, 1976–1990," *Social Psychiatry and Psychiatric Epidemiology, 33* (1998), 181–185.

62. Dermot Walsh, *Report of the Inspector of Mental Hospitals for the Year Ending, 31 December, 1998* (Dublin: Government Publication Sales Office, 1999).

63. Mark Tausig, Janet Michella, and Sree Subedi, *A Sociology of Mental Illness* (Upper Saddle River, NJ: Prentice Hall, 1999), p. 158.

64. B. Cooper, "Epidemiology and prevention in the mental health field," *Social and Psychiatric Epidemiology, 25* (1990), 9–15.

65. Fabrega, "Cultural relativism and psychiatric illness."

66. Marie Jahoda, "Toward a social psychology of mental health," in *Symposium on the Healthy Personality*, Milton Senn, ed. (New York: Josiah Macy, Jr. Foundation, 1950), pp. 211–231.

67. Arno Karlen, *Sexuality and Homosexuality* (New York: Henry Holt, 1945).

68. Ruth Benedict, "Anthropology and the abnormal," *Journal of General Psychology, 10* (1934), 59–82.

69. Otto Klineberg, *Social Psychology* (New York: Henry Holt, 1945).

70. Akhtar, "Four culture-bound syndromes."

71. Heinz Hartmann, "Psychoanalysis and the concept of health," *International Journal of Psychoanalysis, 20* (1939), 308–321.

72. Felix Von Mendelssohn, "On mental illness: A review," *Psychiatric Quarterly, 48* (1974), 357.

73. Akhtar, "Four culture-bound syndromes"; al Issa, "Culture and mental illness."

74. Randolph M. Messe, "Evolution, emotions, and mental disorders," *Harvard Mental Health Letter, 9* (7) (1993), 5–7.

75. Sidney Weissman, Melvin Sabshin, and

Harold Eist, eds., *Psychiatry in the New Millennium* (Washington, DC: American Psychiatric Publishing Group, 1999).

76. Victor R. Adebimpe, "Overview: White norms and psychiatric diagnosis of black patients," *American Journal of Psychiatry, 138* (3) (1981), 279–285.

77. Marti Loring and Brian Powell, "Gender, race, and DSM-III: A study of the objectivity of psychiatric diagnostic behavior," *Journal of Health and Social Behavior, 29* (1988), 1–22.

78. Laura M. Young and Brian Powell, "The effects of obesity on the clinical judgments of mental health professionals," *Journal of Health and Social Behavior, 26* (1985), 233–246.

79. Kendell et al., "Diagnostic criteria."

80. E. Ginzberg et al., *The Lost Divisions* (New York: Columbia University Press, 1959).

81. P. Ash, "The reliability of psychiatric diagnosis," *Journal of Abnormal and Social Psychology, 44* (1949), 271–276.

82. P. Chodoff, "The problem of psychiatric diagnosis: Can biochemistry and neurophysiology help?" *Psychiatry, 23* (1960), 185–191; B. Pasamanick, S. Dinitz, and M. Lefton, "Psychiatric orientation and its relation to diagnosis and treatment in a mental hospital," *American Journal of Psychiatry, 116* (1959), 127–132; R. J. Stoller and R. H. Giertsma, "The consistency of psychiatrists' clinical judgments," *Journal of Nervous and Mental Disease, 137* (1963), 58–66.

83. David Baskin, "Cross-cultural categorizations of mental illness," *Psychiatric Forum, 12* (1984), 36–44.

84. J. E. Cooper, *Psychiatric Diagnosis in New York and London* (New York: Oxford University Press, 1972); Joseph L. Fleiss et al., "Cross-national study of diagnosis of the mental disorders," *International Journal of Social Psychiatry, 19* (1973), 180–186.

85. M. K. Temerlin, "Suggestion effects in psychiatric diagnosis," *Journal of Nervous and Mental Disease, 147* (1968), 349–353.

86. N. Rosenzweig et al., "A study of the reliability of the mental status examination," *American Journal of Psychiatry, 117* (1961), 1102–1108.

87. David L. Rosenhan, "On being sane in insane places," *Science, 179* (1973), 250–258.

88. Ibid., 257.

89. James R. Greenley, "The psychiatric patient's family and length of hospitalization," *Journal of Health and Social Behavior, 20* (1979), 217–227.

90. Henry J. Steadman and Stephen A. Ribner, "Life stress and violence among ex-mental patients," paper presented at the annual meeting of the Society for the Study of Social Problems, New York, 1981.

91. Richard M. Levinson and Georgeann Ramsay, "Dangerousness, stress and mental health evaluations," *Journal of Health and Social Behavior, 20* (1979), 178–187.

92. G. Devereux, "Normal and abnormal; The key problem of psychiatric anthropology," in *Some Uses of Anthropology, Theoretical and Applied* (Washington, DC: Anthropological Society of Washington, DC, 1956).

93. Ari Kiev, "Transcultural psychiatry: Research problems and perspectives," in *Changing Perspectives in Mental Illness*, S. C. Plog and R. B. Edgerton, eds. (New York: Holt, Rinehart & Winston, 1969), pp. 106–127.

94. Allen Francis, Michael B. First, Harold Alan Pincus, Herb Kutchins, and Stuart A. Kirk, "Is the DSM-IV a Useful Classification System?" in Richard P. Halgin, ed., *Taking Sides: Clashing Views on Controversial Issues in Abnormal Psychology* (Guilford, CT: Dushkin/McGraw-Hill, 2000), pp. 2–13.

95. Terry A. Kupers, Ruth Ross, Allen Frances, and Thomas A. Widiger, "Is There Gender Bias in the DSM-IV?" in Richard P. Halgin, ed., *Taking Sides: Clashing Views on Controversial Issues in Abnormal Psychology* (Guilford, CT: Dushkin/McGraw-Hill, 2000), pp. 14–39.

96. Juan E. Mezzick, Arthur Kleinman, Horacio Fabrega, Jr., and Delores L. Parcon, eds., *Culture and Psychiatric Diagnosis: A DSM-IV Perspective* (Washington, DC: American Psychiatric Publishing Group, 1996).

CHAPTER 3

1. Ritske le Coultre, "Splitting of the ego as the central phenomenon in neurosis," *International Journal of Psychoanalysis, 74* (4) 1993, 791–802.

2. For a discussion of integration of the disciplines, see Jerome Rabow, Gerald Platt, and Marion Goldman, *Advances in Psycho-*

analytic Sociology (Malabar, FL: Krieger, 1987).

3. William C. Cockerham, *The Sociology of Mental Disorder* (Englewood Cliffs, NJ: Prentice Hall, 1996).

4. National Research Council, Commission on Behavioral and Social Sciences and Education, Panel on High-Risk Youth, *Losing Generations: Adolescents in High-Risk Settings* (Washington, DC: National Academy Press, 1993).

5. Franca Ongaro Basaglia, "Politics and mental health. II," *International Journal of Social Psychiatry, 38* (1) (1992), 36–39.

6. Terry M. Killian and Lynn Taylor Killian, "Sociological investigations into mental illness: A review," *Hospital and Community Psychiatry, 41* (1999), 902–911.

7. Janice L. Dreshman and Cheryl I. Crabb, "Developing a plan to deal with catastrophe and trauma. One school district's experience," *Healing Magazine, 4* (1999), 6–11.

8. Donald Meichenbaum, "Treating the effects of severe trauma in adults and children: An advanced clinical workshop" (Philadelphia, PA: Institute for the Advancement of Human Behavior, 1999).

9. Michael Goldstein, "The sociology of mental health and illness," *Annual Review of Sociology, 5* (1979), 381–409.

10. Carolyn A. Smith, Christopher J. Smith, Robin A. Kearns, and Max W. Abbott, "Housing stressors, social support and psychological distress," *Social Science and Medicine, 37* (5) (1993), 603–612.

11. Killian and Killian, "Sociological investigations."

12. Lisa F. Beckman, "Which influences cognitive function: Living alone or being alone?" *Lancet, 355* (2000), 1201–1294.

13. Charles Froland, Gerry Brodsky, Madeline Olson, and Linda Stewart, "Social support and social adjustment: Implications for mental health professionals," *Community Mental Health Journal, 36* (2000), 61–75.

14. David Lester, Yukata Motohashi, and Bijou Yang, "The impact of the economy on suicide and homicide rates in Japan and the United States," *International Journal of Social Psychiatry, 38* (4) (1992), 314–317.

15. Robert Perrucci and Carolyn C. Perrucci, "Unemployment and mental health: Research and policy implications,"

Research in Community and Mental Health, 6 (1990), 237–264.

16. Ibid.

17. M. Harvey Brenner, *Mental Illness and the Economy* (Cambridge, MA: Harvard University Press, 1973).

18. Ralph Catalano, David Dooley, and Robert Jackson, "Economic predictors of admissions to mental health facilities in a nonmetropolitan community," *Journal of Health and Social Behavior, 22* (1981), 284–297.

19. Leo Srole and others, *Mental Health in the Metropolis: The Midtown Manhattan Study* (New York: Harper & Row, 1978).

20. Susan Gore, "The effect of social support in moderating the health consequences of unemployment," *Journal of Health and Social Behavior, 19* (1978), 157–165.

21. G. Chimenti, J. Nasr, and I. Khalifeh, "Children's reactions to war-related stress: Affective symptoms and behavior problems," *Social Psychiatry and Psychiatric Epidemiology, 24* (6) (1989), 282–287; Abdelwahab Mahjoub, Jacques Philippe Leyens, Vincent Yzerbyt, and Jean Pierre diGiacomo, "War stress and coping modes: Representations of self-identity and time perspective among Palestinian children," *International Journal of Mental Health, 18* (2) (1989), 44–62.

22. John E. Gedo, "The roots of personality: Heredity and environment," *Harvard Mental Health Letter, 7* (1) (1990), 4–5.

23. Richard C. Day and Samia N. Sadek, "The effect of Benson's relaxation response on the anxiety levels of Lebanese children under stress," *Journal of Experimental Child Psychology, 34* (1982), 350–356.

24. Stevan E. Hobfoll, Charles D. Spielberger, Schlomo Breznitz, Charles Figley, Susan Folkman, and Bonnie Lepper-Green, "War-related stress: Addressing the stress of war and other traumatic events," *American Psychologist, 46* (8) (1991), 848–855.

25. Zahava Solomon, "Does the war end when the shooting stops? The psychological toll of war," *Journal of Applied Social Psychology, 20* (210) (1990), 1733–1745.

26. Theo A. Dorelei and Denis M. Donovan, "Transgenerational traumatization in children of parents interned in Japanese civil internment camps in the Dutch East Indies during World War II," *Journal of Psychohistory, 17* (4) (1990), 435–447.

27. Donna Nagata, "The Japanese-American internment: Exploring the transgenerational consequences of traumatic stress," *Journal of Traumatic Stress, 3* (1) (1990), 47–69.

28. J. David Kinzie and James J. Boehnlein, "Post-traumatic psychosis among Cambodian refugees," *Journal of Traumatic Stress, 2* (2) (1989), 185.

29. Evelyn Lee and Francis Lu, "Assessment and treatment of Asian-American survivors of mass violence," *Journal of Traumatic Stress, 2* (1) (1989), 93.

30. Robert Krell, "Holocaust survivors: A clinical perspective," *Psychiatric Journal of the University of Ottawa, 15* (1) (1990), 18–21.

31. Lawrence A. Labbate and Michael P. Snow, "Post-traumatic stress symptoms among soldiers exposed to combat in the Persian Gulf," *Hospital and Community Psychiatry, 43* (8) (1992), 831–833.

32. Gerald J. Hunt, "Social and cultural aspects of health, illness, and treatment," in Howard H. Goodman, ed., *Review of General Psychiatry* (Norwalk, CT: Appleton and Lange, 1992), p. 88.

33. Sigmund Freud, *Civilization and Its Discontents* (New York: Norton, 1961).

34. Alex Inkeles, "The modernization of man," in *Modernization: The Dynamics of Growth,* Myron Weiner, ed. (New York: Basic Books, 1966).

35. Ernest Becker, "Social science and psychiatry: The coming challenge," *Antioch Review, 23* (1963), 353–366.

36. Albert C. Gaw, *Culture, Ethnicity, and Mental Illness* (New York: American Psychiatric Press, 1993).

37. C. Noel Bairey Meiz, "The secondary prevention of coronary artery disease," *American Journal of Medicine, 102* (1997), 572–581.

38. Carlfred B. Broderick, *Understanding Family Process: Basics of Family Systems Theory* (Newbury Park, CA: Sage, 1993).

39. Michael J. Goldstein, "The family and psychopathology," *Annual Review of Psychology, 39* (1988), 283–299.

40. Judith S. Wallerstein, "The psychological tasks of marriage," *American Journal of Orthopsychiatry, 66* (1996), 217–227.

41. Marian Radke-Yarrow, *Children of Depressed Mothers: From Early Childhood to Maturity* (New York: Cambridge University Press, 1998).

42. John Bowlby, *Child Care and the Growth of Love* (Baltimore, MD: Penguin, 1968), p. 21.

43. Robert Cudeck, Sarnoff A. Mednick, and Fini Schulsinger, "Effects of parental absence and institutionalization on the development of clinical symptoms in high-risk children," *Acta Psychiatrica Scandinavica, 63* (1981), 95–109.

44. H. R. Schaffer, "The too-cohesive family: A form of group pathology," *International Journal of Social Psychiatry, 10* (1964), 266–275.

45. Andrew J. Cherlin, Frank F. Furstenburg, P. Lindsey Chase-Lansdale, et al., "Longitudinal studies of the effects of divorce on children in Great Britain and the United States," *Science, 252* (1991), 1386–1389.

46. Nicholas Zill and Charlotte A. Schaenborn, "Developmental learning and emotional problems: Health of our nation's children; United States, 1988," *Advance Data, 190* (1990), 1–20.

47. "Violence and violent patients," Editorial, *Harvard Mental Health Letter, 7* (12) (1991), 1–4.

48. Films for the Humanities and Sciences, *The Impact of Violence on Children* and *Family Violence: Breaking the Chain* (Princeton, NJ: 1999).

49. Murray A. Straus and Philip Greven, *Family Violence* (San Diego, CA: Greenhaven Press, 1996).

50. Robert Hare, "Predators: The disturbing world of the psychopaths among us," in Joseph J. Palladino, ed., *Abnormal Psychology 98/99* (Guilford, CT: Dushkin/McGraw-Hill, 1998), pp. 124–127.

51. Donald Dutton and Susan Galant, *The Batterer: A Psychological Profile* (Boulder, CO: Westview Press, 1997).

52. James S. House, Karl R. Landis, and Debra Umberson, "Social relationships and health," *Science, 241* (1988), 540–544.

53. Janice M. Steil, "Marital relationships and mental health: The psychic costs of inequality," in Jo Freeman, ed., *Women: A Feminist Perspective* (Palo Alto, CA: Mayfield, 1984), pp. 113–124.

54. Thomas Szaz, "Curing, coercing, and claims making: A reply to critics," *British Journal of Psychiatry, 162* (1993), 797–800.

55. G. W. Albee, "The dark at the top of the agenda," *Clinical Psychologist Newsletter, 20* (1966), 7.

56. Cockerham, *Sociology of Mental Disorder.*

57. Thomas S. Szaz, *The Myth of Mental Illness* (New York: Hoebner, 1961).

58. David Pilgrim and Anne Rogers, *A Sociology of Mental Health and Illness* (Buckingham: Open University Press, 1999).

59. N. Rosenzweig et al., "A study of the reliability of the mental status examination," *American Journal of Psychiatry, 117* (1961), 1102–1108.

60. Thomas J. Scheff, *Being Mentally Ill: A Sociological Theory* (Hawthorne, N.Y.: Aldine de Gruyter, 1999).

61. For a delineation of the differences between the labeling model and the symbolic interactionist view, see Morris Rosenberg, "A symbolic interactionist view of psychosis," *Journal of Health and Social Behavior, 25* (1984), 289–302.

62. Edwin Lemert, *Social Pathology* (New York: McGraw-Hill, 1951).

63. Albert Ellis, *How to Live with a Neurotic* (New York: Crown, 1957), pp. 99–100.

64. B. R. Hergenhahn and Matthew H. Olson, *An Introduction to Theories of Learning* (Englewood Cliffs, NJ: Prentice Hall, 1993).

65. G. T. Wilson, "Clinical issues and strategies in the practice of behavior therapy," in C. M. Franks, G. T. Wilson, P. C. Kendall, and J. P. Foreyt, eds., *Review of Behavior Therapy* (New York: Guilford Press, 1990).

66. J. Dollard and N. E. Miller, *Personality and Psychopathology* (New York: McGraw-Hill, 1950).

67. B. F. Skinner, *Beyond Freedom and Dignity* (New York: Knopf, 1971).

68. B. M. Braginsky, D. D. Braginsky, and K. Ring, *Methods of Madness: Mental Hospitals as a Last Resort* (New York: United Press of America, 1969).

69. Julian B. Rotter, *Social Learning and Clinical Psychology* (Englewood Cliffs, NJ: Prentice Hall, 1954).

70. Albert Bandura, *Social Cognitive Theory* (London: Jessica Kingsley Publishers, 1992); Albert Bandura, "A social learning interpretation of psychological dysfunctions," in P. London and D. Rosenhan, eds., *Foundations of Abnormal Psychology* (New York: Holt, Rinehart & Winston, 1968).

71. Albert Bandura, "Social cognitive theory of moral thought and action," in William M. Kurtines and Jacob L. Gerwitz, eds., *Handbook of Moral Behavior and Development* (Hillsdale, NJ: Lawrence Erlbaum Associates, 1991); Albert Bandura, D. Ross, and S. Ross, "Imitation of film-mediated aggressive models," *Journal of Abnormal Social Psychology, 66* (1963), 3–11.

72. Gordon L. Berry and Joy Keiko Asamen, eds., *Children and Television: Images in a Changing Sociocultural World* (Newbury Park, CA: Sage, 1993); Thomas Skill, Samuel Wallace, and Mary Cassata, "Families on prime-time television: Patterns of conflict escalation and resolution across intact, nonintact, and mixed-family settings," in Jennings Bryant, ed., *Television and the American Family* (Hillsdale, NJ: Lawrence Erlbaum Associates, 1990).

73. Arthur Freeman, Karen M. Simon, and Larry E. Beutler, *Comprehensive Handbook of Cognitive Therapy* (New York: Plenum Press, 1989).

74. Aaron T. Beck and Steve Hollen, "Controversies in cognitive therapy: A dialogue with Aaron T. Beck and Steve Hollon," *Journal of Cognitive Psychotherapy, 7* (2) (1993), 79–93.

75. Albert Ellis, *Using Rational-Emotive Therapy Effectively: A Practitioner's Guide* (New York: Plenum Press, 1991); Wendy Dryden and Raymond DiGiuseppe, *A Primer on Rational Emotive Therapy* (Champaign, IL: Research Press, 1990).

76. Lawrence A. Pervin, *Personality: Theory and Research* (New York: Wiley, 1993); Sigmund Freud, "Formulations of the two principles of mental functioning," in J. Strachey, ed. and trans., *The Standard Edition of the Complete Psychological Works of Sigmund Freud*, Vol. 12 (London: Hogarth, 1911/1958).

77. Robert B. Ewen, *An Introduction to Theories of Personality* (Hillsdale, NJ: Lawrence Erlbaum Associates, 1993); Sigmund Freud, "The ego and the id," in J. Strachey, ed. and trans., *The Standard Edition of the Complete Psychological Works of Sigmund Freud*, Vol. 19 (London: Hogarth, 1923/1961).

78. William C. Crain, *Theories of Development: Concepts and Applications* (Englewood Cliffs, NJ: Prentice Hall, 1992).

79. Sigmund Freud, *The Problem of Anxiety* (New York: Norton, 1936).

80. Herman Nunberg, *Principles of Psychoanalysis* (New York: International Universities Press, 1955).

81. Otto Fenichel, *The Psychoanalytic Theory of Neurosis* (New York: Norton, 1945).

82. Arthur Feiner, Irwin Hirsch, Robert Gordon, and Roberta Shechter, "Pitfalls of the psychoanalytic supervisory process: Interpersonal and self psychological perspectives," paper delivered at the 18th Annual Scientific Conference, Philadelphia, January 1994; Arnold D. Richards, "The future of psychoanalysis: The past, present, and future of psychoanalytic theory," *Psychoanalytic Quarterly, 59* (1990), 347–367.

83. Lawrence S. Wrightman, *Adult Personality Development: Theories and Concepts* (Thousand Oaks, CA: Sage, 1994).

84. Charles H. Zeanah, K. Dommen, and Alicia F. Lieberman, "Disorders of attachment," in C. H. Zeanah, ed., *Handbook of Infant Mental Health* (New York: Guilford Press, 1993), pp. 332–349

85. Carolyn C. Grey, "Culture, character, and the analytic engagement: Toward a subversive psychoanalysis," *Contemporary Psychoanalysis, 29 (3)* 1993, 487–502.

86. Robert Plomin, *Genetics and Experience* (Thousand Oaks, CA: Sage, 1994).

87. William Goldfarb, "The effects of early institutional care on adolescent personality," in Sandra Scarr-Salapatek and Phillip Salapatek, eds., *Socialization* (Columbus, OH: Charles E. Merrill, 1973), pp. 66–101.

88. Evelyn Ellis, "Social psychological correlates of upward social mobility among unmarried career women," in Stephen P. Spitzer and Norman K. Denzin, eds., *The Mental Patient: Studies in the Sociology of Deviance* (New York: McGraw-Hill, 1968), pp. 147–154.

89. Charlotte Krause Prozan, *The Technique of Feminist Psychoanalytic Psychotherapy* (Northvale, NJ: Jason Aronson, 1993).

90. Mardy S. Ireland, *Reconceiving Women: Separating Motherhood from Female Identity* (New York: Guilford Press, 1993); Susan Quinn, *A Mind of Her Own: The Life of Karen Horney* (Boston, MA: Addison-Wesley, 1988).

91. Lisa Appignanesi and John Forrester, *Freud's Women* (New York: Basic Books, 1992); Eva Elisabeth Wright, Dianne Chisolm, and Juliet Flower MacCannell, *Feminism and Psychoanalysis: A Critical Dictionary* (Oxford: Blackwell, 1992).

92. Nancy J. Chodrow, *Feminism and Psychoanalytic Theory* (New Haven, CT: Yale University Press, 1991).

CHAPTER 4

1. For a more complete description of the uncommon psychotic syndromes, see M. D. Enoch, W. H. Trethowan, and J. C. Barker, *Some Uncommon Psychiatric Syndromes* (Bristol, CT: John Wright, 1967); S. Arieti and J. M. Meth, "Rare, unclassifiable, collective, and exotic psychotic syndromes," in S. Arieti, ed., *American Handbook of Psychiatry*, Vol. 1 (New York: Basic Books, 1959).

2. Raquel Gur, "Recent developments in investigating and treating mental illness," paper delivered at monthly meeting of PLAN of Pennsylvania, Wayne, PA, March 1999.

3. Stephen M. Laurie et al., "Magnetic resonance imaging of brain in people at high risk of developing schizophrenia," *Lancet, 353* (January 1999), 30–33.

4. Thomas Bouchard, Jr., David Lykken, Matthew McGue, Nancy Segal, and Auke Telegen, "Sources of human psychological differences: The Minnesota study of twins reared apart," *Science*, October 12, 1990, pp. 223–250.

5. Heinz Häfner, Anita Riecher-Rössler, Kurt Maurer, Brigette Fätkenheuer, et al., "First onset and early symptomatology of schizophrenia: A chapter of epidemiological and neurobiological research into age and sex differences," *European Archives of Psychiatry Criminals Clinical Neuroscience, 242* (2–3) (1992), 109–118.

6. Bryant Furlow, "Children destined to become schizophrenic," *Emory Magazine, 76* (Spring 2000), 1–6.

7. V. F. Druz, "The familial status of elderly schizophrenics: Social and psychological problems," *Zhurnal Neuropatologii i Psikhiatrii, 84* (1984), 731–734; Films for the Humanities and Sciences, *Schizophrenia and Delusional Disorders* (Princeton, NJ, 2001); Films for the Humanities and Sciences, *Schizophrenia: New Definitions, New Therapies* (Princeton, NJ, 2001); www.Eduex.com, *Schizophrenia: The Shattered Mind* (Princeton, NJ, 2000).

8. E. Hartmann et al., "Vulnerability to schizophrenia," *Archives of General Psychiatry, 41* (1984), 1050–1059.

9. S. Gupta, "Cross-national differences in the frequency and outcome of schizophrenia: A comparison of five hypotheses,"

Social Psychiatry and Psychiatric Epidemiology, 27 (1992), 249–252; Geoffrey Der, Sunjai Gupta, and Robin Murray, "Is schizophrenia disappearing?" *Lancet,* March 3, 1990, pp. 513–516.

10. Morton Beiser and William G. Iacono, "An update on the epidemiology of schizophrenia," *Canadian Journal of Psychiatry, 35* (November 1990), 657–667; Jose L. Vazauez-Barquero, Maria J. Cuesta, Sara Herrera Castanedo, Ismael Lastra, Andres Herran, and Graham Dunn, "Cantabria first episode schizophrenia study. Three-year follow-up, *British Journal of Psychiatry, 174* (February 1999), 141–149.

11. Phil Gunby, "Epidemiology indicates a disorder that assaults much of patients' 'humanness' in prime of life," *Journal of American Medical Association,* November 21, 1990, p. 2487.

12. John Horgan, "Overview: Schizophrenia," *Scientific American, 252* (June 1990), 37–38.

13. Health Canada, *Schizophrenia: A Handbook for Families* (Toronto: Schizophrenia Society of Canada, 2000).

14. Leonard L. Heston, *Mending Minds* (New York: Freeman, 1992).

15. There are many excellent books on schizophrenia both for the professional and the lay public. My recommendation for mental health professionals is Philippe A. E. G. Delespaul, *Assessing Schizophrenia in Daily Life: The Experience Sampling Method,* IPSER Series in Ecological Psychiatry, M. W. de Vries, ed. (Maastricht, Netherlands, 1995). A more basic and well-informed source is Richard S. E. Keefe and Philip P. Harvey, *Understanding Schizophrenia: A Guide to the New Research on Causes and Treatment* (New York; Free Press, 1994).

16. William Carpenter, Jr., "Clinical features of schizophrenia," Proceedings of "Schizophrenia as a Brain Disorder," conference at University of Pennsylvania Medical Center, Philadelphia, October 29, 1993, pp. 7–8; Glenn D. Shean, "Syndromes of schizophrenia and language dysfunction," *Journal of Clinical Psychology, 55* (2) (February 1999), 233–240; Philip Tibibo, Peg Nopoulos, Stephan Arndt, and Nancy C. Andreasen, "Corpus callosum shape and size in male patients with schizophrenia," *Biological Psychiatry, 44* (6) (September 1998), 405–412.

17. There are also mental health professionals who believe that categorizing schizophrenia is a large waste of clinical time.

18. Wayne Fenton and Thomas McGlashan, "Positive and negative symptoms and long-term course," *Journal of American Medical Association,* February 19, 1992, p. 924; Ross M. G. Norman, A. K. Malla, L. Cortese, and F. Diaz, "Aspects of dysphoria and symptoms of schizophrenia," *Psychological Medicine, 28* (6) (November 1998), 1433–1441.

19. D. Kibel, I. Laffont, and P. Liddle, "The composition of the negative syndrome of chronic schizophrenia," *British Journal of Psychiatry, 162* (June 1993), 744–750; B. Bower, "'Deficit' schizophrenia follows unique path," *Science News,* March 12, 1994, p. 166; Ashok K. Malla, "Understanding symptoms of schizophrenia," *Canadian Journal of Psychiatry, 40* (3, Suppl. 1) (April 1995), S12–S17.

20. "Positive and negative symptoms: A follow-up," *Harvard Mental Health Letter, 7* (4) (October 1990), 7: A. Eden Evins, Donald C. Goff, "Adjunctive antidepressant drug therapies in the treatment of negative symptoms of schizophrenia," *CNS Drugs, 6* (2) (August 1996), 130–147; Raimo K. R. Salokangas, "Structure of schizophrenic symptomatology and its changes over time: Prospective factor-analytical study," *Acta Psychiatrica Scandinavica, 95* (1) (January 1997), 32–39.

21. Nancy C. Andreasen and Victor D. Sanua, "Is schizophrenia a biological disorder?" in Richard P. Halgin, ed., *Taking Sides: Clashing Views on Controversial Issues in Abnormal Psychology* (Guilford, CT: Dushkin/McGraw-Hill, 2000), pp. 74–85.

22. S. R. Hirsch and D. R. Weinberger, eds., *Schizophrenia* (Washington, DC: American Psychiatric Publishing Group, 1995).

23. M. Siegler and H. Osmond, "Laing's models of madness," *British Journal of Psychiatry, 115* (1969), 947–958.

24. D. A. Soskis, "Aetiological models of schizophrenia: Relationships to diagnosis and treatment," *British Journal of Psychiatry, 120* (1972), 367–373; Richard D. Baxter and Peter F. Liddle, "Neuropsychological deficits associated with schizophrenic syndromes," *Schizophrenia Research, 39* (3) (April 1998), 239–249.

25. Nancy Andreasen, ed., *Schizophrenia: From Mind to Molecule,* American Psychopatho-

logical Association Series (Washington, DC: American Psychiatric Press, 1994); Tyrone Cannon, Sarnoff Mednick, Josef Parnas, Fini Schulsinger, et al., "Developmental brain abnormalities in the offspring of schizophrenia mothers," *Archives of General Psychiatry, 50* (7) (1993), 551–564; Rodney Ford, Shon Lewis, G. Shah Syed, Adrienne Reveley, et al., "Ventricular size and regional cerebral blood flow in schizophrenia: An attempted replication," *Psychiatry Research: Neuroimaging, 50* (2) (1993), 141.

26. J. M. Silverman et al., "Lateral ventricular enlargement in schizophrenia probands and their siblings with schizophrenia-related disorders," *Biology and Psychiatry, 43* (1998), 97–106.

27. Tyrone Cannon, "Hereditary and family studies of schizophrenia," Proceedings of "Schizophrenia as a Brain Disorder," conference at University of Pennsylvania Medical Center, Philadelphia, October 29, 1993, pp. 9–39; Peter F. Liddle, "The multidimensional phenotype of schizophrenia," in Carol A. Tamminga et al., eds., *Schizophrenia in a Molecular Age.* Review of Psychiatry Series (Washington, DC: American Psychiatric Press, 1999), pp. 1–28.

28. Irving I. Gottesman, *Schizophrenia Genesis: The Origins of Madness* (New York: Freeman, 1991); Martin Gallen, Stephen Cohen, and William Pollin, "Schizophrenia in veteran twins: A diagnostic review," *American Journal of Psychiatry, 128* (1972), 939–945; Seymour S. Kety et al., "Mental illness in the biological and adoptive relatives of schizophrenic adoptees: Findings relevant to genetic and environmental factors in etiology," *American Journal of Psychiatry, 140* (1983), 720–727.

29. Richard Suddath, George Christenson, E. Fuller Torrey, Manuel Casanova, and Daniel Weinberger, "Anatomical abnormalities in the brains of monozygotic twins discordant for schizophrenia," *New England Journal of Medicine, 322* (12) (1990), 789–794; Alan Breier, "Brain morphology and schizophrenia," *Journal of American Medical Association,* March 24, 1993, p. 1554.

30. "The abnormal schizophrenic brain," *Harvard Mental Health Letter, 7* (2) (August 1990), 6; Ross M. G. Norman, A. K. Malla, P. C. Williamson, S. L. Morrison-Stewart, et al., "EEG coherence and syndromes in schizophrenia," *British Journal of Psychiatry, 170* (May 1997), 411–415.

31. Suddath, Christenson, Torrey, Casanova, and Weinberger, "Anatomical abnormalities in the brains of monozygotic twins."

32. Tony Dajer, "Divided selves," *Discover, 13* (9) (September 1992), 38–44.

33. Timothy Crow, "Temporal lobe asymmetries as the key to the etiology of schizophrenia," *Schizophrenia Bulletin, 16* (3) (1990), 430–443; R. M. G. Norman, A. K. Malla, S. L. Morrison-Stewart, E. Helmes, et al., "Neuropsychological correlates of syndromes in schizophrenia," *British Journal of Psychiatry, 170* (2) (February 1997), 134–139.

34. F. J. Kallman, *Heredity in Health and Mental Disorder* (New York: Norton, 1953).

34. J. M. Neale and T. F. Oltmanns, *Schizophrenia* (New York: Wiley, 1980).

36. L. L. Heston, "Psychiatric disorders in foster home reared children of schizophrenic mothers," *British Journal of Psychiatry, 112* (1966), 819–825.

37. Carol Prescott and Irving Gottesman, "Genetically mediated vulnerability to schizophrenia," *Psychiatric Clinics of North America, 16* (2) (1993), 245–267; Seymour S. Kety et al., "Mental illness in the biological and adoptive families of adopted schizophrenics," *American Journal of Psychiatry, 128* (1971), 302–306; David Rosenthal et al., "The adopted-away offspring of schizophrenics," *American Journal of Psychiatry, 128* (1971), 307–311; Norman Garmezy, "New approaches to a developmental overview of schizophrenia," paper presented at the annual meeting of the American Psychological Association, Toronto, 1978; Patricia A. Lowing, Allan F. Mirsky, and Robert Pereira, "The inheritance of schizophrenia spectrum disorders: A reanalysis of the Danish adoptee study data," *American Journal of Psychiatry, 140* (1983), 1167–1171; Kenneth S. Kendler, Alan M. Gruenberg, and John S. Strauss, "An independent analysis of the Copenhagen sample of the Danish adoption study of schizophrenia. V. The relationship between childhood social withdrawal and adult schizophrenia," *Archives of General Psychiatry, 39* (1982), 1257–1261.

38. Theodore Lidz, Sidney Blatt, and Barry

Cook, "Critique of the Danish-American studies of the adopted-away offspring of schizophrenic parents," *American Journal of Psychiatry, 138* (1981), 1063–1068.

39. Paul E. Meehl, "Schizotaxia, schizotypy, schizophrenia," *American Psychologist, 17* (1962), 827–838.

40. D. C. Fowles, "Schizophrenia: Diathesis-stress revisited," *Annual Review of Psychology, 43* (1992), 303–336.

41. I. I. Gottesman and J. Shields, "Genetic theorizing and schizophrenia," *British Journal of Psychiatry, 122* (1973), 15–30.

42. Peter R. Breggin, "Schizophrenia is not genetic," in David L. Bender, ed., *Mental Illness: Opposing Viewpoints* (San Diego, CA: Greenhaven Press, 1995), pp. 55–62.

43. R. S. Smith, "A comprehensive macrophage-T-lymphocyte theory of schizophrenia," *Medical Hypotheses, 39* (1992), 248–257.

44. Linda Thompson, "The dopamine hypothesis of schizophrenia," *Perspectives in Psychiatry Care, 26* (3) (1990), 18–23; Steven W. Matthysse, "Current status of biochemistry in schizophrenia," paper presented at the annual meeting of the American Psychological Association, Toronto, 1978: B. Bogerts et al., "Amorphometric study of the dopamine-containing cell groups in the mesencephalon of normals, Parkinson patients and schizophrenics," *Biological Psychiatry, 18* (1983), 951–968.

45. Gavin P. Reynolds, "Neurotransmitter systems in schizophrenia," *International Review of Neurobiology, 38* (195), 306–334.

46. F. Awouters, C. J. Niemegeers, and P. A. Janssen, "'Tardive' dyskinesia: Etiological and therapeutic aspects," *Pharmacopsychiatry, 23* (1990), 33–37.

47. Wagner Gattaz et al., "Low platelet MAO activity and schizophrenia: Sex differences," *Acta Psychiatrica Scandinavica, 64* (1981), 167–174.

48. Judith Hooper, "A new germ theory," *Atlantic Monthly*, February 1999, pp. 41–53.

49. M. Sarnof, A. Mednick, and J. Meggin Hollister, *Neural Development and Schizophrenia: Theory and Research* (New York: Plenum Press, 1995).

50. Corinne Rita, "Schizophrenia and drug abuse," unpublished manuscript, 2002.

51. Malcolm Weller, P. C. Ang, D. T. Latimer-Sayer, and A. Zachary, "Drug abuse and mental illness," *Lancet* (1988), 997.

52. Herbert Meltzer, "New drugs for the treatment of schizophrenia," *Schizophrenia, 16* (2) (1993), 365–385.

53. Bernard J. Gallagher III, Joseph A. McFalls, Jr., Brian J. Jones, and Anthony M. Pisa, "Prenatal illness and subtypes of schizophrenia: The winter pregnancy phenomenon," *Journal of Clinical Psychology, 55* (1999), 915–922.

54. B. J. Gallagher, J. A. McFalls, Jr., and B. J. Jones, "Racial factors in birth seasonality among schizophrenics: A preliminary analysis," *Journal of Abnormal Psychology, 92* (1983), 524–527; P. Woodard and M. Feldman, "Seasonal birthrates and schizophrenia," *American Journal of Psychiatry, 147* (1990), 537.

55. D. Dassa, J. M. Azorin, V. Ledoray, and R. Sambuc, "Season of birth and schizophrenia: Sex difference," *Progress in Neuro-Psychopharmacology and Biological Psychiatry, 20* (2) (1996), 243–251.

56. E. Franzek and H. Beckmann, "Gene-environment interaction in schizophrenia: Season-of-birth effect reveals etiologically different subgroups," *Psychopathology, 29* (1) (1996), 14–26; J. Modestin, R. Ammann, and O. Wurmle, "Season of birth: Comparison of patients with schizophrenia, affective disorders, and alcoholism," *Acta Psychiatrica Scandinavica, 91* (2) (1996), 140–143; E. F. Torrey, R. R. Rawlings, J. M. Ennis, and D. D. Merrill, "Birth seasonality in bipolar disorder, schizophrenia, schizo-affective disorder and stillbirths," *Schizophrenia Research, 21* (3) (1996), 141–149.

57. R. Suddath, G. Christian, E. Torrey, and M. Casathe, "Brains of monozygotic twins discordant for schizophrenia," *New England Journal of Medicine, 322* (1990), 789–794; E. O'Callaghan, T. Gibson, H. A. Colohan, D. Walshe, et al., "Season of birth in schizophrenia: Evidence for confinement of an excess of winter births to patients without a family history of mental disorder," *British Journal of Psychiatry, 158* (1991), 764–769.

58. M. Berk, M. J. Terre-Blanche, C. Maude, and M. D. Lucas, "Season of birth and schizophrenia: Southern hemisphere data," *Australian and New Zealand Journal of Psychiatry, 30* (2) (1996), 220–222.

59. N. Takei, P. C. Sham, E. O'Callaghan, G. Glover, and R. M. Murray, "Early risk factors in schizophrenia: Place and season of birth," *European Psychiatry, 10* (4) (1995), 165–170; N. Takei, P. C. Sham, E. O'Callaghan, G. Glover, and R. M. Murray, "Schizophrenia: Increased risk associated with winter and city birth: A case-control study in 12 regions within England and Wales," *Journal of Epidemiology and Community Health, 49* (1) (1995), 106–107.

60. A. Berquier and R. Ashton, "A selective review of possible neurological etiologies of schizophrenia," *Clinical Psychology Review, 11* (5) (1991), 645–661; E. Franzek and H. Beckmann, "Season-of-birth effect reveals the existence of etiologically different groups of schizophrenia," *Biological Psychiatry, 32* (4) (1992), 375–378.

61. M. A. Roy, M. Flaum, and N. C. Andreasen, "No difference found between winter- and non-winter-born schizophrenic cases," *Schizophrenia Research, 17* (3) (1995), 241–248.

62. National Center for Health Statistics, *Seasonal Variation of Births,* Series 21, No. 9, 1933–1963 (Washington, DC: U.S. Government Printing Office).

63. National Center for Health Statistics, "Births, marriages, divorces, and deaths for 1997," *Monthly Vital Statistics Report, 46* (1997–1998), 1–12; "Update: Influenza activity in the United States, 1995–1996 seasons," *Mortality and Morbidity Weekly Report, 45* (6) (1996), 134–136.

64. J. M. Kane, "Schizophrenia," *New England Journal of Medicine, 334* (1) (1996), 34–41.

65. M. Lyon and C. E. Barr, "Possible interactions of obstetrical complications and abnormal fetal brain development in schizophrenia," in S. A. Mednick, T. D. Cannon, C. E. Barr, and M. Lyon, eds., *Fetal Neural Development and Adult Schizophrenia* (New York: Cambridge University Press, 1991), pp. 134–139.

66. M. Jacobsen, ed., *Developmental Neurobiology* (New York: Plenum Press, 1978).

67. H. A. Nasrallah and D. R. Weinberger, eds., "Neurology of schizophrenia," in *Handbook of Schizophrenia,* Vol. 1 (Amsterdam: Elsevier, 1990).

68. M. Lyon, C. E. Barr, T. D. Cannon, S. A. Mednick, and D. Shore, "Fetal neural development and schizophrenia," *Schizophrenia Bulletin (UDH), 15* (1) (1989),

149–161; M. Lyon and C. E. Barr, "Possible interactions of obstetrical complications and abnormal fetal brain development in schizophrenia," in S. A. Mednick, T. D. Cannon, C. E. Barr, and M. Lyon, eds., *Fetal Neural Development and Adult Schizophrenia* (Cambridge: Cambridge University Press, 1991), pp. 134–139.

69. P. Laing, J. G. Knight, P. Wright, and W. O. Irving, "Disruption of fetal brain development by maternal antibodies as an etiological factor in schizophrenia," in S. A. Mednick, ed., *Neural Development and Schizophrenia* (New York: Plenum Press, 1995), p. 215.

70. B. J. Gallagher III, *The Sociology of Mental Illness* (Englewood Cliffs, NJ: Prentice Hall, 1995).

71. E. O'Callaghan, T. Gibson, H. A. Colohan, D. Walshe, et al., "Season of birth in schizophrenia: Evidence for confinement of an excess of winter births to patients without a family history of mental disorder," *British Journal of Psychiatry, 158* (1991), 764–769.

72. H. Verdoux, N. Takei, R. Cassou de Saint-Mathurin, R. Murray, and M. Bourgeois, "Seasonality of birth in schizophrenia: The effect of regional population density," *Schizophrenia Research, 23* (1997), 175–180.

73. "Higher schizophrenia risk tied to birth timing and flu," *New York Times,* August 7, 1991, p. B7 (N).

74. Suzanne N. Brixey, Bernard J. Gallagher III, and Joseph A. McFalls, Jr., "Obstetrical complications contribute to schizophrenia," in William Barbour, ed., *Mental Illness: Opposing Viewpoints* (San Diego, CA: Greenhaven Press, 1995).

75. Raquel Gur, "Brain structure and function," Proceedings of "Schizophrenia as a Brain Disorder," conference at University of Pennsylvania Medical Center, Philadelphia, October 29, 1993, pp. 40–61.

76. D. J. Castle, K. Scott, S. Wessely, and R. M. Murray, "Does social deprivation during gestation and early life predispose to later schizophrenia?" *Social Psychiatry and Psychiatric Epidemiology, 28* (1) (1993), 1–4.

77. Bernard J. Gallagher III, Suzanne N. Brixey, and Joseph A. McFalls, Jr., "Prenatal insults and schizophrenia," manuscript in preparation.

78. Lyn Pilowsky, Robert Kerwin, and Robin Murray, "Schizophrenia: A neurodevelopmental perspective," *Neuropsychopharma-*

cology, *9* (1) (1993), 83–91; Henry Nasrallah, "Neurodevelopmental pathogenesis of schizophrenia," *Psychiatric Clinics of North America,* *16* (2) (1993), 269–280.

79. Sidney Jortner, "Schizophrenia is usually psychogenic," *American Psychologist,* *45* (4) (1990), 551.

80. Gottesman, *Schizophrenia Genesis,* pp. 133–149.

81. Ibid., pp. 150–165.

82. Leona Bachrach, "The urban environment and mental health," *International Journal of Social Psychiatry,* *38* (1) (1992), 5–15.

83. Richard Hudson, "New Swedish study links big-city life with schizophrenia," *Wall Street Journal,* July 17, 1992, p. B12 (E).

84. Preben Bo Mortensen et al., "Effects of family history and place of season of birth on the risk of schizophrenia," *New England Journal of Medicine,* *340* (1999), 603–608.

85. For further elaboration of the resemblances between schizophrenic thinking and that of young children, see A. E. Goldman, "A comparative-developmental approach to schizophrenia," *Psychological Bulletin,* *59* (1962), 57–69.

86. Thomas Ritzman, "Schizophrenia, its cause and cure," *Medical Hypnoanalysis Journal,* *4* (1) (1989), 27–37.

87. See Samuel F. Klugman, "Differential preference patterns between sexes for schizophrenic patients," *Journal of Clinical Psychology,* *22* (1966), 170–172.

88. Martin S. Willick, "Psychoanalytic concepts of the etiology of severe mental illness," *Journal of the American Psychoanalytic Association,* *38* (4) (1990), 1049–1081.

89. David Miklowitz, Dawn Velligan, Michael Goldstein, Keith Nuechterlein, Michael Gitlin, Gregory Ranlett, and Jeri Doane, "Communication deviance in families of schizophrenic and manic patients," *Abnormal Psychology,* *100* (2) (1991), 163–173.

90. D. Shakow, "Psychological deficit in schizophrenia," *Behavioral Science,* *8* (1963), 275–305; A. McGhie and J. Chapman, "Disorders of attention and perception in early schizophrenia," *British Journal of Medical Psychology,* *34* (1961), 103–117. Also see J. H. Liem, "Effects on verbal communications of parents and children: A comparison of normal and schizophrenic families," *Journal of Consulting and Clinical Psychology,* *42* (1974), 438–450.

91. J. C. Andorfer, "Affective pattern recognition and schizophrenia," *Journal of Clinical Psychology,* *40* (1984), 403–409.

92. Raquel Gur, "Cognitive dysfunction and its rehabilitation," Proceedings of "Schizophrenia as a Brain Disorder," conference at University of Pennsylvania Medical Center, Philadelphia, October 29, 1993, pp. 40–61.

93. Malca Lebell, Stephen Marder, Jim Mintz, Lois Mintz, et al., "Patients' perceptions of family emotional climate and outcome in schizophrenia," *British Journal of Psychiatry,* *162* (June 1993), 751–754.

94. "Study links schizophrenia to upbringing (The Lancet Report)," *New York Times,* July 21, 1992, p. B7 (N).

95. Theodore Lidz and S. Fleck, "Schizophrenia, human integration, and the role of the family," in D. D. Jackson, ed., *The Etiology of Schizophrenia* (New York: Basic Books, 1960).

96. Theodore Lidz, "Schizophrenic patients and their siblings," *Psychiatry,* *26* (1963), 1–18; Theodore Lidz, S. Fleck, and A. R. Cornelison, *Schizophrenia and the Family* (New York: International Universities Press, 1965).

97. L. Nagelburg, H. Spotnitz, and Y. Feldman, "The attempt at healthy insulation in the withdrawn child," *American Journal of Orthopsychiatry,* *23* (1953), 238–252.

98. Elliot Mischler, "Families and schizophrenia," *Harvard Mental Health Letter,* *7* (11) May 1991, 3–6.

99. Gregory Bateson et al., "Toward a theory of schizophrenia," *Behavioral Science,* *1* (1956), 251–264.

100. There is also a minority opinion which holds that the communication deviance originates in the children, not the parents. See Liem, "Effects on verbal communications."

101. Yi-chuang Lu, "Contradictory parental expectations in schizophrenia: Dependence and responsibilities," *Archives of General Psychiatry,* *6* (1962), 219–235; Nancy M. Docherty, "Communication disturbances in schizophrenia: A two-process formulation," *Comprehensive Psychiatry,* *36* (3) (1995), 182–186.

102. Yi-chuang Lu, "Mother-child role relations in schizophrenia: A comparison of schizophrenic parents with nonschizophrenic siblings," *Psychiatry,* *24* (1961), 133–142.

103. H. Barry and H. Barry, "Birth order, family size and schizophrenia," *Archives of General Psychiatry, 17* (1967), 435–440.

104. Bruce P. Dohrenwend and Barbara S. Dohrenwend, "Stress situations, birth order, and psychological symptoms," *Journal of Abnormal and Social Psychology, 71* (1966), 215–223.

105. The preponderance of schizophrenia in the lower class has been reported many times. See Bruce P. Dohrenwend and Barbara S. Dohrenwend, "Social and cultural influences on psychopathology," *Annual Review of Psychology, 25* (1974), 417–452.

106. Melvin Kohn, "Social class and schizophrenia: A critical review and reformulation," *Schizophrenia Bulletin, 7* (1973), 60–79.

107. See M. M. Lystad, "Social mobility among selected groups of schizophrenics," *American Sociological Review, 22* (1957), 288–292; R. J. Turner and M. O. Wagonfeld, "Occupational mobility and schizophrenia," *American Sociological Review, 32* (1967), 104–113; Leigh Silverton and S. Mednick, "Class drift and schizophrenia," *Acta Psychiatrica Scandinavica, 70* (1984), 304–309.

108. See J. A. Clausen and M. L. Kohn, "Relation of schizophrenia to the social structure of a small city," in B. Pasamanick, ed., *Epidemiology of Mental Disorder* (Washington, DC: American Association for the Advancement of Science, 1959); W. H. Dunham, *Community and Schizophrenia: An Epidemiological Analysis* (Detroit, MI: Wayne State University Press, 1965).

109. E. M. Goldberg and S. L. Morrison, "Schizophrenia and social class," *British Journal of Psychiatry, 109* (1963), 785–802.

110. Turner and Wagonfeld, "Occupational mobility and schizophrenia."

111. See C. Bagley, "The social aetiology of schizophrenia in immigrant groups," *International Journal of Social Psychiatry, 17* (1971), 292–304; S. D. Eitzen and J. H. Blau, "Type of status inconsistency and schizophrenia," *Sociological Quarterly, 13* (1972), 61–73.

112. William W. Eaton, "A formal theory of selection for schizophrenia," *American Journal of Sociology, 86* (1980), 149–158.

113. R. E. Faris, "Cultural isolation and the schizophrenic personality," *American Journal of Sociology, 40* (1934), 155–164.

114. Bernard J. Gallagher III, Anthony M. Pisa, and Brian J. Jones, "Social class and type of schizophrenia: An association with the 'winter pregnancy' phenomenon," unpublished manuscript.

115. Soskis, "Aetiological models of schizophrenia."

116. Bernard J. Gallagher III, "The attitudes of psychiatrists toward etiological theories of schizophrenia," *Journal of Clinical Psychology, 33* (1977), 99–104.

117. Bernard J. Gallagher III, Brian J. Jones, and Lamia Barakat, "The attitudes of psychiatrists toward etiological theories of schizophrenia, 1975–1985," *Journal of Clinical Psychology, 43* (4) (1987), 438–443.

118. Harvey Clarizio, *Assessment and Treatment of Depression in Children and Adolescents*, 2nd ed. (Brandon, VT: Clinical Psychology Publishing Co., 1994); Michael Furlong and Douglas Smith, eds., *Anger, Hostility, and Aggression* (Brandon, VT: Clinical Psychology Publishing Co., 1994); Bruce Compas, Sydney Ey, and Kathryn Grant, "Taxonomy, assessment, and diagnosis of depression during adolescence," *Psychological Bulletin, 114* (2) (1993), 323–344; Cornelius Katona et al., "The symptomatology of depression in the elderly," *International Journal of Clinical Psychopharmacology, 12* (1997), 519–523.

119. Dana Crowley Jack, *Silencing the Self: Women and Depression* (New York: Harper Perennial, 1993); Ellen Leibenluft, "Gender differences in mood and anxiety disorders: From bench to bedside," in *Review of Psychiatry* (Washington, DC: American Psychiatric Press, 1999).

120. J. L. Vázquez-Barquero, J. F. Diez Manrique, J. Muñoz, J. Menendez Arango, L. Gaite, S. Herrera, and G. J. Der, "Sex differences in mental illness: A community study of influence of physical health and sociodemographic factors," *Social Psychiatry and Psychiatric Epidemiology, 27* (1992), 62–68; K. Wilhelm and D. Hadzi-Pavlovic, "Fifteen years on: Evolving ideas in researching sex differences in depression," *Psychological Medicine, 27* (1997), 875–883.

121. M. Dewey, C. de la Cámara, J. Copeland, and A. Lobo, "Cross-cultural comparison of depression and depressive symptoms in older people," *Acta Psychiatrica Scandinavica, 87* (6) (1993), 369–373.

122. E. Fuller Torrey, with Ann Bowler, Edward Taylor, and Irving Gottesman, *Schizophrenia and Manic-Depressive Disorder* (New York: Basic Books, 1994).

123. Ibid.

124. Heston, *Mending Minds.*

125. Norman Cameron, "The place of mania among the depressions from a biological standpoint," *Journal of Psychology, 14* (1942), 181–195.

126. Ibid.

127. Leon Grunhaus and John Greden, eds., *Severe Depressive Disorders,* Progress in Psychiatry No. 44, American Psychopathological Association Series (Washington, DC: American Psychiatric Press, 1994); Alan Swann, "Biology of bipolar disorder," in Joseph Mann and David Kupfer, eds., *Biology of Depressive Disorders, Part B: Subtypes of Depression and Comorbid Disorders,* Depressive Illness Series, Vol. 4 (New York: Plenum Press, 1993), pp. 1–35.

128. Films for the Humanities and Sciences, *Depression and Manic Depression* (Princeton, NJ, 2000).

129. Reinhard Heum and Wolfgang Maier, "Bipolar disorder in six first-degree relatives," *Biological Psychiatry, 34* (4) (1993), 274–276.

130. Stanley J. Watson, ed., *Biology of Schizophrenia and Affective Disease* (Washington, DC: American Psychiatric Publishing Group, 1995).

131. Sue A. Marten et al., "Unipolar depression: A family history study," *Biological Psychiatry, 4* (1972), 205–213.

132. E. S. Gershan, S. D. Targum, and L. R. Kessler, "Genetic studies and biologic strategies in the affective disorders," *Progress in Medical Genetics, 2* (1977), 103–125.

133. Neal Swerdlow, "Dopamine and depression: Circuitous logic?" *Biological Psychiatry, 33* (10) (1993), 757.

134. J. J. Schildkraut, "The catecholamine hypothesis of affective disorders: A review of support evidence," *American Journal of Psychiatry, 122* (1965), 507–522.

135. Peter C. Shybrow, "Making sense of mania and depression," in Joseph J. Palladino, ed., *Abnormal Psychology 98/99* (Guilford, CT: Dushkin/McGraw-Hill, 1998).

136. Marleen M. M. Von Eck, *Stress, Mood and Cortisol Dynamics in Daily Life,* IPSER Series in Ecological Psychiatry, M. W. de Vries, ed. (Maastricht, Netherlands: 1996).

137. Peter D. Kramer, *Listening to Prozac* (New York: Viking, 1993).

138. Robert Aseltine and Ronald Kessler, "Marital disruption and depression in a community sample," *Journal of Health and Social Behavior, 34* (3) (1993), 237–251.

139. Films for the Humanities and Sciences, *Depression* (Princeton, NJ, 2000).

140. Sigmund Freud, "Mourning and melancholia," in *Collected Papers* (London: Hogarth Press and the Institute of Psychoanalysis, 1950).

141. Heston, *Mending Minds.*

142. R. Spitz, "Infantile depression and the general adaptation syndrome," in P. H. Hoch and J. Zubin, eds., *Depression* (New York: Grune & Stratton, 1999), pp. 93–108.

143. A. T. Beck, B. B. Sethi, and R. W. Tuthill, "Childhood bereavement and adult depression," *Archives of General Psychiatry, 9* (1963), 295–302; M. J. Abrahams and F. A. Whitlock, "Childhood experience and depression," *British Journal of Psychiatry, 115* (1969), 883–888.

144. Steven Beach, Jack Martin, Terry Blum, and Paul Roman, "Subclinical depression and role fulfillment in domestic settings: Spurious relationships, imagined problems, or real effects," *Journal of Psychopathology and Behavioral Assessment, 15* (2) (1993), 113–128; Diane Spangler, Anne Simons, Scott Monroe, and Michael Thase, "Evaluating the hopelessness model of depression: Diathesis-stress and symptom components," *Journal of Abnormal Psychology, 102* (4) (1993), 592–600.

145. A. T. Beck, *Depression: Clinical, Experimental and Theoretical Aspects* (New York: Harper & Row, 1967); Martin E. P. Seligman and David L. Rosenhan, *Abnormality* (New York: Norton, 1998).

146. Thomas Joiner, "Dysfunctional attitudes and Beck's cognitive theory of depression," *British Journal of Psychiatry, 162* (June 1993), 850–851.

147. J. H. Geer, "Reduction of stress in humans through nonveridical perceived control of aversive stimulation," *Journal of Personality and Social Psychology, 16* (1970), 731–738.

148. Maria Kovacs and Aaron T. Beck, "Maladaptive cognitive structures in depression," *American Journal of Psychiatry, 135*

(1978), 525–533; J. H. Chen et al., "Gender differences in the effects of bereavement-related psychological distress in health outcomes," *Psychological Medicine, 29* (1999), 367–380.

149. G. Parker, "Parental rearing style: Examining for links with personality vulnerability factors for depression," *Social Psychiatry and Psychiatric Epidemiology, 28* (3) (1993), 97–100.

150. See, for example, P. H. Lewinsohn and J. M. Libet, "Pleasant events, activity schedules and depressions," *Journal of Abnormal Psychology, 79* (1972), 291–295; J. M. Libet and P. H. Lewinsohn, "The concept of social skill with special reference to the behavior of depressed persons," *Journal of Consulting and Clinical Psychology, 40* (1973), 304–312.

151. R. W. Gibson, M. B. Cohen, and R. A. Cohen, "On the dynamics of the manic-depressive personality," *American Journal of Psychiatry, 115* (1959), 1101–1107.

152. Parker, "Parental rearing style."

153. Robert L. Leahy and Stephen J. Holland, *Treatment Plans and Interventions for Depression and Anxiety Disorders* (Indianapolis, IN: Behavioral Science Book Service, 2001).

154. Nan Linn Liaolon Ye and Walter M. Ensel, "Social support and depressed mood: A structural paralysis," *Journal of Health and Social Behavior, 40* (1999).

CHAPTER 5

1. NIMH, "The numbers count: Mental illness in America," <http://www.nimh.nih.gov/publicat/numbers.cfm> (2000).

2. Gabriele Maxi et al., "Symptomatology and comorbidity of generalized anxiety disorder in children and adolescents," *Comprehensive Psychiatry, 40* (3) (1999), 210–215.

3. Kjell R. Nilzon and Kerstin Palmerus, "Anxiety in depressed school children," *International Journal of School Psychology, 18* (2) (1997), 165–177.

4. Andrew Meisler, *Understanding Anxiety: Special Focus: Mind Over Mood,* seminar presented by Cor Text/Mind Matters Educational Seminars, Salisbury, MD, November 1, 2000.

5. Deborah C. Beidel and Samuel M. Turner, "Anxiety disorders," in Samuel M. Turner, Michel Hersen, et al., eds., *Adult Psychopathology and Diagnosis* (New York: Wiley, 1997), pp. 282–332.

6. Christer Allgulander and Philip W. Lavori, "Causes of death among 936 elderly patients with 'pure' anxiety neurosis in Stockholm County, Sweden, and in patients with depressive neurosis or both diagnoses," *Comprehensive Psychiatry, 34* (5) (1993), 299–302.

7. Kathleen Brady and Bruce Lydiard, "The association of alcoholism and anxiety," special issue on Contemporary Topics in Drug Dependence and Alcoholism, *Psychiatric Quarterly, 64* (2) (1993), 135–149.

8. Matig Mavissakalian, Mary Hamann, Said Haidar, and Christopher de Groot, "DSM-III personality disorders in generalized anxiety, panic/agoraphobia, and obsessive-compulsive disorders," *Comprehensive Psychiatry, 34* (4) (1993), 243–248.

9. Christian Grillon, Lisa Diecker, and Kathleen R. Merikangas, "Fear-potentiated startle in adolescent offspring of parents with anxiety disorders," *Biological Psychiatry, 44* (10) (1998), 990–997.

10. Tari D. Topolski et al., "Genetic and environmental influences on child reports of manifest anxiety and symptoms of separation anxiety and overanxious disorders: A community-based twin study," *Behavioral Genetics, 27* (1) (1997), 15–28.

11. This thesis, originally developed by Freud, is also the essence of other psychoanalytic views as well. See, for example, Karen Horney, "Culture and neurosis," *American Sociological Review, 1* (1936), 221–230.

12. Robert Bastide, *The Sociology of Mental Disorder* (New York: David McKay, 1972).

13. L. C. Kolb, *Modern Clinical Psychiatry* (Philadelphia, PA: Saunders, 1982).

14. R. Lynn, *Personality and National Character* (Oxford: Pergamon Press, 1971).

15. Peer M. Lewinsohn et al., "Gender differences in anxiety disorders and anxiety symptoms in adolescents," *Journal of Abnormal Psychology, 107* (1) (1998), 109–117.

16. Sherry H. Stewart, Steven Taylor, and Jan M. Baker, "Gender differences in dimensions of anxiety sensitivity," *Journal of Anxiety Disorders, 11* (2) (1997), 179–200.

17. Adrian Furnham, "Overcoming neuroses: Lay attributions of cure for five specific neurotic disorders," *Journal of Clinical Psychology, 53* (6) (1997), 595–604.

18. Edudex.com, *Panic* (Princeton, NJ, 1991).
19. Lester Grinspoon, ed., *Harvard Mental Health Letter*, 7 (3) (1990).
20. Dave A. Clark, Aaron T. Beck, and Judith S. Beck, "Symptom differences in major depression, dysthymia, panic disorder, and generalized anxiety disorder," *American Journal of Psychiatry*, 151 (2) (1994), 205.
21. Andrew Briggs, David Stretch, and Sydney Brandon, "Subtyping of panic disorder by symptom profile," *British Journal of Psychiatry*, 163 (1993), 201–209.
22. David A. Katerndahl and Janet P. Realini, "Lifetime prevalence of panic states," *American Journal of Psychiatry*, 150 (2) (1993), 246.
23. Ewald Horwath, Jim Johnson, and Christopher D. Hornig, "Epidemiology of panic disorder in African-Americans," *American Journal of Psychiatry*, 150 (3) (1993), 465.
24. Gerald Klerman, Robert Hirschfeld, Myrna Weisman, and Yves Pelicier, eds., *Panic Anxiety and Its Treatments: Report of the World Psychiatric Association Presidential Educational Program Task Force* (Washington, DC: American Psychiatric Press, 1993).
25. Janet Borden, Pamela Lowenbraun, Patricia Wolff, and Allison Jones, "Self-focused attention in panic disorder," *Cognitive Therapy and Research*, 17 (5) (1993), 413–425.
26. Justin Kenardy, Leslie Fried, Helena Kraemer, and C. Barr Taylor, "Psychological precursors of panic attacks," *British Journal of Psychiatry*, 163 (1993), 130.
27. Noel K. Free, Carolyn N. Winget, and Roy M. Whitman, "Separation anxiety in panic disorder," *American Journal of Psychiatry*, 150 (4) (1993), 595.
28. Martin E. P. Seligman and David L. Rosenhan, *Abnormality* (New York: Norton, 1997), pp. 148–153.
29. Laszlo A. Papp, Donald F. Klein, and Jack M. Gorman, "Carbon dioxide hypersensitivity, hyperventilation, and panic disorder," *American Journal of Psychiatry*, 150 (8) (1993), 1149.
30. Rene S. Kahn and Herman VanPraag, "Panic disorder: A biological perspective," *European Neuropsychopharmacology*, 2 (1) (1992), 1–20.
31. Lester Grinspoon, ed., "Panic disorder: Part I" *Harvard Mental Health Letter*, 7 (3) (September, 1990), 1–4.
32. M. Katherine Shear, Arnold Cooper, Gerald Klerman, Frederic Busch, and Theodore Shapiro, "A psychodynamic model of panic disorder," *American Journal of Psychiatry*, 150 (6) (1993), 859–867.
33. Mary A. Gogoleski, Bruce A. Thyer, and Raymond J. Waller, "Reports of childhood incest by adults with panic disorder or agoraphobia," *Psychological Reports*, 73 (1) (1993), 289–290.
34. Ahmad Tayseer, Jane Wardle, and Peter Hayward, "Physical symptoms and illness attributions in agoraphobia and panic," *Behaviour Research and Therapy*, 30 (5) (1992), 493–501.
35. Martin B. Keller and Diane L. Hanks, "Course and outcome in panic disorder," *Progress in Neuropsychopharmacology and Biological Psychiatry*, 17 (4) (1993), 551–570.
36. S. Agras, D. Sylvester, and D. Olvieau, "The epidemiology of common fears and phobias," unpublished manuscript, 1969.
37. D. A. Regier, W. E. Narrow, and D. S. Rae, "The epidemiology of anxiety disorders: The Epidemiological Catchment Area (ECA) experience," *Journal of Psychiatric Research*, 24 (Suppl. 2) (1990), 3–14.
38. T. A. Ross, *The Common Neuroses* (Baltimore, MD: Wm. Wood, 1937), pp. 219–223.
39. Ewald Horwath, Jennifer Lish, Jim Johnson, Christopher Hornig, et al., "Agoraphobia, without panic: Clinical reappraisal of an epidemiologic finding," *American Journal of Psychiatry*, 150 (10) (1993), 1496–1501.
40. Chantal I. Dijkman-Caes, Marten de Vries, Herro Kraan, and Alexander Volovics, "Agoraphobic behavior in daily life: Effects of social roles and demographic characteristics," *Psychological Reports*, 72 (3) (1993), 1283–1294.
41. S. Waldfogel, "Emotional crisis in a child," in A. Burton, ed., *Case Studies in Counseling and Psychotherapy* (Englewood Cliffs, NJ: Prentice Hall, 1959), pp. 35–36.
42. Thomas Uhde, Manuel Tancer, Bruce Black, and Terry Brown, "Phenomenology and neurobiology of social phobia: Comparison with panic disorder," *Journal of Clinical Psychiatry*, 52 (1991), 31–40.
43. Harald Merckelbach, Peter de Jong, Arnound Arntz, and Erik Schouten, "The

role of evaluative learning and disgust sensitivity in the etiology and treatment of spider phobia," *Advances in Behaviour Research and Therapy, 15* (4) (1993), 243–255.

44. Sigmund Freud, "Analysis of a phobia in a five-year-old boy," in *Collected Papers*, Vol. 10 (London: Hogarth Press, 1957), pp. 5–149.

45. Walter J. Schneider and Jeffrey S. Nevid, "Overcoming math anxiety: A comparison of stress inoculation training and systematic desensitization," *Journal of College Student Development, 34* (4) (1993), 283–288.

46. Uhde, Tancer, Black, and Brown, "Phenomenology and neurobiology of social phobia."

47. See, for example, H. B. English, "Three cases of the 'conditioned fear response,'" *Journal of Abnormal and Social Psychology, 34* (1929), 221–225; E. L. Thorndike, *The Psychology of Wants, Interests and Attitudes* (New York: Appleton, Century, 1935).

48. A. Bandura and T. L. Rosenthal, "Vicarious classical conditioning as a function of arousal level," *Journal of Personality and Social Psychology, 3* (1966), 54–62.

49. Leon Eisenberg, "School phobia: Diagnosis, genesis and clinical management," in Leslie Y. Rabkin and John E. Carr, eds., *Sourcebook in Abnormal Psychology* (Boston, MA: Houghton Mifflin, 1967), p. 429.

50. Timothy A. Brown, "Diagnostic and symptom distinguishability of generalized anxiety disorder and obsessive-compulsive disorder," *Behavior Therapy, 24* (2) (1993), 227–240.

51. N. Kendler, M. Neale, R. Kessler, and A. Heath, "Generalized anxiety disorder in women: A population-based twin study," *Archives of General Psychiatry, 49* (1992), 707–715.

52. E. Slater and J. Shields, "Genetic aspects of anxiety," in M. H. Lader, ed., *Studies of Anxiety* (Ashford, England: Headley Brothers, 1969).

53. Svenn Torgersen, "Genetics of neurosis: The effects of sampling variation upon the twin concordance ratio," *British Journal of Psychiatry, 142* (1983), 126–132.

54. David Nutt et al., *Generalized Anxiety Disorder: Diagnosis, Treatment, and Its Relationship to Other Anxiety Disorders* (Washington, DC: American Psychiatric Publishing Group, 1998).

55. Cameron, *Personality Development and Psychotherapy*, p. 268.

56. Joseph Wolfe, *Psychotherapy by Reciprocal Inhibition* (Stanford, CA: Stanford University Press, 1958).

57. William Thomas Moore, "Some economic functions of genital masturbation during adolescent development," in Irwin M. Marcus and John J. Francis, eds., *Masturbation: From Infancy to Senescence* (New York: International Universities Press, 1975), pp. 231–276.

58. "OCD: When a habit isn't just a habit. A guide to obsessive-compulsive disorder," (Pine Brook, NJ: Ciba-Geigy Corp., 1993).

59. Films for the Humanities and Sciences, *Obsessive-Compulsive Disorder* (Princeton, NJ, 2000).

60. P. H. Thomsen and H. U. Mikkelsen, "Development of personality disorders in children and adolescents with obsessive-compulsive disorder: A 6- to 22-year follow-up study," *Acta Psychiatrica Scandinavica, 87* (6) (1993), 456–462.

61. Gary A. Christenson, Stephen L. Ristvedt, and Thomas B. Mackenzie, "Identification of trichotillomania cue profiles," *Behaviour Research and Therapy, 31* (3) (1993), 315–320.

62. Isaac Marks, "Exposure therapy for phobias and obsessive-compulsive disorders," *Hospital Practice, 14* (1979), 101–108.

63. Leon Salzman, *The Obsessive Personality* (New York: Jason Aronson, 1973), p. 62.

64. Ibid., pp. 29–30.

65. P. Sachdev and P. Hay, "Does neurosurgery for obsessive-compulsive disorder produce personality change?" *Journal of Nervous and Mental Disease, 183* (6) (1995), 408–413.

66. Obsessive-compulsives typically have favorite numbers that are even. Psychoanalysts consider this to be a symbolic attempt at balancing the demands of id and superego.

67. Ronnie S. Stangler and Adolph M. Printz, "Psychiatric diagnosis in a university population," *American Journal of Psychiatry, 137* (1980), 937–940.

68. Edudex.com, *Obsessive-Compulsive Disorder: The Hidden Epidemic* (Princeton, NJ: 1997).

69. Marvin Karno, Jacqueline Golding, Susan Sorenson, and M. Audrey Burnam, "The epidemiology of obsessive-compulsive dis-

order in five U.S. communities," *Archives of General Psychiatry, 45* (1988), 1094–1099.

70. Andrew L. Stoll, Mauricio Tohen, and Ross Baldessarini, "Increasing frequency of the diagnosis of obsessive-compulsive disorder," *American Journal of Psychiatry, 149* (5) (1992), 638–641.

71. Stuart Montgomery and Joseph Zahar, *Obsessive-Compulsive Disorder-Pocketbook* (Washington, DC: American Psychiatric Publishing Group, 1999).

72. Films for the Humanities and Sciences, *Obsessive-Compulsive Disorder* (Princeton, NJ, 2000–2001).

73. Bruce Bower, "Images of obsession: The peculiar symptoms of obsessive-compulsive disorder appear to be linked to a mismatch in the brain's metabolic activity," *Science News,* April 11, 1987, 236.

74. Lewis R. Baxter, Jr., Jeffrey Schwartz, Kenneth Bergman, et al., "Caudate glucose metabolic rate changes with both drug and behavior therapy for obsessive-compulsive disorder," *Archives of General Psychiatry, 49* (1992), 681–689.

75. U. Meyer and E. S. Chesser, *Behavior Therapy in Clinical Psychiatry* (Baltimore, MD: Penguin, 1970).

76. William S. Sahakian, "A social learning theory of obsessional neurosis," *Israel Annals of Psychiatry and Related Disciplines, 7* (1969), 70–75.

77. A. Kardiner, *The Traumatic Neuroses of War* (New York: Hoeber, 1941), pp. 15–20.

78. Salzman, *Obsessive Personality,* p. 47.

79. Herbert Nunberg, *Principles of Psychoanalysis* (New York: International Universities Press, 1955), p. 315.

80. Ibid., p. 316.

81. Abraham H. Maslow, "Neurosis as a failure of personal growth," in William S. Sahakian, ed., *Psychopathology Today: Experimentation, Theory and Research* (Itasca, IL: F. E. Peacock, 1970), pp. 122–130.

82. DSM-IV (Washington, DC: American Psychiatric Press, 1994), p. 424.

83. Edudex.com, *Post-Traumatic Stress Disorder* (Princeton, NJ, 1991).

84. Films for the Humanities and Sciences, *Post-Traumatic Stress Disorder* (Princeton, NJ, 2000–2001).

85. Films for the Humanities and Sciences, *The Impact of Violence on Children and Rape: The Ultimate Violation* (Princeton, NJ, 2000–2001).

86. Eugene J. Fierman, Molly Hunt, Lisa Pratt, Meredith Warshaw, Kimberly Yonkers, Lisa Peterson, et al., "Trauma and posttraumatic stress disorder in subjects with anxiety disorders," *American Journal of Psychiatry, 150* (12) (1993), 1872–1875.

87. Jon G. Allen, *Coping with Trauma: A Guide to Self-Understanding* (Washington, DC: American Psychiatric Publishing Group, 1999).

88. Earl L. Giller, Jr., ed., *Biological Assessment and Treatment of Posttraumatic Stress Disorder* (Washington, DC: American Psychiatric Press, 1990); Marion E. Wolf and Aron D. Mosniam, eds., *Posttraumatic Stress Disorder: Etiology, Phenomenology, and Treatment* (Washington, DC: American Psychiatric Press, 1990); Lawrence C. Kolb, "The psychobiology of PTSD: Perspectives and reflections on the past, present, and future," *Journal of Traumatic Stress, 6* (3) (1993), 293–304.

89. I. Boaz Milner, Bradley Axelrod, Jay Pasquantonio, and Monica Sillanpaa, "Is there a Gulf War syndrome?" *Journal of the American Medical Association,* March 2, 1994, p. 661; Alan Fontana, "War zone traumas and posttraumatic stress disorder symptomatology," *Journal of Nervous Mental Disorders, 180* (1992), 748–755; Dragica Kozaric-Kovaclc, Vera Folnegovic-Smalc, and Ana Marusic, "Psychological disturbances among 47 Croatian prisoners of war tortured in detention camps," *Journal of the American Medical Association, 270* (5) (1993), 575; Rachel Yehuda, "Exposure to atrocities and severity of chronic posttraumatic stress disorder in Vietnam combat veterans," *American Journal of Psychiatry, 149* (1992), 333–336.

90. Herbert Hendin and Ann Pollinger Haas, "Suicide and guilt as manifestations of PTSD in Vietnam combat veterans," *American Journal of Psychiatry, 148* (5) (1991), 586.

91. Derek Summerfield and F. Hume, "War and posttraumatic stress disorder: The question of social context," *Journal of Nervous and Mental Disease, 181* (8) (1993), 522.

92. Carol S. North, Elizabeth M. Smith, and Edward L. Spitznagel, "Posttraumatic stress disorder in survivors of a mass shooting," *American Journal of Psychiatry, 151* (1) (1994), 82–89.

93. David A. Wolfe, Louis Sas, and Christine Wekerle, "Factors associated with the development of posttraumatic stress disorder among child victims of sexual abuse," *Child Abuse and Neglect, 18* (1) (1994), 37–51.

94. Lester Grinspoon, ed., "Post-traumatic stress. Part II," *Harvard Mental Health Letter, 7* (9) (March 1991), 1–4.

CHAPTER 6

1. Jiri Modestin, B. Oberson, and T. Erni, "Possible correlates of DSM-III-R personality disorders," *Acta Psychiatrica Scandinavica, 96* (6) (1997), 424–430.

2. Nikola Mandic and Jelena Barkic, "Psychosocial and cultural characteristics of personality disorders," *Psychiatric Danubina, 8* (1) (1996), 29–33.

3. Mirjana Divac-Jovanovic, S. Svrakic, and L. Lecic-Toesevski, "Personality disorders: Model for conceptual approach and classification," *American Journal of Psychotherapy, 47* (4) (1993), 558.

4. Gunnar Kullgren, "Personality disorders among psychiatric inpatients," *Nordisk Psykiatrisk Tidsskrift, 46* (1) (1992), 27–32.

5. Quality Assurance Project, "Treatment outlines for paranoid, schizotypal and schizoid personality disorders," *Australian and New Zealand Journal of Psychiatry, 24* (3) (1990), 339–350.

6. American Psychiatric Association, *Diagnostic and Statistical Manual of Mental Disorders,* 3rd ed. (Washington, DC: American Psychiatric Association, 1980), p. 305.

7. Hisato Matsunaga et al., "Gender differences of obsessive-compulsive symptoms and personality disorders in patients with obsessive-compulsive disorder," *Clinical Psychiatry, 40* (8) (1998), 839–845.

8. Carlos Grilo et al., "Gender differences in personality disorders in psychiatrically hospitalized adolescents," *American Journal of Psychiatry, 153* (8) (1996), 1089–1091.

9. Janet D. Carter et al., "Gender differences in the frequency of personality disorders in depressed outpatients," *Journal of Personality Disorders, 13* (1) (1999), 67–74; Carlos Grilo et al., "Gender differences in personality disorders in psychiatrically hospitalized young adults," *Journal of Nervous and Mental Disease, 184* (12) (1996), 754–757.

10. Thomas A. Widiger, "Sex biases in the diagnosis of personality disorders," *Journal of Personality Disorders, 12* (2) (1998), 95–118.

11. Beth M. Rienzi and David J. Scrams, "Gender stereotypes for paranoid, antisocial, compulsive, dependent, and histrionic personality disorders," *Psychological Reports, 69* (3) (1991), 976–978.

12. Bruce Bower, "Piecing together personality," *Science News, 145* (1994), 152–154.

13. W. John Livesley, Kerry L. Jang, Douglas N. Jackson, and Phillip A. Vernon, "Genetic and environmental contributions to dimensions of personality disorder," *American Journal of Psychiatry, 150* (12) (1993), 1826.

14. Kerry L. Jong, John W. Livesley, and Philip A. Vernon, "A twin study of genetic and environmental contributions to gender differences in traits delineating personality disorder," *European Journal of Personality, 12* (5) (1998), 331–344; Kenneth R. Silk, ed., *Biology of Personality Disorder* (Washington, DC: American Psychiatric Publishing Group, 1998).

15. Patricia Cohen, "Childhood risks for young adult symptoms of personality disorder: Method and substance," *Multivariate Behavioral Research, 31* (1) (1996), 121–148.

16. Diana O. Perkins, Elizabeth J. Davidson, Jane Leserman, Liao Duanping, and Evans L. Dwight, "Personality disorder in patients infected with HIV: A controlled study with implications for clinical care," *American Journal of Psychiatry, 150* (2) (1993), 309.

17. Salman Akhtar, "Paranoid personality disorder: A synthesis of developmental, dynamic and descriptive features," *American Journal of Psychotherapy, 44* (1) (1990), 5–25.

18. Elizabeth L. Auchincloss and Richard W. Weiss, "Paranoid character and the intolerance of indifference," *Journal of the American Psychoanalytic Association, 40* (4) (1992), 1013–1037.

19. Ira D. Turkat, Susan P. Keane, and Sue K. Thompson-Pope, "Social processing errors among paranoid personalities," *Journal of Psychopathology and Behavioral Assessment, 12* (3) (1990), 263–269.

20. David P. Bernstein, David Useda, and Larry J. Siever, "Paranoid personality disorder: Review of the literature and recommendations," *Journal of Personality Disorders, 7* (1) (1993), 53–62.

21. Mark F. Lenzenweger and Lauren Korfine, "Identifying schizophrenia-related personality disorder features in a nonclinical population using a psychometric approach," *Journal of Personality Disorders, 6* (3) (1992), 256–266.

22. Gunvant Thaker, Helene Adami, Marianne Moran, Adrienne Lahti, and Shawn Cassady, "Psychiatric illnesses in families of subjects with personality disorders: High morbidity risks for unspecified functional psychoses and schizophrenia," *American Journal of Psychiatry, 150* (1) (1993), 66.

23. Svenn Torgensen, Sidsel Onstad, Ingunn Skre, and Jack Edvardsen, "'True' schizotypal personality disorder: A study of co-twins and relatives of schizophrenic probands," *American Journal of Psychiatry, 150* (11) (1993), 1661.

24. Alfred M. Freedman, Harold I. Kaplan, and Benjamin J. Sadock, *Modern Synopsis of Comprehensive Textbook of Psychiatry* (Baltimore, MD: Williams & Wilkins, 1985).

25. Lawrence C. Kolb, *Modern Clinical Psychiatry* (Philadelphia: Saunders, 1982).

26. David F. Hurlbert, "Voyeurism in an adult female with schizoid personality: A case report," *Journal of Sex Education and Therapy, 18* (1) (1992), 17–21.

27. Remi J. Cadoret, "Toward a definition of the schizoid state: Evidence from studies of twins and their families," *British Journal of Psychiatry, 122* (1973), 679–685.

28. Ibid., 680.

29. Ibid., 679.

30. Salman Akhtar, "Schizoid personality disorder: A synthesis of developmental, dynamic, and descriptive features," *American Journal of Psychotherapy, 41* (4) (1987), 499–518; Oren Kalus, David P. Bernstein, Larry J. Siever, "Schizoid personality disorder: A review of current status and implications," *Journal of Personality Disorders, 7* (1) (1993), 43–52; Norman Cameron, *Personality Development and Psychopathology: A Dynamic Approach* (Boston, MA: Houghton Mifflin, 1963), p. 648.

31. Antonis Kotsaftis and John M. Neale, "Schizotypal personality disorder. I. The clinical syndrome," *Clinical Psychology Review, 13* (5) (1993), 451–472; Marco Battaglia and Laura Bellodi, "Schizotypal disorder," *Hospital and Community Psychiatry, 43* (1) (1992), 82; Larry J. Siever, David P. Bernstein, and Jeremy M. Silverman, "Schizotypal personality disorder: A review of its current status," *Journal of Personality Disorders, 5* (2) (1991), 178–193.

32. Michael Ritsner, Sergei Kara, and Yigal Ginath, "Relatedness of schizotypal personality to schizophrenic disorders: Multifactorial threshold model," *Journal of Psychiatric Research, 27* (1) (1993), 27–38.

33. Rochelle Caplan and Donald Guthrie, "Communication deficits in childhood schizotypal personality disorder," *Journal of the American Academy of Child and Adolescent Psychiatry, 31* (5) (1992), 961–967.

34. Ruth Condray and Stuart Steinhauer, "Schizotypal personality disorder in individuals with and without schizophrenic relatives: Similarities and contrasts in neurocognitive and clinical functioning," *Schizophrenia Research, 7* (1) (1992), 33–41.

35. Larry J. Siever, Farooq Amijn, Emil F. Coccaro, and Robert Trestmen, "CSF homovanillic acid in schizotypal personality disorder," *American Journal of Psychiatry, 150* (1) (1993), 149–151.

36. Marco Battaglia and Laura Bellodi, "Schizotypy in partners of patients with schizotypal personality disorders," *Psychiatry Research, 41* (3) (1992), 283–285.

37. Phillip Coons, "Self-amputation of the breasts by a male with schizotypal personality disorder," *Hospital and Community Psychiatry, 43* (2) (1992), 175–176.

38. Bruce Pfohl, "Histrionic personality disorder: A review of available data and recommendations for DSM-IV," *Journal of Personality Disorders, 5* (2) (1991), 150–166.

39. Ibid.

40. Salman Akhtar, "Further exploration of gender differences in personality disorders," *American Journal of Psychiatry, 153* (6) (1996), 846–847.

41. Ruben M. Basili, "Developments in British psychoanalytic schools regarding severe narcissistic personality disorders: Our experience," *Revista de Psicoanalisis, 47* (5–6) (1990), 1087–1112; Raymond Battegay, "The narcissistic relationship to the object world," *Journal of Independent Social Work, 4* (4) (1990), 35–49.

42. Elsa Ronningstam, ed., *Disorders of Narcis-*

sism: Diagnostic, Clinical, and Empirical Implications (Washington, DC: American Psychiatric Publishing Group, 1997).

43. Paul Wink, "Three types of narcissism in women from college to mid-life," *Journal of Personality, 60* (1) (1992), 24.

44. P. J. Watson, Tracy Little, Steve M. Sawrie, and Michael D. Biderman, "Measures of the narcissistic personality: Complexity of relationships with self-esteem and empathy," *Journal of Personality Disorders, 6* (4) (1992), 434–449.

45. James J. Bourgeois, Molly J. Hall, Ray M. Crosby, and Karen G. Drexler, "An examination of narcissistic personality traits as seen in a military population," *Military Medicine, 158* (3) (1993), 170–174.

46. Anna Higgit and Peter Fonagy, "Psychotherapy in borderline and narcissistic personality disorder," *British Journal of Psychiatry, 161* (1992), 23–43.

47. Films for the Humanities and Sciences, *The Mind of a Killer: Case Study of a Murderer* (Princeton, NJ, 2000).

48. Thomas A. Widiger and Elizabeth M. Corbitt, "Antisocial personality disorder: Proposals for DSM-IV," *Journal of Personality Disorders, 7* (1) (1993), 63–77.

49. Films for the Humanities and Sciences, *Mind of the Assassin* (Princeton, NJ, 2000).

50. S. Williamson, T. J. Harpur, and R. D. Hare, "Sensitivity to emotional valence in psychopaths," paper presented at the 98th Annual Convention of the American Psychological Association, Boston, MA, 1990.

51. David Abrahamsen, *The Psychology of Crime* (New York: Columbia University Press, 1967), p. 135. High intelligence is usually characteristic of the antisocial type of criminal. Criminals with a conscience (such as those who rob out of perceived economic necessity) often have low intelligence.

52. H. Cleckley, *The Mask of Sanity* (St. Louis, MO: Mosby, 1964).

53. Films for the Humanities and Sciences, *The Psychopathic Mind* (Princeton, NJ, 2000).

54. Excerpts taken from interview with Henry Lee Lucas by Sylvia Chase, *20/20*, American Broadcasting Companies, Inc., July 5, 1984. Used with permission of American Broadcasting Companies, Inc.

55. Kathleen M. Carroll, Samuel A. Ball, and Bruce J. Rounsaville, "A comparison of alternate systems for diagnosing antisocial personality disorder in cocaine users," *Journal of Nervous and Mental Disease, 181* (7) (1993), 436–443; Robert K. Brooner, Jeffrey H. Herbst, Chester W. Schmidt, and George E. Bigelow, "Antisocial personality disorder among drug abusers: Relations to other personality diagnoses and the five-factor model of personality," *Journal of Nervous and Mental Disease, 181* (5) (1993), 313–319.

56. S. Kirson Weinberg, "Social psychological aspects of acting-out disorders and deviant behavior," in S. Kirson Weinberg, ed., *The Sociology of Mental Disorders* (Chicago, IL: Aldine, 1967), pp. 150–158.

57. Gail F. Stevens, "Applying the diagnosis antisocial personality to imprisoned offenders: Looking for hay in a haystack," *Journal of Offender Rehabilitation, 19* (1–2) (1993), 1–26.

58. Films for the Humanities and Sciences, *By Reason of Insanity* (Princeton, NJ, 2000).

59. Brian J. Jones, Bernard J. Gallagher III, John M. Kelley, and Thomas Arvanites, "The mental health makeup of a forensic population," *Sociological Practice Review, 2* (1992), 803–812.

60. Charles W. Nuckolls, "Toward a cultural history of the personality disorders," *Social Science and Medicine, 35* (1) (1992), 37.

61. Marshall B. Jones, David R. Offord, and Nola Abrams, "Brothers, sisters and antisocial behaviour," *British Journal of Psychiatry, 136* (1980), 139–145. Some report that the antisocial condition is not more common among males. See Dorothy O. Lewis, Shelley R. Shanok, and Jonathan H. Pincus, "A comparison of the neuropsychiatric status of female and male incarcerated delinquents: Some evidence of sex and race bias," *Journal of the American Academy of Child Psychiatry, 2* (1982), 190–196.

62. Carol S. North, Elizabeth M. Smith, and Edward L. Spitznagel, "Is antisocial personality disorder a valid diagnosis among the homeless?" *American Journal of Psychiatry, 150* (4) (1993), 578–583.

63. Opposing Viewpoints, "What causes crime?" (San Diego, CA: Greenhaven Press, 2001), pp. 285–305.

64. Corrine J. Rita, and Bernard J. Gallagher III, "Biological correlates of psychopathy: An overview," unpublished manuscript.

65. Remi J. Cadoret, Edward Troughton, Jeffrey Bagford, and George Woodworth, "Genetic and environmental factors in adoptee antisocial personality," *European Archives of Psychiatry and Neurological Sciences, 239* (4) (1990), 231–240.

66. Robert B. Graham, *Physiological Psychology* (Belmont, CA: Wadsworth, 1990).

67. Robyn J. Holden, Irwin S. Pakula, and Phyllis A. Mooney, "A neuroimmunological model of antisocial and borderline personality disorders," *Human Psychopharmacology: Clinical and Experimental, 12* (4) (1997), 291–308.

68. S. Williamson, T. Harpur, and R. Hare, "Abnormal processing of affective words by psychopaths," *Psychophysiology, 28* (3) (1991), 260–273.

69. Elizabeth Kandel, "Biology, violence, and antisocial personality," *Journal of Forensic Sciences, 37* (3) (1992), 912–918.

70. Christiana A. Meyers, Stephen A. Berman, S. Randall, and Anne Hayman, "Case report: Acquired antisocial personality disorder associated with unilateral left orbital front lobe damage," *Journal of Psychiatry and Neuroscience, 17* (3) (1992), 121–125.

71. R. J. Ellingson, "Incidence of EEG abnormality among patients with mental disorders of apparently nonorganic origin: A criminal review," *American Journal of Psychiatry, 3* (1954), 263–275.

72. Abrahamsen, *The Psychology of Crime*, pp. 138–139.

73. J. Lange, *Crime as Destiny* (London: George Allen, 1931).

74. H. H. Newman, F. N. Freeman, and K. J. Holzinger, *Twins: A Study of Heredity and Environment* (Chicago, IL: Chicago University Press, 1937).

75. H. Kranz, *Lebenschicksale Krimineller Zwillinge* (Berlin: Springer-Verlag, 1936).

76. Remi J. Cadoret, Colleen A. Cain, and Raymond R. Crowe, "Evidence for gene-environment interaction in the development of adolescent antisocial behavior," *Behavior Genetics, 13* (1983), 301–310.

77. J. Rimmer and Bjorn Jacobsen, "Antisocial personality in the biological relatives of schizophrenics," *Comprehensive Psychiatry, 21* (1980), 258–262.

78. D. T. Lykken, "A study of anxiety in the sociopathic personality," *Journal of Abnormal and Social Psychology, 55* (1957), 6–10.

79. S. Schachter and B. Latone, "Crime, cognition, and the autonomic nervous system," in D. Levine, ed., *Nebraska Symposium on Motivation*, Vol. 12 (Lincoln: University of Nebraska Press, 1964).

80. Kenneth Tardiff et al., "Violence by patients admitted to a private psychiatric hospital. Reply." *American Journal of Psychiatry, 154* (10) (1997), 1481.

81. J. B. Ovvis, "Visual monitoring performance in three subgroups of male delinquents," unpublished master's thesis, University of Illinois, 1967.

82. G. J. Skrzypek, "The effects of perceptual isolation and arousal on anxiety, complexity preference and novelty preference in psychopathic and neurotic delinquents," *Journal of Abnormal Psychology, 74* (1969), 321–329.

83. Herman Nunberg, *Principles of Psychoanalysis* (New York: International Universities Press, 1955), p. 309.

84. Clinton T. Duffy, "Sex as the cause of most crime," in John W. Petras, ed.. *Sex: Male/Gender: Masculine: Readings in Male Sexuality* (Port Washington, NY: Alfred Publishing, 1975), pp. 38–45.

85. S. Greu, "Study of parental loss in neurotics and sociopaths," *Archives of General Psychiatry, 11* (1964), 177–180.

86. R. G. Andry, *Delinquency and Parental Pathology* (London: Methuen, 1960).

87. Mark Zoccolillo, Andrew Pickles, David Quinton, and Michael Rutter, "The outcome of childhood conduct disorder: Implications for defining adult personality disorder and conduct disorder," *Psychological Medicine, 22* (4) (1992), 971–986.

88. Mary E. Griffin, Adelaide M. Johnson, and Edward M. Litin, "The transmission of superego defects in the family," in Norman W. Bell and Ezra F. Vogel, eds., *A Modern Introduction to the Family* (New York: Free Press, 1968), pp. 670–682.

89. Ibid., p. 675.

90. Cameron, *Personality Development and Psychopathology*, p. 654.

91. Kolb, *Modern Clinical Psychiatry*.

92. Remi J. Cadoret and Colleen A. Cain, "Sex differences in predictors of antisocial behavior in adoptees," *Archives of General Psychiatry, 37* (1980), 1171–1175.

93. Mary Schwab-Stone et al., "The effects of violence exposure on urban youth," *Journal of the American Academy of Child and*

Adolescent Psychiatry, 38 (4) (1999), 359–367.

94. Joseph Eaton and Robert J. Weil, "The mental health of the Hutterites," *Scientific American, 189* (1953), 31–37.

95. Films for the Humanities and Sciences, *Teen Killers: Can Psychotherapy Help?* (Princeton, NJ, 2000).

96. Michael J. Engle, Bernard J. Gallagher III, and Joseph A. McFalls, Jr., "Violent sex offenders: The attitudes of members of the Association for the Treatment of Sexual Abusers toward treatment, release and recidivism," (presently under review, *Journal of Interpersonal Violence*).

97. John E. Douglas, Ann W. Burgess, Allen G. Burgess, and Robert K. Ressler, *Crime Classification Manual* (New York: Lexington Books, 1992).

98. Emile Lounsberry, "No simple answers in treating pedophilia," *Philadelphia Inquirer,* June 22, 1997, p. B5.

99. Emile Lounsberry, "Therapy for sex offenders at issue," *Philadelphia Inquirer,* June 8, 1997, p. B2; Rene Denfeld, "Do most sex offenders strike again?" *Philadelphia Inquirer,* July 23, 1996.

100. Denfeld, "Do most sex offenders strike again?"

101. Ibid.

102. V. Quinsey, G. Harris, and M. Rice, "Sexual recidivism among child molesters released from a maximum security psychiatric institution," *Journal of Consulting and Clinical Psychology, 59* (3) (1991), 381–386.

103. John Douglas and Mark Olshaker, *Journal into Darkness* (New York: Scribner's, 1997), p. 177.

104. Paul Story, "Californians track sex offenders by CD-ROM," *Philadelphia Inquirer,* July 2, 1997.

105. John Gibeaut, "Defining punishment: Courts split on notification provisions of sex offender laws," *ABA Journal, 83* (March 1997), 36–37.

106. Cori A. Harbour, "Sex offender legislation and the Constitution: Striking a balance for practical, productive, and promising legislation," *Thurgood Marshall Law Review, 21* (1996), 99–123.

107. John Gibeaut, "Defining punishment: Courts split on notification provisions of sex offender laws," *ABA Journal, 83* (March 1997), 36–37.

108. Aaron Epstein, "Justices say states can keep sexual predators locked up," *Philadelphia Inquirer,* June 24, 1997.

109. Ibid.

110. Stephen J. Schulhofer, "Two systems of social protection: Comments on the civil-criminal distinction, with particular reference to sexually violent predator laws," *Journal of Contemporary Legal Issues, 7* (1996), 69–96.

111. Ibid.

112. Ibid.

113. Stephen J. Schulhofer, "Two systems of social protection: Comments on the civil-criminal distinction, with particular reference to sexually violent predator laws," *Journal of Contemporary Legal Issues, 7* (1996), 69–96.

114. Lounsberry, "No simple answers in treating pedophilia."

115. Richard D. Hare, "Psychopathos: New trends in research," *Harvard Mental Health Letter, 12* (3) (1995), 4–6.

116. Richard D. Hare, *Without Conscience: The Disturbing World of the Psychopaths Among Us* (New York: Simon & Schuster, 1993).

117. Barbara K. Schwartz and Henry R. Cellini, eds., *The Sex Offender: Corrections Treatment and Legal Practice* (Kingston, NJ: Civic Research Institute, 1995); Barbara K. Schwartz and Henry R. Cellini, eds., *The Sex Offender: New Insights, Treatment Innovations and Legal Developments* (Kingston, NJ: Civic Research Institute, 1997).

118. Mary C. Zanarini et al., "Axis II comorbidity of borderline personality disorder," *Comprehensive Psychiatry, 39* (5) (1998), 296–302.

119. Leonard Horwitz et al., *Borderline Personality Disorder: Tailoring the Psychotherapy to the Patient* (Washington, DC: American Psychiatric Publishing Group, 1996).

120. Laura Baker, Kenneth Silk, Drew Western, Joel T. Nigg, and Naomi Lohr, "Malevolence, splitting, and parental ratings by borderlines," *Journal of Nervous and Mental Disease, 180* (4) (1992), 258–264.

121. Mark J. Russ, "Self-injurious behavior in patients with borderline personality disorder: Biological perspectives," *Journal of Personality Disorders, 6* (1992), 64–81.

122. Debra Simmons, "Gender issues and borderline personality disorder: Why do females dominate the diagnosis?" *Archives of Psychiatric Nursing, 6* (1992), 219–223.

123. Dana Becker, *Through the Looking Glass:*

Women and Borderline Personality Disorder (Boulder, CO: Westview Press, 1997).

124. Terri L. Weaver and George A. Clum, "Early family environments and traumatic experiences associated with borderline personality disorder," *Journal of Consulting and Clinical Psychology, 61* (6) (1993), 1068.

125. James Karagianis, "Borderline personality disorder in incest victims," *American Journal of Psychiatry, 149* (9) (1992), 1278.

126. Mary C. Zanarini, ed., *Role of Sexual Abuse in Etiology of Borderline Personality Disorders* (Washington, DC: American Psychiatric Publishing Group, 1996).

127. John G. Gunderson and Alex N. Sabo, "The phenomenological and conceptual interface between borderline personality disorder and PTSD," *American Journal of Psychiatry, 150* (1) (1993), 19–27.

128. R. Van Reekum, "Acquired and developmental brain dysfunction in borderline personality disorder," *Canadian Journal of Psychiatry, 38* (1993), 4–10.

129. Kenneth R. Silk, *Biology of Personality Disorders* (Washington, DC: American Psychiatric Publishing Group, 1998).

130. David Lester, "Borderline personality disorder and suicidal behavior," *Psychological Reports, 73* (2) (1993), 394.

131. Werner Koepp, Sebastian Schildbach, Carola Schmager, and Robert Rohner, "Borderline diagnosis and substance abuse in female patients with eating disorders," *International Journal of Eating Disorders, 14* (1) (1993), 107–110.

132. Royal Grueneich, "The borderline personality disorder diagnosis: Reliability, diagnostic efficiency, and covariation with other personality disorder diagnoses," *Journal of Personality Disorders, 6* (3) (1992), 197–212.

133. John Lauer, Donald W. Black, and Pat Keen, "Multiple personality disorder: Distinct variations on a common theme?" *Annals of Clinical Psychiatry, 5* (2) (1993), 129–134; Jeremy W. Coid, "An affective syndrome in psychopaths with borderline personality disorder?" *British Journal of Psychiatry, 162* (1993), 641–650.

134. Joel Paris, "The treatment of borderline personality disorder in light of the research on its long-term outcome," *Canadian Journal of Psychiatry, 38* (1993), 28–34.

135. James D. Herbert, Debra A. Hope, and Alan S. Bellack, "Validity of the distinction between generalized social phobia and avoidant personality disorder," *Journal of Abnormal Psychology, 101* (2) (1992), 332–339.

136. Theodore Millon, "Avoidant personality disorder: A brief review of issues and data," *Journal of Personality Disorders, 5* (4) (1991), 353–362.

137. James Reich, "Avoidant and dependent personality traits in relatives of patients with panic disorder, patients with dependent personality disorder, and normal controls," *Psychiatry Research, 39* (1) (1991), 89–98.

138. James Reich, "Using the family history method to distinguish relatives of patients with dependent personality disorder from relatives of controls," *Psychiatry Research, 39* (3) (1991), 227–237.

139. Armand W. Loranger, "Dependent personality disorder: Age, sex, and Axis I comorbidity," *Journal of Nervous and Mental Disease, 184* (1) (1996), 17–21.

140. I. Rubino, Sonnino Alberto Alex, and Giovanna Tonini, "Perceptual strategies of isolation in obsessive-compulsive personality disorder," *Perceptual and Motor Skills, 74* (3) (1992), 979–992.

141. Merrill T. Eaton, Jr., and Margaret H. Peterson, *Psychiatry* (New York: Medical Examination Publishing Co., 1969), p. 128.

142. Joseph T. McCann, "A comparison of two measures for obsessive-compulsive personality disorder," *Journal of Personality Disorders, 6* (1) (1992), 18–23.

143. Bruce Pfohl and Nancee S. Blum, "Obsessive-compulsive personality disorder: A review of available data and recommendations for DSM-IV," *Journal of Personality Disorders, 5* (4) (1991), 363–375.

144. Marolyn C. Wells, Cheryl Glickauf-Hughes, and Virginia Buzzell, "Treating obsessive-compulsive personalities in psychodynamic/interpersonal group therapy," *Psychotherapy, 27* (3) (1990), 366–379.

145. Vladan Sarcevic, "Relationship between hypochondriasis and obsessive-compulsive personality disorder. Close relatives separated by nosological schemes?" *American Journal of Psychotherapy, 44* (3) (1990), 340–347.

CHAPTER 7

1. Carol S. Aneshensel and Jo C. Phelan, eds., *Handbook of the Sociology of Mental Health* (New York: Kluwer Academic/Plenum, 1999), p. xii.
2. Assen Jablensky, "Psychiatric epidemiology and the global public health agenda," *International Journal of Public Health, 28* (12) (1999), 6–14.
3. Richard Schweder, *"Thinking Through Cultures: An Expedition in Cultural Psychology* (Cambridge, MA: Harvard University Press, 1991); Suman Fernando, *Mental Health, Race and Culture* (New York: St. Martin's, 1991).
4. Brian Cooper, "Sociology in the context of social psychiatry," *British Journal of Psychiatry, 161* (1992), 594–598.
5. Richard E. Vatz and Lee S. Weinberg, "Is mental illness a myth?" *USA Today Magazine,* August 19, 1993, p. 62.
6. Jerzy Krupinski, "Social psychiatry and sociology of mental health: A view on their past and future relevance," *Australian and New Zealand Journal of Psychiatry, 26* (1) (1992), 91–97; Terry M. Killian and Lynn T. Killian, "Sociological investigations of mental illness: A review," *Hospital and Community Psychiatry, 41* (8) (1990), 902–911.
7. Ronald C. Kessler and Shanyang Zhao, "Overview of descriptive epidemiology of mental disorders," in Aneshensel and Phelan, *Handbook of the Sociology of Mental Health,* p. 127.
8. Melissa J. Perry, "The relationship between social class and mental disorder," *Journal of Primary Prevention, 17* (1) (1996), 17–30.
9. Dana Crowley Jack, *Silencing the Self: Women and Depression* (New York: HarperCollins, 1991).
10. Bruce P. Dohrenwend, Itzak Levav, and Patrick E. Shrout, "Socioeconomic status and psychiatric disorders: The causation-selection issue," *Science, 255* (1992), 946–952.
11. L. N. Robins, "Psychiatric epidemiology: A historic review," *Social Psychiatry and Psychiatric Epidemiology, 25* (1990), 16–26; B. Cooper, "Epidemiology and prevention in the mental health field," *Social Psychiatry and Psychiatric Epidemiology, 25* (1990), 9–15.
12. For a review of this problem, see H. Davidian, "Practical problems in psychiatric field surveys," *Acta Psychiatrica Scandinavica, 65* (1982), 87–93.
13. Graham Thornicroft, "Social deprivation and rates of treated mental disorder: Developing statistical models to predict psychiatric service utilization," *British Journal of Psychiatry, 158* (1991), 475–484.
14. See, for example, E. M. Brooke, "International statistics," in J. K. Wing and H. Hafner, eds., *Roots of Evaluation: The Epidemiological Basis for Planning Psychiatric Services* (London: Oxford University Press, 1973); R. Fink et al., "The 'filter-down' process to psychotherapy in a group medical care program," *American Journal of Public Health, 59* (1969), 245–257; B. Kaplan, R. B. Reed, and W. Richardson, "A comparison of the incidence of hospitalized and nonhospitalized cases of psychosis in two communities," *American Sociological Review, 21* (1956), 472–479; M. Kramer, "Statistics of mental disorders in the United States: Current status, some urgent needs and suggested solutions," *Journal of the Royal Statistical Society, 132* (1969), 353–407.
15. Peter Skrabanek, "The poverty of epidemiology," *Perspectives in Biology and Medicine, 35* (2) (1992), 182.
16. Bruce P. Dohrenwend and Barbara Snell Dohrenwend, "Social and cultural influences on psychopathology," *Annual Review of Psychology, 25* (1974), 423.
17. Leo Srole et al., *Mental Health in the Metropolis* (New York: McGraw-Hill, 1962).
18. D. C. Leighton et al., *The Character of Danger* (New York: Basic Books, 1963).
19. T. S. Langner and S. T. Michael, *Stress and Mental Health* (New York: Free Press, 1963), p. 76.
20. Scott B. Patten, "The specificity of epidemiological correlates of major depression," *Comprehensive Psychiatry, 41* (2) (2000), 92–96.
21. Juan E. Mezzick, "Epidemiological perspectives on the health of New York City," *International Journal of Mental Health, 28* (4), 41–47.
22. Lee N. Robins and Darrel A. Regier, eds., *Psychiatric Disorders in America: The Epidemiologic Catchment Area Study* (New York: Free Press, 1991).
23. Karen H. Bourden, Donald S. Rae, Ben Z.

Locke, William Narrow, and Darrel A. Regier, "Estimating the prevalence of mental disorders in U.S. adults from the Epidemiologic Catchment Survey," *Public Health Reports, 107* (6) (1992), 663.

24. Bruce P. Dohrenwend, "Sociocultural and social-psychological factors in the genesis of mental disorders," *Journal of Health and Social Behavior, 16* (1975), 368.

25. Bruce P. Dohrenwend, "The problem of validity in field studies of psychological disorders," *Psychological Medicine, 20* (1) (1990); Jeffrey D. Blum, "On changes in psychiatric diagnosis over time," *American Psychologist, 33* (1978), 1017–1031.

26. Ronald C. Kessler, Katherine A. McGonagle, Shanyang Zhao, Christopher B. Nelson, Michael Hughes, and Suzann Eshleman, "Lifetime and 12-month prevalence of DSM-III-R psychiatric disorders in the United States," *Archives of General Psychiatry, 51* (1994), 8–18.

27. World Health Organization, "Cross-national comparisons of the prevalences and correlates of mental disorders," *Bulletin of the World Health Organization, 78* (4) (2000), 413–445.

28. Ajita Chakraborty, "Culture, colonialism, and psychiatry," *Lancet, 337* (8751) (1991), 1204.

29. Arthur Kleinman, *Rethinking Psychiatry* (New York: Free Press, 1988); S. Kirson Weinburg, *Society and Personality Disorders* (Englewood Cliffs, NJ: Prentice Hall, 1952).

30. Myrna M. Weissman et al., "Epidemiologic strategies to address world mental health problems in underserved populations," *International Journal of Mental Health, 28* (2) (1999), 15–37.

31. H. Lin and T. Lin, "Mental illness among Formosan aborigines as compared with the Chinese in Taiwan," *Journal of Mental Science, 108* (1962), 134–146.

32. M. A. Kidson, "Psychiatric disorders in the Walbiri of Central Australia," *Australia and New Zealand Journal of Psychiatry, 1* (1967), 14–22; M. A. Kidson and I. H. Jones, "Psychiatric disorders among aborigines of the Australian Western Desert," *Archives of General Psychiatry, 19* (1968), 413–417.

33. J. H. Shore et al., "Psychiatric epidemiology of an Indian village," *Psychiatry, 36* (1973), 70–81.

34. The reader is reminded of Lynn's finding that anxiety levels vary between industrial societies. The countries with the greatest preoccupation with industrial growth, such as Germany and Japan, have the most anxious populations. See R. Lynn, *Personality and National Character* (Oxford: Pergamon Press, 1971), pp. 94–95; Soloman Tafari, Frances E. Aboud, and Charles P. Larson, "Determinants of mental illness in a rural Ethiopian adult population," *Social Science and Medicine, 32* (2) (1991), 197.

35. Lynn, *Personality and National Character,* pp. 91–92.

CHAPTER 8

1. William W. Eaton and Carles Muntaner, "Social stratification and mental disorder," in Allen V. Horwitz and Teresa L. Scheid, eds., *A Handbook for the Study of Mental Health: Social Contexts, Theories and Systems* (Cambridge: Cambridge University Press, 1999), p. 283.

2. R. Collins, *Four Sociological Traditions* (New York: Oxford University Press, 1994); J. E. Farley, *Sociology,* 3rd ed. (Englewood Cliffs, NJ: Prentice-Hall, 1994).

3. Brian J. Jones, Bernard J. Gallagher III, and Joseph A. McFalls, Jr., *Sociology: Micro, Macro, and Mega Structures* (Fort Worth, TX: Harcourt Brace, 1995).

4. G. A. Kaplan and J. W. Lynch, "Editorial: Whither studies on the socioeconomic foundations of public health?" *American Journal of Public Health, 87* (1997), 1409–1415; N. Krieger, D. R. Williams, and N. M. Moss, "Measuring social class in U.S. public health research: Concepts, methodologies, and guidelines," *Annual Review of Public Health, 18* (1997), 341–378.

5. Jane M. Murphy, Donald C. Olivier, Richard R. Monson, and Arthur M. Sobol, "Depression and anxiety in relation to social status: A prospective epidemiologic study," *Archives of General Psychiatry, 48* (3) (1991), 223–229; Norman M. Bradburn and David Caplovitz, *Reports on Happiness* (Chicago: Aldine, 1965).

6. Yan Yu and David R. Williams, "Socioeconomic status and mental health," in Carol S. Aneshensel and Jo C. Phelan, eds., *Handbook of the Sociology of Mental Health* (New York: Kluwer Academic/Plenum, 1999), pp. 151–166.

7. Hugh Drummond, "Power, madness and

poverty," *Behavioral Disorders: Journal of the Council for Children with Behavioral Disorders,* 7 (2) (1982), 101–109.

8. Melvin L. Kohn, *Class and Conformity: A Study in Values* (Homewood, IL: Dorsey, 1969), p. 189.

9. Chris Power, "Social and economic background and class inequalities in health among young adults," *Social Science and Medicine,* 32 (4) (1991), 411.

10. M. Granovetter, *Getting a Job: A Study of Contacts and Careers* (Chicago: University of Chicago Press, 1995).

11. Scott Weich and Glyn Lewis, "Poverty, unemployment, and common mental disorder: Population based cohort study," *British Medical Journal,* 317 (7151) (1998), 115–119.

12. Bernard Schissel, "Coping with adversity: Testing the origins of resiliency in mental health," *International Journal of Social Psychiatry,* 39 (1) (1993), 34.

13. Robert Blauner, *Alienation and Freedom: The Factory Worker and His Industry* (Chicago: University of Chicago Press, 1964).

14. A. Kornhauser, *Mental Health of the Industrial Worker* (New York: Wiley, 1965).

15. Charles M. McCaghy and James K. Skipper, Jr., "Lesbian behavior as an adaptation to the art of stripping," *Social Problems,* 17 (1969), 262–270.

16. P. D. Sorlie, E. Backlund, and J. B. Keller, "U.S. mortality by economic, demographic and social characteristics: The national longitudinal mortality study," *American Journal of Public Health,* 85 (1995), 903–905.

17. This has been confirmed by a number of studies. See, for example, J. Agustin-Ozamiz and J. Duffy, "Age, sex, marital status, and social class in affective disorders treated in the Basque region: A case register study," *Psiquis Revista de Psiquiatria, Psicologia y Psicosomatica,* 13 (2) (1992), 45–50; Richard L. Meile, David Richard Johnson, and Louis St. Peter, "Marital role, education, and mental disorder among women: A test of an interaction hypothesis," *Journal of Health and Social Behavior,* 17 (1976), 295–301.

18. Melissa J. Perry, "The relationship between social class and mental disorder," *Journal of Primary Prevention,* 17 (1) (1996), 17–30.

19. Ibid., p. 19.

20. Derek L. Phillips and Kevin J. Clancy, "Response biases in field studies of mental illness," *American Sociological Review,* 35 (1970), 503–514.

21. R. W. Hyde and L. V. Kingsley, "Studies in medical sociology: The relation of mental disorder to the community socioeconomic level," *New England Journal of Medicine,* 231 (1944), 543–548.

22. Timothy P. Johnson, "Mental health, social relations, and social selection: A longitudinal analysis," *Journal of Health and Social Behavior,* 32 (4) (1991), 408; Leo Srole et al., *Mental Health in the Metropolis: The Midtown Manhattan Study* (New York: McGraw-Hill, 1962).

23. Bruce P. Dohrenwend and Barbara Snell Dohrenwend, "Social and cultural influences on psychopathology," *Annual Review of Psychology,* 25 (1974), 417–452.

24. H. A. Katchadourian and C. W. Churchill, "Components in prevalence of mental illness and social class in urban Lebanon," *Social Psychiatry,* 8 (1973), 145–151.

25. B. B. Sethi and R. Manchandoa, "Social factors and mental illness: An analysis of first admissions to a psychiatric hospital," *International Journal of Social Psychiatry,* 26 (1980), 200–207.

26. Jan Haldin, "Prevalence of mental disorder in an urban population in central Sweden in relation to social class, marital status and immigration," *Acta Psychiatrica Scandinavica,* 71 (1985), 117–127.

27. R. Neugebauer, B. P. Dohrenwend, and B. S. Dohrenwend, "Formulation of hypotheses about the true prevalence of functional psychiatric disorders among adults in the United States," in B. P. Dohrenwend, ed., *Mental Illness in the United States* (New York: Praeger, 1980), pp. 45–94.

28. Carles Muntaner et al., "Social class, assets, organizational control and the prevalence of common groups of psychiatric disorders," *Social Science and Medicine,* 47 (12) (1998), 2043–2053.

29. Eaton and Muntaner, "Socioeconomic stratification and mental disorder."

30. Mary Clare Lennon, "Work and unemployment as stressors," in Horwitz and Scheid, eds., *A Handbook for the Study of Mental Health,* pp. 284–294.

31. D. R. Williams, D. Takeuchi, and R. Adair,

"Socioeconomic status and psychiatric disorder among blacks and whites," *Social Forces, 71* (1992), 179–194.

32. Gyles R. Glover, Morven Leese, and Paul McCrane, "More severe mental illness is more concentrated in deprived areas," *British Journal of Psychiatry, 175* (1999), 544–548.

33. Juan E. Mezzick, "Epidemiological perspectives on the health of New York City," *International Journal of Mental Health, 28* (1999), 41–47.

34. Ann Vander Stoep and Bruce Link, "Social class, ethnicity, and mental illness: The importance of being more than earnest," *American Journal of Public Health, 88* (9) (1998), 1396–1402.

35. Eaton and Muntaner, "Socioeconomic stratification and mental disorder."

36. Daniel W. Phillips III, *Mental Illness, Social Status and Health Care Utilization: A Test of Societal Reaction Theory,* Ph.D. dissertation, Virginia Polytechnic Institute and State University, 1996.

37. Orville R. Gursslin, Raymond G. Hunt, and Jack L. Roach, "Social class and the mental health movement," *Social Problems, 7* (1960), 210–218.

38. Gregg S. Wilkinson, "Patient-audience social status and the social construction of psychiatric disorders: Toward a differential frame hypothesis," *Journal of Health and Social Behavior, 16* (1975), 28–38.

39. Carol S. Aneshensel and Carolyn M. Rutter, "Social structure, stress and mental health: Competing conceptual and analytic models," *American Sociological Review,* 56 (1991), 166–178.

40. Films for the Humanities and Sciences, *Children of Poverty* (Princeton, NJ, 2000).

41. Ramsay Liem and Joan Liem, "Social class and mental illness reconsidered: The role of economic stress and social support," *Journal of Health and Social Behavior, 19* (1978), 139–156.

42. For a review of studies in this area, see Blair Wheaton, "The sociogenesis of psychological disorder: Reexamining the causal issues with longitudinal data," *American Sociological Review, 43* (1978), 383–403.

43. Bruce P. Dohrenwend, Itzak Levav, Patrick E. Shrout, and Bruce G. Link, "Life stress and psychopathology: Progress on research begun with Barbara Snell Dohrenwend," *American Journal of Community Psychology, 15* (6) (1987), 677–715; Bruce P. Dohrenwend and Barbara Snell Dohrenwend, *Social Status and Psychological Disorder: A Causal Inquiry* (New York: Wiley-Interscience, 1969), pp. 71–72.

44. R. C. Kessler, J. S. House, R. Anspach, and D. R. Williams, "Social psychology and mental health," in K. S. Cook, G. A. Fine, and J. S. House, eds., *Sociological Perspectives on Social Psychology* (Boston: Allyn & Bacon, 1995), pp. 548–570.

45. Peter B. Jones, Paul Bebbington, Alice Foerster, and Lewis W. Shon, "Premorbid social underachievement in schizophrenia: Results from the Camberwell Collaborative Psychosis Study," *British Journal of Psychiatry, 162* (1993), 65–71; Melvin L. Kohn, "Social class and schizophrenia: A critical review and a reformulation," *Schizophrenia Bulletin, 7* (1973), 60–79.

46. Bruce G. Link, Bruce P. Dohrenwend, and Andrew E. Skodol, "Socio-economic status and schizophrenia: Noisome occupational characteristics as a risk factor," *American Sociological Review, 51* (2) (1986), 242–252; David Mechanic, "Social class and schizophrenia: Some requirements for a plausible theory of social influence," *Social Forces, 50* (1972), 305–309.

47. R. C. Kessler, C. L. Foster, W. B. Saunders, and P. E. Stang, "Social consequences of psychiatric disorders. I. Educational attainment," *American Journal of Psychiatry, 152* (1995), 1026–1032.

48. Kessler et al., "Social psychology and mental health."

49. H. Warren Dunham, *Community and Schizophrenia: An Epidemiological Analysis* (Detroit, MI: Wayne State University Press, 1965).

50. See, for example, J. Britchnell, "Social class, parental social class, and social mobility in psychiatric patients and general population controls," *Psychological Medicine, 1* (1971), 209–221; E. M. Goldberg and S. L. Morrison, "Schizophrenia and social class," *British Journal of Psychiatry, 109* (1963), 758–802; Lee N. Robins, *Deviant Children Grown Up: A Sociological and Psychiatric Study of Sociopathic Personality* (Baltimore, MD: Williams & Wilkins, 1966); R. J. Turner and M. O. Wagenfeld, "Occupational mobility and schizophrenia: An assessment of the social causation

and selection hypothesis," *American Sociological Review, 32* (1967), 104–113.

51. E. H. Hare, J. S. Price, and E. Slater, "Parental social class in psychiatric patients," *British Journal of Psychiatry, 121* (1972), 515–524.

52. D. Wiersma et al., "Social class and schizophrenia in a Dutch cohort," *Psychological Medicine, 13* (1983), 141–150.

53. John Harkey, David L. Miles, and William A. Rushing, "The relation between social class and functional status: A new look at the drift hypothesis," *Journal of Health and Social Behavior, 17* (1976), 194–204.

54. George Antunes et al., "Ethnicity, socioeconomic status, and the etiology of psychological distress," *Sociology and Social Research: An International Journal, 58* (1974), 361–368.

55. Bruce P. Dohrenwend, Itzak Levav, Patrick E. Shrout, and Sharon Shwartz, "Socioeconomic status and psychiatric disorders: The causation-selection issue," *Science, 255* (5047) (1992), 946–952; Duncan Timms, "Gender, social mobility and psychiatric diagnoses," *Social Science and Medicine, 46* (9) (1998), 1235–1247; Jeffrey G. Johnson et al., "A longitudinal investigation of social causation and social selection processes involved in the association between socioeconomic status and psychiatric disorders," *Journal of Abnormal Psychology, 108* (3) (1999), 490–499; John W. Fox, "Social class, mental illness, and social mobility: The social selection-drift hypothesis for serious mental illness," *Journal of Health and Social Behavior, 31* (4) (1990), 344–353.

56. Jerome K. Myers and Leslie Schaffer, "Social stratification and psychiatric practice: A study of an outpatient clinic," *American Sociological Review, 21* (1954), 307–310.

57. B. Kaplan et al., "A comparison of the incidence of hospitalized and nonhospitalized cases of psychosis in two communities," *American Sociological Review, 21* (1956), 472–479.

58. B. Pasamanick et al., "A survey of mental disease in an urban population: Prevalence by race and income," in B. Pasamanick, ed., *Epidemiology of Mental Disorder* (Washington, DC: American Association for the Advancement of Science, 1959), pp. 183–201.

59. J. N. Morris, "Health and social class," *Lancet, 1* (1959), 303–305.

60. Katchadourian and Churchill, "Components in prevalence of mental illness and social class in urban Lebanon."

61. J. A. Clausen and M. L. Kohn, "Social relations and schizophrenia: A research report and a perspective," in Don D. Jackson, ed., *The Epidemiology of Schizophrenia* (New York: Basic Books, 1960), pp. 295–320.

62. S. Parker et al., "Social status and psychopathology," paper presented at the annual meeting of the Society of Physical Anthropology, Philadelphia, 1962.

63. Hope Landrine, "The social class-schizophrenia relationship: A different approach and new hypotheses," *Journal of Social and Clinical Psychology, 8* (3) (1989), 288–303, J. F. J. Cade, "The aetiology of schizophrenia," *Medical Journal of Australia, 2* (1956), 135–139.

64. E. Kevin Kelloway and Julian Barling, "Job characteristics, role stress and mental health," *Journal of Occupational Psychology, 64* (4) (1991), 291; Ornub Odegaard, "The incidence of psychosis in various occupations," *International Journal of Social Psychiatry, 2* (1956), 85–104.

65. Tsung-yi Lin, "A study of the incidence of mental disorder in Chinese and other cultures," *Psychiatry, 16* (1953), 313–336.

66. William M. Fuson, "Research note: Occupations of functional psychotics," *American Journal of Sociology, 48* (1943), 612–613.

67. Li-yu Song, David E. Biegel, and Sharon E. Milligan, "Predictors of depressive symptomatology among lower social class caregivers of persons with chronic mental illness," *Community Mental Health Journal, 33* (4) (1997), 269–286.

68. Ann B. Goodman, Carole Siegel, Thomas J. Craig, and Shang P. Lin, "The relationship between socioeconomic class and prevalence of schizophrenia, alcoholism and affective disorders treated by inpatient care in a suburban area," *American Journal of Psychiatry, 140* (1983), 166–170.

69. Melvin L. Kohn, "The interaction of social class and other factors in the etiology of schizophrenia," *American Journal of Psychiatry, 133* (1976), 177–180.

70. John W. Fox, "Social class, mental illness, and social mobility: The social selection-drift hypothesis for serious mental illness,"

Journal of Health and Social Behavior, 31 (4) (1990), 344–353; Leo Levy and Louis Rowitz, *The Ecology of Mental Disorder* (New York: Behavioral Publications, 1973), p. 148.

71. Bruce P. Dohrenwend, "Socioeconomic status and psychiatric disorders: Are the issues still compelling?" *Social Psychiatry and Psychiatric Epidemiology, 25* (1) (1990), 41–47.

72. Sigmund Freud, "The loss of reality in neurosis and psychosis," in Leslie Y. Rabkin and John E. Carr, eds., *Sourcebook in Abnormal Psychology* (Boston: Houghton Mifflin, 1967), p. 192.

73. C. Power and O. Manor, "Explaining social class differences in psychological health among young adults: A longitudinal perspective," *Social Psychiatry and Psychiatric Epidemiology, 27* (6) (1992), 284–291; H. A. Jansen, "The nuclear family as a mediator between class and mental disturbance in children," *Journal of Comparative Family Studies, 13* (1982), 155–170.

74. M. Gisermann et al., "Perceived parental rearing practices in depressed patients in relation to social class," *Acta Psychiatric Scandinavica, 70* (1984), 568–572.

75. John J. Schwab et al., "Current concepts of depression: The sociocultural," *International Journal of Social Psychiatry, 14* (1968), 230.

76. Marvin Karno, "The enigma of ethnicity in a psychiatric clinic," *Archives of General Psychiatry, 14* (1966), 516–520.

77. Judith Richman, "Social class and mental illness revisited: Sociological perspectives on the diffusion of psychoanalysis," *Journal of Operational Psychiatry, 16* (1985), 1–8.

78. David W. Rowden et al., "Judgments about candidates for psychotherapy: The influence of social class and insight-verbal ability," *Journal of Health and Social Behavior, 11* (1970), 51–58.

79. Denise Bystryn Kandel, "Status homophily, social context, and participation in psychotherapy," *American Journal of Sociology, 71* (1966), 640–650.

80. Rowden et al., "Judgments about candidates for psychotherapy," p. 56.

81. John H. Marx and S. Lee Spray, "Psychotherapeutic 'birds of a feather': Social class status and religiocultural value homophily in the mental health field,"

Journal of Mental Health and Social Behavior, 13 (1972), 413–418.

82. Sukdeb Mukherjee et al., "Misdiagnosis of schizophrenia in bipolar patients: A multiethnic comparison," *American Journal of Psychiatry, 140* (1983), 1571–1574.

83. Marx and Spray, "Psychotherapeutic 'birds of a feather.'"

84. Ibid.

85. Maxine Springer Stein, "Social class and psychiatric treatment of adults in the mental health center," *Journal of Health and Social Behavior, 18* (1977), 317–325.

86. Roberta Satow and Judith Lorber, "Cultural congruity and the use of paraprofessionals in community mental health work," paper presented at the annual meeting of the Society for the Study of Social Problems, San Francisco, 1978; Peter L. Heller, Gustavo M. Quesada, and H. Paul Chalfant, "Class, perceptions of 'disordered' behavior, and suggestions for therapy: A tri-cultural comparison," *Sociology of Health and Illness, 5* (1983), 196–207.

87. S. A. Stansfeld and M. G. Marmot, "Social class and minor psychiatric disorder in British civil servants: A validated screening survey using the General Health Questionnaire," *Psychological Medicine, 22* (3) (1992), 739–749; Myrna M. Weissman, Effie Geanakoplos, and Brigitte Prusoff, "Social class and attrition in depressed patients," *Social Casework, 54* (1973), 162–170.

88. Judith Richman, "Social class and mental illness revisited: Sociological perspectives on the diffusion of psychoanalysis," paper presented at the annual meeting of the Society for the Study of Social Problems, New York, 1982.

89. See Gary I. Schulman and Joseph Hammer, "Social characteristics, the diagnosis of mental disorders, and the change from DSM II to DSM III," *Sociology of Health and Illness, 10* (4) (1988), 543–560; Julius A. Roth, "Some contingencies of the moral evaluation and control of clientele: The case of the hospital emergency service," *American Journal of Sociology, 77* (1972), 839–856.

90. Fox, "Social class, mental illness, and social mobility."

91. Bryan Rodgers and Susan L. Mann, "Rethinking the analysis of intergenerational social mobility: A comment on John

W. Fox's 'Social class, mental illness and social mobility,'" *Journal of Health and Social Behavior, 34* (2) (1993); P. M. Blau, "Social mobility and interpersonal relations," *American Sociological Review, 21* (1956), 290–295; J. Greenbaum and L. I. Pearlin, "Vertical mobility and prejudice: A social psychological analysis," in R. Bendix and S. M. Lipset, eds., *Class, Status and Power: A Reader in Social Stratification* (Glencoe, IL: Free Press, 1953), pp. 480–491.

92. John Clausen and Melvin Kohn, "Relation of schizophrenia to the social structure of a small city," in Pasamanick, ed., *Epidemiology of Mental Disorder,* pp. 69–86; D. L. Gerald and L. Houston, "Family setting and the social ecology of schizophrenia," *Psychiatric Quarterly, 27* (1953), 90–101; August B. Hollingshead and Frederick C. Redlich, *Social Class and Mental Illness* (New York: Wiley, 1958); R. M. Lapouse, M. A. Monk, and M. Terris, "The drift hypothesis in socio-economic differentials in schizophrenia," *American Journal of Public Health, 48* (1956), 978–986.

93. John W. Fox, "Social class, mental illness and social mobility."

94. Karen Horney, *The Neurotic Personality of Our Time* (New York: Norton, 1937), pp. 80–82, 178–179.

95. Evelyn Ellis, "Social psychological correlates of upward social mobility among unmarried career women," *American Sociological Review, 17* (1952), 558–563.

96. R. J. Turner, "Social mobility and schizophrenia," *Journal of Health and Social Behavior, 9* (1968), 194–203.

97. See, for example, Dunham, *Community and Schizophrenia*; Goldberg and Morrison, "Schizophrenia and social class"; M. Lystad, "Social mobility among schizophrenic patients," *American Sociological Review, 21* (1957), 228–292; Turner, "Social mobility and schizophrenia."

98. B. G. Link, B. P. Dohrenwend, and A. E. Skodol, "Socioeconomic status and schizophrenia: Noisome occupational characteristics as a risk factor," *American Sociological Review, 51* (1986), 242–258.

99. Christopher G. Hudson, "The social class and mental illness correlation: Implications of the research for policy and practice," *Journal of Sociology and Social Welfare, 15* (1) (1988), 27–54; Robert J. Kleiner and Seymour Parker, "Social mobility,

anomie, and mental disorder," in Stanley C. Plog and Robert B. Edgerton, eds., *Changing Perspectives in Mental Illness* (New York: Holt, Rinehart & Winston, 1969), pp. 463–464.

100. Walter T. Martin, "Status integration, social stress, and mental illness: Accounting for marital status variations in mental hospitalization rates," *Journal of Health and Social Behavior, 17* (1976), 280–294.

101. See, for example, H. W. Dunham. P. Phillips, and B. Scinivason, "A research note on diagnosed mental illness and social class," *American Sociological Review, 31* (1966), 223–227; Goldberg and Morrison, "Schizophrenia and social class"; A. B. Hollingshead, R. Ellis, and E. Kirby, "Social mobility and mental illness," *American Sociological Review, 19* (1954), 577–584; Seymour Parker, R. J. Kleiner, and H. G. Taylor, "Level of aspiration and mental disorder: A research proposal," *Annals of the New York Academy of Sciences, 84* (1960), 878–886; J. Tuckman and R. J. Kleiner, "Discrepancy between aspiration and achievement as a predictor of schizophrenia," *Behavioral Science, 7* (1962), 443–447.

102. D. Stanley Eitzen and Jeffrey H. Bair, "Type of status inconsistency and schizophrenia," *Sociological Quarterly, 13* (1972), 61–73.

103. Bryan Rodgers and Susan L. Mann, "Rethinking the analysis of intergenerational social mobility: A comment on John W. Fox's 'social class, mental illness, and social mobility',' *Journal of Health and Social Behavior, 34* (1993), 165–172.

104. Ronald C. Kessler et al., "The U.S. national comorbidity survey: Overview and future directions," *Epidemiology of Social Psychiatry, 6* (1997), 4–16.

CHAPTER 9

1. Adalberto Aguire, Jr. and David V. Baker, *Structured Inequality in the United States: Discussions on the Continuing Significance of Race, Ethnicity and Gender* (Upper Saddle River, NJ: Prentice Hall, 2000).

2. Vivien K. Burt and Victoria C. Hendrick, *Concise Guide to Women's Mental Health* (Washington, DC: American Psychiatric Publishing Group, 1997); Mary V. Seeman, ed., *Gender and Psychopathology*

(Washington, DC: American Psychiatric Publishing Group, 1995).

3. Films for the Humanities and Sciences, *Women: A True Story,* 5-part series (Princeton, NJ, 1997).

4. Insight Media, *Cross-Cultural Comparisons: Gender Roles* (New York, 1994).

5. <http://www.nimh.nih.gov/grants/research/950061.htm>, NIMH PA-95-061: *Women's Mental Health Research.*

6. Tracy Robinson, "The intersections of gender, class, race, and culture: On seeing clients whole," *Journal of Multicultural Counseling and Development, 21* (1) (1993), 50–58.

7. J. L. Vazquez-Barquero, J. F. Diez-Manrique, J. Munoz, J. Menendez Arango, L. Gaite, and S. Herrera, "Sex differences in mental illness: A community study of the influence of physical health and sociodemographic factors," *Social Psychiatry and Psychiatric Epidemiology, 27* (1992), 62–68.

8. Bruce P. Dohrenwend and Barbara Snell Dohrenwend, *Social Status and Psychological Disorder: A Causal Inquiry* (New York: Wiley-Interscience, 1969), p. 13.

9. Bruce P. Dohrenwend and Barbara Snell Dohrenwend, "Sociocultural and social psychological factors in the genesis of mental disorders," *Journal of Health and Social Behavior, 16* (1975), 437.

10. G. Gurin, J. Veroff, and S. Feld, *Americans View Their Mental Health* (New York: Basic Books, 1960).

11. W. Gove and J. Tudor, "Adult sex roles and mental illness," *American Journal of Sociology, 78* (1973), 812–835.

12. See, for example, James Davis, *Stipends and Spouses* (Chicago: University of Chicago Press, 1962); Thomas Langner and Stanley Michael, *Life, Stress and Mental Health* (New York: Free Press, 1963); Derek Phillips, "The 'true prevalence' of mental illness in a New England state," *Community Mental Health Journal, 2* (1966), 35–40.

13. H. Fabrega, Jr., A. J. Rubel, and C. A. Wallace, "Working class Mexican psychiatric outpatients: Some social and cultural features," *Archives of General Psychiatry, 16* (1967), 704–712; T. S. Langner, "Psychophysiological symptoms and the status of women in two Mexican communities," in J. M. Murphy and A. H. Leighton, eds., *Approaches to Cross-Cultural Psychiatry* (New York: Cornell University Press, 1965), pp. 360–392; J. G. Manis et al., "Estimating the prevalence of mental illness," *American Sociological Review, 29* (1964), 84–89.

14. David Pilgrim and Anne Rogers, *A Sociology of Mental Health and Illness* (Buckingham: Open University Press, 1999), p. 42.

15. Edward Jarvis, "On the comparative liability of males and females to insanity, and their comparative curability and morality when insane," *American Journal of Insanity, 7* (1850), 142–171.

16. Gove and Tudor, "Adult sex roles and mental illness," p. 369.

17. Bruce P. Dohrenwend and Barbara Snell Dohrenwend, "Sex differences and psychiatric disorders," *Journal of Health and Social Behavior, 17* (1976),1453.

18. Michael R. Zent, "Sex and mental disorder: A reappraisal," *Sociological Focus, 17* (1984), 121–136.

19. Sarah Rosenfield, "Gender and mental health: Do women have more psychopathology, men more, or both the same (and why)?" in Allan V. Horwitz and Teresa L. Scheid, eds., *A Handbook for the Study of Mental Health: Social Contexts, Theories and Systems* (Cambridge: Cambridge University Press, 1999), pp. 348–360.

20. Ronald C. Kessler and Jane D. McLeod, "Sex differences in vulnerability to undesirable life events," *American Sociological Review, 49* (1984), 620–631.

21. R. C. Kessler et al., "Lifetime and 12-month prevalence of DSM-III-R psychiatric disorders in the United States: Results from the National Comorbidity Survey," *Archives of General Psychiatry, 51* (1994), 8–19.

22. For a comprehensive review of all theories of higher reported rates among women, see Carol C. Nadelson, "The psychology of women," *Canadian Journal of Psychiatry, 28* (1983), 210–218.

23. Gove and Tudor, "Adult sex roles and mental illness"; K. Clancy and W. Gove, "Sex differences in mental illness: An analysis of response bias in self-reports," *American Journal of Sociology, 80* (1974), 205–215.

24. Clancy and Gove, "Sex differences in mental illness," p. 206.

25. Peggy A. Thoits, "Stress, coping, and social support processes: Where are we? What

next?" *Journal of Health and Social Behavior* (extra issue) (1995), 53–79.

26. Shelia R. Cotton, "Marital status and mental health revisited: Examining the importance of risk factors and resources," *Family Relations, 48* (3) (1999), 225–233.

27. Derek L. Phillips and Bernard E. Segal, "Sexual status and psychiatric symptoms," *American Sociological Review, 34* (1969), 58–72; Monica Briscoe, "Sex differences in psychological well-being," *Psychological Medicine*, suppl. 1 (1982).

28. Ruth Cooperstock, "Sex differences in the use of mood-modifying drugs: An explanatory model," *Journal of Health and Social Behavior, 12* (1971), 238–244.

29. John Merowsky and Catherine E. Ross, "Sex differences in distress, *American Sociological Review, 60* (3) (1995), 449–468.

30. Saundra Gardner Atwell and Gerald T. Hataling, "Sex differences in help-seeking behavior: A test of three perspectives," paper presented at the annual meeting of the Society for the Study of Social Problems, San Francisco, 1978; John A. Clausen, "Sex roles, marital roles and response to mental disorder," *Research in Community and Mental Health, 3* (1983), 165–208.

31. Phyllis Chesler, *Women and Madness* (New York: Avon, 1972); David Mechanic, "Perception of parental responses to illness," *Journal of Health and Social Behavior, 6* (1965), 253–257.

32. Lois M. Verbrugge, "Females and illness: Recent trends in sex differences in the United States," *Journal of Health and Social Behavior, 17* (1976), 387–403.

33. Amerigo Farina, "Are women nicer people than men? Sex and the stigma of mental disorders," *Clinical Psychology Review, 1* (1981), 223–243.

34. Derek L. Phillips, "Rejection of the mentally ill," *American Sociological Review, 29* (1964), 679–687; Sherman Eisenthal, "Attribution of mental illness in relation to sex of respondent and sex of rated stimulus person," *Psychological Reports, 28* (1971), 471–474.

35. Sarah Rosenfield, "Sex roles and societal reactions to mental illness: The labeling of 'deviant' deviance," *Journal of Health and Social Behavior, 23* (1982), 18–24.

36. Bruce G. Link, Frances P. Mesagno, Maxine E. Lubner, and Bruce P. Dohrenwend,

"Problems in measuring role strains and social functioning in relation to psychological symptoms," *Journal of Health and Social Behavior, 31* (4) (1990), 354–369.

37. Center for Mental Health Services, "Male-female admission differentials in state mental hospitals, 1880–1990," *Mental Health Statistical Note 211* (Rockville, MD, 1994).

38. I. K. Broverman et al., "Sex role stereotypes and clinical judgments of mental health," *Journal of Consulting and Clinical Psychology, 34* (1970), 1–7.

39. P. L. Hurley and M. Conwell, "Public mental hospital release rates in five states," *Public Health Reports, 82* (1967), 49–60; B. Z. Locke, "Outcomes of first hospitalization of patients with schizophrenia," *Public Health Reports, 77* (1962), 801–805; A. Raskin and R. Golob, "Occurrence of sex and social class differences in premorbid competence, symptom and outcome measures in acute schizophrenia," *Psychological Reports, 18* (1966), 11–22; Terry A. Kupers et al., "Is there gender bias in the DSM-IV?" in Richard P. Halgin, *Taking Sides: Clashing Views on Controversial Issues in Abnormal Psychology* (Guilford, CT: Dushkin/McGraw-Hill, 2000), pp. 14–39.

40. Frederick Kass, Robert L. Spitzer, and Janet B. Williams, "An empirical study of the issue of sex bias in the diagnostic criteria of DSM-III Axis II personality disorders," *American Psychologist, 38* (1983), 799–801. A similar study reports that such biases may still be very much alive. See Marcie Kaplan, "A woman's view of DSM-III," *American Psychologist, 38* (1983), 786–792.

41. Rosenfield, "Gender and mental health," p. 210.

42. Jill M. Goldstein, Ming T. Tsuang, and Stephen V. Faraone, "Gender and schizophrenia: Implications for understanding the heterogeneity of the illness," *Psychiatry Research, 28* (1989), 243–253.

43. R. Thara and S. Rajkumar, "Gender differences in schizophrenia: Results of a follow-up study from India," *Schizophrenia Research, 7* (1) (1992), 65–70.

44. Dohrenwend and Dohrenwend, "Sociocultural and social psychological factors in the genesis of mental disorders."

45. National Institute of Mental Health, *Psychiatric Services and the Changing Institu-*

tional Scene, 1950–1985, DHEW Publication No. (ADM) 77–433 (Washington, DC: U.S. Government Printing Office, 1987), p. 18.

46. Richard R. Lewine, Daniel Burbach, and Herbert Y. Meltzer, "Effect of diagnostic criteria on the ratio of male to female schizophrenic patients," *American Journal of Psychiatry, 14* (1984), 84–87.

47. Richard R. Lewine, "Sex differences in the age of symptom of onset and first hospitalization in schizophrenia," *American Journal of Orthopsychiatry, 50* (1980), 316–322.

48. Jennie Popay, Mel Bartley, and Charlie Owen, "Gender inequalities in health: Social position, affective disorders and minor physical comorbidity" (Special Issue: Women, Men and Health), *Social Science and Medicine, 36* (1) (1993), 21–32; Dohrenwend and Dohrenwend, "Factors in the genesis of mental disorders," 1975, p. 369.

49. Morton Kramer, "Issues in the development of statistical and epidemiological data for mental health services research," *Psychological Medicine, 6* (1976), 185–215.

50. Ellen Leibenluft, ed., *Gender Differences in Mood and Anxiety Disorders* (Washington, DC: American Psychiatric Publishing Group, 1999); Meir Steiner, Kimberly Yonkers, and Elias Eriksson, *Mood Disorders in Women* (Washington, DC: American Psychiatric Publishing Group, 1999).

51. M. J. Prince et al., "Depression symptoms in late life assessed using the EURO-D scale: Effect of age, gender and marital status in 14 European centres," *British Journal of Psychiatry, 174* (1999), 339–345.

52. Richard C. Everson, J. B. Wood, E. A. Nuttall, and D. W. Cho, "Suicide rates among public mental health patients," *Acta Psychiatrica Scandinavica, 66* (1982), 254–264.

53. Raymond Cochrane and Mary Stopes-Roe, "Women, marriage, employment, and mental health," *British Journal of Psychiatry, 139* (1981), 373–381.

54. Martin J. Weich, "Behavioral differences between groups of acutely psychotic (schizophrenic) males and females," *Psychiatric Quarterly, 42* (1968), 108.

55. Ibid.

56. Dohrenwend and Dohrenwend, "Sociocultural and social psychological factors in the genesis of mental disorders."

57. R. C. Benfari et al., "Some dimensions of psychoneurotic behavior in an urban sample," *Journal of Nervous and Mental Disease, 155* (1972), 77–90.

58. F. Engelsmann et al., "Variations in responses to a symptom check-list by age, sex, income, residence and ethnicity," *Social Psychiatry, 7* (1972), 150–156.

59. Christopher Tennant, Paul Bebbington, and Jane Hurry, "Female vulnerability to neurosis: The influence of social roles," *Australian and New Zealand Journal of Psychiatry, 16* (1982), 135–140.

60. Kessler et al., "Lifetime and 12-month prevalence of DSM-III-R psychiatric disorders in the United States"; Dohrenwend and Dohrenwend, "Sex differences and psychiatric disorders," p. 1453.

61. Rosenfield, "Gender and mental health," p. 359.

62. For a review of mental illness among the young, see Walter R. Gove and Terry R. Herb, "Stress and mental illness among the young: A comparison of the sexes," *Social Forces, 53* (1974), 256–265.

63. J. Kagan and M. Lewis, "Studies of attention in the human infant," *Merrill-Palmer Quarterly, 11* (1965), 95–127.

64. Judith Bardwick, *The Psychology of Women* (New York: Harper & Row, 1971); M. Cohen, "Personal identity and sexual identity," *Psychiatry, 29* (1966), 1–14; Eleanor Macoby, *The Development of Sex Differences* (Stanford, CA: Stanford University Press, 1966).

65. Gove and Herb, "Stress and mental illness among the young," p. 258.

66. D. Von Zerssen and S. Weyerer, "Sex differences in rates of mental disorders," *International Journal of Mental Health, 11* (1982), 9–45.

67. Debra Umberson and Kristi Williams, "Family status and mental health," in Carol S. Aneshensel and Jo C. Phelan, eds., *Handbook of the Sociology of Mental Health* (New York: Kluwer Academic/Plenum, 1999), p. 247.

68. Robert H. Coombs, "Marital status and personal well-being: A literature review," *Family Relations, 40* (1) (1991), 97.

69. Allan V. Horwitz, Helene Raskin White, and Sandra Howell-White, "Becoming married and mental health: A longitudinal study of a cohort of young adults," *Journal of Marriage and the Family, 58* (4) (1996), 895–1007.

70. Walter R. Gove, "The relationship between sex roles, marital status, and mental illness," *Social Forces, 51* (1972), 34–44.

71. Ibid.

72. Timothy P. Johnson, "Mental health, social relations, and social selection: A longitudinal analysis," *Journal of Health and Social Behavior, 32* (4) (1991), 408–423.

73. M. S. Forthofer et al., "The effects of psychiatric disorders on the probability and timing of first marriage," *Journal of Health and Social Behavior, 37* (1996), 121–132.

74. C. E. Ross, J. Mirowsky, and K. Goldsteen, "The impact of the family on health: The decade in review," *Journal of Marriage and the Family, 52* (1990), 1059–1078.

75. See, for example, Leonard I. Pearlin and Joyce S. Johnson, "Marital status, life-strains and depression," *American Sociological Review, 42* (1977), 704–715.

76. Ibid.

77. Gove, "Relationship between sex roles, marital status, and mental illness"; Genevieve Knupfer, Walter Clark, and Robin Room, "The mental health of the unmarried," *American Journal of Psychiatry, 122* (1966), 841–851; Joan Busfield, "Gender and mental illness," *International Journal of Mental Health, 11* (1982), 46–66; Ronald C. Kessler and James A. McRae, "A note on the relationships of sex and marital status to psychological distress," *Research in Community and Mental Health, 4* (1984), 109–130.

78. Susan Jean Schenk, *Burning Dinner Is Not Incompetence but War: Marriage and Madness in Contemporary Domestic Fiction,* Ph.D. dissertation, University of Western Ontario, 1989.

79. All of the 17 studies of the rates of mental illness among married men and women reviewed by Gove found that married women have higher rates of mental disorder than married men. See Gove, "Relationship between sex roles, marital status, and mental illness," p. 37. It is also reported that the admission rates to mental hospitals are high for heads of female-headed families and for children who live in such families. See Kramer, "Issues in the development of data for mental health services research," pp. 34–35.

80. Timothy Frank Chapman, *Assortative Mating and Mental Illness,* Ph.D. dissertation, Yale University, 1993.

81. Lisa Drago Piechowski, "Mental health and women's multiple roles: Families in society," *Journal of Contemporary Human Services, 73* (3) (1992), 62–68; Gove, "Relationship between sex roles, marital status, and mental illness," p. 37,

82. Sheri L. Johnson and Theodore Jacob, "Marital interactions of depressed men and women," *Journal of Consulting and Clinical Psychology, 65* (1) (1997), 15–23; Roni Beth Tower, Stanislav V. Kasl, and Deborah J. Moritz, "The influence of spouse cognitive impairment on respondents' depressive symptoms: The moderating role of marital closeness," *Journal of Gerontology,* Ser. D, *52* (5) (1997), 270–278.

83. Judora J. Spanier and Johanna C. Theron, "Stress and coping strategies in spouses of depressed patients," *Journal of Psychology, 133* (3) (1999), 253; Feigin Rena, Sherer Moshe, and Ohry Abraham, "Couples' adjustment to one partner's disability: The relationship between sense of coherence and adjustment," *Social Science and Medicine, 43* (2) (1996), 163–171.

84. Richard L. Meile, David Richard Johnson, and Louis St. Peter, "Marital role, education, and mental disorder among women: Test of an interaction hypothesis," *Journal of Health and Social Behavior, 17* (1976), 295–301.

85. Ibid., p. 295.

86. T. S. Langner and S. T. Michael, *Life, Stress and Mental Health* (New York: Free Press, 1963); J. Veroff and S. Feld, *Marriage and Work in America: A Study of Motives and Roles* (New York: Van Nostrand Reinhold, 1970).

87. Meile, Johnson, and St. Peter, "Marital role, education, and mental disorder among women," p. 299.

88. S. Bellin and R. Handt, "Marital status and mental disorders among the aged," *American Sociological Review, 23* (1958), 155–162; B. Cooper, "Psychiatric disorder in hospitals and general practice," *Social Psychiatry, 1* (1966), 7–10.

89. J. G. Sandberg and J. M. Harper, "Depression in mature marriages: Impact and implications for marital therapy," *Journal of Marital and Family Therapy, 25* (3) (1999), 393–406.

90. Gove, "Relationship between sex roles, marital status and mental illness," p. 38.

91. Leo Srole et al., *Mental Health in the Metrop-*

olis (New York: McGraw-Hill, 1962), p. 186.

92. Knupfer, Clark, and Room, "Mental health of the unmarried," p. 848.

93. R. Fuhrer, S. A. Stansfeld, J. Chemali, and M. J. Shipley, "Gender, social relations and mental health: Prospective findings from an occupational cohort (Whitehall II study)," *Social Science and Medicine, 48* (1) (1999), 77–87.

94. Knupfer, Clark and Room, "Mental health of the unmarried," pp. 845–846.

95. Ibid., p. 846.

96. D. R. Williams et al., "Marital status and psychiatric disorders among blacks and whites," *Journal of Health and Social Behavior, 33* (1992), 140–157.

97. Gove, "Relationship between sex roles, marital status and mental illness," p. 41.

98. R. C. Kessler, E. E. Watters, and M. S. Forthofer, "The social consequences of psychiatric disorders. III: Probability of marital stability," *American Journal of Psychiatry, 155* (1998), 1092–1096.

99. Charles E. Holzer et al., "Sex, marital status, and mental health: A reappraisal," paper presented at the annual meeting of the American Sociological Association, San Francisco, 1975.

100. John W. Fox, "Gove's specific sex-role theory of mental illness: A research note," *Journal of Health and Social Behavior, 21* (1980), 260–267.

101. A. V. Horwitz, J. McLaughlin, and H. R. White, "How the negative and positive aspects of partner relationships affect the mental health of young married people," *Journal of Health and Social Behavior, 39* (2) (1998), 124–136.

102. R. W. Simon and K. Marcussen, "Marital transitions, marital beliefs and mental health," *Journal of Health and Social Behavior, 40* (2) (1999), 111–125.

103. J. R. Earle et al., "Women, marital status and symptoms of depression in a midlife national sample," *Journal of Women and Aging, 10* (1) (1998), 41–57.

104. Xinhua Steve Ren, "Marital status and quality of relationships: The impact on health perception," *Social Science and Medicine, 44* (2) (1997), 241–249.

105. R. W. Bothlander, "Differentiation of self, need fulfillment, and psychological well-being in married men," *Psychological Reports, 84* (1999), 1274–1280.

106. C. E. Ross, "Reconceptualizing marital status as a continuum of social attachment," *Journal of Marriage and the Family, 57* (1995), 129–140.

107. Films for the Humanities and Sciences, *What Is Family? Defining the Tie That Binds* (Princeton, NJ, 2001).

108. K. H. Jockel and K. Bromen, "Sex, ratios, family size, and birth order," *American Journal of Epidemiology, 151* (11) (2000), 1133–1134.

109. K. Pearson, *On the Handicap of Firstborns* (London: Eugenics Laboratory Section Service, 1914).

110. E. H. Hare and G. K. Shaw, "A study in family health: Health in relation to family size," *British Journal of Psychiatry, 3* (1965), 461–466.

111. Almeida Filho Naomar De, "Family variables and child mental disorders in a third world urban area (Bahia, Brazil)," *Social Psychiatry, 19* (1984), 23–30.

112. John Birtchnell, "Sibship size and mental illness," *British Journal of Psychiatry, 117* (1970), 303–308.

113. Erica E. Goode, "Only children: Cracking the myth of the pampered, lonely misfit," *U.S. News & World Report, 116* (1) January (1994), 50; D. M. Levy, *Maternal Over-Protection* (New York: Columbia University Press, 1943).

114. Bernard F. Reiss and Jeanne Safer, "Birth order and related variables in a large outpatient population," *Journal of Psychology, 85* (1973), 61–68.

115. Margaret G. Howe and Maribeth E. Madgett, "Mental health problems associated with the only child," *Canadian Psychiatric Association Journal, 20* (1975), 189–194.

116. W. Vogel and C. G. Lauterback, "Sibling patterns and social adjustment among normal and psychiatrically disturbed soldiers," *Journal of Consulting and Clinical Psychology, 27* (1963), 236–242.

117. Yung-ho Ko and Long-chu Sun, "Ordinal position and the behavior of visiting the child guidance clinic," *Acta Psychologica Tiawanica, 7* (1965), 1016–1062.

118. Howe and Madgett, "Mental health problems associated with the only child," p. 190.

119. H. Richards and R. Goodman, "Are only children different? A study of child, psychiatric referrals: A research note," *Journal of Child Psychology and Psychiatry, 37* (6) (1996), 753–757.

120. James S. Grotstein, "The enigmatic relationship of creativity to mental health and psychopathology," *American Journal of Psychotherapy, 46* (3) (1993), 405; S. Schachter, "Birth order, eminence and higher education," *American Sociological Review, 28* (1963), 757–768.

121. J. C. Stuart, "Data on the alleged psychopathology of the only child," *Journal of Abnormal and Social Psychology, 20* (1926), 441–445.

122. H. V. Ingham, "A statistical study of family relationships in psychoneurosis," *American Journal of Psychiatry, 106* (1949), 91–98.

123. S. Glueck and E. Glueck, *Unraveling Juvenile Delinquency* (Cambridge, MA: Harvard University Press, 1950).

124. Lawrence Nyman, "The identification of birth order personality attributes," *Journal of Psychology, 129* (1995), 51–59.

125. J. Richter, G. Richter, M. Eisemann, and R. Mau, "Sibship size, sibship position, parental rearing and psychopathological manifestations in adults: Preliminary analysis," *Psychopathology, 30* (3) (1997), 155–162.

126. D. E. Ross et al., "Sibling correlation of deficit syndrome in the Irish study of high-density schizophrenia families," *American Journal of Psychiatry, 157* (7) (2000), 1071–1076.

127. H. Barry III and H. Barry, Jr., "Birth order, family size and schizophrenia," *Archives of General Psychiatry, 17* (1967), 435–440.

128. K. L. Gronville-Grossman, "Birth order and schizophrenia," *British Journal of Psychiatry, 112* (1966), 1119–1126; L. Solomon and R. Nuttall, "Sibling order, premorbid adjustment and remission in schizophrenia," *Journal of Nervous and Mental Disease, 144* (1966), 37–46; M. Sundararaj and B.S.S.R. Rao, "Order of birth and schizophrenia," *British Journal of Psychiatry, 112* (1966), 1127–1129.

129. G. Schooler, "Birth order and hospitalization for schizophrenia," *Journal of Abnormal and Social Psychology, 69* (1964), 574–579.

130. Roger Bastide, *The Sociology of Mental Disorder* (New York: David McKay, 1972), p. 161.

131. H. J. Grosz, "The depression-prone and the depression-resistant sibling: A study of 650 three-sibling families," *British Journal of Psychiatry, 114* (1968), 1555–1558.

132. John Birtchnell, "Mental illness in sibships of two and three," *British Journal of Psychiatry, 119* (1971), 481–487.

133. K. Konig, *Brothers and Sisters* (New York: Anthroposophic Press, 1963).

134. Reiss and Safer, "Birth order and related variables," p. 67.

135. Stanley Schachter, *The Psychology of Affiliation* (Stanford, CA: Stanford University Press, 1959).

136. J. M. Darley and E. Aronson, "Self-evaluation vs. direct anxiety reduction as determinants of the fear-affiliation relationship," *Journal of Experimental Social Psychology*, suppl. 1 (1966), 66–79; B. S. Dohrenwend and B. P. Dohrenwend, "Stress situations, birth order, and psychological symptoms," *Journal of Abnormal Psychology, 71* (1966), 215–233; H. B. Gerard and J. M. Rabbie, "Fear and social comparison," *Journal of Abnormal and Social Psychology, 62* (1961), 586–592; I. Sarnoff and P. G. Zimbardo, "Anxiety, fear, and social isolation," *Journal of Abnormal and Social Psychology, 62* (1961), 356–363; L. S. Wrightsman, Jr., "Effect of waiting with others on changes in level of felt anxiety," *Journal of Abnormal and Social Psychology, 61* (1960), 216–222; P. G. Zimbardo and R. Formica, "Emotional comparison and self-esteem as determinants of affiliation," *Journal of Personality, 31* (1963), 141–162.

137. R. A. Zucker, M. Monosevitz, and R. I. Lonyon, "Birth order, anxiety, and affiliation during a crisis," *Journal of Personality and Social Psychology, 8* (1968), 354–359.

138. E. H. Hare and J. S. Price, "Birth order and family size: Bias caused by changes in birth rate," *British Journal of Psychiatry, 115* (1969), 647–657.

139. Herman J. Schubert, Mazie E. Wagner, and Daniel S. Schubert, "Child spacing effects: A comparison of institutionalized and normal children," *Journal of Development and Behavioral Pediatrics, 4* (1983), 262–264.

140. T. Stompl et al., "Sibling orders of schizophrenic patients in Austria and Pakistan," *Psychopathology, 32* (6) (1999), 281–291.

141. Gwendolyn E. P. Zahner and Constantine Daskalakis, "Factors associated with mental health, general health, and school-based service use for child psychopathology," *American Journal of Public Health, 87* (1997), 1440–1448.

142. A. E. Brand and P. M. Brinick, "Behavior problems and mental health contacts in adopted, foster, and nonadopted children," *Journal of Child Psychology and Psychiatry, 40* (8) (1999), 1221–1229.

143. P. Tienari, et al., "Finnish adoptive family study: Sample selection and adoptee DSM-III-R diagnoses," *Acta Psychiatrica Scandanavica, 101* (6) (2000), 433–443.

144. See, for example, Nathan M. Simon and Audrey G. Senturia, "Adoption and psychiatric illness," *American Journal of Psychiatry, 122* (1966), 858–868; H. David Kirk, Kurt Jonassohn, and Ann D. Fish, "Are adopted children especially vulnerable to stress?" *Archives of General Psychiatry, 14* (1966), 291–298.

145. M. D. Schecter, "Observations on adopted children," *Archives of General Psychiatry, 3* (1960), 21–32.

146. Schecter observed only a small group of children seen in private practice by one psychiatrist.

147. P. W. Toussieng, "Thoughts regarding the etiology of psychological difficulties in adopted children," *Child Welfare, 41* (1962), 59–65.

148. M. Bohman and Soren Sigvardsson, "A prospective, longitudinal study of children registered for adoption: A 15-year follow-up," *Annual Progress in Child Psychiatry and Child Development* (1981), 217–237.

149. Byron W. Lindholm and John Touliatos, "Psychological adjustment of adopted and nonadopted children," *Psychological Reports, 46* (1980), 307–310; Soren Sigvardsson et al., "An adoption study of somatoform disorders. 1. The relationship of somatization to psychiatric disability," *Archives of General Psychiatry, 4* (1984), 853–859.

150. Simon and Senturia, "Adoption and psychiatric illness," p. 863.

151. Nancy Greenberg, "A most militant adoptee comes out of the closet," *Evening Bulletin,* Philadelphia, April 7, 1976, p. 6.

152. John G. Looney and Keith D. Grace, "Treatment of the adopted adolescent: Involvement of the biologic mother," *Journal of the American Academy of Child Psychiatry, 21* (1982), 281–285.

CHAPTER 10

1. Jeffrey S. Levin and Linda M. Chatters, "Research on religion and mental health: An overview of empirical findings and theoretical issues," in Harold G. Koenig, ed., *Handbook of Religion and Mental Health* (San Diego, CA: Academic Press, 1998), pp. 33–50.

2. Elizabeth K. Oakes, "Reflection on religiousness and mental health," *Counseling and Values, 44* (2) (2000), 113–117; Andrew J. Weaver et al., "Research on religious variables in five major adolescent research journals: 1992 to 1996," *Journal of Nervous and Mental Disease, 188* (1) (2000), 36–44.

3. John Maltby, Christopher-Alan Lewis, and Liza Day, "Religious orientation and psychological well-being: The role of the frequency of personal prayer," *British Journal of Health and Psychology, 4* (1999), 363–378.

4. Christopher G. Ellison and Jeffrey S. Levin, "The religion-health connection: Evidence, theory, and future directions," *Health, Education and Behavior, 25* (6) (1998), 700–720.

5. Harold G. Koenig, D. B. Larson, and A. J. Weaver, *Research on Religion and Serious Mental Illness* (New York: Jossey-Bass, 1998).

6. W. Larry Ventis, "The relationship between religion and mental health," *Journal of Social Issues, 51* (1995), 33–48.

7. N. Narendra Wig, "Mental health and spiritual values: A view from the East," *International Review of Psychiatry, 11* (1999), 92–96.

8. Harold G. Koenig, ed., *Handbook of Religion and Mental Health* (San Diego, CA: Academic Press, 1998).

9. Christopher G. Ellison, "Religious involvement and subjective well-being," *Journal of Health and Social Behavior, 32* (1991), 80–99; Niels G. Waller, Brian A. Kojetin, Thomas A. Bouchard, David Lykken, and Auke Tellegen, "Genetic and environmental influences on religious interests, attitudes, and values: A study of twins reared apart and together," *Psychological Science, 1* (2) (1990), 138–142; For a review of studies investigating the relationship between religion and mental health, see Gary Lea, "Religion, mental health, and clinical issues," *Journal of Religion and Health, 2* (1982), 336–351.

10. Rodney Stark, "Psychopathology and religious commitment," *Review of Religious Research, 12* (1971), 165–176.

11. Samuel Pfeifer, "Demonic attributions in nondelusional disorders," *Psychopathology, 32* (5) (1999), 252–259.

12. Sigmund Freud, *The Future of an Illusion* (New York: Liveright, 1953).

13. In 1934, Leuba reported that only 13 percent of distinguished sociologists and 12 percent of distinguished psychologists in the United States acknowledged the existence of God. In addition, only 10 percent of the sociologists and 2 percent of the psychologists said they believed in life after death. See James H. Leuba, "Religious beliefs of American scientists," *Harper's Magazine*, November 4, 1934, pp. 291–300. There are indications that the same may be true today. See Susan Sanderson, Brian Vandenberg, and Paul Raese, "Authentic religious experience on insanity," *Journal of Clinical Psychology, 55* (5) (1999), 607–616.

14. Timothy J. Madigan, "Can illusions be mentally healthy?" *Free Inquiry, 13* (3) (1993), 11; David B. Larson, Kimberly A. Sherrill, John S. Lyons, Frederic C. Craigie, Samuel B. Theilman, et al., "Associations between religious commitment and mental health reported in the 'American Journal of Psychiatry' and 'Archives of General Psychiatry': 1978–1989," *American Journal of Psychiatry, 149* (4) (1992), 557; Robert L Sevensky, "Religion, psychology, and mental health," *American Journal of Psychotherapy, 38* (1984), 73–86.

15. Kathleen M. Clark et al., "A longitudinal study of religiosity and mortality risk," *Journal of Health and Psychology, 4* (93) (1999), 381–391.

16. Carl E. Thoresen, "Spirituality and health: Is there a relationship?" *Journal of Health and Psychology, 4* (3) (2000), 291–300.

17. Kenneth S. Kendler, Charles O. Gardner, and Carl A. Prescott, "Religion, psychopathology, and substance use and abuse: A multimeasure, genetic-epidemiologic study," *American Journal of Psychiatry, 154* (1997), 322–329.

18. Kenneth I. Pargament and Curtis R. Brant, "Religion and coping," in Koenig, ed., *Handbook of Religion and Mental Health*, pp. 111–128.

19. Marc Galonter, "Unification church ('Moonie') dropouts: Psychological readjustment after leaving a charismatic religious group," *American Journal of Psychiatry, 140* (1983), 984–989.

20. Daniel G. Brown and Warner L. Lowe, "Religious beliefs and personality characteristics of college students," *Journal of Social Psychology, 33* (1951), 103–129.

21. Allen E. Bergin, "Values and religious issues in psychotherapy and mental health," *American Psychologist, 46* (4) (1991), 394; Stark, "Psychopathology and religious commitment," pp. 168–169.

22. P. P. Yeung and S. Greenwald, "Jewish Americans and mental health: Results of the NIMH Epidemiologic Catchment Area study," *Social Psychiatry and Psychiatric Epidemiology, 27* (6) (1992), 292–297.

23. James A. Thorson, "Religion and anxiety: Which anxiety, which religion?" in Koenig, ed., *Handbook of Religion and Mental Health*, pp. 147–160.

24. Leo Srole and Thomas S. Langner, "Protestant, Catholic and Jew: Comparative psychopathology," in Stanley C. Plog and Robert B. Edgerton, eds., *Changing Perspectives in Mental Illness* (New York: Holt, Rinehart & Winston, 1969), pp. 422–440.

25. William P. Wilson, "Religion and psychoses," in Koenig, ed., *Handbook of Religion and Mental Health*, pp. 161–173.

26. Itzhak Levav, Robert Kohn, and Jacqueline M. Golding, "Vulnerability of Jews to affective disorder," *American Journal of Psychiatry, 154* (1997), 941–947.

27. A. Zieba et al., "Religiosity and intensity of endogenous depression symptoms: A follow-up study," *Psychiatry in Poland, 33* (94) (1999), 575–584.

28. Gary J. Kennedy, "Religion and depression," in Koenig, ed., *Handbook of Religion and Mental Health*, pp. 129–145.

29. Keith G. Meador, Harold G. Koenig, Dana C. Hughes, Dan G. Blazer, Joanne Turnbull, and Linda K. George, "Religious affiliation and major depression," *Hospital and Community Psychiatry, 43* (12) (1992), 1204.

30. S. L. Varma and Azhar Zain, "Religion and psychiatry," *Australian and New Zealand Journal of Psychiatry, 31* (4) (1997), 604–606.

31. Dinesh Arya, "Religion and psychiatry," *Australian and New Zealand Journal of Psychiatry, 31* (4) (1997), 606–607.

32. Jeffrey S. Levin and Linda M. Chatters,

"Research on religion and mental health: An overview of empirical findings and theoretical issues," in Koenig, ed., *Handbook of Religion and Mental Health*, pp. 33–50.

33. Marco Cinnirella and Kate Miriam Loewenthal, "Religion and ethnic group influences on beliefs about mental illness: A qualitative interview study," *British Journal of Medical Psychology, 72* (4) (1999), 505–524.

34. Vicky Genia, "Religiousness and psychological adjustment in college students," *Journal of College Student Psychotherapy, 12* (3) (1998), 67–77.

35. Stephen Cornell and Douglas Hartmann, *Ethnicity and Race: Making Identities in a Changing World* (Thousand Oaks, CA: Pine Forge Press, 2001); Richard T. Schaefer, *Racial and Ethnic Groups* (Upper Saddle River, NJ: Prentice Hall, 2000).

36. Henry L. Tischler, *Debating Points: Race and Ethnic Relations* (Upper Saddle River, NJ: Prentice Hall, 2000).

37. Rodney A. Samaan, "The influences of race, ethnicity, and poverty on the mental health of children," *Journal of Health Care for the Poor and Underserved, 11* (1) (2000), 100–110.

38. Derege Kebede, A. Alem, and E. Rashid, "The prevalence and socio-demographic correlates of mental distress in Addis Ababa, Ethiopia," *Acta Psychiatrica Scandinavica, 100* (1999), 5–10.

39. Cinnirella M. Loewenthal, "Religious and ethnic group influences on beliefs about mental illness: A qualitative interview study," *British Journal of Medical Psychology, 72* (4) (1999), 505–524.

40. Jennifer Alvidrez, "Ethnic variations in mental health attitudes and service use among low-income African American, Latino, and European American young men," *Community Mental Health Journal, 35* (6) (1999), 515–530.

41. Lonnie R. Snowden, "Racial differences in informal help seeking for mental health problems," *Journal of Community Psychology, 26* (5) (1998), 429–438.

42. Robert G. Malgady and Luis H. Zayas, "Cultural and linguistic considerations in psychodiagnosis with Hispanics: The need for an empirically informed process model," *Social Work, 46* (2001), 39–54; Steven P. Cuffe et al., "Race and gender differences in the treatment of psychiatric disorders in young adolescents," *Journal of the American Academy of Child and Adolescent Psychiatry, 34* (11) (1995), 1536–1543.

43. Pauline Agbayani-Siewert, David T. Takeuchi, and Rosavinia W. Pangan, "Mental illness in a multicultural context," in Carol S. Aneshensel and Jo G. Phelan, eds., *Handbook of the Sociology of Mental Health* (New York: Kluwer Academic/Plenum, 1999), pp. 19–36.

44. Bruce P. Dohrenwend, "Social status and psychiatric disorder: An issue of substance and an issue of method," *American Sociological Review, 31* (1966), 14–34.

45. D. M. Kole, "A cross-cultural study of medical-psychiatric symptoms," *Journal of Health and Human Behavior, 7* (1966), 162–173.

46. D. L. Crandell and Bruce P. Dohwenrend, "Some relations among psychiatric symptoms, organic illness, and social class," *American Journal of Psychiatry, 23* (1967), 1527–1538.

47. Maria Luisa Uidaneta, Delia Huron Saldana, and Anne Winkler, "Mexican-American perceptions of severe mental illness," *Human Organization, 54* (1) (1995), 70–77.

48. E. G. Jaco, *The Social Epidemiology of Mental Disorder—A Psychiatric Survey of Texas* (New York: Russell Sage Foundation, 1960), p. 474.

49. Georges J. Casimir and Barbara Jones Morrison, "Rethinking work with multicultural populations," *Community Mental Health Journal, 29* (6) (1993), 547.

50. Samuel Ramos, *Profile of Man and Culture in Mexico* (Austin: University of Texas Press, 1962).

51. William Madsen, "Mexican-Americans and Anglo-Americans: A comparative study of mental health in Texas," in Stanley C. Plog and Robert B. Edgerton, eds., *Changing Perspectives in Mental Illness* (New York: Holt, Rinehart & Winston, 1969), p. 238.

52. Jan Sundquist, "Ethnicity as a risk factor for mental illness: A population-based study of 338 Latin-American refugees and 996 age-, sex-, education-matched Swedish controls," *Acta Psychiatrica Scandinavica, 87* (3) (1993), 208–212; Horacio Faberga, Jr., Jon D. Swartz, and Carole Ann Wallace, "Ethnic differences in psychopathology: Specific differences with emphasis on a Mexican-American group," *Journal of Psychiatric Research, 6* (1968), 221–235.

53. Madsen, "Mexican-Americans and Anglo-Americans," p. 239.

54. David Halpern, "Minorities and mental health," *Social Science and Medicine, 36* (5) (1993), 597.

55. Daniel L. Dolgin, Renee C. Grosser, Martinez Salvador Cruz, and Ignacio Garcia, "Discriminant analysis of behavioral symptomatology in hospitalized Hispanic and Anglo patients," *Hispanic Journal of Behavioral Sciences, 4* (1982), 329–337; David H. Staker, Louis A. Zurcher, and Wayne Fox, "Women in psychotherapy: A cross-cultural comparison," *International Journal of Social Psychiatry, 15* (1969), 5–22.

56. Bertram H. Roberts and Jerome K. Myers, "Religion, national origin, immigration, and mental illness," *American Journal of Psychiatry, 110* (1954), 760–761.

57. Benjamin Malzberg, "Are immigrants psychologically disturbed?" in Stanley C. Plog and Robert B. Edgerton, eds., *Changing Perspectives in Mental Illness* (New York: Holt, Rinehart & Winston, 1969), p. 408.

58. Tony N. Brown, Sherrill L. Sellers, Kendrick T. Brown, and James S. Jackson, "Race, ethnicity, and culture in the sociology of mental health," in Carol S. Aneshensel and Jo G. Phelan, eds., *Handbook of the Sociology of Mental Health* (New York: Kluwer Academic/Plenum; 1999), p. 167.

59. S. D. Sue et al., "Psychopathology among Asian Americans: A model minority?" *Cultural Diversity and Mental Health, 1* (1995), 39–51.

60. David R. Williams and Michelle Harris-Reid, "Race and mental health: Emerging patterns and promising approaches," in Allen V. Horwitz and Teresa L. Scheid, eds., *A Handbook for the Study of Mental Health: Social Contexts, Theories, and Systems* (New York: Cambridge University Press, 1999), pp. 295–314.

61. Harry H. L. Kitano, "Changing achievement patterns of the Japanese in the United States," *Journal of Social Psychology, 58* (1962), 257–264.

62. Theodore Millon and Renee Millon, *Abnormal Behavior and Personality: A Biosocial Learning Approach* (Philadelphia: Saunders, 1974), pp. 149–166.

63. Bernard B. Berk and Lucie Cheng Hirata, "Mental illness among the Chinese: Myth or reality?" *Journal of Social Issues, 29* (1973), 149–166.

64. Ibid., p. 164.

65. Ibid., p. 161.

66. Ibid., p. 164.

67. J. Babcock, "The colored insane," *Alienist and Neurologist, 16* (1895), 423–447; M. O. Malley, "Psychoses in the colored race," *American Journal of Insanity, 71* (1914), 309–337; T. Powell, "The increase in insanity and tuberculosis in the southern Negro since 1860 and some of the supposed causes," *Journal of the American Medical Association, 27* (1896), 1185–1188; A. Witmer, "Insanity in the colored race in the United States," *Alienist and Neurologist, 12* (1891), 19–30.

68. Edward Jarvis, quoted in Seymour Leventman, "Race and mental illness in mass society," *Social Problems, 16* (1968), 73.

69. Bruce P. Dohrenwend and Barbara Snell Dohrenwend, *Social Status and Psychological Disorder: A Causal Inquiry* (New York: Wiley-Interscience. 1969), p. 16.

70. Ibid., p. 76.

71. George J. Warheit, Charles E. Holzer III, and Sandra A. Arey, "Race and mental illness: An epidemiologic update," *Journal of Health and Social Behavior, 16* (1975), 243–256.

72. William C. Cockerham, *Sociology of Mental Disorder* (Upper Saddle River, NJ: Prentice Hall,1996), pp. 186–205.

73. R. Redick and C. Johnson, "Statistical note 100: Marital status, living arrangements and family characteristics of admissions to state and county mental hospitals and outpatient psychiatric clinics, United States, 1970," Department of HEW, Public Health Service, NIMH, Office of Program Planning and Evaluation, Biometry Branch, Survey and Reports Section.

74. E. A. Gardner et al., "A cumulative register of psychiatric services in a community," paper presented at the annual meeting of the American Public Health Association, 1962.

75. David R. Williams, David T. Takeuchi, and Russell K. Adair, "Socioeconomic status and psychiatric disorder among blacks and whites," *Social Forces, 71* (1) (1992), 179; Warheit, Holzer, and Arey, "Race and mental illness," p. 245.

76. John J. Schwab, Nancy H. McGinnis, and George J. Warheit, "Social psychiatric impairment: Racial comparisons," *Ameri-*

can Journal of Psychiatry, 130 (1973), 183–187.

77. Victor R. Adebimpe et al., "Racial and geographic differences in the psychopathology of schizophrenia," *American Journal of Psychiatry, 139* (1982), 888–891.

78. B. Malzberg, "Mental illness among Negroes: An analysis of first admissions in New York State," *Mental Hygiene, 43* (1959), 422–459; A. Pronge and M. M. Vitols, "Cultural aspects of the low incidence of depression in southern Negroes," *International Journal of Social Psychiatry, 110* (1954), 759–764.

79. George J. Warheit, Charles E. Holzer III, and John J. Schwab, "An analysis of social class and racial differences in depressive symptomatology: A community study," *Journal of Health and Social Behavior, 14* (1973), 291–299.

80. Dohrenwend and Dohrenwend, *Social Status and Psychological Disorder*, p. 71.

81. Benjamin Pasamanick, "A survey of mental disease in an urban population. VII. An approach to total prevalence by race," *American Journal of Psychiatry, 119* (1962), 304.

82. Albert C. Gaw, *Culture, Ethnicity and Mental Illness* (Washington DC: American Psychiatric Press, 1993), p. 162.

83. Matthew Figelman, "A comparison of affective and paranoid disorders in Negroes and Jews," *International Journal of Social Psychiatry, 14* (1968), 277.

84. Constance Holden, "New center to study therapies and ethnicity," *Science, 251* (4995) (1993), 748; Michael Breen, "Culture and schizophrenia: A study of Negro and Jewish schizophrenics," *International Journal of Social Psychiatry, 14* (1968), 282–289.

85. This group was aptly termed the "black bourgeoisie" by E. Franklin Frazer. See E. Franklin Frazer, *Black Bourgeoisie* (London: Collier-Macmillan, 1957).

CHAPTER 11

1. Alessandra Sannella, "Transculturation, discomfort and religion," *Critica Sociologica, 131–132* (1999), 74–89.

2. M. G. Madianos, N. Bilanakis, and A. Liakos, "Acculturation, demoralization and psychiatric disorders among repatriated Greek immigrants in a rural area,"

European Journal of Psychiatry, 12 (2) (1998), 95–108; E-da-S-Freire Coutinho et al., "Minor psychiatric morbidity and internal migration in Brazil," *Social Psychiatry and Psychiatric Epidemiology, 31* (3–4) (1996), 173–179.

3. Manuel Carballo, "International centre for migration and health," *World Health, 48* (6), 1–22.

4. Barbara L. Nicholson, "The influence of pre-emigration and post-emigration stressors on mental health: A study of Southeast Asian refugees," *Social Work Research, 21* (1) (1997), 19–31.

5. Benjamin Malzberg, "Are immigrants psychologically disturbed?" in Stanley C. Plog and Robert B. Edgerton, eds., *Changing Perspectives in Mental Illness* (New York: Holt, Rinehart & Winston, 1969), pp. 397–398.

6. Robert E. L. Faris and H. Warren Dunham, *Mental Disorders in Urban Areas* (Chicago: University of Chicago Press, 1939).

7. Benjamin Malzberg, "Mental disease among English-born and native-whites of English parentage in New York State, 1949–1951," *Mental Hygiene, 48* (1964), 54.

8. Malzberg, "Are immigrants psychologically disturbed?" pp. 409–410.

9. Bertram H. Roberts and Jerome K. Myers, "Religion, national origin, immigration, and mental illness," *American Journal of Psychiatry, 110* (1954), 761–762.

10. U. Sanua, "The sociocultural aspects of schizophrenia: A review of the literature," in L. Bellak and L. Loeb, eds., *Schizophrenia: A Review of the Syndrome* (New York: Grune & Stratton, 1969).

11. Christopher Bagley, "The social aetiology of schizophrenia in immigrant groups," *International Journal of Social Psychiatry, 17* (1971), 292–304.

12. Bruce Boman and Maurine Edwards, "The Indochinese refugee: An overview," *Australian and New Zealand Journal of Psychiatry, 18* (1984), 40–52.

13. Malzberg, "Are immigrants psychologically disturbed?" p. 419.

14. Ibid., p. 418.

15. Roland Littlewood and Maurice Lipsedge, "Some social and phenomenological characteristics of psychotic immigrants," *Psychological Medicine, 11* (1981), 289–302.

16. Harrison G. Pope, Martin P. Ianescu, and

Todd D. Yurgelun, "Migration and manic-depressive illness," *Comprehensive Psychiatry, 24* (1983), 158–165.

17. William W. Dressler and Henrietta Bernal, "Acculturation and stress in a low-income Puerto Rican community," *Journal of Human Stress, 8* (1982), 32–38.

18. Roger Bastide, *The Sociology of Mental Disorder* (New York: David McKay, 1972), p. 146.

19. David Lackland Sam, "Psychological acculturation of young visible immigrants," *Migration World Magazine, 23* (3) (1992), 21–24.

20. Robert S. McKelvey, John A. Webb, and Roddy M. Strobel, "The prevalence of psychiatric disorders and Vietnamese Americans: A pilot study," *American Journal of Orthopsychiatry, 66* (3) (1996), 409–415.

21. Ihsan Al-Ihsan, ed., *Mental Illness in the Islamic World* (Madison, CT: International Universities Press, 2000).

22. Javier I. Escobar, Constanza-Hoyas Nervi, and Michael A. Gara, "Immigration and mental health: Mexican Americans in the United States," *Harvard Review of Psychiatry, 8* (2) (2000), 64–72.

23. Josephine J. Danna, "Migration and mental illness: What role do traditional childhood socialization practices play?" *Culture, Medicine and Psychiatry, 4* (1980), 25–42.

24. Leo P. Chiu and Ranan Rimon, "Relationship of migration to paranoid and somatoform symptoms in Chinese patients," *Psychopathology, 20* (1987), 203–212.

25. Ingrid Sinnerbvink et al., "Compounding of premigration trauma and postmigration stress in asylum seekers," *Journal of Psychology, 131* (5) (1997), 463–470.

26. Raymond Cochrane, "Mental illness in England, in Scotland and in Scots living in England," *Social Psychiatry, 15* (1980), 9–15.

27. David Morrison, "Intermediate variables in the association between migration and mental illness," *International Journal of Social Psychiatry, 19* (1973), 60–65.

28. Alexander Ponizovsky and Eliezer Perl, "Does supported housing protect recent immigrants from psychological distress?" *International Journal of Social Psychiatry, 43* (2) (1997), 79–86.

29. Michael Ritsner and Alexander Ponizovsky, "Psychological distress through immigration: The two phase temporal pattern?" *International Journal of Social Psychiatry, 45* (2) (1999), 125.

30. Goeran Roth, Solvig Ekblad, and Sjukhus Huddinge, "Migration and mental health: Current research issues," *Nordic Journal of Psychiatry, 47* (3) (1993), 185–189.

31. Max W. Abbott et al., "Chinese migrants' mental health and adjustment to life in New Zealand," *Australian and New Zealand Journal of Psychiatry, 33* (1) (1999), 13–21.

32. Peter J. Guarnaccia and Steven Lopez, "The mental health and adjustment of immigrant and refugee children," *Child and Adolescent Psychiatric Clinics of North America, 7* (3) (1998), 537–553.

33. Benjamin Malzberg, "Rates of mental disease among certain population groups in New York State," *Journal of American Statistical Association, 31* (1936), 545–548.

34. Locke, Kramer, and Pasamanick analyzed rates of hospital admissions among migrant and native-born populations of Ohio and found lower rates among natives of Ohio. See B. Z. Locke, M. Kramer, and B. Pasamanick, "Immigration and insanity," *Public Health Reports, 75* (1960), 301–306.

35. R. Freedman, *Recent Migration to Chicago* (Chicago: University of Chicago Press, 1950).

36. Specifically, that study found that approximately one in four of the patients were migrants. Translated differently, there were at least two and a half times as many migrants in the patient population as in the general population of Los Angeles County. See Arnold W. Wilson, Gordon Saver, and Peter A. Lachenbruch, "Residential mobility and psychiatric help-seeking," *American Journal of Psychiatry, 121* (1965), 1108–1109.

37. Mildred B. Kantor, "Internal migration and mental illness," in Stanley C. Plog and Robert B. Edgerton, eds., *Changing Perspectives in Mental Illness* (New York: Holt, Rinehart & Winston, 1969), p. 379.

38. A. O. Wright, "The increase of insanity," *Conference on Charities and Corrections* (1884), 228–236.

39. See C. Tietze, P. Lemkau, and M. Cooper, "Personality disorder and spatial mobility," *American Journal of Sociology, 48* (1942), 29–39; Rema Lapouse, Mary A. Monk, and Milton Terris, "The drift hypothesis and socioeconomic differentials in schizophre-

nia," *American Journal of Public Health, 46* (1956), 979–986.

40. Robert J. Kleiner and Seymour Parker, "Migration and mental illness: A new look," *American Sociological Review, 24* (1959), 687–690.

41. Hilliard E. Chesteen, Veronica Bergeron, and William P. Addison, "Geographical mobility and mental disorder," *Hospital and Community Psychiatry, 21* (1970), 43–44.

42. Ibid., p. 44.

43. James R. Greenley and Susan L. Dottl, "Sociodemographic characteristics of severely mentally ill clients in rural and urban counties," *Community Mental Health Journal, 33* (6) (1997), 545–551.

44. Lee N. Robins et al., "Lifetime prevalence of specific psychiatric disorders in three sites," *Archives of General Psychiatry, 4* (1984), 949–958.

45. B. J. L. Vazquez, P. E. Munoz, and J. V. Madoz, "The influence of the process of urbanization on the prevalence of neurosis: A community survey," *Acta Psychiatria Scandinavica, 65* (1982), 161–170.

46. Susan L. Dotti and James R. Greenley, "Rural-urban differences in psychiatric status and functioning among clients with severe mental illness," *Community Mental Health Journal, 33* (1997), 311–321.

47. W. W. Eaton, "Residence, social class, and schizophrenia," *Journal of Health and Social Behavior, 15* (1974), 289–299.

48. Sharon Louise Larson, *Rural-Urban Comparisons of Item Response in a Measure of Depression,* Ph.D. dissertation, University of Nebraska, 2000.

49. Erkki Isometsae, "Differences between urban and rural suicides," *Acta Psychiatrica Scandinavica, 95* (4) (1997), 297–305.

50. U.S. Department of Health, Education and Welfare, National Center for Educational Statistics, *Digest of Educational Statistics* (Washington, DC: U.S. Government Printing Office, 1970), p. 13.

51. Leo Srole, "Urbanization and mental health: Some reformulations," *American Scientist, 60* (1972), 576–583.

52. R. E. L. Faris and H. W. Dunham, *Mental Disorders in Urban Areas* (New York: Hafner, 1960).

53. Leo Levy and Louis Rowitz, *The Ecology of Mental Disorder* (New York: Behavioral Publications, 1973).

54. Ibid., p. 5.

55. J. A. Clausen and M. L. Kohn, "Relation of schizophrenia to the social structure of a small city," in B. Pasamanick, ed., *Epidemiology of Mental Disorders* (Washington, DC: American Association for the Advancement of Science, 1959).

56. Michael Rutter, "The city and the child," *Annual Progress in Child Psychiatry and Child Development* (1982), 353–370.

57. F. Engelsmann et al., "Variations in responses to a symptom check-list by age, sex, income, residence and ethnicity," *Social Psychiatry, 7* (1972), 150–156.

58. Neal Krause, "Mental disorder in late life: Exploring the influence of stress and socioeconomic status," in Carol S. Aneshensel and Jo C. Phelan, eds., *Handbook of the Sociology of Mental Health* (New York: Kluwer Academic/Plenum, 1999), pp. 183–184.

59. John Mirowsky, "Analyzing associations between mental health and social circumstances," in Carol S. Aneshensel and Jo C. Phelan, eds., *Handbook of the Sociology of Mental Health,* (New York: Kluwer Academic/Plenum, 1999), pp. 105–123.

60. Walter T. Martin, "Status integration, social stress, and mental illness: Accounting for marital status variations in mental hospitalization rates," *Journal of Health and Social Behavior, 17* (1976), 290. If impairment among age groups is measured by psychiatric screening of people in the community, the relationship is much weaker. In one such study, few age-related differences were noted in people's responses to instruments used to measure mental health. The researchers were at a loss to explain their findings. See Charles M. Gaitz and Judith Scott, "Age and the measurement of mental health," *Journal of Health and Social Behavior, 13* (1972), 55–67.

61. Sunipa Sinha, "Psychiatric problems of old age," *Samiksa, 37* (1983), 20–35; Films for the Humanities and Sciences, *Aging* (Princeton, NJ, 2001).

62. Shevy Healey, "Confronting ageism: A must for mental health," *Women and Therapy, 14* (1993), 41.

63. L. N. Robins and D. A. Regier, *Psychiatric Disorders in America: The Epidemiologic Catchment Area Study* (New York: Free Press, 1991).

64. S. Meeks, S. A. Murrell, and R. C. Mehl, "Longitudinal relationships between depressive symptoms and health in normal older and middle-aged adults," *Psychology of Aging, 15* (1) (2000), 100–109.

65. Frederick L. Coolidge et al., "Personality disorders in older adult inpatients with chronic mental illness," *Journal of Clinical Geropsychology, 6* (1) (2000), 63–72.

66. Harry H. L. Kitano, "Japanese-American mental illness," in Stanley C. Plog and Robert B. Edgerton, eds., *Changing Perspectives in Mental Illness* (New York: Holt, Rinehart & Winston, 1969), pp. 265–266.

67. Joseph L. Fleiss et al., "Cross-national study of diagnosis of the mental disorders: Some demographic correlates of hospital diagnosis in New York and London," *International Journal of Social Psychiatry, 19* (1973), 180–186.

68. Gordon Johnson, Joseph Cooper, and Jack Mandel, "Expectation of admission to a Canadian psychiatric institution," *Canadian Psychiatric Association Journal, 14* (1969), 295–298.

69. Kimmo Pahkala, Sirkka Liisa Kivela, and Pekka Laippala, "Relationships between social and health factors and major depression in old age in a multivariate analysis," *Nordisk Psykiatrisk Tidsskrift, 45* (4) (1991), 299–307.

70. Celine Mercier, Normand Peladeau, and Raymond Tempier, "Age, gender and quality of life," *Community Mental Health Journal,* 34 (5) (1998), 487–200.

71. John Mirowsky, "Sex differences in distress: Real or artifact?," *American Sociological Review, 60* (1995), 449–468.

72. Krause, "Mental disorder in late life," p. 199.

73. E. R. Mackenzie et al., "Spiritual support and psychological well-being: Older adults' perceptions of the religion and health connection," *Alternative Therapies in Health and Medicine, 6* (6) (2000), 37–45.

74. John Mirowsky and Catherine E. Ross, "Well-being across the life course," in Allan V. Horwitz and Teresa L. Scheid, eds., *A Handbook for the Study of Mental Health: Social Contexts, Theories, and Systems* (New York: Cambridge University Press, 1999), p. 347.

75. Kenneth Heller, "Prevention activities for older adults: Social structures and personal competencies that maintain useful social roles," *Journal of Counseling and Development, 72* (2) (1993), 124.

76. Sharon Y. Moriwaki, "Self-disclosure, significant others and psychological well-being in old age," *Journal of Health and Social Behavior, 14* (1973), 226–232.

77. George J. Warkeit, Charles E. Holzer III, and John J. Schwab, "An analysis of social class and racial differences in depressive symptomatology: A community study," *Journal of Health and Social Behavior, 14* (1973), 291–299.

78. S. A. Stansfeld, J. E. Gallagher, D. S. Sharpe, and J. W. Yarnell, "Social factors and minor psychiatric disorder in middle-aged men: A validation study and a population survey," *Psychological Medicine, 21* (1) (1991), 157–167.

79. Patricia B. Moran and John Eckenrode, "Gender differences in the costs and benefits of peer relationships during adolescence," *Journal of Adolescent Research, 6* (4) (1991), 396–409.

80. M. Carlos Grilo et al., "Frequency of personality disorders in two age cohorts of psychiatric inpatients," *American Journal of Psychiatry, 155* (1) (1998), 140–142.

81. Blair Wheaton, "Life transitions, role histories, and mental health," *American Sociological Review, 55* (2) (1990), 209–223.

82. Catherine Ross and C. L. Wu, "Education, age and the cumulative advantage in health," *Journal of Health and Social Behavior, 37* (1996), 104–120.

83. Krause, "Mental disorder in late life."

84. Anand Chabra et al., "Mental illness in elementary-school-aged children," *Western Journal of Medicine, 170* (1), 28.

85. Marcia Valenstein et al., "Psychiatric diagnosis and intervention in older and younger patients in a primary care clinic: Effect of a screening and diagnostic instrument," *Journal of the American Geriatrics Society, 46* (12) (1998), 1449–1455.

86. James Walkup and Sally K. Gallagher, "Schizophrenia and the life course: National findings on gender differences in disability and service use," *International Journal of Aging and Human Development, 49* (2) (1999), 79–105.

87. Dean G. Kilpatrick et al., "Risk factors for adolescent substance abuse and dependence: Data from a national sample," *Journal of Consulting and Clinical Psychology, 68* (1) (2000), 19.

88. T. A. Tuma, "Outcome of hospital-treated depression at 4.5 years: An elderly and a younger adult cohort compared," *British Journal of Psychiatry, 176* (2000), 224–228.

89. Alison M. Langley, "The mortality of mental illness in older age," *Reviews in Clinical Gerontology, 5* (1) (1995), 103–112.

CHAPTER 12

1. Carol S. Aneshensel, "Mental illness as a career: Sociological perspectives," in Carol S. Aneshensel and Jo C. Phelan, eds., *Handbook of the Sociology of Mental Health* (New York: Kluwer Academic/Plenum, 1999), pp. 585–603.

2. Bernice A. Pescosolido and Carol A. Boyer, "How do people come to use mental health services? Current knowledge and changing perspectives," in Allan V. Horwitz and Teresa L. Scheid, eds., *A Handbook for the Study of Mental Health: Social Contexts, Theories and Systems* (New York: Cambridge University Press, 1999), pp. 392–411.

3. Bernice A. Pescosolido, C. B. Gardner, and K. M. Lubell, "How people get into mental health services: Stories of choice, coercion and 'muddling through' from 'first timers,'" *Social Science and Medicine, 46* (2) (1998), 275–286.

4. Bernice A. Pescosolido, Carol A. Boyer, and Keri M. Lubell, "The social dynamics of responding to mental health problems: Past, present, and future challenges to understanding individuals' use of services," in Aneshensel and Phelan, eds., *Handbook of the Sociology of Mental Health,* pp. 441–460.

5. R. H. Rahe et al., "Life crisis and health change," in P. R. A. May and J. R. Wittenborn, eds., *Psychotropic Drug Responses: Advances in Prediction* (New York: Charles C. Thomas, 1969).

6. Barbara Snell Dohrenwend et al., "Exemplification of a method for scaling life events: The PERI Life Events Scale," *Journal of Health and Social Behavior, 19* (1978), 205–229.

7. Joanne C. Gusten et al., "An evaluation of the etiologic role of stressful life-change events in psychological disorders," *Journal of Health and Social Behavior, 18* (1977), 228–244; Daniel P. Mueller, Daniel W. Edwards, and Richard M. Yarvis, "Stressful life events and psychiatric symptomatology: Change or undesirability?" *Journal of Health and Social Behavior, 18* (1977), 307–317.

8. Sverker Samuelsson, "Life events and mental disorder in an urban female population," *Acta Psychiatrica Scandinavica, 65* (1982), suppl. 29.

9. John Gillis, "On the critical role of cognition in stress and mental illness," *Social Science International, 6* (1) (1990), 1–10.

10. Eugene S. Paykel and Zafra Cooper, "Life events and social stress," in Eugene S. Paykel, ed., *The Handbook of Affective Disorders* (New York: Free Press, 1992), pp. 149–170.

11. Nan Lin and Walter M. Ensel, "Depression-mobility and its social etiology: The role of life events and social support," *Journal of Health and Social Behavior, 25* (1984), 176–188; Howard B. Chaplain, Cynthia Robbins, and Steven S. Martin, "Antecedents of psychological distress in young adults: Self-rejection, deprivation of social support and life events," *Journal of Health and Social Behavior, 24* (1983), 230–243.

12. Nan Lin, Mary W. Woelfel, and Stephen C. Light, "The buffering effect of social support subsequent to an important life event," *Journal of Health and Social Behavior, 26* (1985), 247–263.

13. For a comprehensive review of the role of social networks and social support, see Lambert Maguire, *Understanding Social Networks* (Beverly Hills, CA: Sage, 1983).

14. C. G. Nuckolls, J. Cassel, and B. H. Chaplain, "Psychosocial assets, life crises and the prognosis of pregnancy," *American Journal of Epidemiology, 95* (1972), 431–441.

15. Suzanne C. Kobasa, Salvatore R. Maddi, and Sheila Courington, "Personality and constitution as mediators in the stress-illness relationship," *Journal of Health and Social Behavior, 22* (1981), 368–378.

16. J. H. Johnson and I. G. Sareson, "Life stress, depression and anxiety: Internal-external control as a moderator variable," *Journal of Psychosomatic Research, 22* (1978), 205–208.

17. Michael D. Newcomb, George J. Huba, and Peter M. Bentler, "A multidimensional assessment of stressful life events among adolescents: Derivation and corre-

lates," *Journal of Health and Social Behavior, 22* (1981), 400–415.

18. Stephen Hansell, "Student, parent, and school effects on the stress of college application," *Journal of Health and Social Behavior, 23* (1982), 38–51.

19. William D. Bowden, "The onset of paranoia," *Schizophrenia Bulletin, 19* (1) (1993), 165–167.

20. Roberta L. Payne, "My schizophrenia," *Schizophrenia Bulletin, 18* (4) (1992), 725–727.

21. John V. Lavigne et al., "Correlates and predictors of stable case status," *Journal of the American Academy of Child and Adolescent Psychiatry, 37* (12) (1998), 1255–1261.

22. William R. Avison, "The impact of mental illness on the family," in Aneshensel and Phelan, eds., *Handbook of the Sociology of Mental Health,* p. 506.

23. See, for example, Harold Sampson et al., "Family processes and becoming a mental patient," *American Journal of Sociology, 68* (1962), 88–96; Marion Yarrow et al., "The psychological meaning of mental illness in the family," *Journal of Social Issues, 11* (1955), 12–14; Charlotte G. Schwartz, "Perspectives of deviance: Wives' definitions of their husbands' mental illness," *Psychiatry, 20* (1957), 275–291.

24. Sampson et al., "Family processes and becoming a mental patient." p. 88.

25. Ibid.

26. Ibid., p. 92.

27. Gerald J. Hunt, "Social and cultural aspects of health, illness, and treatment," in Howard H. Goodman, ed., *Review of General Psychiatry* (Norwalk, CT: Appleton-Lange, 1992), pp. 83–91.

28. I. Zola, "Illness behavior of the working class" in A. Shostak and W. Gomberg, eds., *Blue Collar World: Studies of the American Worker* (Englewood Cliffs, NJ: Prentice Hall, 1964), pp. 351–361.

29. David Mechanic, *Medical Sociology: A Selective View* (New York: Free Press, 1968).

30. J. Clausen and M. Yarrow, "Introduction: Mental illness and the family," *Journal of Social Issues, 11* (1955), 25–32.

31. Pescosolido et al., "The social dynamics of responding to mental health problems," p. 445.

32. Egon Bittner, "Police discretion in apprehending the mentally ill," *Social Problems, 14* (1967), 278–292.

33. Reprinted from Clarence J. Rowe, *An Outline of Psychiatry* (Dubuque, IO: William C. Brown, 1975), p. 147. By permission of publisher.

34. Ibid., p. 127.

35. It is reported that there is a greater consensus as to what constitutes mental illness in communities that are culturally homogeneous as measured by (1) political consensus (2) common economic interests, and (3) radical-ethnic homogeneity. In this type of setting, there is a greater consensus because social similarity causes a prompt rejection of deviants. See Arnold S. Linsky, "Community homogeneity and exclusion of the mentally ill: Rejection versus consensus about deviance," *Journal of Health and Social Behavior, 11* (1970), 304–311.

36. Virginia Aldige Hiday, "Mental health problems in primary care: A new study," paper presented at the annual meeting of the Society for the Study of Social Problems, San Francisco, 1978.

37. Milton Mazer, "Two ways of expressing psychological disorder: The experience of a demarcated population," *American Journal of Psychiatry, 128* (1972), 933–938.

38. Derek L. Phillips, "Rejection: A possible consequence of seeking help for mental disorders," *American Sociological Review, 29* (1963), 963–972.

39. Maxwell Jones, *Social Psychiatry* (Springfield, IL: Charles C. Thomas, 1962), p. 31.

40. J. K. Hall et al., *One Hundred Years of American Psychiatry* (New York: Columbia University Press, 1944), p. 538.

41. Paul S. Applebaum, "What are the prospects for insurance coverage of mental disorders?" *Harvard Mental Health Letter, 7* (6) (1990), 8.

42. Thomas J. Scheff, *Being Mentally Ill* (Chicago: Aldine, 1966).

43. David L. Rosenhan, "On being sane in insane places," *Science, 179* (1971), 250–258.

44. William A. Rushing, "Individual resources, societal reaction, and hospital commitment," *American Journal of Sociology, 77* (1971), 511–525.

45. William A. Rushing, "Status resources, societal reactions, and type of mental hospital admission," *American Sociological Review, 43* (1978), 521–533.

46. Beverly Ann Baldwin, H. Hugh Floyd, Jr.,

and Dennis R. McSeveney, "Status inconsistency and psychiatric diagnosis: A structural approach to labeling theory," *Journal of Health and Social Behavior, 16* (1975), 257–267.

47. See, for example, E. G. Mishler and N. E. Waxler, "Decision processes in psychiatric hospitalization: Patients referred, accepted, and admitted to a psychiatric hospital," *American Sociological Review, 28* (1963), 576–587; Allen D. Wade, "Social agency participation in hospitalization for mental illness," *Social Service Review, 26* (1967), 27–43.

48. Mishler and Waxler, "Decision processes in psychiatric evaluation."

49. G. E. Hogarty et al., "A critical evaluation of admissions to a psychiatric day hospital," *Journal of Psychiatry, 124* (1968), 934–944.

50. Mechanic, *Medical Sociology.*

51. Scheff, "Societal reaction to deviance," p. 412.

52. Ibid.

53. Phillip J. Hilts, "U.S. defines mental illness as standard for treatment," *New York Times,* May 22, 1993, p. 1.

54. See Chapter 13 for an elaboration of the negative aspects of life in a mental hospital.

55. Charles W. Lidz, "Legal rights vs. how staff process patients," paper presented at the annual meeting of the Society for the Study of Social Problems, San Francisco, 1978.

56. Ruta J. Wilk, "Federal legislation for rights of persons with mental illness: Obstacles to implementation," *American Journal of Orthopsychiatry, 63* (4) (1993), 518–525.

57. Frederick K. Goodwin, "Mental illness in health-care reform," *National Forum, 73* (3) (1993), 25; Peter Huxley and Joseph Oliver, "Mental health policy in practice: Lessons from the All Wales Study of Mental Illness," *International Journal of Social Psychiatry, 39* (3) (1993), 177.

58. Stephan Haimowitz, "Americans with Disabilities Act of 1990: Its significance for persons with mental illness," *Hospital and Community Psychiatry, 42* (1) (1991), 23–24.

59. John Petrila, "Redefining mental health law: Thoughts on a new agenda," *Law and Human Behavior, 16* (1) (1992), 89–106; Steven B. Bisbing, "Recent legal developments and psychiatry," in Robert I. Simon, ed., *American Psychiatric Press Review of Clinical Psychiatry and the Law,* Vol. 3 (Washington, DC: American Psychiatric Press, 1992), pp. 285–330.

60. Editor, "Health care reform for Americans with severe mental illnesses: Report of the National Advisory Mental Health Council," *American Journal of Psychiatry, 150* (10) (1993), 1447.

61. Ibid.

62. Wilk, "Federal legislation for rights of persons with mental illness," p. 520.

63. John Q. LaFond and Mary L. Durham, *Back to the Asylum: The Future of Mental Health Law and Policy in the United States* (New York: Oxford University Press, 1992).

64. Eric Turkheimer and Charles D. H. Perry, "Why the gap: Practice and policy in civil commitment hearings," *American Psychologist, 47* (5) (1992), 646.

65. David B. Wexler, "Putting mental health into mental health law: Therapeutic jurisprudence," *Law and Human Behavior, 16* (1) (1992), 27–38.

66. Rosalyn Carter, "Mental health policy and health care reform," *National Forum* (Winter 1993), 13.

CHAPTER 13

1. Michael F. Polgar and Joseph P. Morrissey, "Mental health services and systems," in Carol S. Aneshensel and Jo C. Phelan, eds., *Handbook of the Sociology of Mental Health* (New York: Kluwer Academic/ Plenum, 1999), p. 463.

2. Ronald W. Manderscheid et al., "Contemporary mental health systems and managed care," in Allan V. Horwitz and Teresa L. Scheid, eds., *A Handbook for the Study of Mental Health: Social Contexts, Theories and Systems* (New York: Cambridge University Press, 1999), pp. 412–426.

3. There is some controversy as to whether drugs directly effected a drop in hospital populations or did so indirectly by encouraging policy changes that hastened the mass release of patients (*deinstitutionalization*). See William Gronfein, "Psychotropic drugs and the origins of deinstitutionalization," *Social Problems, 32* (1985), 437–454.

4. David A. Rochefort, "Mental health policy

making in the intergovernmental system," in Horwitz and Scheid, eds., *A Handbook for the Study of Mental Health*, pp. 467–483.

5. Harriet P. Lefley, "Mental health systems in cross-cultural context," in Horwitz and Scheid, eds., *A Handbook for the Study of Mental Health*, pp. 566–584.

6. C. Kiesler, "U.S. mental health policy: Doomed to fail," *American Psychologist, 47* (1992), 1077–1082.

7. Paul D. Cleary, "The need and demand for mental health services," in Carl A. Taube, David Mechanic, and Ann A. Hohmann, eds., *The Future of Mental Health Services* (Rockville, MD: National Institute of Mental Health, 1989), pp. 161–184.

8. James A. Kennedy, *Fundamentals of Psychiatric Treatment Planning* (Washington, DC: American Psychiatric Press, 1992); John A. Talbott, Robert E. Hales, and Stuart L. Keill, *Textbook of Administrative Psychiatry* (Washington, DC: American Psychiatric Press, 1992).

9. Michael Goodman, Janet Brown, and Pamela Deitz, *Managed Mental Health Care: A Mental Health Practitioner's Survival Guide* (Washington, DC: American Psychiatric Press, 1992); Ellen Leibenluft, Allan Tasman, and Stephen A. Green, *Less Time to Do More: Psychotherapy on the Short-term Inpatient Unit* (Washington, DC: American Psychiatric Press, 1993).

10. Bruce Lubotsky Levin and Jay H. Glasser, "Comparing mental health benefits, utilization patterns, and costs," in Judith Feldman and Richard Fitzpatrick, eds., *Managing Mental Health Care: Administrative and Clinical Issues* (Washington, DC: American Psychiatric Press, 1992), Chapter 3.

11. Charles A. Kiesler, "Changes in general hospital psychiatric care, 1980–1985," *American Psychologist, 46* (4) (1991), 416–417.

12. Douglas L. Leslie and Robert Rosenheck, "Changes in inpatient mental health utilization and costs in a privately insured population, 1993 to 1995," *Medical Care, 37* (1999), 457–468.

13. Mark Schlesinger, "Ethical issues in policy advocacy," *Health Affairs, 14* (1995), 23–29.

14. Sharon A. Salit and Luis R. Marcos, "Have general hospitals become chronic care institutions for the mentally ill?" *American Journal of Psychiatry, 148* (7) (1995), 892.

15. Raymond A. Johnson, "Adapting the chronic disease model in the treatment of dually diagnosed patients," *Journal of Substance Abuse and Treatment, 9* (1) (1995), 63.

16. Mary Ellen Fromuth and Barry R. Burkhart, "Recovery or recapitulation? An analysis of the impact of psychiatric hospitalization on the child sexual abuse survivor," *Women and Therapy, 12* (3) (1992), 81.

17. Andrew P. Ho et al., "Achieving effective treatment of patients with chronic psychotic illness and comorbid substance dependence," *American Journal of Psychiatry, 156* (11) (1999), 1765–1770.

18. Michael J. Long, Steven T. Fleming, and James D. Chesney, "The impact of diagnosis related group profitability on the skimming and dumping of psychiatric diagnosis related groups," *International Journal of Social Psychiatry, 39* (2) (1993), 108.

19. G. S. Norquist and D. A. Regier, "The epidemiology of psychiatric disorders and the de facto mental health care system," *Annual Review of Medicine, 47* (1996), 473–479.

20. Robert A. Dorwart, Mark Schlesinger, Harriet Davidson, Sherrie Epstein, and Claudia Hoover, "A national study of psychiatric hospital care," *American Journal of Psychiatry, 148* (2) (1991), 204.

21. Michael J. McCue and Jan P. Clement, "Relative performance of for-profit psychiatric hospitals," *American Journal of Psychiatry, 150* (1) (1993), 77.

22. Mark Schlesinger and Bradford Gray, "Institutional change and its consequences for the delivery of mental health services," in Horwitz and Scheid, eds., *A Handbook for the Study of Mental Health*, pp. 427–448.

23. Joseph P. Morrissey, "Integrating service delivery systems for persons with a severe mental illness," in Horwitz and Scheid, eds., *A Handbook for the Study of Mental Health*, pp. 449–466.

24. M. L. Durham, "Can HMOs manage the mental health benefit?" *Health Affairs, 14* (1995), 116–122.

25. Barbara Shapard, "The human toll: Managed cases restriction of access to mental health services," *Psychoanalytic Inquiry,* suppl. (1997), 151–161.

26. Sarah E. Rosenblatt, "Insurer liable for cost containment program: Wilson v. Blue Cross of Southern California," *Law, Medicine and Health Care, 20* (4) (1992), 408–410.

27. Glen O. Gabbard, Tetsuro Takahashi, Joyce Davidson, Marceil Bauman-Bork, and Kenneth Ensroth, "A psychodynamic perspective on the clinical impact of insurance review," *American Journal of Psychiatry, 148* (3) (1991), 318.

28. David Mechanic, "Emerging issues in international mental health services research," *Psychiatric Services, 47* (1996), 371–375.

29. Susan M. Schappert, "Office visits to psychiatrists: United States, 1989–90," *Advance Data, 237* (1993), 1–16; Bruce Bower, "Mental disorder numbers outpace treatment," *Science News, 143* (1993), 134.

30. Lawrence Appleby, Prakash N. Desai, Daniel J. Luchins, Robert D. Gibbons, and Donald R. Hedeker, "Length of stay and recidivism in schizophrenia: A study of public psychiatric hospital patients," *American Journal of Psychiatry, 150* (1) (1993), 72.

31. Frank Holloway, Marisa Silverman, and Tony Wainwright, "Not waving but drowning: Psychiatric inpatient services in East Lambeth 1990," *International Journal of Social Psychiatry, 38* (2) (1992), 131.

32. Charles A. Kiesler and Celeste Simpkins, "The de facto national system of psychiatric inpatient care: Piecing together the national puzzle," *American Psychologist, 46* (6) (1991), 579.

33. Mary E. Sullivan, Charles E. Richardson, and William D. Spaulding, "University-state hospital collaboration in an inpatient psychiatric rehabilitation program," *Community Mental Health Journal, 27* (6) (1991), 441; Robert D. Coursey, Elizabeth W. Farrell, and James H. Zahniser, "Consumers' attitudes toward psychotherapy, hospitalization, and aftercare," *Health and Social Work, 16* (3) (1991), 155.

34. Lawrence Appleby et al., "Institution-centered and patient-centered mental hospitals: A comparative analysis of polar types" in *The Sociology of Mental Disorders*, S. Kirson Weinberg, ed. (Chicago: Aldine, 1967), pp. 212–218.

35. Sally-Wai-chi Chan and Ka-fai Wong, "The use of critical pathways in caring for schizophrenic patients in a mental hospital," *Archives of Psychiatric Nursing, 13* (3) (1999), 145–153.

36. Ruth E. S. Allen and John Read, "Integrated mental health care: Practitioners' perspectives," *Australian and New Zealand Journal of Psychiatry, 31* (4) (1997), 496–503.

37. Morris S. Schwartz and Charlotte Green Schwartz, *Social Approaches to Mental Patient Care* (New York: Columbia University Press, 1964), p. 198.

38. Richard W. Redick, Michael J. Witkin, Joanne E. Atay, and Ronald W. Manderscheid, "Specialty mental health system characteristics," in *Mental Health United States, 1992* (Rockville, MD: U.S. Department of Health and Human Services, 1993).

39. Richard W. Redick, Atlee Stroup, Michael J. Witkin, Joanne E. Atay, and Ronald W. Manderscheid, "Private psychiatric hospitals, United States: 1983–84 and 1986," *Mental Health Statistical Note, 191* (1989), 1–10.

40. Leon Eisenberg, "Is psychiatry more mindful or brainier than it was a decade ago?" *British Journal of Psychiatry, 176* (2000), 1–5.

41. Aaron Rosenblatt, "Providing custodial care for mental patients: An affirmative view," *Psychiatric Quarterly, 48* (1974), 14–25.

42. Elisabeth I. Severinsson and Ingalli R. Hallberg, "Systematic clinical supervision, working milieu and influence over duties: The psychiatric nurses viewpoint—A pilot study," *International Journal of Nursing Studies, 33* (4) (1996), 394–406.

43. Robert Perrucci, *Circle of Madness: On Being Insane and Institutionalized in America* (Englewood Cliffs, NJ: Prentice Hall, 1974), p. 47.

44. Olive M. Stone, "The three worlds of the back ward," *Mental Hygiene, 45* (1961), 22.

45. Marge Stringer, "Therapeutic nursing intervention following derogation of the nurse by the patient," *Perspectives in Psychiatric Care, 3* (1965), 36–46.

46. William G. Bye and Martha E. Bernal, "The effects of two patient behaviors upon psychiatric nurses' ratings of the patient," *Nursing Research, 17* (1968), 251–255.

47. J. M. Bordeleau et al., "Authoritarian-humanitarian index in a large mental hos-

pital," *Disorders of the Nervous System, 31* (1970), 166–174; John F. Leckwart, "Social distance: An important variable in psychiatric settings," *Psychiatry, 31* (1968), 352–361.

48. L. C. Toomey et al., "Attitudes of nursing students toward psychiatric treatment and hospitals," *Mental Hygiene, 45* (1961), 589–602. Attitudes toward psychiatric treatment have also been linked with shift work. Day-shift staff members report more improvement in patient functioning over time as opposed to those working other hours. It is believed that this is because most therapy is scheduled during the day. See Edmund G. Doherty and Joseph Harry, "Structural dissensus in the therapeutic community," *Journal of Health and Social Behaviors, 17* (1976), 272–279.

49. Rose Laub Coser, "Suicide and the relational system: A case study in a mental hospital," *Journal of Health and Social Behavior, 17* (1976), 318–327.

50. Michael P. Leiter, Phyllis Harvie, and Cindy Frizzel, "The correspondence of patient satisfaction and nurse burnout," *Social Science and Medicine, 47* (10) (1998), 1611–1617.

51. Barry S. Brown and Toaru Ishiyoma, "Some reflections on the role of the student in the mental hospital," *Community Mental Health Journal, 4* (1968), 509–518.

52. Philip C. Boswell and Edward J. Murray, "Depression, schizophrenia, and social attraction," *Journal of Consulting and Clinical Psychology, 49* (1981), 641–647.

53. John M. Meyer, "Collective disturbances and staff organization on psychiatric wards: A formalization," *Sociometry, 31* (1968), 180–199.

54. Thomas P. Holland, "Organizational structure and institutional care," *Journal of Health and Social Behavior, 14* (1973), 241–251.

55. William B. Hawthorne et al., "Comparison of outcomes of acute care in short-term residential treatment and psychiatric hospital settings," *Psychiatric Services, 50* (3) (1999), 401–406.

56. K. Bhaskaran and N. Dhawan, "A comparison of the effects of hospitalization on long-stay and recently admitted female schizophrenic patients," *International Journal of Social Psychiatry, 20* (1974), 72–77.

57. Stuart A. Kirk, "Instituting madness: The evolution of a federal agency," in Aneshensel and Phelan, eds., *Handbook of the Sociology of Mental Health,* p. 539.

58. Erving Goffman, *Asylums: Essays on the Social Situation of Mental Patients and Other Inmates* (New York: Anchor Books, 1961).

59. Lawrence S. Linn, "The mental hospital from the patient perspective," *Psychiatry, 31* (1968), 213–223.

60. Madeline Karmel, "The internalization of social roles in institutionalized chronic mental patients," *Journal of Health and Social Behavior, 11* (1970), 231–235.

61. Seija Raitasuo et al., "Social networks experienced by persons with mental disability treated in short-term psychiatric inpatient care," *British Journal of Developmental Disabilities, 44* (87) (1998), 102–111.

62. Julia S. Brown and Powhatan J. Woolridge, "Interpersonal attraction among psychiatric patients: Patterns of interaction and choice," *Journal of Health and Social Behavior, 14* (1973), 299–311.

63. G. W. Gilliland and R. A. Sommer, "A sociometric study of admission wards in a mental hospital," *Psychiatry, 24* (1961), 367–372.

64. Julia S. Brown, "Sociometric choices of patients in a therapeutic community," *Human Relations, 18* (1965), 241–251.

65. E. J. Murray and M. Cohen, "Mental illness, milieu therapy, and social organization in ward groups," *Journal of Abnormal and Social Psychology, 58* (1959), 48–54; W. G. Shipman, "Similarity of personality in the sociometric preferences of mental patients," *Journal of Clinical Psychology, 13* (1957), 292–294.

66. Robert Perrucci, "Social distance strategies and interorganizational stratification: A study of the status system on a psychiatric ward," *American Sociological Review, 28* (1963), 952–962.

67. William Gardner et al., "Patients' revisions of their beliefs about the need for hospitalization," *American Journal of Psychiatry, 156* (9) (1999), 1385–1391.

68. Nan Greenwood et al., "Satisfaction with in-patient psychiatric services," *British Journal of Psychiatry, 174* (1999), 159–163.

69. Raymond Sobel and Ardis Ingalls, "Resistance to treatment: Explorations of the patient's sick role," *American Journal of Psychotherapy, 18* (1964), 562–573; Committee

on Government Policy, *Forced into Treatment: The Role of Coercion in Clinical Practice* (Washington, DC: American Psychiatric Press, 1993).

70. Rose Laub Coser, "A home away from home," *Social Problems, 4* (1956), 3–17.

71. Frank A. Petroni, "Correlates of the psychiatric sick role," *Journal of Health and Social Behavior, 13* (1972), 47–54.

72. Michael F. Polgar and Joseph P. Morrissey, "Mental health services and systems," in Aneshensel and Phelan, eds., *Handbook of the Sociology of Mental Health,* pp. 461–479.

73. Susan A. Pickett, Judith A. Cook, and Lisa Razzano, "Psychiatric rehabilitation services and outcomes: An overview," in Horwitz and Scheid, eds., *A Handbook for the Study of Mental Health,* pp. 484–492.

74. David T. Takeuchi, Edwina Uehara, and Gloria Maramba, "Cultural diversity and mental health treatment," in Horwitz and Scheid, eds., *A Handbook for the Study of Mental Health,* pp. 550–565.

75. Kevin Walker, "Lawyer sees mentally ill ill-served by system," *Philadelphia Inquirer,* July 26, 1999, p. B5.

76. S. D. Imber et al., "A ten-year follow-up study of treated psychiatric outpatients," in Stanley Lesse, ed., *An Evaluation of the Results of the Psychotherapies* (Springfield, IL: Charles C. Thomas, 1968), pp. 70–81; Ronald Maris and Huell E. Connor, Jr., "Do crisis services work? A follow-up of a psychiatric outpatient sample," *Journal of Health and Social Behavior, 14* (1973), 311–322.

77. Gale Miller, *Becoming Miracle Workers: Language and Meaning in Brief Therapy* (New York: Aldine, 1997).

78. Masahisa Nishizono, John P. Docherty, and Stephen F. Butler, "Psychotherapy is effective," in David L. Bender, ed., *Mental Illness: Opposing Viewpoints* (San Diego, CA: Greenhaven Press, 1995), pp. 91–100.

79. James Hillman and Michael Ventura, "Psychotherapy is counterproductive," in Bender, ed., *Mental Illness,* pp. 101–109.

80. James P. Le Page, "The impact of a token economy on injuries and negative events on an acute psychiatric unit," *Psychiatric Services, 50* (7) (1999), 941–944.

81. For a review of research on the efficacy of token economy programs, see Jesse B. Milby, "A review of token economy treatment programs for psychiatric inpatients,"

Hospital and Community Psychiatry, 26 (1975), 651–658.

82. J. P. Wincze, H. Leitenberg, and W. S. Agras, "The effects of token reinforcement and feedback on the delusional verbal behavior of chronic paranoid schizophrenics," *Journal of Applied Behavior Analysis, 5* (1972), 247–262.

83. R. F. Heap, "Behavior-milieu therapy with chronic neuropsychiatric patients," *Journal of Abnormal Psychology, 76* (1970), 349–354.

84. R. F. Gripp and P. A. Magaro, "A token economy program evaluation with untreated control ward comparisons," *Behavior Research and Therapy, 9* (1971), 137–149; L. Krasner, "Assessment of token economy programs in psychiatric hospitals," in R. Porter, J. London, and A. Churchill, eds., *The Role of Learning in Psychotherapy* (London: Ciba Foundation, 1968), pp. 155–173; G. D. Shean and Z. Zeidberg, "Token reinforcement therapy: A comparison of matched groups," *Journal of Behavior Therapy and Experimental Psychiatry, 2* (1971), 95–105.

85. Gary Fischler and Nan Booth, *Vocational Impact of Psychiatric Disorders: A Guide for Rehabilitation Professionals* (Gaithersburg, MD: Aspen Publishers, 1999).

86. Schwartz and Schwartz, *Social Approaches to Mental Patient Care,* pp. 122–123.

87. Julia S. Brown and Sharon K. Tooke, "On the seclusion of psychiatric patients," *Social Science and Medicine, 35* (5) (1992), 711.

88. Heino Kaltiala et al., "Coercion and restrictions in psychiatric inpatient treatment," *European Psychiatry, 15* (3) (2000), 213–219.

89. Bert Lendemeiyer and Lillie Shortridge-Baggett, "The use of seclusion in psychiatry: A literature review," *Scholarly Inquiry for Nursing Practice, 11* (4) (1997), 299–315.

90. Ruth Gallop et al., "The experience of hospitalization and restraint of women who have a history of childhood sexual abuse," *Health Care for Women International, 20* (4) (1999), 401–416.

91. Steven K. Hoge et al., "Family, clinician, and patient perceptions of coercion in mental hospital admission: A comparative study," *International Journal of Law and Psychiatry, 21* (2) (1998), 131–146.

92. Jeremy Cord et al., "Patients with personality disorder admitted to secure forensic psychiatry services," *British Journal of Psychiatry, 175* (1999), 528–536.

93. David Reiss, Don Grubin, and Clive Meux, "Institutional performance of male 'psychopaths' in a high-security hospital," *Journal of Forensic Psychiatry, 10* (2) (1999), 290–299.

94. Deborah L. Finfgeld, "Psychotherapy in cyberspace," *Journal of the American Psychiatric Nurses Association, 5* (4) (1999), 105–110.

95. Dale E. McNeil, "The role of violence in decisions about hospitalization from the psychiatric emergency room," *American Journal of Psychiatry, 149* (1992), 207–212.

96. Merton J. Kahne, "Suicide among patients in mental hospitals: A study of the psychiatrists who conducted their psychotherapy," *Psychiatry, 31* (1968), 32–43.

97. Ibid.

98. Meyer, "Collective disturbances and staff organization on psychiatric wards."

99. Shailesh Kumar, Bradley Ng, and Elizabeth Robinson, "The crowded ward," *Psychiatric Services, 50* (11) (1999), 1499.

100. Murray Melbin, "Behavior rhythms in mental hospitals," *American Journal of Sociology, 74* (1969), 650–665.

101. Raymond B. Flannery and Walter E. Penk, "Cyclical variations in psychiatric patient-to-staff assaults: Preliminary inquiry," *Psychological Reports, 72* (2) (1993), 642.

102. Raymond B. Flannery et al., "The Assaulted Staff Action Program (ASAP) and declines in roles of assault: Mixed replicated findings," *Psychiatric Quarterly, 71* (2) (2000), 165–175.

103. William Gardner et al., "Clinical versus actuarial predictions of violence in patients with mental illness," *Journal of Consulting and Clinical Psychology, 64* (3) (1996), 602–609.

104. Wesley D. Allan, Javad H. Kashani, and John C. Reid, "Parental hostility: Impact on the family," *Child Psychiatry and Human Development, 28* (3) (1998), 169–178.

105. Karl R. Beutner and Russell Branch, "The psychiatrist and the patient's relatives," *Psychiatric Quarterly, 33* (1959), 4.

106. Marsha Vannicelli et al., "Family attitudes toward mental illness: Immutable with respect to time, treatment setting, and outcome," *American Journal of Orthopsychiatry, 50* (1980), 151–155.

107. Norman W. Bell and Robert A. Zucker, "Family-hospital relationships in a state hospital," *Mental Hygiene, 51* (1967), 201.

108. Robert Rosenheck, "The delivery of mental health services in the 21st century: Bringing the community back in," *Community Mental Health Journal, 36* (1) (2000), 107–124.

109. David W. Harder and Deborah F. Greenwald, "Parent, family interaction, and child predictors of outcome among sons at psychiatric risk," *Journal of Clinical Psychology, 48* (2) (1992), 151.

110. Francine Cournos, Karen McKinnon, and Barbara Stanley, "Outcome of involuntary medication in a state hospital system," *American Journal of Psychiatry, 148* (4) (1991), 489.

111. Debby Tsuang and William Coryell, "An 8-year follow-up of patients with DSM-III-R psychotic depression, schizoaffective disorder, and schizophrenia," *American Journal of Psychiatry, 150* (8) (1993), 1182.

112. Lonnie R. Snowden and Jane Holschuh, "Ethnic differences in emergency psychiatric care and hospitalization in a program for the severely mentally ill," *Community Mental Health Journal, 29* (4) (1992), 281.

113. Goffman, *Asylums.*

114. Mike Hazelton, "Psychiatric personnel, risk management and the new institutionalism," *Nursing Inquiry, 6* (4) (1999), 224–230.

115. John K. Wing, "Institutionalism and institutionalization," *Journal of Forensic Psychiatry, 11* (1) (2000), 7–10.

116. Norma Baldwin, John Harris, and Des Kelly, "Institutionalisation: Why blame the institution?" *Aging and Society, 13* (1) (1993), 69.

117. J. K. Wing, "Institutionalism in mental hospitals," *British Journal of Social and Clinical Psychology, 1* (1952), 38–51.

118. Schwartz and Schwartz, *Social Approaches to Mental Patient Care,* p. 124.

119. Madeline Karmel, "Total institution and self-mortification," *Journal of Health and Social Behavior, 10* (1969), 134–141.

120. A. R. Goldman, R. H. Bohr, and T. A. Steinberg, "On posing as mental patients: Reminiscences and recommendations," *Professional Psychology, 2* (1970), 427–434.

121. Goffman, *Asylums,* pp. 61–62.

122. Ibid., p. 150.

123. B. M. Craginsky, D. Braginsky, and K. Ring, *Methods of Madness: The Mental Hospital as a Last Resort* (New York: Holt, Rinehart & Winston, 1969); Joint Commission on Mental Illness and Health, *Action for Mental Health* (New York: Basic Books, 1961); D. J. Levinson and E. B. Gallagher, *Patienthood in the Mental Hospital* (Boston: Houghton Mifflin, 1964); J. M. Townsend, "Cultural conceptions, mental disorders and social roles: a comparison of Germany and America," *American Sociological Review, 40* (1975), 739–752.

124. Karmel, "Total institution and self-mortification."

125. Ann Sloan Devlin, "Psychiatric ward renovation: Staff perception and patient behavior," *Environment and Behavior, 24* (1) (1992), 66.

126. Robert E. Drake and Michael A. Wallach, "Mental patients' attraction to the hospital: Correlates of living preference," *Community Mental Health Journal, 28* (1) (1992), 5.

127. Maxwell Jones, *The Therapeutic Community* (New Haven, CT: Yale University Press, 1953).

128. Norma C. Ware et al., "An ethnographic study of the meaning of continuity of care in mental health services," *Psychiatric Services, 50* (3) (1999), 395–400.

129. Scott Simon Fehr, ed., *The Therapeutic Modality of Group Therapy* (Binghamton, NY: Haworth Press, 2000).

130. Kathleen M. Kelly, Frederick Sautter, Karen Tugrul, and Michael D. Weaver, "Fostering self-help on an inpatient unit," *Archives of Psychiatric Nursing, 4* (3) (1990), 161–165.

131. Swaran P. Singh, "Three-year outcome of first-episode psychoses in an established community psychiatric service," *British Journal of Psychiatry, 176* (2000), 210–216.

132. Kam-shing Kip, "The community care movement in mental health services: Implications for social work practice," *International Journal of Social Work, 43* (1) (2000), 33–48.

133. Richard K. McGee, "Community mental health concepts as demonstrated by suicide prevention programs in Florida," *Community Mental Health Journal, 4* (1968), 144–152.

134. Bert Pepper, Michael C. Kirshner, and Hilary Ryglewicz, "The young adult chronic patient: Overview of a population," *Psychiatric Services, 51* (8) (2000), 989–995.

135. G. L. Paul, "The chronic mental patient: Current status-future directions," *Psychological Bulletin, 71* (1969), 81–94.

136. Judy Harrison et al., "Open all hours: Extending the role of the psychiatric day hospital," *Psychiatric Bulletin, 23* (7) (1999), 400–404.

137. Eamon O'Shea et al., "An economic evaluation of inpatient treatment versus day hospital care for psychiatric patients," *Irish Journal of Psychological Medicine, 15* (4) (1998), 127–130.

138. Richard H Lamb, "The new state mental hospitals in the community," *Psychiatric Services, 48* (10) (1997), 1307–1310.

139. Randy Borum et al., "Consumer perceptions of involuntary outpatient commitment," *Psychiatric Services, 50* (11) (1999), 1489–1491.

140. G. Vaslamatzis, K. Katsouyanni, and M. Markidis, "The efficacy of a psychiatric halfway house: A study of hospital recidivism and global outcome measure," *European Psychiatry, 12* (2) (1997), 94–97.

141. Mike Gorman, "Community mental health: The search for identity," *Community Mental Health Journal, 6* (1970), 353–354.

142. For a more detailed analysis of the problem of caring for psychotics in the community as well as other weaknesses of community mental health clinics, see Jonathan L. Borus, "Issues critical to the survival of community mental health," *American Journal of Psychiatry, 135* (1978), 1029–1035.

143. J. P. Morrissey et al., "Service system performance and integration: A baseline profile of the ACCESS demonstration sites," *Psychiatric Services, 48* (3) (1997), 374–380.

144. Teresa L. Scheid-Cook, "Changing models of community care for the chronically mentally ill," paper presented at the annual meeting of the Society for the Study of Social Problems, Pittsburgh, PA, 1992.

145. Alan I. Levenson and Shirley R. Reff, "Community mental health center staffing patterns," *Community Mental Health Journal, 6* (1970), 118–125.

146. Ronald Maris and Huell E. Connor, Jr.,

"Do crisis services work? A follow-up of a psychiatric outpatient sample," *Journal of Health and Social Behavior, 14* (1973), 311–322.

147. T. E. Boosher et al., "Vagrancy and psychosis," *Community Mental Health Journal, 19* (1983), 27–41.

148. "Madness on the streets: The need to keep mentally disturbed drug addicts off city streets," *National Review,* March 1, 1993, p. 20.

149. Roy Clymer, "Reacting to inmate behavior requires insight and caring," *Corrections Today, 55* (7) (1993), 22; Joel A. Dvoskin and Raymond Broaddus, "Creating a mental health care model," *Corrections Today, 55* (7) (1993), 114.

150. Michael J. O'Sullivan, "Criminalizing the mentally ill," *America, 166* (1) (1992), 8.

151. Malcolm Dean, "Bedlam lives on," *Lancet, 340* (1990), 1398.

152. David Braddock, "Community mental health and mental retardation services in the United States: A comparative study of resource allocation," *American Journal of Psychiatry, 149* (2) (1992), 175–183.

153. Jae Kennedy, "Policy and program issues in providing personal assistance in providing personal assistance services," *Journal of Rehabilitation, 59* (3) (1993), 17.

154. Karin Tetlow, "Supportive housing: A growing field where design counts in supporting populations at risk," *Interiors, 152* (11) (1993), 66; Committee on Occupational Psychiatry, *Introduction to Occupational Psychiatry* (Washington, DC: American Psychiatric Press, 1993).

CHAPTER 14

1. Ota De Leonardis and Diana Mauri, "Social enterprise programs would benefit the mentally ill," in David L. Bender, ed., *Mental Illness: Opposing Viewpoints* (San Diego, CA: Greenhaven Press, 1995), p. 283.

2. Deborah Kelly, "Coping with mental illness," *Richmond Times–Dispatch,* December 12, 1996, pp. 1–4.

3. The reader would be informed by glancing at a current issue of the *American Journal of Psychiatry.* A large portion of each issue contains ads for drugs to help psychotic patients. On the back of each ad sheet is a list of "adverse reactions." It is amazing how many undesirable effects a single drug can produce. Some side effects of antipsychotic medications include drowsiness, motor restlessness, muscle group contraction, blurring vision, nausea, dry mouth, urinary retention, constipation, cardiovascular changes, skin rash, dyskinesia, and even death! Dyskinesia is characterized by rhythmical involuntary movements of the tongue, face, mouth, or jaw and includes protrusion of tongue, puffing of cheeks, puckering of mouth, and chewing movements. There is no known effective treatment for dyskinesia.

4. Mid-Atlantic Addiction Training Institute, *High-Risk Children, Familes, and Behavioral Health,* annual meeting, Indiana University of Pennsylvania, July 2001.

5. Nancy Kratzer Worley and Barbara Jean Lowery, "Deinstitutionalization: Could it have been better for patients?" *Archives of Psychiatric Nursing, 2* (3) (1988), 126–133.

6. Lindsay Prior, "Community versus hospital care: The crisis in psychiatric provision," *Social Science and Medicine, 32* (4) (1991), 483; Ota De Leonardis and Diana Mauri, "From deinstitutionalization to the social enterprise," *Social Policy, 23* (2) (1992), 50.

7. John A. Talbott, "The care of the chronically mentally ill: Deinstitutionalization and homelessness in the United States," *Psychiatric Hunarica, 7* (6) (1992), 615–626.

8. George Ulett, "Hospitals without walls," *Hospital and Community Psychiatry, 44* (1) (1993), 82–83.

9. George B. Palermo, Edward J. Gumz, and Frank J. Liska, "Mental illness and criminal behavior revisited," *International Journal of Offender Therapy and Comparative Criminology, 36* (1) (1992), 53–61; George B. Palermo, Maurice B. Smith, and Frank J. Liska, "Jail versus mental hospitals: A social dilemma," *International Journal of Offender Therapy and Comparative Criminology, 35* (2) (1991), 97–106; Georgia Sargeant, "Back to Bedlam: Mentally ill often jailed without charges," *Trial, 28* (12) (1993), 96.

10. Leona L. Bachrach, "The biopsychosocial legacy of deinstitutionalization," *Hospital and Community Psychiatry, 44* (6) (1993), 523–524.

11. Deborah Deas Nesmith and Stephan McLeod Bryant, "Psychiatric deinstitution-

alization and its cultural insensitivity: Consequences and recommendations for the future," *Journal of the National Medical Association, 84* (12) (1992), 1036–1040.

12. Gregory B. Saathoff, Jorge A. Cortina, Ronald Jacobson, and Knight C. Aldrich, "Mortality among elderly patients discharged from a state hospital," *Hospital and Community Psychiatry, 43* (3) (1992), 280–281.

13. Anton Aggernaes, "How schizophrenic patients experience treatment and quality of life as inpatients and outpatients," *Nordic Journal of Psychiatry, 46* (26) (1992), 29–34; Anette Gjerris, "Is handling of schizophrenia a hospital task?" *Nordic Journal of Psychiatry, 46* (26) (1992), 17–19.

14. Catherine O'Driscoll, "The TAPS project: Mental hospital closure: A literature review of outcome studies and evaluative techniques," *British Journal of Psychiatry, 162* (19) (1993), 7–17.

15. Richard H. Lamb, "Lessons learned from deinstitutionalization in the U.S.," *British Journal of Psychiatry, 162* (1993), 587–592.

16. Michael Goldacre, Valerie Seagroatt, and Keith Hawton, "Suicide after discharge from psychiatric inpatient care," *Lancet, 342* (8866) (1993), 283.

17. G. Dix, " 'Civil' commitment of the mentally ill and the need for data on the prediction of dangerousness," *American Behavioral Scientist, 19* (1976), 318–334; D. G. Langsley, J. T. Barter, and J. M. Yarvis, "Deinstituionalization—The Sacramento story," paper presented at the annual meeting of the American Orthopsychiatric Association, Atlanta, 1976.

18. Joan Sall, William W. Vosburgh, and Abby Silverman, "Psychiatric patients and extended visit: A survey of research findings," *Journal of Health and Human Behavior, 7* (1966), 20–28.

19. Shirley H. Heinemann, Lee W. Yudin, and Felice Perlmutter, "A follow-up study of clients discharged from a day hospital aftercare program," *Hospital and Community Psychiatry, 26* (1975), 752–754.

20. John Cumming and Elizabeth Markson, "The impact of mass transfer on patient release," *Archives of General Psychiatry, 32* (1975), 804–809.

21. Edmund G. Doherty, "Are differential discharge criteria used for men and women psychiatric inpatients?" *Journal of Health and Social Behavior, 19* (1978), 107–116.

22. A. Keskiner and J. J. Zalcman, "Advantages of being female in psychiatric rehabilitation," *Archives of General Psychiatry, 28* (1973), 689–692.

23. James R. Greenley, "The psychiatric patients's family and length of hospitalization." *Journal of Health and Social Behavior, 13* (1972), 25–37.

24. James R. Greenley, "The psychiatric patient's family and length of hospitalization," 34–35. By permission of publisher.

25. James R. Greenley, "The negotiating of release from a mental hospital: Substantive and methodological considerations," paper presented at the annual meeting of the Midwest Sociological Associations, Milwaukee, Wisconsin, 1973.

26. Ozzie G. Simmons, James A. Davis, and Katherine Spencer, "Interpersonal strains in release from a mental hospital," *Journal of Health and Human Behavior, 7* (1967), 20–28.

27. Charles W. Lidz, "The accuracy of predictions of violence to others," *Journal of the American Medical Association, 269* (8) (1993), 1007.

28. Janet Ford, Dale Young, Barbara C. Perez, and Robert L. Obermeyer, "Needs assessment for persons with severe mental illness: What services are needed for successful community living?" *Community Mental Health Journal, 28* (6) (1992), 491–503.

29. Deena White, "(De)-constructing continuity of care: The deinstitutionalization of support services for people with mental health problems," *Canadian Journal of Community Mental Health, 11* (1) (1992), 85–99.

30. Roberto Mezzina, Pierpaolo Mazzuia, Daniela Vidoni, and Matteo Impagnatiello, "Networking consumers' participation in a community mental health service: Mutual support groups, 'citizenship' and coping strategies," *International Journal of Social Psychiatry, 38* (1) (1992), 68–73.

31. Sean Conneally, Grainne Boyle, and Frances Smythe, "An evaluation of the use of small group homes for adults with a severe and profound mental handicap," *Mental Handicap Research, 5* (2) (1992), 146–168; Phyllis Levine, "Supported hous-

ing programs in Michigan: Variations of the theme of independence," *Adult Residential Care Program, 5* (4) (1991), 277–292; Barry L. Hall, J. Mobashar, and Robert M. Wong, "Cooperative housing as a component of aftercare for long-term mentally ill residents: A Canadian experience," *Adult Residential Care Journal, 5* (4) (1991), 263–275.

32. William H. Fisher, Jeffrey L. Heller, Doris T. Pearsell, and Lorna J. Simon, "A continuum of services for the deinstitutionalized, chronically mentally ill elderly," *Administration and Policy in Mental Health, 18* (6) (1991), 397–410.

33. National Institute of Mental Health, "Deinstitutionalization: An analytical review and sociological perspective," DHEW Publication No. (ADM) 76-351 (Washington, DC: U.S. Government Printing Office, 1976), p. 11.

34. Paul Becker and Christopher Bayer, "Preparing chronic patients for community placement: A four-stage treatment program," *Hospital and Community Psychiatry, 26* (1975), 448–450.

35. S. A. Purvis and R. W. Miskimins, "Effects of community follow-up on post-hospital adjustment of psychiatric patients," *Community Mental Health Journal, 6* (1970), 374–382.

36. Morris S. Schwartz and Charlotte Green Schwartz, *Social Approaches to Mental Patient Care* (New York: Columbia University Press, 1964), Chapter 15.

37. One study estimates that only one-third of patients referred to aftercare programs actually enter the programs. See George H. Wolkon, "Effecting a continuum of care: An exploration of the crisis of psychiatric hospital release," *Community Mental Health Journal, 4* (1968), 63–73.

38. George H. Wolkon, "Characteristics of clients and continuity of care into the community," *Community Mental Health Journal, 6* (1970), 215–221.

39. Teresa L. Scheid-Cook, "Outpatient commitment as both social control and the least restrictive alternative," *Sociological Quarterly, 32* (1) (1991), 43.

40. Fiona Shaw, "Mistaken identity," *Lancet, 352* (9133) (1998), 105.

41. Gabriel Constans, "This is madness: Our failure to provide adequate care for the mentally ill," *USA Today*, August 19, 1991, p. 77.

42. "Mental Illness Awareness Week," *Weekly Compilation of Presidential Documents, 29* (40) (1993), 2009.

43. Raymond M. Weinstein, "Labeling theory and the attitudes of mental patients: A review," *Journal of Health and Social Behavior, 17* (1976), 35–44.

44. Richard James Bord, "Rejection of the mentally ill: Continuities and further developments," *Social Problems, 18* (1970), 497.

45. J. C. Nunnally, *Popular Conceptions of Mental Health* (New York: Holt, Rinehart & Winston, 1961).

46. J. M. Giovannoni and L. P. Ullmann, "Conceptions of mental health held by psychiatric patients," *Journal of Clinical Psychology, 19* (1963), 398–400.

47. J. M. Giovannoni and L. Gurel, "Socially disruptive behavior of ex-mental patients," *Archives of General Psychiatry, 17* (1967), 146–153.

48. Dorothy Miller and William H. Dawson, "Effects of stigma on re-employment of ex-mental patients," *Mental Hygiene, 49* (1965), 52–53.

49. M. Yvonne Dudgeon, "The social needs of the discharged mental hospital patient," *International Journal of Social Psychiatry, 10* (1964), 52–53.

50. Roy Porter, "Can the stigma of mental illness be changed?" *Lancet, 352* (9133), 1049–1052.

51. Linda L. Shaw, "Stigma and the moral careers of ex-mental patients living in board and care," *Journal of Contemporary Ethnography, 20* (3) (1991), 285.

52. L. H. Kaiser, "Decentralization: The solution for patient stigmatization?" *Tijdschrift voor Psychiatrie, 35* (1) (1993), 33–44.

53. L. Allen, "Study of community attitudes toward mental hygiene," *Mental Hygiene, 27* (1943), 248–254.

54. See, for example, the following studies, which are chronologically ordered: G. V. Ramsey and M. Siepp, "Attitudes and opinions concerning mental illness," *Psychiatric Quarterly, 22* (1948), 428–444; G. Gurin, V. Veroff, and S. Feld, *Americans View Their Mental Health: A Nationwide Interview Survey* (New York: Basic Books, 1960); J. K. Meyer, "Attitudes toward mental illness in a Maryland community," *Pub-*

lic Health Reports, 79 (1964), 769–772; W. J. Edgerton and W. K. Bentz, "Attitudes and opinions of rural people about mental illness and program services," *American Journal of Public Health, 59* (1969), 470–477.

55. Guido M. Crocetti, Herzl R. Spiro, and Iradj Siassi, *Contemporary Attitudes Toward Mental Illness* (London: University of Pittsburgh Press, 1974), pp. 121–122.

56. Donald W. Olmsted and Katherine Durham, "Stability of mental health attitudes: A semantic differential study," *Journal of Mental Health and Social Behavior, 17* (1976), 35–44.

57. H. P. Halbert, "Public Acceptance of the mentally ill," *Public Health Reports, 84* (1969), 59–64; Lervin R. Lieberman, "Attitudes toward the mentally ill, knowledge of mental illness, and personal adjustment," *Psychological Reports, 26* (1970), 47–52.

58. American Psychiatric Association, "Position statement on discrimination against persons with previous psychiatric treatment," *American Journal of Psychiatry, 135* (1978), 643.

59. Walter J. Johannsen, "Attitudes toward mental patients: A review of empirical research," *Mental Hygiene, 53* (1969), 218–228; David Schroder and Danuta Ehrlich, "Rejection by mental health professionals as a possible consequence of not seeking appropriate help for emotional disorders," *Journal of Health and Social Behavior, 9* (1968), 222–232.

60. Bruce P. Dohrenwend and Edwin Chin-Shong, "Social status and attitudes toward psychological disorder: The problem of tolerance of deviance," *American Sociological Review, 32* (1967), 417–433; Howard E. Freeman and Ozzie G. Simmons, "Feelings of stigma among relatives of former mental patients," *Social Problems 8* (1961), 312–321; Olmsted and Durham, "Stability of mental health attitudes"; Derek L. Phillips, "Rejection of the mentally ill: The influence of behavior and sex," *American Sociological Review, 34* (1964), 679–687.

61. S. A. Star, "What the public thinks about mental health and mental illness," paper presented at the annual meeting of the National Association for Mental Health, 1952.

62. Robert M. Swanson and Stephen P. Spitzer, "Stigma and the psychiatric patient career," *Journal of Health and Social Behavior, 11* (1971), 45–51.

63. Vytautas J. Bieliauskas and Harvey E. Wolfe, "The attitude of industrial employers toward hiring of former state mental patients," *Journal of Clinical Psychology, 16* (1960), 256–259.

64. Dorothy Miller, "Is the stigma of mental illness a middle class phenomenon?" *Mental Hygiene, 51* (1967), 182–184.

65. Swanson and Spitzer, "Stigma and the psychiatric patient career."

66. Miller, "Is the stigma of mental illness a middle class phenomenon?"

67. Dohrenwend and Chin-Shong, "Social status and attitudes toward psychological disorder."

68. Josephine A. Bates, "Attitudes toward mental illness," *Mental Hygiene, 52* (1968), 250–253; A. W. Clark and Noel M. Binks, "Relation of age and education to attitudes toward mental illness," *Psychological Reports, 19* (1966), 649–650.

69. Edwin Chin-Shong, "Rejection of the mentally ill: A comparison with the findings of ethnic prejudice," Ph.D. dissertation, Columbia University, 1968; Swanson and Spitzer, "Stigma and the psychiatric patient career," p. 48.

70. Bernard J. Gallagher III, David F. Bush, and Wendy Weiner, "Intergenerational patterns of authoritarianism," paper presented at the annual convention of the Society for the Study of Social Problems, San Francisco, 1978.

71. J. M. Bordeleau et al., "Authoritarian-humanitarian index in a large mental hospital," *Diseases of the Nervous System, 31* (1970), 166–174.

72. Howard Freeman and Ozzie G. Simmons, *The Mental Patient Comes Home* (New York: Wiley, 1963), p. 162.

73. Johannsen, "Attitudes toward mental patients," p. 220.

74. Editorial, "Hiding mental illness," *British Medical Journal,* 314 (7093) (1997), 1559–1560.

75. Mollie Grob and Golda Edinburg, "How families view psychiatric hospitalization for their adolescents: A follow-up study," *International Journal of Social Psychiatry, 18* (1973), 14–21.

76. Miller and Dawson, "Effects of stigma on re-employment of ex-mental patients," p. 285.

77. Howard E. Freeman, Ozzie G. Simmons, and Bernard J. Bergen, "Residential mobility inclinations among families of mental patients," *Social Forces, 38* (1960), 320–324.

78. Huntley Collins, "At conference on mental illness, the focus is self-help," *Philadelphia Inquirer,* December 12, 1992.

79. Bureau of Justice Statistics, *Mental Health and Treatment of Inmates and Probationers: Special Report* (Washington, DC: U.S. Department of Justice, July 1999).

80. Alan F. Fontana and Barbara Noel Dowds, "Assessing treatment outcome. II. The predictions of rehospitalization," *Journal of Nervous and Mental Disease, 161* (1975), 231.

81. Lesley Cotterill and Richard Thomas, "A typology of care episodes experienced by people with schizophrenia in an English town," *Social Science and Medicine, 36* (12) (1993), 1587–1595.

82. Rael Jean Issac and Virginia C. Armat, *Madness in the Streets: How Psychiatry and the Law Abandoned the Mentally Ill* (New York: Free Press, 1990).

83. Rene C. Grosser and Phyllis Vine, "Families as advocates for the mentally ill: A survey of characteristics and service needs," *American Journal of Orthopsychiatry, 61* (2) (1991), 282.

84. George Serban and Christina B. Gidynski, "Significance of social demographic data for rehospitalization of schizophrenic patients," *Journal of Health and Social Behavior, 15* (1974), 117–126; R. Jay Turner and John W. Gartrell, "Social factors in psychiatric outcome: Toward the resolution of interpretive controversies," *American Sociological Review, 43* (1978), 368–382.

85. Robert H. Richart and Lawrence M. Millner, "Factors influencing admission to a community mental health center," *Community Mental Health Journal, 4* (1968), 27–35.

86. Ozzie G. Simmons and Howard E. Freeman, "Familial expectations and post-hospital performance of mental patients," in S. Kirson Weinberg, ed., *The Sociology of Mental Disorders: Analyses and Readings in Psychiatric Sociology* (Chicago: Aldine 1968), pp. 248–254.

87. Simmons and Freeman, "Familial expectations and post-hospital performance of mental patients," pp. 251–252.

88. Richart and Millner, "Factors influencing admission to a community mental health center," p. 31.

89. Mary H. Michaux et al., "Relatives' perceptions of rural and urban day center patients," *Psychiatry, 36* (1973), 203–212.

90. Allan V. Horwitz, "Sibling participation in social support for the seriously mentally ill," unpublished manuscript, 1993.

91. Joanne L. Riebscleger, "Families of chronically mentally ill people: Siblings speak to social workers," *Health and Social Work, 16* (2) (1991), 94.

92. Jack L. Franklin, Lee D. Kettredge, and Jean H. Thrasher, "A survey of factors related to mental hospital readmissions," *Hospital and Community Psychiatry, 26* (1975), 749–751; L. Guel and T. W. Lorei, "Hospital and community ratings of psychopathology as predictors of employment and readmission," *Journal of Consulting and Clinical Psychology, 39* (1972), 286–291; R. Williams and R. Walker, "Schizophrenics at time of discharge," *Archives of General Psychiatry, 4* (1961), 87–90.

93. Dinitz et al., "Instrumental role expectations and post-hospital performance"; Richard L. Wessler and Donna Iven, "Social characteristics of patients readmitted to a community mental health center," *Community Mental Health Journal, 6* (1970), 69–74.

94. Cumming and Markson, "The impact of mass transfer on patient release."

95. Steven H. Miles, "A challenge to licensing boards: The stigma of mental illness," *Journal of the American Medical Association, 280* (10) (1998), 865.

96. Norman Frost, Keshav Chander, and Steven H. Miles, "Licensing boards and the stigma of mental illness," *Journal of the American Medical Association, 281* (1999), 606.

97. Patrick W. Sullivan, "Reclaiming the community: The strengths perspective and deinstitutionalization," *Social Work, 37* (3) (1992), 204–209.

98. James Angelo Forte, "Operating a member-employing therapeutic business as part of an alternative mental health center," *Health and Social Work, 16* (3) (1991), 213.

99. This is true for both men and women. See Richart and Millner, "Factors influencing

admission to a community mental health center," pp. 30–32.

100. Wessler and Iven, "Social characteristics of patients readmitted to a community mental health center."

101. Films for the Humanities and Sciences, *Myths About Madness: Challenging Stigma and Changing Attitudes* (Princeton, NJ, 2001).

102. Robert Walker and James McCourt, "Employment experience among 200 schizophrenic patients in hospital and after discharge," *American Journal of Psychiatry, 122* (1965), 316–319.

103. Simon Olshansky, "Some assumptions challenged," *Community Mental Health Journal, 4* (1968), 153–156.

104. Johannsen, "Attitudes toward mental patients," p. 221.

105. P. Rothaus et al., "Describing psychiatric rehospitalization: A dilemma," *American Psychologist, 18* (1963), 85–89.

106. Lawrence C. Hartlage, "Factors influencing receptivity to ex-mental patients," *American Psychologist, 21* (1966), 249–251.

107. Karl Easton, "Boerum Hill: A private long-term residential program for former mental patients," *Hospital and Community Psychiatry, 25* (1974), 513–517.

108. Jerome K. Myers and Lee L. Nean, *A Decade Later: A Follow-Up of Social Class and Mental Illness* (New York: Wiley, 1968), Chapters 6–9.

109. Howard E. Freeman and Ozzie G. Simmons, "Social class and post-hospital performance levels," *American Sociological Review, 24* (1959), 345–351.

110. H. Richard Lamb, "The homeless mentally ill need assertive treatment," in Bender, ed., *Mental Illness,* p. 167.

111. Leona L. Bachrach, "What we know about homelessness among mentally ill persons: An analytical review and commentary," *Hospital and Community Psychiatry, 43* (5) (1992), 453–464.

112. Ezra S. Susser, Shang P. Lin, and Sarah A. Conover, "Risk factors for homelessness among patients admitted to a state hospital," *American Journal of Psychiatry, 148* (12) (1991), 1559–1664.

113. Ezra S. Susser, Shang P. Lin, Sarah A. Conover, and Elmer L. Struening, "Childhood antecedents of homelessness in psychiatric patients," *American Journal of Psychiatry, 148* (8) (1991), 1026–1030.

114. John R. Belcher, "Moving into homelessness after psychiatric hospitalization," *Journal of Social Service Research, 14* (3–4) (1991), 63–77.

115. For a comprehensive review of social policy issues in mental health care, see Phil Brown, ed., *Mental Health Care and Social Policy* (Boston: Routledge and Kegan Paul, 1985).

116. A. M. Rosenthal and Richard Cohen, "The homeless mentally ill should be institutionalized," in Bender, ed., *Mental Illness,* p. 181.

117. P. M. Roman and H. H. Floyd, Jr., "Social acceptance of psychiatric illness and psychiatric treatment," *Social Psychiatry, 16* (1981), 21–29; Fred E. Markowitz, "Modeling processes in recovery from mental illness: Relationships between symptoms, life satisfaction, and self-concept," *Journal of Health and Social Behavior, 42* (2001), 64–79.

118. Films for the Humanities and Sciences, *Mistreating the Mentally Ill* (Princeton, NJ, 2001).

Photo Credits

Index